Mysticism and Alchemy
through the Ages

ALSO BY GARY EDSON

*Masks and Masking: Faces of Tradition and
Belief Worldwide* (McFarland, 2005; paperback 2009)

*Shamanism: A Cross-Cultural Study of
Beliefs and Practices* (McFarland, 2009)

Mysticism and Alchemy through the Ages

The Quest for Transformation

Gary Edson

McFarland & Company, Inc., Publishers
Jefferson, North Carolina, and London

LIBRARY OF CONGRESS CATALOGUING-IN-PUBLICATION DATA

Edson, Gary, 1937–
Mysticism and alchemy through the ages : the quest for transformation / Gary Edson.
    p.   cm.

Includes bibliographical references and index.

ISBN 978-0-7864-6531-6
softcover : acid free paper ∞

1. Religions — History.　2. Spirituality — History.
3. Spiritual life — History.　4. Mysticism — History.
5. Alchemy — History.　I. Title.
BL80.3.E37 2012   204'.2—dc23   2012031030

BRITISH LIBRARY CATALOGUING DATA ARE AVAILABLE

© 2012 Gary Edson. All rights reserved

No part of this book may be reproduced or transmitted in any form or by any means, electronic or mechanical, including photocopying or recording, or by any information storage and retrieval system, without permission in writing from the publisher.

Front cover: Page from alchemic treatise of Raimundus Lullus, 16th century; borders © 2012 Shutterstock

Manufactured in the United States of America

McFarland & Company, Inc., Publishers
Box 611, Jefferson, North Carolina 28640
www.mcfarlandpub.com

To Master Chiang Min-Chi

Acknowledgments

Alchemists of old describe their laboratory work in anthropomorphic terms. They were particularly inclined to equate the development of gold to the process of gestation of the human fetus. It was their belief that all metals would be gold if allowed to reach full maturity in the womb of the earth. Following that logic, this book has had a long gestation process, and whether it emerges as gold or lead is yet to be determined. Any deficiencies in the writing are those of the author, not the earth below or the heavens above.

A number of people contributed to making the book a reality. Some assisted by telling about experiences or identifying sources for further investigation. Personnel at the Library of Texas Tech University and Ottawa Public Library were especially helpful. Both locations assisted with locating important research materials.

My gratitude is due to three people who specifically aided in the generation of this book. Master Chiang Min-Chi allowed me to photograph pieces in his collection. Access to those objects stimulated my thinking and enhanced my understanding of mystical beliefs and practices, particularly as they relate to Tibetan Buddhism. I am also indebted to Professor Wanchen Liu of the Tainan National University of Arts in Taiwan. Professor Liu contributed expertise in identifying and translating Chinese texts about Taoism, Buddhism, and Yoga. The help of Professor Liu was very beneficial in sorting through the different spellings and pseudonyms of Chinese authors, scholars, and historical figures. Finally, I thank Andrew Wheatcroft, author and scholar. Andrew is a constant reminder that writing is about writing. He is also a sounding board and a fountain of information.

Table of Contents

Acknowledgments — vi
Preface — 1

One. The Great Mastery — 5
Two. Searching for the Absolute — 27
Three. Mysticism and the Harmony of Order — 50
Four. The Nature of Phenomena: Mysticism, Magic, and Myths — 76
Five. Secret Language of Mysticism — 108
Six. Principles and Techniques of Transformation — 137
Seven. The Transformers — 155
Eight. *Prima Materia* — 192
Nine. Secret Messages of the Mind — 213
Ten. Transformation and Transcendence — 238

Chapter Notes — 255
Bibliography — 279
About the Illustrations — 293
Index — 295

Preface

[Life] is a scrap of time in which whilst we reap the fruits of today's good and evil action, limitless possibilities open up to man's [or woman's] free choice.[1]

Thinking about transformation is not new. It has been the subject of conjecture since humans first started to wonder about existence and the conditions in which they found themselves. Once humankind acknowledged the Self, transformation became an issue for speculation, study, and pursuit. No issue has been more rigorously pursued than identification and transformation of the Self. Transformation evolved from a personal concern into organized group practices and eventually into religions.

The mystical union with the Absolute is one way of considering the transformation issue and modification of material whether mineral or corporal is another. Such issues are veiled by the questions about permanence and impermanence that have concerned humanity since before societal incorporation. There can be no clear starting point for spiritual awareness, and no method of assessing the importance of such abstract thought in the evolution of human beings. Life requires belief as the foundation of hope. To deny belief is to eliminate the possibility of change — transformation — from one state of being to another. All organized belief systems are based, for the most part, on promoting hope. Life everlasting, enlightenment, immortality, and a place in paradise are commonly stated objectives of the church, temple, or mosque.

Transformation is the key element of belief. The change from one state of being to another — loser to winner, poor to rich, sinner to saint, mortal to immortal, unworthy to worthy, and impure to pure — are symbolic manifestations of deliverance into the realm of the Absolute. Whether alchemy began as the search for spiritual emancipation or the quest for earthly riches is not clearly defined by the historical record. There can, in fact, be no identifiable time to mark the moment when the concept of transformation first entered the human mind.

Topics like mysticism, shamanism, alchemy, and various other approaches to transformation are often abstract and general. Although dealing with issues relating to transformation, mysticism, shamanism, and alchemy, in particular, are not the same in basis or direction. Each of these practices has an articulated approach to practice just as Christianity, Hinduism, Islam, and Buddhism do. All these systems may be called religions, but each travels its own path toward a defined goal. Each has its own validity.

Mysticism and alchemy are often viewed as Western phenomena primarily because mysticism is associated with established religion and alchemy is viewed as a process to change base metal to gold. The two activities are generally considered as weird, or appropriate for parlor games that are not taken too seriously. Ouija boards, séances, card tricks, fortune telling, and various feats of skill and magic were intended to confuse the senses and baffle the audience. These performances were, at times, truly remarkable, but they must be considered as only entertaining activities and hardly represent the true nature of magic or mysticism.

> We should never get any truth at all if we try to eliminate all possibility of error at the outset; such complete rational detachment is to be secured only by ceasing to live.[2]

About This Book

This is the third book in what I view as a series that looks into the mystical motivations and actions of humanity. The books call attention to beliefs and traditions that cross cultural and social horizons. All people need to believe in something and the process of believing includes certain mystical assumptions. They look to the heavens for escape from life and salvation from death.[3] It is human nature to seek answers to unanswerable questions about the creation of the world and the origin of the first human. Religions provide answers based on belief—not fact—because there are no facts to validate such issues. There is no intellectual or physical knowledge to guarantee the truth of such beliefs. Consequently, people assume an attitude of passive acceptance of the feelings and attitudes associated with such beliefs.

Mysticism, a form of religion that advocates transformation, has had a primary role in the lives of humans from the earliest times. The topics of these books are therefore but aspects of a larger belief system that is inherent in humanity. The need for self-realization, however it is defined, is a necessary part of life. Mystic insight gives attention to the fundamentals of human existence. It attempts to address crucial questions about the creation of the world and the first person, survival after death, proper principles of living, and personal fulfillment. When these elements are lacking, hope is abandoned and life ceases to have value.

The first of the three books, *Masks and Masking: Faces of Tradition and Belief Worldwide*, considers the mask and masking as a type of mystical as well as social expression. Masks alter the person. They are a form of temporary physical transformation. The book calls attention to the different ways humanity has developed to modify the human body in addition to covering the face. The book describes the mask as a way of changing an individual's outward appearance as well as transforming the societal role of the person behind the mask. The book deals with forms of belief and the mystical elements of masking.

The second book, *Shamanism: A Cross-Cultural Study of Beliefs and Practices*, gives consideration to the spiritual activities of humanity as influenced by belief. It also looked at the role of the shaman within the social setting. The book considers the various tools and methods used by the shaman in performing his role as a communicator of social necessities. Shamanism is about the unity of the visible and invisible worlds, and the host community normally endorses this concept because it reinforces an identifiable sense of security. They also approve of the specific acts, practices, and beliefs required to support and maintain that definable feeling.

The methods devised to determine and evaluate the relationship between humanity and the external world are numerous and include not only mysticism and alchemy but also a wide range of activities called by different names. People want and need reassurance and exoneration, and for those benefits they endorse the most accommodating mystical practice.

This third book continues along the same path as the first two. It gives attention to the idea of transformation through different practices, especially mysticism and alchemy. The notion of direct contact with the Absolute (the acknowledged God or godhead), the search for the elixir of immortality, and the quest for the magical (or mystical) philosopher's stone reflect a commonality of purpose. Spiritually, physically, or socially the human is in constant need of reinforcement and validation. The mystic helps to satisfy that craving based on an inherent belief system.

The three books might have been written as one in that each attempts to give insight into the purposeful beliefs and associated activities of humanity. The books consider, in a non-scientific way, the psychological and physiological motivations of people as defined by the objectives they pursue. Those activities inspired by belief, heritage, and survival and are normally focused on elements that appeal the most to people: wealth, longevity, and immortality. They may be configured as religions, rituals, and practices that include a wide range of behavioral patterns from the most inhuman and cruel to the most loving and beneficial.

I wrote in the Preface to *Masks and Masking*, "No one book can adequately describe, define, explain, and detail the importance of the mask as a part of the history of humankind."[4] The same can be said about the other books in this triad. Shamanism, mysticism, and alchemy are so pervasive in the lives of humanity that it is not possible to ignore their roles in historical or contemporary society, nor is it possible to define every way they influence our lives.

Life often gives exposure to a number of experiences that in retrospect are difficult to understand or explain. These situations are not issues of superstition but circumstances or events in our lives that have no logical basis for their occurrence. We may look back at our personal history and wonder why those events happened as they did. They may have been lucky or unlucky, but they shaped the activities that followed. For example, like many people who lived during the fifties and sixties, I had my first exposure to Buddhism as an undergraduate student in 1956 or 1957. The English-born writer Alan Watts, Buddhist scholar and thinker Daisetz Teitaro Suzuki, and Indian scholar, art historian, and interpreter of Indian culture Ananda K. Coomaraswamy were the writers of choice at that time as a renewed interest in Eastern religion found an audience in Western young people. That first exposure remained as a guide to further study that eventually led me to Korea and Japan in the 1960s and more recently to Taiwan, China, and Mongolia.

The study of Asian art history during my graduate program at Tulane University, in the early '60s, reinforced my interest in Hinduism, Buddhism, Jainism and Taoism. It infused an attitude that remains and has found its way into these three books. My research and study attempts to draw from all sources and to show the central theme relating to transformation, spiritual and physical, as demonstrated by practices of mysticism and alchemy. However, the points of reference, the choice of data and images are mine. When dealing with material that draws from different times and cultures, it is easy to make assumptions based on unintended personal bias or beliefs, and such errors are not easy to discover and correct.

Ultimately, this book, like the other two mentioned above, is about people and the methods they develop to deal with challenging occurrences that influenced their lives. My purpose is not to condemn or endorse any belief; rather, it is to reference certain similarities, differences, and conditions that are the basis for transformation.

A Note About the Illustrations

The book includes four types of illustrations. Information about their sources is found in the About the Illustrations section at the back of the book. Identifying them from the beginning should cause less confusion when attempting to decipher why some illustrations are called one thing and some another.

First, there are drawings that come from various sources. The model(s) I used for each drawing is identified in the *Drawings* subsection of the About the Illustrations section. The pieces depicted were selected to give a representation or visualization of a particular style or form of object. The drawings are not intended to be true copies of the work, but simplifications to allow easier understanding of the object.

Second, there are figures that are to give visual manifestation of a concept. This is not to say the concepts are complicated; instead, the figures are to enhance the readability of the ideas being expressed. The figures are simple liner arrangements in most cases with direct reference to the text. Their source information is in the *Figures* subsection.

Third, there are photographs that are to provide exact images of identified objects. These objects have or had a specific role in particular activities and it seems important to provide that image for the reader as a means of connection. The images are intended to make the text more understandable. Most of these images relate to mystical practices. Source information is in the *Photographs* subsection at the back of the book.

Fourth, there are plates that are bookplates from early publication relating to alchemy. The images come from the Library of Congress or the British Museum and are copied (with permission) from old manuscripts. The original use of the plates as illustrations was not to clarify the message of the text to the uninitiated reader, but to provide symbolic references to the initiated. They are included in this book as representations of a style of imagery that had an important role in alchemy up to the early eighteenth century. Information is in the *Plates* subsection.

> Wisdom is the fruit of communion; ignorance the inevitable portion of those who "keep themselves to themselves," and stand apart, judging, analyzing the things which they have never truly known.[5]

CHAPTER ONE

The Great Mastery

"For there is suffering, but none who suffers"[1]

Mysticism is, in general, a spiritual quest for hidden truth or wisdom, the goal of which is union with the divine or sacred [the transcendental realm]. Forms of mysticism are found in all major world religions, by analogy in the shamanic and other ecstatic practices of non-literate culture, and in secular experience.[2]

The quest for truth has been a mission of humanity for centuries; however, the definition of that objective has changed. Many early people viewed the human plane of existence (the middle ground) as mundane, unreal, and subject to the manipulation of a range of contravening elements. All phenomena were illusions. Life was made difficult and challenging by malevolent entities. It was only in the spirit world that truth and reality existed, and the methods for attaining spiritual oneness differed from culture to culture. Nevertheless, transcendence, the existence above and apart from the material (mundane) world was a commonly acknowledged pursuit.

The search for truth that corresponded with spiritual reality makes a distinction between reason and belief. Where reason as a condition dictated by the mundane world is ineffectual, people substitute emotion and imagination. They sense the divine, and imagine the direct and immediate possession of benevolent spirit beings. They also envision an obliging universe and the necessary human nature that will make possible a human-deity union. People have for centuries promulgated belief systems to facilitate interactions in which the universe and the human soul are considered a part of the supernatural, or at least containing something of the divine essence. The outcome of this unification is inevitably a form of mysticism—the belief in personal communication with the divine through faith, ecstasy, or insight.

Bertrand Russell wrote in *Mysticism and Logic* (1929) that truth might be both annoying and trivial; therefore, in the pursuit of it, kindness and sublimity must be equally ignored.[3] Nonetheless, all peoples, at one time or another, "have fallen in love with the veiled Isis whom they call Truth."[4] People believe that by spiritual discipline they can change their lives and the lives of others within their immediate family or community. That belief often finds endorsement in practices involving the placation of spirits to divert their energy for benevolent purposes.

"Within the bounds of sensing and knowing, we can perceive neither nothing nor everything, but only something," according to Robert Paul.[5] Among Tibetan Buddhists it is believed that a dedicated and devout person will have the capacity to see the "transcendental bodies (Tibetan: *lang-ku*; Sanskrit: *sambhoga-kaya*) of Buddhas and Bodhisattvas, which are the power of light,"[6] and may only exist as a faint idea within the mind. Logic and reason have no relevance in an attitude of ardent belief. When the transcendental bodies become real in what is normally believed to be the "material world" then it is possible to understand that the "reality of the inner and outer world are interchangeable."[7]

This concept divides the universe into two distinct realms, the seen and the unseen, the physical and the metaphysical (or the sacred and the profane). The same divisions continue today, and in a bipartite environment people often subscribe to traditional values that are more relevant than scientific truths because they represent seemingly real solutions to personal problems. The acceptance that something is true or real is the basis for an emotional or spiritual sense of certainty. Sociologically, participation in communal belief practices identifies a person as a member of the community and integral to the group that accepts that system. This attitude is particularly relevant when working within the mystic realm, because the real world that exists beyond the mundane is highly significant. Therefore, attempts are made, in the form of prayer, ritual, trance, and ceremony to gain admittance to the spiritual world and to exercise an influence upon it.

People turn inward to identify an energy source when assistance is needed to deal with supernatural as well as natural issues. It is a question of belief, not science or reason, and people get excited and fanatical when they are presented with facts or conditions that do not fit their prescribed frame of reference. This reality is often demonstrated by conflicts between different sects of the same belief system. Nonetheless, belief in the supernatural allows people to escape their menial, sometimes frightening, and normally difficult lives by allowing them to imagine a better existence in the sanctum sanctorum of the spirit world.

The mystic, like the alchemist, seeks energy that is beyond the power of ordinary humans and outside the common processes of nature. The essence of this power is identified with and inherent in specific applications (trance, prayer, ecstasy, etcetera) and supportive systems of belief. Peoples in all areas of the world recognize the foundational relevance of mysticism and its meaning in society.

Belief in the supernatural has been a part of the human psyche for as long as people have observed the changing cycles of nature, and attaining immortality is a part of a fundamental rejuvenation process. The sun sets and is reborn in the morning just as nature is resurrected with the spring or following a rain. Believe with enough commitment and the imagined is true or real. (Reality is believed to be a form of truth in this instance.) Belief generally refers to the attitude that believes something to be true. It gives reason and understanding to those circumstances that appear to be beyond human control. People believe because they wish to believe and because not believing would create a void and deny hope. Belief in the phenomenal acknowledges a force that addresses basic questions about existence that are unanswerable in other ways.

It is certain mysticism and alchemy are a part of life, and whether there is real power that resides within these practices is irrelevant. That people believe there is power is sufficient. Belief is a significant element in the rationalization of those actions that support or enhance desired results. Deliverance from the frailties of the human body and the search for immortality are laudable objectives, as much as the pursuit of gold or material objects. Such beliefs are natural and need no empirical verification or intellectual corroboration. The alchemist, although often a social curiosity and an assumed delver into magical formulas, is generally acceptable by those persons guided by societal norms.

As an example: mystical practices may include activities related to psychometry. This so-called object reading process is thought to provide impressions about a person through contact with an object associated with that individual. Psychometry has been defined as the "faculty of divining from physical contact or proximity to the qualities of an object or of it."[8] It is probable that matter can be impregnated with psychic energy, and a "reading" may bring visions to the mystic's (psychometrist's) mind that relate to facts, sometimes in the future of the subject. A state of near trance is considered to improve the consistency of psychometric readings.

It would seem that although certain objects or practices can be psychometrically effective, that is, endowed with spiritual or emotional content, it is likely that without mindful co-operation by the human element (belief), no benefit "can be gained through any mechanical or material device."[9] Nevertheless when linked with activities such as rituals, ceremonies, incantations, or symbols, the psychometeric charged object or activity can be very effective in helping to focus the mind and energy on specific outcomes. It is the related power of belief.

Whether it is believed that matter has psychometric properties or that it is possible to attach to a substance certain qualities through conscious concentration, there is a constant interaction between mind and matter. Diverse phenomena in an endorsing society are connected on the assumption that they originate from outside the natural world. Humans reflect the environment in which they live; therefore, they assign the forces they encounter different names and influences. The people are, in that way, constantly investigating and assessing their surroundings. They are at once the same but different with their world, because the energy that activates their physiological and intellectual essence — the soul, spirit, consciousness — and identifies them as who they are, is derived from their universe and modified by their beliefs and practices.

A tendency so universal and so persistent as that of mysticism, which appears among all peoples and influences philosophical thought more or less throughout all centuries, must have some real foundation in human nature.[10] People are people; that is to say that it is human nature to want to understand the circumstances that influence our lives. Closely aligned with this thinking is the equally ubiquitous concept of alchemic transformation. John Maxson Stillman wrote in the 1924 publication *The Story of Alchemy and Early Chemistry* that "the human mind is so constituted that it finds a need to attempt to account for observed phenomena, so that theory and practice are inseparable."[11] He speculates that humans have a natural curiosity about what the "earliest natural philosophers thought about the nature and changes of substances."[12]

The early acknowledgment of the mind as an active element of the human cognitive system is significant. It assumed that the mind is the source of thought, but because of the ambiguity of thought, it does not aid in defining the essence of the mind. It is also assumed that the mind is involved with knowledge and includes consciousness in that function. It is in consciousness that a distinction is made between truth and falsity, between knowledge and belief, hope and fear. This distinction further implies a degree of self-knowledge or self-consciousness. These complex duties support the notion that the mind is capable of planning a course of action with foreknowledge. The mind may seek knowledge but depend on belief to deal with the unknown, to promote truth and hope, and to dissuade falsity and fear.

The mind refers to consciousness as described in *Tantra in Tibet*.[13] The book defines the six consciousnesses as eye, ear, nose, tongue, body, and mental consciousness. "Consciousness is based on two functions: awareness and the storing up (or preservation) of the fruits of experience, which we call memory."[14] This is a consciousness that is non-physical but is capable of being aware of things. Joseph Conrad wrote in *Heart of Darkness* (1967), "The mind of man is capable of anything — because everything is in it, all the past as well as all the future. What was there after all? Joy, fear, sorrow, devotion, valor, rage — who can tell? — but truth — truth stripped of its cloak of time."[15] The mind may assert that the everyday physical reality is illusory and that the commonly perceived world is a figment of our imagination.

Carl Jung (1875–1961), the Swiss psychologist and psychiatrist, addressed the issue of illusion as it relates to alchemy in a different way. He advocated the idea that alchemy had both an esoteric and an exoteric manifestation. He believed that the esoteric or popular aspect of alchemy was centered on the preparation of the Philosophers' Stone — a magical substance capable of changing base metal silver and gold. Exoteric or mystical alchemy regarded the transmutation of metal as "symbolic of the devotional system by which sinful man could be transformed into a perfect and immortal being."[16] The focus of exoteric alchemy was on "a pill or elixir prepared from minerals and metals, which might confer immortality."[17] The interweaving of mystical and alchemic ideas was an inherent part of the intellectual as well as the emotional and psychological processes.

> Movement is the nature of the mind as much as it is the nature of light. All that tries to arrest, to hinder, or to confine the free, infinite movement of the mind, is ignorance — whether is it caused by conceptual thought, desire, or attachments.[18]

Alchemy is often viewed as a specialized form of transformational practice; however, mysticism or the mystical faculty of perceiving transcendental reality is available to all individuals.[19] It is identified with the human quest for direct physical and mental communication with the divine. This pursuit occurs outside ordinary experience and therefore is not restricted by logic or the limitations normally imposed on belief. This fundamental urge of humanity — the search for reality — may have been stronger or more pervasive in early society but it continues today. It was during the initial stages of social development that people interacted with nature in direct ways so obstacles were overcome by physical and mental ability. People in that environment understood that existence was predicated on numerous factors, many of which were beyond their control. This realization carried the seeds of hope and fear, and laid the foundation for belief in omnipresent deities. The divine was present in all things; consequently, there was a need to regulate those phenomenal beings.

Truth and Infinite Good

Mysticism is a process of seeking truth (wisdom) and union with the sacred. It is an integral part of all faith-based systems including shamanism and other ecstatic practices. Although considered different than prophetic religions, mysticism is founded on psychic transformation in which the mystic communicates with a world beyond normal experience. Therefore, the essence of mysticism is its transcendent reference, but society and the specific environment in which it is practiced regulate the circumstances by which it is known and the ways it is expressed.

There is within the human psyche a basic need for truth, the absolute truth, as well as the infinite good. The attainment of material objects does not give the fullness of truth or the perfection of serenity that completely satisfies human desires and aspirations. There is for most people a motivation for more truth — wisdom or meaning — and perfection than can be acquired through tangible (material) things. The search for truth as well as unification with the divine confirms the essential nature of mysticism. The ability to perceive transcendental reality, as confirmed by the mystic experience, may be available to everyone, but few persons make use of this opportunity.

Pursuant to the search for truth and wisdom, Buddhism distinguishes three kinds of wisdom (*prajna*): "wisdom as language, wisdom as insight, and wisdom as true appearance. According to this conception, language provides the means by which insight arises, and insight perceives true appearance."[20] Chen-k'o (1543–1603) a Chinese monk recognized for his knowledge of Taoism, agreed with this assessment. He illuminates his statement by explaining, "The *prajna* [wisdom] of true appearance is the mind possessed by all beings. The *prajna* of insight is the light of the mind."[21] The monk added, "Once someone awakens [is enlightened], the light of the mind shines forth. And anything composed of words and phrases, regardless of its length, if it contains the wisdom of the ancients and dispels the darkness of ignorance, is called the *prajna* of language."[22]

It can be said that people of most cultures are guided by spiritual and religious beliefs and practices that have evolved from earlier times. Such traditions often instill everything with a spirit (a form of animism). The mystic believes that the universe exists on, above, and below ground, and that it has the ability (power) to communicate with the spirits on all three levels. This belief configuration (trinity) is consistent with most organized religions. (For example: the Father, Son, and Holy Ghost symbolize this arrangement in Christianity.) In Christian belief, specifically Catholicism, the third person of the Trinity, the Holy Ghost (or Holy Spirit), is associated with healing, prophecy, the expelling of demons, and speaking in tongues. The Council of Constantinople gave special attention to the Holy Spirit in 381 C.E. attempting to define the exact nature of this spiritual (supernatural) element of the Trinity.

Humans, in this tri-parted arrangement (up, down, and middle), exist on the surface (middle world) plane while heaven and hell — salvation and damnation — constitute the upper and lower worlds respectively. The spiritual life of many people appears to center on beliefs and practices emanating from this divisional arrangement that involves supernatural forces. A balance has to be achieved and harmony maintained between the ethereal and material worlds for people to survive. This equilibrium is sought through ceremonies and related activities that include various forms of mysticism.

Such fundamental transcendental practice (the search for the higher truth) extends beyond mundane experience and allows emotional interpretation to moderate an imperfect reality. The acceptability of this practice on both the physical and mental levels is continually modified to accommodate group tradition and practice. A sympathetic understanding such as found in the Christian congregation or Buddhist *sangha* must exist between the elements for the transformational process to be effective. (A *sangha* refers to a community of practitioners including monks, nuns, and lay people. It is one of the three objects of refuge in Buddhism.[23])

The truths of this world (physical) are believed understandable through communication with other worlds (mystical). It is this concept that stimulated the notion that the real world exists beyond the mundane. This belief is highly significant in achieving and maintaining emotional and spiritual balance; therefore, attempts are made, in the form of the trance, prayer, and other forms of devotion, to gain access to the spiritual world and influence it.[24] Mystics work to maintain harmony among the powers in the universe. The goal of the mystic is to acquire the power inherent in the unseen dimension of reality and mediate it for a practical benefit.[25]

A mystic or magician must make others (believers and when possible non-believers) see what he sees or believe what he believes (or says he believes) to communicate truth, and magical or mystical demonstrations help viewers to see reality reflexively, that is, the way it is intended to be seen. As an example, shamanic practice interprets the natural and supernatural influences people encounter as a form of truth that is indispensable to the environment in which they live. That truth may explain that all objects have an existence that extends beyond human knowledge. It may make clear that objects great or small possess universal importance no matter how limited that universe might be. The shaman may sing, dance, and appear to fly though the air to demonstrate the validity of the truth being proffered. Mystic intervention not only seeks the message, it provides the means for transmitting that message.

Certain styles or forms of Buddhism and mysticism promote the belief that the universe consists of seen and unseen dimensions, that it is animated by spirit forces, and that those spirits cause suffering as the result of disharmony or negative interactions between humans and their social and natural worlds. Ritualized activities are performed to promote harmony by changing the participant's sense of space and time, reality and fantasy, and in some instances life and death. There is a linking of the natural and supernatural worlds during ritual acts. This connection occurs in ways that establish empathy between the two spheres, and for the believers, reality and belief are joined. This transformation is in essence an activity performed by the mystic.

Reality as a Concept

> Like the philosopher's stone, the Great Symbol purges from the mind the doss of Ignorance (*Avidyā*); and the human is transmuted into the divine by the spiritual alchemy of *yoga*.[26]

The sky, humans, sticks and stones, the wind as well as human-made artifacts existing in the universe of matter, and phenomena are assigned their own form of causal force or energy. Natural objects — plants or animals — have an identity that exists externally (outside their physical structure), and that reality — the natural and spiritual life — represents a universal meaning for a particular culture.[27] Therefore, the notion of reality must be gauged against the anthropocentric attitude that perceives it.

The activities of the mystic and alchemist are associated with the culture in which he lives. Beliefs, like ideas and actions, are determined to be real when they satisfy and nourish the interests and needs of a specific person or people. Some individuals require only a limited (external) form of spiritual assistance to gain domination over worldly circumstances. Advancements of this nature might be a successful hunt (domination of animals, objects, or events), a safe voyage (domination of the elements), or a victorious clash with an enemy (domination of others). Other acts of domination may be substituted for these activities depending on the time and place. These manifestations of power are found in all cultures and during all ages. Domination (power) reinforces the ego and enforces a sense of personal or group security and superiority.

The assertion of domination (power) often required the mystic's spirit to search the cosmos for assistance. This extraterrestrial journey may not be required when the culture has no confirming belief whereas traveling into the outer world to confront a malevolent ancestor or angry deity is a routine requirement in other cultures. Similarly, the host community might require the mystic to search the dark regions of the earth to retrieve a lost soul from the land of the dead — the inner world. The mystic's energies are outwardly oriented and directed toward the community, so the visionary journey is a means of communication between the natural and supernatural settings. The mystic as well as the endorsing participants are integral elements of this mystic travel.

Not all belief systems rely on the same type of spiritual communication. Western religious convictions tend to request assistance by "sending a message through an intermediary." (Modes of western mysticism are exceptions to this generality.) Nevertheless, in eastern practices, such as mysticism, shamanism, and forms of Buddhism, the practitioner seeks direct contact with the divine: it is "a vertical relationship." The same can be said of Sufi (practitioners of Sufism). They aspire to achieve a state in which they are in direct communion with God. Sufi believe that "ultimately the individual human personality passes away and the Sufi feels his soul is absorbed into God."[28] The idea of being absorbed or joined physically with God has its roots in many spiritual practices. An example of personalized absorption relates to the *Virasaivas* or *Lingâyats* (lingam-bearers) of the Hindu tradition in southwestern India. The *Lingâyat* is absorbed into the lingam (phallus or cosmic pillar); as a result, his body (the male practitioner) is not cremated but interred in a way similar to ascetics of other groups.[29]

The mystic might call upon mystical beings to normalize the real world by joining the sacred with the profane in ways that are governed by unnatural circumstances. The mystic in this role is a narrator of myths and tradition during a mystical journey (ecstatic episode) that takes the participants to find truth. The mystic and the participants often experience phenomena beyond their imagination and outside their time and place. This type of miraculous experience helps the believer to see reality reflexively, in much the same way the mystic sees it. This experience presents itself as authoritative and real, no matter how much it is in variance with natural law or ordinary experience.

Mystics often seek physical and mental balance through reconciliation (balance or harmony) to accommodate the connections between opposites. The balance between being and non-being or existence and non-existence characterizes this approach. Consistent with this thinking, there is a different view of life and death (non-life). Western cultures hold firmly to traditional belief based on the perception of opposites such as good and evil, right and wrong, black and white. Life and death are definable opposites. Death is the absence of life; therefore, the two (life and death) cannot exist simultaneously. The opposing elements are by necessity given an equal measure of importance in establishing and maintaining emotional or logical stability. This idea depends on the acknowledgment of a beginning (birth) and an end (death), a straight line of existence connecting the two points. This concept does not apply in Eastern thinking that follows a cyclical approach to existence. There is no beginning so there can be no end. The cycle of renewal is continual until the human consciousness is released.

The activities associated with death (or the end of one cycle before the start of another) are of great significance in most cultures. All people have ways for dealing with this inevitability. There is for some peoples a particular concern that the consciousness of the deceased may wander in the time between death of the mortal body and rebirth. ("Buddhist philosophy teaches that when you change your body [die], your body's consciousness continues."[30]) "[L]ife and death are in the mind and nowhere else."[31] (Tibetan Buddhists call this time *Bardo*, an intermediate state of existence — a transition between death and enlightenment or rebirth into one of the six worlds of transmigration.)

The protective process of physical death and consciousness trans-positioning often requires the services of a mystic. This preparatory process can be accomplished in different ways depending of the ability of the mystic and the requirements of the deceased. One method requires the co-operation of the dying person. For the well disciplined individual "[t]he most difficult but effective way of all is to become proficient in the Yoga of Consciousness Transference, which will enable the consciousness [spirit or soul] to depart from the body just prior to [physical] death."[32] This procedure allows the dying man or woman to select the person to whom the consciousness will be transferred.

Note: There is no concept of spirit or soul — no soul substance — in most forms of Buddhism. There is instead the notion of consciousness. It is the consciousness that is transferred at the time of reincarnation. This distinction, although it may be semantics, redefines the self.

Life and death can be viewed as two sides of the same reality. The sameness of this state of being is exemplified by the Tibetan Buddhists' belief in reincarnation (transmigration or metempsychosis). This conviction endorses the notion of rebirth of the individual consciousness in one or more successive existences. The Egyptians espoused a similar attitude of transcendent faith that sanctioned a spiritual reality for the dead relinquishing earthly presence for a sustained existence in a state of perpetual ecstasy. Buddhism, however, recognizes no garden of delights at the end of their quest for nirvâna. The status to achieve is enlightenment and a release from cyclical renewal. A concept of paradise is not shared by all cultures despite the ever-present adoration of immortality. Some people view the first stop after death as simply an intermediate resting place for righteous souls awaiting resurrection. Death is an imperfect state of being for all people, regardless of the ultimate outcome; it is suspension between two worlds.

> [A]lthough the body dies, the mind — since it is not destructible, like physical matter — continues on and eventually comes into a new body, within your mother's womb as you are to be born as a human [Khen Rinpoche Geshe Lobsang Tharchin].[33]

A life and death phenomenon peculiar to "Tibet and Mongolia is the prevalence of *Tulkus*—the recognized incarnations of departed dignitaries."[34] Tibetans contend that a young child "can be recognized as the incarnation of a particular individual."[35] They believe that a spiritually advanced lama is capable of choosing the conditions of his next incarnation including where he will be reborn. Although the specific child is not indicated, the prediction is sufficiently accurate to allow discovery of his incarnation. The directed reincarnation is not the same as *samsâra*, the cycle of rebirth — the wheel of existence, "which arises out of ignorance and is marked by suffering."[36] Reincarnation is controlled transformation.

An Imperfect Reality

The human species lives in a profane state that is made understandable by a paradigmatic, mythically sacred setting. It is an environment where reality is contextually defined, and where humans may alter or circumvent the circumstances that blocked the way when achieving a particular goal became too difficult. Often the process of circumvention includes determining that the connection between the objective and accomplishment of that objective is not governed by reality but by the supernatural. Consequently, different beliefs and contraventions are devised to deal with challenging situations, and to address the inconsistencies of life.

Life forces are manipulated by power, and the world is full of power. Power often takes the persona of a deity or spirit, and that kind of power is difficult to control because it has a will of its own.[37] The wish to control spirits and the actions they represent stimulated the development of magic; however, the concept of spirit can be defined in different ways. It is often viewed as being interchangeable with soul. The words reflect the principle of life as related to breath and air (ether), which in turn was associated the idea of life. The cessation of breath is regarded as the loss of spirit or soul and an indication of death.

Traditional beliefs often endorse the notion that an abundance of spirits inhabits the world, and their presence is reflected in every aspect of life. The spirits are thought to dwell in the trees, sky, and rain, as well as in most animate and inanimate objects with which the people interacted directly or indirectly. This mystically defined environment is the source of positive and negative occurrences. It promotes life but brings physical death for humans, animals, and nature. Every object, action, or person is subject to the authority of paranormal forces. Everything possessed a form of associated power that emanated from the supernatural. It is in this realm that "[t]he things of the world have the function of stabilizing human life."[38] They address the metaphysical as well as the physical questions about the relationship of the people and the spirits that hold an essential position in the concept of individual and group identity.

The belief that human consciousness (soul or spirit) is quasi-physical and can exist outside the mortal body, can be transferred from one mortal body to another, and persists after physical death by reincarnation is found in many cultures. Such thinking is a part of the process of spiritual consolidation in which beliefs and deities are unified and incorporated into culturally defined forms (rituals, symbols, and practices) that are methodical. This consolidation makes the belief system stable and more easily maintained. It is can be formalized, in that form, with a hierarchical structure, systematic rituals, and predictable practices. These activities are the foundation blocks of organized religion.

There are, in the patterns of human existence, many elements subsumed under the notion of culture that evade direct understanding, including magic and mysticism. Such beliefs endorsed by the Tibetan Buddhists are exemplified by the shrine called *U Khang*, and described by Alexandra David-Neel in *My Journey to Lhasa* (1986 [1927]). The name of the shrine means House of the Vital Breath. It is believed that the breath of "every being who dies on the earth is carried to it."[39] There are, according to David-Neel, numerous stories told about the struggles of the "tortured 'breath' [deposited in the shrine] against the ferocious beings of another world."[40]

Such stories reinforce and give credibility to popular beliefs. Tibetan Buddhists believe that careful observance of everyday activities strengthens the possibility of advancement by reincarnation to a "higher position in the life after death." The "doctrine of metempsychosis [reincarnation] and karma and the potency of acquiring merit by good deeds enter into the ordinary habits and speech of the people."[41] John Blofeld reinforces this notion in his book *The Tantric Mysticism of Tibet: A Practical Guide* (1974): "Buddhism is perhaps the one widespread religion that, in theory at least, is wholly mystical, for it recommends to all its followers the practice of mind control and the attainment of intuitive wisdom."[42]

The notion of intuitive wisdom touches on the idea of consciousness, and "the experience of consciousness is entirely subjective."[43] Nevertheless, the physiological and emotional needs of people generally exceed the limits of their understanding of the spiritual and material worlds. The stimulants of belief, hope, and anxiety are transcendental methods for finding acceptable solutions for challenging situations in an adverse environment. (These elements include the possibility of elevating expectations without generating a corresponding response.) Awareness of the possibilities inherent in belief must find its way into the psyches of people through their sensibility and receptivity. The most effective aid for transmission of these values often includes a visual or physical signs, symbols, or actions. This level of help normally extends beyond commonplace experience and provides opportunities for faith (belief) to enhance an imperfect reality. The acceptability of this attitude on both the physical and mental levels is continually modified by group tradition, myth, and experience.

Mysticism, in contrast with formalized belief practices, is a practical process for dealing with impractical situations in a constantly changing world. It is not based on comprehensive knowledge of the infinite, but as a direct and immediate insight into the finite. It can be considered by the principles that apply to the values associated with the transcendental world of belief and tradition. Such practices interpret the natural and supernatural influences encountered as a form of truth that is indispensable to the environment in which humanity exists. Because all natural objects have an existence that extends beyond human knowledge, they possess universal importance no matter how small that universe is.

The things of daily existence, tangible or intangible, are a blending of elements that can be altered, refined, or rejected. This flexibility allows people to develop new attitudes about existence and to give substance to basic feelings once they have transferred their emotional insecurity to the supernatural.[44] Belief is often the deciding factor in determining the balance between thought and action. There is in most circumstances no clear separation of the physical and the mental, or the mental and the emotional.[45] An extra-human force such as mysticism is often necessary to ally regressive thinking, that is, returning to a state of fear and emotional atrophy, and to explain the unknown elements that influence human survival both physically and emotionally.

Transformation and Belief

> Belief in transformation was associated with the practice of journeying into the land of the spirits. That transitory act did not presume that the person became a spirit/deity, but that they passed beyond the mirror (the barrier between worlds) and entered the space occupied by spirits.[46]

Mystic insight often caused Taoist adapts to question those individuals who sought longevity and immortality through physiological practices. The mystic way of thinking transcends the ordinary distinctions between mundane elements to become one with the energy that manifested itself in a powerful and beneficial influence on the surroundings. It is likely that physical immortality was a Taoist goal before the adoption of Taoist mysticism, because the distinction between this vital energy and spirituality (consciousness) is not clearly defined. Nonetheless, it was the practice for those following the mystic path to choose from among different methods for restoring the "pure energies possessed at birth." The objective of this process was to transform the adept's body into pure *yang* energy, and allow him (most often a male but not always) to become an immortal (*hsien*) if he wished.[47]

Life and death for most early Chinese were manifest in the eternal transformation from Non-Being to Being and back to Non-Being, the underlying primordial unity was never lost.[48] It was the physical transformation, which confirmed death as the ultimate transitional state of being. This occurrence was regarded of great significance in most early Chinese societies, and mystics (shamans, monks, or oracles) had a primary role in the ritual-related activities associated with the transition. However, because there was no clear boundary between life and death, many early peoples viewed death as simply a condition of non-life. Among populations that recognized death as a conclusive physical condition, the cessation of life was seen as a release from one cycle of existence and the beginning of another.[49]

This concept of transformation has a common and often powerful role in established belief systems. Alchemy as a method of spiritual purification and transformation therefore had a prominent role in the mystical traditions of both East and West. The basis for the idea of transformation is found in every aspect of nature — young to old, day to night, life to death. It is exemplified in the traditional belief that in certain circumstances humans can change (transformed) their body to become an animal or bird. This belief is very old and is found nearly worldwide.[50] Gods, sorcerers, magicians, shamans, and legendary heroes are said to have this shape-changing power by virtue of magical knowledge or special quality. The Greek god Zeus transformed himself into a swan, a bull, a ram, a serpent, a dove, and eagle, and a shower of gold according to legend.

Tibetan Buddhism maintains that transformation and the creative power of the mind establish a conscious continuity between consecutive lives. Therefore, "according to the law of Karma (Pali: *Kamma*) none of our actions and thoughts is lost. Each of them leaves its imprint on our character, and the total of one life creates the basis for the next."[51] (The *Law of Karma* refers to an ancient Indian (Hindu) law of cause and effect. It is a law that is inviolable — not open to change. This law defines "the inequities that are observed among creatures."[52] *Karma* as it relates to Buddhism "becomes the moral law of the universe by which men reap good for good, or evil for evil. The idea is linked with that of rebirth."[53])

Consistent with the belief in physical transformation, it was thought that injuries inflicted upon a shape-changing being would appear on the person once that individual returned to his original form. Stories tell of persons being struck by sword, spear, or shot, and finding another human with a similar wound. The idea of this type of transformation met the need of explaining observed or imagined phenomena. It is an easy transition from transformation of human form to transformation of material. The Egyptians used their skills to make alloys and dyes, as well as to embalm the dead, thus exemplifying this transitory concept. They transformed materials and arranged the dead for an afterlife. Both of these processes were transformational.

Much of what is known about early alchemical practice in China comes from the period of the Warring States (the fifth to the third century before the current era). That practice was associated with Taoism, a system of metaphysics and ethics, believed to have been the founded by Lao-tzu (Laozi) in the sixth century B.C.E. in which mysticism is a fundamental element. However, the Chinese search for immortality (or as proposed, enhancement "of spiritual qualities on a level sufficient to allow a transcendence of human morality"[54]) appears to go back to the eighth century before the current era. Belief in the possibility of obtaining unending existence either in body or spirit with the use of mind enhancing substances (drugs) came about in the fourth century B.C.E.

The Chinese mystic envisioned the universe as being constantly reshaped and transformed out of primordial chaos, and where the cycle of life and death was endless. The parts of the universe were joined as with a rhythmic pulsation in which everything was subject to change; nothing was static. Change was systematic due to its consistency in this arrangement. The search for the unchanging — the permanent — the Tao — led the mystic to seek a magical drug (elixir of life) referred to as "drinkable gold" that prolonged life. These practitioners in the cult of Spirits were called *wu* in ancient China. (The magician was *hua-*

jen.) They are characterized "as experts in exorcism, prophecy, fortune-telling, rain-making and interpretation of dreams."[55] Alchemists, East and West, sought the means for transforming life into the divine.

"The general term used for alchemy in Chinese literature is '*lien tan.*' Its literal meaning is, the pill, or drug, or transmutation."[56] The oldest known Chinese alchemical writing is the "'*Chou-i ts'an t'ung ch'i*' or '*Commentary on the I Ching.*'"[57] The most famous Chinese alchemical book, however, is the *Tan chin yao chüeh* (*Great Secrets of Alchemy*).[58] This book was probably written by Sun Ssu-miao during the middle years of the 6th century of the current era. It expounds on the process for creating elixirs made of mercury, sulfur, and the salts of mercury and arsenic to attain immortality. This treatise also includes cures for certain diseases and instructions on how to make precious stones.[59]

Tantric Buddhism as developed within Buddhist practices in India and neighboring countries, particularly Tibet where the style is known as *Vajrayâna* (also called *Mantrayâna* or Mantra Vehicle) endorsed a form of alchemy. This type of Buddhism was a transition from "speculative thought to the enactment of Buddhist ideas in individual life."[60] Tantric practitioners, therefore, embrace a process of internal alchemy to bring body functions under the control of the human will. "The alchemy expounded in the tantric texts, like its counterpart in the writings of the Western alchemists, is replete with esoteric passages and little can be made of their jargon."[61]

The Search for Immortality

The quest for immortality is not a uniquely mystic or alchemic activity. John Oman wrote in *The Natural & the Supernatural* (1931), that humans won three victories over the fluctuation of experience with the distinction of sacred and profane. He states that the first victory is that "death is not an absolute end, but a part of man continues to exist; the second, that his conduct is not measured by the immediate situation, but has a relation to a wider society of the living and the dead."[62] Oman believes that the third victory is the recognition of an "invisible reality, which, though of uncertain and various manifestations, is more continuous and more reliable than mere material events, and is akin to man himself and responsive to his purposes, whereby purposes, otherwise impossible, may be realized."[63]

Regardless of the supposed victories won or the theories proposed all major belief systems have personified death as a way of calling attention to his (usually a male) presence. The Grim Reaper is acknowledged in some countries as the purveyor of the ultimate transitional state of being. Yama is the god of death in ancient Indian literature. He is the judge of the dead in Tibetan, Chinese, and Japanese Buddhism (**see drawing 1.a**). "An Assyrian text of about 650 B.C.E. actually describes the dread enemy in an account of the underworld, and pictures a grim figure with the hands of a man and the feet of serpents."[64] Some cultures view death as the expression of life, and that continuity cannot exist without interruption, therefore there is no need to cling to one status (life) and fear the other (death). Nevertheless, most humans agree that life, despite its difficulties, is good whereas death, despite its apparent peace, is not a desirable alternative for life.

It is an observable phenomenon that death follows life and out of death, life is created. The cessation of life, among cultures that recognize death as a conclusive physical condition, is a release from one cycle of existence and the beginning of another. Death for other peoples is an opportunity for renewed life through the transfer of guilt, sin, and other social transgressions, a concept reflecting the mingling of the material and spiritual worlds.⁶⁵ It is, for some persons, part of the life cycle that allows them to alter their status among the living, whereas for others, it is an opportunity to become one with their deities.

Although change (transformation) is a necessary part of the human experience, it is often unpredictable and seldom regulated by logic or reason. The author Alice Beck Kehoe observed that early anthropologists attempted to identify laws of human behavior that were as qualified as the laws of physics and chemistry,⁶⁶ but belief as a ubiquitous characteristic of human behavior defies empirical classification. However, it is embodied in the so-called Law of Progress, assuming progress can be found in various forms. For example, "Greek philosophers before Plato and Aristotle, particularly the Sicilian Empedocles (492–432 B.C.E.), had theories about the nature of matter, the elements of which it was composed, and how one could change into another."⁶⁷ The Law of Progress endorsed the notion that "things change." Alchemy and mysticism attempted to regulate or control the nature of that change.

This concept of transformation as the essence of Western alchemy appears to have come from Egypt. History tells us that Alexander the Great of Macedon conquered the Persian Empire in 334 B.C.E., and although he died eleven years later in 323 B.C.E., the Macedonians remained in control of large areas of the Middle East. This period, called the Hellenistic Age, in the eastern Mediterranean and Middle East continued from 323 B.C.E. to 30 B.C.E. It ended with the conquest of Egypt by Rome. There was a mingling of Western (Greek) and Asian elements during three hundred years of the Hellenistic Age including an exchange of information about alchemy.

Ptolemy Soter, one of Alexander's generals, established a kingdom in Egypt in 323 B.C.E. and founded the Ptolemaic dynasty. The city of Alexandria was the capital. Ptolemy and his son, Ptolemy II Philadelphus, built a temple to the Muses in Alexandria about 280 B.C.E. Today the temple-museum-library might be called a university because the greatest library of ancient times was a part of the temple. It was in this setting that "Egyptian mastery of applied chemistry met and fused with Greek theory."⁶⁸ It was here that alchemy gained a scholarly presence. The temple-museum-library was destroyed in 272 C.E. in a civil war instigated by the Roman emperor Aurelian. The education and research functions of the institution continued into the current era, but the trove of written documents was destroyed.

The Greeks were impressed with the chemical knowledge of the Egyptians, although

Drawing 1.a: Yama, god of death, originated in Indian mythology. He is represented in the Vedas and early myths as a king of departed ancestors, but he later becomes the just judge (*Dharmarâja*) who passed judgment on the good and evil of the dead. Yama moved into Buddhist mythology in Tibet, China, and Japan where he is viewed as the guardian of the land of the dead. Yama is often represented in Tibetan Buddhist imagery to call attention to the impermanence of existence and the ultimate fate of all beings. The escape from the cycle of life and death is enlightenment by following the Four Noble Truths.

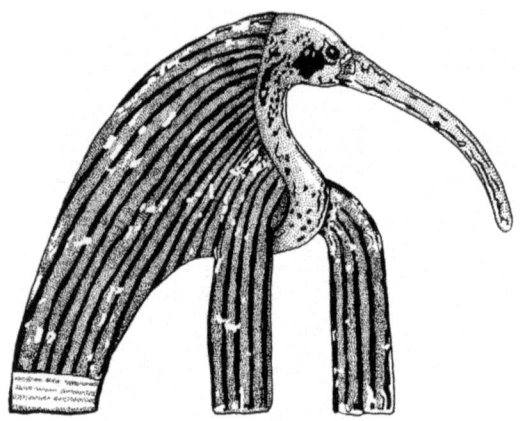

Drawing 1.b: Thoth (Egyptian *Djhuty* also written *Djhowtey*), god of wisdom and god of the moon. Thoth has many guises but is usually represented as a man with the head of an ibis (as shown). He was also identified as a baboon. "He is credited with inventing writing, the calendar, science, music, magic and arts, medicine, math and astronomy." J. Forty, *Mythology: A Visual Encyclopedia*, p. 117. He is associated with alchemy because of his knowledge and skills. He is identified with the Greek god Hermes. The Greeks called him Hermes, the thrice great (Hermes Trismegistos). Important writing on alchemy, medicine, and astronomy are attributed to him.

much of that knowledge was closely related to preserving the dead and related religious rituals. The Egyptians believed that Thoth, the god of wisdom (**see drawing 1.b**), was the source of all chemical knowledge; consequently, the Greeks identified Thoth with the God, Hermes (son of Zeus and Maia and associated with Mercury), and integrated much of the information into mystical and alchemic practice.

The Egyptian ibis headed god, Thoth, is credited with being the founder of alchemic art in the Western world. He was patron of all the arts and renowned for his wisdom and skill. Hermetic writing (also called *Hermetica*) is ascribed to him as the god of leaning and writing. These works of revelation on theology and philosophy (astrological philosophy first noted in 150 B.C.E.), as well as the occult greatly impressed the Greeks. They identified Thoth with their god Hermes and called him *"Hermes Trismegistus"* (Hermes the Thrice Greatest). The surviving documents ascribed to him are the *Emerald Tablet (Tabula Smaragdina)*, the *Asclepian Dialogues*, and the *Divine Pymander*.

The earliest works attributed to *Hermes Trismegistus* were primarily on astrology. Treatises on medicine, alchemy (the *Emerald Table*, a favorite source for medieval alchemists), and magic were added later. The basic concept of astrology as defined by *Hermes Trismegistus* was that the "cosmos constituted a unity and that all parts of it were interdependent."[69] This idea of the unity of parts is fundamental to the occult sciences. The alchemic thesis also calls upon the laws of sympathy and antipathy by which the parts of the universe are related. Because these affinities do not exist in tangible form and cannot be confirmed by normal scientific methods, validation is sought from divine revelation. Hence, the objective of *Hermetism* is the "deification or rebirth of man through the knowledge of the one transcendent God, the world, and men."[70] It is a concept based on the unity of parts.

Unity of Purpose

There was little mysticism in the first schools of Greek philosophy, but it had a major place in the thinking of Plato (428 or 427–348 or 347 B.C.E.). It is well represented in "his theory of the world of ideas, of the origin of the world soul and the human soul, in his doctrine of recollection and intuition."[71] Plato's concepts parallel those found in the Hindu religion where the world of Brahman equates to the Universal Soul. It is through the migration of the soul that humankind is drawn into the circle of animals and plants.[72]

The Greek philosopher and scientist Aristotle (384–322 B.C.E.) is best known for his writing on metaphysics, however, he also investigated alchemic practices. He wrote extensively on matter and form, substance and essence, change and generation, actuality and potentiality.[73] According to Aristotle, "an element is an irreducible constituent of material things, actually or potentially present in them and into which they can be divided."[74] He believed that all bodies were "composed of these elements in different proportions and combinations" and that to "change the proportions and combination of these elements in a body would be to make a different body."[75] This transformational process was infused with the philosophical theories of the Greeks including the "element and atom ideas of the nature-philosophers and of Plato and of Aristotle,"[76] as well as the religious views of the Neoplatonists.

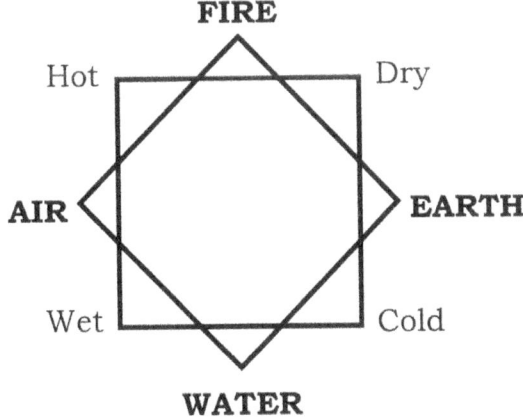

Figure 1.1: The four elements and four related conditions theory was advocated by Aristotle 300 years before the current era. The concept he proposed was based on the work of Plato as described in his writing titled Timasus. Aristotle contended all bodies were made of the same four elements in different proportions. He believed that since elements combine to form composite substances it should be possible to alter any substance by increasing and decreasing the amount of one or more of the four elements. This concept was to reinforce alchemic belief for nearly two thousand years.

Aristotle theorized there are "four elementary qualities to matter — hot, moist, cold and dry; and four elements: fire, water, air, and earth"[77] [see figure 1.1]. These elemental properties were identified as principles and not "actual flames or drops of water."[78] They were composed of defining qualities. "The idea of four elements, fire, air, water and earth, as the basis of matter was ... already in place in Plato's *Timaeus* (written c. 360 B.C.E.), which has a claim to be the first treatise on theoretical chemistry and was the only dialogue of Plato's which was known in Europe before the late twelfth century."[79]

It is in this elemental arrangement that woman is identified as cold and moist and associated with the moon, while man is considered hot and dry and allied with the sun. (The idea that female qualities relate to the moon — silver — and male traits are aligned with the sun — gold — is found in various cultures.) The androgynous being is believed to contain all four qualities at once.[80] Consequently, the androgynous figure was given a special place in many cultures.

The androgynous being is complete and is associated with the creation of the first people. Versions of this myth are found in Tahiti, Greece, China, Egypt, Japan, India, and parts of Africa. The Buddha was conceived when his mother had a dream of a white elephant, and Jesus Christ was born of the Virgin Mary. The Greek gods were able to change from one sex to another or to maintain the characteristics of both sexes at the same time. The Inuit, Arctic peoples of Canada and Greenland, identified shamanism as a third gender — neither male nor female but having both masculine and feminine traits (androgynous). The androgynous being personified the duel elements — the two halves of the whole — necessary to create life.

Johannes Fabricius commented on the four elements. He wrote in *Alchemy: The Medieval Alchemists and Their Royal Art* (1976), the "alchemical idea that the variety of things depends on the proportions in which the four elements are present in them may be illustrated by the process of transmutation undergone by a piece of green wood when heated." Fabricius explains, "Drops of water form at the cut end of the wood, therefore wood contains water; steam and vapor are given off, therefore wood contains air; the wood burns, therefore it contains fire; and an ash is left, therefore wood contains earth."[81]

A further example of the alchemist's belief in the process of metallic transmutation is based on the four elements concept as it relates to the sulfur-mercury theory. This theory is composed of the opposite or contrasting elements fire and water in a different form. Fire is sulfur with hot and dry qualities, and water is represented by mercury containing cold and moist qualities. Sulfur exemplified combustibility or the spirit of fire, and mercury is the fusibility or the mineral spirit of metals.

According to this theory, when sulfur and mercury are combined in different proportions and different degrees of purity, various metals and minerals are formed. When the two ingredients are perfectly pure, and combined in correct portions, the outcome is the production of the perfect metal — gold. However, when the sulfur or mercury is impure or in errant proportions the results may be silver, lead, tin, or copper.[82] Alchemists believe any type of substance can be transformed into any other type by simply changing the elemental conditions through burning, calcinations, solution, evaporation, distillation, sublimation, and crystallization.[83] This approach also reflects the idea of the *yin* and *yang*. (Yin is like a rock and yang is like water or air, rock is heavy and hard and air is soft and energetic.) "[T]hat anything can be described in terms of only two basic elements is beautiful in its simplicity."[84]

Alchemists seek a "grand mastery" of elements that is "universal." They want to transform all metals into gold and heal all diseases. The true alchemists experiment with the transmutation of metals, not for gain, but to add material proofs "in the interests of science."[85] Other practitioners pursue a more constrained approach that focuses on a special metal and cures for only one disease. Unity, order, and harmony as well as belief are necessary aspects of both ways of thinking. The foundation of alchemy is the joining of theory and practice, knowledge and belief in ways that promote mindfulness and a sense of achievement.

Tibetan astrological and medical practices follow a scheme based on five elements — wood, fire, earth, metal, and water.[86] (The five elements concept reflects Taoist logic, that is, the natural law determined by the yin and yang division of the universe. Taoists follow the art of *wu wei* (non-action), which may be translated "let nature take its course." Tibetans believe that "all visible objects are composed of these five elements. Even the wind contains five elements."[87] The elements reportedly constituted the foundational components of the world. It is therefore possible to consider Tibetan medical practice as an alchemic process that transforms the physical condition of patients from sickness to health by adjusting the elements, as physiological energy, to achieve a harmonious balance.

Contrary to the five element concept noted above, Tenzin Gyatso (the Fourteenth Dalai Lama) wrote in *The Universe in a Single Atom* (2005), that "early Buddhist theory of atoms, which has not undergone any major revision, proposes that matter is constituted by a collection of eight so-called atomic substances: earth, water, fire, and air,"[88] the four elements, and "form, smell, taste, and tactility"[89] the four derivative substances. This thinking is probably derived from early (two centuries before the current era) Indian schools of thought. The Dalai Lama explains that the "earth element sustains, water coheres, fire enhances and air enables movement."[90] Based on this Buddhist assessment an atom is considered the smallest part of matter and a composite of these eight substances.

There is a close affinity between the fundamental natures of certain materials (elements) according to alchemic theory. The "changes between elements is easier when they share a common characteristic; as in the case of fire and air which are both hot, and air and water, which are both moist."[91] There is a balancing between materials based on their characteristics that allow easier transfer from one alchemic state to another. Cold water treated with heat is transformed (transmuted) into hot air (vapor). In contrast, hot air when cooled produces water (condensate). Air is moist because it draws vapor (called exhalation) from the earth that is hot and dry. However, as Aristotle explains,[92] there are some elemental "manifestations" which are opposites and cannot be transmuted directly into another. A dead thing, as an example, cannot be restored directly into a living thing. The dead thing must first return to matter (decompose) before it can be changed into its opposite. The logic of this process is quite basic.

The most organized attempt at a philosophical system of a mystical nature in the western world came with the Neoplatonic School of Alexandria, especially in the "Enneads" of Plotinus (205–270 C.E.), a collection of writing arranged by Porphyry. (Neoplatonism was the last school of Greek philosophy.) Plotinus viewed mysticism and the occult from a philosophical perspective instead of a practical one. His system is therefore a combination of different philosophies based on mysticism, and organized as an emanative and pantheistic explanation for everything — except the absolutely Good.[93]

The mystical nature of alchemic theory and practice is, in general, outside the realm of most people. Nevertheless, the concepts of magic and superstition held an important role in many societies. Magic is a label that is often used to describe activities or practices in the mundane world for which no word or its conceptual equivalent existed. Superstition and magic fill the void perpetuated by lack of knowledge and fear. Consequently, various phenomena are linked on the assumption that they fulfill personal, social, and spiritual needs. This arrangement constitutes a unity of parts — a balanced blending of need and response. This notion of magic is also defined in relation to what it is not — science or religion. Although superstition is a personal part of every individual, the distinction of what magic is not is important in determining its role in society.

The theories and practices of mysticism and alchemy maintain the nature of the developing culture, nevertheless, there is a ubiquitous nature to the resulting processes. For instance, Greek alchemy in theory resembled the practices of China. They shared similar characteristics; however, a major difference is that the Greek objectives included (some say focused on) gold making, whereas the Chinese alchemists generally regarded the transformation of base metals into gold or silver of secondary importance. The Chinese gave greater attention to physical transformation, the curing of ailments and the quest for immortality — the elixir of life.

The Great Transformer

Humans have always felt that the mystery of life required explanation. Alchemists, in this respect, were "men [and women] inspired by a vision, a vision of [hu]man[ity] made perfect, of [hu]man[ity] freed from disease and the limitations of warring faculties both mental and physical, standing godlike in the realization of power."[94] To become a god or to be godlike may be the objective of both alchemists and mystics not necessarily in the sense of being divine, but being able to control the matters and substances of the universe.

Transformation as with the cycle of life is a basic aspect of the physical world and a reality about which all humans are concerned. Every culture has a method for dealing with the inevitability of death — the ultimate transformation, and whether or not there is something beyond the grave. Heaven and hell (or their equivalents) are necessary concepts for every belief system (**see drawing 1.c**).

All things, tangible and intangible, are potential sources of mystical or transformational intervention. The intermingling of the physical and metaphysical, human and animal, external and internal, or life and death provided an abundant range of opportunities for paranormal influence. Death, as an example, is a transformation of life that includes the translocation of energy from one source to another. Death as a permanent metamorphosis is the complete separation from the world of the living, and a change of the elemental composition of the human body.

The alchemist is the great transformer intent on acquiring the knowledge to change or rearrange the essence of matter. Turning base metal into gold is one aspect of alchemic practice, but formulating the elixir of life is an equally significant part of the alchemist's craft. It is possible to view the transmutation of metal as basic compared with the search for knowledge about life after death, a question that has challenged every culture since humans first walked the earth. The question of eternal life in some form, and how to achieve immortality are the necessary elements of every religious or quasi-religious experience. The accompanying dogma generally identifies the processes required for gaining the desired transformational results.

Concern about the unknown aspects of existence is a consuming human condition, and there is a great fear is that nothing exists after death. Therefore, death is for many people a metaphor for the unimaginable transformation that penetrates the protective barriers of the rational mind — the eternal void. It is the con-

Drawing 1.c: Death is an acknowledged factor in the cycle of human existence. It is an element of renewal that can move an individual forward or backward in their mortal quest; however, the major religions have different attitudes about death and afterlife. Buddhists view death as a natural transition and employ various means of granting people insight into the process of dying. Integrating death into daily life is a way of acknowledging the impermanence of existence and dispelling the fear of the dying process. The Skeleton Dance is one of the ways Tibetan Buddhists celebrate the reality of death. The dance is performed as part of monastic activity calling attention to the skeleton figures (*citipati*) as acolytes of the Lord of Death. C. Levenson, *Symbols of Tibetan Buddhism*, p. 115–117.

cept of resurrection that provides a way of renouncing the discontinuation of life due to death. People, in their search for immortality, seek recourse in the supernatural to find a measure of protection against the forces that constituted physical and emotional dangers. The power of belief energized a force far stronger than reality.

> Christ has been raised from death, how can some of you say that the dead will not be raised to life? If that is true, it means that Christ was not raised, and if Christ has not been raised from death, them we have nothing to preach and you have nothing to believe. More than that, we are shown to be lying about God, because we said that he raised Christ from death. And if Christ has not been raised, then your faith is a delusion and you are still lost in you sins. (Paul's First Letter to the Corinthians 15:12–18)

A culturally guided event that requires mystical attention is the disposition of the soul after death — the transformation from the living to the non-living. This activity is of extraordinary concern for many people. There is an equal fear that a living person's soul (consciousness) might be lost, or the soul that descends to the land of the dead might be one that causes illness by its departure. These are complex and critical issues, and special skills are required to locate the errant soul. Only a qualified person might overtake the truant spirit, determine its nature, and return it to its body

Life after death is one of the earliest mystical conjectures and preservation of the body is central to all concerns about an afterlife. The ancient Egyptians, for example, focused much of the alchemic investigation on properly preparing the physical remains of the deceased for the ethereal journey. The jackal-headed god Anubis (**see drawing 1.d**) was the psychopomp (guide of the dead) in Egypt, while the shaman fulfilled that role in Siberia, and a Buddhist monk performed those duties in Tibet and elsewhere. The successful transition from life to death was an important social issue because the dead might inflict misfortunes on the living. The living were equally concerned that when they died those in the next world might oppose their entry into it as newcomers who might displace the less recently dead.[95]

The dynamic paradox of life and death is not easy for people to understand or explain. However, examples of natural transformation are abundant in nature as some organisms are consumed so others can live. Reasons to believe in renewed life can be found in natural cycles that appear to be inspired by spiritual intervention. Seasons change, crops return, the sun reappears, the ill recover, and the complex process of childbearing for humans and

Drawing 1.d: This mask of Anubis, Lord of Sacred Lands is from the Early Kingdom in Egypt. Embalmers wore (carried on their shoulders) these masks to protect against odors, thus, they becoming jackal-headed gods of the dead. The original mask for this drawing is made of clay and weighs over seventeen pounds. It was most likely a model for making lighter papier-mâché masks. This mask is believed currently in collection of the Roemer und Pelizaeus Museum in Hildesheim, Germany. R-M Hagen, and R. Hagen, *L'Egypte: Les hommes, les dieux, les pharaons*, p. 147.

animals are phenomena most easily explained by the intervention of spirits and the notion of death and rebirth by spirit transfer.

Egyptian myths include the concept of a dying and rising savior god who has the power to grant devotees the gift of immortality. The ritualistic process involving death and resurrection is also common heritage of the peoples of Central Asia and Siberia. People have a need to embrace the idea of salvation and resurrection because of their anxieties about life after death. Stories, beliefs, and practices endorsing the transformational concept of reemergence or life after death can be found in all cultures regardless of intellectual or sociological development. Although the conviction may not apply to every individual, people as a communal body hold strongly to the belief in some form of life beyond the grave.

The mythical heritage of most cultures includes a legend about the gift of immortality undoubtedly because of this preoccupation with life after death. It is commonly believed that the first people were immortal but because of their unkind or selfish actions, they lost that privilege. A version of the immortality myth involves the shedding of the skin (like snakes and some lizards) to recover a youthful healthy body. The idea of skin changing is particularly prevalent in South-East Asia, but it is also found in Africa. This transformation was available to all humans until they lost immortality. (This loss is not related to spiritual immortality but bodily renewal or eternal life.)

There is a story related in Volume Four of *Man, Myth & Magic: The Encyclopedia of Mythology, Religion, and the Unknown* (1995) that comes from North American Indian legacy explaining events relating to death and transformation by magic. The story explains that the first man and first woman discussed the possibility of (physical) immortality. They were to make a choice — eternal life or prescriptive death for humanity. The first man wanted immortality, but the first woman thought death was better. She reasoned that without death the world would become too crowded. They decided, after extensive discussion, to leave the decision to chance. They threw a bone into the water and if it floated, humans would be immortal but if it sank, they would die after a time. The first woman had power, so she transformed the bone to stone causing it to sink. Thereafter, death was a part of human destiny because of this magical intervention.[96]

A transformational event that ritualizes life after death is the Medicine Dance of the Winnebago people (*Ho-chungra*).[97] This ceremony is a complex representation of death and rebirth as an act of reincarnation. The participants in the ritual experience symbolic death and are reborn on a higher level. "The critical feature of the live world [is] the horizon of death which present[s] the ultimate limit."[98] The primary symbolic references in the mystical practices of people relate to death and rebirth. In almost all cultures when a person passed from one level of existence to another, as exemplified by events from birth to death, the transmigration of the inner being followed a culturally defined path.

The concept behind culturally motivated ritual activities emphasizes spiritual or physical transformation, including the losing and gaining of personal identity. This idea is not limited to antiquity; instead, it is apparent in many (most) contemporary ritualized events. The recognition of death (qua: the end of an event, cycle, or status) and the perpetuation of life (qua: renewal, a new beginning, or starting over) are the two primary rituals (occasions) observed by people. Every object, action, or person is subject to the inevitability of transformation. The most commonly practiced event of change is the group directed rituals related to the continuation of life in all its manifestations.

Searching for Inspiration

Although the Arabs added to the alchemic practices of the Western World, they were most likely the "preservers of Greek-Hellenistic knowledge."[99] According to tradition, and as already noted, the legendary ancestor of alchemical practice is the Egyptian god Thoth, who was "identified with Hermes in the time of the Ptolemies."[100] The Arabic alchemists acknowledged this viewpoint, although their perspective was significantly different from that of the Greeks. There appears to have been, nevertheless, an active exchange of information between these two centers of alchemic investigation.

It is the opinion of some scholars that Arabic alchemy was likely derived from a western Asiatic school, but as far as is known, that source was not Chinese or Indian related. Researchers support the notion that Arabic alchemy was associated with the city of Harren in Syria.[101] This location appears to have been a primary source of Arabic alchemical thinking. Greek alchemy, on the other hand, resembles, in theory and practice, that of China and India. The Greek objectives, however, included gold making; consequently and as noted, it remained fundamentally different from the Asian practices.[102]

The Greeks considered the treatise call *Physica et Mystica* (Natural and Mystical Things) thought to have been written in 200 B.C.E. by a Hellenized Egyptian, Bolos of Mende, to be of singular importance.[103] This document is a type of "recipe book for dyeing and colouring but principally for the making of gold and silver."[104] These recipes are stated imprecisely and explained with references to the Greek theory of elements and to astrological theory. The writings of Bolos of Mende speak of killing base metals and resurrecting them as ennobled. His theories give considerable attention to "drawing the spirits from bodies and binding the spirits within bodies."[105]

The early alchemist search for inspiration was, in most instances, based on past knowledge. They believed that ancient gods, priests, or conjurers knew the secrets of the alchemic processes and were able to perform them. The alchemists' focus was therefore to understand the writings of earlier practitioners and to unlock the secrets to their success. *The Emerald Tablet* (*Tabula Smaragdina*) of Hermes exemplified this thinking. It is the primary document of alchemy. It had similar importance for Arabic alchemists as *Physica et Mystica* for the Greeks. Perhaps because of its importance, there are numerous stories of the origin of this text. One account is that Alexander the Great discovered the emerald slab upon which the principles were written in Phoenician characters in the tomb of Hermes.

It should be noted that *The Emerald Tablet*, probably dates from the middle of the first to the end of the third century C.E., well after the time of Alexander. It is also generally believed to be a part of a larger work called *Book of the Secret of Creation*. This Latin and Arabic manuscript is usually attributed to Hermes Trismegistos, but it might have been written by the Muslim alchemist ar-Razi during the reign of Caliph al-Ma'mun (813–833 C.E.). It has also been attributed to the first century pagan mystic Apollonius of Tyana.[106]

The authentication of authorship of *The Emerald Tablet* is difficult as with many early documents. Time and the loss of pertinent documentation have obscured specific details about its origin. The existing versions (copy) of the *Book of the Secret of Creation* that include the *Emerald Tablet* have been traced only to the 7th or 6th century, but they are believed to represent much earlier writing. An Arabic edition of this manuscript was discovered in the works attributed to Jabir ibn-Hayyan (c.760-c.815 C.E.), who was known to Europeans as Geber.

It is documented that alchemy was widely practiced during the third century of the current era. It was also during that time, in the year 296, that the Roman Emperor Diocletian (284–305 C.E.) destroyed all the Egyptian books on alchemy and the other Hermetic sciences. All evidence of alchemic progress made up to that date was consequently lost. The Egyptian-born writer Zosimos, the Panopolis, wrote his treatise on *The Divine Art of Making Gold and Silver* (an encyclopedia of twenty-eight volumes) in the fourth century. The encyclopedia includes all the information about alchemy produced in the preceding five or six centuries, and some person foresaw a danger in revealing the secrets of alchemy to the common people.

Adding to the difficulty of aligning particular individuals with their alchemic undertakings is the tendency to maintain privacy. Most alchemists conducted their activities in private, and kept the records of their experiments in a secret language. Ar-Rāzi (c.850–923–924 C.E.) was an exception to this practice, and consequently, he is the best-known Arabic alchemist. Ar-Rāzi was a Persian physician who lived in Baghdad. His achievements include classifying the "materials used by the alchemist into 'bodies' (the metals), stones, vitriols, boraxes, salts, and 'spirits,' putting into the latter those vital (and sublimable) materials, mercury, sulfur, orpiment, and realgar (the arsenic sulfides), and sal ammoniac."[107]

The alchemists were often viewed as philosophers, and indeed, they often considered themselves in those terms, because they were the repositories of an advanced science. The source of the special knowledge, "the mother of all the sciences,"[108] was as revealed to humanity by the god Hermes (the Egyptian Thoth). Alchemy was a practical art based on a body of theories "concerning the composition of matter, the formation of living and inanimate substances, and so on."[109] It was on these concepts that the alchemist based his experiments.

> There is a kind of ease that comes when we comprehend the illusory nature of reality, the dreamlike quality of life, this impermanence that pervades everything[110] (quoting H.E. Chagdud Tulku Rimpoche).

Chapter Two

Searching for the Absolute

"Many people are victims of their own self-deception."[1]

We bring trouble upon ourselves by mistaking the true nature of people, but also mistaking what is impure for pure, what is a state of pain for pleasure, and what is impermanent for permanent.[2]

The mystic world is essentially of its own making and governed by the needs and expectations of the community in which it evolves. However, the mystic event does not express one emotion at a precise time; mysticism is the essence of all emotions about a specific activity — a social expression without time. It is the ability to understand, assimilate, and project a particular attitude or emotion from an inclusive perspective that makes mysticism an appealing instrument of society and a part of the human life cycle from birth to death.

Mysticism is considered to be of a monistic religious nature that seeks unity and identity with a universal principle. This monistic attitude is shared with Hinduism, Jainism, and Buddhism. These belief systems do not include belief in intermediaries as the primary divulgers of the truth. Instead, they believe in direct contact with the sacred source and rely upon their own strength to overcome their own flaws. Carl Jung describes this attitude as a "connection to something metaphysical."[3] Jung continues his commentary by saying psychology treats such thinking (metaphysical) as not "absolutely valid or even capable of establishing a metaphysical truth."[4] Nevertheless, he acknowledges in the same writing that "faith enables man[kind] to know God."[5] All the same or perhaps because of Western thinking, mysticism is considered an element of the occult that involves a belief in supernatural forces to achieve specific aims.

The complex nature of mystic belief as an intuitive and ecstatic union with the divine is a part of every major religion, and perhaps every basic thinking process, particularly the imagination. It is an element of the history of religion (as an organized belief system) and fundamental to contemporary religious practices. Mystical experience is as old as humanity. The same can be said of alchemy if the transformational process is considered from a broader perspective that includes changes in body and mind resulting from attitude and belief. All things change, therefore time is itself an element of transformation.

Although the concept of time is critical in human life, the time duration process is conceptual instead of real. Life is measured by events and regulated by the abstract notion of time. Therefore, the passage of time depends on other means of measure to judge its progress. Days, weeks, and months are common measuring factors for communal time, whereas, personal time is measured by birthdays, anniversaries, and standardized events.

Time is only a related factor. Mysticism has an invariable role in the understanding of time, since time has no naturally preferred direction (forward or backward). Time can be taken out of context (and often is), thereby causing the event or sequence of events to converge or diverge. The shaman, soothsayer, conjuror, oracle, or mystic transcends time by moving forward or backward (intellectually or emotionally) to live or relive relevant activities. Thus, mystic thinking may question "whether future events pop into existence as the 'now' reaches them or are there all along?"[6]

This puzzlement calls attention to one of the peculiarities of mystical activity: the shifting sense of time as it relates to the physical or metaphysical events. Things often occur earlier or later than believed. They are real or imagined; therefore, they are frequently confusing. The imagined or believed may become visible even to the experienced eye and the normal, that is, the usually experienced shapes of familiar objects, may be transformed. The mystic in this process is the transformational link that joins the physical with the metaphysical. He or she is the vehicle for the displacement of time and place and a means for creating or reestablishing psychic harmony (belief) within the individual or community. Knowing and understanding the means to transfer information becomes less complicated when belief is a part of the collective value system.

Chinese myth includes a story about the Titan K'ua Fu and his efforts to capture the sun and thereby to put an end to time.[7] This myth is but one of many that references the traditional revolt of humanity against the omnipotence of time. The myth calls attention to the estrangement between the death and the rebirth of the day with the passage of the sun as a constant reminder of the certain end that awaits all life. "Since no revolt against time (to allude death) can succeed, it follows that temporal tensions should be moderated by the desire for reconciliation with time, a wish fulfillment for the timeless state which was man's before the estrangement [between heaven and earth]."[8]

Mircea Eliade, in the 1991 edition of *Images and Symbols: Studies in Religious Symbolism*, describes the time for rituals and other mystical activities as "sacred time."[9] He reasons that such activities place everyday life in suspension, that is, into a different time. It is possible with ritual practice to recreate the fundamental relationship between humans and deities and to reorder that relationship. The passage from profane to sacred time brought about by a ritual also implied a transitional relationship, as liturgical time is an extension of the period when the mystical event was last carried out.[10]

Sacred time and the related events help to preserve the eternal structure through which humans have life. It is the model and source of power in the present. People occasionally need to move away from the illusory nature of the mundane world and into sacred and indestructible time — the eternal reality. This psychological transformation into the enduring sacred environment makes survival possible in the profane (common) time necessary for daily life. People use their traditions selectively to influence the conditions in which they exist.

The symbolic meaning and emotional significance of time as a cultural feature is implicit in many elements of daily life. For instance, there is an assumption that motion is a time related function. The duration of individual life, the passage from one cycle (phase) of existence to another (the states of childhood, youth, maturity, and old age), or the gestation of new life, are time-measured events. The people seek reassurance that time as reality transcends daily activities. They want answers to unanswerable questions, and they prefer to be guided by belief instead of fact. The methods of responding to this situation are varied; however, dependency on the supernatural is universal.

The mystic may have abilities that exceed the limits (time, space, or understanding) of the normal individual. He has a special gift that can be described as supernatural. Perhaps the mystic fills the void in human sensibilities that is vacant due to lack of knowledge, or as likely, he provides a means of expression for human wants, needs, and desires. The mystic may grant protection from known and unknown enemies, predict the successful transaction, foretell life and death, and prophesy feast or famine. The extremes of most circumstances are seen in a vision received during a state of ecstasy, meditation, conjuring, or prayer.

Although mysticism is a part of every major religion and unites most religions in the quest for divinity, it manifests itself in different ways and with different objectives. As examples, "[W]hat Christian mystics call the Godhead ["Godhead is a term used by some mystics to refer to the absolute, unknowable Essence of the Deity, by contrast with the term God which stands for the Deity in His revelation of Himself."[11]], "Buddhists think of divine reality not as a person to be adored but as a state to be attained."[12] Buddhists regard delusion (i.e., the universe as currently viewed) "not as a creation of divine reality because it does not proceed from a divine source but from our own ignorance."[13] Buddhism endorses mystic thinking, but is not a religion in the same meaning as Western belief systems. Buddhism promotes the notion of advancement through meaningful conduct, and teaches liberation from the world and release from the cycle of suffering.

"The transience of the body and of physical pleasures is a commonplace of all mystics, East and West."[14] Buddhists believe that everything is transient, and that all things arise from prior causes, only to fall away again. The purpose of meditation is to break through the seeming solidity of the world and to "see things 'as they really are'—unsatisfactory, impermanent, devoid of essence."[15] (Death, disease, and old age were the three experiences that persuaded the bodhisattva to abandon the pursuit of eternal happiness and to search instead for truth.)

Everything is impermanent according to the Buddhist doctrine of emptiness, or *sunyatâ*. Everything is made of ephemeral components in a state of continuous change and shared condition. Nothing has an ultimate reality or ultimate stability "because the quality of the projections [that] arise from the mind is continual impermanence, change and flux, where nothing remains the same because there is nothing to remain the same." Consequently, physical elements as well as mental attitudes are impermanent, but in the mundane world, these attributes are believed by un-enlightened individuals to be real and constant. Enlightened awareness (*nirvâna*) is realized when the impermanent nature of these components is fully understood and ignorance, craving, and hatred are eliminated.[16]

True mystics, regardless of religious background, have always sought intuitive wisdom and believed intellectual knowledge to be unhelpful, just as scientists have favored intellectual knowledge and considered intuitive wisdom with caution. I. M. Lewis wrote in *Ecstatic Religion: A Study of Shamanism and Spirit Possession* (1989) that "mystical experience, like any other experience, is grounded in and must relate to the social environment in which it is achieved."[17] The activities that follow the experience reflect how different societies and cultures treat ecstasy and the rituals associated with spirit possession. "It is [always] necessary to differentiate between how phenomena appear to us and how they actually exist in fact."[18]

Tibetan Buddhism exemplifies the phenomenal contradictions, complexities, and values of a belief system that is both old and new. It is a religious system, which incorporates many elements of mysticism and alchemy in both form and function. Tibetan Buddhism can be considered on two very different levels. One level is theoretical or intellectual that calls for an understanding of the subtleties of teaching and practice. The second level is one of belief based on ardent faith. Both levels acknowledge a tradition that has a mystical basis drawn from indigenous practices. However, the theorist may refute the significance of the mystical foundation because Buddhism in principle does not seek or endorse the absolute. In contrast, the faithful are not concerned with such equivocation — belief is belief. The faith is not defined by intellectualism.

Tibetan Buddhism, particularly the Tantra (identified with the continuity between Spirit and matter[19]), is associated with mystery and secret knowledge or secrets of the mind. The mystical experience is identified with a consciousness that is not precisely focused or clearly divided into a subject-object consciousness. The subject and object are in most instances joined into an undivided single concept, activity, or action. They constitute a succession of idea. Alexandra David-Neel wrote in the 1927 edition of *Magic and Mystery in Tibet*, "The field of the occult seems boundless in Thibet [sic]."[20] David-Neel insists, in the Author's Preface to the 1965 edition of the same book, "the Tibetans do not believe in *miracles*, that is to say, in *supernatural* happenings."[21] She explains, "They [Tibetans] consider the extraordinary facts which astonish us to be the work of *natural* energies which come into action in exceptional circumstance, or through the skill of someone who knows how to release them."[22] (The italics in these two quotations are as written by David-Neel). Reflecting on the same topic, Giuseppe Tucci wrote, "The thing to talk of in Lamaism [Tibetan Buddhism], then, would be marvels, not miracles."[23]

Mysticism and alchemy are emotive processes, and emotional receptivity influences what people believe. It is therefore normal for what they believe to reinforce their observance of an established spiritual scheme. The circular concept of this process is contrary to the linear progression that regulates most commonplace activities. (The everyday activity [*samâra*] has a definable beginning and an identifiable end.) The non-linear approach supports the two principles of mysticism and alchemy. The imagined can be made real, while the real remains an illusion.

When the transcendental bodies become real in what is normally believed to be the "material world" then it is possible to understand that the "reality of the inner and outer world are interchangeable."[24] The individual may decide, at that time, in which of the two worlds he wishes to live, whether he wishes to be "a slave to the one or the inheritor and master of the other."[25] The decision is subject to the will of the observer.

Buddhism and especially the Buddhism as practiced in Tibet is an excellent example of the integration of mysticism and alchemy into activities of an applied religious nature. There is a joining — an amalgamation — of the sacred and the mundane, the subject and the object. The human relationship with the spirit world gives creditability to both. The giving and the receiving are the same in this unity. The Tibetans believe in "communication between the worlds of gods and men: it allows the possibility of supernatural forces taking possession of a person in order to reveal what is to be done in perilous times, or what the future holds."[26]

Such possessions may be enigmatic rituals that combine two intended functions; one generates new power or energy, as well as truth, for the world, and the other purifies the corrupted (dishonest and unharmonious) facets of human existence. Rituals whether for individuals or a group are a socializing effort to return to a sacred time that came before the structured existence of contemporary humanity. Early "Sanskrit-Buddhism speaks of the 'Cloud of Truth' or the 'Cloud of the Universal Law' (*dharma-megha*), from which descends the rain of bliss and liberating knowledge upon the world burning with passion."[27]

Joining Spirit and Matter

> All veritable and first-hand apprehensions of the Divine obtained by the use of symbols, as in the religious life; all the degrees of prayer laying between meditation and the prayer of union; many places of poetic inspiration and "glimpses of truth," are activities of the illuminated mind.[28]

The main preoccupation of humanity has been interaction with the physical environment from the beginning of life on the earth. It was necessary for men and women to deal with natural world and the elemental powers that inhabit it before attention could be given to issues such as morality and spiritual liberation. Joan Halifax observes that "shamanic knowledge is remarkable consistent across the planet. In spite of cultural diversity and the migration and diffusion of peoples across the earth, the basic themes related to the art and practice of shamanism form a coherent complex."[29]

The shaman's vision, like that of the mystic, is a holistic one where the difference between the outer physical environment and the inner human consciousness is blurred. This mindset allows no radical distinction between outer phenomena and inner noumena (logic or common sense). It is a transcendent understanding that considers what lies beyond the limits of experience. Belief in transformation as a mystical experience is associated with the practice of interacting with the spirits. These transitory activities do not presume the participant becomes a spirit or deity, but that he passes beyond the mirror (the barrier between worlds) and encounters the space occupied by spirits.

The transcendent function of such actions is, according to C. G. Jung, one that facilitates the transition from one psychic condition to another by means of the mutual confrontation of opposites.[30] The opposites in this instance are the inner and outer elements that influence the lives of people. They are also those aspects of human existence that seek to find release from the conditions that pervade the mundane world by knowing the sacred.

People have sought transformation by mystical means in all ages, and to facilitate that process the assistance of special beings (mystics, shamans, prophets or deities) were sought. Often the expression of that special being was by use of a unique symbol or marker that both confirmed and acknowledged belief. The symbolic as well as the actual manifestation of that transformational assistance was given great importance. The symbol implied something more than is obvious and immediately known or understood. For instance, the alchemist's effort to transform base metal into gold was more than a means of gaining a valuable resource. It symbolizes alchemic achievement, and represents "the elevation of the individual to the Good, the True, and the Beautiful; the perfection of the archetype that each man [or woman] contains within himself [or herself]."[31]

Transformation often involves some form of religious or mystical experience that includes submission to a metaphysical (supernatural or abstract) authority. People, however, are often constrained by overdependence on intuitive thinking and accumulated physical experience. It is belief that is the determining factor in this conundrum because there is no verifiable means "for distinguishing metaphysical factors from psychic ones."[32] Metaphysics in this context has no limitations. It is, therefore, inclusive of all beings and all realities. It embraces mystic realization and does away with the distinction between the self and the universe. It is in this realm that Buddhism, as an example, embraces the metaphysical concept of the absolute.

"[In Tibetan Buddhism] as in all religious institutions, there is adaptation to the needs of the common man, with his simplicity and his fears of the many forces he imagines to be working around him."[33]

The Buddhist religion that migrated into Tibet had its beginning in India in an environment of contrasting religious and social beliefs. The history of that development is well documented whether beginning with Brahmanism or the early teaching of Siddhartha Gautama. The canonical accounts of the Buddha's activities and doctrine are embellished by legend as with all systems of belief. Nevertheless, the narrative of the Buddha's life when divested of embellishment seems remarkably meaningful.

A simple account of the life of the Buddha (the "enlightened one" of this age) is that sometime between the sixth and fifth centuries before the current era (possibly 460 B.C.E., but the exact dates of his life, historically speaking, continue to be debated), Siddhartha appeared in India as an original thinker and teacher. The beginning of Buddhism can be viewed as a process of transformation. Siddhartha was also called *Śākyamuni* (Sage of the *Śākya*)[34] confirming he was of the *Śākya* people. That he was born on the northern edge of the Ganges River basin into a warrior (*ksatriya*) caste family conforms to most accounts. (Some scholars suggest that his father was only a petty lord or chief and not a king or raja. Archaeologically there is no indication of grand palaces or large centralized communities in this region.[35]) It is known that the caste system was prevalent among the peoples of the *Śākya* at that time. That the young Siddhartha was concerned about the degrading system that was firmly entrenched by Brahmanism is accepted narrative. The essence of his early dedication was the search for a way of escaping an existence that involved suffering and sorrow.

Therefore, historically, Buddhism should be viewed as an active living tradition, receiving its momentum from a great religious teacher about the year 500 B.C.E.[36] (The [*manushi* earthly] Buddha was born in 483 B.C.E. according to Japanese experts quoted in *The Secret Message of Tantric Buddhism*.[37] However, due to the accumulation of myths, legends, and traditions that have developed about him, there is no hope in isolating the historical truth from the accumulated fiction.[38]) The book *Indian Mythology: Myths and Legends of India, Tibet and Sri Lanka* written by Rachel Storm, for instance, states, "566 or 563 B.C.E. [b]irth of Siddhartha Gautama, founder of Buddhism, in Kapilavastu in the Himalayas."[39]

Siddhartha renounced his birthright, as well as his wife and child to become an ascetic and to seek the means for deliverance from suffering according to tradition. He followed the practices of the ascetic through isolation and self-mortification in search of spiritual insight. Legends tell he eventually retired into solitude and self-communication (meditation), and it was in that posture that he found a final success and the realization of his quest.

As Gautama Buddha, "the Enlightened One," and an incarnate eternal principle,[40] he traveled from town to town spreading the secrets of deliverance. He protested against the sacrifice of animals (as practices by the Brahmans), and sought relief for the "suffering inflicted upon helpless animals and humans beings, in the name of religion."[41] This attitude exemplifies the message of wisdom and compassion. Buddhism in its original form was more of a code of ethics and conduct than a religion. The worship of gods and deities was not a primary part of Buddhist dogma. Individuals sought salvation (enlightenment) through meditation and personal observance of the teaching of Buddha.[42]

The Buddha selected suffering of the three universal characteristics of humanity as the starting point of his teaching.[43] (The word "*duhkha*" is translated as "suffering," however it has a wider connotation.[44]) His message was optimistic in that it placed the possibility of salvation and the escape from a cycle of suffering within reach of every person, and "pointed the way to the permanent destruction of suffering."⁴⁵ *Nirvâna* ("*beyond suffering*," the final realization of the Buddha-nature potential in all humans) as a refuge from suffering and sorrow was attainable through individual dedication and meditation. The Buddha's doctrine of universal compassion and tolerance as exemplified by a pure and noble lifestyle appealed to people of all classes. It promoted hope for salvation among all persons regardless of status; consequently, it quickly gained many converts.

Buddhism is not a belief system that depends on the book or the written word, as do Christianity, Islam, or Judaism.⁴⁶ The message is conveyed as the teaching of the Buddha, and for the devoted, belief is an act of faith. Even the words of the Buddha were qualified by the caution "not to put blind faith in his teachings but to test their validity."⁴⁷ The Buddhist practitioner in the pursuit of liberation from suffering must depend on their own efforts, and the characteristics of that self-efficiency are "restraint, compassion, self-awareness and wisdom."⁴⁸

After Gautama Buddha's death (c. 486 B.C.E.), the *sangha*, the brotherhood of monks (some accounts limit these devotees at that time to monks while others include nuns), was subject to a succession of patriarchs selected from within the ranks of the senior monks. They followed the doctrine (*Dharma* or Law) of the Buddha, begging for food, and living a simple life of meditation and teaching. They moved from location to location as determined by the weather and by the needs of the group or laity. Consequently, there was no centralized hierarchal power and no fixed location of authority.

The first Buddhist Council was held in c. 483 B.C.E., shortly after the death of the Buddha. King Ajatasattu reportedly sponsored the council, and the detailed account of this meeting is found in the *Cullavagga* of the *Vinaya Pitaka* (Disciplinary Rules for the Disciples). The reported reason for the council was to clarify certain rules for monastic discipline. The second Buddhist Council (between 388 and 370 B.C.E.),⁴⁹ held more than a century after the Buddha's death (*Mahaparinibbana*—passing away to the un-conditional) was to resolve concerns about the relaxed practices including begging and eating after the prescribed time. The council voted against the relaxed practice causing a schism in the Theravâda tradition.⁵⁰

Buddhism, although popular among certain peoples, remained one of many ascetic sects until the Indo-Aryan emperor Asoka (264–227 B.C.E.⁵¹; or 290–232 B.C.E.⁵² the exact dates of his reign as ruler differ according to scholarly interpretation) adopted it as his official state religion in the third millennium B.C.E. and spread the faith throughout India. He also sent missionaries into other lands, including Burma, Ceylon, and Nepal to disseminate the belief.

None of the Buddha's teaching was transcribed during his lifetime. His doctrine was transferred orally from monk to monk (individual votaries) or presented in lectures or sermons to the *sangha*. Each time the message was repeated, consistence with the original commentary depended on the speaker's recollection and interpretation. King Asoka is reportedly the first to collect and record the sayings and legends of the Buddha and to form them into the first Buddhist scriptures. This compilation became greatly expanded and overlaid by later priests and prophets prompted by divine inspiration, divine revelation, and self-interest.

King Asoka's zealous endorsement changed the nature of Buddhism. It became a quasi-popular religion under his patronage, which repressed the pessimism of Buddhist doctrine and the notion of escape into *Nirvâna*. Asoka is reported to have "optimistically praised the Law of Piety as the bringer of happiness both in this world and in the next to come, which he sometimes called 'Heaven,' and 'Bliss.'"[53] He sought to make Buddhism a religion that could and should be accepted by all persons.

Asoka established many Buddhist temples and endowed Buddhist monasteries. He not only transformed the basic doctrine, he erected and endowed beautiful shrines and instituted festivals and masked plays on Buddhist holy days to make the religion more popular with the people. Buddha overpowered demons and had traditional Hindu gods as devotees and disciples in these plays.[54]

Indian Buddhist monks were once again wholly dependent on the largesse of the laity with the fall of Asoka's dynasty just before the beginning of the current era. Buddhism was changed (transformed) to meet the needs of both the advocates and the devotees. The evolving theistic form of Buddhism included popular superstition and addressed the need for a god that could hear and grant prayers. The Buddhist priests created an everlasting Buddha in the heaven (the Western Paradise), and identified Bodhisattvas *Avalokita* (The Lookingdown Lord or the Savior) and *Tara* (the Queen of Heaven and the Overhead Sky or the Goddess of Mercy[55]) as intermediaries between heaven and earth to address the popular need. This arrangement allowed Gautama Buddha to be an incarnation of the celestial Buddha.

Early in the Christian era, Indian Buddhist priests expanded the number of gods to five to include all directions of the universe in the theistic assembly. This transformation was to seek converts among the non–Buddhist population.

This theistic form of Buddhism was called *Mahâyâna* or the Great Vehicle for the transportation of many to salvation (*yâna* means vehicle). *Mahâyâna* Buddhism offered a way for the laity to find deliverance from the cycle of suffering without the piety and austerity advocated by the more traditional approach generally referred to as *Hînayâna* or Little Vehicle for the salvation of a few.

There are different sects of Buddhism. They are, however, divided into two great schools of practice, *Hinayâna* and *Mahâyâna*. Both of these sects are mentioned in this text. For clarification, *Mahâyâna* Buddhism is as stated above the Greater or Superior Vehicle. It is considered an altruistic approach where "taking part in this spiritual activity [is] not simply for our own benefit, but to benefit others."[56] Whereas, *Hinayâna* Buddhism is called the Little, Lesser, or Imperfect Vehicle, because it "abandons worldly concerns to dedicate energy to an austere spiritual practice."[57] It focuses on the transport of a few to *Nirvâna* (Tibetan: *Nyangenle-de*[58]). While there are other difference such as meditation, behavior, and ethics, between *Hinayâna* and *Mahâyâna* Buddhism, this one aspect (altruism) exemplifies the major distinction between the two forms of belief. The only surviving Hinayâna School is the Theravâda.

It is the determination of the method for gaining access to nirvana that defines the fundamental difference between *Mahâyâna* and Theravâdin practice. The Theravâda school emphasized personal enlightenment, as exemplified by the *Arhat*. (An *Arhat* is a monk identified as a foe or enemy destroyer. The term "designates a level of accomplishment where the enemy, dualistic ego-cling, has been conquered."[59] He is a person who has transcended passion and desire to know the bliss of Nirvâna.[60]) The *Arhat* practices monastic discipline in accordance with the Sutra of the Buddha and meditates on the impermanent nature of reality to realize nirvana and transcend the cycle of rebirth (*samâra*) (**see drawing 2.a**). In contrast, the *Mahâyâna* practitioner follows the example of the Bodhisattva, and strives for the salvation of all sentient beings.[61]

Supernatural power and legendary attributes were assigned to the Buddha, and Buddhism became more metaphysical and ritualistic as it changed to meet the needs of the monks and the laity. Worship of the Buddha figure started around the first century of the current era. There was only symbolic reference to the Buddha such as the wheel (dharma), footprint, and stupa until that time. "Different forms of Buddha's image, originally intended to represent different epochs in his life, were afterwards idealized into various Celestial Buddhas."[62]

Indian Buddhism embraced Yoga in the fifth century of this era as the "ecstatic union of the individual with the Universal Spirit."[63] The importation of this pantheistic cult supported the notion of meditation and reinforced the mystical and theistic development of *Mahâyâna* Buddhism. Yogis also enjoyed a much freer lifestyle than the Buddhist monks. They embraced the practice known as Tantra that employed magic spells and formulas.[64] (Tantra "refers to methods of spiritual practice, ways of transforming the ordinary work into a divine one, by weaving an enlightened universe in place of the realm of suffering."[65])

Monks mastering the Yogic system

Drawing 2.a: The *arhat*, Bhadra the Elder (arhat means "a perfected person" or "worthy one"). He is said to be a "Buddha-to-be" that continues in the physical realm out of compassion to work for salvation of others. Bhadra the Elder is the sixth of sixteen great *arhats*. He is identified as the "Arhat Who Crossed the River." The crossing of the river is symbolic recognition of attaining the exalted spiritual state. "On an island in the Yamuma river is the noble elder Bhadra, surrounded by 1,200 *arhats*; homage to the One performing [the gestures] of Dharma explanation and meditation."

were called *Yogâeârya* Buddhists. This mystic system increased the appeal of *Mahâyâna* Buddhism. It is within the *Yogâeârya* practice that traces of early *Tantrism* are found.[66] The basic nature of *Mahâyâna* Buddhism was transformed by the end of the sixth century with the introduction of these mystical elements.

Buddhism thrived in Ceylon, Burma, Thailand, and Cambodia, and its influence spread to China although it declined in India from the fifth to the eighth century. The Buddhist missionaries made known the latest developments of the *Mahāyāna* in distant lands. It was in those locations that the essence of Buddhism continued to flourish.

The idealization of Buddha as professed by the *Mahâyâna* School led to the creation of metaphysical Buddhas as well as the "introduction of innumerable demons and deities as objects of veneration, with their attendant idolatry."[67] Buddhism in India included many images and symbols by the middle of the seventh century. *Tantric* mysticism endorsed the worship of female energy as spouses of the Hindu god Shiva. It also allotted consorts (Sanskrit, *shakti*) to celestial Bodhisattvas (Tibetan: *changchup-sempa*) and most of the other gods and demons.[68] The consorts symbolize the female energy of the deity[69] (see photographs

2 and 7). Many of the figures were given monstrous forms and endowed with supernatural power. Myths and ceremonies invested the dominant form of Buddhism (in early India) with organized litanies and rituals. The images and ritual objects have special meaning and a complex symbolism that is guided by tradition. "Every pose of the hands, every object carried, even the color and type of garment and ornament has a special significance."[70]

The rituals performed were explained or justified as the way the celestial Buddha did things in the beginning. Such imitative rituals were seen as a repetition of the creative act of the Buddha and a return to the beginning. This type of ritual supported the theory that all rituals either repeat myths or the basic motifs in myths. Such practices seem contrary to the attitude of individual emancipation and salvation advocated by Buddhist doctrine; however, their formality gave a confirming presence to abstract mystical concepts.

Several monastic universities developed in northwest India during the latter year of Buddhist prominence in that country. The academic curriculum of those institutions included philosophy, as well as the study of logic, disputation, and monastic disciplinary code. The faculty of these institutions were mostly ordained monks. The universities were therefore considered a part of the monastic community that had existed from the earliest days of Indian Buddhism.[71]

"The universities were also ... to become centers of Tantric practice,"[72] and the most significant Indian academic figures for the Tibetans were persons associated with these institutions. "At the beginning of the eighth century the most important centre of esoteric Buddhism was the monastery of Nâlandâ in north-east India. Buddhist 'theologians' effected at this time a synthesis between the two main current of Mâhâyanist thought — the 'School of Wisdom' and the 'School of Mind-Only'—declaring that the Ultimate Reality of the Universe can only be a product of our own minds and that it can only be the Void, since no component of the human mind has any substantial reality."[73] Monks from Nâlandâ, the most famous of the institutions, and Vikramasila, a second university in the same region, were of particular importance in promoting this dogma.[74]

There have been many voices speaking of the Buddha and Buddhist practice over the years. The author David Snellgrove wrote in *Buddhism Himalaya* (1957), "Buddhism is not just the word of one master, promulgated, and fixed for all time. It was part of India's religious experience, changing, adapting, [and] developing through the centuries, yet at the same time retaining a certain continuity and independence in its traditions"[75] Professor Snellgrove continued by saying, "However far we go back in time, we can never discover such a thing as pure Buddhism, for it inevitably shared its philosophical concepts, its moral and ascetic practices with the rest of the religious life of India."[76]

Buddhism as a living doctrine in India declined over time until the spiritual and regenerating influences were moribund. The religion, already weakened by internal manipulation and dilution, was dealt a final blow when the followers of Islam invaded India in the latter part of the twelfth century of the current era. (There were, in fact, a number of invasions over almost two hundred years, and each took its toll on the population, both Buddhists and Hindus.) The invaders destroyed the idol-rich temples and monument of the Buddhists and massacred the monks. The fanatical destruction influenced much of the religious life of India including the scriptures, canons, commentaries, and symbols of *Mahâyâna* Buddhism.[77]

Buddhism, as is its nature and appeal, depended on the monks for its energy and purpose; consequently, with the monks gone, it ceased to have means for transmission. It disappeared as a viable spiritual practice in India except for the more remote locations that were not influenced by the Muslim invasion.

Impermanent Existence

> Natural man is not a "self"—he is the mass and a particle in the mass, collective to such a degree that he is not even sure of his own ego. That is why since time immemorial he has needed the transformation mysteries to turn him into something, and to rescue him from the animal collective psyche, which is nothing but an assortment, a "variety performance."[78]

According to C. G. Jung, "The psyche creates reality every day. The only expression [Jung] can use for this activity is *fantasy*. Fantasy is just as much feeling as thinking, as much intuition as sensation. There is no psychic function that, through fantasy, is not inextricably bound up with the other psychic function."[79] Jung continues, "It is, pre-eminently, the creative activity from which the answers to all answerable questions come; it is the mother of all possibilities, where, like all psychological opposites, the inner and outer worlds are joined together in living union."[80]

Different interpretations of the nature of reality and *nirvâna* after Sakyamuni's death led to the formation of different schools of Buddhism. *Theravâda*, an early school, maintains that nirvâna is distant from the mundane world. The *Mahâyâna* tradition avows that *nirvâna* can be achieved in this world, and is not fundamentally different from *samâra* (the cycle of rebirth). The *Mahâyâna* view *nirvâna* and *samsâra* as two aspects of the same phenomenal world—it is a matter of perspective. If the doctrine of emptiness, which explains the complex nature of the phenomenal world, is fully understood, then individuals can live in a state of nirvâna while in this physical body.[81]

The spoken or written word as invoked in religious activities is not generally considered symbolic. Instead, it is viewed as a form of rational communication, that is, the transfer of thought. A holy writing may represent the divine in some way. The record of Buddhism depends on text written in the form of *sutras* and *tantra*. This documentation is not to be confused with the book, the *Bible*, *Qur'ân*, or *Âdi Granth* that is the basis for organized religions such as Christianity, Islam, and Sikhism. The meaning of these two words (*sutra* and *tantra*) is much the same—"threads (of discourse)"—according to David Snellgrove.[82] He also points out that the words are applied to different, but not mutually exclusive, types of literary works.[83] The *sutras* are considered doctrinal and historical in character. They are representative of the instructions given by the Buddha to his followers. The later *sutras* are to explain the "new philosophies with its goal of buddhahood for all beings."[84] The older, as well as the newer *sutras*, are to reinforce the same type of spiritual practice.

The *tantras*, in contrast with the *sutras*, make no claim to historical authenticity. They are said to come from the Buddha in a "transcendent sphere of existence, and they differ from the sutras ... by telling of an entirely different kind of practice, by means of which buddhahood can be gained in this very day."[85] Snellgrove states that the *tantru* contain "magical spells, descriptions of divinities and sets of divinities arranged for meditational and ritual use, instructions in sacramental worship and the bestowing of consecrations."[86] There are, however, times where the two types of text overlap. As an example, "Magical spells appear in several of the *sutras*, and at least two famous texts which are known as sutras in the Sanskrit versions ... were firmly classed as *tantras* by the Tibetans."[87]

Allowing for the Buddhist documentation that came out of India, there is scant written record of the history of religious practices in Tibet. This may be attributed to the oral tradition particularly as applied to certain forms of religious instruction. It is, consequently, difficult to know exactly what is myth or legend, and what is real in the development of the

Tibetan Buddhism. Various contemporary writers have contributed their version of this intriguing story offering a range of facts, many of which confuse rather than enlighten. Nevertheless, each writer and each publication has contributed to the picture of this interesting land. Alexandra David-Neel wrote about her encounter with Tibet more than 80 years ago as a "face to face [encounter] with a world still more amazing than the landscapes I had beheld from the high passes through which one enters Thibet [sic]."[88]

The Tibetans, David-Neel wrote in *Magic and Mystery of Tibet*, "tend to believe that everything which one imagines can be realized. They claim that if the imagined corresponded to no external reality, one could not conceive of their image."[89] Nevertheless, if such belief is not based on an underlying principle, the pleasure (or truth) derived from that belief is false. Not only does a false belief deceive, it gives a sense of power that is invalid and corrupt, because it is in defiance of humanity. Therefore, when a belief does not consist of meanings that are acceptable to the authorities of that conviction (religious doctrine or belief), but on questions asked and answers that generate more questions, then the value of that belief must be questioned. The very sanctity of a belief imposes a responsibility upon society to test its validity and thereby to purify it or to acknowledge it's unacceptable.

"Traditional Buddhism, though rational in the sense that no dogmas are imposed, does not lack a powerful supernatural element which makes it a religion in the full sense of the word."[90] Tibetan Buddhism, for example, was greatly influenced by indigenous shamanic practices. The ancient attitudes and beliefs give Tibetan Buddhism a unique character that places special values on both practical and spiritual practices. Although Tibetans do not believe in supernatural occurrences, they acknowledge the work of natural energies that come into use in exceptional circumstances.[91] David-Neel adds that sometimes an individual "unknowingly contains within himself the elements apt to move certain material or mental mechanisms"[92] thereby producing extraordinary phenomena.

"Tibetan religion is basically Buddhism, incorporating elements from the indigenous more primitive religion of Bön; a principal feature is belief in Bodhisattvas."[93] Giuseppe Tucci wrote in *Tibet: Land of Snow* (1967) that under the influence of Miwo Sherrap, Bön "absorbed some of the rites of neighbouring countries, particularly Kashmir and Gilgit, and was probably influenced by popular forms of *Shivaism*."[94] The validity of this statement depends on the perspective and knowledge of the reader. Certainly, there is a blend of Buddhism with traditional practices, but Buddhism is the dominant influence. The *Vajrayâna* or Adamantine Vehicle school of *Mahâyâna* Buddhism is prevalent in Tibet and Mongolia. (*Vajrayâna* is the "Diamond or Indestructible Vehicle. This vehicle is based on the teachings of *Shakyamuni* manifested in the form of *Vajradhara*, the *Dharmakaya* Buddha."[95]) *Vajrayâna* (sometimes called *Mantrayana*) is a practical form of mysticism that includes techniques for subduing the ego and allowing the individual to achieve his spirituality.[96]

Buddhism was not an established belief system in Tibet until relatively late, perhaps not before the latter half of the seventh century or early eighth century of the current era. Even so, Buddhism was already practiced in Kashmir, Nepal, Mongolia, China, Japan, Korea, and across the southern regions of the area by the early years of the current era. Buddhism, as a dominant influence, guided the religious and social practices of Asia from the early days of Emperor Asoka's reign. Tibet (*Khang Yul*, "the land of snows" was an exception to this generalization. It remained inwardly focused and influenced by what are identified as shamanistic and folkloric beliefs.

The geographic isolation of Tibet caused the people to pursue their own beliefs in their religion and social life. Hence, before the introduction of Buddhism, Tibet was a nation of people guided by shamans and following an animistic belief system. Such practices were normal for a people living with and off the land. The human capacity for direct physical and mental communication with nature was believed to be much greater in agrarian societies. During the early stages of social development, people had to interact with nature with direct means so natural obstacles and difficulties were overcome by physical and mental capacities.

Alexandra David-Neel wrote in the author's preface of *Magic and Mystery in Tibet*, "The belief in psychic phenomena, in miracles, and in magic is as alive in our days as in was in the Middle Ages. What we have gained is the freedom to speak of these things and to attempt the experience of them without having to fear the stakes of the Inquisition."[97]

Indian monks (mainly from the Pala kingdom of northeastern India and Kashmir) introduced Buddhism into Tibet in the year 640 of the current era according to author Austine L. Waddell.[98] (David Snellgrove contends Buddhism reached Tibet in c. 625 C.E.).[99] G. Tucci states that according to traditional accounts "Buddhism was introduced into Tibet during the lifetime of *Song btsan sgam po (Songtsen-gampo)*, who died in 649 [C.E.]."[100] Other scholars propose a somewhat later date for the religious transmission, and it is certainly possible that an earlier penetration of Buddhism reached Tibet from Central Asia, China, or Nepal. It is generally agreed, nevertheless, that Buddhism was firmly established in Tibet under royal patronage by the eighth century of the current era. It carried with it the practices that dominated Indian Buddhism at that time including the images and symbols. The Buddhism that was established in Tibet "included elements of the old '*Hinayâna*' tradition, such as the monastic ordination lineages that had continued to provide the framework within which *Mahâyâna* Buddhist religious practice, yoga, and ritual had developed."[101]

Hence, the Buddhism practiced in Tibet was not a radical transformation of Indian Buddhism, and in many ways the Tibetans remained faithful to the Indian prototype.[102] It was essentially a form of theistic or *Mahâyâna* Buddhism that was prominent in India between the seventh and twelfth centuries. The practices called *Vajrayâna* or Vehicle of the Diamond or Thunderbolt was incorporated into Buddhist practice in Northern India, Kashmir, and Nepal in the tenth century of the current era. *Vajrayâna*, also known as the Third Vehicle, offered humankind the change of attaining deliverance from the world of endless cycles of rebirth (*samsara*; wandering) in the course of their present lives. The followers of this polydemonist doctrine were identified as *Vajrâ-cârya*, or Followers of the Thunderbolt.[103]

Vajra is a Sanskrit word meaning diamond and is sometimes translated as thunderbolt (**see photograph 1**). It is to "signify the absolutely real and indestructible in man, as opposed to the fictions an individual entertains about himself and his nature."[104] *Vajrayâna* is a mystical style (also called Tantric Buddhism) that incorporates Tibetan mythology and spirit-worship. The meaning of *yana* refers to the spiritual pursuit of the "ultimately valuable and indestructible."[105] *Vajrayâna* includes the belief that enlightenment occurs with the recognition that seemingly opposite principles are in truth one. Acknowledgement of the basic difference between opposites and their resolution is often expressed using symbols of sexuality.

The male deity in sexual embrace with his female consort as seen in Tibetan Buddhist art expresses the mystical union of opposites, which illustrates a basic principle of Tantric thinking. This coupling is viewed as the joining of active force, the male element, with wisdom, the female element, with energy. The *yab-yum* images in Tibetan symbolism exemplify this concept is reflective of Indian imagery (**see photograph 2**). Appeals made to a deity in the company of his consort are believed more effective. This notion of opposites is akin to the androgynous ideal expressed in Western symbolism (see Chapter One).

The phenomenal world is the materialization of the divine thought, but since thought is nothing if it is not action, the inseparable couple. Thought-Action, Cause-Effect, is represented in terms of the god and his consort, his *sakti*, his creative energy.[106]

These manifestations of oneness (god and consort) are not attained through the intellectual or the practical expression alone, but through a unified respond to belief acknowledged stimulants. The need to render these initiatives in visual forms led to the depiction of paired images frequently found in Tibetan art (*yab-yum* = Father-Mother) (see photographs 2 and 7). The intertwined forms should not be viewed as simply an erotic fixation; "the male symbolizes 'Means' or active compassion, and the female stands for Higher Knowledge. Similar assumptions inspired the ecstasies of Tibetan ascetics who, like the Indian yogis in whose steps they followed, reached that state after prolonged exercises."[107]

The early Tibetan Buddhist sects coexisted with the indigenous religion, Bön, during the tenth and eleventh centuries. The history of Tibet, however, shows the Bön spiritual tradition was practiced long before the arrival of Buddhism, and it continues today. Bön, as noted, is generally described as the shamanistic and animistic tradition of the Himalayas before Buddhism's rise to prominence,[108] and in that capacity, it served the interests of many Tibetans. S.C. Das wrote in his *Tibetan-English Dictionary with Sanskrit Synonyms* in 1903 and reprinted in 1985 that "Bön is an ancient religion of Tibet which was fetishism, demon worship, and propitiation by means of incantation."[109] Das continues by stating, "Bön signifies the kind of Shamanism which was followed by Tibetans before the introduction of Buddhism and in certain parts still exists [in 1903]."[110] This reference to mystical practices might be said about all early forms of belief.

The religious beliefs of Tibet may be divided into two parts. One part gives special attention to internally engendered practice, Bön, a tradition that had a large number of local varieties. The second part of the religious equation is Bud-

Photograph 1: The vajra (Tibetan: *dordje*) or Adamantine Scepter of cast bronze is a ritual implement. Originally the symbol of the Hindu deity Indra, it may be made of bronze, silver, or gold. It once signified a thunderbolt and is still sometimes associated with that symbol. The Buddhist *dordje* symbolizes the impermanence of absolute reality. When held in the right hand of a peaceful deity with the tongs at the end of the *dordje* closed, it is a peaceful scepter, but in the right hand of a wrathful god with the tongs open, it is a wrathful weapon. Philosophically, it is the supreme principle of wisdom (*prajna*) by which everything can be penetrated and transcended. It is also the male generative force and the esoteric name of the penis.

Two. Searching for the Absolute

dhism. Alexandra David-Neel wrote in *My Journey to Lhasa*, "Their [Bön-po, followers of Bön] beliefs may originally have been much like those of the shamanists of Siberia, but it is most difficult to be certain of this, for at the time when primitive Bön doctrines existed in Thibet [sic], writing was probably not known in the country."[111] (The written language was not introduced into Tibet until the ninth century. It is based on Sanskrit.)

It is difficult to trace specific spiritual practices in Tibetan history because there is little information about the beliefs of pre–Buddhist Tibet, however, it is believed that the universe was conceived as being divided into three levels. This reasoning is consistent with Siberian and Mongolian shamanist beliefs. The level above (upper or outer) was for the gods, the earth level (middle or surface) for human inhabitants, and the level below (lower or inner) was for "a class of beings known as *klu*."[112] The *klu* were viewed as a constant danger to the people who lived and worked on the middle level. The plowing or digging of the earth's surface was believed to annoy the *klu*.[113]

Photograph 2: Indian Couple in coital embrace. This embracing position symbolizes the divine strength of creation. The practice of sexual union as a symbolic act of mystical fulfillment developed from Indian Tantric belief. "Since the inner sexual energy of humanity is identified in India with the cosmic energy, images which represent the outward appearance of sexual energy are worshipped as its emblems." The act of sexual unification is viewed as necessary to rise above the false duality of the world in an effort to achieve spiritual enlightenment. © The Trustees of the British Museum. All rights reserved.

Some scholars are of the opinion that Bön appeared one thousand years before Buddha, and others contend that *gShen-rab* or *Son pa Gshen rab* (*Tonpa Shenrap*), the legendary founder (or primary proponent) of Bön, was a contemporary of Buddha.[114] It is generally claimed by Bön-po that *gShen-rab* could control the spirits and foretell coming events.[115] He reportedly could tell the location of spirits and knew which types of offerings would be beneficial to the people. He is said to have shown the people methods for performing rituals to make offerings, cure illness, and appease evil spirits. These practices gradually developed into a ritualistic system.[116]

According to Snellgrove and Richardson writing in *A Cultural History of Tibet*, "The religion itself was not called Bon, but simply 'sacred conventions' or 'the pattern of heaven and earth.'"[117] Although some researchers referred to this early religion as *Bön*, "the word never seems to appear with any other meaning but 'priest' in really early Tibetan literature. Later on the term 'Bön' came to be applied to the new religious developments, which incorporated some old beliefs and a very great deal of Buddhism."[118]

There were many sects among the followers of Bön (*Bön-po*) in Tibet. The two better-known sects are Black Bön (*Bon-chhal-nag*), the original or traditional form closer to shamanism, and White Bön with Treasure Bön (*Bon-chhal-kar* with *Bon-terma*), the transformed or new form very similar to Buddhism.[119] *Gshen-rab* (or *Shenrab Miwo*) is believed to have taught Black Bön (*Bon-chhal-nag*). His followers altered the original form later by introducing other materials into the Tibetan language and practice. The heavenly spirits of Bön were called *bDud*. The Buddhists viewed these spirits as devils that were black and lived in castles.[120]

The Tibetan king, Srong btsan sgam-po[121] (also written Srong Tsan gam-po and Songtsen Gampo) ruled from c. 627 to c. 649 C.E.[122] He was reportedly supportive of Buddhism due in part to the influence of two of his wives who were Buddhist. Nonetheless, Buddhism as a popular belief system made little progress against the widespread Shamanist practice.[123] (If these are the actual dates of his reign, it supports the earlier arrival of Buddhism as advocated by Per-Arne Berglie in *Shamanism: An Encyclopedia of World Beliefs, Practices, and Culture*.) It was King Srong btsan sgam-po's son, Khri-srong-Ide-btean[124] (also written: Trhi-Sron-de-tsan) (740–786 C.E.), who sent to India for a Buddhist priest to establish a religious order in Tibet. The person responding to the request (in 747 C.E. according to legend) was Guru Padmasambhava (Chinese: *Lian-hua-sheng-da-shi*), a member of the *Yogâcârya* School and a master adapt at the *Vajrâyâna* or Tantric path of Buddhism.[125] He is said to have "subdued all the evil spirits and local gods of Tibet by means of his *Siddhi* power."[126]

> The law of dependent origination whereby one condition arises out of another, which in turn arises out of prior conditions. Every mode of being presupposes another immediately preceding mode from which the subsequent mode derives, in a chain of causes.[127]

Padmasambhava (the lotus born) was said to be a *mahâsiddha* (master of miraculous powers).[128] He explained the fundamental teachings of Buddhism, promoted the Tantric doctrine, and gave new energy to the development of Buddhism in Tibet. He is called Guru (teacher) Padmasambhava or Guru Rimpoche (the Precious Guru or the Precious One), and is recognized as the primary promulgator of Buddhism in Tibet.[129]

Ten Buddhist sects were eventually established in Tibet. They came into being with a "view to preserving the purity of Buddhist teaching and doing away with the degrading practices, superstitions, beliefs then prevalent."[130] The four main sects, accounting for the majority of the Buddhist population, are divided into two groups. Three sects are identified as Red Hat (the *Nyingmapa, Kargyupa,* and *Sakyapa*[131]) and one is called Yellow Hat (*Ge-lug-pa or One of the Virtuous System*). The Red Hat sects are older and are considered the most faithful to the ancient traditions; however, each of the three sects follows its own practices. The Yellow Hats are identified with discipline and learning. The proponents of this sect follow the benevolent doctrine advocated by the *Mahâyâna* Buddhism; whereas, the Red Hats are more closely associated with *Hinayâna* practices. Most Mongolian Buddhists are *Gelugpas*—Yellow Hats.

Lama is derived (some say mistakenly) from the Tibetan word *bla ma*[132] meaning the Superior One or Supreme One. It corresponds with the Sanskrit word *Uttara*. It was originally limited to ecclesiastical dignitaries such as *tulku* (lamas of high rank; reincarnates), the abbots of the monastery or great monastic colleges, and monks who hold high university degrees.[133] All other monks (*grva pa*) even those ordained as *gelong* (or *gelung*) are called students (*trapas*). However, lama is often used to refer to all Tibetan Buddhist monks. The lamas have no special term for their form of Buddhism. They simply call it "the religion" or "Buddha's religion." Those persons following the Buddhist way are called Insiders, or "within the fold," in contradistinction to the non–Buddhists or Outsiders. The word Lamaism has no counterpart in the Tibetan language. (According to David Snellgrove, L.A. Waddell coined the word lamaism= to correspond in a disparaging way with papism.)[134]

One of the unique features of Tibetan Buddhism is that it preserves many of the philosophical and ethical tenets of the Buddhist system as taught by the Buddha. The teachings of Buddha are read and revered. Tibet is said to preserve the greater body of early Buddhist material, because only a relatively few examples of Buddhist doctrine were safeguarded in Nepal, Mongolia, and China, and most of the related material in India was destroyed by the Moslem invaders.[135] Tibetan archives include such important documents as the *Kanjur* collection consisting of 106 volumes regarded as the words of the Buddha, and the *Tanjur*, 225 volumes of treaties and commentaries by Indian masters.[136]

The Expression of Emptiness

> The art of esoteric Buddhism is the expression of Form, it being of course understood that Form is none other than Emptiness. If Emptiness is expressed by Form, it is simply because beings, living as they do in the universe of Forms, are incapable of apprehending Emptiness directly.[137]

Several schools of *Mahâyâna* Buddhism were active in Central Asia and China by the seventh century. The conversions were gradual but consistent since the inception of the *Mahâyâna* teaching in approximately 100 C.E. The essential nature of Buddha became increasingly abstract as the practice of *Mahâyâna* spread. The Buddha of the current age, Sâkyamuni, was determined to be but one of a thousand or more Buddhas that are to appear in this era. The Buddha of the future age was identified as Maitreya. The idea of successive Buddhas in this world was extended further in India during the first to second centuries of the current era. This idea accommodated a plurality of Buddhas in one time epoch. Five main Buddhas manifest the idea of Buddhahood as a universal principle: Vairocana (Resplendent) is at the center, with Amitabha (Infinite Light), Aksobhya (Imperturbable), Amoghasiddhi (Infallible Success), and Ratnasambhava (Jewel born), radiating out as the four cardinal points (see figure 2.1). Each direction is a Buddha family, with Bodhisattva attendants, and wrathful guardians as protectors.

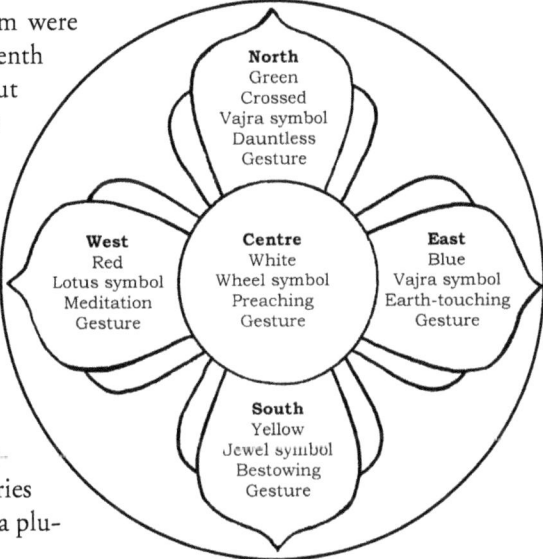

Figure 2.1: The pattern of the five mystic Buddhas or Jinas (Spiritual conquerors) arrangement within four lotus petals grouped around the fifth symbolizing a powerful type of energy-wisdom. The Jinas appear together in the "Mandala of the Five Jians," and are known collectively as *Dhyanibuddhas* or "Meditation Buddhas." The mandala is often configured with the images of five Buddhas each of which is seated in a meditative position with his hand in the appropriate gesture as described in this figure. A mandala is a symbolic picture of the universe.

"*Mahâyâna* Buddhists have no one name for divine reality."[138] This exclusion is perhaps because reality is real only in the context of time, that is, only in a relative sense. Lama Anagarika Govinda wrote in *The Way of White Clouds* (1966), "The creation of the 'image' of our highest ideals is the real 'magic,' namely the power that acts, forms, and transforms."[139] Lama Govinda believes, "An ideal, therefore, can only act if it is represented by a symbol — not merely a conventional sign or a mere allegory, but a valid, living symbol that can be visualized, experienced, felt, and realized by our whole being."[140] Tibetan Buddhism places stress on visualization of the symbols of Buddhahood for this reason. The symbols are not so much objects of worship but instruments of visualization, through which the practitioner "becomes one with his ideal, is transformed into it, becomes its embodiment."[141]

As people gain awareness of themselves and their relationship with other human beings and nature, they transform that encounter to meet their purposes. This transformation accounts for one of the greatest changes in human existence — the extraordinary revelation of self-awareness. The declaration of the ego altered human thinking. The Buddhists believe that the root of all suffering is found in the ego that separates the individual from other humans (in the sense of spiritual responsibility and caring based on manifestations of the ego) and subsequently from the source of reality.

Although the influences on Tibetan Buddhist art during the years after the tenth century came from China, this influence pertained to the details of religious painting, such as "cloud-motifs, waterfalls, the representation of houses and temples, and sometimes the general arrangement of the main figures."[142] David Snellgrove states the Chinese influence "scarcely affected the form of the Buddha image, which has remained faithful to the canons of Indian Buddhist art as received mainly through Kashmir and Nepal."[143] The symbolic reference was retained.

Psychologically, both belief and art invoked an emotional response that has no clearly explainable logic though there is an identifiable intellectual element. Giuseppe Tucci states, "Buddhism came to Tibet not merely as a body of doctrine, but with a highly developed art whose business was to teach the same thing in visual form."[144]

The actual development of a Tibetan style of art did not begin until the end of the tenth century despite the fact that the first Tibetan kings (the so-called Yarlung Valley kings) embraced Buddhism in the seventh century.[145] There was major importation of Buddhist sculpture into Tibet from India and other locations in the early years of Buddhism in Tibet. The Buddhist missionaries and masters promoted this activity by bringing images of protective deities. Many statues, according to tradition, were imported into Tibet after the time Buddhism was first introduced. The sculpture of Tibet comes from those countries from which it drew its religion.

The Tibetans embraced Buddhism during the last years of its organized existence in India. Because so much Buddhist art and iconography was destroyed in India, the images and symbols in Tibet tend to be treated as uniquely Tibetan. Though the art of Tibet is a blend of influences from various cultures including China, India, Nepal, Sikkim, and Bhutan, Tibetan art, once firmly established, became a tradition so distinctive and vital that it influenced the arts of other locations.

In reality, "Few of the major subjects and characteristics of Tibetan Buddhist art are known from the formative years, the period before the tenth century."[146] Much of the early Tibetan art came from India, and very little was added other than a few local saints, divinities, and religious leaders. The Buddha forms were mainly inspired by Indian examples that the Tibetans simply reproduced.[147] Nevertheless, the influence of Tibetan art extended not only to those lands immediately adjacent to Tibet, but as far as Mongolia and the imperial court of China.[148]

Tibetan symbolism and art are essentially an expression of religious belief, and although they mostly are derived from borrowed influences, they are an important part of Tibet's religious and mystical vocabulary. Tibet "accepted and freely elaborated the elements of both [Chinese and Indian art] and although its sources of inspiration are clearly evident, Tibetan art has retained a marked individuality."[149] This is to say that Tibetan art is a manifestation of belief. It is a means of bringing practitioners into contact with the divine. Therefore, to understand Tibetan art, it is necessary to reflect upon Tibet's religion.

The portrait as a representative image is of major importance in Tibetan art probably because of the number of Tibetan deities. Many of the portraits have been granted the status of icons, and include "inscriptions indicating that the spirit remain[s] within the portrait."[150] Some of the paintings include the handprints of the subject, thus assigning a timeless association between the image and the viewer. "Such linkage between a high lama and his portrait remain an especially potent form of imagery ... a further connection with the shamanistic heritage of Tibet."[151] The image is the person. This tradition is found throughout much of Asia.

While the portrait has significance, depicting the Buddha had a special set of concerns. It was questioned even in India whether to represent the Buddha in a deified human form or to represent the *dharma* symbolically. There is no evidence of images of Buddha (Gautama) during his lifetime, and there are no instructions for depicting the Buddha in early writings. Scholars have suggested there may have been a prohibition against showing the Buddha in human form thereby deifying the person and not the message. This approach is consistent with early Christian practices of representing Christ and Christianity symbolically. It is only in later years that the two symbols have been joined to represent one meaning.

The footprints of the Buddha are symbolic of his presence, the Bodhi or Bo tree (*Ficus religiosa*) indicated his enlightenment, the wheel was the sign of his first teaching, and the miniature stupa his final nirvâna. The lion was associated with the royal birth of Sakyamuni Buddha,[152] and is revered in many Asian locations. "Sign systems produced by people always constitute means of social connection, but these connections are very intricate. For better orientation society has accepted 'different languages' such as e.g., the colloquial language, gestures, games, etiquette, [and] religion."[153]

Writing in *Tibetan Religious Art*, Antoinette Gordon states, "In the past most of the ritual objects were made in the monasteries by the monks and their acolytes."[154] Gordon notes that occasionally a painting will have the "imprint of the hand of a high lama on the back, and at times also an invocation or the Buddhist creed."[155] Three-dimensional images and ritual objects often have a hollow space in which to insert prayers and invocations. The prayer or invocation makes the objects sacred.

Because certain mystical ideals stirred emotions and dictated group activities, it was natural that the symbolic references to those idealizations should have similar properties. When a people follow certain ideals and give special attention to the representative symbols, they often do so because their ancestors did. However, at times, the ideal is so deeply rooted in the cultural group that it exceeds the limits of its original purpose. The purpose may be forgotten or modified by time, but the symbol remains as a remembered reference.

The symbols found in Tibetan Buddhist art may seem erotic or gruesome at first view; however, many of the same symbols are found in Christian art. "[T]he iconography of Christian painting [includes] the symbolism of skulls and skeletons as the symbols of mortality and impermanence. These concepts pervade the religious and spiritual systems of the world, because there is this common or fundamental quality to them."[156] Such symbols are generally accepted as a kind of reality or true representation of the sacred. This relation to reality (or truth) is defined within the terms of belief. The relationship between believer and symbol is a type of cultural exchange. The believer grants the symbol power or authority, and in return, the act of believing confirms the believer's faith. The more ardent the belief, the stronger the symbol and the more pious the faith.

> Despite its visual richness and vast complexity, Tibetan art remains at the service of the most simple of acts within the religion, as an implement of meditation.[157]

It is normal for meditation to include the recitation of the traditional Buddhist words *Aum mani padme hum* (see drawing 2.b). David-Neel contends that the "six syllables of the formula are connected with the six classes of sentient beings and are related to one of the mystic colours."[158] Writing in the book *Magic and Mystery in Tibet*, David-Neel states:

"*Aum* is white and connected with gods (*Iha*)
Ma is blue and connected with non-gods (*Ihamayin*)
Ni is yellow and connected with men (*mi*)
Pad is green and connected with animals (*tudo*)
Me is red and connected with non-men
Hum is black and connected with dwellers in purgatories."[159]

The Tibetan religious books, the *Tanjur* or *Commentaries*, are reference documents that describe the "various deities and how they are to be depicted in painting and sculpture. Everything must be done according to these rules."[160] Consequently, the artist has very little latitude for imaginative innovation and self-expression in traditional Tibetan art. The colors, for example, are symbolic and allow for no deviation from the established code. The composition, motif, line, and color in painting are the result of years of practice in creating the ideal Buddha-image. The quality of the art is judged by the degree to which it follows the traditional constraints of the craft and only as an afterthought by the quality of artistic treatment and composition.

The pictorial displays in monasteries (*gompa*) are designed to enhance religious practice by presenting images and symbols of the Buddhist tradition. The images that cover the walls follow a sacred, ritual logic inspired by the devotional or mystical vision to be induced in the particular location. The pictures are not decorative. They are to bring the place to life, esoterically, by transforming the monastery or temple into a non-human dimension, and imbuing it with the sacred character required to fulfill its task.[161]

Drawing 2.b: The mantra *Om mani padmi hum* as written in the Tibetan alphabet. It is said that all the teachings of the Buddha are contained within this mantra. It is the most commonly used of all Buddhist mantras, because it is available to anyone who wishes to practice it. The six syllables of the mantra are pronounced Om Mani Padme Hum and Om Mani Padme Hom. This mantra originated in India, and it is pronounced differently in different location. Common pronunciation is: Om (ohm) Ma (mah) Ni (nee) Pad (pahd) Me (may) Hum (hum or hom).

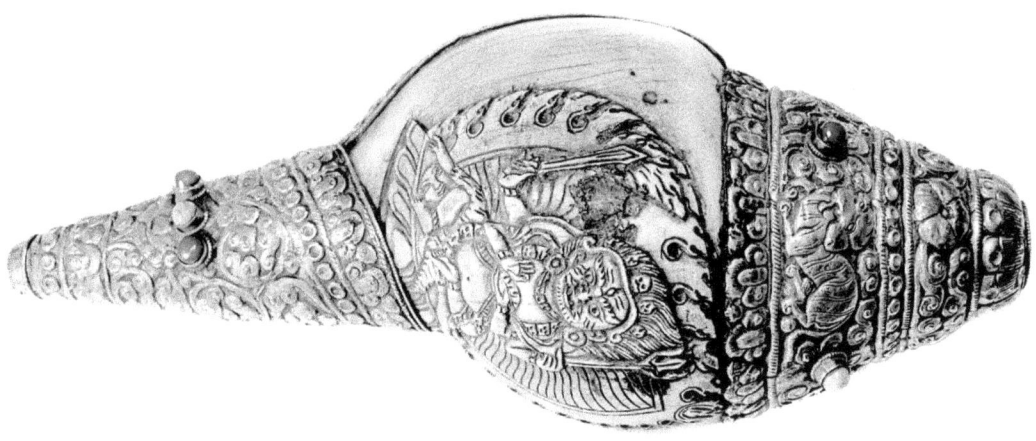

Photograph 3: The white right-spiraling conch shell trumpet (Sanskrit: *shankha;* Tibetan: *dung dkar*) has a long tradition in Hindu and Buddhist practices. It has been a sacred instrument for centuries as a signal horn to begin meditation or for the summoning of spirits. The sound of the *shankha* is believed to put fear in the hearts of enemies and causes poisonous snakes and animals to stay away. The *shankha* pictured has an elaborately worked silver overlay with semiprecious stones. The central figure carved on the lip of the conch holds a sword of wisdom to cut through ignorance. The flame design at the end of the upraised sword indicated the figure is Manjushri, the bodhisattva of wisdom. The silver overlay on the lower end of the conch turns to the right following the twist of the shell. The conch shell is one of the eight auspicious signs of the Buddha.

"A great variety of substances and instruments are required in order to carry out the manifold ceremonies whose purpose it is either to please or to pacify the deities and their acolytes, or to engage their help for achieving a good or sometimes an evil purpose."[162] Figures made of "bones and ashes take the ritual object to a level of reality beyond that of a symbolic image."[163] Such objects bring the worshipper as close as possible to the venerated person. Ritual objects are employed to spiritually reinforce the living as well as to influence spirit beings.

The conch shell, as an example, is a widely used ritual object. The shell is often ornamented with tooled silver overlays that are enriched with semiprecious stones, particularly carnelian and turquoise (**see photograph 3**). The distinctive sound of the conch is believed to drive away evil spirits. Tibetan altars pieces generally include silver bowls and butter lamps, and a variety of vessels. Other ritual objects are reserved for special ceremonial practices.

Robert Fisher wrote in the book *Art of Tibet*, "Few Tibetan ritual implements can be more difficult to understand than the human skull cup (Sanskrit: *kapala*), filled with blood or sometime with brainmatter."[164] Fisher continues by writing, "The traditional ceremonial use of human bones, including skulls, bone aprons, and human thighbone trumpets, often to frighten away evil spirits, was a practice found throughout much of Asia, including in pre–Buddhist Tibetan ancestor worship."[165] The Tantric Buddhist practices in Tibet have an Indian source, although the Tibetan use of human bones in ceremonies is more extensive than in India.

The use of human skeletal elements is a natural part of Tibetan Buddhist practice. Life and death are not contradictory opposites for the Tibetan Buddhist. They are two sides of

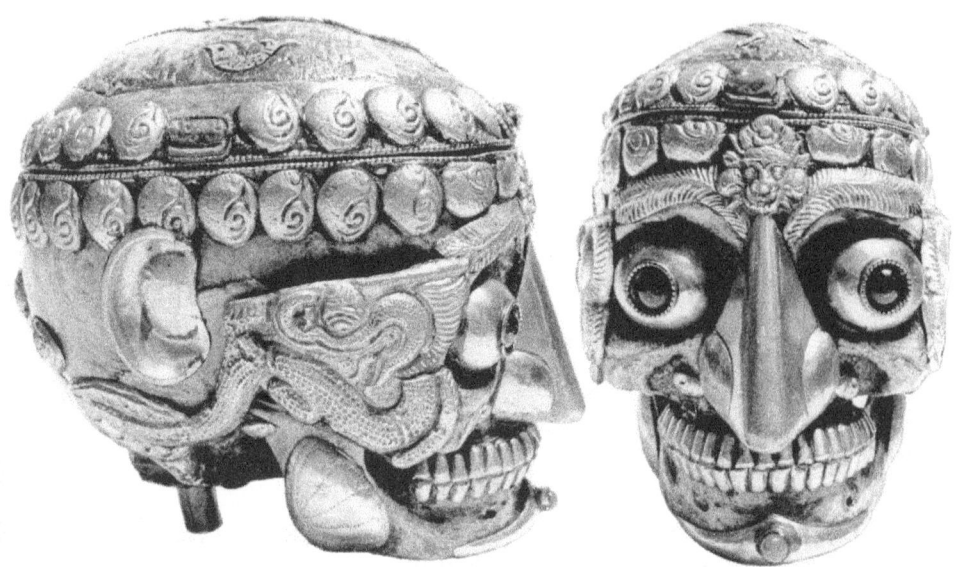

Photograph 4: A dead person's bones are thought to retain elements of the soul. The bones are considered the seeds of renewed life, and although there are more than 200 different bones in the human body, the skull is considered of primary importance. The skull has an important role in Tibetan Buddhism. It symbolizes the impermanence of life and the inevitability of death. Because of the "sky burial" practice in Tibet, there is an availability of skull and other bones, and unlike some cultures, the remains of the body have no particular significance to Tibetan Buddhists. The body is the shell in which the spirit/soul resides, and once that element departs, at time of death, the remainder is empty. This skull is overlaid with silver, copper, and brass decorative elements. The crown of the skull is hinged so it can open to expose a place (a sliver tray) for prayers or sacred messages.

the same reality. "The necromantic aspects of prehistoric religions and their survival in certain traditions and rituals of Tibetan Buddhism — in which symbols of death, like skulls, skeletons, corpses, and all aspects of decay and dissolution, are impressed upon the human mind — are not means to create disgust for life but means to gain control over the dark forces which represent the reverse side of life."[166] These symbols have power as long as they are feared (**see photograph 4**). The acknowledgment of the dark forces is not to pacify them; rather, it is to give them a place in our mind and to place them within the order of the universe as a necessary part of reality.

A Tibetan practice that relates to death as well as the availability of human bones is the method of disposing of the corpses of laypersons. Due to the scarcity of wood, cremation is not always possible; consequently, the bodies of the dead are cut up and left in remote places to be devoured by vultures. This means that bones are plentiful, and their use in ritual activities enhances belief in the transient nature of human life.[167]

The transitory element is inherent in the idea of reincarnation and the veneration of *tulku*. This belief is a "major subject in Tibetan art, as painting displaying the spiritual linage of a particular order provided a visual authority for legitimacy."[168] It is understood that this process of reincarnation will continue until all sentient beings are saved. That the incarnate dedicates his spiritual being to the liberation of all being is a concept at the heart of Mahâyâna Buddhism. It is therefore an often-rendered subject in Buddhist art. Perhaps of equal importance are the paintings and sculptures of guardian deities that are among the gods and goddesses of the Tibetan Buddhist pantheon. The guardian figures are often represented as fearsome entities in an angry pose surrounded by fire or human remains. They are, in fact, protectors of the Dharma, and their attitude is a warning to those who might challenge the teaching of Buddha.

"Tibetan paintings and sculptures are considered offerings, prayers for the well-being of all living things."[169] Sanctity is added to the paintings by a formal rite of consecration that generally includes an inscribed general prayer that the work benefits all sentient beings. The inscription is written on the back of the piece and may be accompanied by the handprint of the monk or lama invoking the blessing. Sculptures often contain sacred substance or written mantra. These blessings are to bring merit to all. The blessing of a living Buddha is especially important because it endows an object with his meditative essence, and this merit (spirit) can be transmitted to the person worshiping the art. The symbolic and pictorial representations are brought into connection with dogma and theological concepts.

Although the Buddha image as presented in Tibetan art is an assemblage of symbols, it has the power to instill Buddha-attributes in the adept's mind. The complete image is therefore a symbol of an archetypical deity that includes the appropriate posture, gestures, ornamentation, clothing, and the symbols. The objects the Buddha holds are to promote a mind-state in which the adept finds identity with the Buddha or Buddhism. It is understood that a primary goal of the Tibetan artist is the "visualization of inner qualities, the transcendent nature of the subject, rather than the creation of a record of a time-bound world."[170]

The power of the image (the visual material or seen element) is greatly increased when it is used as an element of a ritual activity to influence spiritual (unseen) entities. Symbolic numbers, colors, sounds, gestures, names, and places have an affiliation with magic. Although there is nothing particularly magical in most magic activities, the psychological influence of magico-religious manifestations has a tremendous impact upon receptive participants.

> Life amid the impermanence of everything and being themselves impermanent, human beings search for the way of deliverance, for that which shines beyond the transitoriness of human existence.[171]

CHAPTER THREE

Mysticism and the Harmony of Order

"We cannot journey to a real goal along an unreal road."[1]

> Mystical experience is as old as humanity, is not confined to any one racial stock, is undoubtedly one of the original grounds of personal religion, and does not stand or fall with the truth or falsity of the metaphysically formulated doctrine of mysticism.[2]

The spiritual history of humanity exhibits two distinct and basic attitudes towards the unseen (supernatural) and two methods people have used to get in touch with those powers. Evelyn Underhill identifies the two attitudes as "the way of magic" and the "way of mysticism."[3] Underhill also concedes that although the two approaches may strongly contrast in method and attitude, their lines of demarcation are not clearly defined. She believes they (magic and mysticism) represent the "opposite poles of the same thing: the transcendental consciousness of humanity."[4] She further notes that the fundamental difference between the two is that "magic wants to get" whereas "mysticism wants to give."[5]

There continues to be discussion about the nature of mysticism and the mystical experience; for that reason, there seems to be as many definitions of the terms as there are writers. The problem of definition comes, in part, from the fact that some scholars contend all mystical practices have the same objectives, while other researchers acknowledge the unique nature of each mystical undertaking. There are those that view mysticism as a form of religious devotion while others, theologians and scholars alike, consider it to be no more than a personal experience that has little or no residual meaning. Writings about mysticism generally agree that the intention of the mystic is to gain an immediate awareness of God through a direct and intimate consciousness of the Divine Presence. This emphasis on personal communion with the God figure (or metaphysical reality) is both a positive and negative aspect of mystical practice. That man might become one (spiritually) with God (the Absolute) is the foundational element for those endorsing mysticism and the primary criticism for the detractors. For one (the mystic) it is love and truth, and for the other (the critic), it is often heresy.

Because it is an inclusive concept, it is possible to consider mysticism from either the practical or theoretical perspective. A practical interest may lead the individual to follow the mystic path and to gain self-realization, while the theoretical concern may satisfy the need for knowledge about maintaining equilibrium in a chaotic world. Scholars and philosophers as well as laypersons from across the cultural and social horizons have given thought and attention to mysticism, and every religion has a mystical element. The mystical experience may be life changing and grant the recipient indisputable certainty of higher personal life. It also may reveal an extraordinary addition of life functions and a new acknowledgment of truth.

"[T]he mysticism of all times and all nations has its source in the same spiritual attitude and reveals the same trends. And that is why it often arrives at similar conclusions."[6] It is incorrect to assume that mystical activity is limited to the quest for a "pantheism in which God, Nature, and Man are merged into a whole."[7] There is also the need to deal with mundane misfortunes (the things of life) and the conditions that relate to such situations. Every human society is limited by the methods it has developed for the maintenance and endorsement of those things that contribute to its permanence. When forces beyond the control of the group threaten vital interests, such as, life, health, property, etc., the people find ways to deal with those situations without succumbing to hysteria. Hence, people often seek mystical inspiration to deal with such unpredictable circumstances.

Mysticism in its narrow and exact historical meaning is a doctrine of merging with (or love of) the Absolute — the one (metaphysical) reality also called *truth*. It declares a particular metaphysical idea about God and the soul, and includes a mystic methodology of achieving union with the Absolute. Mystics may view the mystical occurrence as part of a larger experience intended to result in transformation. For them, the "state of the inward man, the 'unrealness' of him when judged by any transcendental standard, is their centre of interest."[8] His transformation is the primary objective, if he is to achieve a level of spiritual perfection. The truth of faith has to be more infallible than human reason and logic to fully activate this process.

Consistent with the changing nature of human needs, mysticism has many forms. People had an intuitive admiration for nature and a feeling of unity with their surroundings from the earliest times. Prompted by this respect, they assigned spiritual significance to plants, trees, rocks, and all the tangible and intangible elements they encountered on a daily basis. The need to communicate with these spirits caused people to direct their attention inward as they received signs of a magical and spiritual nature. Regardless of whether the intention was to gain practical benefits or to sense communion, people sought to interact with these mystical beings. It was occasionally necessary to seek the assistance of a specialist to achieve the desired outcome. These especially valued individuals — the communicators — fulfilled a communal need. It may be said, "The essence of mysticism is the assertion of an intuition which transcends the temporal categories of the understanding."[9] Consequently, cultural groups often formed around the individuals who possessed extraordinary powers and insights.

This congregational aspect of mysticism gradually assumed a religious nature. Mystical elements influenced the religious experience when religious feelings exceeded rational thinking, that is, when the non-rational and often subconscious elements dominated and directed the emotional life and intellectual attitude of the practitioner. Theistic or religious mysticism is greatly influenced by the belief that the human spirit is not pure and simple but weighted down by passions, possessed by demons, and obsessed by evil, because man is in the world but does not belong to it. Consequently, the personal religious experience has its roots in mystical states of consciousness. Evelyn Underhill wrote, "No deeply religious man is without a touch of mysticism; and no mystic can be other than religious, in the psychological if not in the theological sense of the word."[10]

The mystics in all spiritual traditions seek to be transported beyond speculative dogma of daily existence to experience profound knowledge of Truth — the Absolute. Kaj Birket-

Smith observed in the book *The Paths of Culture* (1965), "Mysticism issued from the human mind.... In the mystical experience the boundaries between man and the supernatural are wiped out; one is gripped and elevated to the deity, merges with it, or becomes completely charged with it."[11] This consuming motive originates from the desire to join or understand those elements or qualities of existence that fall outside ordinary experience. Such experiences, although illusive, are believed available to anyone who desires them. True believers contend that all humans are granted a glimpse into the heart of the real world, which they can pursue or ignore.

> Adepts who send forth their minds to dwell in those high places day after day, night after night for years on end ceased to be as other men. Their personalities, thoughts, words, and actions are permeated through and through with the brilliant, objectless, attachment-free consciousness of [individuals] approaching the holy state of Liberation.[12]

The mystical quest for the Buddha-nature of all sentient beings as the representational character of reality is not the same as the "Christian mystic's experience of the Trinity, Christ, or the Godhead," nor the "Jewish mystic's experience of *En-sof* [the hidden God]," nor "the same as the Vedantist's experience of the identity of *atman* and Brahman."[13] It may also be said that the goals of mystical practices are not always the same or have stayed the same. For example, the goal of mystical and ecstatic practices in the Han dynasty (206 B.C.E.—220 C.E.) changed from limited pursuit of an experience of oneness with the Tao or following a free-flowing course of existence to the attainment of an eternal and perfect life. They (Taoists) wanted to become immortal.[14] The objective was changed from daily advancement to immortality.

Mysticism is a constant source for renewal and development concurrent with the notion of change. It shares a "common world with magic, theurgy (power of persuading the supernatural), prayer, worship, religion, metaphysics (transcendent levels of reality), and even science."[15] It often implies a certain metaphysical conception of the Absolute (God or the Truth) and of the soul (spirit). It normally proffers a mystic way of attaining union with the Absolute. Mysticism, among the many forms of experience, confirms the claims of religion by providing a foretaste of life after death.[16] The mystical connection is dynamic and may be described as a means of perpetual transformation—the transcendence of the self.

Although mysticism has many manifestations, the similarity of mystic practice "in all religions points to the fact that there is only one Inner Way, the experience of which is expressed differently in the respective cultural and religious environments."[17] Mysticism should not however be defined as religion. It is experience of a wider, more inclusive reality that extends beyond the limits of normal comprehension. The relationship of mysticism to religion can be described as a living revelation that brings life to a dead tradition, only to fall into religious convention.[18]

> Mystical power is believed in different societies to be gained in a great variety of ways; by inheritance or purchase, by psychedelic drugs, by use of medicine bundles, by special temporary or permanent social status, by killing (as in headhunting), by use of powerful words.[19]

The mystic maintains that the nature of humans is not single but dual, and that every being has two selves. A person is vested with an extraordinary ego that is the surface or temporary manifestation. This persona is generally regarded as the true self. There is also a non-phenomenal, eternal self, an inner being, sometimes called the spirit or soul that is actually the *true self*. It is possible for an individual, if he or she wishes and is willing to make the effort to align himself or herself with the *true self*, to attain a consciousness of the Absolute.

Beyond the quests associated with the theistic point of view, it is possible to describe mysticism as a practical psycho-philosophical approach to self-development and self-integration. The intention of the mystic "is wholly transcendental and spiritual."[20] (Spiritual in this instance is viewed as self-realization.) Mysticism is not intended as an addition too, re-arrangement, or improvement of the visible universe; in fact, the mystic bypasses that universe, even in its extraordinary manifestations to remain focused upon the Absolute. The genuine mystical experience has a striking unanimity that includes "a perception of all-pervading unity in which the duality of subject and object, of worshipper and worshipped"[21] is subsumed.

Two psychogenic aspects of humanity appear to be universal. People are uncomfortable with the unknown and they have a limitless capacity for belief. The primary human motivating force for thousands of years was probably emotion, and the most dominant emotion is fear. The world is cruel. It inflicts many forms of suffering, both natural and human-made, on every person. The root of all suffering, according to Buddhist doctrine, is found in the ego that separates the individual from other humans in the sense of spiritual responsibility and caring based on manifestations of the ego. (Buddhist doctrine is founded on elimination of suffering.)

A cultural phenomenon, such as fear, that originates under one set of circumstances and continues into a time when those conditions no longer exist alters human stability and reasoning. It is, therefore, understandable that people invested much of their time and energy in avoiding situations that promoted fear and suffering. The avoidance process often results in psychological and spiritual paralysis that aggravates the fear factor.

The Maya (Meso-American people) believed that fear "keeps the soul off balance so that it cannot feel centered or express itself with dignified grace."[22] The Chinese addressed such issues by advocating the importance of balance and the equalizing forces of the yin and yang. They reasoned that a response to fear that caused aggression would shift the balance in the other direction; thus, perpetuating disharmony. People in all regions of the world assign their fears to the deities or demons to avoid emotional distress, and with that transfer, beliefs were formed to avoid imbalance. Reason and logic are seldom employed in response to fear.

Belief is a powerful element of the human psyche. It is the attitude that most often refers to the perspective that a situation or circumstance is real, honest, or true. People believe because they want to believe and because believing complements their life or lifestyle. Furthermore, not believing often creates an emotional void and denies hope. Belief identifies answers to basic questions that cannot be answered in other ways. Mystical practices encompassing belief offer the means for responding to circumstances that challenged a people's mental or physical well-being. Moreover, beliefs recognize and reinforce existing conditions and further the attitudes that influenced previous generations, thus, reinforcing social and cultural heritage.

Belief is a part of the biological composition of humans, and as such, it is always relative to an individual's intellect and range of experience. Nevertheless, the connection between ideas and outcomes (causes and effects) is true (valid) only for experiences at a particular moment. The relating logic or belief in other circumstance may not correspond with specific intellectual understanding, however, that is not sufficient cause to abandon the role of reason by which fundamental truths are intuitively known. Both the positive and negative facets of human reality (truth) are embedded in belief.

Belief in the supernatural is a universal condition, as is the tripartite structure of the universe — heaven, paradise, or outer world (the place of the gods), earth or middle world (the place of humans), and purgatory or the inner world (the place of the dead and demons). Humans endorse some form of spiritual reverence to this structure as a concept for dealing with the social, physical, and emotional environments. Purgatory must exist as a balance for paradise. Admission to the first (paradise) and third (purgatory) worlds is generally controlled by mystical beings and entry is supposedly determined by activities in the second world (surface). The shaman or mystic may be employed to enter the realm of the spirits and personally carries the messages of reconciliation to the deities. Thus, the intermediary is the messenger between the invisible realm of the spirits and the manifest world of human life. The practice of placating the spirits is reinforced by the belief systems of many cultural groups.

Such beliefs as these are determined to be real when they satisfy the interests and needs of the people. There may be little meaningful difference between the physical and spiritual worlds for most cultures; consequently, a profusion of spirit beings is often present in every aspect of life. Beliefs, once accepted, galvanize a societal energy that is both emotional and physiological. Humans responding to the energized environment assign their fears and concerns to the deities or demons and with that transfer, beliefs are reinforced to give balance to daily activities. A sympathetic understanding must exist between all elements (humans, nature and deities) for this arrangement to be effective. Belief provides a balancing or harmonizing influence to ensure acceptable outcomes.

Doctrine of Unification

Because mysticism is a doctrine of unification, it can be said that the mystical experience is a psychological matter, and that the doctrine of mysticism is essentially a metaphysical response to personal circumstances. The mystical experience may include unusual phenomena, such as voices or visions, extraordinary body changes, swoons, or ecstasies.[23] It may also include a sense of awareness that is not sharply focalized, or clearly differentiated into a subject-object relationship. The subject and object — in this case, the human and the divine — may be merged into a single entity. Such ecstasy is defined by belief and reinforced by myths, traditions, and customs that give a sense of empowerment to individuals and communities.

Whatever is seen, heard, or felt in mystical or transcendent occurrences is thought filled with an infusion of persistent energy from that aspect of internal life called the spirit or soul. The inner energy (power) that is activated as protection against compartmentalization of inner life is consequently set aside. External energies fill the inner self with consciousness as an enveloping presence at the same time. The whole sense of being is an integral and undivided experience that defines itself. John Alexander Stewart, in his translation of the *Myths of Plato* (1970 [1905]), identified these experiences as "transcendental consciousness."[24]

Perhaps because the definitions of mysticism and the mystical experience are varied and range from the biological through the psychological to the theological, this diversity aptly qualifies mysticism as "the science of a hidden life."[25] All mystics undoubtedly do not have the same experiences; they do, however, all take part in the same mystery. It is possible that even this concept is limiting. Though there are similarities, mysticism is different from prophetic religions as well as from shamanism (a belief system built around psychic transformations).[26] The deeper the understanding, the more the seemingly different elements of the mystical experiences cease to matter. The bizarre and fantastic are of little interest to mature mystics, and may be viewed as little more than distractions. Mystics strive to discover something simpler and more substantial that is beyond the extraordinary — an all-consuming Oneness.[27]

Magic, although at times marginalized as superstition, is also a part of human history and an undeniable ingredient in the development of social order. It, like power, is an aspect of survival. Hutton Webster stated in *Magic: A Sociological Study* (1948), "Spiritual beings are often credited with a knowledge of magic. They handed it down to men and sometimes use it in their relations with men."[28] The endorsement of magic as a social ingredient confirms (at least from Webster's perspective) the notion that invisible forces influence or change events or human actions. Mysticism and magic may have evolved together. Though they employ different methods, they are practical activities used to achieve desired results or to avoid unwanted outcomes.

Magical activities may be viewed as mystical, religious, or scientific. They occur in various ways and with differing degrees of depth. They look to invisible forces to influence events or change material conditions such as those that happen at the time of extreme stress, an absorbing intellectual experience, or the sudden insight into the meaning of truth. The magical event may occur in conjunction with some types of experience that transcends understanding and in which the individual consciousness and divine reality are joined into an undifferentiated union. This connection may be illusionary, but it conveys the belief that the self and the object are inseparable.

> *Mysticism*, according to its etymology, implies a relation to mystery. In philosophy, Mysticism is both a religious tendency and desire of the human soul towards an intimate union with the Divinity, or a system growing out of such a tendency and desire.[29]

Humans often seek interaction with the divine as a part of the mystical experience. They pursued unification with gods or goddesses on celestial ground and with expectation to be transformed into godlike figures themselves.[30] This form of mystical realization has two primary categories: the temporary and the permanent.[31] It is believed that some persons transported to the otherworld, the place of gods and goddesses, may never return to the mundane world. They might be sequestered forever in the celestial landscape or trapped at some point of their travel and unable to continue or return. Whereas, other persons may make the journey and return bringing knowledge back to the host environment.

A Talmudic adage explains, "There are as many ways to Truth as there are human faces."[32] Each method used in this quest is believed to be a way of arriving at truth by unbiased means. Therefore, there is in the true mystic a greater than normal consciousness, a discharge of suppressed energy, and an expansion of vision, so that elements of truth overlooked by the rational intellect are exposed. The mystic discovers the universal nature of the temporal in the eternal and the eternal in the temporal by both feeling and through.[33] The religious mystic may have, in such circumstances, a direct encounter with God, but is unable to describe the experience, nor can he logically demonstrate its validity. Such experiences for the mystic are nevertheless fully and absolutely authentic.

> This phenomenal world of matter and individual consciousness is only a partial reality and is the manifestation of a Divine Ground in which all partial realities have their being.[34]

Mysticism relies upon the assumption that people need to communicate with a higher being in a personal search for truth. They may seek in addition to union with the Absolute, the means for immortality, and the essence of everlasting life. The restrictive boundaries between humans and the supernatural are eliminated by mystical practices. Through mysticism, mortals may be elevated to deity status, merged with the divine (the transcendent realm), or be completely charged with mystical energy. It is a means for returning to the source of being. The essential sign of mysticism is a sense of ecstasy that elevates the spirit and reaffirms the power of belief.

There are mystics and mystical philosophers. Mystical experience is undoubtedly one of the foundational aspects of personal religion, and does not maintain its validity based on the fact or falsity of the doctrine of mysticism. Gershom G. Scholem wrote in 1941, "There is no such thing as mysticism in the abstract." He stated, "There is no mysticism as such, there is only the mysticism of a particular religious system, Christian, Islamic, Jewish mysticism and so on."[35] Whereas the 2004 edition of Encyclopædia Britannica describes mysticism as "a spiritual quest for hidden truth or wisdom, the goal of which is union with the divine or sacred (the transcendent realm)."[36] It notes, "Forms of mysticism are found in all major world religions, by analogy in the shamanic and other ecstatic practices of nonliterate cultures, and in secular experience."[37]

Mysticism should be viewed as an organic process that is active and practical regardless of the objective sought or the motivating ideology. It is a movement toward a higher level of reality, and although it can be described as one of the foundations of religion, it plays an important role in the "defense of psychic integrity of the community."[38] Mircea Eliade contends rational mystical experiences are possible in every type of cultural and religious circumstance.[39] "[M]etaphysical knowledge and doctrine," according to Allan Watts, "is quite distinct from religious knowledge, but not at all in conflict with it. As religion begins with revelation, metaphysical knowledge begins with actual realization, which is the basis for all that follows."[40]

Shamanic Mysticism

> The shaman as a mediator is placed at those very critical points where the human sphere and the superhuman sphere do overlap. His activity covers the liminal spheres of the world, which are dangerous for ordinary human beings and for shamans as well.[41]

Most forms of shamanism fall within the sphere of mysticism. The mystical element in this process is the presence of the divine essence in the shaman and his distribution of it to others. This action constitutes a union with the divine (the spirit world in this instance). The shaman achieves an altered state of consciousness to establish a relationship with the supernatural world, and by that means gains power and knowledge to help members of his community. Shamans are believed visited by spirits when in an ecstatic trance. The spirits may speak through the shaman's mouth, and guide him in performance of his social and cultural responsibilities.

Although people often believe they are powerless to deal with the perilous and unpredictable forces that surround them, certain individuals have a unique ability — a power — that allows them to overstep the boundary between the known and unknown. This ability does not rely on physical strength or mental dexterity; it is of a different nature that often is acquired at the expense of physical well being. The power transcends ordinary limitations and is beyond normal understanding. "A limited number of people [are] inspired by stronger spirit powers than others.... They [are] an elite [group] since the number of men and women with shamanistic abilities [is] very small, and they [are] sometimes considered as outsiders to the community."[42]

The shaman as transformer and mediator has a special gift that is described as mystical or supernatural power. He often fills the gaps in human sensibilities left vacant by lack of knowledge and circumstantial understanding. The shaman might grant protection from known and unknown situations, predict successful or unsuccessful activities, foretell life and death, and prophesy feast or famine. The extremes of these conditions are viewed in visions or experiences during ecstatic episodes. Describing the shaman's communal role Mariko Namba Walter and Eva Jane Neumann Fridman wrote in *Shamanism: An Encyclopedia of World Beliefs, Practices, and Culture*, volume I (2004), "The shaman knows the spirit world and human soul through 'ecstasy,' the power of an altered state of consciousness, or trance, which is used to make a connection to the world of the spirits in order to bring about benefits to the community."[43]

The shaman's activities are rooted in mysticism. The term shaman normally identifies someone who has access to other spiritual dimensions; however, it is often used as an inclusive name for persons with mystical knowledge. The true shaman may be a healer or diviner but generally performs a greater service to the community by reducing anxiety. Shamanic power is believed to come from supernatural forces. However, the division of the force or power into natural and supernatural realms is not restrictive, because the shaman does not make this distinction.[44] A spirit, sometimes called a familiar, is said to take possession of the shaman and give him extraordinary powers, often after transposition to a spirit world. It is the shaman's function through rituals or transcendental activities to regulate (balance) relations between the spirits and humans, thereby ensuring equilibrium within the community.

Shamanic practice implies something more than prescribed action. It is an encounter with human mortality and the forces that influence reality. Endorsement of the mystical realm has been a part of the human psyche for as long as people have observed the changing cycles of nature. Cyclical transformations are reasons for concern because they are beyond human control. Consequently, subjective reasoning accepts the supernatural as a primary influence upon the lives of people. No other force is remotely equivalent to the impact on the existence of individuals and communities as that generated by acknowledgment of the transcendental world — the unity of all creation. The phenomena that occur outside the rule of natural law are both wondrous and terrifying because they reinforce the belief that life as a transcendental concept has meaning.

The shaman has a range of powers in an altered state of consciousness that he does not possess in mundane surroundings. The shaman sees spirits and souls and communicates with them. He makes magical flights to the Outer World as an intermediary between the deities and the people. The mystic in the form of a shaman also descends to the land of the dead (the Inner World). This activity is thought performed while riding a mythical horse, traveling in a spirit boat, or being transformed into a bird. It is also commonly believed that entering the circle enhances the mystical experience of being united with the gods. The circle is a universally accepted symbol of perfection. It exemplifies isolation and freedom from surroundings influences. It is also believed to consolidate energy and provide a focus for ritual activity.

Shamans use magic (a pseudo-action as a substitute for true action) to demonstrate the illusory quality of projected reality and direct awareness to the spirit world. This purposeful deception is a way to demonstrate the falsity of human apprehension about the future or future events. The shaman's role is identified with anxiety and the amelioration of that condition. Similar shamanic demonstrative activities and the pacifying influence of magic also appear in Tantra and other more esoteric sects of Hinduism and Buddhism that use mystical signs and symbols in ritual events. The notion of magic as an activity, especially relating to its communal dimension, is influenced by the cultural context in which it is used.

The imagined becomes real when magic is employed as an invisible force to influence events, effect change in material conditions, or present the illusion of change. Shamanism might be said to include an element of magic when a phenomenon occurs, or a need is realized. Certain shamanic activities such as divination, spirit intervention, and some forms of curing appear to have magical elements, and the same might be said of Hindu, Buddhist, and Taoist activities. All material life is an illusion and therefore, subject to manipulation by cosmic forces. The real world is in the imagination, whereas, the mundane is a world governed by unnatural circumstances. The shaman guides the participating audience to see and believe what he sees as a way of conveying truth. Miraculous (magical or mystical) routines are also used to assist uninitiated persons to see reality in the way the shaman sees it.

Shamanism in the strict sense is a religious phenomenon of Siberia and Inner Asia including Tibet and Mongolia. "Both shamanic and Buddhist traditions, therefore, share a social purpose, even if the community of those to be served is understood differently."[45] The magico-religious life of society may center on the shaman; however, shamanism should not be considered just by the principles that apply to reality as everyday life, but by the standards that identify with the transcendental world of belief and tradition. Shamanic practice is practical. It interprets the natural and supernatural influences people encounter as a form of truth that is indispensable to the environment in which the host community exists.

Shamanic transformation is a process that grants certain individuals the sacred essence of life, and consequently, the shaman's actions are believed communicated from a divine source. Similarly, human life is about transformation. Celebrations are held to mark the changing of the seasons, major events in life, and the beginning or ending of a cycle. Life to death and life after death are transformational issues that occupy the thinking of contemporary society much as they did in earlier times. The unique role of the shaman in this process is evident from the earliest times. Human remains discovered in Stone Age graves were often buried with flowers and the bodies sprinkled with red earth. This ritual burial can be viewed as the preparation for rebirth — the anticipated transformation to a new life.

Life and death are contained in this eternal transformation from Non-Being into Being and back to Non-Being, but the underlying primordial unity is never lost.[46]

Belief in the ability to be transformed is related to the practice of voyaging into the land of the spirits. Belief in such activity does not presume that the shaman or mystic actually becomes a spirit, but that he or she passes beyond the mystical barrier between worlds and enters the realm occupied by spirits. A number of methods are used to achieve a transformational state including group activities such as singing and dancing, ritualistic ceremonies involving fasting and sun gazing, or consuming various kinds of stimulants or hallucinates. (Ancient Persians were believed to drink a hashish-based concoction [*Cannabis sativa*], and various South American tribal groups consumed vast amounts of tobacco to induce a trance.) However, the only way of actually passing beyond the limits of terrestrial space — the middle ground — is spiritual or physical death. The body (corpse) stays behind while the spirit journeys to where it is transformed and remains, or where it is rejected and returned to reunite with its material body.

Shamanism and magic are recurrent elements in the ritual events that assure the successful outcome of the sociological exercises. There are similar recurrent transformational occasions in all societies that are connected with the critical events of in the human life cycle. The practice of transformational release is also a part of most cultures. It serves various objectives including the purging of sins and maladies that are conveyed to deities as well as animate and inanimate objects. The weaknesses of the body may be transferred to a stone, stick, plant, or effigy, and casting the object away eliminated fatigue or pain. Alternatively, social misconduct, misfortune, illness, and sin can be transferred to deities, humans, or animals. The act of confession is a similar transformational practice that relieves the confessor of unacceptable acts. The shaman, priest, mystic, diviner, or soothsayer performs the appropriate ritual in the presence of the errant person and accepted the malady or sin to facilitate the exculpation process.

Like other psychophysical concepts that have been incorporated into beliefs, the idea of transformation extends across cultures and centuries. The spirit possesses the shaman's body during possession ecstasy, and he is transformed into an agent of the spirit. Whereas, the shaman's soul departs to travel into the realm of the spirits in wandering ecstasy. The body of the shaman is transformed in both of these ecstatic states. "Shamanic thought postulates a distant past when there was no difference between humans and animals, when they could talk to one another and even transform themselves from human to animal form at will."[47] Robert McGhee writing in *Ancient Peoples of the Arctic* (1996) states, "The transformations and communications are thought to occur in the present under special circumstances, such as in a dream or when a human soul journeys to one of the other planes of existence, where the animals live as humans do in the mid-world."[48]

References to life transformed by death and dismemberment, transformation of male to female (and vice versa), and the changing roles of the sexes are common to many cultures. The processes of change found in the context of natural and human activities fascinate people. The physiological and psychological complexities associated with daily existence challenge traditional existential practices adding uncertainty and insecurity. Transformation of the ordinary — mundane — into the extraordinary gives greater importance to socio-cultural activities and supports the creation of ritual events that can be controlled by designated intermediaries.

Evelyn Underhill wrote about the role of the mystic in 1911. She stated, "Only the mystic can be called a whole man." She made this assessment on the premise that in others "half the powers of the self always sleeps."[49] This attitude of wholeness particularly as it relates to experience is an important part of mystical activity. Mircea Eliade reinforces this idea in *Shamanism: Archaic Techniques of Ecstasy* (1974) where he states, "A shaman was a man who had immediate, concrete experiences with gods and spirits, he saw them face to face, he talked with them, prayed with them, implored them — but he did not 'control' more than a limited number of them."[50]

Mystics in all cultures seek physical and mental balance through reconciliation to accommodate the connections between opposites. The opposing elements are by necessity given an equal measure of importance to establish and maintain stability. As an example, to give too much importance to a positive situation is to devalue the negative. Thereafter, the negative has little meaning and that in turn lessens the importance of the positive. The concept of equal value is a significant aspect of balance (harmony). An example of this balance is the relationship between salvation and damnation. The appeal of salvation is enhanced by the repulsion of damnation.

The supernatural is often viewed as the real extension of daily life, and as the central figure, the shaman (mystic) must merge with the universe as a harmonious whole. The supernatural is the source of all positive and negative occurrences. It gives life and brings death for humans, animals, and nature. Every object, action, or person is subject to the power of external forces. Everything possesses a form of associated power that emanates from the supernatural, and it is the shaman's role to be the intermediary between the distinct yet closely joined natural and supernatural influences and to ensure harmony. The mystic (shaman) facilitates the exchange between the two domains by locating and consolidating supernatural influences, and reconciling the positive influences of a particular deity with the suffering in the world.

A form of transformation that is critical to shamanistic orientation is the opening of the mind to know things not known to others. This transformational practice demonstrates that similar trends of thought have influenced communities so diverse that they might belong to different worlds. Opening the mind to greater understanding or knowledge — enlightenment (as with Buddhists) — is an inherent element in many belief systems. The mystical transformation is the means to cross the boundaries of the natural and supernatural worlds and thereby to gain access to critical knowledge.

Yogic Mysticism

> Mysticism is inextricably bound up with, dependent upon, and usually subservient to the deeper beliefs and values of the traditions, cultures, and historical milieux which harbour it.[51]

In the Hindu belief relating to the creation of the world and man, the "Universal Self becomes divided immediately after conceiving and utters the pronoun "I" (Sanskrit *aham*). This illustrates the fundamental Indian conviction that a sense of ego [small self] is the root of the world illusion."[52] The I always includes conditions, always influences behavior, and always reacts to circumstantial conditions. The concern with I-ego — imprisonment of the soul (spirit) — is reflected in Buddhist belief that suffering is one of the basic characteristics of existence. Joseph Campbell wrote, "Ego generates fear and desire, and these are the passions that animate all life and even all being; for it is only after the concept 'I' has been established that the fear of one's own destruction can develop or any desire for personal enjoyment."[53] Campbell proposes, "The aim of Indian yoga, therefore is to clear the mind of the concept 'I' and therewith dissolve both fear and desire."[54]

Yoga is an early form of mystical practice that originated in India. It is believed that yoga was taught as early as the sixth century B.C.E., but the prehistory of the yogic tradition is not clearly recorded. Campbell suggests "figures in yoga posture dating from c. 2000 B.C.E. that have been found in ancient ruins of the Indus Valley might indicate a very early initiation of yogic practice."[55] In addition, ascetics mentioned in early Vedic writings may be the predecessors of the later yogis. Although yoga is divided into different schools, it influenced (and continues to influence) many belief systems. Yoga (sometimes described as a mental-psychological-physical meditation system) is a way of achieving union with God. According to Gershom G. Scholem in the general history of religion this fundamental experience is know as *unio mystica*, or mystical union with God.[56] Yoga is also used, as described in the epic poem the *Bhagavad-Gita* ("Divine Song" or "Song of the Lord"), to identify alternate paths to such a union. The *yogi* (yoga practitioner) believes that spiritual liberation occurs when the self is freed from the bondages of matter that is the result of ignorance and illusion.

Yoga in Sanskrit means union. It is a fundamental form of mysticism in India relating to the desire for individual *union* with a force or power greater than the self. This greater power may be defined as an inclusive belief that spreads across the universe or the exclusivity of a personal god. Hindu mysticism includes both these objectives; however, the essence of Hindu mystical thought is the "functional principle that knowing is being." Therefore, it is acknowledged that knowledge is "more than analytical categorizing: it is total understanding. Knowing can also mean total transformation."[57] It is believed that if the practitioner truly knows something (love and devotion for example), he is transformed into that being.

Yogic mysticism recognizes the importance of controlling the mind and body as a means of realization as described in the *Yoga-sutra* said to have been written or compiled by Patanjali between the second century B.C.E. and fifth century C.E. The true authorship of the sutra has not however been verified. The process of controlling mind and body takes the form of extreme asceticism and mortification at times. It may be, at other times, in the form of cultivation of mind and body so their energies are properly directed. The understanding imparted by yogic practice may be purely intellectual, and some such attitudes equate to the final goal with omniscience — an inclusiveness that joins mind, body, and spirit free from karmic obstruction. The yogi or yogini (female yoga practitioner) in the transformed state is thought to be in an immediate and loving relationship with the deity.[58]

The *tantra* (Sanskrit, meaning the warp or weft of a fabric or loom) are numerous texts dealing with esoteric practices closely associated with yoga and its influence on Buddhism. Forms of tantra differ significantly from each other; however, the basic attitude deals with the spreading of knowledge. Tantra refers to a group of post–Vedic treatises that deal with such topics as spells, rituals, and religious practices. They are secret books of teaching that contain knowledge of theology, techniques of concentration (yoga), and such practical religious activities as the making of images, the building of temples, ways of worship, and the hierarchy of living beings. The books also include instructions on the drawing of *yantras* and *mandalas* (ritual diagrams), and the use of mantras (secret formulas) and *mudrâs* (mystic gestures).

Tantrism is an important part of both Buddhism and Hinduism. It influenced many religious practices from the fifth century C.E. Tantrism advocates new ways to achieve higher goals through mystical speculation and divine energy.

The *Sakta Tantras* relate to yoga and subsequently to Buddhism. Manuscripts relating to the *Sakta Tantra* date to about the seventh century C.E. (650 or earlier), and they "emphasize the goddess Sakti (Shakti) as the female personification of the creative power or energy of god."[59] She is also symbolizes shamanic healing energy, and is identified with *kundalini*, the coil of energy at the base of the spine that is infused into the body by yogic discipline. The dragon is associated with the *Sakti* as a representative of *kundalini* power in Tantra Buddhism.

Yogic practices include several features borrowed from the magical and mystical traditions of both Aryan and aboriginal India that incorporate shamanic elements. Mircea Eliade calls attention to shamanic practices such as "flying through the air, disappearing, becoming extremely tall or extremely short"[60] that are found in early yogic techniques. The yogi is, however, said to be a "higher transformation of the shamanistic techniques and experiences of ecstasis."[61] Numerous instructional texts warn against the dangers of being seduced by the "magical sense of boundless capability that they (various techniques and narcotic stimulants) produce and that can make the yogin forget his true aim—final liberation."[62]

Yogic mysticism is one of the six orthodox systems of Indian philosophy. It is a system of physical and mental discipline wherein the union with the Absolute is realized through self-control. This control emphasizes spiritual liberation from the physical and intellectual constraints of matter that are the result of ignorance and illusion. Perfected body control leads to control of both natural and divine forces. Hatha Yoga (Sanskrit for Union of Forces), as an example of this philosophy, emphasizes mastery of the body as a method of gaining spiritual perfection.

"The central mystical experience of enlightenment is aptly symbolized by Light in most of the numerous forms of mysticism."[63] The color of light (or the lack of light) is also considered an important factor. Light of different colors indicates the success of particular meditations and yogic techniques, especially those of the Buddhist schools. The *Tibetan Book of the Dead* also assigns great significance to the light (color) of the dying person's soul during his final hours and immediately after death. The individual's destiny (deliverance or reincarnation) depends on the purity of the chosen light—described as the Clear Light of Reality.[64]

In contrast with the light of destiny there is the so-called dark night of the soul that is due, according to Evelyn Underhill, to the "double fact of the exhaustion of an old state [of being], and the growth towards a new state of consciousness."[65] John Lee Maddox explains in one further example that the priests and exorcists (shamans) in China possessed a special power, "the so called 'Yang power' of good [light side], through which they were expected to avert droughts and other troubles by rendering harmless the evil-force of darkness or 'Yin'"[66]

> The human body is like a rootless tree and relies solely on the breath as root and branches. A lifetime is just a dream, like an out breath which does not guarantee the in breath after it, and today does not ensure the morrow.[67]

There are differences between the mystical nature of shamanism and yoga. Mircea Eliade notes that the final goal of shamanism is "always ecstasy and the soul's ecstatic journey through the various cosmic regions, whereas Yoga pursues *ecstasis* [as the] final concentration of the spirit and 'escape' from the cosmos."[68] When there is harmony between body and mind, self-realization can be achieved. Yoga teaches that the obstacles in the way of self-realization are apparent in the physical or mental condition. That is, when the physical condition is not perfect, the mental state is placed in a condition of imbalance know in Sanskrit as *chittavritti*. The practice of yoga assists in ameliorating that imbalance.[69] Consistent with this attitude, Tibetan Buddhists (a practice that incorporates elements of yoga) contend that the "mind is not merely a product of physical functions or chemical reactions,"[70] but the essential factor of life. It builds the body, and consequently, good health is ascribed to a "balanced, harmonious mind and diseases to mental disorder or spiritual disharmony."[71]

Taoist Mysticism

> Taoists honor balance [harmony] above all and the masculine *yang* energy, but they are aware that it is through what the *Tao Te Ching* calls the valley spirit — the spirit of the sacred feminine, the Mother, the *yin* energy — that the deepest realization is attained.[72]

"Existence — the Way — the Nameless — Ultimate Reality — the Void — Emptiness — the Absolute — all of these are Tao and yet none of them are, for the Tao is beyond description by the human mind."[73] Though words cannot exactly explain what *Tao* actually is, it constitutes the foundation of existence for Taoists. The way of the Tao may be described as simple. It demands no exceptional talents or achievements, no specialized training or expertise. Ambition, luxury, wealth, or pleasure must not be a part of the life-attitude of the Taoist. The only requirement is complete self-abnegation. It is everything and nothing that only a person with an open mind and in complete forgetfulness of self is capable of understanding beyond its surface layer. Tao is the source from which all things originate and toward which all things proceed. It is the Way.

The Tao is a mystical approach to transcending everyday life. Its goal is to find the *path* or the way of nature.[74] Taoism, like other forms of Eastern mysticism, distinguishes itself from Western mysticism by its conscious techniques of mind and body designed to induce trance and to give access to mystical experience.[75] It is, in the broadest sense, the way the universe functions, and is characterized by the alternations (transformations) of phenomena, such as day followed by night, that proceed without effort.[76] "Between man and universe there exists a system of correspondences and participations that the ritualists, philosophers, alchemists, and physicians have described but certainly not invented."[77]

There are two principal approaches to Taoism. One is mystical philosophy (*Tao-chia*) in which the mystic seeks to find Tao or truth by living a disciplined life of denial and poverty devoted to meditation and matters of life and death. This practice endorses the belief that man is God, therefore, "the only way to know God or Tao is to know oneself, and that knowledge comes only from the deep recesses of the mind or the 'spirit self,' discovered through the medium of meditation."[78] The other path is liturgical Taoism (*Tao-chiao*) in which the common person relies on traditional methods of accessing God's wisdom, that is, through the involvement of intermediaries, rituals, and organized religious institutions. (A possible third approach advocated by contemporary scholars includes a communal or social element.[79])

Regardless of the path followed, "Taoism has no dogma, for the ever-changing flow and growth of life itself cannot be bound by rules nor by man-made intellectual categories."[80] The Taoist mystic aspires to attain both an orderly and organic life joined into one harmonious existence. The mystic might acknowledge different aspects of the Tao to understand truth and the fulfillment of the Way. He (most often a male) might marvel in the seasons, contemplate the celestial bodies, or just glorify the personal needs for food and sleep. The objective is to reach into the center of the world and to find the essence of the Tao. "The realm of Tao is the realm of man's inner spirit, his Reality; to live in accord with the Tao is to live at one with one's being."[81]

Livia Kohn defines Chinese mysticism in the book *Early Chinese Mysticism: Philosophy and Soteriology in the Taoist Tradition* (1992) as "the worldview that seeks the perfection of the individual through union with an agent or force conceived as absolute."[82] The absolute in this reference is the Tao. It is in this way that the Tao is fundamental to all existence. "It makes the world function, brings all beings to life, and orders the entire universe, ever transforming and changing continuously."[83] It is "ineffable and defies all sensual definition; it cannot be seen, heard, or felt. Yet it can be reached."[84]

> The conception of the universe common to all Chinese philosophy is neither materialistic nor animistic (a belief system centering on soul substances); it can be called magical or even alchemical.[85]

Taoism is believed to have been established by Lao-tzu in the sixth century B.C.E., and it is considered more mystical than philosophical. (*Lao* means old or elder and *tzu* is "knowledgeable person" and is sometimes translated to identify a teacher. Lao-tzu's family name is thought to be Li and his given name Tan.[86]) Although the Tao, literally translated road or way is a difficult and complex concept, it represents the cosmic order, and is an important aspect of Chinese religion. The cosmic order is about total order. It is composed not only of all natural things but also social and moral rules. The Tao as advocated by Lao-tzu was the primordial unity—the One. It is the oneness which is fundamental to all phenomena.

The cosmic principle in Taoism is more than order. It is the concept that gives existence meaning, and it is used to designate a high deity in some instances. Taoism is a mystic religion, and the *Tao-te Ching* (*Classic of the Way and Its Power*) is a mystic discourse in which the essential nature of the Tao is elucidated in stories and metaphors because it is difficult to explain in logical terms. The complexity of the writing is acknowledged by the first words of the *Tao-te Ching*, "The Tao that can be trod is not the enduring and unchanging Tao, and the name that can be named is not the enduring and unchanging name."[87] Nevertheless, the *Tao-te Ching* expresses the fundamental concepts of early Chinese mysticism.

Taoists believe that the interaction of yin and yang (as described in the *I Ching* [also written, *Yi Ching*], the *Book of Changes*, the ancient Chinese guidebook) holds the world in balance (harmony), because they are interdependent and acknowledged as always being in relationship. The bad must be given the same value as the good for that reason. If this is not done, for example, a person is a hostage of his good or bad side, unable to acknowledge it as part of himself, and thus not free to integrate it with the opposite value. "The Tao is thus described in a pattern of outer and inner, yin and yang, dark and light. Opposed to it is the reality of everyday life as interpreted by the human mind."[88]

Although the notion of integration of opposites is essential to Taoism, Carl Jung commented on this concept as it relates to Christian mysticism. He wrote, "Ascent and descent, above and below, up and down, represent an emotional realization of opposites, and this realization gradually leads or should lead, to their equilibrium."[89] Jung calls this equilibrium the "'liberation from opposites,' the *nirdvandva* of Hindu philosophy."[90]

The concept of change is the basic nature of yin and yang, which always change into each other. When yin dominates for too long, it "grows old" and renews itself by changing into yang, and vice versa. As described in the *I Ching*, change means the yin and yang reflect each other, affront each other, and restore each other. Anne Bancroft wrote in *Religions of the East* (1974), "The Tao has no opposites; it is the Absolute Ground, pure, eternal and unchanging. But once it is manifest into the duality of Yin and Yang, there is no absoluteness ... in any manifestation; all pairs of opposites can become each other."[91] This sense of duality is exemplified by occurrences in daily existence: Happiness turns to sorrow, life becomes death, day turns into night, desire converts to hatred, and rejection replaces acceptance. Each occurrence gives birth to the other, eliminates the other, and maintains balance.

The *I Ching* deals with the cosmic forces, and through its pronouncements has universal validity. Used originally for divination, its influence on Chinese thinking relates to a system of cosmology that incorporates humans and nature in a single system. The *I Ching* offers a clear distinction between "separate duties to the family, to the state, and to the Gods — all of them being considered as overlapping parts of a single whole."[92] The cosmic order, in this context, is viewed as benevolent in that the individual feels safe and his existence is assured because such an order is different than the personal relationship between the individual and his god. The cosmic order is in clear contrast with the disorder of chaos. It is *total order* that includes all natural things as well as social and ethical rules.[93]

Taoism is the most characteristic Chinese form of practical mysticism. Mystical philosophy, a kind of thinking distinctive from that of the early philosophers, includes instructional writings and a practical manual developed in the fifth century with the establishment of Taoism as a religion.[94] The Taoist mystic views the universe as a structured environment in which each part replicates the whole. It is in this context that the mystic considers the Tao as nature, but as more than nature. It is the essence of nature. It is that quality — that essential character — that makes things what they are. "The Taoist mystic ... not only adapts himself ritually and physiologically to the alternations of nature but creates a void inside himself that permits him to return to nature's origin."[95]

Taoism has a tradition of thaumaturgy (performance of miracles) and magic as well as scholarly pursuits. The Tao can be considered an inspirational thesis or a mystical doctrine. It can also be viewed as one of the primary sources of Chinese magic, including the search for the elixir of life (alchemy). Theistic Taoism includes the idea of balance and interaction of cosmic forces (natural energies). Taoism has a diversity that lends itself to considerations from philosophy to pseudo-science to magic.

The mystical practices in ancient China gave special attention to three activities:

1. Maintenance of the emperor's health and vitality;
2. Correction and maintenance of the standards of time, of space, of weight, and of pitch; and
3. Perception and interpretation of omens foretelling the future, illuminating obscurities of the present, and guiding the policies of the government toward those that would gain the favor of heaven.[96]

According to mystical Taoist tradition the true sage is a person who abides by the way of heaven and earth without seeking personal goals. He views success or misfortune equally and follows the natural order of all things. Flexibility, long life, and even spiritual immortality are regarded as the outcome of living without conflict and strife. The concepts of mystical Taoism inspired many Chinese scholars, poets, artists, recluses, and artisans.[97]

The ideal person must live in accordance with the Tao, and in harmony with the natural course of things. Because opposites are relative and interdependent, a Taoist does not struggle, oppose, or strive. Even so, the ego or self are not completely dormant in the Taoist mystics. "They have roused the dweller in the innermost from its slumbers, and round it have united their life. Heart, Reason, Will are there in full action, drawing their incentive not from the shadow-show of sense, but from the depths of true Being."[98]

> The aim of religious practice is to be rid of the delusion of ego, thus freeing oneself from the fetters of this mundane world. One who is successful in doing so is said to have overcome the round of rebirths and to have achieved enlightenment. This is the final goal — not a paradise or a heavenly world.[99]

Jewish Mysticism

> Prior to the penultimate state of being, before total union with the Absolute, the universe and mankind have to pass through many stages. According to one view, the human race as a whole is less than half way in its development.[100]

Though the mystical nature of all religions developed over time, western religions and mystical practices tend to emphasize obedient response to the Word of God. In contrast, Eastern religions are, for the most part, concerned with humanity's struggle to understand and deal with the conditions of its existence and to achieve liberation, enlightenment, and unity with the Absolute.[101]

Anne Bancroft wrote in her book *Religions of the East* (1974), "Mysticism is realizing the Self, or God, as one's inner Being, more truly oneself than one's manifest self." Accord to her thinking, "The eastern religions are mystical, while the three religions which have their origin in the Near East—Judaism, Christianity, and Islam—are not, for they believe that God is to be found 'out there,' somewhere infinitely beyond man."[102] However, Dion Fortune insists, "The mysticism of Israel supplies the foundation of modern Western occultism. It forms the theoretical basis upon which all ceremonial is developed. Its famous glyph, the Tree of Life (*Etz haChayim* in Hebrew), is the best meditation-symbol we possess because it is the most comprehensive"[103] (**see figure 3.1**).

> The Tree of Life, as cannot too often be emphasised, is not so much a system as a method; those who formulated it realized the important truth that in order to obtain clarity of vision one must circumscribe the field of vision.[104]

The Jewish Kabbalah (for the original version, Cabala signifying the Christian version, and Qabalah indicating the Hermetic version) is the most prominent form of alleged theurgic (the power to perform supernatural or magic

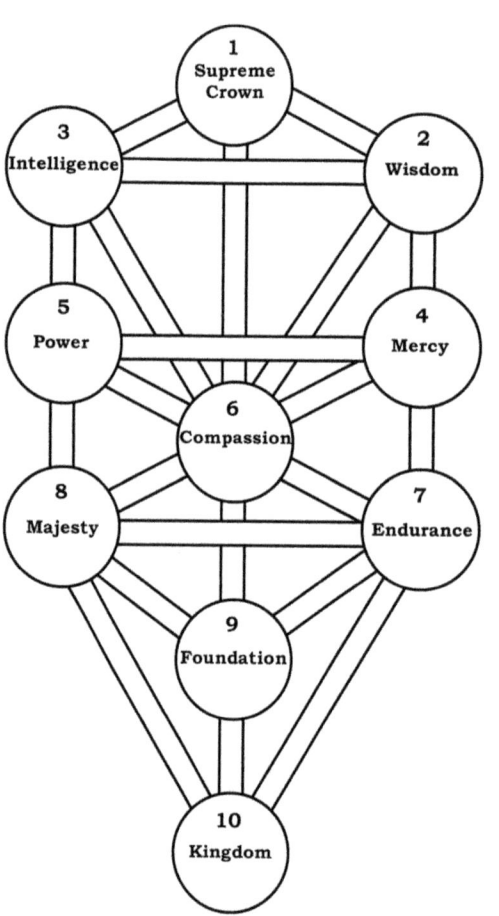

Figure 3.1: The Kabbalah Tree of Life (Hebrew: *Etz haChayim*) is a meditative device and a symbol of the progression of wisdom. The tree represents any ten manifestations or powers by which by God as the Creator becomes manifest. The relationship between the ten elements and their meaning is believed to represent the rhythm of creation. It was perhaps this transformational element—the moving from one stage to another—that inspired Jewish alchemists.

things) mysticism.[105] The Hebrew word "*kabbalah* means 'receiving' or 'that which has been received.' On one hand, Kabbalah may also be translated as a reference to tradition, ancient wisdom received and treasured from the past. On the other hand, if one is truly receptive, wisdom appears spontaneously, unprecedented, taking you by surprise."[106]

Although the mystic quest takes different forms — spiritual, physiological, or material — the goal is communication with the Godhead for the purpose of unification (oneness) with the supreme truth. David Ariel wrote in the book *The Mystic Quest: An Introduction to Jewish Mysticism* (1988), "The Jewish mystical conception of human psychology is based on a spiritual theory of the origin and destiny of the human soul."[107] Ariel contends, "Unlike modern psychology, Jewish mysticism posits the existence of a spiritual realm beyond the individual that animates and energizes the life of the soul."[108]

The message of the Kabbalah begins (conceptually), according to Z'ev ben Shimon Halevi, with the name given to Moses as he stood before the burning bush on Holy Mountain. Moses was told he should tell the people of Israel that EHYEH ASHER EHYEH had given him instruction about leaving Egypt. It is this name of names, *I AM THAT I AM*, that sets out the Absolute's Will (also see Exodus 3:13).[109] The implications of this name give a key to why the universe and its inhabitants exist. Everything between the limits of harmony above and disarray below is part of a process of spiritual fulfillment. The realization of this process will be achieved when "the mirror of the macrocosm reflects the name *I AM* back as a fully conscious image to its Divine origin."[110]

The Kabbalah is esoteric Jewish mysticism as it was represented in the twelfth century. It is an oral tradition, and a personal guide is needed to conduct initiates through the labyrinth of doctrines and practices to avoid the dangers inherent in mystical experience. Esoteric Kabbalah claims to include secret knowledge of the unwritten Torah that was communicated by God to Moses and Adam. It provides the means for approaching God directly. The roots of Kabbalah can be traced to *Merkava* mysticism, an ecstatic and mystical consideration of the moving throne or chariot as seen by the prophet and described in Ezekiel 1. The *Sefer Yetzirah* (*Book of Creation*), the earliest known book on magic and cosmology, also influenced the Kabbalah. The *Book of Creation* tells that God created the world using thirty-two secret ways of knowledge that are the ten Sephira and the twenty-two letters in the Hebrew alphabet.

Merkava mysticism began in Palestine during the first century of the Common Era. The Merkava mystics apparently sought a visionary glimpse of the divine throne situated on its chariot. The initiates fasted to prepare for the rigorous journey and used certain magical formulas (called seals) to placate the angelic gatekeepers of each of the seven heavenly dwellings through which they had to pass. It was believed that use of an incorrect seal could result in injury or death.[111] The Merkava movement continued through the eleventh or twelfth century. It was centered in Babylonia at that time.

Early Jewish mystics described their experience as an "ascent of the soul to the Celestial Throne where [he] obtains an ecstatic view of the majesty of God and the secrets of His Realm."[112] The objective of the Kabbalist is to be a purposeful agent of transformation between the eternal and transient worlds. That is to say, to guide the raising of energy, matter, and awareness from the ordinary level to a higher state, and to transmit power and consciousness from the realm of the soul, so that the natural world may experience paradise.[113] Similarly, the material quest seeks to transform one material into another as exemplified by the transformation of base metal into fine metal. The truth sought in this (alchemic) process is the defining origin (composition) of materials.

Although many persons want to return to the Light and to escape the lessons of the lower world, before access is allowed certain tests must be undergone. Fundamental to the learning process, the methods of the Kabbalah cannot really be taught; they must be experienced. Its metaphors and history make it a uniquely Jewish form of spiritual practice. Nonetheless, the Kabbalistic experience is universal in that it seeks to realize the No-thingness of all things."[114] This effort and objective are similar to the doctrine associated with the Tao.

The Kabbalah is a guidebook for the soul on its path upward in the way of the Tibetan and Egyptian books of the dead. It is also a book of wisdom similar to the *I Ching*, which can be studied for its own sake. Kabbalah is a primary means for individuals wishing to shorten the time to self-realization by self-improvement. The spiritual traditions, such as Kabbalah, are to help such individuals, because "to overcome the forces of nature, rise above fatal patterns, avoid the tricks of tempters, and tactfully move among the angels on the ascent of Jacob's Ladder, is not [an] easy matter."

Judaism in its classical form is defined as faith in a sole God who created the universe and who revealed himself to a select group by means of a rule of life. Consequently, Jewish mysticism as the search for direct contact with the divine may seem to be incompatible with Judaism. Nevertheless, the book *The Occult: A History* (1971) by Collin Wilson describes the Kabbalah as "one of the oldest systems of mystical thought in the world; it was regarded for many centuries as the key to all the mysteries of the universe."[115] (Some scholars believe the Kabbalah is derived from Gnostic doctrine and the first book *Sepher Yetzirah* was written in the second century of the common era.) Kabbalists became heirs to Gnostical symbolism in the thirteenth century thus reinforcing the connection between the two belief systems.

The Kabbalah is viewed as being related to Gnosticism (having gnosis or secret knowledge), in that God withheld sacred knowledge from humanity in both beliefs. Eventually, the withheld knowledge was given to man by God's rival, the serpent in the Garden who tempted Eve, and the fallen angels who gave the Kabbalah. It is knowledge of God, that is the important factor in both instances, and to know God is the purpose of the Kabbalah.

Knowledge in the form of the written word has been essential to Judaism from its beginning as a religion. The texts are central to Jewish life and culture. Mysticism is also a meaningful element of Judaism. It represents belief in the direct vision of divine resources and a way to experience things and events other than through our ordinary senses. The mystic element is defined in the *Zohar*, a writing that is described as the *Talmud* of Jewish mysticism.[116] This book written in the thirteenth century is of historical importance. It expands upon the Torah by literal, allegorical, and expository techniques and, most important, by mystical insight.

> Kabbalistic hermeneutics may be said to be founded upon a defined numerical system: the units of ten, and the twenty-two letters, each letter having a number in the letter-numeral relationship of Semitic notation, constitute the raw material, comprising the "thirty-two marvelous tracts of wisdom" upon which the whole system is built.[117]

Jacob's Ladder and the great Tree of Existence (the center pole) are reminiscent of the shamanist practices of Siberia and areas of Asia. The shaman climbs a ladder to reach the upper world, and the center of the world is marked by a tree around which the shaman dances or upon which he sits. The Chinese diviner or soothsayer drives a stake into the ground to mark the center location of a new house before it can be built. Granted the Jacob's Ladder and Tree of Existence endorsed by the Kabbalists is much more complicated than the simple spirit enhancing elements used by the indigenous shaman and diviner, however the similarities exist. The teachings of the Kabbalah were popular in the countries of the eastern Mediterranean starting around the first century of this era.

It may be said that Kabbalist thinking was due to the influence the semi–Gnostic Manichaeism — the universal message to replace all other religious expounded by Mani, in Persia during the third century C.E. — that a universal dualism between soul and matter was formalized. This doctrine complements the dogma represented in the Kabbala. Manichaeism is a type of Gnosticism that views the world as painful and offers salvation through knowledge of spiritual truth. Those persons following either belief (Manichaeism or Gnosticism) thought they were the chosen because they possessed knowledge of the divine.

Adolphe Franck notes in *The Kabbalah: The Religious Philosophy of the Hebrews* (1940) that the borrowing of material from the ancient Persians "did not destroy the originality of the Kabbalah for [the theology of the ancient Persians] substituted the absolute unity of cause and substance for the dualism in God and nature."[118] Franck contends, "Instead of explaining the formation of beings as an arbitrary act of inimical [contrary] forces, it presents them as divine forms, successive and providential manifestations of the Infinite Intelligence."[119] Franck believes that the similarities between the Kabbalah and the texts of "several sects in Persian" (presumably including Manichaeism) fall within the "general law of the human mind. No absolute originality, but also no servile imitation between nations and centuries."[120]

Christian Mysticism

> Rationalism and superstition are complementary. It is a psychological rule that the brighter the light, the blacker the shadow; in other words, the more rationalistic we are in our conscious minds, the more alive becomes the spectral world of the unconscious.[121]

It is often assumed that people in different parts of the world believe in different gods and spirits and that the validity of their beliefs can neither be confirmed nor denied. Such thinking is always relative to a people's intellect and range of experience. The connection between ideas and outcomes is true and lasting only for the experience prevailing at a particular time and place. Adding to these tenuous sociological conditions are the difficulties imposed by conventional church leadership; thus, it is easy to understand the strong attraction that religious ecstasy has always had within the Christian community. The mystic, as a religiously motivated person, wishes to grasp the divine essence or ultimate reality by actually speaking with God. It may be said, however, that in the "case of Christian mystical experiences, how those experiences are interpreted seems to be more important than the experiences themselves."[122]

Charles Morris Addison wrote extensively about Christian mysticism, and in his book titled *The Theory and Practice of Mysticism 1918*, he gave attention to the meaning of the word mysticism. He surmises that "sometimes we have a knowledge that is not easy to put into words. So Mysticism almost defies definition. It is as undefinable [sic] and yet as recognizable as Beauty, or Love — or God, yet still it is possible to get a better understanding of it and to approach some sort of definition which will be true as far as it goes."[123]

Theistic mysticism, or mystical theology, is considered "a communicable and inexpressible knowledge and love of God or of religious truth received in the spirit without precedent effort or reasoning."[124] Mystics, in accordance with this definition, have often claimed to have secret knowledge of God that has been conveyed to them in a covert manner. They have subsequently undertaken to share that special information for the good of humanity. This exchange entails a reliable metaphysical perception of God and an equally astute view of the human soul (spirit).

The great mystics of Christianity and other religions of the world have often received their first illumination either in circumstances of extreme adversity, or in a form that appeared initially as a severe affliction. The conception of this first mystic revelation, though viewed as a dreaded sickness, is recognized as a prerequisite for mystical authentication. This test of surviving a seemingly fatal illness is found among many peoples, and it is particularly true for shamans of northeast Asia. The shaman must die, have his bones removed and washed by spirits, and be reassembled. The articulated skeleton is sheathed with flesh, and the restored shaman is returned to serve the needs of his community. A similar concept is found in Egypt where Osiris was dismembered and the parts of his body were scattered. His wife, Isis, collected and reassembled the pieces. It was her magical power that brought him back to life (c. 2350-c. 2100 B.C.E.).

David Knowles gave attention in his book *What Is Mysticism* (1967) to both the notion of mysticism and the specific nature of theistic mysticism as related to Christian mystical practices. He believes, "Ardent love, self-sacrifice, wisdom and clarity of vision are the signs of true Christian mysticism — above all, perhaps, the abiding realization of union with a transcendent, infinite Being beyond all knowledge."[125] Knowledge is the reoccurring theme in these commentaries on mysticism. Carl Jung also wrote about the nature of Christian mysticism in *Mysterium Coniunctionis* (1970). He noted, "Only the mystics bring creativity to religion. That is probably why they can feel the presence and the workings of the Holy Ghost, and why they are nearer to the experience of brotherhood in Christ."[126] Jung emphasizes in this statement the idea of union between humanity and the Godhead.

The belief in the mystical realm is significant to all religions regardless of definition or explanation. Evelyn Underhill wrote in *Practical Mysticism* (1960), "Since it is of the essence of the Christian religion to combine personal and metaphysical truth, a transcendent and an incarnate God, it is not surprising that we should find in Christianity a philosophical and theological basis for this paradox of the contemplative experience."[127] Underhill continues, "Most often ... the Christian mystic identifies the personal and intimate Lover of the soul, of whose elusive essence he is so sharply aware, with the person of Christ; the unknowable and transcendent Godhead."[128]

Mysticism has played an important role in the history of Christian religion. The Virgin of Guadalupe, for example, is said to have appeared in a vision to a Mexican Indian named Juan Diego in 1531 and commanded that a church should be built. That mystical episode was very important to the conversion of the indigenous population of Mexico to Christianity. Similarly, when Christianity was introduced into Korea, it had to consider the cultural setting in which shamans had served indigenous populations for five thousand years. Christian mystical experiences that are confirmed throughout the Bible had to be examined in relation to traditional Korean shamanistic practices.[129] These mystical acknowledgments seemed especially relevant in that environment because they related to an abundant spirit world.

Early church leaders recognized the significance of traditional beliefs and developed Christian philosophy, principally Neoplatonic theology, that incorporates all the better aspects of Grecian, Indian, and Egyptian spiritual perception to support and explain the revelations of the mystic. It reiterates the values of metaphysics in terms of personality and proposes a living mediator between the Unknow God and the conditioned (expectant) self. This concept resolves the conundrum researchers encounter when considering the conditions that are beyond sensual perception, the compatibility of infinity and intimate — conditions known and felt, but not understood. The living mediator (mystic, priest, or spiritual advisory) is essential if the mystical concept is to reach an active union (God and self), that is its objective, and develop from a ecstatic rapture into fulfilling and selfless love.[130]

People pursuing a personal quest for intellectual and spiritual fulfillment often encounter not one truth but several truths, and not one but several views of reality. They are thereby conscious of a conflict in the agreement of things, in that to endorse one truth is to deny another. Consequently, to know spiritual truth men and women must in their basic nature be spiritual, and to know their God, there should be at least some kinship between God and the human soul.[131]

"Mysticism is concerned with the possibility of personally encountering a spiritual reality which is hidden from our normal awareness."[132] It acknowledges a supernatural force that explains fundamental questions regarding existence that are unanswerable in other ways. The "nostalgia for paradise"[133] is a compelling force found in all organized religious experiences. It is the garden of life (paradise) extolled by Judaism, Christianity, and Islam and the golden age of human society marking the beginning of each cycle of human existence recognized by Buddhism and Hinduism. It is a final state of bliss conceived as a heavenly afterlife by Islam and Christianity, the Hinduism's union with the divine, and the eternal condition of peace and changelessness embraced by Buddhism.[134] All aspects of a paradisiacal setting is an illusion that reinforces mystical references and religious dogma.

People at different cultural plateaus separate their social conditions into subsections and arrange those elements into an order of preference. Emotion and passion in that differentiated state are tempered by basic experience and reason, and individual reaction is moderated by group requirements. Every object, action, or person is subject to the power of supernatural forces — mystical energy. Everything possesses a form of associated power that emanates from the supernatural, and it is the mystic's role to be an intermediary between distinct, yet closely joined, natural and supernatural influences. This role — the unification of the natural and the supernatural — is regularly re-enacted within Christian religious practice. The laity is directed to partake of the bread and wine that are transubstantiated into the body and blood of Christ.[135] The practitioners are taught that Jesus is spiritually as well as physically present in the Eucharist, and by participation in this communion they are unified with the Son of God.

Although orthodox Christianity has endeavored to minimize the mystical interpretations of trance or an altered state of consciousness where there are claims of divine revelation, there have been many visions by mystic Christians. "The mystic claims contact with an order of reality transcending the world of the senses and the ordinary forms of discursive intellectual knowing."[136] When the church is obliged to recognize or honor these individuals, they have done so for different reasons. The concept of heresy is a strong deterrent for mystical experimentation within the Christian environment.[137]

Consistent with the beliefs of other major religions, mysticism refers to direct experience or consciousness of reality, and this concept of mystical acknowledgment is understood to refer to God within the Christian faith.[138] The essential nature of mysticism, as previously described, is contact in some form with the divine or transcendent, as exemplified by union with God. The New Testament describes several instances of mysticism in various forms.

The earliest known manifestation is called Christ-mysticism, and it related to the writings of the apostles. This mysticism is also present in the activities of the church. The priest in the Catholic Church presents himself as an earthly manifestation of Christ, and people are instructed to experience God through the one Christ—to be one with and in Christ.

Rufus Jones includes a quotation from Canon R.C. Moberly in his book *Studies in Mystical Religions* (1970 [1909]) that speaks to the issue of Christian mysticism. Canon Moberly said, "Christian mysticism is the doctrine, or rather the experience, of the Holy Spirit—the realization of human personality as characterized by, and consummated in the indwelling reality of the Spirit of Christ, which is God."[139] The alignment of the physical and spiritual reaffirms belief and grants creditability to the supernatural.

Dissident groups have criticized the lack of freedom, charity, or vitality in the institutional Christian church. Their concerns have included many issues, but, in particular, they called for a greater sensitivity to the mystical practice attributed to the Holy Spirit. The fifth book of the New Testament, Acts of the Apostles, gives attention to the numerous manifestations of the Holy Spirit. Acts defines the activities of the Spirit as healing, prophesying, expelling demons (exorcism), and speaking in tongues. These mystical activities are linked to the Old Testament reference to the Spirit of Yahweh; however, there is no explicit belief in the spirit as a separate anthropomorphized manifestation. It (the spirit) is ethereal. The actual nature of the Holy Spirit as the intercessor (*paraclete*) or helper spirit (familiar) though described in the Gospel According to John has been an issue within the Catholic Church for centuries.

Christ-mysticism includes the special contact (relationship) Jesus enjoyed with God (Luke 10:21–22)—a union of ultimate reality.[140] Jesus said, "The Father and I are one" (John 10:30). In addition, Colossians 2:9–10 describes the unification of the human spirit with the body with Christ. It states that Christ embodies the "full content of divine nature [with God]"; and that "He is supreme over every spiritual ruler and authority." Jesus states in John 14:7–11, "I am the way, the truth, and the life; no one goes to my Father except by me. Now that you have known me," he said to them, "you will know my Father also, and from now on you do know him and you have seen him." Colossians 2:11 explains, "In union with Christ you were circumcised, not with the circumcision that is made by men, but with the circumcision made by Christ, which consists of being freed from the power of this sinful self." The Oneness of Christ with God and humankind with Christ emphasize the mystic concept of union with the Absolute.

All aspects of religious doctrine are subject to interpretation. The universal nature of religion is consequently difficult to define, although attempts continue to be made to determine the essential elements. Beyond describing religion as a system of practices related to the divine, almost all descriptions refer to belief in transcendental power, that is, the acknowledgment of mystical or supernatural experience that is outside the material world. As an example, there is mystical implication associated with the devotions of the cult of saints. Although the Catholic Church does not endorse this practice, it does indicate understanding of it as an extension of belief in the communion of saints, and a simple and pleasing familiarity with the world of the supernatural.[141]

The mystic experience vastly transcends the "richness of life" according to Rufus Jones.[142] He describes the experience as being "marked by the emergence of a sort of undifferentiated consciousness like that well known to us when we rise to a high appreciation of the beautiful in nature or art or music."[143] Jones explains that "at the highest moments of appreciation there comes, not a loss of consciousness, but the emergence of a new level of consciousness in which neither the *I* nor the *object* is focused in perception or thought."[144]

Islamic Mysticism

> [T]he roots of Islamic mysticism formerly were supposed to have stemmed from various non–Islamic sources in ancient Europe and even India, it now seems established that the movement grew out of early Islamic asceticism.[145]

F. C. Happold contends "Islam is the most transcendent of all the higher religions; in no other is the complete 'otherness' of God so strongly emphasized. Yet out of it came one of the most beautiful and profound upsurges of mystical insight in the whole history of mysticism."[146] He explains, "In Sufism ... one finds a most subtle blending of the experience of God as the Divine Lover and of utter self-loss in Him."[147]

The Sufis distinguish three organs of spiritual communication: the heart (*qalb*), which knows God; the spirit (*ruh*), which loves him; and the inmost ground of the soul (*sirr*), which contemplates him.[148] Sufi relies on the Holy Qur'an as the source of faith, but its adherents gave it a different interpretation, including the mystical union with God that is the foundation of Sufi belief.

Sufism as the spirituality and mysticism of Islam is a way of love, and its doctrine is about the way of submission to God — the ecstatic passage of the spirit into union with him. It is written, "[f]or thousands of years, Sufism has offered a path on which one can progress toward the 'great end' of Self-realization, or God-realization. Sufism is a way of love, a way of devotion, and a way of knowledge."[149] It is believed that Islamic mysticism evolved out of early asceticism, and that Râbi'ah al Adawiyah introduced the element of love that changed asceticism into mysticism. Rabi'ah, an eighth century writer and poet, is credited as being the one who "first formulated the Sufi ideal of a love of God that was disinterested, without hope for paradise and without fear of hell."[150]

Sufis "rebelled against the era of sumptuous luxury and corrupt power which followed the death of the Prophet Muhammed, and they became desert wanderers and ascetics, dressed in garments made from coarse wool."[151] Therefore, Islamic mysticism is called *tasawwuf* in Arabic (literally, to dress in wool or it can be translated to mean self-purification[152]), but it is known as Sufism in Western languages.[153] The term Sufi was applied to Muslim ascetics and mystics because they wore garments made of *suf or soof* (wool). It is also possible, as believed by some persons, that word sufi is derived from *sa fá* meaning he was pure. (This translation is reinforced by the fact that initiates called themselves *Asfiá*, pure.)[154]

Sufis are also often known as the poor, *faqará'*, plural for the Arabic *faqir*, and in Persian they are called *darvish*. (*Dar* means, door and probably refers to a person who goes from door to door, as when begging for food or lodging.) These terms are the source of the English words fakir and dervish.

The word Islam is said to come from the Arabic root *s-l-m*, which can be translated as peace and surrender [submission] and at its heart is the mystical concept of surrendering to God — the abandoning of self and its personal will, and embracing the divine will.[155] A literal translation of Islam might be "that peace that comes when one's entire being and life are surrendered to God."[156] A definition of Sufism drawn from tenth century documentation and quoted by James Fadiman and Robert Frager is, "The Sufis are people who prefer God to everything, and God prefers them to everything else."[157]

Although Islam and Sufism both love the Absolute, the One True God, Islam does not encourage the ascetic life. The good Muslim need not have a mystical experience with God, but must only obey the teachings of the Qur'an. In contrast, the Sufi expresses an eagerness for communication with God and the "status of the heart." Sufis are, in general, devout

Muslims. They pray five times a day, give to charity, fast, and adhere to the traditional values of Islam. They are, however, different from other Muslims in cultivating their spiritual principles. While the orthodox Muslim teachers emphasize the formal and legal aspects of Islam, the Sufis speak of the emotional and mystical aspects of the religion. Islam is rigid. Sufism is not. Sufism has a broad outlook and believes in tolerance. Therefore, the Sufi approach had great appeal to the common people.

> Both Moslem and Sufi declare that God is one, but the statement bears a different meaning in each instance. The Moslem means that God is unique in His essence, qualities, and acts: that He is absolutely unlike all other beings. The Sufi means that God is the One Real Being which underlies all phenomena.[158]

Sufism is the mystical belief and practice in which Muslims seek to find the truth through direct contact of God. This central concept of Sufism came from earlier generations of Islamic mystics who concentrated their efforts upon *tawakkul*, the "absolute trust in God."[159] (The word *tawakkul* is defined literally to mean "a habitual state of mind, which is impaired only by self-pleasing thoughts."[160]) Sufis believe that Islamic knowledge should be learned directly from teachers and not entirely from books because of its esoteric nature. They promote the idea that the mystical union with the deity is not confined to a single moment but is a continuous, transformative process. It is said that Sufis put their trust in God to such an extent that even thoughts about tomorrow were considered inappropriate.[161]

Simply stated, Sufis are men and women of religious learning who seek to be close to Allâh. The understanding of spiritual mysteries and love are the same for the Sufis, and they are the same message and the greatest goal. Sufism defines the way to spiritual realization through increased perceptions and deeper mystical grace. They believe the Prophet, his companions, and their first three successive generations personify Islamic mysticism, but that the manifestation is too general to have a specific name. Sufism internalizes the essential nature of Islamic belief, whereas, later generations of Muslims are often distracted by worldliness. Sufis in this unsympathetic environment increasingly emphasized "the pre-eternal covenant between God and man, and the introduction of the idea of mutual love between God and man."[162] They are dedicated to worshipping Allâh and often use the metaphor of lovers to express their admiration and devotion.

Belief in Essence is part of the essential character of Sufism. The term Essence refers to the quality Buddhists might call Suchness and Hindus Thatness. It is the inner nature of the individual and an aspect of reality that cannot be seen but is known and felt. The Sufi aids the person to discover his own Essence — his own Reality — by advocating certain exercises and practices as defined by a teacher. Sufis contend that every individual has created his personal obstructions, such as desire, hypocrisy, greed, and sloth, which hide that individual's Essence. Hence, exercises were configured to remove these self-imposed obstructions and thereby to allow the hidden Essence of an individual to manifest itself.[163]

Fadiman and Frager wrote in *Essential Sufism* (1987), "To understand Sufism, we must understand mysticism."[164] Sufism represents a dimension of Islamic religious life that includes different mystical ways to determine the essential nature of man and God and to facilitate the presence of divine love and wisdom in the world.[165] Sufis are self-defined pilgrims on the road that leads to the truth.[166] The goal of a Sufi is to be so close to God that he loses his own identity and feels himself transformed and absorbed into God. They seek a state of being, through a series of devotional practices, in which they are in direct communion with God. Ultimately, the practitioner's personality is emotionally and spiritually suppressed, and he feels his soul drawn into God.

Dervish is the name given to some members of the Sufi fraternity in the twelfth century. Dervish initiates had to be trained before being granted access to mystical experiences, many of which the undedicated mind could not accept. These experiences are intended to awaken the five centers of illumination (divine light or clarity), called the *lataif*. The process for accomplishing this goal is to concentrate on specific locations in the head and the body and linking each place with a *latifa*.[167] The *latifa* is activated when consciousness penetrates that area. This interaction changes consciousness and expands the mind. Such concentration, often verging on self-hypnosis, gradually relieves the restrictive attitudes of the disciple's mind and allows him to become free to encounter his Essence (spirit, soul, or inner being). The five centers of activation are the Heart, awakened by concentration on the area of the physical heart, the Spirit, located on the side opposite of the chest; the Secret, between the Heart and the Spirit; the Mysterious, in the forehead; and the Deeply Hidden, in the brain.[168]

Dervish practices are restricted to those persons who have a genuine desire to devote themselves to God. They must also undergo extensive training once a dervish teacher accepts them. Breathing techniques are some times used to teach the disciples self-control as are exercises designed to break old habits of thought. A common exercise in general use is called *zikr* (translated as remembrance). This practice involves repetition of a devout incantation, or one of the names of God of which there are ninety-nine to correspond to the Sufi rosary.[169] One of the names of the Prophet is Dhikr Allah (Remembrance of God). Dhikr as practiced by Sufis is the invocation of Allah's divine names, verses from the Qur'an, or sayings of the Prophet in order to glorify Allah. Dhikr may be practiced individually or in groups and is a source of serenity for Sufis. Dhikr manifests in the heart with the result that the outward appearance is composed, while the inner being is obsessed with divine love.

These training activities have counterparts found in Eastern religious tradition. Yogis and Buddhists practice breath control and Hindus and Buddhists (as well as Christians) repeat the name of their gods as a way of devotion. "[L]iberation [from the mundane] cannot occur if one is not first 'detached' from the world, if one has not begun by withdrawing from the cosmic [universal] circuit. For without doing so, one could never succeed in finding or mastering oneself."[170]

Through education and increased awareness, Sufism has played a primary role in the formation of Muslim society. Muhammad ibn Ali al-Qassab (died 888–89 C.E.) said, "Sufism consists of noble behavior (*akhlaq karima*) that is made manifest at a noble time on the part of a noble person in the presence of a noble people."[171]

CHAPTER FOUR

The Nature of Phenomena: Mysticism, Magic, and Myths

> Our danger lies not in committing ourselves to certainty with the inevitable risk of error, but in refusing to bring our several certainties together so that they may suffer mutual correction or enjoy mutual reinforcement."[1]

Human beings construct myths to explain their world as long as there are unanswered questions about their existence and the environment in which they live. They may create myths to find temporary or permanent solutions to daily challenges. "[A]s long as human beings are aware of the contingency of their existence in the face of what often appears to be a capricious universe, they must construct myths to orient themselves within that universe."[2] The human mind will fulfill this function even if it must "generate gods, demons, or other 'power sources.'"[3]

Mysticism

> Mysticism is usually viewed as being of a religious nature, and can be either monistic or theistic. The objective of monistic mysticism is to seek unity and identity with a universal principle; while theistic mysticism seeks unity, but not identity, with God.[4]

Life is full of contradictions, consequently, the search for and the understanding of reality (truth) is a complex and demanding process. There is no common ground on which to base this investigation for most persons. When life is continuous and death indecisive as Buddhism proposes, or when the individual can receive absolution for immoral and illegal activities as Christianity allows, then the idea of one truth seems an abstract concept. If right and wrong are identical, they cannot be related; if they are altogether different then they also cannot be related, for they would have no common ground. Logic and reason often find no common ground on which to base their theses.

Mysticism is the "freedom of the human spirit to seek out, in all ways possible to it, the means of union with ultimate reality—God."[5] This attitude shows how, "like many other psychological concepts, mysticism, no matter of what brand [manifestation], scarcely admits of rigid definition."[6] It is so complex and so integrated into the lives and attitudes of a culture that it is difficult to identify where it begins and ends. The validation of this notion is that believing reality (truth) is both permanent and changing is to make a metaphysical assertion that is as incorrect as believing that reality (truth) is neither permanent nor changing.

Like many words and expressions commonly used and understood today, not all were used in the distant past. Although it seems an obvious statement, Frederick C. Happold explains in the book *Mysticism: A Study and an Anthology*, "The word 'mysticism' did not become current until the late Middle Ages, and [therefore], 'mysticism' is indeed quite a modern word."[7]

The concept of mysticism is ubiquitous. "[A]s the worldview that describes the attainment of an absolute through overcoming the limitations of human sensual and intellectual faculties [it] is certainly present in all high civilizations of the world."[8] Nonetheless, H.H. Brinton wrote in *The Mystic Will: Based on a Study of the Philosophy of Jacob Boehme* (1930), "Mysticism has, as a rule, been treated by its interpreters and historians as a type of reply to either or both of two problems, of which one is theoretical, the other practical."[9] Brinton questions the theoretical issue: "'Can absolute truth be known?' or [from the] ethical [perspective]: 'Can desire be completely satisfied?' Mysticism replies that a kind of experience is possible through which both questions are answered in the affirmative."[10]

Mysticism is a universal constant. Its variations are observable as practices shaped by the belief systems upon which they are based.[11] People constantly seek ways to connect with the Absolute regardless of culture or location. The process often relies on practices that are beyond the normal sensual perceptions yet interpreting and building on the material world. This spiritual search may include various forms of occult knowledge regardless of how they are derived. The spiritual worldview of many cultures includes belief that mystics or shamans can provide healing, or spiritual and emotional guidance by achieving an altered state of consciousness.

Although the world is generally divided into two realms, the sacred and the secular, the two spheres are more closely aligned than separated. Perhaps because of the bipartite assumption, the mystical (supernatural) temper plays an important role in human life. "Mysticism has always held — and parapsychology also seems to suggest — that the discovery of a nonphysical element in man's personality is of utmost significance in his quest for equilibrium in a world of apparent chaos."[12] Acknowledging this idea, shamans, priests, mystics, and magicians are necessary elements of society for promoting an understanding of how humans related to the spiritual world. The sense of the reality of the spiritual has intellectual and emotional content, and in most societies, the two characteristics are closely related and effortlessly blend into one consciousness. Society generally accepts the phenomenal nature of mysticism because it gives added meaning to life values.

Mystics are found in all ages, in all places of the world, and in all belief systems. Mysticism manifests itself in similar or identical forms wherever the mystical consciousness is present.[13] Although no spiritual truth is amenable to logical proof, humanity generally wants to believe the psychomental life, the activity of the senses, feelings, thoughts, and wishes is identical with Spirit and with the Self.[14] Consequently, the individual is frequently confused by the seeming superimposition of the temporary and the eternal, the material and the spiritual.

"Hinduism teaches the sublime mystical truth, that at the heart of every man and woman is a divine soul."[15] This concept places great importance on *dharma* (the cosmic order), the duties and responsibilities of the individual that take precedence over the desire for transcendentalism. Dharma calls attention to the belief that everything connected with the material world and physical life is transient and culminates in a hunger for knowledge of what is eternal. Mircea Eliade explains these are "two wholly autonomous and opposed realities, for the psychomental experience does not belong to Spirit, it belongs to nature;

states of consciousness are the refined products of the same substance that is at the base of the physical world and the world of life."[16] Belief proclaims there is a superior authority above humanity from which everything emanates and from which people may acquire extraordinary power.

The unique aspects of belief determine how different societies respond to the practices and attitudes associated with mysticism. "In the *Tao Te Ching* [for example] three elemental teachings are discernible—the metaphysical, the ethical, and the political. These three are frequently interwoven, presenting a strange mixture of the mystical, the ideal, and the practical."[17] The early Chinese philosopher, developer, and proponent of orthodox Confucianism, Meng-tzu, is reported to have remarked, "All things are complete within us."[18] (Meng-tzu is known in the West as Mencius, c.372–289 B.C.E.) The author of *A Short History of Chinese Philosophy* (1948), Yu-Lan Fung, speaking about mysticism, interprets this statement to mean, "Through the full development of his nature, a man can not only know Heaven, but can also become one with Heaven."[19] Mencius believed that the feelings of right and wrong were inborn in humans, and that "man possessed intuitive [*a priori*] knowledge and intuitive ability and that personal cultivation consisted in developing one's mind."[20]

The idea expressed by Mencius is consistent with the Webster Dictionary definition of mysticism as the doctrine that declares it is possible to achieve communion with God through contemplation and love without the medium of human reason.[21] It also agrees with the concept that *a priori* (intuitive) knowledge is the foundation for mystical practice. This assumption reinforces the notion that it is possible to attain knowledge of spiritual truths through contemplation and love without the medium of human reason.[22] Mencius believed, "He who has developed his mind to the utmost, knows his nature. Knowing his nature, he knows Heaven."[23]

Assumptions of faith are mystical or metaphysical. It can be said, therefore, that religion (theology) depends on the basic premise—a foundation—of mysticism or metaphysics to advance certain beliefs. Such beliefs may not be the basis of supernatural faith, but often lead to a discussion of the existence and nature of the Absolute. It is here that the metaphysical and the mystical come together since the search for the Absolute (God) is the objective of religion. Religion depends on the metaphysical in this quest.

Such metaphysical occurrences may be viewed as either natural or supernatural phenomena, and therefore, beyond the realm of science, which limits its attention to naturalism and does not give credence to supernatural occurrences because they cannot be investigated empirically. Religious miracles are usually considered as supernatural assertions as are divination and ideas relating to the afterlife. There are few (some say none) ways of validating phenomenal claims, as they are not reproducible by scientifically controlled processes. Nonetheless, the supernatural realm is closely related to religious spirituality and occultism or spiritualism, this is to claim, that anything that exists naturally is not supernatural. It may be equally possible that those things considered supernatural are simply occurrences not yet understood by human reasoning.

The mystical elements that appear in Tantra and other more esoteric sects of Hinduism and Buddhism include the use of mystical signs and symbols as expression of veneration. This mysticism is the effort of people to gain the ultimate reality of enlightenment or direct communion with the higher spiritual world. Mysticism maintains a relationship with the gods is possible by introspection and meditation in conjunction with a purified life outside the ordinary religious channels. This practice culminates in the awareness that the individual can unify the self with something greater than the self, whether that is defined as a principle that pervades the universe or as a personal God.[24] Although mysticism is often identified with pantheism, it is not necessarily connected with a specific philosophical or theological point of view.

Metaphysics is a distinctive discipline that is often considered as relating to mystical activities—defining the indefinable. It is a "branch of philosophy that deals with first principles and seeks to explain the nature of being or reality and of the origin and structure of the world; it is closely associated with a theory of knowledge."[25] Aristotle referred to metaphysics as "wisdom" and sometimes "first philosophy" and even as "theology." He is said to consider metaphysics as "describing the most general or abstract features of reality."[26] His was a search for "truth" according to the standards and conditions of the time. The objective of metaphysics, as a philosophical study, according to Aristotle is to determine the real nature of things—the defining of truth.

Metaphysical knowledge is the knowing of ultimate realities. "It is valued and sought, because it alone procures liberation. It is by 'knowledge' that man, casting off the illusions of the world of phenomena, 'awakens.'"[27] Knowledge means finding the "center" so the practitioner will be in agreement with his "true spirit." The knowledge must be "transformed into a kind of meditation, and metaphysics becomes soteriology."[28] When metaphysics is considered from the ideal of salvation by concentrated adherence to the doctrines of any specific religion, the alignment with mysticism becomes apparent.

Belief systems that endorse the concept of salvation (also called redemption) are motivated by a mystical concept. The relationship between mysticism and religion is closely aligned based on this perspective. However, mysticism is generally different from religion. The institutionalized religion emphasizes reverential submission to the deity and the ethical dimension of life; whereas, mysticism focuses on attaining a personal unification with the divine source. The mystic wants to be close to God, and a part of the divine spirit, whereas the ordinary religious devotee simply wishes to follow in God's way and obey his or her will.

Way of the Mystic

> [Mysticism] is a temper, a spirit, rather than a clearly definable attitude of the universe, but it is a temper and spirit that under various aspects appears among all races and in all periods whenever religion and the relation of the soul to the unseen powerful occupy the attention of men.[29]

"The mystic insight begins with the sense of a mystery unveiled, of a hidden wisdom now suddenly become certain beyond the possibility of a doubt. The sense of certainty and revelation comes earlier than any definite belief."[30] The mystic seeks an enhanced form of life. The way of spiritual and emotional enhancement involves the "remaking of character and the liberation of a new, or rather latent, form of consciousness; which imposes on the self the condition which is sometimes inaccurately called 'ecstasy,' but is better named the Unitive State."[31] (Ecstasy may be considered as meaning, "to stand outside." The mystic, in a state of ecstasy, stands outside his normal awareness and discovers he or she is more than he or she imagined.[32])

Whatever means used to achieve mystical experiences, the visions received speak of direct insight into the mystery of life. Mystical experience gives deeper meaning to the realities of the everyday—the commonplace—world. A period of retreat from everyday life is often helpful in disengaging from the fears, desires, and egoism of mundane existence. The ideals of isolated disengagement are the same, although expressed differently, in much of the world. The early Christian philosophers, ascetics, and monastics that established the foundation for Christian mysticism exemplify this common purpose concept in the West. The goal of ascetic and monastic life in fourth century Europe was "the conquest of self through renunciation so that, once purified from all obstacles, the soul might live the perfect life face to face with God, in direct communication and union with him."[33]

Mystic communion with the divine takes many forms and often involves sacred sounds, syllables, and expressions. The most generally used method for this communication with the supernatural is prayer and chant. The recitation of prayers or chants is one of the most ancient expressions of belief. Prayers often call upon mystical beings to give hope to the living and accompany the deceased to their preferred final resting.

Mysticism often includes a type of religious experience that happens when a person is deeply conscious of the void that separates him or her from God, understands that his or her predecessors had a relationship that he or she does not have, and tries to cross the chasm that divides the two.[34] There are different ways of addressing the mystical dilemmas of the world, although many such issues have a religious basis delineated by the adherent's beliefs. Most mysticism pursuits include what is considered a mystical relationship with an identified sacred element that may differ from group to group. Mystical communication also varies and may include dance, song and chant, fasts, dreams, vision quests, and the use of psychotropic drugs.[35]

William James is quoted in *The Encyclopedia of Religion and Ethics* as identifying "four marks" being distinctive of the mystic state. He contends the four distinguishing qualities are "ineffability, noetic quality, transiency, and passivity."[36] The characteristic of ineffability is found in any deeply felt and vivid experience of the divine nearness. It may be found in theistic as well as pantheistic religion. Both these types of mystical experience are found in Hinduism. The "noetic quality" (existing in the intellect) of Hinduism demonstrates a certain relationship with mysticism, while passivity is an obvious characteristic of a part of the religion of the *Upanishads*.[37] The transient quality is defined by the impermanence of all things. Nothing is permanent. This notion is an acknowledged part of Hinduism and Buddhism.

> Buddhists think of divine reality not as a person to be adored but as a state to be attained. They regard delusion (i.e. the universe as we see it now) not as a creation of divine reality because it does not proceed from a divine source but from our own ignorance.[38]

More than addressing a certain number of marks as identified above, "Mysticism is realizing the Self, or God, as one's inner Being, more truly oneself than one's manifest self."[39] This state of being is exemplified by either an insight into the world of the mysterious bordering on the supernatural, or as stated by Eugene d'Aquili and Andrew Newberg in *The Mystical Mind: Probing the Biology of Religious Experience* (1999), "a sense of attaining absolute reality, union with God or the Absolute, a sense of either bliss and utter tranquility, and, perhaps more important of all, a lack of fear of death."[40] D'Aquili and Newberg assert, "What we are talking about ... is the mystical phenomena or altered state of consciousness generating a sense of ... interaction with another and mysterious world perceived in some way as ultimate or transcendent."[41]

Mystics in the East and West may withdraw from the everyday life to enhance mystical progress, thus people follow a path of solitude and a life of prayer and meditation. China has a long tradition of hermits, people who retired from society to live in solitude. Bill Porter wrote about Chinese hermits in *Road to Heaven: Encounters with Chinese Hermits* (1993). He states, "Distant and insignificant, they were the most respected men and women in the world's oldest society."[42] The first Christian hermits (also called Eremite meaning, "living in the desert") were reported in Egypt near the end of the third century. These recluses were reacting to the persecution of Christians by the Roman emperor Decius. They reportedly went into the desert to lead a life of prayer and penance.[43]

The Essene brotherhood existed in Palestine from about the second century B.C.E. to the end of the first century C.E. It was in essence a hermit community. This monastic sect scrupulously observed the Law of Moses, shunned Temple worship, and was content to live ascetic lives. They professed belief in immortality but denied the resurrection of the body.[44]

Hermit mystics (Sanskrit: *vanyâsana*) have a long tradition in India that included ascetics, yogins, seers, and ecstatics among others. The *rsis* [seers] of Vedic India (pre–800 B.C.E.) were among the first hermits. Each hermit group or order had its unique approach to pursuing a defined goal. Some hermits went into the forest with or without their wives; some wore clothing and some did not; some ate by begging and others ate only what was found on the earth. One of the more interesting hermit groups, according to Mircea Eliade is the Paramahamsas. This group "represents an extremely ancient, aboriginal, anti–Brahmanic ascetic tradition and foreshadow certain 'extremist' yogico-tantric schools."[45] These hermits "live under trees, in graveyards, or in deserted houses.... In their view, 'there is no good and evil, no holiness or wickedness, or any other similar dualism.[46]

Belief has always created an ideal towards which people direct their energies, vows, and sacrifices. It is an ideal bolstered by ritualized activities and reinforced by physical and mental control. The mystic way and the path to liberation are often severe; therefore, mystics are sometimes accused of escapism, retreating from the responsibilities of everyday life to seek refuge in a private world. The austerities associated with mystic or hermetic life can be extreme. For instance, Tibetan Buddhist monks spend a period of three years, three months, and three days in hermitage as a part of their traditional training.[47]

The objectives of Buddhism demonstrate the idealistic nature of belief. The goal is to transcend the world of suffering by realizing through meditation the essential truth of the individual's being. This insight is often the result of years of patient, thoughtful meditation. "The greatest seats of learning in Tibet [are] the humble hermitages, tucked away in the folds and cracks of mighty mountains, or in lonely valleys and in inaccessible canyons, or perched on high cliffs like eagle's nests...."[48] The most dedicated Tibetan monks spend much of their life in seclusion where they meditate and seek enlightenment.

Monasteries often have different hermitage arrangements. Some monks and nuns spend their time secluded in especially built huts where they are given one meal each day. Other sects require monks and nuns to sit in a meditation box during their time in hermitage. They remain in the box constantly except for short periods to allow time for personal necessities. The box is only large enough for the monk or nun to sit in a lotus or simplified position with the legs crossed. The sides of the box are tall enough for the occupant to lean back, to relax, and if necessary to sleep, but he is to focus his time and energy on meditation. Other practitioners simply go into the forest or mountains where they live in isolation and forage for much of their food.

> Recognition of the fact of suffering (Sanskrit: *duhkha*) as one of three basic characteristics of existence — along with impermanence (*anichcha*) and the absence of a self (*anatta*) — constitutes the 'right knowledge.'[49]

The monastery and convent provided a (cenobite) common life community for monks and nuns. The monastic environment was established in the fourth century, and from the beginning, the emphasis was on living alone. The monastic ideal developed in Europe to facilitate the solitary life sought by ascetics ("*monos*" means "alone" in Greek.)[50] The purpose for isolation was the same as for the hermits living in the mountains. Monasticism is said to be "the most magnificent example of that heterogeneity of aims and consequences which govern the historical development of Christianity."[51]

"[T]he basic concepts of Chinese mysticism, the alternation between yin and yang, forms the theoretical reason why withdrawal from the world and solitary meditation ultimately means intense involvement in the world."[52] The assumption of retirement from social involvement to pursue the serenity of the monastery or a more reclusive environment often begins when the Chinese adepts realize "that life is short and that there is no self worth laboring for."[53] These practitioners are identified as "'accomplished ones' (*daren*), an old Chinese expression for someone close to sagehood, someone who penetrates and pervades the deeper reaches of the universe."[54] It is in this attitude of commitment that the accomplished ones pursue the life of a mystic.

Yoga is also associated with the mystical notion of joining and breaking the bond of the spiritual essence with that of the universe. Separation is predicated on of self within the cosmic complex. "Liberation cannot occur if one is not first 'detached' from the world, if one has not begun by withdrawing from the cosmic circuit. For without doing so, one could never succeed in finding or mastering oneself."[55] The emphasis in yogic practice is placed on the individual whether classic yoga, Hindu or Buddhist. The adherent must maintain self-discipline and concentration of spirit before seeking assistance from the mystic realm.

An additional mystical element of yoga is the existence of the god Isvara. This yogic deity, identified by Patanjali (author or one of the authors of the *Yoga-Sutra*), is not a creator but an advocate. He (Isvara is described as a male probably because early yogic practice was limited to males) is believed to "hasten the process of deliverance; he helps them [adherents] toward a more speedy arrival at *Samadhi* [ecstasy]."[56] It is believed that Isvara can assist only yogins, that is, male practitioners who have already made a commitment to yoga. "According to Patanjali, this divine aid is not the effect of a 'desire' or a 'feeling'—God can have neither desires nor emotions—but of a 'metaphysical sympathy' between *Isvara* and the *purusa* [yogin Self], a sympathy explained by their structural correspondence."[57]

Prânâyâma, the yogi breathing technique, has a mystic nature that is identified with the three Hindu gods. "Brahma is said to be inhalation, Vishnu suspension [of breath], Rudra [the 'Howler,' one of the names of Shiva] exhalation."[58] Mysticism and the gods are connected with various elements of Hinduism and Buddhism. For example, mudra and mantra, symbolic gestures and sacred syllables, are believed to have mystical power, that is, they connect with deities that have the power to initiate and enforce change. The OM (pronounced a + u + m), the most commonly used mantra has a mystical color for each letter, and each evokes a different god[59] (see Chapter Two).

The Hindu mystic and ascetics may be identified by the term *mantrik* or mantric. This designation is synonymous with magician in India, and associated with persons who often specialize in reciting mantras. The *mantrik* is believed to obtain his or her powers from charms, mantras, spells, and other methods. Knowledge of mantras is contained within the *Atharvaveda* that deals with magical prayers or spells for a long life, and curses used for or against forms of magic, as well as love charms. The hymns and prose passages of the *Athar-

vaveda reflect the mystical (magical-religious) concerns of everyday life. It is an important source of knowledge regarding religion and magic.

Mystics, after long periods of meditation focusing on salvation and liberation, including a process of mind-body transformation, are believed to reach a state where they can use mystical (supernatural) powers. However, many mystics choose not to use such ability and instead they concentrate on transcending physical power into the realm of spirituality. Mystics are sometimes called yogi in Tibet referring to their spiritual discipline instead of the physical ability. Yogic powers are called siddhis (spiritual perfection or paranormal power). Those who acquire siddhis are called *Sid has* (Sanskrit: saint). Many persons, yogi or mystics, are believed capable of controlling and transcending the barriers of time and space by meditation. Some practitioners are said to have the ability to perform miracles that are normally impossible.

People generally recognize a concept of occult power for which they have specific applications and unique systems of belief. *The Encyclopedia of Religion and Ethics* (1994) states, "Most forms of shamanism come within the sphere of mysticism."[60] Shamans, like mystics, are social functionaries. They are capable of attaining an altered state of consciousness to establish a relationship with the supernatural world, and by that means, obtain power and knowledge to help members of their communities. Nevertheless, shamanism is something more than prescribed sacred action. "It is an intimate, mystical encounter with the fields of life and death and the forces that fuse these realms."[61] The psychological and physiological elements are unified in shamanic activities.

Shamans are in a similar way separated from the rest of the community by the strength of their spiritual experience. Therefore, it is correct to describe shamans as mystics in the sense of their dedication to achieving union with the divine. Mircea Eliade attributed to shamanism a special role relating to mysticism. He wrote in *Shamanism: Archaic Techniques of Ecstasy* (1964), "[S]hamanism is important not only for the place that it holds in the history of mysticism. The shamans have played an essential role in the defense of the psychic integrity of the community."[62] Eliade described shamans as "pre-eminently the antidemonic champions that combat not only demons and disease, but also the black magicians."[63]

There is a distinctive shamanistic element in the Bön religion that influences Tibetan Buddhism. Early in the eighth century, Buddhism gained popularity with the Tibetans, Mongols, and Manchu, peoples with a strong shamanic tradition. The shamanistic practices integrated with Tibetan Buddhism and became institutionalized under the Mongolian Yüan dynasty (1206–1368) and the Manchurian Qing dynasty. It was generally believed by Bönpo (advocates of Bön) that the shaman communicated directly with the supernatural world, and that connection was thought to give the shaman power to make things happen. It gave him or her control over the forces of nature.

Generations of humans have endeavored to reach into the regions of spirituality in pursuit of essential knowledge, and to understand the forces that influenced the tangible environment. All experiences, mystical or mundane, are grounded in and must relate to the social environment in which they are achieved.[64] There was, for example, in late Chou dynasty (1050–256 B.C.E.), a class of people called the *wu* (mystics, diviners, sorcerers, and soothsayers), whose abilities resembled those typically attributed to shamans. This indigenous tradition incorporated alternative forms of mysticism including shamanism. However, shamanism entered a new phase in ancient China with the development of literacy and a sedentary society. "By the twelfth century B.C.E., in the early part of the Chou dynasty, kings and nobles employed shamans as advisers, diviners, and healers. Shamanism became an institution, and shamans were expected to exercise their ability as a duty."[65] Shamans employed by the Chinese emperor or by individuals "were expected to fulfill certain functions, and failure in an assignment was often punishable by death."[66]

Buddhism, like other forms of mysticism, offers to those prepared to master the long and difficult task of controlling the mind an unimpeded flow of intuitive wisdom.[67] However, if adhering to the definition of mysticism in its purest form — love of the Absolute, the One Reality, Truth, or God, then, Buddhism is not truly mystical. Buddhism has no Godhead, no Absolute; therefore, the fundamental concept of mysticism cannot be achieved. However, mysticism is normally considered in a less formal manner allowing that Buddha's revelations came by mystical enlightenment through meditation. The mystical nature of Buddhism is an inherent part of the concept of meditation. The meditative process to help the seeker transcend his or her separate life and discover his or her Buddha nature is mystically founded. The mindful outcome of Buddhist consciousness (mystical contemplation) is not rejection of worldly matters but the willful intent to help free the Self and others from suffering. "Merging into nothingness is, in Buddhism, the counterpart of the 'merging into the One' of the Vedânta or New-Platonism."[68]

It is acknowledged that although Buddhism has a mystical foundation, it is a non-theistic religion. It is not atheistic, since like the other religions it is based on the idea of a transcendent Absolute.[69] Mahâyâna Buddhism has no one name for divine reality. It may be called nirvâna or Buddhahood, but it is so exalted and so subtle that any name must demean it. All names imply a limitation. In addition, things named are thought to exist, whereas this divine reality is above the concepts of existence and non-existence.[70]

The mystical element is found in much Buddhist practice. For instance as Mircea Eliade writes, "to obtain the state of unconditioned — in other words, to die completely to this profane, painful, illusory life and to be reborn (in another 'body') to the mystical life that will make it possible to attain nirvâna — the Buddha employs the traditional yogic techniques, but correcting them by the addition of a profound effort to 'comprehend' truth."[71]

> Mysticism is a perpetual return to the vision of God, to the original datum, a return therefore to the old; but to the old not as an exhausted but as an inexhaustible datum from which may be drawn out new suggestions, new dogmas — not in the form of pure metal but in the form of ore.[72]

Although mystical practice often has a religious motivation, this determination is culturally defined. The use of mystical means for nonreligious purposes such as repulsion of demons and divining to determining physical conditions is consistent with the objectives of shamanism, astronomy, divination, and soothsaying. Whether these are truly mystical practices is another social determination that gives greater attention to experiencing mysticism through or from nature. An authentic experience of mysticism derived from such activities is essentially the unity of the subject and the object. The mystic is unified with the objective. The boundaries that separate the person and activity disappear.

Evelyn Underhill wrote in *Practical Mysticism* (1943), "More than the apprehension of God, then, more than the passion for the Absolute is needed to make a mystic."[73] Underhill believes, "These must be combined with an appropriate psychological make-up, with a nature capable of extraordinary concentration, an exalted moral emotion, a nervous organization of the of the artistic type."[74] Mysticism, like revelation, is personal. It is not simply a beautiful experience, which in the "words of Plotinus [third century philosopher], is the soul's solitary adventure: 'the flight of the Alone to the Alone.'"[75]

Mysticism operates in a historical context; however, it also tends to reveal a timeless attitude. The mystic is undoubtedly both in and out of time. The perpetual now (the present regardless of time or place) is a type of release from the temporal order. Such a release may lead to a shift from the local to a universal attitude, and a growing sense of unity of all experience. Though not a conscious objective, this result can be viewed as a praiseworthy goal as well as a practical criterion.

> We are trapped in *maya* [an illusionary existence] by our karma — the universal laws of cause and effect. The goal of the spiritual journey is to achieve *molsha* — liberation from karma. Karma is often interpreted as a form of cosmic justice — for each good action a person performs he will reap good fortune, and for each bad action misfortune.[76]

Magic

> There's a kind of ease that comes when we comprehend the illusory nature of reality, the dreamlike quality of life, this impermanence that pervades everything. (H.E. Chagdud Tulku Rinpoche)[77]

"In the beginning was the nonexistent, from which the existent arose" (*Rigveda* 10.72.2.). Practices classified as magic include divination, astrology, incantations, alchemy, sorcery, spirit mediation, and necromancy.[78] Malinowski wrote in 1962, "Magic is obviously further from our comprehension even than primitive religion. Those acquainted with ethnological literature know how much attention has been devoted to magic. It is usually regarded as a primitive form of mental aberration and as a typical symptom of savagery."[79] He quotes James George Frazer's *Golden Bough* (1958) theory that "magic [is] a perverted from of primitive pseudo science."[80] Malinowski quickly adds, "In truth, magic is nothing of the sort."[81] He offered the following as his view of the real function of magic:

> On the psychological side it [magic] leads to a mental integration, to that optimism and confidence in the face of danger which has won to man many a battle with nature or with his human foe. Socially, magic, by giving leadership to one man, establishes organization at a time when organized and effective action is of supreme importance.[82]

The topic of magic is often analyzed from a sociological or anthropological perspective. It is viewed as the cause or cure for almost all activities from cooking fires to immortality. It is most often assigned as a phenomenon of the illiterate or primitive. It is probably true that magic was employed to ensure a successful hunt, an abundant crop, or the renewal of animal life; it is equally true that all ages and cultures have sought the aid of magic in dealing with a full range of personal activities. There is, in fact, no limit to the possibilities of magical intervention.

Magic is essentially the same wherever it is found. It is in essence the "belief that the external world reflects the inner spiritual realms," and that the forces originating within the spirit realm, that is, from within human consciousness, can influence the external world. It can also be said, "The underlying principles of magic can be found in alchemy, which also has a long and universal history on this planet. Alchemy is about perfection — taking an imperfect thing and making it perfect."[83] Magic is an attempt by humankind to understand and control the external world. It helps people create a personalized transformation process by identifying the means by which their desires can be achieved. It also acknowledges and accepts self-delusion when circumstances are too impractical to attain the desired outcome.

Magic is a "superior power that arises from harnessing inner power and supernatural forces and brings to effect change in the physical world."[84] It relates to power that is a part of human history and an undeniable ingredient in the development of social order. It, like power, is an aspect of survival. "Spiritual beings are often credited with a knowledge of magic. They handed it down to men and sometimes use it in their relations with men."[85] Magic is considered an art so ancient that there is no known originating source other than revelation by a power associated with magic itself—a spirit being or deity.

There was a time when religion, science, and magic formed a unity, and then religion and science developed separately. The term magic is generally used to describe a form of supernatural energy that is beyond the normal powers of humans and outside the ordinary processes of nature. It is not unique to one people or place. Peoples in all areas of the world recognize the power of magic, for which they have special uses and unique forms of belief. The manifestations of magic are as simple as a prayer or as complex as a ritual. People know and respect the forces of the supernatural and therefore have ritual practices for acknowledging the powerful and often volatile forces, both positive and negative. "The highest form of magic is mystical, a path of illumination and enlightenment that adepts pursue with as much intensity as adepts in traditional religion."[86]

> Magic is an integral part of the socio-cultural framework, but has its own tasks to perform. It has a value for humanity and for culture, and in all this activity its realm and its function are different from those of science and religion. It is a process of cause and effect, and the basis of human reasoning and experience. "Magic is a way of manipulating the forces of Nature, whereas spirituality is about the transcendence of the manipulative ego-personality."[87]

The actual application of magic can differ according to the time and place in which it is practiced. It may be viewed as evil, helpful, religious, bizarre, or simply curious. However, James George Frazer believes that by analysis it can be determined there are two principles upon which magic is based: "first, that like produces like, or that an effect resembles its cause; and second, that things which have once been in contact with each other continue to act on each other at a distance after the physical contact has been severed."[88] Frazer's theory identifies the two principles as the Law of Similarity and the Law of Contact or Contagion.[89] This assessment may be acceptable but like all generalizations there are circumstances that challenge this categorization, as exemplified by divination. The process of divining is used to discover the answer to an arbitrary question.

Nonetheless, the concepts associated with these two Laws are relatively straightforward. The first, the Law of Similarity, implies that by simply imitating an effect it can be produced. Water is sprinkled to imitate rain and clay models of cattle are made to increase the herd. In the Law of Contact or Contagion a commonly used example is the molding an effigy figure (Tibetan; *linga*) to represent a particular individual, wrapping it in a piece of cloth from a garment owned by the intended victim and the subsequent stabbing, burning, or burying of the figure to inflict pain or death on the represented person. The standard of probability for the success for either course of actions is good. A normal increase in animals, a drop of rain, or an injury of any type can be claimed as successful magical intervention; failure can be blamed on to social or cultural wrongdoing—a taboo broken.

There is often a pragmatic side effect to the magic invoking process such as aiding humans to overcome a feeling of helplessness. As long as magic is practiced within basic limitations (similarity or contact and culturally defined measures), it is on a reasonable and secure foundation. People in difficult situations can confidently seek assistance in dealing with personal, societal, or economic issues. Prayers or incantations in such circumstances are an acceptable approach to gaining aid with personal problems. It is in this realm that magic and mysticism become one with religion. An appeal is made to a superhuman (omnipotent) authority or power (the One God) to intercede in an issue based on a personal request. Religion assumes the "variability of natural phenomena as determined by the will of supernatural personalities."[90]

All cultural systems include magic, in some form, as a means of relating to the supernatural beings that are omnipresent and influence daily activity. Yogis, in the magical folklore of India, are described as being able to raise the dead from their bones and ashes. Magic is the basis for a belief system to accommodate the mystical beings that influence the uncertain world of humans and a method for dealing with problems that have no socially accepted solutions. Magic in most societies is a part of a belief system that seeks both direct and indirect interventions on behalf of the requesting individual or group. It requires no spiritual intermediary to transmit the request for action; therefore, magical intervention is thought to be the automatic outcome of properly performed rites or rituals and correctly stated recitation.

Magic, regardless of the application, can be viewed as false and only intended for the ignorant or gullible, or as Rosemary Guiley writes in *The Encyclopedia of Magic and Alchemy* (2006), it can be considered "a superior power that arises from harnessing inner power and supernatural forces and beings to effect change in the physical world."[91] Every society determines a particular level of magico-religious sophistication within the context of their beliefs and institutions. Magic is a part of maintaining an endorsed belief system, and its importance as a sustaining factor ultimately depends upon the practices and values transmitted from preceding generations. Time and place influence perception.

Magic is an element of survival that blends aspects of intimidation, manipulation, mollification, and delusion. It is formed by the basic instincts of the ego as a means of achieving a desired objective. The application of magical influence from a strictly practical perspective has primary importance in satisfying the need for the most essential elements of human existence. Different applications of magic are recognition of the metaphysical powers capable of being controlled, directed, and used by humans. Therefore, magic, as a practice, is the application of that power for personal or public purposes, and its importance differs according to the values granted by a particular society at a specific time.[92]

Examples of the comingling of spiritual attitudes (magic, mysticism, and religion) are abundant. For instance, human skulls have been found in Switzerland with perforations probably used as suspension holes. This suggests they were used in some type of ceremony or ritual. Perhaps the skulls were hung around a priest or shaman's neck, mounted on a shrine, or used in some form of veneration. Other human skulls in the same area, as well as in France, were shaped into drinking cups.[93] This conversion suggests they were used for a magical, mystical, or religious purpose. In addition, pieces of human skull were worn as amulets or talisman in regions of Western Europe. A similar practice is found in Tantric Buddhism where the human skull-cup (Sanskrit: *kapala*, Tibetan: *thod pa*) is used as a ceremonial object to symbolically represent the impermanence of human life, and rosaries (*mala*) of human bone are worn for devotional purposes (see Chapter Five and **photograph 5**).

The skull is a regular part of paintings depicting the "defenders of the religious law" (Sanskrit: *dharmapāla*). This group of eight Tibetan Buddhist divinities, derived from Bön and shamanic tradition, are shown in paintings, sculptures, and masks used by dancers during dances ('cham). They are considered benevolent but are represented by ferocious images to instill terror in evil spirits. The Great Black One (Sanskrit: *Mahākāla*; Tibetan: *Mgonpo*) and the Conqueror of Death (Sanskrit: *Yamāntaka;* Tibetan: *Gshin-rje-gshed*) are shown with crown of skulls as a reminder of the impermanence of life (see drawing 1.a, 5c, and 5d). It is said that the magician-saint Padmasambhava (Lian-hua-sheng-da-shi) conquered the malevolent deities and made them take an oath to protect Buddha and the Buddhist faith.[94]

> All values are relative, so what purpose do concepts of good and evil have? Life and death are not opposites states of being, for death is only the continuation of life.[95]

The skull was thought to be the center of psychic power; therefore, it played a principal role in medicine as well as magic. An elixir known as the Spirit of Human Skull was used to treat epilepsy, a physical condition regarded with supernatural awe. The elixir was prepared from the unburied skull of a criminal. Other magical formulas required drinking water from the skull of a suicide.[96] A violent death was a prerequisite for a skull to be used for medicinal purposes. "Severe head-aches were said to be cured by an inhalation of snuff made from skull-scrapings, and in order to relieve toothache the sufferer had only to bite a molar out of a freshly disinterred churchyard skull."[97] Eastern and Western myths relating to the human skull are numerous.

Magic is often associated with activities inherited from the past and are viewed as important cultural traditions. Myths as historical references are used to verify and reinforce the foundational elements of all major religions. Buddhism, Christianity, Hinduism, and Islam are "firmly rooted in supernatural myth and divine revelation."[98] For instance, "Esoterically, *Chritsos* or *Christ* refers not to one specific individual but to the divine *individuality* within every human begin.... Exoterically, *Christ* means *Jesus of Nazareth*, historically a shadowy figure, the myth of whose miraculous birth, life, death, and resurrection underlies the Christian religion."[99] Whereas in Islam, "Mohammed the Prophet received the Koran from God via the archangel Gabriel, whom he described in anthropomorphic terms, and through various forms of superstitious belief survived in the new religion."[100]

Buddhism is configured on avoiding

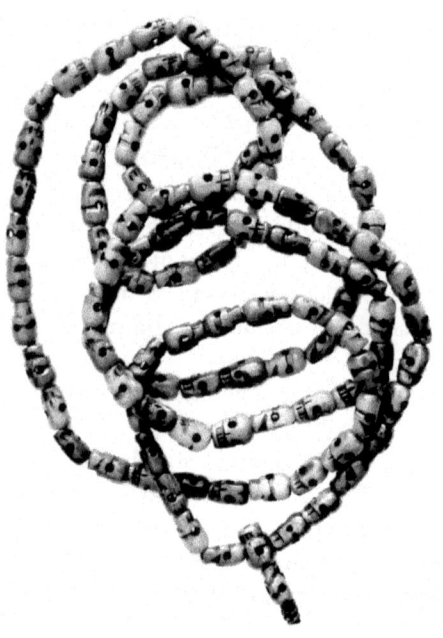

Photograph 5: The rosary (Sanskrit: *mala*; Tibetan: *'phreng-ba*) is used for counting repetitions of mantras or the saying of the name of a particular deity. *Malas* may be made of wood, bone, seeds, stones, and shells. The Buddhist mala consists of 108 beads (for purification) and may have secondary strings of counting beads. The counting beads are to remember the number of repetitions of the rosary cycle. The mala is usually held in the right hand for counting and wound around the left wrist when at rest. Some wrathful gods, such as Mahakala, hold or wears beads made from human bones carved in the shape of skulls when performing special ceremonies.

extremes and the pursuit of the Middle Way (Sanskrit: *Madhyama-pratipadâ*). It is the myth of the current Buddha's life that "includes magical contests with wizards of other beliefs."[101] Although Hinduism is a religion without a founder, the thinking of early advocates was gathered and passed by word of mouth until formed into the *Vedas* (sacred book) that includes instructions on many subjects including meditation and mystical transcendence. The *Mahâbhârata* is a mythical discussion about the nature of God and the means by which man can know him.

Magic, whether beneficial or malevolent, is defined by socially authorized activities and recognized by beliefs, practices, and superstitions. It is associated with tradition and unregulated by science or logic. Magical power is often associated with prescriptive elements such as symbolic colors, sounds, gestures, names, charms, and talismans. For example, the word (oath, chant, and mantra) and related symbol often have special power. The initiating society understands the relationships of these sounds and symbols but their meanings may be unknown to persons outside the group. This exclusiveness is the language of the initiated as exemplified by the use of Latin for the Catholic mass and the *mantra* of Tibetan Buddhism. Equally recognizable are protective charms, such as the mystical eye, the Hand of Fatima, or the mustard seed.

The uniqueness of the symbol often adds to the magical or mystical quality. Once a connection between the known (object or symbol) and the unknown (message) is made, the relationship between the media and the message (material to spiritual) is understandable. The power of the visual material (object or symbol) is greatly enhanced when the message is used in the context of a culturally defined activity.

Magic is not an externally imposed belief; it is validated by the daily experiences of the host culture. The magical intervention may be called upon to deal with seemingly mundane events or activities — finding lost objects, recovering from illness, determining right or wrong, ascertaining the outcome of future events, and resolving seemingly overwhelming situations. Magic, like mysticism, is a search for the truth, and as always, truth is subject to the understanding of the searcher. How the results are accomplished is not a relevant factor. The supplicant makes no inquiry into the laws of chance or probability, the powers of suggestion, or the natural course of events. Magical intervention is sought, and the desired results are believed accomplished. There is a successful transformation of an issue or there is not. Belief prevails. However, what is called belief for some is superstition for others.

The human mind (psyche), regardless of time, place, or circumstance, needs to believe that corporal existence has meaning and some form of a universal reference. Belief is therefore a necessary part of existence, and magic is both the foundation and the enhancement of that belief. "People have been doing magic for thousands of years, and they do it still today in hopes of improving their circumstances and lives."[102] Individuals and social groups are what they believe themselves to be, and that belief is always relative to communal intellect, experience, and condition. The connection between expectation and the outcome is normally based on the group experience, and the level of the belief in magic.

Although some cultures make a distinction between magic and ordinary activities, it is seldom entirely separated from most aspects of life. It is a common way to pursue desired goals and results. Prayers are said, lucky charms are worn, goals are visualized, chances are taken, and thoughts are projected. Magic gives expression to the desires and wishes of an individual or a group of people. It has universal appeal because it falls within the acceptable psychological framework of all cultures and the accepted social patterns of group mentality.

Magic includes a number of symbols, as do most human activities. Religion, mysticism, alchemy are esoteric activities that involve related symbols, but daily life also includes a full range of other symbols that are culturally defined. Magic often appears to be a celebration of the symbolic energy that includes chants, songs, and power words as elements of a magical action to achieve specific results. Magic is also a communal event that involves practices recognized by a particular society for achieving acknowledged results or a personal search for assistance. It is a "real and valuable resource. Misused, it creates imbalance and havoc; used properly, it contributes to the holistic balance of all things."[103]

"Magical Taoism, the Way of Power, is the oldest form of Taoism."[104] This power is derived from the natural elements and from the spirits, immortals, and deities, and channeled through the practitioner.[105] The power of magic energizes a unique force stronger than reality. It reinforces emotional resolve and provides the confidence to accomplish challenging tasks. The intensified self-confidence gained through magical intervention can influence daily existence, because numerous activities, real and imagined, can be ascribed to magical influence. Unexplainable phenomena that alter daily activities can be attributed to the will of a god or to the benevolence or malevolence of sorcery, witchcraft, or magic. The great mysteries of life and death can be defined as magical manifestations unexplainable in human terms.

Magic is a way of dealing with everyday activities. All things, great and small, are potential sources of magical energy. Magic offers a view of life that is less complex. It mingles the physical and the supernatural, human and animal, external and internal, and life and death, thereby providing an abundant range of opportunities for magical influence. People in need of material insight or physical security often rely on magic as a way of influencing personal circumstances. Magic provides the means to accommodate the uncertainties of daily existence. Nevertheless, "magic only steps in where knowledge has declared its inability to deal with the situation."[106]

Almost everything can be viewed as a message or sign from mystical beings, and beliefs about such beings influence the interpretation of those signals. When positive events occur, social, cultural, or physical achievements as well as good health, they can be attributed to mystical influence. The good things are viewed as the positive endorsement by the gods. When negative events occur, it is thought to be a sign of improper action by individuals or the community and the disapproval of mystical forces.

It is human nature to desire a positive outcome before initiating an activity. A planned undertaking can be cancelled with foreknowledge of failure. Disruption of plans is an inherent possibility; consequently, divination as knowledge of the future is a desirable method for planning activities. Magic in the form of divination is often employed to assist in making decisions about future events. The practice is exemplified by reading sticks, bones, and signs as well as horoscopic astrology, crystal gazing, and dream interpretation. "Some of the interpretation of events may be spontaneous; gross catastrophe might anywhere invite a supposition of divine ill will."[107] Other interpretations require cultural understanding as a practical glossary of the meaning of events that everyone in the resident community has learned and relies upon.

Divination takes many forms. Augury is the art of interpreting omens. It is the ability to discover divine will in phenomena of animated nature. This practice includes examination of the entrails, particularly the liver, of humans and animals sacrificed to the gods. It also extended to scapulimancy, the study of the cracks in the shoulder blades of sheep, ox, or goats. One Chinese technique of divination involved study of the tortoise shell. This form of forecasting related the round upper part of the shell, the heavens, to the flat lower part, the earth. The lower part, the earth, was heated to reveal signs that could be read by professional diviners.[108]

Omens are often viewed as simply positive or negative predictions. A flight of birds might include more white birds than black — a good omen. It is a good day to travel. The smoke from the chimney curls to the right — that is a bad omen. It is a bad day to purchase new clothing. A rooster crows three times before the sun rises — it is a sign someone will die that day. Some religions viewed omens and divination as a form of magic and objected to the practice believing that it interfered with divine authority.

Divination as an aspect of mysticism is found in all civilizations, ancient and modern. Consulting the magic of the oracle can be described as a practice or process of determining the hidden causes of events, often including foretelling the future, by different natural or psychological methods or techniques. "The various techniques of divination often yield contradictory outcomes."[109] Consequently, "the trust placed in them depends on the reputation of the technique and of its practitioner."[110]

Oracular divination is ancient and numerous techniques have been developed for its practice. An oracle is a person who practices divination and prophecy by allowing deities or supernatural beings to speak through him or her. Deities are said to "take possession of men or women who act then as their mouthpieces; through these persons the deities make their wishes known or give prophetic answers to question which are submitted to them."[111] Such prophetic ceremonies are of a sacred (transcendental) nature since the consulted deity is in temporary residence in the oracle.

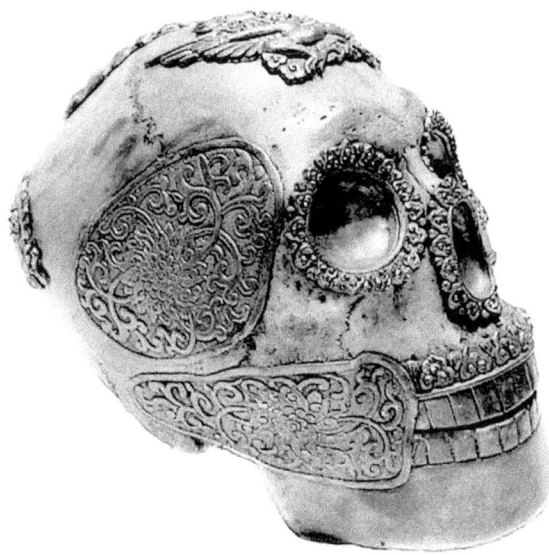

Objects are also used for divination and as oracles. Cards, sticks, bones, and tea leaves are said to aid in the process of predicting future events, identifying wrongdoers, and prescribing remedies for illness. The human skull is an often used for oracle purposes. The mystical significance of the skull for divination purposes is not restricted to one region or culture; Greeks, Jews, Semites, and Norsemen reportedly kept human heads as oracles in early times. Tantric Buddhists also employ the human skull for predicting future events. These skulls are often elaborately embellished with silver, copper, brass, and precious and semi-precious gemstones (see photograph 6). The use of these oracle skulls is normally limited to persons (monks or lamas) of superior ability and position.

The oracle skull is used for divination. Such powers are used to predict the outcome of future events as well as for diagnosing and treating illness. The practice of divination is very old and the use of oracles can be traced to earliest times in East and West. Both human and animal skulls, along with other part of the body are favored mediums for gleaning information. The skull shown is enhanced with patterned brass and copper elements. A figure of the *garuda* is affixed to the forehead. Only qualified lamas or officially sanctioned diviners are to use skulls such as this type.

Dreams were considered powerful sources of divination. Egyptian dream interpretation is recorded as early as the twelfth dynasty (1991–1786 B.C.E.), and the Old Testament includes numerous references to dream prophecies.[112] The *I Ching* (traditionally assigned to the twelfth century B.C.E.) is described as the ancient Chinese guide to wisdom and fortunetelling. The *I Ching* is a complex form of divination that has a systematic foundation. When properly interpreted the 64 symbolic hexagrams provide meaningful information applicable to daily life. "The *I Ching* is the only book of ancient wisdom that makes CHANGE itself the centre of observation and recognizes TIME as an essential factor in the structure of the world and the development of the individual."[113]

Magic, as is the circumstance with divination and rituals, is a part of a complex belief system that seeks both direct and indirect interventions on behalf of the petitioners. It is about changing emotional attitudes to reflect the anticipated outcome of the magical procedure and providing explanations that meet the human need for an understandable and responsive world. Magical procedures may be in the form of a ritual act performed to bring about a practical result people are unable to achieve without assistance. Such ritual acts are based on the belief that "by strict observance of traditionally prescribed behavior, bodily and verbal, [an individual] can influence the course of nature and the rulings of fate."[114]

Rituals are a connection between the natural and the supernatural worlds. The religious ceremony is an example of this relationship. It is a ritual process conducted by ordinary humans seeking connection with the extraordinary deities. Such ritualistic forms of worshipful practices are objective in that the outcome is expected to benefit the petitioner. They are an expression of individual or group needs and the endorsement of the myths or traditions of a particular people or culture. Rituals focus attention on creating conditions favorable for supernatural interaction. They emphasize and perpetuate life-values as determined by traditions and beliefs. Speculative thought and ritual in Indian Mahâyâna Buddhism were linked; consequently, that aspect of Buddhism was adopted in Tibet, due, in part, to the magical propensities already present in Indian activities.[115]

Divination in Tibetan Buddhism is closely aligned with traditional medical practice; thus, mystical assistance is regularly sought when dealing with illness. Using divination methods, the lama, shaman, or astrologer is called upon to determine whether the disease can be cured and what type of medicine should be used.[116] Divination, in practical practice, is a way to know things that are hidden from normal understanding. It should be remembered that people exist in the *samsaric* realm (a finite world of change); therefore, their perceptions are incomplete and imperfect. Human inability to recognize the relationships between phenomena, such as signs pointing to the presence of a disease, does not mean that such a relationship does not or cannot exist.[117] It only indicates that due to lack of adequate knowledge people are unable to recognize that relationship.

Magic is about power and the ability to enact change. It is not simply about bringing communal equilibrium through affirmation of underlying social values. Power is spiritual energy that allows the individual or group to relate to the forces of the supernatural world. That power is believed to give the receiver the ability to influence certain aspects of the physical and spiritual worlds. The concept of power, in this application, means the ability to cause something to happen by bringing about a particular act, action, or sequence of events. For example, the power associated with sympathetic magic is the most commonly endorsed belief. People believe that performance of an act or event with passion and devotion will cause a like event to occur. The successful completion of the ceremony is thought to assure the desired results will be achieved.

Magic as a socially accepted process is a practical way for sustaining and perpetuating life and a means for dealing with anomalies. It is considered an alternative to a more structured belief system (religion). It should not, however, be assumed that people rely on magic to do what they can achieve with knowledge, skill, or physical effort. Magic may be used to reinforce those abilities, but it is not a substitute for personal or group action. There are undoubtedly times when no viable action is apparent and magic in the form of prayer, incantation, or plea is called upon. Nonetheless, these entreaties normally follow basic socially acknowledged practice.

Beliefs and magic are necessary and purposeful parts of the practices of survival. Ancient Vedic worshipers seeking good fortune and material benefits from the gods believed their offerings could be made more acceptable if accompanied by songs of praise and other invocations of the gods' might and power. The rituals described in the *Vedas* are believed to have originated in this way. The actual form of the ritual may have included the symbolic enactment of natural or imagined events in which individuals, priests or shamans performed representative roles.

Belief as a cultural phenomenon is described as acceptance of an idea without the intellectual knowledge required to determine its truth. Knowing something is true simply requires believing it is true. The essential nature of belief is located in the mind, since it is not lost because a person is not consciously thinking about it. Belief is an attitude that may be plainly expressed infrequently but often has a powerful influence on the activities of an individual. Beliefs, like other psychological occurrences, reflect the influence of both the secular and spiritual worlds.

Every belief system is satisfactory to those persons who know its values. Life often depends on the ability of people to adapt to their surroundings and their capability of dealing with unknown forces. Beliefs are critical to that process. They are the basis for mystically formulated ritual activities that assure a level of security. The ritual as a magical enactment is an energizing venue for expressing and suppressing fears and desires that reflect irrational concerns about life and death that conventional means do not answer. Rituals may petition ancestors, supernatural beings, and deities for help with critical issues. Culturally dictated rituals are to ensure the powers of the universe are sufficiently honored that they will not withhold the things requested by petitioners.

The rituals most commonly practiced relate to the continuation of life and most rely on mystical assistance, supernatural intervention, or spiritual transformation. They are practices associated with belief, and a system of symbolic acts based upon rules established by the endorsing community as a way of soliciting the help of mystical beings believed to be a necessary part of the survival process. Ritual practice promotes the creation of a supportive relationship between humans and deities and the reordering of that affiliation to gain the desired results. Ritual activities temporarily place mundane aspects of life in suspension, thus, facilitating the passage from profane (the realm of time, space, and cause and effect) to sacred time (the transcendental realm).

Beliefs are the foundation for truth within the social order, and eventually those truths became the rules of the society. The identity of the group is formed out of that beginning, and subsequently, those beliefs became the rudiments of their cultural heritage. Organized forms of religion, Taoism, Buddhism, Christianity, Judaism, and Islam, among others, exemplify this process. Mystical observances of this type are important because they reinforce a bond between the supplicants, and the ensuing rituals are a way of demonstrating unity.

The inherent value of magic, that is, the ability to do good or bad, depends to the social situation in which it is evoked. Intellectual and emotional endorsement is an aspect of that process and absolute dedication is necessary for it to be meaningful. Practitioners (lamas, priests, shaman or astrologers) must believe in the effectiveness of their technique, the associated individual must believe in the power of the practitioner, and the resident group must believe in the outcome of the magical process.[118]

Magic is a socially recognized activity for contacting supernatural beings and initiating ritual actions to seek the intervention of those forces for supportive purposes. Magic acknowledges the causes of human suffering and offers hope for deliverance from the often devastating conditions. It is a way for humans to deflect or redirect the forces of fate. Magical practices provide the group with a scheme of social control that results in a sense of equanimity. Magic in its various forms is an effective and accepted method for explaining, empowering, and manipulating both the material and spiritual elements of human existence. It is a practical way to achieve an identified purpose.

Magic, like religion, is concerned with invisible, non-empirical forces. It often depends on the symbolic energy originating in chants, songs, power words, and other symbols are a part of magic to initiate a proposed action. The symbols announce the intention of the mystic, shaman, or priest, and it is through those actions that magic becomes a social event involving methods recognized by society for achieving established goals. As examples, there is the call to worship, the ringing of bells, liturgical music (including the responsorial), Vedic chant, mantras, mudras, oaths, curses, images, signs, *milagros*, and many others. Magic in all its manifestations promotes the idea that there is more to the universe than is normally believed, and that power over all things natural and supernatural is a realizable goal.

Although magic belongs to a domain where the things that happened appeared to be the result of chance or accident and where human activities are never certain of fulfillment, it is believed capable of influencing a wide range of events. It calls upon supernatural or mystical powers beyond ordinary comprehension to influence the actions of humans and nature. This ability to employ the power of magic is vested in certain individuals who have special abilities and can function as intermediaries between supernatural powers and human beings.[119]

Myth

> Ancient myths of every culture tell the same story of our search for wholeness. As the mind explores its own depths, it uncovers archetypal images that sustain and guide the journey inwards. These are the signposts on the old road home, half-remembered from long ago.[120]

As integral elements of the transformational process, myths and magic are closely interwoven. Myths inspire the beliefs and symbolism of the mystical world as well as the commonplace. "Getting into harmony and tune with the universe and staying there is the principal function of mythology."[121] The mythological past is a time when the world was shaped and humanized by ancestral beings. It was a time when the world was transformed for the benefit of humanity. Faith in that notion is the foundation of belief, because such thinking transcends ordinary consciousness. Myths are of particular importance in cultures where the idea of rebirth or reincarnation exists. They are the memory of both the divine and the ordinary. Myths verify faithfulness, whether of the spirits towards humanity or of humanity toward the supernatural.

The myths of Jewish tradition describe the soul of the deceased as passing through many trials before reaching its final destination. "If the soul is not worthy of an afterlife, it may be 'tossed around like a rock in a sling' and transmigrated into another body."[122] The transmigration of the soul from the deceased person to another body is an issue of dispute among Jewish mystics. One group insists that transmigration is a form of punishment, and another group views the process as a way to repair sins committed in a previous life.[123]

Myths are a necessary part of spiritual and intellectual development for all cultures. They provide the foundation from which change can evolve. Myths transport the believing mind from ordinary time and space into mystical time and space that is located beyond the horizon of human authority. "[T]here has been no age nor civilization that has not attempted to understand and interpret the mysteries of this strange life."[124] This search for understanding is facilitated by mystical time that is revisable. It can be extended or shortened to meet the requirements of a particular situation. The complex nature of mythical times, beings, and places contain the "archetypes of [humanity's] various evolutionary states that combine to work our conscious minds through the new thresholds of transformation."[125]

Myths as mediums of transformation may be described as "bridges between the intellect and emotion, between the mind and heart."[126] They are a symbolic narrative relating to events, especially those associated with sacred beliefs. They often provide specific accounts of deities or superhuman beings involved in extraordinary events or activities occurring in unspecified times but which are believed to have happened apart from ordinary human existence. Myths are generally implausible narrations of mythical circumstances that are represented as factual accounts of social or cultural history. They may also refer to ideological beliefs that are thought the basis for social practices, such as rituals or rites, although they have no factual basis. Myths are often the validating basis for the changes that take place in people, places, or things. Such myths emanated from the distant past and were generally held to be true because they were thought to convey socially accepted history.

Malinowski quoting Ruth Benedict wrote in 1963, "Myth is among some peoples the keystone of the religious complex, and religious practices are unintelligible, except by way of their mythology."[127] In fact, myths are used in organized religions at different emotional and intellectual levels to give symbolic as well as quasi-historical expression to assumed truths. All religious belief has a supernatural foundation in that it is based, either directly or indirectly, on myth. For example, without a Buddha to reveal them, the truths of Buddhism would remain unknown. Only after the neophyte receives revelations can he or she proceed by his or her own efforts. Similar circumstances are apparent in Christianity. The revelations of Jesus Christ founded and confirmed the beliefs. The Old Testament identified the time "in the beginning" and established the basis for the evolving myth to be detailed in the New Testament. The teaching of Jesus and Buddha was more precise in early times when the revelation was thought of as historically related to Christ or Sakyamuni's mission in the world.

Myths cannot be viewed as simply creations of the psyche; they are a response to a need and therefore fulfill a function that brings to light a people's hidden values as well as their fears. Myths are messengers of social and psychological exchange from person to person and from generation to generation. Through myths, people explain life conditions and forces that influence their lives in ways they can accept. Myths illuminate the hopes and aspirations that comprise the shared beliefs of the people.

"Myths are made to explain the world, to make sense of it."[128] They are seldom a search for reality, although their meanings often embody inherent truth. They may be both profane and sacred. Myths are most often a means for explaining the unexplainable, or at least they were at the time of their inception. The cosmic egg, for example, is viewed by many cultures as the beginning of life. It is also considered the symbol of procreation, rebirth, and new life. The egg creation myth is found in Dogon, Tahitian, Chinese, and Japanese mythology. Egg references are also found in Buddhist, Greek, and other myths. Hindu mythology includes a story about the ancient goddess of India, *Ammavaru*, who existed before the beginning of time. The myth explains that she laid an egg that hatched revealing the divine trinity of Brahma, Vishnu, and Shiva.

It is true that there is no agreement regarding the origination, meaning, or purpose of myths. Claude Lévi-Strauss wrote in *Structural Anthropology* (1963), "Some claim that human societies merely express, through their mythology, fundamental feeling common to the whole of mankind, such as love, hate, or revenge or that they try to provide some kind of explanations for phenomena which they cannot otherwise understand."[129] Myths often are an imaginative expression in narrative form of what is believed an aspect of reality. Equilibrium (harmony, balance, or order) is also a considered purpose for myths. This application, the idea of an orderly existence, may be used to explain excesses or deficiencies. For example, belief that there are sacred (mythical or mystical) powers in the form of spirits that can guide human activities is found in most cultures. This mythology balances the imperfect abilities of humans in dealing with natural conditions.

C. A. Burland wrote in *Myths of Life and Death* (1974), "[Myths] reflect the hopes and fears, and dreams experienced by our fellow humans from many place and in many ages. They are stories which are told, and often acted, with some sense that they are reflections of reality."[130] Burland states, "In detail myths vary widely; though they may reflect archetypal themes, they are conditioned by our experience of life and by the cultural level of the society within which we live."[131]

Clyde Kluckhohn believes mythology "answered the insistent human how? And why? How and why was the world made? How and why were living creatures brought into being? Why, if there was life must there be death?"[132] It seems certain that although there are similar myths in most cultures, the purpose they serve may vary dramatically. Belief, application, and practice ensure different values for local myths according to societal needs. "Man for the most part conceives of that which is remote, unknown, or difficult to understand in terms of what is near, well known and self-evident," according to Ernst Topitsch in the article "World Interpretation and Self-Interpretation: Some Basic Patterns."[133]

Myths may serve as the essential memory for all life from birth to death and beyond. Such myths confirm a point of view that is "basic to all human life; initiation of youths, reproduction and death ... all is seen in the light of the myth and is supposed to reflect its events."[134] The question of how the universe came into being is a central concern. Creation myths (generally called cosmogonic myths) are subscribed to by all cultures. They mark the beginning of things. Myths that concentrate on the origin of a people or the world normally reflect the prevailing cultural tradition. Myths tell the history of a people beginning with the creation of the world, the origin of the first people, and the foundation of their survival-related belief system.

The most commonly endorsed myth is the one referencing the creation of the world and humans. "Myth describes the acts and beings whose appearance shaped material existence in all its concrete specificity."[135] The cosmogonic myth is inevitably an elaboration of the primal myth of creation advocated within a religious community. Genesis 1:1 states, "In the beginning, when God created the universe, the earth was formless and desolate. The raging ocean that covered everything was engulfed in total darkness, and the power of God was moving over the water."[136] This type of creation is the formation of the universe out of non-matter by the will and intent of one omnipotent albeit supernatural being. He or she is the wise person who may be viewed as a creator as well as the helper and guide of the human soul. Consistent with this origination is the acknowledgment that the creator is also the transformer and possible terminator of the world who may be subject to manipulation by human activities such as prayer and ritual.

Many creation myths define the basis of cultural belief. They immediately establish the foundation for their societal origination. For example, "In the beginning there was nothing. In the process of time, matter came into existence as formless ether. It was known as the 'T'ai Chi'—primal matter,"[137] according to Chinese belief in the time of Lao Tzu. It was thought this primal matter gradually "began to gyrate, and during the process divided into two parts. The part which was gross and heavy precipitated and formed the earth, while the part which was fine and light remained in suspension and formed the heavens."[138]

Some cultures have complex creation myths that record the development of the earth from existing conditions. Often such myths include duel entities, male and female as well as preexisting conditions that allowed the formation of the earth and sky. An interesting example of this type story is the Shinto myth that explains that the world was originally a chaotic collection of gases. The gases separated after a time, and the earth and sky were formed. It is believed that a bud appeared floating in the sea from which two gods appeared. The gods, Izanagi and Izanami, were brother and sister, as well as husband and wife. Eventually, they created the islands of Japan, the gods, and the people. "By standing on the floating bridge of heaven [*Ama-No-Uki-Hashi*] and stirring the primeval ocean with a heavenly jeweled spear, they created the first land mass."[139] It is believed that from the left eye of Izanagi the sun goddess was born and from his right eye the moon god.[140]

"When the gods were human" is the open statement for many myths addressing the creation of both the universe and humans. A number of myths document the creation of humans from clay or dust. Khnum the Egyptian potter god that is represented as a ram or a ram-headed man is said to "fashion the bodies of all living things" on the potter's wheel[141] **(see drawing 4.a)**. Myth describes the Sumerian god Enki as the creator of humans. It is said he made the first humans from clay mixed with an extraordinary liquid sometime described as the blood of the gods or divine spittle. Chinese mythology includes the story that the first humans were shaped from clay by the goddess Nüwa. However, after she "created a hundred people, she

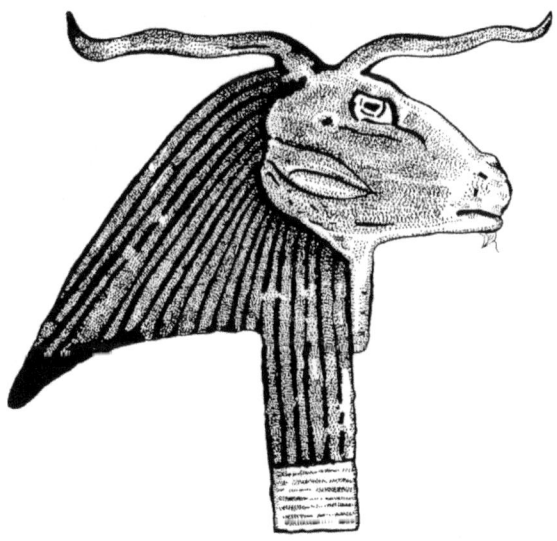

Drawing 4.a: Khnum the Egyptian God of Creation and guardian of the Nile is regarded as the son of the sun god Ra. He is represented as a ram with horizontal horns and was worshiped in association with water and procreation. Myth relates that he created the humankind from clay using a potter's wheel. He is the god of Elephantine Island and the first Cataract of the Nile River. This drawing is from the twelfth century B.C.E. painting found in the Valley of the Queens.

grew tired. She took a long, climbing plant, dipped into the clay, and shook it vigorously. As the lumps of clay fell to the ground, they came to life."[142] Myth maintains the Mayan gods tried to make people out of mud but gave up the practice because they melted easily.[143]

The Bible includes the Judeo-Christian myth of human origination. It describes how God "took some soil from the ground and formed a man out of it; he breathed life-giving breath into his nostrils and the man began to live" (Genesis 2:7). The myth asserts, "Man is created in the image of God. He declares that God has given man a soul, capable of reaching up into Heaven itself and inspiring the human mind to its noblest achievement, the quest after God."[144] The myth informs man, "You were made from soil, and you will become soil again" (Genesis 2:19). This is an indication of the power of the omnipotent creator. He gives and he takes away.

Mythology also gives special attention to the idea of duality, that is, one becoming two. This notion is perhaps the basis for the recurring myth of the androgynous being (see Chapter One). The self-creating deity is found in many cultural traditions. The serpent was believed to be androgynous and therefore was a symbolic reference to self-creating activity as was the transformation from one sex to another. A male deity, for example, might change into a female and vice versa. This sexual transformation, especially as it concerns powerful deities, cannot be explained on a purely spiritual basis. It is often a matter of cultural recognition and practice.

An example of the trans-sexuality of a god or goddess, the *Kuan Shi Yin*, Chinese Goddess of Compassion, and Mercy (the One Who Hears the Cries of the World), is also embodied as *Avalokitesvara* (bodhisattva), known in Tibet as *Spyan-ras gzigs* ("With a Pitying Look"). Kuan Shi Yin is the Chinese translation of the Sanskrit Avalokitesvara. This male deity is "self-born," and often associated with his consort the goddess *Târâ*. *Avalokitesvara* "guards the world in the interval between the departure of the historical Buddha, Gautama, and the appearance of the future Buddha, Maitreya."[145] It is believed he has the ability to assume whatever form is required to relieve suffering. "Around the end of the Tang dynasty (early tenth century C.E.), [*Avalokitesvara/Kuan Yin*] changed sex and became a woman — the form in which she is revered and venerated to this day."[146]

The Kuan-yin cult was imposed onto the bodhisattva qualities of a mother-goddess from about the tenth century. Representations of the Kuan-yin generally have an understated sexual identity. The body is normally depicted in such a way to offer no reference to breasts or other specifically female characteristics. The Kuan-yin has a counterpart in Christianity with the Mary, Mother of Christ, cult that reflects the practices associated with the "great mother" and the "divine virgin" cults of the pre–Christina era. Mother goddess figures are found in almost every ancient religion.[147] A Buddhist myth features the mother of Gautama, the future Buddha. It is said that the Buddha Sakyamuni leaves heaven to incarnate himself in the shape of a white elephant in his mother's womb. Queen *Mâyâ* retires to the Lumbini Garden near Kapilavastu, lifts her right hand and the baby emerged from her right hip. The myth states the gods *Brahamâ* and *Indra* were there to receive the child.[148] Similar myths about miraculous conceptions and births are found in many cultures.

Myths about the androgynous nature of gods and goddesses fulfill important functions in society; they express, classify, and in many ways clarify attitudes related to human sexuality. Those beliefs reinforce a concept of morality, and in some cultural settings, they provide explanations to verify traditional beliefs and customs.[149] C.G. Jung writing about the Immaculate Conception and birth of Jesus Christ states, "Myth is the primordial language natural to these psychic processes, and no intellectual formulation comes anywhere near the richness and expressiveness of mythical imagery."[150]

The concept of spiritual oneness and the inclusion of both aspects of gender in one being correspond with Hermetic teaching. The same concept is included in numerous myths that feature a hero or heroine capable of exchanging identity (and gender) according to the circumstances.[151] The notion of oneness is not limited to gender or identity, it considers spiritual inclusiveness as well. Christianity speaks of the oneness of Father and Son — "the Son became the mediator of the glory of the Father to those who believe in him."[152]

Transformation beliefs relating to the changing nature of the gods and goddesses come from the distant past, and are generally held to be true because they express a history of social acceptance. These beliefs are often represented by symbols, and they are transmitted by traditional methods. These activities are primary elements of the culture validating process, and over time they became more idealized and less directly influenced by the originating beliefs. Nonetheless, they normally retain important elements of the traditional meaning as exemplified by the androgynous gods or goddess and the idea of oneness.[153]

Early Christian myths endorsed "the ancient Asian concept of the combined male/female deity, the Primal Androgyny."[154] The Jewish mystical tradition includes the belief that the original Jehovah was an androgynous and that his and her name was "composed of Jeh (*jod*) and the pre–Hebraic name of Eve, Havah or Hawah, rendered *he-vau-he* in Hebrew letters."[155] Though there are many myths related to religious ideals and activities, including the origins of saints, it is a misconception to believe that religion and mythology are the same, or that mythological concepts evolved into religion. There are examples that would support this idea; however, there are opinions contrary to this notion. Belief may be argued as a common factor, but the ideology is different.

Drawing 4.b: Ganesha (also called Ganapati) is revered as the Remover of Obstacles. He is the son of Shiva and Parvati. The legendary account of his birth is that Parvati formed him from the rubbings of her body and dust. He has a potbelly and is usually shown with four arms that may hold a noose, a goad or an axe, a pot of sweets or jewels, and his broken tusk or a book. Ganesha is considered to create obstacles as well as remove them. He is also a patron of letters and learning, and is the legendary scribe of the *Mahabharata*. He is important in the art, myth, and rituals of Buddhist Asia.

Numinous Transformations

Human and animal forms are mixed in many myths. Many Egyptian gods, for instance, are represented as humans with animal heads, while in Semitic mythology the animal bodies often have human heads. Indian mythology includes the son of Shiva and Parvati, Ganesha, an important god, with a human body and an elephant head (**see drawing 4.b**). The story of Ganesha explains that he was made from the dew of Parvati's body mixed with dust. The myth describes how this handsome young man was Pravati's *dvârapâla,* or guardian. When he confronted Shiva, Pravati's husband, and refused to allow him to enter his wife's apartment, Shiva called a troop of demons to destroy the upstart. The *dvârapâla* was decapitated in the ensuing battle. Shiva eventually agreed to replace the head to appease Pravati's anger for the decapitation of her son and guardian. Shiva directed the gods to bring the head of the first animal they met as a replacement for the headless youth. The first animal encountered was an elephant, hence, the "Elephant-face" god, Ganesha.[156]

Tibetan mythology also includes the story of the Bodhisattva Avalokitesvara's (*Spyan-ras gzigs*) transformation into a white horse, and in that manifestation, he went to the aid of those in purgatory. The horse, Bahala, was also responsible for saving merchants that had fallen under the power of monsters as well as performing a series of miracles at the request of his devotees.[157] Other mythical animals are the goats that pulled the war chariot of Thor, the Viking god of thunder. The myth maintains the goats could travel over land and sea, as well as through the air. The rolling sound of the chariot is the thunder.

The origin of the Goddess Târâ (Tibetan: *Sgrol-ma*) is a widely acknowledged myth in Nepal, Tibet, and Mongolia. She is also considered the feminine counterpart of the bodhisattva Avalokitesvara and especially venerated in Tibet where she is the goddess of sublimated compassion. Târâ came into existence from the tears of the All-Compassionate Avalokitesvara. The tears fell on the ground and became a lake. Out of the water grew a lotus, which, when opened revealed the goddess. "She is the protectress of navigation and earthly travel, as well as of spiritual travel along the path to Enlightenment."[158]

The sexual union of male and female is a symbol of completeness and totality in forms of Hinduism and Buddhism. The Hindu deity Vishnu is given great attention in Nepal. He is often depicted in two- and three-dimensional forms with his wife Lakshimi and accompanied by his mount the mythical Garuda (**see drawing 4.c**). The body of Vishnu is often divided showing the masculine embodiment on one side (half) and that of Lakshimi, representing the creative energy on the other side. The androgynous representation of the Lord

Drawing 4.c: The Garuda is an Indian bird-god or mythical sunbird with outstretched wings. Hindu mythology describes the Garuda as the *vâhara* (mount or vehicle) of Shiva, and he is known as the filth eater. Hindu myths include the story that the Garuda's mother was held captive by the naga (snakes, cobras), but they would release her in exchange for a drink of the elixir of immortality. The Garuda reportedly got the elixir and attained the release of his mother. It is for this reason that he is a destroyer of snakes. The Garuda in the snake destroying posture plays a role in Tibetan Buddhism where he is known as *Khyung.* The Khyung is often seen in Tibetan thangka with a snake in his beak held taunt in his upraised hand. This piece from which this drawing was made originated in the fifteenth or sixteenth century. It is of gilt bronze, inlaid with turquoise.

Four. The Nature of Phenomena: Mysticism, Magic, and Myths

Photograph 7: Yab-Yum is the father/mother image identified with Tantric Hinduism and Tantric Buddhism. It represents a male deity in sexual union with his female consort. Often, as in this image, the male is seated in a lotus position with the female sitting in his lap. The male figure is linked to compassion and skillful means and the female is associated with wisdom and insight. This union is generally understood to represent the primordial (or mystical) joining of wisdom and compassion. Tantric practitioners realize the union as a mystical experience within their own body. The yab-yum figures are not intended for general use. They are held in reserve for those persons who have received appropriate guidance concerning their esoteric importance.

Vishnu is an iconography developed in Nepal, whereas, in India, Vishnu and Lakshimi are generally represented as the divine couple. Androgyny is considered a sign of perfection. Krishna, an avatar of Vishnu, states in the *Bhagavad-Gita*, "I am the father, mother, maintainer and grandfather of all this universe" (8:17).

Transformation myths extend into the earliest time of human existence. Communal beliefs are often founded on the idea of duality and the physiological and psychological ability to change — to be transformed. Mythical beings often cross the physical boundaries that separated humans, animals, spirits, and in many instances, gender. There was Osiris and Isis in Egyptian mythology; the Greeks had a pantheon of mythical pairs including Dionysus and Demeter, Zeus and Hera, and Uranus and Gaia; and in Tibet, the duel nature of regeneration was embodied in Yab and Yum (see photograph 7).[159]

Osiris, the mythical Egyptian deity, was the god of fertility and the embodiment of the dead and resurrected king. "According to myth ... Osiris was slain or drowned by Seth [his brother], who tore the corpse into fourteen pieces and flung them over Egypt." Isis gathered the body parts and with the assistance of Anubis, god of mummification, preserved the body of Osiris. Anubis or Anpu is often represented as a jackal or a human with the head of a jackal (see drawing 1.e). He was lord of the dead during the Old Kingdom (c.2575-c.2130 B.C.E.). Anubis is associated with the funerary cult and care of the dead. He is credited with being the inventor of embalming because of this relationship. He is also recognized as a conductor of souls to the afterlife.[160]

Myths of dismemberment and resurrection are found in many cultures. It is often a necessary part of gaining supernatural or mystical status. Shaman often underwent a ritual death, dismemberment, and resurrection before gaining their full ability. Mythology explains that in addition to Osiris, Dionysus and Attis were dismembered in sacrifice for rebirth. "[C]reation [could] not take place except from a living being who is immolated — a primordial androgynous giant, or a cosmic Male, a Mother Goddess or a mythic Young Woman."[161] The process was the same in most instances. Creation was not possible without sacrifice. Myths told the people how their world was created out of the body of a primordial deity and other myths told how the human race came into being from an ancestor or sacred being that was sacrificed, dismembered, and in most culture resurrected as a deity in human form. Myth captured emotional attitudes that people perpetuated in life.

Some mythic explanations about the creation process are simple and direct. "'At the beginning there was nothing,' the Chinese philosophers taught their pupils. 'Long ages passed by, then nothing became something.'"[162] The transformation of nothing into something is a reasonable explanation of creation. Other creation myths relate to the division of the body or physical elements to ensure development. An example of this type of creation is found in Tibetan mythology. The myth declares that in the beginning, there was only one man and he had three children who lived with him (there is no explanation about the source of the children). The man died after many years, and the children could not agree about what to do with the body of their father. Each child had a different plan for disposal of the corpse. Eventually, they decided to divide the body into three parts. "The eldest had the body and arms; he was the ancestor of the great Chinese family [...] the second son had the breast; he was the father of the Tibetan family [...] from the third, who had the inferior parts of the body, are descended the Tartars."[163]

The creation myth endorsed in Egypt starts with *Nun*, the waters of chaos, and the primeval state represented by four divine couples. The couples were known as the *Ogdoad*, and they came together to form a cosmic egg that was fertilized by the god Amon in serpent form or perhaps Thoth (also known as Hermes) in ibis form.[164] "The creator sun god was hatched from this egg, so *Hermopolis* claims to be the site of the first sunrise [...] Like other sacred sites to which creation myths were attached, *Hermopolis* was famous as a centre of magical knowledge."[165]

Myths about defining forces are easily understood and emotionally satisfying; that is, myths that explain coming and going (in the spiritual sense), good and evil, etc. Opposing elements are a necessary part of human existence because one aspect cannot be recognized without the other as a counter-balance. Numerous myths dramatized the conflict in which the giver and taker of life are represented in the single character transformed by magical or spiritual intervention. This transformation, the real to the unreal or vice versa — the same but different — is an important component of myths and mythmaking. It keeps alive the traditions of the peoples with whom the myths are associated. The mythical point and counterpoint approach is a necessary ingredient in religions.

"[T]hroughout the mythologies and religious systems of the world, the same images, the same themes are constantly recurring, appearing everywhere."[166] The book *In Search of the Cradle of Civilization* (1995) by George Feuerstein, Subhash Kak, and David Frawley notes the cross-cultural nature of myths. For examples, myths relating to the night sky include similar figures. "Varuna (India), Ouranos (Greece), and Osiris (Egypt) are identical in fundamental ways. All three were born to the Great Mother Goddesses and typically represent the night sky. More specifically, they symbolize the constellation of Orion."[167] It is said that when the army of Alexander the Great entered India in the fourth century B.C.E. they "recognized the same gods that they were themselves worshiping. And they made correlations. Krishna is now identified with Heracles, Indra with Zeus, and so forth."[168]

Myths are often associated with power and the supernatural authority of certain deities and humans. Myth tells of the struggle between a Buryat shaman (Buryat are Mongol people living south and east of Lake Baikal in Siberia) and the high god of the dead, Erlen Khan. The shaman reportedly bit the cheek of Erlen Khan in that encounter and subsequently, Buryat shamans are thought to have lost much of their power.[169] Myths generally focus on

Four. The Nature of Phenomena: Mysticism, Magic, and Myths   103

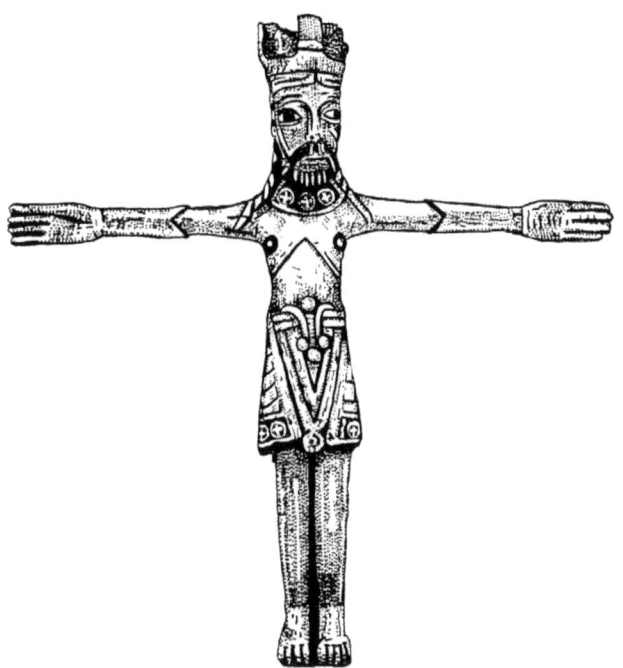

Drawing 4.d: The cross is viewed as the principal symbol of the Christian religion. It is intended to recall the Crucifixion of Jesus Christ. The cross has come to symbolize both Christianity as a faith and Jesus Christ as the redeemer. Cross forms were used symbolically before the Christian era. The Egyptian symbol of life — the *ankh*, is a cross with a loop on top. This symbol is commonly called a Coptic cross. The swastika is a cross-form called the *crux gammata* because it is compose of the Greek letter gamma. It, *crux gammata*, was commonly used during the early Christian era to mark tombs.

superhuman characters, and acknowledge the power such deities command. The Hindu myth recounts the destructive nature of time as a god regulated element. "Everything dies in time: 'Time ripens the creatures, Time rots them'" (*Mahabhalata* 1.1.188). "Time" (*kala*) is thus another name for the god of death, Yama. The name is associated with Shiva in his destructive aspect as Mahakala and is extended to his consort, who may be known as the goddess Lali or Mahakali."[170]

Myths rely on belief. Religion as a concept has no creditability and nothing remains but a reportedly historical figure with no special message to impart without the corroborating belief or faith. The Buddha would be a wandering ascetic in ancient India; Christ a carpenter and preacher in Nazareth; and Muhammad a camel-driver in Mecca. Each of these revered persons reportedly conveyed a message of hope based on faith, and each is symbolically acknowledged by the associated belief. Nonetheless, the origin of religion is not restricted to mythological concepts nor is the origin of myth fixed in religion. The two are intertwined and cross generating.[171] Religion meets a need and myth helps to validate both the need and the solution. The Absolute is defined by cultural acceptance in the form of belief.

Just as beliefs are often expressed in myths endorsed by a culture, they are also expressed in the symbols made and used by people. Symbols inspired by myths are normally abstractions of ideas that elicit emotion or belief. The Christian cross (see **drawing 4.d**), the Hand of Fatima, the Hammer of Thor, the Wheel of the Law, and the Wadjet eye of Horus (see **drawing 4.e**) are but a few of the myth inspired symbols commonly used. Other examples of such symbols are found in the indigenous traditions of civilizations from pre-historic times. The fierce guardians of the law and Buddhist faithful are mythical demons associated with Bön and the indigenous beliefs of Tibet (see **drawing 4.f**).

Other principal issues on which myths focus, aside from the creation concerns, are death and the afterlife. The ideas and fantasies relating to death and the associated suffering humans might be destined to endure are the source of many prominent myths. Yama (Tibetan: Gshin-rje) is the lord of death in India mythology. He is described in the *Vedas*

Left: Drawing 4.e: The Eye of Horace or Wadjet (also written Udjat) resembles the eye of a hawk. It is said to represent the right eye of the Egyptian god Horace. Egyptian mythology tells that in the battle with Seth, Horace lost both his eyes. (Some persons say just his left eye was removed.) The left eye represented the moon and with it removed, the night sky was empty. The eye was reportedly found by Thoth and returned to its proper place. This act is believed to symbolize the restoration of cosmic order. The wadjet is a symbol of good luck. *Right:* Drawing 4.f: Vajrapâni is a mythical demon, protector of the Mahâyâna master of the secret, leader of the bearers of knowledge mantras. He fulfills an important role in Vajrayâna Buddhism. Vajrapâni is the mother, father and son of all Conquerors in that "he is the essence of all wisdoms; he take the form of spiritual guides and causes beings to generate an altruistic aspiration to highest enlightenment; and he assumes the form of Bodhisattvas as he did within Sakyamuni Buddha's retinue."

as the first man who died. Yama is represented in Vedic writing as a "cheerful king of the departed ancestors, not as a punisher of sins, but in later mythology he became known as the just judge (*Dharmaraja*) who weighs the good and evil deeds of the dead and determines their retribution."[172] The god Yamantaka is the mythical Conqueror of Yama, or Death (**see photograph 8**).

The counterpart to Yama in Aztec mythology is the god Mictlantecuhti. He rules Mictlan, the underworld and is usually depicted with a skull face (**see drawing 4.g**). Mictlantecuhti and his wife Mictecacihuatl are the parents of Quetzalcoatl, the god of life. The journey of the "soul of those whose manner of death failed to call them to various paradises (i.e., for those dead by war, sacrifice, childbirth, drowning, lightning, and certain diseases)"[173] is four years in duration. It involved passing through the nine hells of Mictlan. "[D]eath [is] a passage from earthly life to another existence on a different plane in a multilevel universe."[174] Aztec mythology also includes an opportunity for reincarnation. Huitzilopochtli, god of the sun, occasionally sent souls back to the land of the living as hummingbirds.[175]

The wish for immortality or a long life is documented by various myths. Ancient Egyptians believed in an afterlife long before the advent of writing and a formalized state

Four. The Nature of Phenomena: Mysticism, Magic, and Myths   105

Left: Photograph 8: The Dharmapala figure carved in the crown of a skull is that of Yamantaka "the destroyer of Yama (death)." He is known in Tibet as Vajrabhairava "The Diamond Terrifier." He is the wrathful manifestation of the Bodhisattva Manjushri. He is normally depicted as a multi-armed and multi-legged being with a large bull's head surrounded by flame. He may be represented as a single figure or with his consort, Vajravetali. The figure is to "chase away the three kinds of death: outer, inner, and secret." Yamantaka is worshipped as the Tutelary Deity of the Ge-lug-pa Sect. *Right:* Drawing 4.g: This figure made of fired clay is the Aztec god of the dead, *Mictlantecuhti*, ruler of Mictlan, the underworld. He and his wife, *Mictecacihuatl*, kept watch over the souls of those whose manner of death failed to grant them access to various paradises. He could grant the soul rest or damnation. *Mictlantecuhti* and *Mictecacihuatl* are the parents of Quetzalcoatl. It is said the emperor Montezuma feared the return of Quetzalcoatl and the prophesized ensuing disaster. Montezuma reportedly longed for the peace of *Mictlan* because he believed nothing could change the foretold path of events.

religion.[176] The myth of Osiris is the foundation for hope of a new life after death; consequently, special attention was given to preserving the body and reanimating the corpse. An important occurrence in connection with the process of reanimation was "the opening of the mouth." This process is to ensure the ability to talk. "It was believed that the reanimated corpse should speak with 'the true voice' and justify itself in the court of Osiris, judge of the dead, when the heart was weighed in the balance."[177] It is in the afterworld that this critical judgment is made. The heart is weighed against the feather of truth.

Egyptian myth also maintains that the scarab amulet is a guarantee of immortality. Amulets with inscribed spells were of particular importance. It was believed they "prevented the heart from testifying against its owner"[178] at the time of the weighing. "Heart scarabs" (*Scarabaeus sacer*) were placed in the mummy wrappings during the New Kingdom (1539–1075 B.C.E.), and symbolically identified with the heart of the deceased. They were believed to protect the heart (mind) and tongue of the dead and to ensure resurrection.

Chinese records relating to ancient burial customs include instructions to preserve the body from decay. However, instead of mummifying the body in a manner similar to the Egyptians, the Chinese believed the bodies could be preserved by magic.[179] "If there is gold and jade in the nine apertures of the corpse, it will preserve the body from putrefaction."[180] Pearls were placed into the mouth of the dead during the Han Dynasty (206 B.C.E.—C.E. 220). Pearls are identified in Chinese literature as "depositories of Yang matter [...] and can be useful for recalling to life those who have expired, or are at the point of dying."[181] Similar customs are found in other cultures, including the placing of coins (gold) on the eyes of the dead.

> For him there is no birth and death, nor joy or sorrow worth mentioning. Such is the true condition of an immortal, to which even the most gifted cannot easily attain, for it is not to be found through knowledge, whether human or divine.[182]

Physical immortality was a Taoist goal, probably before the development of Taoist mysticism. Aspirants seeking immortality had a choice among many methods that were intended to eliminate the ailments latent in the body and restore the pure energies possessed at birth.[183] The Taoist idea was to extend life; whereas, Christians consider immortality in terms of spirituality and resurrection. Christians professed the hope of life everlasting in the sense that they might be reborn as an indissoluble psychophysical unit — mind and body. This concept is configured on the notion that the soul leaves the body at death to dwell in a disembodied state. The souls of the righteous are re-embodied on Judgment Day to live eternally in the heavenly kingdom. Similarly, "The vision of heaven and hell in the Koran, the sacred book containing the teachings of the prophet Muhammad, is much like that of the Christians. Heaven is for the true believers; hell is for the infidel or the sinner."[184]

The Hindu notion of immortality involved a complex cycle of birth and rebirth moving toward an absolute condition that is freedom for the cycle. Hindus seek reincarnation as the "rebirth of the soul in one or more successive existences, which may be human, animal, or, in some instances, vegetable."[185] The belief in reincarnation is shared by different religions including Hinduism, Jainism, Buddhism, and Sikhism.

Acceptance of death as the definitive end of human life is difficult for most peoples. The belief that something of the individual survives continues despite the decomposition of the physical remains of humans. Myth, belief, or hope for life everlasting includes transformation of the soul and a place in paradise. The journey between worlds is expressed in the beliefs of many religions. Among the oldest records of this activity is the Egyptian *Pyramid Text* written about 2,375 years before the current era. The *Text*, often inscribed on the walls of the inner chambers of the pyramids included mortuary prayers, hymns, and protective spells.[186]

> The mystic is not always amorous of the beyond, leaving an unredeemed world to its own ways. Not escape but, rather, victory is mysticism's inner urge and promise. The more sober among the mystics do not merely withdraw; they also return to the base and attempt the ancient alchemy, the transformation of men. A solitary salvation does not satisfy either head or heart.[187]

Myths, rituals, and religion are often closely aligned in the death practices of Tibet as they are in many religions. The *Bardo Thödrol* ("Liberation by Hearing on the After-Death Plane") of the Tibetan Buddhists is considered unique among the sacred books. It is a "mystic manual for guidance through the Otherworld of many illusions and realms, whose frontiers are death and birth."[188] The *Bardo* is read for a period of 49 days to cover the time between death and rebirth. If a soul is transferred to an identified source for rebirth, as sometime occurs, there is no need for the *Bardo*. When no transfer has been prearranged, the body and consciousness separate at the time of death, and it is necessary for the lama or a trusted brother of the faith to read the *Bardo* to direct the soul to its proper destination.

It is generally acknowledged that myth has a specific and meaningful role to play in every human culture. Myth, like religion, is connected with identity, mortality (or immortality), and the moral sense of the world. Myth seeks a means for expression and therefore manifests itself in the ritual activities of a people. The ritual outlet may be religious in nature, that is, prayers and processions, or secular such as observances of the vernal and autumnal equinoxes. These are times when mythological forces are acknowledged and propitiated.

The ritual as a manifestation of a myth is a transformational link that joins the physical with the metaphysical. It is a vehicle for the displacement of time and place and a means for creating or reestablishing psychic harmony within the universe. The ritual reinforces belief and reaffirms the power of both the mystic and the divine by strengthening the omnipresence of the spirit world. The ritual as an expression of mythic belief is a mingling of the natural and supernatural worlds in ways that established empathy between the two realms.

Myths, based on concepts about supernatural beings or deified forces, are often difficult to convey as meaningful information. Consequently, the myths may be performed as ritual to establish a working relationship between the physical and metaphysical worlds. This practice is best exemplified by religious ceremonies. The religious ritual is associated with the transfer of information, and purveying information is often identified with power — the power of right thinking and right action. These rituals also grant a transitional relationship, as liturgical time is an extension of the period when the ritual was last performed.[189]

"Each kind of ritual is a patterned process in time. The units of which are symbolic objects and serialized items of symbolic behavior."[190] Although there are differences in their expression, the significance of religion-like activities is probably similar to all people and to all groups of people. One group may appear more spiritual, another less. One people may strive to placate local ghosts, another may worship a distant god, and a third may rely on magic to open the rain clouds, grow the crops, and ensure the successful birth of a progeny. However, all cultures give signs of satisfaction with their own observances.[191]

CHAPTER FIVE

Secret Language of Mysticism

"To age with the sun and moon and be renewed by spring and summer."[1]

> Order is intrinsic to the universe. Images and sounds are an expression of these underlying patterns. Life is a meaningful expression of this universal harmony beyond any one individual conscious conception.[2]

Visual comprehension for most cultures is a relational process. Symbols are associated with a particular deity, ritual, or event and through that association the symbolic prototype evolves. The relationship between the symbol and its purpose ensured easy recognition within the social confines. Symbols convey information and enhance understanding.

The symbolic message is an active ingredient of communication that is inherent to all forms of devotional belief. Although symbols may express ideas that are beyond the range of human understanding, they are also used to enhance commonly held beliefs. The human psyche requires constant reinforcement and recollection reactivation. Mystical activities often depend on psychological fulfillment that reinforce tradition and commonly held beliefs. "There are ... unconscious aspects of our [human] perception of reality. The first is the fact that even when our senses react to real phenomena, sights, and sounds, they are somehow translated from the realm of reality into that of the mind."[3]

Through the centuries, cultures have had differing attitudes toward symbolism. In some locations, particularly Europe, symbols were employed to signify different activities and events. An example of this conspicuous use of symbolism is heraldry. Later, such "invented" symbols were discarded as being on the "fringe of life." The fact that such symbols could be acquired in one era and disregarded in another testified to their superficial nature.[4]

Early people probably worshiped the natural forces without temples or symbols. These forces may have included the sun, moon, wind, fire, and water among other things. They gave recognition to those elements as through they were animated beings. They may have treated those forces as divine, offered sacrifices for propitiating them, and prayed for life sustaining resources. This was a religion of sacrifice and praise to various spirits. It dealt with forces that were considered alive and animated. It may be that over time the sacrifice became the symbol or that other images or objects were viewed as representative of the animated beings. Such symbols were a connection between humans and the divine, and for some persons they acquired mystical value.

The human mind is functioning symbolically when certain elements of its experience elicit consciousness, beliefs, emotions, and usages, representing other aspects of its experience. These elements may be described as the symbols, while the components constitute the meaning of the symbols.⁵ This is to say that the symbol, like the written word, must have a reference if it is to have meaning. According to Alfred North Whitehead, "This symbolic reference is the active synthetic element contributed by the nature of the percipient."⁶ However, the relationship between the symbol and the meaning must be based on some common factors such as those found in forms of belief and similarity of language.

The symbols of cultural heritage reflect the interests, traditions, and beliefs of the people. They often identify the unique character of a particular group and that distinction is essentially psychological. The power of the image (the visual material or seen element) is greatly increased when it is used as an element of a ritual activity to influence the spiritual (unseen) entities. Symbolic numbers, colors, sounds, gestures, names, times, and places have an affiliation with magic. Although there is nothing particularly magical in most magic activities, the psychological influence of magico-religious manifestations has a tremendous impact upon receptive participants.

Francis Huxley considered the issue of the difference between the symbol and the sign in his 1974 book titled *The Way of the Sacred*. He wrote, "A symbol is the image of a relationship in which the knower and the known share a common factor; a sign is rather a mark placed upon the known to distinguish it from the knower."⁷ Huxley explains the secondary relationship that is to be "intuited in a symbol constantly tends to take the form of the knower, which means that it is personified."⁸ Symbols are intricately woven into a people's ongoing perception of the reality. It is therefore a mark, element, or sound considered a primary element of the psychic life of the participating culture.

Almost every society has a symbol system that includes unusual objects and odd types of behavior. This seemingly irrational conduct may evoke peculiar, unwarranted mindfulness and emotions when encountered by the outside observer. It is that each symbol system has a particular cultural logic, and every symbol communicates information between members of that culture in much the same way as normal language. Symbols, however, are not a language by themselves. They are a means to express ideas thought too difficult, complex, or inconvenient to speak about in conventional language.

Symbols are a hidden reality that may be shared with others. They may be read as what they are, that is, the image, word, or element they appear to be, or as that element of information revealed to those persons having knowledge of a particular attitude or emotion. Writing about symbolism, Heather Child and Dorothy Colles state, "It can come to the eye as a visual image, it can come to the mind as an intellectual parallel between two ideas, but its truest value is when it flowers in the spirit in a sudden uprush of rich understanding."⁹

Speaking the name of an object or repeating a mantra (words that liberate and protect) is the expression of an individual's inner thoughts. The spoken word as the symbolic manifestation of the inner thought is the same for people of all beliefs. When a person thinks of an object, the image or idea is the same whether called to mind by the object itself or by the utterance of its name. It is for this reason that a mystic or dedicated believer acknowledges symbols as the embodied presence of the sacred regardless of what the essential nature of the symbol may be. Symbolic thinking is an integral element of human existence. "It came before language and discursive reason. The symbol reveals certain aspects of reality — the deepest aspects — which defy any other means of knowledge."¹⁰

"The symbol translates a human situation into cosmological terms and reciprocally, more precisely, it discloses the interdependence between the structure of human existence and cosmic structures."¹¹ This means that humanity does not feel isolated in the cosmos, that he or she is open to a world that is symbolically familiar. Symbols acknowledge certain common values and aid in sustaining an emotional commitment to those objects and ideas that are important to a people or culture. Symbols add a new or different meaning to objects or expression without violating related immediate or historical validity. The recognition of the symbol is an amenable experience that has immediate authenticity for the resident community. This acknowledgment corresponds with the idea of a symbol representing or causing something to be recalled due to related qualities or associations in fact or thought.

A mystical experience may occur as the result of different forms symbolic reference. Some allusions are direct and informal while others are indirect and may require the services of a messenger or intermediary. A word, song, prayer, or image may be adequate to promote a trancelike condition that enhances a mystical episode for some persons and situations. However, experiences relating to the symbolism of divine messengers most often are communicated through sanctified sources such as yogis, shamans, mystics, saints, and spiritual masters of the inner life. This process of communicating through human agents has generated a number of divine messengers including angels, intermediaries, and incarnations.

> Prayer consists of the silent recitation (*japa*) of sacred formulae (*mantra*) which are repeated indefinitely. The mantra are composed of from one to a hundred or more syllables. Here we find a tribute to the word as form, for many of the syllables (notably in the religious practices of Tantrism) have no meaning while others consist of a simple mention of the divine name such as Râm(a) Râm(a)![12]

Symbols come from different cultural and societal occurrences. The visionary experience of the mystic evolves from his or her need for a meaningful means of communication. Symbols often reflect belief or value systems that are familiar to the related culture. However, because they may have unique cultural references, the symbol often has another meaning in a different belief system. All religions have a mode of symbolic veneration recognized by different names — prayer, devotion, observance, meditation, etc. Meditative processes frequently include sounds, objects, or gestures such as the lotus flower, wheel, ladder, heart, cross, music, incense, and other supportive symbols to enter into a mystical union.

Sounds, objects, and gestures have a definite symbolism, and a culture uses a range of such symbols to convey both positive and negative meaning. Objects normally acquire their symbolic reference from their association with certain practices of social and cultural life and from the transference of specific ideas and qualities. Symbols commonly associated with rites and rituals communicate group-recognized messages and thereby stimulated group acknowledgment and response. Consequently, the relationship between the symbol and the idea or emotion it represents has definable mystical or symbolic implications.

The mystic maintains that mystical knowledge is above reason; however, it must be reasonably acceptable if it is to be communicated to others. Evelyn Underhill wrote on this issue in *Mysticism: A Study in the Nature and Development of Spiritual Consciousness* (2002 [1911]), She states, "The mystic, as a rule, cannot wholly do without symbol and image, inadequate to his vision though they must always be; for his experience must be expressed if it is to be communicated."[13] Underhill continues, "Its actuality is inexpressible except in some side-long way, some hint or parallel which will stimulate the dormant intuition of the reader, and convey, as all poetic language does, something beyond its surface sense."[14]

> In the beginning, God is too awesome for the human mind to grasp and only later can Divine Energy be perceived in its pure form, so the human mind needs to establish a link with a personal aspect such as Krishna or Siva in the Indian religions, or Jesus or Mary in Christianity. Adults who are still spiritual children need to have a personal concept of God until they can see the Divine Energy in its pure form.[15]

A symbol may represent several ideas and may be interpreted in different ways. This possibility is not exceptional considering the fundamental significance of the symbol and the idea with which it was associated when selecting from an infinite number of possibilities. Certain symbols are "intensely powerful because they enshrine and express the highest values and relationships of life."[16] However, for the religious person, the world always presents a supernatural facade, that is, it shows a vision of the sacred. Each element of the natural world is transparent (or transformed), because its means of existence reflects the believer's attitude, and hence, the sacred. The sacred or sacred consciousness is the full manifestation of life for such a person.

Symbols develop according to human need. They are not manufactured in the sense that immediate symbolic recognition is granted a sound, object, or gesture. It is because of the common needs of people that certain symbols evolved in different locations without interrelated influence. Nonetheless, the multi-cultural endorsement of a symbol does not alter its originality or relevance. The objects or sounds created to meet specific needs gradually gain recognition as symbolically representing the related activity. The symbol may be altered in this process to gain greater acceptability, but it normally retains it original message. Common understanding is eventually granted the symbol, and it is aligned with human interests such as those found in ritual activities or other communally endorsed practices.

An example of a multi-cultural symbol that developed in different locations is the Cosmic Tree. It is also called the world pole, god-pillar, Tree of the World, Tree of Life, lingam, and various other names. The tree or pole is the symbolic link between earth (the middle world) and the two other worlds. The tree is believed to grow upward through all layers of the natural and spiritual upper worlds while the roots reach the lower world. Climbing the tree (actually or symbolically) signified the ascent to heaven and a connection with the deities. A ladder is used to symbolize the tree, or an actual tree was prepared with steps to aid in the climb.

The use of symbols is a general human attribute that enters into the mental and physical activities of all groups. Symbols are valid references for analyzing cultural attitudes when examined in relation to fundamental beliefs and the way they are conceived and formulated. An element of conceptual thinking is the ability to utilize symbols and to recognize the idea of one thing or image as representing another. Although people normally communicate in orally sounded words with commonly endorsed meanings, non-literal symbols are also used. Symbols must have the same or similar value to both parties — the presenter and the receiver — to function as elements of communication.

Mircea Eliade[17] describes a symbol as an "autonomous mode of cognition" since it aids the viewer or listener in seeing or hearing both what is represented and what is perceived. Human sensibilities in most circumstances are inclined to recognize the anticipated objects or sound disallowing the overriding authority of reason.[18]

Symbolism plays important roles in society because symbols express beliefs, desires, expectations, affiliations, and loyalties. Symbolic representations have many forms from the simplest reference to the most complex expression. They may be a one-word *mantra* passed from guru to student or a large-scale painting or sculpture of a venerated religious figure. Some symbols are broadly recognizable and only a few people know others. Culturally acknowledged figures, shapes, and colors are enhancing elements of differing importance to people, as are sound symbols. However, nonverbal language is the universal reference for defining the spiritual and emotional content of most cultures.

> Whether the symbol [is] a spoken word, a drawing in the sand, or a mimetic dance, the principle [is] the same, the act of symbolizing, particularly when ritualized, actually "re-present" its object, that means "bringing it before us by calling it back from whatever place it may have reached."[19]

Different symbolic systems are generated as elements of social connection, but the linkages are often very complicated. Societal messages can differ one from another according to their content, form, and affiliation. They are, however, the same in two aspects: people want to establish contacts with other beings even when that communication is one-sided, and the message is conveyed not just in one type of language, but in more than one code at the same time. An example of this communication is the ceremony in which the Buddhist monk uses the chant as a language to make connection with a deity. The monk's robe, incense, and a thanka add to the possibility of communication as symbols, because a recognized value (belief) is assigned to those symbols.

The mystical experience is a renewal of life, that is, a rediscovery of the forgotten language of symbols and symbolism. The mystic is a part of two worlds, the profane and the sacred. Rituals, ceremonies, and symbols are the way of joining with a higher reality and consciousness. However, like rituals and ceremonies, symbols cannot be deliberately produced, nor do they make an arbitrary system. The symbol foretells its essential nature, its unity. It points beyond itself and participates in that to which it points. It opens levels of reality that are otherwise closed to humanity. The profound symbol may open dimensions of the inner being (soul or spirit) that might otherwise remain dormant. An example of such inspirational symbolism is the Buddhist incantation *om mani padme hum* ("the jewel in the lotus") (see drawing 2.b).

Symbolism is a language, and from the perspective of basic communication, it discloses dimensions that are not provided by the tangible object or the fully enacted activity. The need to make visible the invisible led to the creation of symbols, and the symbols became elements of the communication process. The symbols of mysticism evolve as representations of the social sphere and function to unite the individual or activity with society. Such symbols may have originated in the unconscious, but were integrated into tradition.[20] Each mystical object or activity was patterned by time as an inclusive element of symbolic behavior.

Symbolism is a part of human society because it has a primary role in social life of most people.[21] Symbols define certain values common to people and aid in sustaining an emotional commitment to that which is determined to be of significance to the group. Symbols add value to objects and acts without violating related historical importance. The activity with symbolic meaning is an open event that has immediate reality for the resident community.[22] That immediacy validates the belief that a symbol represents or causes something to be recalled due to analogous qualities or associations in fact or thought. Symbols, in this context, are a fundamental part of society and the socializing processes. They were aligned with human interests when formulated as a formal or informal ritual activity acknowledged by circumstances and practices.

The use of symbols is a general human attribute that enters into "all mental activity and the physical activity it empowers and guides."[23] Symbolic reference is consequently a tool for analyzing cultural attitudes when examined in relation to fundamental beliefs and the way they are conceptualized and formulated. Jung viewed symbol development as a millennial process that pushes "toward consciousness, beginning in the darkness of prehistory with primordial and archetypal images, and gradually developing and differentiating these images into conscious creations."[24]

Symbols as the embodied presence of the sacred have societal influence regardless of what the essence of reality of the symbol may be. The use of symbols is one of the most distinctive of all human characteristics.[25] Mircea Eliade describes a symbol as an "autonomous mode of cognition" since it aids the viewer in seeing both what is represented and what is perceived.[26] Human sensibilities in most circumstances are inclined to see or recognize the objects anticipated disallowing the overriding authority of reason.[27] The symbol, although a facsimile (a representation), is granted validity and purpose because it is similar to the associated mental image of the ideal.

The Word as Symbolic Language

> Symbols ... integrate the social and personal dimensions of religion, enabling individuals to share certain commonly held beliefs expressed by symbols, while also giving freedom to read private meaning into them.[28]

There was the word in the beginning, and the word was truth. The divine truth was at times revealed symbolically to the mystic. These revelations might be in visions or dreams complete with colors and sounds. "Speech is man's most constant expression, his greatest performance, and the barometer of his emotions."[29] Consequently, the mystic had to rely upon terminology of worldly experience, such as that relating to love and intoxication, to covey these seemingly indescribable experiences to others. All natural elements were viewed in relation to God—the Absolute. "For spiritual education, symbols taken from medicine (healing of the sick soul and alchemy, [the] changing of base matter into gold) were also used."[30]

Sufi mystics often relied on the written word and in particular poetry as a means for delivering his or her message of truth. The passionate writing expressed the hope for the union of the soul with the divine. The theistic emotion was often conveyed by symbolic reference to human yearning and love. The allegories and parables spoke of eternal beauty in terms of female pulchritude and described the soul as the loving wife. Sufi poetry depicted physical union as the "submersion of the drop in the ocean, the state of the iron in the fire, the vision of penetrating light, or the burning of the moth in the candle."[31]

> All kinds of symbolic language come naturally to the articulate mystic, who is often a literary artist as well: so naturally, that he sometimes forgets to explain that his utterance is but symbolic—a desperate attempt to translate the truth of that world into the beauty of this.[32]

It is commonly understood that language and the written word are forms of symbolism. C. G. Jung wrote in *Symbols of Transformation*, "[L]anguage, in its origin and essence, [is] simply a system of signs or symbols that denote real occurrences or their echo in the human soul."[33] Language is a symbolic form of communication that involves understanding of the words as well as the expression of feelings. The spoken sound of a word in the English language corresponds roughly to the combined sounds of the letters of the alphabet. These letters are also symbols. This identification is not applicable to all languages or all writing styles. The Chinese written language, as an example, is often considered pictographic or ideographic, however, logographic, a symbol or sign used to represent a word, is the term that best describes the Chinese writing system.

Alfred North Whitehead wrote in *Symbolism: Its Meaning and Effect* (1927), "A word is a symbol. But a word can be either written or spoken. Now on occasions, a written word may suggest the corresponding spoken word, and that sound may suggest a meaning."[34] North explains the issue by saying, "The written word is a symbol and its meaning is the spoken word, and the spoken word is a symbol and it meaning is the dictionary meaning of the word, spoken or written."[35]

All forms of visual expression depend on symbols as modes of informational transfer. "The Power of symbols lies in the ability to unite fellow-believers into a community."[36] Consequently, symbolism plays an important role in societies because people use symbols to express beliefs, desires, expectations, affiliations, and loyalties. Symbolic representations have many forms from the simplest reference to the most complex expression. Some symbols are generally known and understood while only a few individuals recognize others. Use of symbolic elements may have contradictory meanings to people unfamiliar with specific cultural values.

Mantras are symbolic utterances found in Hinduism and Buddhism. They are a combination of sacred syllables (words and sounds) formulated as a nucleus of spiritual energy. They are not prayers that are selected or defined by the aspirant; instead, they are a combination of a particular kind of consciousness that focuses spiritual vibrations. They are sound symbols that promote meditation. "According to the *Upanishads*, the ancient scriptures of India, the original abode of the mantra was the *Parma Akasha* or primeval ether, the eternal and immutable substratum of the universe, out of which ... the universe itself was created."[37] The mantra leads the spirit that is lost in trivialities and misdirection back to the Pure Essence.

Mantras may have no apparent verbal meaning, but they are believed to have a profound underlying importance that is the distillation of spiritual wisdom. They are the essence of the guru's (teacher) understanding of the Truth and their vibrations create the right conditions around the worshipper for his or her chosen deity to respond.[38] Mantras are transmitted from generation to generation and from teacher (guru) to disciple. This process of repetition adds power, and is believed to activate spiritual forces that promote harmony in all parts of the human being each time they are repeated. The worshipper is gradually transformed into a living center of spiritual vibration that is connected to other, more powerful center of vibration. The energy produced by this process can be gathered and directed for the benefit of the person who initiates it and for others.[39]

Swami Sivnanda Radha states, "The power, the consciousness within the mantra, is *Sakti*, Divine Mother, the Goddess of the Spoken Word. The male aspect of God is energy in a state of equilibrium; the female aspect is dynamic energy that manifests as creation."[40] The Swami explains, "Chanting a mantra with devotion and concentration attunes the individual through Divine melody and has a harmonious influence over the whole body and mind."[41] Each *raga*, according to the Swami, is a specific blending of sounds that reflects the laws of the universe and therefore is in perfect harmony with the universe at the time it is sounded.

The six-syllable mantra—*Om Mani Padme Hum*—is the principal mantra of Buddhism. It is most famous mantra in the world (see drawing 2.b). It is a symbol of blessing and a request for acknowledgment. Said to calm fears, soothe worries, and answer prayers, it is a call to the "Buddha of Compassion, known as the Buddha *Chenrezig* in Tibet, as the Goddess of Mercy, *Kuan Yin*, by Chinese all over the world, as *Avalokiteshvara* in India, and as the Goddess *Kwannon* in Japan."[42] The first syllable, *Om*, is equally important in Hindu and Jaina rituals. It is composed of three sounds "a-u-m" (**see drawing 5.a**). It is pronounced in three locations, the back, middle, and front of the mouth. *Om*, for the Hindus, represents

Five. Secret Language of Mysticism

the three worlds (upper, middle, and lower); the three major Hindu gods, Brahma, Vishnu, and Siva; and the three sacred *Vadic* scriptures, *Rg*, *Yajur*, and *Sama*. Om mystically embodies the essence of the entire universe.[43] *Om* is used in the practice of yoga and is commonly spoken in techniques of meditation.

> Nothing is meaningless or neutral: everything is significant. Nothing is independent, everything is in some way related to something else. The quantitative becomes the qualitative in certain essentials which, in fact, precisely constitute the meaning of the quantity. Everything is serial. Series are related on to another as to position, and the components of each series are related as to meaning.[44]

Drawing 5.a: Om mystically represents the essential nature of the whole universe. The three sounds of the Om, a-u-m, have sacred meaning in Hinduism, Jainism, and Buddhism. It represents the three worlds, the three major Hindu gods, and the three sacred Vedic scriptures. It is considered the greatest of all mantras (sacred formulas). It is believed to represent the primordial sound that created the existential world—the divine word and the mantra of mantras. "'*Aum*' (OM) is known as the *pranava* mantra. The fusion of a, u, and m into the single, complete syllable of *aum* (the *pranava*) represents the integral totality of the microcosm as well as the macrocosm. The process of gradually transcending all three states of phenomenal existence leads to the fusion of the three parts of *aum* into the transcendent integrality of *aum*." Each letter of the word has an associated mystical color.

The *yantra* (meaning instrument) expresses thought-form in visual symbols in the same way the mantra communicates in sound. *Yantras*, used in Tantric Hinduism and Vajrayâna, are geometrical figures for meditation. They are drawings of basic linear elements—straight lines, crosses, circles, and triangles, and although two-dimensional, they are always thought of as three-dimensional. "To the Hindu, there are innumerable *yantras* in the world; for every natural shape, such as a flower or a leaf can be meditated upon as a *yantra*, its meaning being the story of creation itself."[45] *Yantras* are called *mandalas* when they are in elaborate or pictorial forms.

Thangka, *thanka*, or *tangka* come from the Tibetan "*thang yig* meaning 'written word,' with the sense of a painting or written record."[46] These often elaborate and usually colorful images represent timeless, universal, and cosmic realities. "The shamans of Nepal are certain of the fact that shamans were the first people to paint *thangkas*."[47] The images depicted on thangkas are to give belief a visible form and to serve as symbolic references to "train the visionary powers and thus assist [believers] in the ability to move about more purposefully in the three worlds."[48] *Thangka* are "paintings for healing, teaching, and meditation. Those who immerse themselves in them are healed and edified, and they are led back to what is essential by the contemplation of images that have been created to aid in meditation and concentration."[49]

The symbolism seen in most religious depictions is not a graphic representation of the universe but a means of creating places in which the observer can find a haven that is safe from the surrounding chaos and, from that refuge, discover a connection to the celestial being that governs it throughout.

The Soul as a Symbol of the Self

> Plato believed in the immortality of the human soul. The soul was, he thought, an entity that was fundamentally distinct from the body although it could be and often was affected by its association with the body, being dragged down by what he called in one passage "the leaden weight of becoming."[50]

The soul, in religion and philosophy, is the intangible (ethereal) feature or essence of a human being. The soul is thought to confer individuality and humanity, elements often viewed as the same as the mind or self. The soul from the perspective of theology is viewed as that aspect of a person that has a religious nature and is believed to survive physical death. "Mongolians believe that man, besides his body, consists of a soul, even of several souls. Man also has a mirror soul, which can be seen when looking into water, and a shadow soul, which is visible when the sun is shining."[51]

The soul may be viewed as a mystical symbol in that it is a fundamental element of faith. It represents to the adherent his or her essential nature and it resides within each of his or her actions. Further, the soul of the incarnate deity is believed to transfer at death into another incarnation; and if this takes place when the death is a natural one, there is no reason why it should not take place when the death is by violence. The idea that the soul of a dying person may be transmitted to his or her successor is an accepted conviction for certain cultural groups.[52]

Many cultures acknowledge an incorporeal principle of human life or essence analogous to the soul, and many ascribe souls to all living things. The number of souls often relates to the mystic numbers endorsed by the culture. The Plains Indians of North America, as an example, associate the mystic number four with peculiar potency; consequently, some tribes maintain the notion of four souls. The ancient Egyptians believed people had two souls. One, the *ka* (breath) remained near the body after death; whereas, the spiritual soul (*ba*) traveled to the land of the dead. The ancient Chinese also recognized duel souls. They make a distinction between a lower, sensitive soul, which ceases to exist at death, and the second soul, the *hun*, that remain after death, and is the object of ancestor worship.

The early Hebrews apparently had a concept of the soul but did not separate it from the body. The Old Testament refers to the soul in relation to the concept of breath and assigns no difference between the ethereal soul and the corporeal body. St. Augustine (C.E. 354–430) spoke of the soul as a "rider" on the body in later Christian theology. He made clear the division between the tangible and the intangible, with the soul representing the "true" person. Though the body and soul were believed separate, it was not possible to envision of a soul devoid of its body. Later Christian mystics spoke of the "dark night of the soul" and the purification necessary to ready for divine reunion.[53]

The Hindus believe each *atman* (breath, or soul) is created at the beginning of time and confined in an earthly body at birth. The atman is thought to pass into a new body at the death of the resident body. The nature of that transfer is determined by *karma*, or the collective results of personal action. Buddhism refutes the Hindu concept of *atman*, believing instead that any impression of the individual soul or self is illusory. The Muslim belief seems to correspond with the Christian concept of the soul. They, Muslims, maintain the soul comes into being at the same time as the body; thereafter, it has a life of its own. They contend that its relationship with the material body is but a temporary condition.

Time as a Transparent Symbol

> The sacred manifests itself in time and space, so that time and space themselves become diaphanous indications of the holy.[54]

It is said in Indian philosophy that no one can interfere with fate or destiny (*daiva*) except a yogi. Swami Rajarshi Muni wrote about *daiva* in *Yoga: The Ultimate Spiritual Path* (2001). He stated, "*Daiva* is closely related to the other two determinative forces of the universe, *desha* or *sthala* (space) and *kala* (time)."[55] The Swami also noted, "The mysterious force of *daiva* (destiny) drives forward the evolutionary process, working out changes in the mundane world that is engulfed in the immense space and struggle for existence through the tides of time."[56] The Swami believes that "such matters cannot be brought down to the scale of ordinary human understanding or imagination."[57]

Time is a transparent symbol of the sacred. It is represented by the cycle of the sacred year as exemplified by traditional practices such as celebration of the solstices and equinoxes. Time sequence also may be represented in signs and pictures. Cosmic, mythical, sacred time, and destiny are shown, for example, in the Tibetan Buddhist symbol the wheel of life, *bhava-cakra*; there are three creatures in the center: "a cock signifying craving and greed; a snake signifying wrath and passion; and a pig signifying ignorance and delusion"[50] (**see drawing 5.b**). The symbols and the message are clear.

Drawing 5.b: The middle circle of the ***bhava-cakra*** (Wheel of Life) showing the three basic evils (faults or spiritual poisons) of humanity symbolized by the cock signifying craving and greed, the snake representing wrath and passion, and the pig manifesting ignorance and delusion. They are symbolic of the fires of evil that make sentient beings victims of Avidhya — primordial delusion. Hindus and Buddhists acknowledge the message of the Wheel's multi-layers representing the endless cycle of rebirths. Yama, God of Death, holds the wheel symbolizing the impermanence of life. Following the path of the basic evils as depicted on the Wheel is to pursue damnation and bad rebirths, whereas, the opposite direction leads to better rebirths and progression toward final liberation.

Humans are seemingly unable to live without the concept of time; consequently, time has symbolic meaning in most societies. There is secular and sacred time, and among some peoples, time has a profound mystical nature. Time is measured by sequence and duration, but it is not real. It is an impression that must be defined in relative terms. Much Eastern thought views time as a process of constant renewal. Such thinking follows the notion of illusion and impermanence resulting in change and death. These conditions are the functions of time. Time means change. The concept of time as a symbolic element of mysticism should not be confused with the passing of conventional time. It refers to the highest goal of spiritual existence. "A person who succeeds in escaping karma and the flux of time through the power of liberating awareness is known among other things, as a *maha-siddha*, or 'great adept' who has transcended or 'cheated' time."[59]

Life is calculated from beginning to end by factors acknowledged by a measure of time. Time is cyclical in Eastern belief, not linear as in Western thinking. Samsâra for Hindus is the cycle of birth, death, and rebirth to which every human is subject so long as he or she lives in ignorance. It is for some Buddhists the cycle of existence that humans must endure until they attain liberation and enter nirvâna. It is the continuous cycle that is conditioned by the three unwholesome roots, wrath (hatred), greed (desire), and delusion (ignorance). The Mahâyâna Buddhists views samsâra and nirvâna as the same since both are mental representations. However, for all Buddhists, neither has real substance, and therefore, cannot be realized by time or place. Samsâra is above all about time. The beginning of samsâra is speculative because it evolves with the individual cycle of incarnations, and the end (nirvâna) can be achieved only during rebirth as a human being, which in turn depends on karma.[60] "To be trapped in samsâra means to be doomed endlessly to repeat oneself, that is, one's karmic patterns."[61]

All belief systems (religions) have a fundamental time sequence — past, present, and future. All have a mystical initiation that is to personify (humanize by example) the basic principles of belief. As in the distant past gods were given human characteristics that they might be more closely identified with their devotees. Christ, Buddha, Muhammad, Lao Tzu, and Confucius are examples of this practice. They are the source, "in the beginning," that gives an initial time reference for devotees who live in the present and prepare for the future (life after death). Hinduism, however, does not evolve from a single source. It integrates a variety of elements involving religious, social, economic, literary, and artistic aspects. It is a composite of diverse doctrines, cults, and ways of life. Nevertheless, the foundational belief inherent in Hinduism comes for the distant past.

Time in most societies is divided into separate realities — the sacred and the secular. The two spheres overlap to a greater or lesser degree depending on individual belief and practice. The Sufis, as an example, reacted against separation of attitudes that seemed contrary to the basic tenets of Islam. They sought to instill the mystical (devout) nature of Islam into the all aspect of life. In contrast, other cultures viewed secular time as an illusion and sacred time as reality. There is in most cultures a sharing of sacred information in stages (present time) beginning with the coming of age of group members and continuing through adulthood. The information is disclosed in culturally defined steps according to tradition (past time honored practices).

People identify with the present time, but socio-culturally they recognized the past and anticipated the future. Ethereal time is, in contrast, continuous and unlimited by concepts of past, present, and future. Events relating to sacred time are described as being from a time when all things were created. "This mythic or sacred time is qualitatively different from profane time, from the continuous and irreversible time of our everyday, de-sacralized existence."[62] The attitude of sacred time makes possible the transmission of the mythological history of a people and formalized the belief system. This practice is exemplified by sacred documentation: the Bible, Torah, Qur'an, Veda, and Sutra.

The Tantric view of time gives special attention to the figure of the Divine Female or Shakti in her manifestation of the Hindu goddess Kali (Sanskrit "She Who is Black"). The color black symbolizes her all-embracing and transcendental nature. The name Kali is the female form of Kala, and Shiva is called Kala — the eternal time — past, present, and future. Since Kali is Shiva's consort, her name also means time, death, and black. Hence, Kali is considered the goddess of time and change. These connotations are fused in the symbolism of the goddess Kali.[63] She is worshiped as the ultimate reality in Tantric beliefs, and as Bhavatarini (literally "redeemer of the universe"). Kali is depicted standing or dancing on the supine body of Lord Shiva. She destroys ignorance, maintains the world order, and blesses and frees those who strive for the knowledge of God. Kali is the foremost among the Dasa Mahavidyas — the ten fierce Tantric goddesses.

Kali is commonly associated with death, sexuality, and violence as well as time. She is often shown completely or partially nude with a girdle of human hands and around her neck a necklace of 50 human heads (some say 51 heads), and dancing on her husband, the god Shiva. "The skulls stand for the fundamental energies of the cosmos (also represented by the fifty letters of the Sanskrit alphabet); the hands symbolize action and its karmic fruition. In the middle of her forehead is a third eye, indicating her omniscience."[64] She is usually shown with four arms. The book, *Tantra: The Path of Ecstasy* (1998), by Georg Feuerstein writes about one of Kali's left hands holding a severed human head by the hair, signifying human ego that must be slain by divine knowledge; the other left hand holding a bloody sword that signifies divine knowledge to cut all bondage to the world. One right hand is in the fear-dispelling gesture (*abhaya* mudra), the other in the gesture of blessing (*varada* mudra).[65] Feuerstein describes the commonly depicted image of Kali as including snakes encircling her ankles, wrists, and upper arms as "symbols of both temporal cycles and the arcane knowledge that liberate the initiate from space and time [may be] dangerous to the uninitiated."[66]

Kali became popular with the composition of the *Devi Mahatmya*, a manuscript of the fifth or sixth century C.E. She is depicted in that text as having been born from the brow of the goddess Durga during a battle with the evil demon Raktabija (Blood Seed). The legend contends that Kali entered the fray, killed the demon, and became so involved in destroying evil that she began a frenzied cosmic dance that demolished everything. Lord Shiva threw himself under her feet to stop her dance. Shocked at this sight, Kali stuck out her tongue in surprise, and stopped her destructive dancing.

Nepalese shamans view the goddess Kali as an important deity to whom the whole of creation can be traced.[67] She provides protection from dangers that come from the west, and fulfills a primary role in shamanic healing. This association (goddess and practitioner) is an example of the symbol as primarily intended for a circle of initiates (large or small) which invokes the acknowledgment of the experience that it expresses.

Time is also a primary factor in Taoist belief. A measure of time, age, is an important factor in acknowledging Taoist teachers and devotees as immortals. Lao-tzu, the first major patriarch of Taoism, was thought to be 150 to 200 years old. It was natural for Taoists to credit their masters with uncommon longevity. The legend, in the case of Lao-tzu, relates that he was an old man when he was born. He was conceived by a shooting star, and is said to have exited the womb after 72 years with white hair and long whiskers in 604 B.C.E. Other legends contend he was born at the foot of a plum (*li*) tree. Lao-tzu was considered a mythical figure that was worshiped by the people by the time of the Eastern, or late, Han dynasty (C.E. 25–220).

Living in harmony with the laws of the universe is cause for tranquility of mind and Taoists considered this a requirement for normal life, whereas living by rules was viewed as a way of false security. If rules are followed, there may be a superficial feeling that all is well but in reality "life cannot be structured in a rigid way and volcanoes will inevitably erupt from underneath."[68] Taoists believe all things are interdependent; therefore, there was no division between the sacred and the secular.

The Head as Symbolic Seat of the Soul

People endorsed the belief that possession of human bone, particularly the skull, brought the protection and help of the dead at some time in ancient history.[69] The skull was, from that time forward, apparently viewed as a primary symbol of mortality in many localities. The head bone was a part of two very prevalent beliefs; (1) bones were centers of psychic energy, and (2) the head was the dwelling place of the spirit.

Early people placed the spirit or soul in the skull rather than the heart. This notion relates to ancestor worship where the heads of ancestors are retained as objects of spiritual importance, and a demonstration of respect. In contrast, headhunting took the heads of enemies to demonstrate superiority and to deny a resting place for adversarial spirits. Skulls were often decorated or covered with clay to give a likeness of the deceased, and thereby, to ensure the retention of ancestral spirits. However, the skulls of enemies were normally left unadorned to be unattractive and unrecognizable to the potentially combative spirit.

The magic head symbolically stands for many things. It is the astral light as described in the *Sefer ha-zohar* (Hebrew: "Book of Splendor"). The *Zohar*, as the book is generally called, is a classic writing of esoteric Jewish mysticism (Kabbalah) that deals with the inner (mystical, and symbolic) meaning of biblical texts. This thirteenth century book is believed to be based on supernatural revelations and it serves as support and reference for all the Jewish theosophies. It speaks of universal harmony among other attitudes related to observance of the biblical and rabbinical precepts. "The method of symbolic representation used by the writings of the Zoharic corpus was supported by a system of interpretation that made use of the originally Christian concept of the fourfold meaning of Scripture: literal, moral, allegorical (philosophical), and mystical."[70] Many Jews turned to the *Sefer ha-zohar* as a guide for mystical speculations.

Christians viewed the head as the seat of life, and the controller of the rest of the body. Therefore, Christ was viewed as the spiritual head of the Christian church "not only in eminence and influence but in that He communicates life and strength to every believer."[71] The head is also used as a symbol associated with other biblical persons. Often it is a severed head in the hands of a hero or heroine. David cut of the head of Goliath, Judith is often shown holding the head of Holofernes, and Salome carried the severed head of John the Baptist on a platter. "A head on a platter is sometimes employed as an attribute of St. John the Baptist."[72] Another severed head, this one belonging to Chinnamasta, symbolizes the transcendence of the body through Tantra.

The head as the primary part of the body is sometimes used in Christianity to symbolically represent the whole person, whereas the skull is an important part of Tantric ritual. The skull-cup (Sanskrit: *kapala*, Tibetan: *thod phur*) made from the upper portion of a human skull is used in ritual activities for Vajrayana deities as a drinking container. The symbolic meanings placed upon the skull-cup in the hands of wrathful and protective deities (*yidam, dakinis, saddhas*, and tantric linage holders) and their human emanations are complex and multifaceted.[73] The skull cups are often decorated with silver and brass or copper grinning death heads. The cups may also be carved with protector figures, skeletons, or demons

Photograph 9: A protector figure carved into the outer surface of a skull cup (kapala). The central image is a horned figure with a fierce expression. He has multiple arms and he is holding a bowl (*kapala*) in his left hand and a ritual cleaver (*trigug* or *kartika*) in his right. The cleaver is to cut the bonds of ignorance. The arms hold various tools and symbols of Tantric Buddhism. This roughly carved but powerful figure is the ferocious *Yamantaka*, the fierce expression of Manjushri, the God of Learning, to whom the people of Tibet appealed when *Yama*, the God of Death, was ravishing the country. *Yamantaka* assumed this fierce form and conquered *Yama*, limited his powers, by making him Judge of the Dead and a Defenders of Buddhism.

(see photograph 9). The *kapalas* are used by shamans and are very important invocations and meditations.

The quality of the skull from which the skull-cup is made, is of particular importance. Robert Beer reports in *The Handbook of Tibetan Buddhist Symbols* (2003), "The skull of a murderer or execution victim is believed to possess the greatest tantric or spirit power; the skull of one who has died from a violent or accidental death, or from a virulent illness, possesses a medium magical power."[74] In contrast, "the skull of a person who died peacefully in old age has virtually no occult power."[75] Great mystic potency is found in the "skull of a child who died during the on-set of puberty, as do the skulls of a miscegenated or misbegotten child of unknown paternity, born from the forbidden union of castes, out of wedlock, from sexual misdemeanor, or particularly from incest."[76] The greatest power in certain tantric rituals resides in the skull of a seven or eight-year-old child born from an incestuous union.[77]

The skull is used as a symbol of the transitory nature of life on earth in Western imagery. It is also thought to signify the upper world — the heavens.[78] The skull is the receptacle of life as well as thought in the East. It has significant symbolic meaning in alchemy because it is what survives of the living being once the body is destroyed. The skull is symbolic of impermanence and the momentary essence of existence; consequently, it is often worshiped long after death. The cross on Golgotha, "the place of the skull," is said to rest on the skull and bones of Adam according to Christian belief. (There are those who believe that Adam carried the philosopher's stone with him when he left Paradise and that it is now present within everyone.)

A more direct method of acknowledging the head as the symbolic seat of the soul is headhunting. "[T]he decapitation of corpses in prehistoric times marked Man's discovery of the independence of the spiritual principle, residing in the head, as opposed to the vital principle represented by the body as a whole."[79] The practice of removing and preserving the human head to capture the soul of the deceased was known in many parts of the world and may have started in Paleolithic times. Among those cultures practicing headhunting the acquired soul matter was believed to add to the general wellbeing of the community. The accumulated souls (heads) were thought to contribute to the fertility of humans, animals, and crops. Headhunting survived until the early 20th century in Europe, and in China, the Wa people of Yunnan are thought to have continued the practice into the mid–20th century.

The Hand as Symbol of Mystic Awareness

The imprints of the human hand are found in numerous caves in Spain and France. Aurignacian man (25,000 B.C.E.) placed his hand against the surface of the cave wall and sprayed by mouth black or ocher pigment to give a negative imprint. He also applied pigment to the palm and made a series of positive impressions. Handprints have been left in locations in South Africa, Mexico, India, and the American Southwest. Although the meaning is not clear, these hands prints are not believed to be art but elements of magic or mystical ritual often associated with shamanism.

The hand has a special place in mysticism as well as alchemy and magic. "A vast number of symbolic hands have been discovered in the ruins of Pompeii and elsewhere in Europe."[80] The hand was a symbol of strength and power in ancient Egypt. The right hand signifies the masculine principle and rational conscious thought in alchemy; whereas, the left hand signifies the feminine principle, and intuitive, unconscious thought. "The clasping hands in alchemy symbolize the mystic marriage of opposites to create wholeness and also the communication between the conscious and unconscious."[81]

The Old Testament includes commentary about the imposition of hands. The ritual act of placing one or both hands on a person is a form of symbolic blessing or the amelioration of sin, sickness, or infirmity. The imposition of hands—"the laying on of hands"—was first practiced in Judaism and was later adopted by Christianity.[82] Jesus laid his hands on the dead child and brought her back to life according to writing in the New Testament. He touched the blind man and restored his sight (Matthew 9:18–29).

The imposition of hands is associated in Christianity with the anointing of the sick. This practice began in apostolic times as a sacramental rite 'to covey a blessing, recover from illness, or with the last communion to fortify the believer safely on his new career in the fuller life of the eternal world."[83] It was not until the eighth and ninth centuries that extreme unction, another term for the final anointing of the sick, become one of the seven sacraments. "Extreme unction is also coupled with exorcism for the restraint of the power of evil—a practice taken over from Judaism by the early church."[84]

The Hand of God is viewed as a Jewish symbol of strength and power. This hand is also worn as a good-luck charm. The Hand of God is known in Islam as the Hand of Fatima after Mohammed's daughter. The five fingers represent the Five Pillars of Islam. The Roman Hand of the Future was linked to the cult of Bacchus and was used for divination.[85] A traditional method for looking into the future in Arab countries is to read the pattern of a pool of ink or oil in the palm of the hand.[86]

The Hand of Glory is a reoccurring symbol associated with bewitchment and black magic. The right hand of an executed felon must be severed and preserved to be suitable for casting spells according to legend. The hand must be prepared by draining the blood, pickling for fifteen days in a mixture including saltpeter, and drying in the sun or in an oven. "The dried hand is either dipped in wax so the fingers will burn as candles, or else ...

fitted with one or more candles placed between the fingers."[87] If candles are used, they should be made from the fat of a hanged man. Once the hand is properly prepared, it can be used to render the owner invisible and to cast a sleeping spell on people, thus allowing a thief to burglarize a home.[88]

Buddhist iconography includes many *mudra* (seal or sign), hand gestures used with the recitation of a *mantra* (mystic invocation) during meditative sessions to convey different offerings. Mantras are combinations of sacred syllables that form a focus of spiritual energy. Tom Lowenstein wrote in *Treasures of the Buddha: The Glories of Sacred Asia* (2006), "All people [are] capable of realizing their identity with the Buddha in body, speech, and mind through ritual hand gestures (*mudras*), the repetition of mystic syllables (*mantras*), and meditation on *mandalas*, or sacred diagrams." Mudras are specific gestures and each is identified by name. The most commonly recognized is the *anjali mudra*, the greeting and veneration symbol with hands joined vertically high on the chest. Other examples of often seen mudras are: *abhaya mudra* (fear-allaying), *dharmachakra mudra* (preaching), and *dhyana mudra* (meditating).

The Dance as a Symbol of Spiritual and Social Life

The Order of Whirling Dervishes a Sufi organization created by Jalaludin Rami, the thirteenth-century poet and teacher, came to ecstasy by dancing. The exact movements of the dance are unknown to persons outside the Sufi world. The dance is configured on the movements of the sun and planets. The individual dancer rotates according to the secret pattern, and the whole group swirls in rapid circular movements. The dance continues, sometimes for hours, until "the dervishes individually fall into a trance of ecstasy and 'pass away into God.'"[89]

Sherpa (also called Sharwa) shamans perform a masked dance in which they transform themselves into Mahâkâla (Sanskrit meaning the Great Black One) the shamanic god. The Mahâkâla is one of eight *dharmapala*, defenders of Tibetan Buddhist religious law. Their grotesque appearance is to instill terror in evil spirits, and to promote an attitude of worshipful recognition of Mahâkâla (**see drawing 5.c**). "Whatever was represented by the mask [is] made present in reality, and [has] a visible body."[90] The dance and the costume are to symbolically join the two worlds — the spiritual and the mundane.

Performance arts also play an important role in the spiritual and social life of Central Asia. Tibetan monks perform healing and longevity dances, *Khadro Tenshug Garham* (the Dance of

Drawing 5.c: Mahâkâla is called the "Great Black One." He is described as a fierce protector of the Law and faithful defender of the Buddha. Mahâkâla is lord of time and transcendent wisdom. He symbolizes the strength that destroys illusion.

the Rainbow Space Travelers), at times of senior lama illnesses. Five monks wearing rainbow costumes perform to music played on drums and cymbals. The sacred dance to exorcise negative forces is the Black Hat Dance that most likely came from the pre–Buddhist tradition of Bön. Monasteries perform this dance on the last day of the year to eliminate negative energy. Each performer carries a mystical dagger (*phurba*) with which to pierce the ego, the force that carries old negativities into the present moment, and each also carries a skull cup filled with blissful wisdom, the ambrosia by which ego is transcended.[91]

A ritualistic dance called '*cham* developed as a event in Buddhist monasteries. The origin of the dance may be an older form of shamanic ceremonial ritual. The '*cham* appears to come from a time before the introduction of Buddhism. According to legend, it was initially performed as a type of exorcism to expel evil spirits and to mollify guardian spirits. It was believed that these activities would assure a favorable and prosperous new year. However, after years of residence within a Buddhist-dominated society, the roles and themes of the '*cham* were transformed in keeping with Buddhist dogma. The ancient dance was reinterpreted as symbolizing the victory of Buddhism over shamanism.

The '*cham* spread across Central Asia with the establishment of Buddhist monastic communities. Monasteries of adequate size maintained the requisite masks, costumes, props, and musical instruments, and in all locations the performance of '*cham* was essentially the same. The setting for the performance was in the courtyard of the monastery. Horns and drums provided the music, and performers wearing wide-brimmed black hats topped with a simulated human skull moved about the '*cham-ra* (dance enclosure).[92]

Some '*cham* performers wear large masks depicting evil spirits that bother humans, and others in skeleton costumes wearing skull masks. There are also masked dancers representing various deities of Buddhism (**see drawings 5.d**). The most impressive performer is normally the King of the Religion, who wears a mask resembling the head of a bull, to symbolically represent the deity that conquered of Yama, the Lord of the Dead (see drawing 1.a). The performance also includes a dancer wears a mask portraying an old man who acts the part of a clown.[93]

The '*cham* performance is based on the

Drawing 5.d: This '*chum* mask is a nineteenth century papier-mâché mask used in Mongolian traditional New Year '*chem* performances. The dancers enact the roles of Buddhist deities to ward off evil. The '*chem* performance spread across Asia with Buddhism and it was particularly implanted in Mongolia where it became a regular part of monastic practice. The masks used in these performances are attention-fixing elements but often the exact meaning of each color, design, or shape are unclear to all observers; nonetheless, they are seldom without meaning. '*Chem* masks are made and used based on ideological design and purpose.

fear of demons and grotesque creatures and the way Buddhism lessen that anxiety. The audience is reassured that the good forces of religion have vanquished the evil spirits to ensure a favorable new year.

The Rosary as a Symbol of Devotion

A rosary is a religious practice involving saying a prayer or recitation numerous times and counting the repetitions on a string of beads or knots. It is believed to be an antidote to heresy and sin. The beads or knotted string used in this process is also called a rosary. The string of beads or knots is a memory device, and it is symbolically associated with the act of prayer and devotion. This form of ritual acknowledgment is widespread and can be found in virtually every major religion in the world: Hinduism, Buddhism, Islam, Roman Catholicism, Eastern Orthodoxy, and Judaism.

Most religions use something as prayer-counters. Eastern Christian monks adopted the practice of "reciting the beads" or "saying the rosary" in the third century C.E. The rosary became a popular way of public and private prayer following that time. The most common prayer is the Rosary of the Blessed Virgin. The beads of the chaplet (circular string of beads) for this rosary are normally arranged in five decades (set of ten) or 50 beads in total. The traditional recitation of the Rosary of the Blessed Virgin requires three progressions around the chaplet or 150 Hail Marys; consequently, Roman Catholic rosaries may have 150 beads made of various materials. Other rosaries are performed to reinforce meditation of particular mysteries, that is, the 15 mysteries representing the events from the life, death, and glorification of Jesus Christ.[94]

The Eastern Orthodox (Orthodox Catholic Church) prayer rope (the *kombologion*, or *komboschoinion*, a cord with a hundred knots to count genuflexions and signs of the cross) predates the Catholic rosary. It is mainly for monastic devotion. Brahmanic and Buddhist (Tibetan: *mala*) rosaries have 108 beads, the Islamic rosary (*subha* or *subh ah*) has 100, 33, or 25 beads and used for many centuries to counting devotionally the names of Allah. The Japanese Buddhist rosary has 112 wooden beads. The Russian Orthodox rosary is made of 103 beads and is strung in such a way to symbolize a ladder, thereby, reminding the devout of the climb toward greater devotion and virtue.

Swami Sivananda Radha writing in the book *Mantra: Words of Power* explains the 108 beads in the Buddhist rosary. According to the Swami, "[One] 1 means one line, symbolizing God, and the Supreme Energy, the power from which all other line, circles, or movements come. [Zero] 0 is completeness, a circle representing God's creation as complete and perfect. [Eight] 8, as the sign of eternity, brings in the time element, for creation goes on eternally."[95]

The Tibetan *mala* (sometime referred to as chains) is, like other rosaries, used for reciting or evoking prayer or formula of veneration to a particular deity. It is also used in some funerary rites. The *mala* enjoys great favor among Tibetan Buddhists and is widely used to increase the practitioner's merit. "*Malas* are commonly made of wood but can be made of any material, including seeds, glass, precious or semi-precious stones, ivory, jade, coral, turquoise, and mother of pearl."[96] Claude Levenson wrote in the book *Symbols of Tibetan Buddhism* (2003), "For some secret rites, Tantric masters formerly used chaplets [*marensi mala*] composed of beads carved out of bone, sometime even — it is alleged — out of 108 skulls"[97] (see photograph 5). The *naga mala* is made from the vertebra of a snake (*naga*) as a "symbol of the sacred Nagas and Naginis, the necklace or garland of Shiva."[98] Only shamans wear the *naga mala*. The number of beads, vertebra, in this instance, is not important as long as the *mala* is made from the complete spine of the reptile and the bones are threaded in the original sequence.[99]

The Tibetan *mala* also may be used for divination. A preliminary spell or prayer must be chanted then the rosary is taken in the hands and rolled between the palms. The diviner closes his or her eyes and grasps some portion of the rosary between the thumb and finger of both hands. "The intervening beads are then counted off in threes, starting from both ends, and the result of the divination depends on whether one, two or three beads are finally left."[100] The number is interpreted according to the description written in a book of divinations.

The Wheel as a Symbol of Personal Purification

The devout Tibetan Buddhist monk or layperson hopes to repeat their personal prayer one million times and thereby to gain purification and favor in the next life. Consequently, they carry and rotate a prayer wheel much of their waking hours. The prayer wheel (*mani chos 'khor*) is a common feature of Tibetan Buddhism. There are smaller hand-held prayer wheels (**see photograph 10**) and large wheels or drums that are place in strategic location near a temple. The prayer wheel is a hollow metal cylinder. Hand-held wheels have a handle; whereas, the large cylinders are mounted in a wooden framework. The prayer wheel is normally embossed with sacred words or symbols and contains a scroll with an inscribed *mantra*. Each turn of the wheel is equivalent to the oral recitation of the prayer written on the scroll.

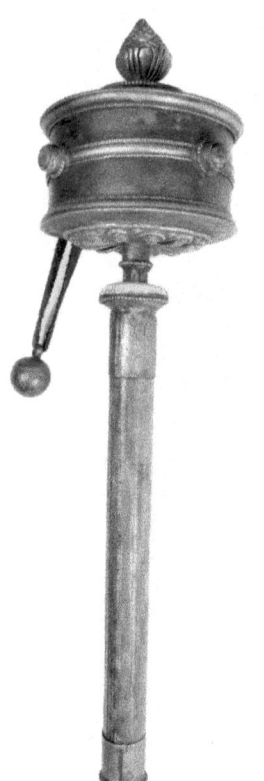

The Wheel of Life is an especially important symbol in Tibetan Buddhism. It consists of three concentric circles held by Yama, the god of the Underworld. It signifies samsâra, the cycle of existence. The innermost circle contains symbols of the three sources of suffering: the pig (delusion or ignorance), the snake (hate), and the cock (desire) (see drawing 5.b). The next circle is divided into six sections, each depicting one of the six states of being (existence). The highest three are the gods, the *asuras* (titans), and human beings; they result from good karma. The lowest three are animals, hungry ghosts (the result of rebirth between heaven and hell), and demons (hell-dwellers); they result from bad karma. The outside ring of the wheel is divided into twelve sections, each representing a symbol of one of the twelve factors of conditioned arising (death, birth, craving,

Photograph 10: The prayer wheel (Tibetan: 'khor-lo) is a device for presenting prayers. Prayers are written on strips of paper and placed inside the upper chamber of the prayer wheel and with each revolution, the prayers are sent (communicated) to the appropriate god or goddess. Tibetan people of all social levels send prayers using prayer wheels. Large cylinders containing prayers are placed on the roof of homes to be turned by the wind, and larger prayer wheels are positioned outside temples to be turned by passing laypersons and monks.

ignorance, consciousness, becoming, contact, sensation, the six senses, grasping, the power of formation, and mind and body.)[101] The wheel is a guide to life.

The eight-spoked Wheel of Sacred Law (dharma-cakra) is often used to symbolize the presence of the Buddha (see drawing 5.e).

Yin-Yang a Symbol of the Soul of the Universe

Chinese mystics used various techniques including fasting, purification, and meditation to empty themselves of the "senses and the intellect that continuously boost a separate notion of ego through emotions and desires."[102] They reach at the same time to that mystical resolve that is hidden within the Tao.

Much of Chinese traditional thinking, and some say character, evolves around the concept of the yin-yang. These two cosmic forces are regarded as the soul of the Universe. This principle of dualism is a potent factor in Chinese thought, and permeates both the material and the moral worlds.[103] It is believed that since humans are a part of the Universe, it is logical that humanity shares in the properties and manifestations of yin and yang. People are believed to be a product of the two forces, a combination of the qualities of each element.

The concept of a personified deity is foreign to Taoism, as is belief in the creation of the universe. Taoists view many gods as the manifestation of the one Tao; consequently, there is no single image to symbolically represent the Godhead. Therefore, they do not pray as Christians do. There is no God to hear the prayers or to act upon them. Taoists seek answers to life's problems through meditation and observation. The symbol most commonly associated with Taoism is the interconnected yin and yang surrounded by the eight trigrams (see drawing 5.f). The perpetual transformation of the universe by the alternations of yin and yang as opposing forces is the external aspect of the Tao.

The yin and yang is associated with the five elements: metal, wood, water, fire, and earth. These agents are of primary importance in Chinese alchemy because they relate to the belief in a cyclical concept of becoming and dissolution as well as the interdependence

Drawing 5.e: Wheel of Law (*dharma chakra*) is an ancient Indian symbol that was later used to represent the Buddha. The wheel with eight spokes, representing the Eightfold Path, was designated by King Ashok to represent the Buddha as "a spiritual world ruler who 'set in motion the wheel of law.'" The figurative images of the Buddha were not made until the beginning of the current era. It is believed they originated in the Gandhâra region due to the influence of Greek invaders. (Alexander of Macedon invaded India in 327 B.C.E. His army entered India through Gandhâra and he proceeded as far as the Beas River. It was there that his troops refused to continue fighting. Many of the soldiers remained in India and while they endorsed the concepts of Buddhism, they required an image to which they could direct their worship, as was the practice in Greece. The result of this situation may have been the creation of the first images of the Buddha.)

between nature and human events. "Yin is conceived of as earth, female, dark, passive, and absorbing; it is present in even numbers, in valleys and streams, and is represented by the tiger, the colour orange, and a broken line [in the I Ching]."[104] In contrast, "Yang is conceived of as heaven, male, light, active, and penetrating; it is present in odd numbers, in mountains, and is represented by the dragon, the colour azure, and an unbroken line [in the I Ching]."[105] The yin-yang is called *In-yō* in Japan.

The documents associated with the Tao are the *Tao-te Ching* (*Classic of the Way of Power*), the *Chuang-tzu* (book of Master Chuang), the *Lieh-tzu* (book of Master Lieh), and the *I Ching* (Classic of Changes or Book of Changes). The eight trigrams of the *I-Ching* are said to be the symbols of all that happens on earth. They continually change into each other "just as phenomena become one another in the physical world (coal becomes ash; ice become water)."[106] The trigrams are symbolically concerned with transformation, that is, the change from one state of being or condition to another. This interchange can remake one force into another or can alternate connecting phenomena. Each action gives birth to corresponding reaction. "Security and danger trade place with each other, bad and good fortune give birth to each other, tense time and relaxed ones buffet one another, gathering-together and scattering bring it all to completion."[107]

Drawing 5.f: The eight trigrams of Taoism include all the possible combinations of a full and a broken line. They combine the polarity theory with the Chinese art of prophecy as emphasized in the *I Ching*. The cosmic symbol acknowledges the alternating and mutually complementary functions of the male and female forces. The trigrams symbolize the cyclic of the male and female energy found in the yin-yang that maintains the created world in a state of equilibrium. The symbol was configured between 2,852 and 2,737 B.C.E. as a graphic expressions of the forces of the universe. Each of the forces is present inside the other and each contains the other. It replaced the divinatories practices that consisted of reading the bones and tortoise shells. The eight trigrams express the two principles of yin and yang acknowledged by the symbol in the center of the wheel.

The *yang* element is cosmic and pertains to heaven, whereas, pure *yin* relates to earth; therefore, there must be a way for them to connect. It is believed there are "dragon veins," invisible lines running from the sky to the mountains and along the earth.[108] The function of the veins is "rather similar to that of the psychic channels within the human body which play such an important part in acupuncture and in yoga, whether Chinese, Indian, or Tibetan."[109] These veins carry *yang* cosmic vitality (*ch'i*) to mingle with yin earth vitality (*ch'i*). Although the dragon veins are invisible to ordinary persons, they are clearly seen by those individuals knowledgeable of the science of *yin* and *yang*. The cosmic energy associated with the dragon veins generated the application known as *fêng-shui*.[110]

The interconnectedness of the yin and yang elements is exemplified by the symbol commonly associated with this concept. The white dot or eye in the black field emphasizes the point that there is an element of yang in the yin and vice versa (**see drawing 5.g**). The old symbol for the yin-yang (**see drawing 5.h**) shows more clearly the relationship between the two elements.

The Tree as a Symbol of the Unity of Worlds

The tree has different symbolic meanings. In general, it symbolizes the time when the worlds of spirits and human were closely located. It was believed that humans might climb the tree to enter the realm of deities. Later the two worlds separated leaving humans in isolation. Numerous myths and cultural practices are based on ascending or descending a real or symbolic tree to interact with gods or spirits. The tree of knowledge is the vertical center of the earth and binds together heaven and earth; whereas, the tree of life is at the horizontal center and is as the name implies the source of life.

"The Mayas and other people of Central America always represented their sacred trees with two branches shooting horizontally from the top of the trunk, thus presenting the appearance of a cross."[111] Harold Bayley commented in *The Lost Language of Symbolism* (1996 [1912]), "The first Spanish missionaries in Mexico found to their great astonishment that the cross was already in use there 'as symbolizing a Tree of Life.'"[112] Bayley also notes that the Egyptians believed "in the East of Heaven stands that high Sycamore-tree upon which the gods sit, the tree of life by which they live, whose fruits also feed the blessed."[113]

The Bible recounts the story of Adam and Eve and the "tree of knowledge of good and evil" (Genesis 2:15–17). The vertical tree tradition is considered the connection between the gods and humans. Joseph Campbell speaks of the holy tree in his book *The Mystic Image* (1974). Quoting from Dante and describing the paradise found at the summit of the mountain where heaven and earth come together, he notes, "And to this arid tree there

Top: Drawing 5.g: The "new" Yin-Yang symbol represents the opposite principles of the yin and yang. The symbol also represents the interdependence of the two forces in that each contains the "seed" of the other. Yin is associated with darkness (hence the black form), water, and the female. Yang is representative of the light (the light or white form), activity, air, and the male. The two parts manifest the duality of the universe and represent the opposing but mutually dependent qualities of life. *Bottom:* Drawing 5.h: The "old" Yin-Yang symbol is a part of the *Wu-chi* progression. Everything begins with the Tao and returns to the Tao. This going and coming is described by the *Wu-chi* (limitless) process in which creation and desolation are viewed as occurring continuously. "If we understand the underlying nature of the change, we will know what has occurred in the past and what will come in the future." The beginning of the Tao is nothingness, an empty circle. The positive and negative energies are added allowing the intermixing of the five elements (fire, water, earth, wood, and metal). The male and female principles as represented in the "new" yin-yang symbol emerge from this mixing of elements.

came, as he declares, a chariot symbolic of the church, drawn by a griffin whose dual nature at once bird and beast, was a likeness of the dual nature of Christ, at once God and man."[114] The Bible also speaks of the "sacred tree of Moreh, the holy place at Shecham" (Genesis 12:6). This entry in the Old Testament refers to the return of Abram and his wife, Sarai, to the land of Canaan.

The *Zohar*, a Kabbalah text (see Chapter Three), refers to the inverted tree. Campbell wrote, "Happy is the portion of Israel, in whom the Holy One, blessed be He, delights and to whom he gave the *Torah* of truth, the Tree of Life."[115] Campbell speculates, "Whoever takes hold of this achieves life in this world and in the world to come. Now the Tree of Life extends from above downward, and it is the Sun which illumines all."[116] Elsewhere, the Buddha legend includes the Bo or Bodhi tree as the tree of Waking to Omniscience. The legend tells that it was under the Bo tree (pipal, species *Ficus religiosa*) that Buddha found enlightenment (bodhi). The Bo tree is often used in early Buddhist art as a symbol of the Buddha.

The Cosmic Tree like the world pole, god-pillar, Tree of the World, or Tree of Life is also a symbolic link between earth and the upper sphere for the Central and Northern Eurasian shamans. The tree is believed to grow through all layers of the natural and spiritual worlds. Climbing the tree is a symbolic ascent to the realm of the deities. A tree was sometime prepared for ritual purposes with seven to nine notches or steps to facilitate the climb. As the shaman climbs, he or she declares that he or she is going up to heaven and describes all that could be seen at each step. The shaman might also use the roots of the tree to descend into the lower world in search of the dead. The tree and the ascent or descent is symbolic, but the ideology is real and the ritual has real meaning within the endorsing community.

The Kabbalist *Book of Splendour* (*Sefer ha-zohar*) deals with the mystery of creation and the functions of the *sefirot* or *seriroth*. "The ten *Seriroth* constitutes the mystical Tree of God or tree of divine power each representing a branch whose common root is unknown and unknowable (see figure 3.1). But *En-Sof* is not only the hidden Root of all Roots, it is also the sap of the tree."[117]

The Dragon as a Symbol of Primordial Consciousness

"The dragon is one of the most important shamanic animals"[118] in the East. He (the dragon is generally referred to as male) lives in the clouds and is the rainbow that connects the three worlds. "The dragon is a hybrid creature, or in other words, a shamanic being. He has horns like the Stone Age and prehistoric shaman gods."[119] The dragon assists shamans to travel in the lower world. He is thunder and lightening, and his body is a spiritual elevator that protects and helps the shaman. "[T]he dragon helps to bring justice to the agitators of evil disease, to clear away poisonous and deadly animals such as snakes, scorpions, and millipedes, through visionary methods. In addition, the dragon signifies the *kundalini* power, also called shakti"[120] (see Chapter Six).

The dragon has the characteristics of the four elements: earth, air, fire, and water. It symbolizes light and dark, sun and moon, male and female as well as the unity underlying opposing forces. It is a symbol for rain and fertility of the earth. The dragon was viewed as a helpful creature in pre–Christianized Europe. The fire-breathing dragon in Greek legends is symbolically associated with the "genius of man — the ancestral principle embodies in his head, brain, spinal marrow, and penis."[121] It was believed that when a man died his "genius took the form of a bearded serpent that haunted the *omphalos* or navel tomb where

Five. Secret Language of Mysticism   131

Drawing 5.i: The horned dragon is a part of Taoist mysticism and ancient-Chinese myth. It symbolizes the search for wisdom, happiness, and immortality. It is also described as the self-willed spirit, which is derived from nature. The dragon represents yang the principle of heaven, activity, and maleness in the yin-yang. Gods are said to take the form of dragons, therefore, it was both the emblem of the imperial family and a symbol of devotion. The dragon is a deified force of nature in Taoism.

he lay buried."[122] Christianity eventually determined the dragon was related to the serpent and therefore a symbol of evil.

The dragon is the quintessential symbol of Taoism (see **drawing 5.i**). It is believed, perhaps a legend, that Confucius called Lao Tzu a dragon. The story told in Ored Johnson's book is that following a visit to Lao Tzu, Confucius said, "I know how birds can fly, fishes swim and animals run. But the runner may be snared, the swimmer hooked, and the flyer shot by the arrow."[123] The story goes on to say, "But there is the dragon — I cannot tell how he mounts on the wind through the clouds, and rises to heaven. Today I have seen Lao Tzu, and can only compare him to the dragon."[124]

The dragon represents the yang (male energy) in the yin-yang of Chinese cosmology. It is a "powerful symbol of psychic transformation. Like the serpent, the dragon represents primordial consciousness, underworld powers, the feminine, the womb, the unformed *Prima Materia*, and wisdom and knowledge."[125] Rosemary Ellen Guiley states in *The Encyclopedia of Magic and Alchemy* (2006), "In Alchemy, the dragon especially represents the treasure of the Great Work, the Philosopher's Stone, and also the alchemical process from chaos to the Stone via countless transformations."[126]

A common factor in many myths is a battle between man and a serpent. (The conflict is usually described as being between man and beast.) This struggle is reflected in the encounter between Eve and the serpent in the Garden of Eden. Later mythological encounters included the serpent as a dragon. This conflict is found in the *Rig-Veda* where the battle is between Indra and Vrtra, and in the *Bhagavad-Gita* the contest is between Krishna and Kaliya. Greek mythology includes many conflicts between man and dragon or serpent: Zeus vs. Typhon, Kronos vs. Ophion, Apollo vs. Python, and Heracles vs. the Hydra. Similar struggles are found in painting (St. George and the Dragon) and sculpture (Laocoön).

Other Important Symbols

Certain symbols used in Buddhist rituals which were originally of Indian origin are of major importance. Foremost of these is the ritual vase (ghata, kalasa) that is thought of as realizing all the Buddhas and attendant divinities, and therefore it can replace all other symbols at the centre of a diagrammatical mandela.[127] Buddhism gives special attention to the eight auspicious objects: The parasol, conch shell, vase, banner, double fish, mystic knot, lotus, and wheel. Each object has symbolic meaning related to the Buddha or Buddhism, and it is common to see one or more of these images represented in sculptures, *mandelas*, *thangks*, and wall paintings, or on altars. Attention is also given to the bell, *vajra*, drum (*denguru*) (**see photograph 11**), and *phurba*.

The three-edged *Vajrakilaya* is a ritual (magic) dagger also called a *phurba or vpurba*. It is used to pierce the heart of negativity. The phurba (**see photograph 12**) is a dagger that represents the fifth tutelary god, *Phurba*. This deity is said to be of Indian origin. The phurba (magic dagger) corresponds to the world tree for the Nepalese shamans. It is the center of the shamanic universe and is found on the altar of every shaman.[128] "It is stuck vertically, point down, into a basket filled with rice that sits in front of the shaman."[129] The phurba

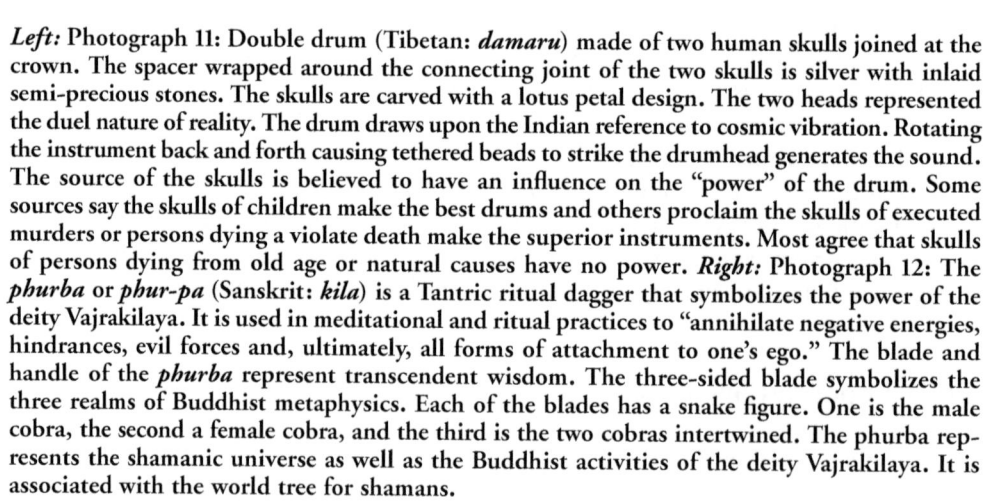

Left: Photograph 11: Double drum (Tibetan: *damaru*) made of two human skulls joined at the crown. The spacer wrapped around the connecting joint of the two skulls is silver with inlaid semi-precious stones. The skulls are carved with a lotus petal design. The two heads represented the duel nature of reality. The drum draws upon the Indian reference to cosmic vibration. Rotating the instrument back and forth causing tethered beads to strike the drumhead generates the sound. The source of the skulls is believed to have an influence on the "power" of the drum. Some sources say the skulls of children make the best drums and others proclaim the skulls of executed murders or persons dying a violate death make the superior instruments. Most agree that skulls of persons dying from old age or natural causes have no power. ***Right:*** Photograph 12: The ***phurba*** or ***phur-pa*** (Sanskrit: *kila*) is a Tantric ritual dagger that symbolizes the power of the deity Vajrakilaya. It is used in meditational and ritual practices to "annihilate negative energies, hindrances, evil forces and, ultimately, all forms of attachment to one's ego." The blade and handle of the ***phurba*** represent transcendent wisdom. The three-sided blade symbolizes the three realms of Buddhist metaphysics. Each of the blades has a snake figure. One is the male cobra, the second a female cobra, and the third is the two cobras intertwined. The phurba represents the shamanic universe as well as the Buddhist activities of the deity Vajrakilaya. It is associated with the world tree for shamans.

Left: Photograph 13: Vajra, the "Diamond Scepter," (Tibetan: ***dorje***) and bell (***ghantâ***) are used in most Tantric rituals. They are held in the right and left hands, respectively, to convey the mystical union of compassion with wisdom. The Vajra has six prongs and lotus pedals decorating the central cup. The bell handle has a similar design but has eight prongs. "The vajra represents the path of supreme wisdom and the bell symbolizes the truth of emptiness. Together they also represent the Buddha's "masculine" compassion and skilful means, and "feminine" wisdom.
Right: Photograph 14: The ***Vishvavajra*** (double thunderbolt, crossed vajra, or universal vajra) design is carved into the center portion of the inverted ***kapala***. The crossed three-pronged ***vajras*** marks the four cardinal directions and symbolically represent absolute stability. Because the vajra are flat, there are only three prongs showing on each for a total of twelve. The number twelve symbolizes the "purification of the twelve links of dependent origination and the twelve continents and subcontinents that surround Mt. Meru." Mount Meru is the center of the universe and the axis of the world according to Hindu mythology.

is used for healing purposes to pull negative energy out of a patient. It is used to destroy or divert the destructive forces that cause disease.

The bell is an essential symbol that is used in place of the lotus. "The bell is a symbol of Kali and the yoni [the female essence]. Positive energy is attracted by the sound of the bell or bells. The ringing also makes the shamanic journey easier."[130] It is often seen in combination with the *vajra* (**see photographs 13**). "Most of the ritual objects derive from Indian religions, including the most widely known of all, the thunderbolt (*dorje* or *rdo-rje* in Tibetan and *vajra* in Sanskrit) and the bell [made of metal] (*ghanti* in Sanskrit)."[131] The thunderbolt is a divine weapon with overwhelming power derived from pre–Buddhist Indian tradition. It is a personal guardian of "Sakymuni, known as Vajrapani, 'Thunderbolt-in-Hand,' who appears in many sculptures. In later Buddhism tradition the vajra becomes the symbol of the supreme 'adamantine' truth, essentially indestructible as a 'diamond'"[132] (**see photograph 14**).

One of the eight auspicious objects is the conch shell trumpet (*shanka*). The conch shell instrument is found in many parts of Oceania (except Australia), and is generally closely associated with the supernatural. The sound of the Tibetan conch shell trumpet is a part of Tantric belief and thought to be a gift from Shiva. It is a call to meditation that resonates with spiritual power. The conch trumpet may be either plain or elaborate in design. Only Tibetan lamas use the conch shells decorated with artful gold or silver findings set with coral or turquoise stones (see photograph 3).

The thighbone trumpet (Tibetan: *nalihar*) made from a human bone, preferably from a buried shaman or lama, is a important element of Tibetan Buddhism as well as shamanic practice. Lamas prefer the thighbone for the trumpet while shamans use the large bone of the forearm.[133] Both lamas and shaman use the bone trumpet (**see photograph 15**) for healing ceremonies and meditation. The use of human bone to make an instrument calls to mind the impermanence of all things. Life ends in death to allow its perpetuation.

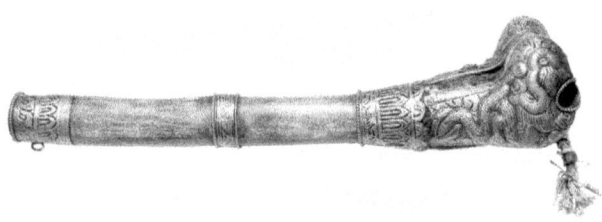

[S]ymbolism has the power to change the human heart. The strength and sensory richness of a symbol, when linked to some ideological message could affect a transfer of energy and heal the patient.[134]

The first symbol to represent the human nature of the Buddha was the footprint (Sanskrit: *buddhapada*) (**see drawing 5.j**). This is the same symbol used to represent the Hindu god Vishnu in cakra (or chakra) seven. The Buddha had no symbolic references during his lifetime, and no human representation was created for hundreds of years following his death. The stupa (in Tibet, chörten or mChod-rten) is among the earliest and most common symbols associated with Buddhism (**see figure 5.1 and photograph 16**). It is a shrine for relics of the Buddha. However, this

Top: Photograph 15: Human thighbone trumpet is fitted with elaborately decorated silver covering on the lower extremity. The upper end, toward the pelvic joint has been cut and fitted with a silver mouthpiece. Thigh bone trumpets are said to make a sound that it pleasing to the gods and spirits; therefore, they are used in Tantric rituals. *Bottom:* Drawing 5.j: This second century stone carving is the ***Buddhapada***, the Buddha's footprints as an ancient form of memorial. The followers of Buddha probably adopted it in remembrance of their leader. The carving depicts the wheel of the law, and other sign of the Buddha including the lotus, the mark of superiority on the toes, and swastikas as signs of good luck. The three pointed symbol on the heel represents the Three Jewels: the Buddha, the Dharma, and Sangha, which preserve and promote the words of the Buddha. This piece is reportedly housed in the British Museum.

Five. Secret Language of Mysticism 135

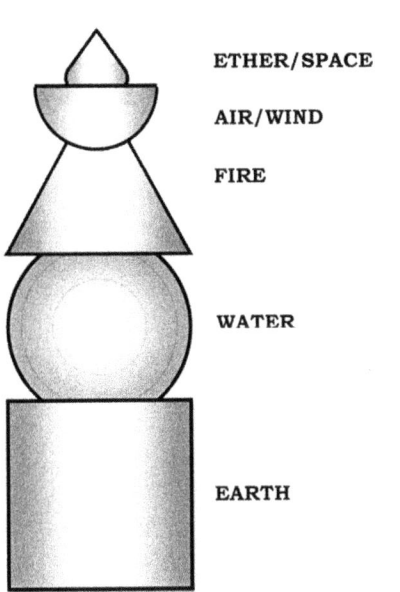

Left: Figure 5.1: Chörten a reliquary tower that represents the mind of the Buddha and often holds physical relics. It may be used on private altars or placed in a temple. The structural parts of the *chörtan* are believed to represent the five elements. Starting at the top, the first element is "ether," the second "air," third "fire," fourth "water," and the base is "earth." The configuration is also associated with a meditation posture. Stone arrangements of this type are seen in Japan. *Right:* Photograph 16: Chörten (Sanskrit: stupa; Tibetan: ***chörten*** or ***mchodrten***) is generally described as a smaller version of the stupa. It is used as an element of an altar to show respect and reverence to the Buddha. It usually contains a prayer, mantra, or spiritual elements sealed within the metal figure. The chörten is, in this way, a reliquary containing a precious relic. Chörten are normally made of bronze, brass, or copper. They may be plated with gold or silver and adorned with precious or semi-precious stones. These reliquaries may contain fragments of significant material or carefully written sayings attributed to the Buddha or an important spiritual leader.

symbol was not recognized until the first century of the current era. The lotus was used as early as the second century C.E. as a Buddhist symbol to represent the mind and the opening of the mind to Buddhism. It was, in time, associated with purity and enlightenment. The wheel with eight spokes (*dharmacakra*) came to be representative of the dharma possible as late as the third century C.E. The eight spokes refer to the Noble Eightfold Path and the teaching of the *buddhadharma*.

The noble eightfold path is the middle way to open eyes and bestow understanding. It "leads to peace of mind to the higher wisdom, to full enlightenment."[135] It is "Right views; Right aspirations; Right speech; Right conduct; Right livelihood; Right effort; Right mindfulness; Right contemplation."[136] Other symbols relating to Buddhism include the diamond rod and the representation of "the Buddha, the dharma, and sangha" the three jewels. The swastika (an often misunderstood design) is a traditional symbol used by both Hindus and Buddhists. It is a very ancient sign that relates to the sun and is considered good luck. When used as a general symbol of Buddhism, the swastika may face to either the left or right.

Symbolic Language

It is well known to mystics that if a man meditates upon a symbol around which certain ideas have been associated by past meditation, he will obtain access to those ideas, even if the glyph has never been elucidated to him by those who have received the oral tradition "by mouth to ear."[137]

All things possess universal importance because they have an existence that extends beyond human knowledge. Symbols activate a sense of commitment that safeguard religious teachings and express them in tangible ways. They bring the believer into a practical relationship with abstract ideas. People need symbols to motivate activity. It is as though theoretical concepts need to be expressed symbolically before individuals are motivated to act upon them. Conversely, when an effort is made to turn symbols into assertions of truth, this essential trigger of the emotions can easily be lost.[138]

Cultural symbolism reveals events and attitudes that occur in another world and therefore could not be compared or explained by experiences in the material world.[139] The use of symbols evokes two worlds at the same time — the sacred and the profane. A symbol might represent in a metaphysical sense an entity of a higher order, that is, a thing or attitude of extraordinary emotional or sentimental value. Words, sounds, objects, and gestures have a definite symbolism, and cultures use a range of symbols to convey both positive and negative meaning.

Although symbols are used to express ideas that are beyond the range of human understanding, they are also used to bolster commonly held beliefs. The human psyche requires constant reinforcement and recollection reactivation. "There are ... unconscious aspects of our [human] perception of reality. The first is the fact that even when our senses react to real phenomena, sights, and sounds, they are somehow translated from the realm of reality into that of the mind."[140] Symbolic and physical aids aside, the greatest factor influencing the role of the mystic among people in all societies is belief.

Most communication skills are learned, often by imitation, therefore, it is probable that imitating the actions of others within the sustaining cultural group is fundamental to learning the symbols associated with societal activities. Symbolic culture consequently can be viewed as a product of past social action although its initiators are not always easily identified. Nevertheless, such acquired symbols often regulate people's religious consciousness including the claim of the holy. "Religion is a system of relationships, a system of reciprocal challenges and responses the principal correspondents of which are the sacred or holy and man."[141]

Shamanic symbolism and practices were well known in Tibet and China. The Bön shamans were believed to use their drums as vehicles to convey them through the air. Their cures included seeking the patient's soul, a shamanic ceremony also popular with the Tibetan exorcists. The practitioner offers his own flesh to be eaten by demons in the Tantric rite named *Gcod*. They (the demons) decapitate him, hack him to pieces, then devour his flesh and drink the blood. This ritual is an enactment of symbolic death before rebirth and regenerated health. Since sickness is interpreted as the flight of the soul, the Lolo shamans of southern Yunnan, as well as the Karen doctors of Burma, read a long litany imploring the patient's soul to return from the distant mountains, forests, or fields.

The symbol translates a human situation into cosmological terms, and reciprocally, more precisely, it discloses the interdependence between the structures of human existence and cosmic structures. This means that man does not feel isolated in the Cosmos, that he is open to the world which is symbolically familiar to him.[142]

CHAPTER SIX

Principles and Techniques of Transformation

"Help others do not harm them."[1]

The magical consciousness [...] present in those aspects of Yoga that involve extreme inward concentration, [leads] to loss of body awareness. Of course, it also is the cognitive basis for all forms of sympathetic magic, which is an ingredient of some yogic paths, notably those schools of Tantrism that emphasize the cultivation of paranormal powers, or *siddhis*.[2]

The quest for an improved physical, spiritual, or intellectual life has appealed to humanity from the beginning of time. Generations of humans have endeavored to reach into the regions of spirituality to gain release from the pains, passions, and ignorance of the finite condition. An individual often seeks contentment by "retreating into the inner depths of his being where he becomes wholly absorbed in the infinite God [deities] whom he finds there."[3] Transcending the mundane in search of the divine is a challenging and often unattainable goal. This demanding physical and psychological condition is the central concern of all religious and philosophical systems.

The notion of transformation as the change from one situation or condition to another has extraordinary appeal. Alchemic revitalization of the physical or spiritual essence as an expression of an undying and limitless vastness is the goal of all life. That personal vastness is defined by yoga as the Self. "According to yoga, we suffer because we live in ignorance. We are ignorant of our real nature."[4] The desire to know the Self and to achieve wholeness is inherent in all humans and in that reality to gain a universal meaning for a particular culture. "Yoga is a way to restore our lost wholeness, our integrity as complete humans beings, by unifying the personality around a centre which is silent and unbounded."[5]

Transformation is the dying of the old and the resurrection into a new state of being. "Yoga is an alchemical process of balancing and transforming the energies of the psyche."[6] It is renewal. Yoga as a transformative process implies a detachment from matter, a search for pure consciousness, and dedication to freedom from suffering. Compassion frees the mind from mundane restrictions, and although it is the essential energy animating all existence, it is obscured by false conceptions of the Self. The practice of yogic methods is an accepted way for eliminating obstructions and attaining perfect vital force. Yoga depends on human effort and relies on the individual's self-discipline, by virtue of which the individual can obtain concentration of spirit.

"[T]he path of Yoga is not a single path, but a path of many paths, all leading to the

One Goal."⁷ The path is manifest in different forms and following different regimen. Forms of yoga place greater emphasis on different aspects of the yogic process; however, all have their beginning in the ancient annals of India and in the *Yoga-Sutra* attributed to Patanjali. "The *Yoga-Sutra* says that each person gets different things from the same teaching based on his or her own perspective. There is nothing wrong with this. This is how it is."⁸

> I doubt that there is anyone who really does not want to improve himself, and even if our first step springs from the desire to become better and is therefore rooted in the ego, it is still a right step because it takes us on to the first rung of the yoga ladder.⁹

The Path of Yoga

The *Bhagavad-Gita*, "The Song of the Blessed One," is the essence of Vedic knowledge. The date of origination of this important document is unknown. It may have been written, as previously noted, as early as the fifth century B.C.E. or as late as the first century C.E. It is designed as an informative dialogue between Lord Krishna (representing the deities) and Arjuna (representing humanity), which deals with the essential nature of human existence including yogic practice. For example, Krishna attempts to explain "material manifestation" and "karma-yoga" to Arjuna in chapter eight. He states (*Bhagavad-Gita* 8:12), "The yogic situation is that of detachment from all sensual engagements. Closing all the doors of the senses and fixing the mind on the heart and the air of life on the top of the head, one establishes this situation."¹⁰

The *Gitā* is a necessary document for understanding the essence of yoga. It defines the connection between classical yoga and the metaphysical references and metaphors that expand the scope of yogic practice. Lord Krishna tells Arjuna (*Bhagavad-Gita* 6:8) "A person is said to be established in self-realization and is called yogi [or mystic] when he is fully satisfied by virtue of acquired knowledge and realization. Such a person is situated in transcendence and is self-controlled. He sees everything — whether it be pebbles, stones, or gold — as the same."¹¹

Krishna directs Arjuna to practice yoga, and explains (*Bhagavad-Gita* 6:11–12), "one should go to a secluded place and should lay *kusa* grass on the ground and then cover it with a deerskin and a soft cloth. The seat should neither be too high nor too low and should be situated in a sacred place."¹² Once this arrangement is made, "The yogi should then sit on it [the seat] very firmly and should practice yoga by controlling the mind and the senses, purifying the heart and fixing the mind on one point."¹³ Krishna instructs Arjuna (*Bhagavad-Gita* 2:48), "Be steadfast in your duty, O Arjuna, and abandon all attachment to success or failure. Such evenness of mind is called yoga."¹⁴ (The word yoga is used at times in early writings to mean meditation.)

Yoga originated in India and is of great age, and legend contends that Lord Shiva is the originator. Hindu tradition maintains the first man, Vaivasvat Manu, knew yoga. The myth claims Vaivasvat Manu learned yoga from his father Vaivasvat (the Sun) 120.53 million years ago.¹⁵ The oldest written record of yoga is the *Rig-Veda* (*Wisdom of the Verses*); a reference that dates circa 2,000 B.C.E. This document includes "sacred mantras [empowerment syllables] and hymns with mystical meanings and effects. It is with the *Rig-Veda* that knowledge of yoga, which was traditionally transmitted orally through the ages, found its place into written Sanskrit."¹⁶

The founding principles of yoga are very basic. The gods saw that life was difficult and happiness often elusive as was common for most early cultures. The people got sick, grew old, and died. They fell prey to the illusion that such an existence was all that could be expected. Parvati, Shiva's wife, understood how hard it could be to maintain focus; therefore, to aid humanity, she asked her husband to "invent a system that would help people to deal with the inevitable suffering that comes with life as a human, and he did."[17] It is said that Shiva (Siva or Siwa), the Auspicious One and the Lord of Yogis, invented yoga out of compassion. Consequently, he is often depicted in paintings and sculptures as a yogin.

The legacy of the yoga tradition has endured for more than four thousand years and spanned the teaching of many Indic schools of thought. It was influential in the development of Hinduism, Buddhism, Jainism, and Sikhism.[18] Although the exact origin of yoga as a systematized practice and the date of its initiation are unknown, traces of yoga activities were discovered during excavation at the Mohenjo-Daro site in 1922. A clay piece uncovered at that location on the right bank of the Indus River shows a male figure in what appears to be a lotus position (a possible cross-legged proto–Shiva). The date for this site is the third millennium B.C.E., and if the piece is a representation of yoga, as is professed, it establishes an early and definable date for the practice. Similar pieces were found at Harappa on the left bank of the Ravi River. The excavation of this site began in 1921. The two locations are similarly configured. They are alike in many aspects.

An obvious difficulty in tracing the history of yoga is that it leaves nothing behind except myths and legends of miraculous powers possessed by some of the more accomplished practitioners of the art.[19] Early Vedic texts refer to ecstatics, who may have been early yogis. Vivian Worthington wrote in *A History of Yoga*, "[Yoga] is more intuitive than reasonable, more experimental than formalistic, more other-worldly than of this world and more akin to art than to science."[20] It is spiritual liberation that is the goal of yoga, and although all yogis have the same goal, release from all limitations is an individual process.

> At the apex of the hierarchy of being is the transcendental Reality, the Self or Spirit (Sanskrit: *purusha*). For Classical Yoga, as for the other schools of Indian spirituality, the Self is the principle of pure Consciousness or sheer Awareness.[21]

The word yoga is frequently reported to come from the Sanskrit root *juj*, meaning, yoking or union.[22] It is sometime referred to as spirituality or mysticism in the Western world. B.K.S. Iyengar, a recognized international yoga master, referring to the concept of union, believes, "In philosophical terms, the union of the individual self, *jivatma*, with the universal self, *paramatma*, is yoga."[23] This idea of the joining of the self and the universe is an often-expressed concept in Hinduism. It is demonstrated by the touching the tip of the thumb with the first finger in the *shanti mudra*, a sign of peace. This gesture of symbolic linking of the self with the universe, a combining of vital elements, is often used during meditation (see **drawing 6.a**).

Jean Varenne, writing in

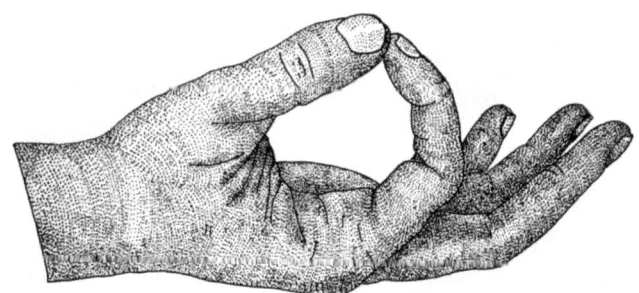

Drawing 6.a: The Shanti mudra is described as the mudra of universal peace. It is dedicated to the relationship between the teacher (*guru*) and the student. A mudra is a hand gesture, also called a seal that is a symbol of energy. The shanti mudra may be done with either hand or both. It involves bringing together the tip of the first finger with the tip of the thumb, and extending the remaining three fingers. The contact between the finger and thumb is a point of focus to clear the mind and generate energy.

Yoga and the Hindu Tradition (1976) offers another opinion about the origin of the word. "Yoga," he says, means to harness and its primary meaning is "the action of harnessing."[24] Varenne states, "in the oldest of the Vedic hymns we read of the horses that are harnessed to the chariots of gods such as Indra [chief of the Vedic gods and personification of warlike strength] or Surya (god of the sun)."[25] He believes, "Such contexts have the advantage of emphasizing the values of violence and constraint that have remained fundamental to its [yoga's] meaning through the word's history."[26] Varenne stresses, "despite the existence of the Latin noun *jugum* (English 'yoke') from the same Indo-European source, yoga has never meant 'yoke' in Sanskrit: the tranquil operation of yoking oxen evokes a peaceful, pleasant way of life that has nothing in common with yoga."[27]

A secondary meaning of the word yoga, also reported by Varenne, is magic recipe or method. He uses an example from the *Yogatattve Upanishad* (1.74) that states, "[B]y means of yoga ... with the help of a little mud mixed with urine transmute brass into gold."[28] The word yoga is given the meaning of magic recipe in this very alchemic application. "This aspect [transmutation] of the discipline [yoga] is so important in the view of its masters that one of the four books of the *Yoga-Sutra* is entirely given over to it."[29] Swami Rajarshi Muni, referencing the transformation nature of the practice, describes yoga as the "joining of a healthy body and a disciplined mind for spiritual development."[30]

Evelyn Underhill calls attention to an interesting correlation in Christianity when she writes about "yoke-fellows with Christ" in the book titled *The Way of the Spirit* (1990). Underhill notes, "The central act, the election of the soul that cares for God, must be deliberate in arranging itself in one way or another with those who accept the discipline, the yoke, the Christ-appointed means of the soul's growth and testing."[31] Underhill writes about the decision (election) to receive the "energy and purifying Spirit" of Christ and to "surrender entirely to His service and with Him for the redemption of the world."[32] The yoke of union between humanity and god may be viewed as spiritual or intellectual.

Although the foundation of yoga is obscured by time, the concepts associated with the practice are basic and reflect the human need for liberation from suffering. The pursuit of physical and spiritual transcendence employs various techniques including, "meditative trance, philosophical inquiry, naturalistic observation, hyper-mortality, or self-mortification."[33] The various approaches reflect a belief that it is possible for individuals to rid themselves of the circumstances that bind them to an unending cycle of birth and death. This state of liberation, once achieved, allows the self to reenter its original state of purity and consciousness.

The central message of all forms of yoga — bhakti-yoga, hatha-yoga, jnâna-yoga, karma-yoga, mantra-yoga, râja-yoga, sahaja-yoga, tantra-yoga, or târaka-yoga — is self-transformation to attain enlightenment.[34] These different forms of yoga have developed because of different emphases on one aspect or another. However, "in general, the goal of all these yoga forms is the same as that of the central Yoga [râja-yoga] even when expressed in terms of the particular metaphysics and metaphors of their own schools."[35] The central element of yoga is transcendental reality.

Yoga was elevated to a school of philosophy nearly 1,000 years ago, acknowledging it metaphysical and spiritual nature. It is one of the six orthodox schools (*darshana*) of Hindu philosophy.

Yoga-Sutra

The *Upanishads* are among the more significant Hindu documents dealing with yoga. The Brahmanic tradition regards them as an integral part of the Veda; however, they are more closely connection with non–Vedic texts such as the *Bhagavad-Gita* or the *Yoga-Sutras*. (The word *Sutra* means thread.) "It is possible they [the *Upanishads*] were written to provide a Vedic acknowledgment for post–Vedic teachings. The Upanishads may be the product of yoga academies formed around gurus of high reputation and made up of followers from the diverse backgrounds.[36] They are, nevertheless, of great importance to the field of yoga, because neither the *Bhagavad-Gita* nor the *Yoga-Sutra* includes information about the *cakra* (Sanskrit: wheels or rings; focal points of the psychosomatic energy also written chakra) or the *kundalini* (the feminine form of *kundala* meaning ring or coil) that are of primary importance to the understanding and practice of yoga. The *kundalini*, the divine cosmic energy, is generally represented in the form of a snake coiled at the base of the spine.

The basic text of yoga, the *Yoga-Sutra* is attributed to Patanjali. (It is possible that Patanjali compiled the *Sutra* drawing upon existing documents.) The word Yoga, as described in the *Sutra*, has at its center the concept of attaining union with the spiritual essence of humanity. It seeks the spiritual liberation by releasing the Self from the bondages of matter that come from ignorance and illusion. Attaining this goal is believed to be by returning the Self to its original state of purity and consciousness.

The essential nature of yoga is stated most clearly in the *Yoga-Sutra,* traditionally believed to have been composed as early the second century B.C.E. or as late as the 5th century C.E. The *Yoga-Sutra* appears to have been written over a long span of time. The first three volumes are thought to have been written in the second century B.C.E. and the last book in the fifth century C.E. It is possible (likely) several authors used the same name.[37] (Some scholars are of the opinion that the *Yoga-Sutra* was written between 100 and 300 C.E.) The *Yoga-Sutra* defines the purpose of yoga as self-liberation from suffering, the same attitude that is conveyed in Buddhist doctrine. The *Sutra* as prescribed by Patanjali is a non–Buddhist guide to liberation; nevertheless, it includes many key Buddhist teachings.

It is said that Shakyamuni Buddha was not only exposed to diverse yoga practices, he was also an accomplished yogi. He refused, however, to accept the doctrine of others, preferring to rely on his own experience.[38] He is said to have "wandered from the known cultural milieu of his time into the dense forests and open deltas of the Ganges seeking to bring an end to his relentless existential questions."[39] He disapproved of the conventional metaphysics of Vedic-based yoga practices; nevertheless, his own teaching and practice are based on the yoga tradition. Although the Buddha taught a variety of practices, it is his emphasis on mindfulness (*smrti*) and methods of cultivating it which has had the greatest impact.[40]

> In Patanjali's yoga, we have instructions on how to remove from consciousness everything that is not compatible with the enlightenment that is our natural state. We don't become someone else, someone enlightened; we become our most authentic self, which is to say, someone who is enlightenment itself, once our self-imposed beliefs in limitations are put into proper perspective.[41]

The *Yoga-Sutra* is instructive. It reminds the yogi, "Wrong knowledge is a false conception of a thing whose real form does not correspond to such a mistaken conception" (*Yoga-Sutra* I:8).[42] The world offers many deceptions. It is a mirage in which there is no true happiness. The external world is created by our thoughts; it is imaginary (impermanent).

Yoga seeks to eradicate the illusionary world by which all unenlightened persons constrain themselves. "It endeavors to systematically remove all those binds that help maintain the illusion. This endeavor can be viewed as an extensive process of disentanglement, or purification, or relaxation."[43] When the idealization of the mind (the sense of individualization) is overcome in favor of truth, the perfect tranquility, *samâdhi* (ecstasy), can be realized.

Georg Feuerstein wrote in *The Shambhala Guide to Yoga* (1996), "The yogic path can be viewed as a lengthy process of physical and mental purification, or catharsis."[44] According to the *Yoga-Sutra* (III.55), the "Self shines forth when the highest aspect of the mind, the *sattva*, approximates the Self in purity."[45] Lu K'uan Yü wrote the Taoist yogin views "laying the foundation (*chu chî*) and 'self-purification' (*lien-chî*)"[46] as the basis for causing life to "last as long as heaven and earth and leading to the acquisition of the supernatural powers possessed by all [Taoist] immortals."[47] Establishing a foundation of positive energy is a means of "stopping the positive generative force from draining away, and thus producing the golden elixir.... This foundation will lift you from the worldly to the saintly plane."[48]

The *Yoga-Sutra* identified traditional yoga's preparatory and secondary role of *âsanas* (yogic posture or positions) in the quest of liberation from the cycle of rebirth. *Âsanas* are the third limb (*anga*) of Patanjali's eightfold Yoga. The concepts defined by Patanjali follow closely the basic teaching of Buddha. "[T]he *Yoga-Sutra* clearly owes much of its organization and trust to the Buddhist traditions both ancient and contemporary up to the second and third century [of the Common Era]."[49] Patanjali's yogic concept followed the eightfold path or eight limbs (*astânga*) (see drawing 6.b). The eight limbs are *yama* (general ethical principles), *niyama* (self-restraint, individual morality and behavior), *âsana* (yogic postures), *prânâyâma* (breath control and discipline the body), *pratyâharâ* (detachment from external world), *dhâranâ* (concentration and focus), *dhyâna* (prolonged concentration and desolation of energy), and *samâdhi* (loss of self as a separate existence).

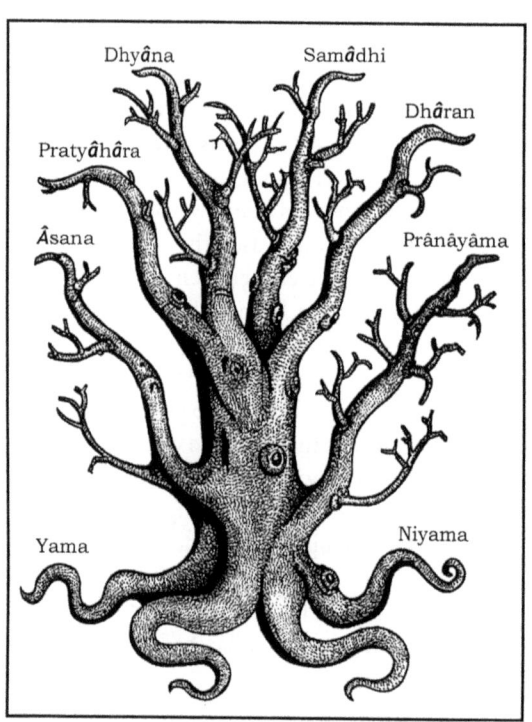

Drawing 6.b: The practice of yoga is built in layers or "limbs." The "tree" of yoga is the core or trunk and the limbs are the stages for ascending the true nature of the practice. The first three limbs are the foundation, the next two are the physical elements, and the last three are the intellectual elements of transformation. Movement upward through the limbs is a part of the learning process of yoga.

The first five *anga* are the outer group of the eight limbs, and the remaining three are the inner limbs. The first limbs are preparatory in nature, but they are not completely necessary. They are to train the body and mind to be receptive to meditation and spiritual growth. However, "A right physical posture or moral conduit may aid internal development but it does not guarantee it."[50] The three inner limbs, *dharana, dhyana,* and *samadi* "constitute what is called *samyama* (discipline, constraint)."[51] The attitude that exists in a state of samyama can be focused on any aspect of *prakrita* (nature that is devoid of sensation, a transcendental perspective) that includes everything that can be an object of perception.

B.K.S. Iyengar describes *prânâyâma* (the fourth limb — regulation and expansion of the breath) as the "link between the physiological and the spiritual organism of man."[52] The practice of *prânâyâma* is transformative. It brings together the elements of fire and water, and this contact in the body "with the help of the element of air, releases a new energy, called by yogis divine energy, or *kundalini sakti*, and this is the energy of *prâna* [life, life force]."[53]

The yoga depends on breath control (*prânâyâma*). It reduces the rate of breathing to make it a slow as possible. The yogin or yogini extends the time between breaths by developing the ability to hold his or her breath for extraordinary lengths of time.[54] It must be stressed, however, that reducing yoga to any one of its various aspects (metaphysics, physical exercise, breath control, etc.) is to alter it radically. If the novice determines the metaphysical aspect of yoga is not of interest, or that the "physiology of the 'vital breath' is just plain silly, but that 'there is an element of validity in the breathing exercise and the postures,' [the neophyte] is guilty of ideological imperialism."[55] ("In Hindu mythology, [a yogini is] one of the eight female demons created by and attendant upon Durgha."[56])

Sufi fraternities, in particular the *Naqshbandi* (an orthodox fraternity of Muslim mystics), borrowed the *prânâyâma* practice from Vedic sources as a means of bringing about realization (the outcome of constant practice of justice and charity). The *Yoga-Sutra* was translated into Arabic at the beginning of the eleventh century; subsequently, they (Arabs and particularly Sufis) imitated the "Hindu doctrine of *Kundalini*" by teaching practices related to the six great centers of light [*cakra*] of various colors in the body of humans.[57] The contemplation of these lights is said to "extinguish the sense of 'otherness.'"[58]

Cakra are an important part of yogic practice. Hindu tradition contends there are 88,000 *cakra* located throughout the human body. Different schools of yoga give attention to a selected number of the *cakra* from four to eleven. Most schools recognize six major *cakra* located along the spine plus a seventh just above the crown of the skull (**see drawing 6.c**). "The tantric model developed around the eleventh century and described as the *Sat-Cakra-Nirupana*, is the most widely accepted, giving seven chakras described as emanations of divine consciousness."[59] B.K.S. Iyengar describes *cakra* as invisible because they are not composed of matter. He states, they are "tangible only through their effects.... The most important is the *Sahasrara cakra* [located at the top of the head], where *prakriti shakti* or energy unites with *purusha shakti*, or soul."[60]

Drawing 6.c: Chakra or cakra are psychic-energy centers of the body that are important in forms of Hinduism, Tantric Buddhism, and yoga. The seven major chakras are associated with a specific color, shape, sense organ, natural element, deity, and mantra.

Gautama Buddha tied six knots in a silk handkerchief and asked a disciple how they could be undone. By tying the six knots, Buddha was showing how our individual identities are bound together by the knots of the ego self in each of the lower six chakras. He taught that we must untie them in the reverse order from which they were tied.[61]

Yogic practice incorporates transformational purification practices that include body postures (*âsana*), breathing (*prânâyâma*), and meditation exercises (*dhyâna*). The cosmic energy in Tantric yoga is believed to exist within everyone in the form of the coiled serpent (*kundalini*). This energy (power), identified with the Shakti, rests at the base of the spine in the lowest psychoenergetic center (*mûlâdhara-cakra*). The *kundalini* is released by yogic practice, and moves upward from *cakra* to *cakra* along the spine until it reaches the head.[62] Activating this process is the central goal of Tantric and Hatha-yoga (also called Laya-yoga). The fire of yoga ignites the cosmic energy of the kundalini, and once activated, it passes through the six centers (cakra) before arriving at the seventh cakra (*sahasara*, the "thousand-petaled lotus") at the crown of the head. The aspirant experiences, at that time, a feeling of bliss that mystically represents incorporation with *âtman*, or the eternal essence of the transcendent Self.

These nerve centers exist in a definite portion of the spinal cord and relate in special ways to systems both sensory and motor that influences specific physiological actions (**see photograph 17**). "It is the subtle aspect of such centers as expressions of Consciousness embodied in various forms of Maya-Sakti which is ... called Cakra."[63] It is the state of consciousness that creates, sustains, and destroys the world. "Brahma, Vishnu, and Shiva are the names for functions of the one Uni-

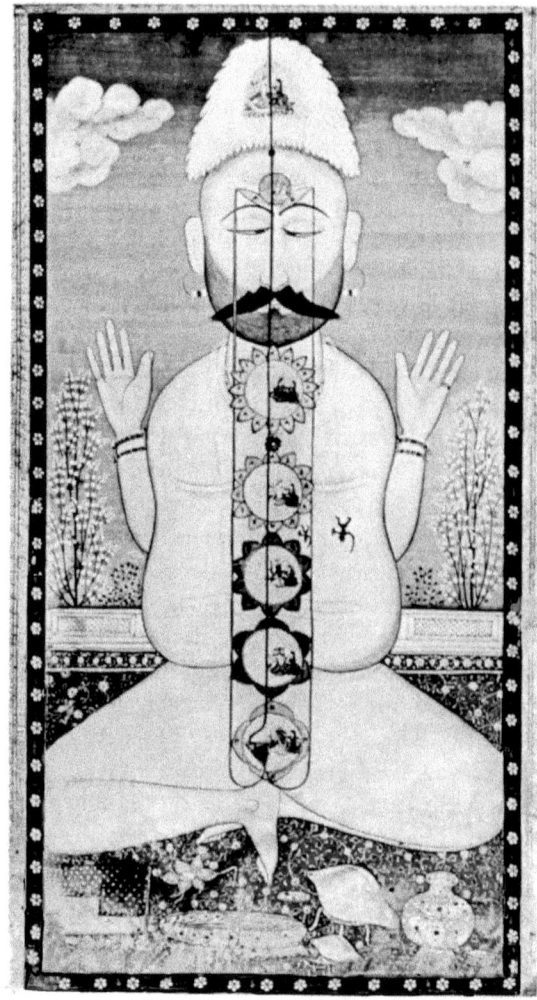

Photograph 17: This eighteenth century painting illustrates the placement of the six cakra in the subtle body leading to the seventh located at the crown of the head (the lotus of the head). The term "subtle" is applied when the yogin has attained total mastery over his or her body. The cakra are psycho-energetic centers within the body that are activated by yogic activity. The cakras are places where psychic forces and bodily functions come together and interact with each other. The Hindus consider six cakra plus the one at the head as important, whereas, the tantric Buddhists speak of only four. This painting is described as a "Diagram of the six cakras in the subtle body. Kalngra, Himachal Pradesh, 18th century. Gouache on paper."

versal Consciousness operating in ourselves."[64] Whatever the means used, it is the transformation of the "lower" into "higher" states of consciousness that is the process and benefit of Yoga and the cause of all its experiences.[65]

The breath and emotions are more concentrated in areas along the central axis of the body, and over the centuries, these platforms (*cakras*) were given different names. Each is associated with a specific color, shape, sense organ, natural element, deity, and mantra. The cakras are stopping places along the upward movements along the spine. They are places that focus on the energetic, emotional, and psychological patterns that occur within the yogi's body. Cultivation of internal energy involves yogic practice, meditation, and inner focus.

"The body and the mind are in a state of constant interaction. Yogic science does not demarcate where the body ends and the mind begins, but approaches both as a single integrated entity."[66] The yogic principle is that the human mind is not totally located in the brain, it is distributed throughout the body; therefore, it is not an isolated function. The mind is a complex organ that draws energy for different sources, and provides guidance and power to all physical resources. The mind in more general terms incorporates a variety of elements including sensation, sense perception, feeling, emotion, dreams, traits of character and personality, the unconscious, and the volitional aspects of human life, as well as thought, memory, and belief.[67] The goal of the yogi (or yogin, yogini) is to gain control of the mind functions to such a degree that they can be directed to transform body and attitude.

Three substances (energies) of great importance in Taoist yoga are known collectively as the Three Treasures: essence (*ching*), vitality (*ch'i*), and spirit (*shên*).[68] It is believed by Taoists that humans are filled with an amount of these treasures due to the effects of passion and extraordinary desire. However, this endowment is of a baser nature and requires refinement to restore it to purity. It is by breathing that the subtle *ch'i* resides in the body. It has a role in the transmutation of both *ching* and *shên*. The process of transmutation "involves both mental visualization and certain muscular movements; but not all versions of the internal alchemy stress the need for arousing psychic heat."[69]

Yoga as Transformation

> The human body is like a rootless tree and relies solely on the breath as root and branches. A lifetime is just a dream, like an out breath which does not guarantee the in breath after it, and today does not insure the morrow.[70]

"The fundamental mystical tradition that developed in India during the Upanishadic period has appeared in modified form in Buddhism, Jainism, and, of course, Hinduism.... But the basic tradition of Oriental mysticism is that of yoga."[71] Each group endeavored to implement yogic practices on a theoretical basis as emanating from its own doctrine. There are many forms of yoga consequently, and the practices differ according to the stage of advancement of both the concepts and the practitioners.

Yoga is transformation. It is a way of transforming the living self—the body, mind, and spirit or soul—from the personal Self to the universal Self. It is a return to the natural state of being. Yoga is a path of spiritual alchemy or esoteric alchemy, based on the transformation of the "Yoga practitioner from a base, corrupted personality into the luminous, nonlocal Self beyond space and time."[72] It is a means for generating a new state of being, and a method for recovering true identity, as well as ending suffering and confusion. Yoga is an acknowledgment that the human body is a microcosm of the universe. "What is here [within the body] is elsewhere. What is not here is nowhere."[73]

The alchemy of the human body, according to yogic tradition, includes the five elements: earth, water, fire, air, and ether. (Some document include only four elements excluding ether.) The earth element is responsible for the producing of the elixir of life (prāna) or energy (life force). "The element of air is used as a churning rod, through inhalation and exhalation (prânâyâma), and distribution is through the element of ether."[74] B.K.S. Iyengar explains, "Two elements remain: water and fire. If there is a fire, water is used to extinguish it. This gives us the idea that fire and water are opposing elements."[75] The elements of earth, air, and ether, create a friction between water and fire that generates energy and releases it. "Earth and ether are eternal; they change when they come into contact with air, fire, and water."[76]

The universe — objective or subjective — is only the evolution of an initial stage of human nature (the I-maker, *ahamkâra*) according to Yogic doctrine. This homogeneous and energetic mass first produced the consciousness of individuality and a comprehension demonstrated by the ego. The ego (Latin for I), in this evolutionary process, is theoretically that part of the human personality that connects with the external world through perceptions. Thought or thinking is therefore considered to mediate between inner activity and external stimuli.[77] The ego remembers, evaluates, and plans. It also responds in various ways to the surrounding physical and social world. It is the capacity of the ego to change — to be transformed — that involves interaction with yogic practice.

The emotional, spiritual, and intellectual lines of human existence develop as parallel concepts. They remain as parallel elements for most individuals. When there is equal development in the three concepts the individual maintains an acceptable equilibrium — a normalcy within the host society. When one element develops with greater strength or energy (power), the person is often considered abnormal. This anomaly may be viewed as either positive or negative. The great artist, writer, scholar, or spiritualist is often viewed as being beyond the limits of the normal — an eccentric or saint. The shaman or mystic, for example, is generally considered an abnormal person. The gifted person may have difficulty in adjusting to the societal notion of normalcy. An individual with acute underdevelopment of one or more of the three elements is viewed as abnormal to the opposite extreme. These conditions are not metaphysical but psychological.

The yogi is dedicated to causing the developmental lines to merge, and thereby to create a synergistic balance of the energies. This union is achieved through physical control and the process of gradual fusion of the parts into the transcendent integrality of *oneness* (the Absolute). The unified whole, in this transformation, is not identical with the sum of its parts. It is different. The attitude formed by this amalgamation represents a specific reality that has its own characteristics. It is a detached consciousness that is empty yet full.

The Absolute is completeness and voidness (*shûngatâ*), everything and nothing. It is the source and receptacle of all energy, but totally inert. The person obsessed with the void as the emptiness of existence, fills the time and space with illusions. The word void (*shûnyata*) literally means emptiness, but it has a subtle connotation when used in Buddhist philosophy.[78] The concept of voidness relates to the experience, realized in meditation, that there is no abiding principle in things.[79] It has meaning only for an ego that holds to the illusory reality of things. "The empty skull (void) is too awesome for the average being to conceive. The mind resists a vacuum and does its best to fill it with its own creations."[80] Such deceptive impressions take many forms and are stimulated by the ego. The person who is not aware of this tendency imagines the emptiness to be reality and the illusion is allowed to grow until the Self (*âtman*) is transfixed into a delusional existence. Liberation from the world of illusions is the goal of the yogin or yogini; "to achieve this he must make use of the double path of higher cognition and meditation, of ethical and cognitive accumulation and of practical exercise."[81]

The concepts of yoga, alchemy, and transformation are closely connected physically and spiritually. They are often viewed as identical attitudes in Eastern practice. The ideas are separated in the Western world where alchemy focused more on the material and far less on the spiritual. This redirection (or some say misdirection) undoubtedly is due, in part, to the route and methods of information exchange between the various cultural elements. John Blofeld comments on the communication issue in the 1985 publication *Taoism: The Road to Immortality*, "This misunderstanding [between the material and the spiritual] arose from the esoteric language of the Taoist yogic manuals, the effect of which was that, among the Taoists themselves, there were not a few who failed to recognize the true spiritual purpose of the [alchemic] texts."[82]

"The primary aim of Yoga is to restore the mind to simplicity, peace and poise, to free it from confusion and distress. This simplicity, this sense of order and calm, comes from the practice of *âsanas* [postures] and *prânâyâma* [breath control]."[83] Yoga is the ultimate form of physical, mental, and spiritual transformation. It is thought the "greatest philosophy of India."[84] It addresses the mysteries of life as well as universal concepts, especially those aspects that are beyond the understanding of normal human intellect. Yogic principles are "based on spiritual experiences, and so they appeal more to intuitive discrimination rather than to intellectual understanding."[85] Yoga should not be viewed as theoretical philosophy or simple calisthenics; instead, it is a time-honored practical discipline based on personal spiritual experience.

It is said that Shiva invented eighty-four basic yogic postures (*âsanas*) to help people purify their bodies and prepare them for meditation.[86] This form of yoga, called *hatha-yoga*, is concerned with the transmutation of the human body into a vessel immune from mortal decay.[87] (The word "Hatha" is composed of two syllables "ha" and "tha," meaning the sun [male] and the moon [female]—*prâna* and *apâna*). Hatha-Yoga is closely related to *rasâyana* (alchemy) "The knowledge (*vidya*) of *hatha-yoga* was first taught by Shiva to his consort Parvati [Sanskrit: Daughter of the Mountain], the Universal Mother"[88] (see plate A).

Although the body and the mind are an inseparable unity, raja-yoga deals with gaining control of the mind while *hatha-yoga* works with the *prâna* and *apâna* (two life-force forms). "The Hatha-yoga practitioner wants to construct a "divine body" (*divya-sharira*) or "adamantine body" (*vajra-deha*) for himself or herself, which would guarantee immortality in the manifest realms."[89]

"Yoga is an initiatory wisdom that has come to us from the very depths of time."[90] It is the oldest known science of physical and mental self-development, caring for the body under the intelligent control of the mind.[91] Swami Sivananda Radha believes "Yogis recognized man's basic need for discipline to counteract the physical and spiritual deterioration caused by the mere fight for survival."[92] The swami maintains the yogis "were aware that when the positive and negative currents by which the human body is enlivened are in equilibrium, we [humanity] enjoy perfect health."[93]

Although psychic powers are often associated with yogic practice, the object of practicing hatha-yoga is to prepare for raja-yoga, and not to attain such powers. Hatha-yoga is to gain control over the bodily organs and the mind so the yogi can maintain good health while pursuing raja-yoga. While hatha-yoga concentrates of physical control, raja-yoga is intended to control the thoughts during meditation. The objective is to stop arbitrary or random thoughts. However, when such control is not possible, the yogi concentrates on regulating the physical breath.[94] The purpose of prânâyâma (the fourth limb of Patanjali's eightfold yoga) is to "reduce breathing to an effortless, even rhythm, thus helping to free the individual's mind from attention to bodily functions."[95]

The Jewish mystic doctrine professed by Abraham Abulafia, a thirteenth century Kabbalist, is viewed as a Judaized version of the spiritual techniques practiced by Indian mystics that follow the yoga system. An important instrument of mental discipline in Abulafia's practice was played by the technique of breathing (qua *prânâyâma*), to cite only one instance out of many.[96]

An advanced raja yogi is one who controls his or her thoughts, and once that is achieved, everything can be controlled—prâna and the body. However, a person with this ability is rare. An advanced raja yogi is an individual who has full control over the emotions: lust, anger, greed, hatred, jealousy, envy, and fear. Most persons are not so accomplished and must practice hatha-yoga to reach raja-yoga competency.[97]

Returning to a system of equilibrium is an important aspect of yoga. It is both a limiting and empowering factor. Ordinary life, according to the yogic perspective, involves the accumulation of pleasurable and painful experiences, and often results in the narrowing of consciousness. Consciousness, in its pure form, as the transcendental self (*âtman*), is unimpeded and free. "Self-realization is a consummation of self-consciousness."[98] This form of relaxation refers to perception of opening or loosening the body as well as the recharging of the body system. It is directly connected with prânâyâma (breath control). Restored equilibrium refers to

Plate A: Pârvati, wife of Shiva, is being approached by Vishnu, Shiva, Brahma, and others who are climbing toward the shrine where she is seated on top of a steep hill. The hill is covered with depictions of sadhus (holy men) seated in yoga asana. Surya and Chanddra, the sun and moon gods, are seated in celestial chariots in the sky. Shiva is said to have invented the basic yogic postures to help people purify their bodies and to transform the human body into a vessel immune from mortal decay. Parvati, the Universal Mother was the first to be taught this practice. © The Trustees of the British Museum. All rights reserved.

releasing the tension that creates "the illusion of the ego's individuality and separateness. Thus, relaxation is not merely relaxation of the body but also of the mind—our opinions, concerns, hopes, and attitudes. It is the master key of all levels of the yogic enterprise."[99]

Although the healing nature of yoga can be profound, it is not personal. The object of yoga is correct internal order. Tranquility of the psyche allows the *purusha* (the transcendental Self, Spirit, or pure Awareness) to hear and be heard. The aspirant must remove interfering mental activities and eliminate attachment to material objects before he or she is about to enter *Samadhi,* a state of deep concentration and the eighth stage or level of yogic practice. *Samadhi* is a Sanskrit term meaning, "'to direct towards' signifying a profound depth of meditation and focus on the ultimate unity of things. It involves the abstraction of consciousness from mental as well as worldly concerns [ecstasy], total control of every faculty and complete conscious union with the divine source [embodied enlightenment]."[100]

Tantric Yoga Tradition

> Tantric Yoga teaches certain practices and mystical rites which, if followed with pure motives, gradually transform the desires of the senses into love of God. In this way, says Tantra, the very chains that bind man to the world are used to free him.[101]

The early form of Buddhism introduced into Tibet (*Yogâcâra,* one who practices yoga, also called *Vijñânavâda*—Doctrine of Consciousness) was strongly influenced by yoga. This influential school of Buddhist philosophy and psychology did not appeal to the common people, because it was too intellectual. It included ten stages of spiritual development to reach Buddhahood, and defined pure consciousness as the ultimate reality. *Yogâcâra* "attaches importance to the religious practice of yoga as a means for attaining final emancipation from the bondage of the phenomenal world. The stages of yoga are systematically set forth in the treatises associated with this tradition."[102] *Yogâcâra* is an idealistic school of Mahâyâna Buddhism that opposes the realistic approach of Theravâda Buddhism (Hinâyâna), as well as the provisional practical realism of the *Mâdhyamika* school of Mahâyâna Buddhism.[103]

The tantric Buddhism that spread to Tibet is strongly influenced by Hindu *Shaktism* in which the Absolute is represented in the form of a sexual union. This Buddhism involved the recognition of the goddess Kali or Durga as the female energy Sakti to consort of Shiva. Various forces of nature were deified and defined at that time as goddesses of magical power—Divine Mother and Yogini. Subsequently, consorts were allotted to several celestial gods and demons.[104] The art of Tibet includes the *yab-yum* (mother-father) figure in which the female element plays the active role (see photographs 2 and 7).[105] "*Kundalini* is *Sakti* power symbolized by Divine Mother. She is pure blissful consciousness. She is the Mother of nature. *Sakti* is always with *Shiva*. They are inseparable like fire and heat."[106]

Yogis following the Tantric traditions of India, China, and Tibet turned their bodies into places of pilgrimage and charted the "energetic channels (*nadis*), platforms (*cakra*), psychophysical point of meditation (*bandhas*), and other features of the mental, emotional, and physical landscape."[107] They practiced *laya*-yoga (hatha-yoga), a form of yoga that gives special attention to the female natural-energy, the serpent (*kundalini*). The serpent is the uncreated and once awakened it rises through the *cakra* (also called *Padma*—lotuses) located along the central feature, the energy source (centers of consciousness) of the human body. The kundalini passes from the root of the lotus (the base of the spine) to the thousand petals at the top of the head.[108]

Anne Bancroft states Tantra yoga "worships the Divine as two principles, male and female, Being and Becoming. Shiva, the masculine, is eternal Being, pure perfection and timeless wisdom, Shakti, the Supreme Mother, is the creative power of Becoming."[109] Because Shakti is present in all living things, Bancroft writes, "She mediates between the Absolute and the relative, between eternity and the flow of events in time. Thus it is to her that men turn when practicing this yoga, for help and guidance in their journey towards perfection."[110]

"Tantra is a profoundly yogic tradition, and the Tantras call themselves *sâdhanâ-shâstras* or books of spiritual practice."[111] The Sanskrit word "'yoga' can be translated as 'unitive discipline.' It stands for what in the West is called spirituality or mysticism."[112] Tantric yoga found in both the Buddhist and Hindu traditions is a "unitive discipline based on the expansion, or intensification of wisdom by means of the beliefs and practices promulgated in the Tantras and the exegetical literature that has crystallized around them."[113] Sâdhanâs are to bring about the union of wisdom and means, of void and non-void consciousness, to be prepared for the task of assisting the liberation of all beings. Georg Feuerstein writes, "By 'unifying' the mind — that is, by focusing it — Tantra Yoga unifies the seemingly disparate realities of time-space and the transcendental Reality."[114]

Tantra yoga emphasizes the point that tantra is not something separate in relation to humanity. Tantra is the same in time and space as the human being's. It is a process like life itself. Tantra, like traditional yoga, is not concerned to be scientific. "It addresses itself to man's uniqueness as a living being, and not to any theoretical scheme."[115] Shiva (Siva) is said to be pure consciousness; therefore, he is an expression of power (*Sakti* or *Shakti*). "The object of Sâdhanâ or Worship and Yoga is to raise this power to its perfect expression, which is perfect in the sense of unlimited experience."[116] Through the practice of yoga, the individual exchanges his or her limited experiences for that which is the unlimited Whole (*pûrna*, a manifestation of the ultimate Reality) or Perfect Bliss.

The physical body (*deha*) is an essential instrument of salvation in all yoga schools.[117] The tantric *Vajrayâna* is directed to obtaining a "body of diamond that is incorruptible, and not susceptible to change, that is, to age or disease. Hatha Yoga strengthened the body to prepare it for the final 'transmutation' and make it fit for 'immortality.'"[118] The goal is to gain awareness in all areas of the body, the senses, and the mind.[119] Therefore, like the alchemist, the yogi regulates and transforms substance, eliminates impurities, and makes them better. Substance in India, *prakrti* [energy source], is the responsibility of Shakti (also called Pârvatî), the consort of Shiva represented by the *yoni* (the female sex organ, the holder), or *Mâyâ*, archetype of the magician.[120] *Prakrti* is defined as primeval stuff, that is, the *Prima Materia* commonly associated with alchemy, and *Mâyâ*, the magician, has powerful wizardry that god uses to make humans believe in illusions, an element of mysticism and magic.

Tantric *sâdhanâ* (the path to spiritual realization) is based on the initiation of death, since every spiritual discipline implies the initiatory process in some form — that is, the experience of ritual death and resurrection. This transformation is exemplified by the ubiquitous rites of passage. The tantrist, in this respect, is a "dead man in life," because he or she has experienced his or her death in advance. He is twice born, in the initiatory sense. However, he or she may not have gained this new birth on a purely theoretical level, but by means of a person experience. Hatha-yoga references to yogin or yogini immortality, stem from the experiences of such "dead men in life."[121] This concept of death is similar to the initiatory process experienced by shaman. The notion of death, dismemberment, and regeneration is a common transformation scenario.

The Tantras believe it is within the power of the individual to accomplish all he or she wishes by centering his or her will on that objective. The human being, according to Tantric doctrine is in his or her essence one with the Supreme Beings and the more he or she manifests spirit, the greater he or she is endowed with its power. The hindrances of power restrict the human action. Patanjali addresses the issue of the nine hindrances in the *Yoga-Sutras*. ("This doctrine of the removal of hindrances became part of Brahminism in the first century of the Common Era."[122])

The transcendent body (*jiva*) is composed of three layers or bodies according to yogic philosophy: the casual (*kârana-sarira*), subtle (*suksma-sarira*), and gross (*sthula-sarira*). Each layer has a causal relationship to the others. The casual body is the spiritual that lasts until liberation, and is the cause of the other bodies that evolve from it. "The second and third bodies (subtle and gross) are the differentiations through evolution of the casual body, from which first proceeds the subtle body, and from the latter is produced the gross body. The subtle body comprises the physiological, psychological, and intellectual elements."[123] "The gross body is the body of 'matter,' which is the gross particular object of the senses derived from the supersensibles."[124]

B.K.S. Iyengar wrote there are four ways to self-realization (transformation). He described those ways as "*jnana marg*, or the path to knowledge, when the seeker learns to discriminate between the real and the unreal; *karma marg*, the path of selfless service without thought of reward; *bhakti marg*, the path of love and devotion."[125] Iyengar describes the final method as, "*yoga marg*, the path by which the mind and its actions are brought under control. All these paths lead to the same goal; *samdhi*."[126] These paths are open to everyone.

Mircea Eliade believes there is a "a definite point where Yoga and shamanism meet. They join in 'emergence from time' and the abolition of history. The shaman's ecstasy recovers the primordial freedom and bliss of the ages in which, according to the myths, man could ascend to heaven physically and converse with the gods."[127] Eliade also said, "For its part, Yoga results in the non-conditioned state of *samadhi* or of *sahaja* [innate, non-conditioned existence], in the perfect spontaneity of the *jtvan-mukta*, the man 'liberated in this life.'"[128]

> To prolong the life span and virility, the medical Tantras advocate practices of inner alchemy, relying on supreme elixirs made from purified essences of mercury and gold, as well as the unequalled nectar of a qualified consort.[129]

A lesser-known form of yoga practiced in Tibet is called *Kum Nye*. It is a "series of simple but effective healing exercises that work to relieve stress, transform negative behavioural patterns, promote balance and health, and increase our enjoyment and appreciation of life."[130] The spreading of information about *Kum Nye* was a predominately oral tradition; however, it is referenced in Tibetan medical texts as, "ways of healing diseases that result from energy blockages."[131] It is likened to a form of meditation in that it is a way to relieve tension and to gain a sense of release and relaxation.

The origin of *Kun Nye* (subtle body awareness), which is similar to yoga, Tai Chi, Qi Gong or therapeutic massage, can be traced to early Buddhist teaching in India where it was used as a guide for the conduct of monks and nuns. It was particularly useful in that it suggested "ways to relieve the fatigues experienced during long periods of meditation."[132] It is a part of the medical and spiritual practices that link Tibetan with Indian and Chinese medicine.[133]

Kun Nye is reflective of an approach to yogic practice that gives greater attention to the spiritual element of the Self instead of assigning primary attention to the physical. This is not to say that the physical element is ignored, rather, that the spiritual is given equal or greater prominence. It is a balance of the physical and the psychological — a balance of the vital life forces. Control of the body is a process by which the physical and emotional worlds can be transformed. "Our bodies are part of a universal body, our minds an aspect of a universal mind."[134]

"The physical body is a by-product of the more subtle aspects of our existence. By influencing these subtle levels we begin to transform our sense of who and what we are."[135] The healing powers may be viewed as miraculous or deceptive unless the relationship between faith and spiritual force is understood. Faith is a conductor that permits spiritual power to become effective. Tibetans endeavor to address the cause of all disease by curing the mind instead of attempting to cure physical symptoms.[136] "The art of healing is achieved when all our actions are inspired by a higher reality in which our individual identity is inseparable from the creative forces of the Cosmos."[137]

The life forces are known in Tibetan medicine as the three humors — wind, bile, and phlegm. These humors are "principles of life energy that govern all the processes of the body, physiological, mental, and emotional. They encompass both the constituents of the physical body and the energy networks of the subtle body."[138] The human body is recognized as a repository of ecstasy in the Buddhist Tantras. It is a place of undeveloped power that, when correctly cultivated will transform into a body of light. This transformation is the result of "an inner alchemy in which the base constituents of the body/mind are purified...."[139]

Ian Baker writes in *The Tibetan Art of Healing* (1997), "Derived from the Indian medical system of *Ayurveda*, the threefold division of bodily energy based on the Five Elements (earth, water, fire, air and space [ether]) is central to all aspects of Tibetan medicine."[140] Irritation of these inner elements caused by dietary irregularities or environmental stress may lead to illness and death.[141] Evoking the healing process "involves creating and maintaining a dynamic equilibrium between these three divisions of human physiology and the corresponding realms of thought, will, and emotion."[142]

Tantric *sâdhanâs* [path of spiritual realization] transform ordinary experiences of pleasure and pain into radiant awareness of our innermost being. As the Tantras proclaim, "Great wisdom dwells with the body," and Tibetan doctors continually profess that the bliss which arises from within, is the only medicine that can cure the ailment from which all others arise — ignorance of our own true nature.[143]

Yogic Meditation

Yogic transformation (alchemy) may follow different paths. The object is not the method but the results, although some yogic internal alchemy texts describe human anatomy in terms of external alchemy, furnace, cauldron, etc., and describe meditational practices by referencing ingredients such as mercury, lead, water, etc.[144] The approach is, however, spiritual instead of material. Though physical and mental health is of primary importance, the ingestion of drugs is a practice that has been eliminated from yogic practice. Meditation is an example of the spiritual focus of yoga. This practice is undertaken to recognize the illusory nature of the human body, as well as all the objects in the universe.[145]

It is very important to help the seeds of mindfulness, forgiveness, and compassion to grow, and the way to do this is to help them be present in your mind consciousness as long as possible. This is called transformation at the base — *ashraya paravritti*. This is the true meaning of *virya paramita*, the perfection of diligence.[146]

Meditation (*dhyâna*) is the seventh limb of the eightfold path. It helps the yogi settle his or her mind into silence, and only when the mind is silent can the yogi realize his or her true nature, the effortless Being of the Self.[147] The fundamental nature of the yogic process is that things dissolve into that from which they originate.[148] Laya-yoga is the way of achieving desolation — *laya* — through meditation, and with that practice, the yogi achieves self-realization. Sir John Woodroffe wrote in the book *The Serpent Power*, "The bases of this [*Laya*] Yoga are of a highly metaphysical and scientific character. For its understanding there is required a full acquaintance with Indian philosophy, religious doctrine and ritual in general."[149]

The moral, physical, and mental aspects are important elements of yoga, however, the purpose of the effort is beyond the body and mind. The objective of yoga is transcendent — beyond the limits of experience. The most significant aspect of yoga and the one that distinguishes it from ordinary physio-psychotherapy, is its transcendent nature.[150] The whole of the physio-psychological effort is preparation of the body to make it physically and mentally suitable for the descent of the spirit.[151]

Meditation is not separate from yoga. It is the heart of yoga, and what is called meditation in raja-yoga is called "stopping the impulses" in hatha-yoga.[152] Tibetan meditative practices seek to "evoke a particular deity as a transcendent aid to help clear away the obstacles to ultimate understanding."[153] Yogic practice includes meditation as a means for purification of the body, mind, and soul (Sanskrit: dhyana). Meditation is the seventh limb (*anga*) of Patenjali's eightfold yoga (*Yoga-Sutra*). Meditation is deeper than mental concentration (dhâranâ). It (meditation) has no point of focus. It considers the true nature of reality or the conditioned and unconditioned *dharmas* (divine laws) that are the basis for all phenomena. Ch'an Master Niu-t'ou Fa-yung states, "I have also heard that there are those who falsely take concentration for enlightenment."[154]

Mantra-yoga is said to be the "'yoga of magic formulas' that deals with the magical efficacy of the specific words or phrases employed to help concentrate the mind etc."[155] Practitioners of yoga acknowledge four states of consciousness — "waking, sleep with dreams, sleep without dreams, and a state resembling cataleptic consciousness — each of which has its own respiratory rhythm."[156] Yogic concentration often focuses on the center cakra (at the navel) or the lotus of the heart. It is important, however, to remember that concentration is not meditation. It is a part of the meditative process and often a necessary first step toward focusing the mind.

"Yoga is the transformation into the Divine, and of the Divine into everything. Meditation is the key."[157] The yogi lives within *dharma* (the cosmic law), as the *dharma* lives within the yogi. Meditation as a method of focus — controlling the mind — occupies a central place in yogic practice. It is an effort to create continuity within discontinuity by making the successively occurring ideas similar to each other. "*Dhyâna* [meditation] is that particular phase of yogic introversion in which the presented-ideas are consistently associated with the object of concentration until no foreign thought intrude and complete restriction is achieved."[158]

A form of meditation that relates to yoga involves a process of moral and intellectual purification and development in four stages. The aspirant achieves detachment from sensual desires and impure states of mind in the first phase, and thereby attains an emotional state of satisfaction and joy. Intellectual activities are abated to a complete inner serenity in the second stage, and the mind achieves one-point concentration (ekâgratâ), a single focus of enjoyment and pleasantness. Emotions disappear in the third stage causing the aspirant to be indifferent to emotional awareness. The fourth stage is the abandoning of the sense of satisfaction, pain, or serenity. The aspirant thus enters a state of supreme purity.

K. Taimni writes in the Fourth Section of his translation of the Yoga-Sutra, "Concentration is the confining of the mind within a limited mental area (object of concentration)."[159] Taimni believes the greatest distraction to the conscious mind (citta), and therefore to concentration, is likely uncontrolled reactions to the environment, to what people do and to the societal conditions to which people are subjected. The normal person has no well-defined means for the controlling these responses. He or she (the practitioner) may react to disturbances in a chaotic manner according to hostile emotions. People often find these emotional outbursts unpleasant, and subsequently, decide not to react at all. They gradually become indifferent to those around them.[160]

The first five *angas* [limbs] of yoga are intended to eliminate these external causes of mental distraction from concentration, according to Taimni. He states, "*Yama* (restraint) and *Niyama* (discipline) eliminate the disturbances that are caused by uncontrolled emotions and desires. *Âsana* and *prânâyâma* eliminate the disturbances arising from the physical body."[161] *Pratyâhâra* (withdrawal) detaches the sense organs from the mind, thereby cutting off the external world and the impact it has upon the mind. "The mind is thus completely isolated from the external world and the *Sâdhaka* (spiritual practitioner) is thus in a position to grapple with it without any interference from the outside."[162]

"The yogin's ultimate purpose, however, is to go beyond the subtle levels of existence and to realize the transcendental Being, which is trans-dimensional and unqualified, and which the yogin knows to be his innermost identity."[163] The yogin is primarily a transcender, that is, he or she goes beyond the limits of experience. However, the yogin is likely to gather a great deal of knowledge about the subtle realms (*sûkshma-loka*) in the spiritual ascent to the transcendental Reality. The transcendent nature plus this "gathering of knowledge" explains why "many yogins have demonstrated extraordinary abilities and have long been looked upon by the Indian people as miracle workers and magicians."[164]

Concentration, meditation, and transformation are aspects of yoga that had a major influence as it moved across Asia. Jean Varenne states, "Indian Buddhism spread throughout Asia (before disappearing from India itself in about the eighth century after Christ), some ideas from yoga were carried with it into Tibet, Mongolia, China, and from there, on into Japan."[165] Varenne underscores the influence of Buddhism and yoga in Japan. "Indeed," he writes, "*Zen* is a specific form of yoga's *dhyana* or 'transcendental meditation,' and the very word '*zen*' (like its Chinese equivalent *tchan*) is a simple phonetic development from Sanskrit *dhyana*."[166]

> When the mind is free from distraction, it is possible for all the mental processes to be involved in the object of inquiry. As one remains in this state, gradually one becomes totally immersed in the object. The mind, like a flawless diamond, reflects only the features of the object and nothing else.[167]

CHAPTER SEVEN

The Transformers

"To be rich forever: to die never"[1]

Everything observable (matter and energy) is subject to change but never to creation out of nothing nor to total extinction, and it seems more likely than not the same laws apply to what is not observable.[2]

Gold is one of the few elements that appear in nature uncombined with other elements. "About 40,000 years ago, in what is now Spain, Paleolithic cave dwellers gathered bits of the metal and hoarded them in their caverns. Sparkling brightly, the nuggets must have seemed like condensed motes of sunshine."[3] The Inca called gold "the sweat of the sun." They made a wide range of objects, common and ceremonial, from the bright material. The Hindu sages called gold "the mineral light." They believed the mineral was a physical token of divine intelligence. Pindar the Greek lyric poet wrote in the fifth century B.C.E. that gold was "the child of Zeus." The chemical symbol for gold is Au, derived from the Latin word for "shining dawn" (*aurum*).[4]

Jay Ramsay writing in *Alchemy: The Art of Transformation* (1997) contends, "The recorded beginnings of alchemy are in Egypt, and the earliest alchemists, although writing in Greek, were Egyptian and Jewish."[5] Ramsay was speaking primarily about Western alchemic thought because there is some doubt about the origin of the earliest writing of alchemy. Current thinking assigns the earliest references to China. Alchemy is said to have emerged in China during the Warring States Period (fifth century to the third century B.C.E.). It was associated with Taoism at that time. Nevertheless, the exact date of the first alchemic experiment may have come much earlier as Gareth Roberts suggests in *The Mirror of Alchemy*. Roberts writes, "In Eden before the Fall, Adam was thought to have possessed an unique knowledge of the wonderful secret of nature, including that of the Philosophers' Stone."[6] Belief has a way of adjusting the hands of time when reason cannot.

Mark Stavish acknowledges other lands have contributed to the development of alchemy, but identifies "the land of Khem" or the "black earth," Egypt as "the home of alchemy and its god Thoth, or Hermes in his Greek incarnation, with being the father of alchemy."[7] Mircea Eliade, however, sees the interconnected nature of shamanism, mysticism, magic, yoga, and alchemy.[8] The origins of all these phenomenal activities are obscured by the necessities of society, and each has at one time during their existence acquired a quasi-religious quality.

Another version of the legend regarding alchemy in Egypt refers to a "legendary adept" named "Chemes, who supposedly passed on his wisdom in a book he called *Chema*. Some scholars believe this adept's name provided the root for the word alchemy."[9] Mircea Eliade writing in *The Forge and The Crucible* references to a 1959 article by S. Mahdihassan that proposes the origin of alchemy to be China and Egypt.[10] The article contends the founder was an aging ascetic who was searching for a means of longevity. Alastair Baxter, referencing the Indian author Bhudeb Mookerji, advances the belief that alchemy originated in India 1,950,000,000 years ago.[11]

A different perspective is stated in a 1988 article published in the *American Journal of Chinese Medicine*. The article contends the word alchemy is derived from a practical process in which the ascetic had tried ground jade, then gold and cinnabar as an aid to immortality, but believed "the ideal was a drug which was red like cinnabar and fire-proof like gold. But what was actually prepared was red colloidal gold or 'calcined gold,' by grinding gold granules in a decoction of an herb of longevity."[12] This mixture was called "*Chin-I*." The word *chin* means gold and *I* means plant juice (liquid). In South China, Fukien Province, the word *Chin-I* is pronounced *Kim-Iya*. This expression was "Arabicized," by pre-Islamic Arabs trading in China as *Kimiya* to which they added the Arabic article *Al* meaning the to say *Al-Kimiya* and finally *alchemy*.[13]

The *American Journal of Chinese Medicine* article elaborates on the evolution of alchemy by stating that the Copts in Egypt transliterated *Kimiya* to *Chemeia*, pronouncing it as the Arabs did. The journal article contends, "The Chinese also went to Alexandria and helped the Greeks to translate *Chin-I* as *Chrusozomion* meaning, gold (making) ferment, instead of gold making plant juice."[14] This article states, "A consumer of *Chin-I* or *Chemeia* became "a drug-made immortal" called *Chin-Jen*, Golden-Man."[15]

Another article also considers the possibility of a Chinese origin for the term chemistry. The article states, "It [the term] may have been derived from the Hakka term *Kim-mi* or the Cantonese term *Kem-mai*, which signifies 'gone astray in search of gold' or 'secret of gold.'"[16] These terms are suggested as the possible origin of the Greek *chemeia* and the Arabic word *alchemy*. The Chinese and Indians usually refer to alchemy as the Art or by terms meaning change or transformation.

Some historians contend that the earliest mention of alchemy was in China in 144 B.C.E., and other scholars point to a book written at about 200 B.C.E. by the Egyptian Democritos as the beginning.[17] Although the beginning of alchemy might be claimed by either China or Egypt, the two-pronged approach to the art was defined from the earliest times (although it may be claimed that in the beginning the two alchemic objectives were the same). One method pursued the transformation of substance as exemplified by turning base metal into gold, while the second method focused on the quest for the elixir of life. Both branches drew from roots firmly fixed within the beliefs of the related social and cultural systems from which they evolved.

Addressing the issue of alchemy and spiritual attainment, Mark Stavish wrote in *The Path of Alchemy* (2006), "Alchemy offers us the opportunity to relieve suffering, ignorance, and fear of death through direct experience of the invisible worlds and understanding how they relate to the physical world of matter."[18] Stavish writes in the next paragraph, "In alchemy, inner transformation is accomplished by using a dual process of transpersonal and technical methods. The transpersonal methods are meditations, prayers, studies, and inner work that the alchemist undertakes."[19] Stavish describes the technical methods as being the "physical techniques and preparations the alchemist uses to produce herbal and mineral tinctures, which can be used as ritual aids and medicinally."[20]

Pursuing the Art

Hope, imagination, and belief are complex attitudes that encourage or discourage humans. All people, regardless of social or cultural environment, are subject to the influences of these feelings. People hope for happiness, riches, fame, and beauty. They imagine a life free from suffering, a carefree and successful existence without responsibility. They embrace their beliefs and attempt to impose them on others, and most of all, they believe in life everlasting. Considering these common traits of the vast majority of humanity, endorsement of mysticism and alchemy as transformational arts should not be viewed as unusual.

Alchemy is nevertheless often considered a strange or exotic activity practiced by unusual or semi-demented persons inhabiting the fringe of lunacy. Alchemists are generally pictured as wizardly men with long white beards laboring in a cluttered laboratory attempting to make gold from a range of base metals or unusual materials. Alchemy is, in truth, a process of transformation that relates to many activities, and it continues to be practiced by a number of persons.

Alchemy appears to have the characteristics of "an art that [is] occult, secret, and exclusive to a few initiates, and that [can] never be divulged to ordinary people."[21] The basis of alchemy "[lies] in ancient secrets handed on in an emblematical literature and in revelations; the alchemist learned nothing new, but, rather, re-discovered secrets."[22] It is for that reason that alchemy changes relatively little through the centuries. "Though its symbolism changed somewhat, and it developed in several ways during the Middle Ages, and even as late as the sixteenth century, its fundamental theories about the composition of matter did not alter after the end of the ancient world."[23]

The logic or reasoning of alchemy is relatively simple. It seemed reasonable to assume that all matter was composed of certain elements and therefore, it should be an easy matter to arrange or rearrange those elements in a way to transform one material into another. Water when heated to the proper temperature was transformed into air (vapor), and water could be made from air by decreasing temperature (condensation). Reducing the temperature further and the water was transformed into a stone like substance (ice) that could be shattered by a forceful blow. This is but a very basic example of the notion of transformation that fascinated early people. The idea of transformation was also applied to early religious thinking. The righteous person might be transformed into a god, or the person might experience the ultimate transformation by achieving eternal life (immortality). (Most texts refer to male alchemists, but there is no reason to assume that all persons experimenting with the transformation process were one gender or the other.)

People have been transforming one substance into another from early times. Some scholars believe the first alchemists were early peoples experiencing with fire to change the states of matter. They used it to harden clay and to transform iron-bearing earth (FeO) into red iron (Fe_2O_3; red-ocher). They toughened wood, calcined bone, limestone, and shells, transformed water to steam, burned wood to ash, and turned darkness into light. These acts of transformation are fundamental to the alchemic process because they lay the foundation for the reality that natural substances can be altered—converted or transformed—by interaction with an external energy source. Early humanity placed these activities within a mystical realm.

E. J. Holmyard wrote about the duel nature of alchemy, exoteric and esoteric, in his book, *Alchemy* (1990). Holmyard states, "Exoteric alchemy is concerned with attempts to prepare a substance, the philosophers' stone, or simply the Stone, endowed with the power of transmuting the base metals lead, tin, copper, iron, and mercury into the precious metals gold and silver."[24] Esoteric alchemy is a more complicated process of transmutation because it deals with the indefinite prolonging of human life. Holmyard explains that prolonged life was believed possible only through divine grace, and this assumption "led to the development of esoteric or mystical alchemy, and this gradually developed into a devotional system where the mundane transmutation of metals became merely symbolic of the transformation of sinful man into a perfect being."[25]

The duality of the alchemic process, the exoteric and esoteric, offers interesting insight into the thinking — the ideals — of the alchemist. This notion of duality is further amplified by the fact that the two types of alchemy were often intermixed. "However, in some of the mystical treatises it is clear that the authors are not concerned with material substances but are employing the language of exoteric alchemy for the sole purpose of expressing theological, philosophical, or mystical beliefs and aspirations."[26]

Parallel to the practical element of alchemy there was in the West a form of alchemy described as mystical (esoteric). The alchemic connection with occultism is very much a Western way of thinking; whereas, in the East, theosophic doctrines were incorporated, to a degree, into so-called official religions. Teaching of this type in the West was secreted from the ecclesiastical and secular authorities, and was often thought to be a form of "secret science."[27] It was believed that these mystical alchemists did not pursue material gold. They were thought to pursue the purification of the soul and the mystical transformation of the spirit. The "base metals" for these alchemic practitioners were thought to represent "earthly desires and passions,"[28] and other matters that might deter the advance of true human existence.

The transformational nature of alchemy can be observed as changing base metal to precious metal and altering the ordinary path of individuals to attain longevity and immortality. The philosopher may argue which of the two processes has the greater value, but this transformational perspective challenged human thinking centuries before the current era.

The Story of Alchemy and Early Chemistry, a 1924 publication by John Maxson Stillman, supposes, "The human mind is so constituted that it finds a need to attempt to account for observed phenomena, so that theory and practice are inseparable."[29] Stillman speculates that humans have a natural curiosity about what the "earliest natural philosophers thought about nature and changes of substances."[30]

Mary Ann Atwood wrote a treatise titled *Hermetic Philosophy and Alchemy* in 1850. She stated in that book, "The pseudo–Alchemists dreamed of gold, and impossible transformations, and worked with sulphur, mercury, and salt of the mines, torturing all species, dead and living, in vain, without rightly divining the true Identity of nature."[31] She stated, "The means they [the pseudo-alchemists] employed were from literal readings of receipts; they had no theory whereby to direct their research, and making trial of nature, as if she were a thing to change, by chance, found nothing."[32]

The alchemists also call the grand mastery the universal. It tinctures all metals to gold and heals all diseases (universal medicine). Many alchemists sought a grand mastery of elements that was universal. They wanted to transform all metals to gold and heal all diseases. The true alchemists experimented with the transmutation of metals, not for gain, but to add material proofs to "in the interests of science."[33] Other practitioners pursued a more constrained approach that focused on special metal and cures for only one disease.

M. A. Atwood quotes Arnald di Villanova (also written: Arnald de Villenueve, Arnold of Villa Nova, and Arnau de Villanova) in her book *Hermetic Philosophy and Alchemy* (1960

[1850]. Di Villanova was a theologian and an alchemist born in 1245 and died in 1310 (also listed as c.1235 -1312 and c.1240 -1311). He wrote in his book, *Flower of Flowers (Flos florum)*, "That there abides in nature a certain pure matter, which, being discovered and brought by art of perfection, coverts to itself proportionally all imperfect bodies that it touches."[34]

> [O]ne can scarcely dismiss so lightly the science — or art, if you will — that won to its service the lifelong devotion of men of culture and attainment from every race and clime over a period of thousands of years, for the beginnings of alchemy are hidden in the mists of time.[35]

Egyptian Alchemy

> The ancient Egyptian language did not have a word for religion, as we know it, only magic [Egyptian: *heka*] — and more precisely, magical power. Everything in Egyptian life was classed according to its perceived amount of magical power.[36]

Egyptian magicians were involved in an array of activities relating to all aspects of life. They were often called upon to deal with supernatural beings "from major deities and their emanations or messengers, to creatures of the underworld, foreign demons, and malicious ghosts."[37] Magic included spells for treatment of the sick, the formulation of medicines, solutions for infertility, and the means to gain spiritual protection both in this world and in the afterlife. Magic and mysticism had a particularly important role at the time of death. Spells and incantations were a necessary part of the embalming and mummification processes, and interment of the body required recitation of passages from the funerary text.

Magical spells, rites, and talisman, like alchemy, often required the gathering and preparation of the proper ingredients. This material had to be newly gathered for each occasion to prevent contamination from past uses. The rules and recipes for these processes were often specific and involved a number of objects. "Freshly-picked herbs are to be used in remedies. Fresh oil is to be poured into divination bowls. Virgin parchment and fresh ink are to be used for writing charms."[38] Geraldine Pinch writes in *Magic in Ancient Egypt* (1994), "Some of [the ingredients] are bizarre, such as bat's blood or the hair of a murdered man; some exotic, such as Syrian honey, and some expensive, like frankincense, gold leaf or real lapis-lazuli."[39]

Transformation (the passage of the dead person to the glorified person) was an important element in the spiritual life of ancient Egypt that involved magic and myth, as well as quasi-scientific methods. The transformational process related to concerns about the afterlife, and the transition from one physical manifestation to another. The possibility of a disembodied existence was unacceptable, therefore there was a need for preserving the bodily remains that they might be revived or resurrected at the appropriate time. The mummification practice developed because of the belief that the survival of the body was necessary to be reborn into the afterlife that existed in the land to the west where the sun went down. A complex system of preservation techniques was consequently developed to facilitate this process of renewal.

Burial preparations probably originated in early Predynastic times (c.5500-c.3100 B.C.E.), and are described by some researchers as the beginning of alchemy in Egypt. The ancient Egyptians believed in the existence of an afterlife based on the resurrection myth pertaining to Osiris. (The myth relating to the death, dismemberment, reassembly, and mummification of Osiris was mentioned earlier.) The mummified body of the dead was subjected to the rituals that made it like the god (Osiris). This idea of immortality evolved before Pharaonic Egypt, and well before the emergence of the formulation of sophisticated mummification techniques. The methods were different but the objectives were the same. Predynastic burials often included objects of ordinary life, probably signifying the anticipation of an after death experience. Bodies were buried in the fetal position suggesting the expectation of rebirth — resurrection.

Sir Wallis Budge wrote. "For about five thousand years men were mummified in imitation of the mummied (sic) form of Osiris; and they went to their graves believing that their bodies would vanquish the powers of death, and the grave, and decay, because Osiris had vanquished them."[40] Budge observed that the Egyptians "had certain hope of the resurrection in an immortal, eternal, and spiritual body, because Osiris had risen in a transformed spiritual body, and had ascended into heaven."[41]

The process of preparing the body of the deceased required not only the skills necessary for removal and preservation of the internal organs, but also the assistance of the gods. The *ka* was the individual's double; "it was endowed with the person's qualities and faults."[42] (The *ka* is often seen in wall paintings as a miniature version of the principle figure.) The *ka* signifies affluence and power. It was believed the *ka* could eat, drink, and enjoy the odor of incense. (Strong incense was used to disguise the stench of putrefied flesh.) The *ka* was believed to give comfort to the deceased. The care and feeding of the *ka* was assigned to a special group of priests.

The *ka* also appeared as the principle aspect of the human soul in ancient Egyptian religion (magic), and the *ba* was the bird form used to express the mobility of the soul. Originally written with the sign of the *jabiru* bird (a type of stork), the *ba* was later represented as a human-headed hawk. This bird form (**see drawing 7.a**) is often depicted hovering over the body of the deceased for which it is responsible. Burial places are often provided with openings for visits by the *ba*.[43]

The heart had an important role in how the Egyptians viewed the functioning of the body. The Ebers papyrus[44] (a type of medical encyclopedia from the early part of the eighteenth dynasty that ended in 332 B.C.E.) offers an interesting view of the Egyptian understanding of human anatomy and the functioning of the heart. The heart as the primary organ was said to "speak out of the ves-

Drawing 7.a: The *Ba* often shown in bird form with a human head is described as the soul or manifestation of a dead person. It is said to retain the characteristics of the deceased and to journey to the underworld after death of the material body where it is in danger of dying again. The ba is believed to reside in the tomb of the deceased and sometimes to fly up the tomb shaft to visit the world of the living by day. The *ba* of the deceased might attain *akb* status as a "transfigured spirit" if it survived the many challenges associated with the Afterlife, Transfigured spirits live with the gods and are granted semi-divine powers.

sels of every limb. But the vessels were thought to convey a mixture of air, blood, tears, urine, saliva, nasal mucus, semen, and at times even feces."[45] The Taoist Chinese considered the heart as the seat of fire, and they believed it should not be stirred or upset by emotions.

The ancient Egyptians had no interest in the "function of the brain; they apparently believed that the heart was the seat of thought and emotion in the human body."[46] It seems that the brain was considered "stuffing for the head."[47] The idea of thinking with the heart appears frequently in Egyptian writing.

It is generally believed, as noted, that the Western alchemic tradition began in Egypt. One legend reports the secrets of alchemy were taught by a fallen angel. Other stories contribute the origination to Isis, and another mentions Miriam, the sister of Moses, as the source of alchemic instruction. Tradition also grants the beginning of alchemy to the philosopher Democritos (also sometimes identified as Bolos of Mendes) from the Egyptian delta town of Mendes. He reportedly wrote a recipe book in four parts titled *Phusika kai mustika*, loosely translated to mean *Natural and Mystical Things* (see Chapter Nine). One part of the book deals with the making of gold, the second part the making of silver, the third the making of gems, and the forth the making of purple.[48] The recipes are vaguely stated and include references to Greek theories about elements and astrology. Most of the recipes (formulas) end with the phrase, "One nature rejoices in another nature; one nature triumphs over another nature; one nature masters another nature."[49]

The recipes speak of the ennobling of base metal by killing and resurrecting them as gold. Bolos' alchemical practices are described in terms of distillation and sublimation, and he appears to be obsessed with spirits. Other recipes give detailed instructions for dealing with alloying, dyeing, and gold copying, including coloring, coating, and plating.

Geraldine Pinch wonders about the extent of alchemical practice in Egypt. She states in *Magic in Ancient Egypt* (1994) there is a difference of opinion about the "proper significance of alchemy [in Egypt], the art of transmuting base metals into gold. In the late third or early fourth centuries C.E., Zosimus of Penopolis (Akhmin) wrote a treatise in which he claimed that many Egyptian priests practiced alchemy."[50] Pinch notes, "He describes visiting a special alchemical furnace in a temple at Memphis. This was probably a furnace for baking or incinerating magical figurines."[51] "It is doubtful," at least for Pinch, "whether alchemy had any real roots in Egyptian culture, but books on the subject were frequently attributed to Hermes Trismegistus."[52]

It is not possible to attribute the origination of alchemy to one person — or possible one country. There are, however, surviving recipes for making silver and gold that seemingly originated in Egypt, including some that are described as methods for deceiving silver or goldsmiths. Other recipes are for making alloys of gold using silver, copper, tin, zinc, and even iron. Pure gold is soft and although easily shaped, it is equally easy to distort. Amalgams, mixtures of gold and other metals, were stronger and allowed the goldsmith to make new gold by adding the lesser metals during the forming process. The blends were reportedly admired because of their different coloration, durability, and uniqueness.

Tradition promotes the belief that Egypt gave her name to early alchemy, as Egypt is known as the land of Khem or the black soil of the Nile delta. Some researchers have suggested, as already mentioned, that the name is associated with a legendary Egyptian sage named Chemes who supposedly passed on his wisdom in a book called *Chema*.[53] (The idea is that the Arabs added the article al to Chema to form the word al chema.) Although Egypt is generally considered the home of alchemy (at least in the West) and its god Thoth or Hermes in his Greek incarnation, the father of alchemy, other lands and people have contributed as well. China and India have highly developed alchemical traditions that have been practiced for centuries [see below]."[54]

Thoth (or Hermes as he was called by the Greeks) is the Egyptian god of writing, the creator of languages, and representative of the sun god Re. The legendary Thoth (Egyptian: *Djhuty*) or Hermes Trismegistus (Thrice Great) is often considered the founder of alchemy in the Western world. Some historians believe he was an Egyptian priest during the first century of the current era while others contend he lived during the second millennium B.C.E. "Other accounts hold that he was the human incarnation of Thoth the god of wisdom and scribe of the underworld, who came to earth and reigned as pharaoh for 3,226 years."[55] Hermes Trismegistus is credited with writing "36,525 books, comprising all possible human knowledge."[56] The more imaginative researchers have added to the mystical origin of the art by attributing the beginning of alchemy to Moses, King Solomon, or Isis.

"The wisdom of Hermes Trismegistus was thought to encompass all the occult arts, especially astrology and alchemy. Astrology developed in the late first millennium B.C.E. from a fusion of Greek science with Egyptian and Mesopotamian star lore."[57] Researchers have theorized Hermes was call Trismegistus because of his reported knowledge in the three parts of wisdom: alchemy, astrology, and theurgy. He was also thought to be a great priest, great king, and great philosopher (three times great). Some persons believe that Abraham may have learned a portion of his mystical knowledge from Hermes, but there is no conclusive information that Hermes Trismegistus was an actual person or if he was, when he lived.

An important work attributed to Hermes Trismegistus is the Emerald Tablet (*Tabula Smaragdina*) on which he reportedly inscribed the basic principles of astrology as well as occultic and theological topics. One legend assigns the discovery of the emerald tablet to Alexander the Great, and another contends the tablet was found in a cave on the west bank of the Nile possibly in the clutches of the skeletal remains of Hermes Trismegistus. Interestingly, the Emerald Tablet does not specifically address the topic of alchemy, nor does the *Book of the Secret of Creation,* the work of which the Tablet is thought to be a part.

The Tablet (or Table) is believed inscribed with secret formulas for transforming all levels of matter — physical, mental, and spiritual; however, the original of this extraordinary table is not known to exist. A number of reported copies have appeared over the years and all have been carefully translated into several languages. All the copies seem to have a like message that is written in a style to allow for selective interpretation. An often-cited example of the Tablet message is: "That which is above is like that which is below, and that which is below is like that which is above, to accomplish the miracles of one thing."[58] (This passage is much like a Taoist dictum.)

Whatever the meaning of the cryptic writing of the Table, and regardless of the true author (some believe it was Jâbir ibn Hayyân or Apollonius of Tyana), the Table is an integral part of alchemic lore. E. J. Holmyard wrote in *Alchemy* (1990 [1957]), "From the clouds of myth surrounding the early history of the Table, it is not possible to discern the original authorship."[59] Holmyard stated, "There is no doubt that the Emerald Table is [accepted as] one of the oldest and most long-lived of all alchemical documents."[60]

The *Corpus Hermeticum*, another important writing attributed to Hermes Trismegistus, is purported to include secret wisdom. The *Hermeticum* was compiled during the Renaissance but the exact dates of the various texts are difficult to determine. However, it is accepted that segments of the writing correspond with the dialogue style common during Pharaonic Egypt. This type of question and answer exchange between teacher and student was a common format for imparting information at that time.

An Egyptian alchemist regarded by most authorities as authentic is Zosimos of Panopolis who lived during the third century of the current era (see Chapter One). This alchemist and writer reportedly wrote an encyclopedia of twenty-eight books detailing all the knowledge about alchemy that had accumulated in the previous five or six centuries.[61] Zosimos is one of forty authors included in a compendium of alchemical writings that was probably collected in Byzantium in the seventh or eighth century C.E. He promoted the theory there existed a substance that could transform matter instantly. Zosimos called this magical material "the tincture" or "the powder," which was translated to "elixir." It was eventually called the Philosopher's Stone (*Lapis Philosophorum*), "a stone that is not a stone, a stone unknown and known to all."[62]

Egyptian Metallurgy

Alchemy, like magic, sought to demonstrate the reality of cosmic truths in the daily life of its practitioners.[63] Herbert Silberer and Smith E. Jelliffe wrote in *Problems of Mysticism and its Symbolism*, 2009 [1917], "The tradition of craftsmanship in metallurgy, an art that was practiced from the earliest times, was during the speculative period of human culture, saturated with philosophy."[64] Silberer and Jelliffe saw this as especially "the case in Egypt, where metallurgy, as the source of royal riches and especially the methods of gold mining and extraction, were guarded as a royal secret."[65]

The Egyptians metallurgists recovered immense quantity of gold from locations in the deserts near the Nile. One deposit was in Nubia (the name of the region was derived from *nub*, the Egyptian name for gold). The other deposit was in the east between the Nile and the Red Sea. These two locations have been mined for 5,000 years and are the oldest gold mines on earth. It is believed that as much as 1.4 million pounds of gold came from these deposits.[66] Nevertheless, every ounce of the bright metal inspired the desire for more. It was a commodity of trade, a reason for war, and "increasingly, through the ages, kings and commoners alike solicited the aid of supernatural agencies to obtain it."[67] Metallurgists also experimented with plating and lustrous patinas to give the appearance of gold. It is said that some products were so cleverly made that even other goldsmiths could not tell whether the pieces were made of gold.

Color was important in alchemical work and Maria (sometimes called "the Jewess," Mary the Prophet, or Maria Prophetissa) is thought to be among the first to stress this idea. The processes used for coloring metal and the symbolic interpretation of the processes is not possible for the uninitiated to understand. There were various stages in the coloring technique, but "what these stages refer to is at once a chemical procedure related to the changing colours of the matter being worked upon, and the symbolic stages that the alchemist goes through on an inner level."[68] Maria's writings indicate an understanding that the methodology was "both physical and non-physical at the same time."[69]

Maria was considered an alchemical authority and is credited with inventing laboratory equipment used in coloring metals.[70] She is credited with being the mother of Egyptian alchemy, and was sometimes called Miriam and identified as the sister of Moses. The *balneum Mariae* (the bath of Maria) an apparatus of particular importance used in warming ingredients in the formulation of elixirs is attributed to her, as is the *tribikos*, a still. Great attention was given to regulating the fire (heat) during the manufacture of elixirs used in metal patinas and plating. The chemical process is said to require a gentle heat, which was apparently difficult to achieve and maintain before the *balneum Mariae*.

Maria has a saying that appears at the end of receipts attributed to her. She wrote: "*One becomes two, two becomes three, and out of the third comes the one as the fourth.*"[71] The intended message of this passage is unclear. It may relate to the mixing of ingredients, or it may refer to the four elements—fire, air, water, and earth.

Egyptian alchemists interacted with Greeks, Romans, Jews, Arabs, and a range of other believers and non-believers in Alexandria during the centuries immediately before and after the beginning of the current era.

The city of Alexandria, founded in 332 B.C.E, was the capital of Egypt. It was considered a great city open to all manner of ideas and the center of Hellenic scholarship and science for almost one thousand years. The Alexandrian library and museum (Mouseion) was an institution of learning that included the great writings of the time. The Mouseion is described as a large complex of buildings that included the Library of Alexandria. The library housed translations into Greek of major writings from across the Mediterranean, Middle East, and India. It seems likely that it had a major influence on the development of the alchemic process in Egypt.

A second factor contributing to the supportive intellectual environment of Alexandria was the number of religious beliefs and practices centered in the city. The population of the Alexandria included followers of esoteric Egyptian rites and cults of Romans, as well as Jews from the Middle East, and Christians. These belief systems exerted influence on the practices of alchemy along with "a number of competing sects, and various mystery cults from the East [that] introduced secret rituals of rebirth and purification and an orientation toward mystical union with God."[72]

The Roman emperor Aurelian (c.215 – 275) reportedly banned the practice of alchemy to stabilize the value of silver used for making coins. The Roman emperor Diocletian (284–305) destroyed all the texts on the subject of alchemy in the third century of this era. The emperor believed according to various legends, that by banning the practice of alchemy he could deprive the citizenry of Egypt of revenue and thereby control their revolt against Rome. The destruction of the alchemic texts along with other historical documents was undoubtedly a deleterious factor for the development of alchemy in the Western world.

Alchemy in ancient Egypt generally fell into two classes or types. One class was technical and not influenced by mystical ideals. The other class started from the practical perspective but was, from the beginning, intermingled with mystical thoughts. Neither class progressed significantly in the years following the ban on alchemic practice by Diocletian. Time passed without the alchemists being any closer to the "solution of the eagerly sought mystery, speculations and fantastic hallucinations overlay the practical nucleus in ever increasing masses, until toward the end of the Middle Ages the writings of the adapts had become one vast farrago of allegories."[73] The center of alchemic study shifted to Spain and eventually to Latin Europe by the end of the tenth century.

The Arabs subdued Alexandria in 642 C.E. and there is no indication that the lure of the alchemist's laboratory like the popular dependency on magic was forgotten. Communities in ancient Egypt were believed to have at least one wise person or *hekau* (magician) to assist the local people in times of need. These individuals, male and female, were trusted and thought capable of offering advice and performing rituals, using *heka*, or magic, to solve people's problems.[74] The community magician was often the local priest who was responsible for performing magical rituals and "reciting the spells in the temple and during the embalming process and funerals."[75] Magical practices were sometime used for spiritual purposes as well as for practical ends.

The Syrian philosopher Iamblichus (c.250-c.330 C.E.) wrote a book *On The Mysteries of Egypt* (*De Mysteriis*) in which he spoke about the art of theurgy, the magical conjuration of the gods. Egyptian priests were renowned for their theurgic skills. "Iamblichus writes about theurgy as a profound spiritual experience, a secret method by which initiates could encounter, and unite, with the divine."[76] Iamblichus believed that a higher "One" exists outside the range of human knowledge and stresses the virtues by which humanity might attain ecstatic union with the "One."[77] This attitude has the same objective of other forms of mysticism.

Greek Alchemy

> Given the paucity of external evidence, any attempt to construct an account of early western alchemy must consequently use the earliest Greek alchemical texts: texts that are pseudonymous, apocryphal, and dubious.[78]

The *History of Philosophy: Great Thinkers from 600 B.C. to the Present Day* (1999) by Martyn Oliver includes the statement, "The relationship between mythology and philosophy in Greek thought is a complex and irreducible one. Mythology was a fundamental part of Ancient Greek life and very often the focus for philosophy."[79] This relationship was made more important by the lack of historical records before the advent of a sophisticated language in c. 700 to 100 B.C.E. Greek history and philosophy consequently have a great deal of myth and mysticism.[80]

Charles A. Bennett wrote in *A Philosophical Study of Mysticism* (1923), "Mysticism seems to me to have priority in this relationship [with philosophy]. It is not only the completion of philosophy; it is its presupposition. Reason may establish our certainties; it does not initiate them."[81] The task of philosophy might be defined, according to Bennett "as the problem of showing how reality and appearance belong together. Philosophy therefore begins with a distinction that it did not create, with a problem: 'Things are not what they seem. How can this be?'"[82]

Philosophy in Ancient Greece came out of such curiosity instead of secularism although it is often thought that it was the result of a conflict with religion. Curiosity caused philosophers such as Plato and Aristotle to study the question of matter and to draw conclusions about the elements of which matter is composed. Questions such as these were the same as those being considered by alchemists and the theories relation to transformation of the corresponding elements had obvious implications for the alchemic process. As Johannes Fabricius declared in 1976, "The first scientists of the West were philosophers and mystical types to whom practical alchemy was a branch of a comprehensive philosophical system."[83]

The earliest known (Western) alchemical texts are on papyrus and written in Greek perhaps by Egyptians or persons living in Hellenic Alexandria. One papyrus proffers "101 practical recipes for making gold and silver, for purifying and assaying metals, for the whitening and bronzing of metals, for attempts to 'increase' metals by changing the colour of other metals so that they will seem gold."[84] The writing describes the technical process for alloying gold and silver and making imitation precious gems. These were but some of the hermetical concepts that the Greeks received from Alexandria and subsequently integrated within the philosophies of Pythagoreanism, Ionianism, and Gnosticism.

The subject matter in these early documents is representative of the cultural and philosophical setting influencing early alchemy. The documents develop and define technological processes and practical techniques of metallurgy that were originally Egyptian. They incorporated theories of matter and change from the Greek philosophers including "the notion that entities and events in the heavens were mirrored by those on earth; a mystical cast to religious beliefs, with a belief in spirit intermediaries, magic, astrology, and other esotericisms."[85]

The practical nature of Greek philosophy was strong, but in the Hellenistic age, there was a distrust of traditional Greek rationalism primarily due to a breakdown of the distinction between science and religion. Hellenic Alexandria also contributed the god Hermes or Thoth to the Greek pantheon but he was but one of the gods and prophets to who people turned for a divinely revealed wisdom. There was, consequently, no religion governed by fixed creeds in Ancient Greece, nevertheless, advice from the gods was sought for most public and private matters. It was generally believed that gods represented all aspects of life.[86]

Various cults emerged in the inclusive Greek environment. Ionianism, for example, was based on the belief that the universe could be explained through concentration on natural phenomena. This was a theme developed by Plato and Aristotle. Other ritual activities related to nature and renewal. Dionysus was of particular importance as the god of fruitfulness and vegetation. Most Greeks joined in the activities of the Dionysiac cult that included a special consideration of fertility and the production of prodigy. The attention to reproduction was not wholly separated from the idea of death; therefore, the worshipers of Dionysus were attracted to mystic communion with the ancestors, the current generation, and the future members of the community.[87]

Gnosticism, a philosophical and religious movement during the second century, combined a number of different elements and may have introduced the influence of Mithraism into the philosophical thinking of the Greeks. Mithra or Sanskrit Mitra (the word can be translated as either friend or contract) is the god of light and a feature of ancient Indo-Iranian mythology. He was called the mediator. The soldiers of Alexander the Great spread the cult of Mitra throughout the Hellenic world after the defeat of the Persians, and later it became the chief rival to the newly developed religion of Christianity.[88] The Greeks considered Mitra a sun god and the god of justice. The Vedic Mitra was first mentioned about 1400 B.C.E. Legend described Mitra as a child of the earth. He is said to have "killed the life-giving cosmic bull, whose blood fertilizes all vegetation."[89]

The worship of Mitra was not particularly popular in the Greek world, because of its association with the Persians; in spite of this history, the mythical killing of the cosmic bull was an often-depicted image in Hellenic art. The myth tells that with the death of the bull, the creatures of the world emerged from darkness and good and evil began, thus initiating the conditions of human life (a version of partaking of the tree of knowledge). The raven, a messenger in the myth, symbolizes air. The myth included a lion, a serpent, and a bowl to catch the blood of the slain bull. The lion symbolically represented fire, the serpent earth, and the bowl water. The story identifies the four elements (air, fire, earth, and water) and from this beginning, all things were created.[90]

Early myths established the thinking from which later Greek philosophy emerged, and although the lives and work of both Plato (427–347 B.C.E.) and Aristotle (384–322 B.C.E.) predate the Hellenistic Age (beginning roughly 322 B.C.E. and ending, by some accounts, as late as 323 C.E.), the philosophical foundation they inherited and promoted influenced the social, material, political, and spiritual life of the region for centuries. It seems certain that the center for Western alchemic activity in the years before and after the beginning of the current era was Hellenistic Alexandria. The impulses felt in Greece came from that city and included both Greek and Egyptian thinking. It is also likely that "Greek philosophers before Plato, Aristotle, and particularly the Sicilian Empedocles (490–430 B.C.E.), had theories about the nature of matter, the elements which make it up, and how one could change into another."[91]

Empedocles was a philosopher, politician, and poet admired by Aristotle. He advocated the theory that all matter was composed of the four essential ingredients, fire, air, water, and earth, and that nothing could be made or destroyed but merely transformed, depending on the relation of basic substances to one another. (This is obviously the same idea advocated by many later alchemists.) Like Heracleitus (540–480 B.C.E.) before him, Empedocles held that two forces, love (attraction; positive energy) and strife (repulsion; negative energy), either bring together or separate the four substances. (This interaction calls to mind the energetic interplay of the yin and yang.) Strife makes the elements withdraw from the others; Love makes them commingle. The world, according to Heracleitus, was at a stage in which neither force dominated. Love was dominant in the beginning, and the four substances were mixed; later, during the formation of the cosmos, strife caused the elements to separate. The four elements were again arranged in partial combinations in certain places after a time. Volcanoes, for example, show the presence of both water and fire in the earth.[92]

Though there is no record that Heracleitus was an alchemist, he promoted a philosophical perspective that was very much in accordance with alchemists' thinking. He reasoned there was an underlying connection between opposites and that a single substance might be perceived in different ways. Heracleitus wrote that the "world order is an 'ever-living fire kindling in measures and being extinguished in measures.' He extended the manifestations of fire to include not only fuel, flame, and smoke but also the ether in the upper atmosphere."[93] His theory was that "part of this air, or pure fire, 'turns to' ocean, presumably as rain, and part of the ocean turns to earth."[94] The concept of turning to and reverting demonstrates the dynamic equilibrium that maintains an orderly balance in the world. It also acknowledges the transformation of the four basic elements by passing through different stages or conditions.

The metaphysical thinking for which Aristotle is renowned describes the most general or abstract features of reality and the principles that have universal validity. The question of substance therefore allows for both the material and the immaterial. He stated it is not necessary to presume the existence of a discrete sphere of transcendent thoughts of which the separate elements that humanity understands with their senses are but flawed copies, that the world as perceived is the real world. He declared, "It is necessary merely to be able to say that something is generally true of certain types or groups of things in order to build up a system of knowledge about them."[95]

Aristotle's writings covered many topics ranging from physics and poetry to ethics and zoology. His metaphysics, as the philosophical understanding of reality, distinguishes between the "'universal' and that which is merely a particular 'form' or 'substance' and the distinction he makes between the three different substances which make up reality."[96] Aristotle was concerned about analyzing the patterns of reasoning and the nature of life, as well as the importance of knowledge. He studied and wrote about form and matter, substance and essence, change and generation, actual and potential.[97] He questioned what constituted substance, as well as the fundamental elements of the world (see figure 7.1).

Sensible/Perishable	Sensible, Not Perishable	Highly Authority
Animals/Plants	Man	God
Private Sphere	Public Sphere	Religion/Morality
Household/Women	Rational Debate/Politics	Absolute Knowledge
Slaves	The Citizen	The Priest

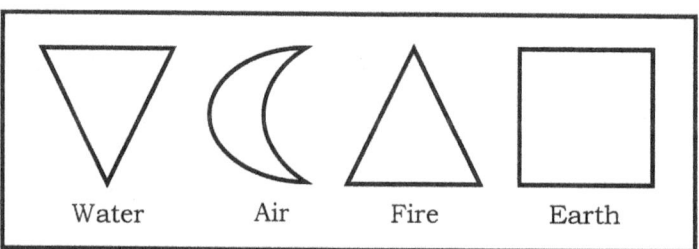

Water   Air   Fire   Earth

Top: Figure 7.1: Aristotle reasoned that aspects of the natural world could be placed in different categories. He studied and wrote about form and matter, substance and essence, change and generation, actual and potential. Aristotle contended that all substances were either perishable or eternal. His theory was the relevant element could be divided into three categories. He believed that "sensible" substances were changeable (not fixed in status or condition) and that there were different types of change including quantity and quality, increase or decrease, generation or destruction. These changes or transformations occur when the state of a substance become something contrary to its nature. *Above:* Figure 7.2: The idea of the four earthly elements as recognized by Plato and Aristotle was very important to the theorizing of alchemists. Aristotle added a fifth element, ether, which related to the heavenly sphere. The four "earthly" elements were believed to have a "natural" place whereas ether as a divine substance was in continuous movement.

In addition to this concept of substances, Aristotle endorsed the notion of the four earthly elements as envisioned by Empedocles and elaborated on the original theory: "According to Aristotle, an element is an irreducible constituent of material things, actually or potentially present in them and into which they can be divided."[98] He believed that all bodies were "composed of these elements in different proportions and combinations" and that to "change the proportions and combination of these elements in a body would be to make a different body."[99] This subdivision of reality into basic elements is the same process advocated by early alchemists. While Aristotle drew certain conclusions about the world by placing selected elements in particular forms, he used the same logic or reasoning in formulating the "four elementary qualities to matter — hot, moist, cold and dry; and four elements: fire, water, air, and earth"[100] (**see figure 7.2**).

Aristotle theorized there are elemental properties identified as principles and not "actual flames or drops of water,"[101] they were composed of defining qualities. He contended each element had a realm to which it belonged and to which it would return if left undisturbed (see Chapter One).

This idea of four earthly elements, fire, air, water and earth, as the basis of matter was therefore already in place in Plato's *Timaeus* (written c. 360 B.C.E.), which has a claim to be the first treatise on theoretical chemistry and was the only dialogue of Plato's which was known in Europe before the late twelfth century."[102] Aristotle recognized a fifth element, ether, which is a divine substance that composes heavenly spheres. The four earthly elements have a natural place, whereas ether is in perpetual motion.

It was not possible for any one of the four earthly elements to change into another. Fire could not become air, water, or earth, etc. They had to pass through the medium of the quality they shared. Air, for example, when linked with fire was hot, however, when linked with water, it was moist (see drawing 1.1). Two opposing elements can be joined to form a third by removing one quality from each. This is exemplified by connecting fire and water and eliminating the cold and dry qualities, the resulting element is earth. Regardless of the manipulation, the prime matter of the elements does not change. Only the form is altered.[103]

There is a close affinity between essences of certain materials (elements). The "changes between elements is easier when they share a common characteristic; as in the case of fire and air which are both hot, and air and water, which are both moist."[104] There is a balancing between materials based on their characteristics. Fire and air are hot, whereas water and earth are cold. Fire and earth are dry while air and water are moist. These characteristics allow easier transfer from one alchemic state of being into another. Cold water treated with heat is transformed (transmuted) into hot air (vapor). In contrast, hot air when cooled produces water (condensate). Air is moist because it draws vapor (called exhalation) from the earth that is hot and dry. However, as Aristotle explains[105] there are some elemental manifestations that are opposites and cannot be transmuted directly into another. A dead thing, as an example, cannot be restored directly into a living thing. The dead thing must first return to matter (decompose) before it can be changed into its opposite. The logic is direct and easily calculated.

Aristotle supposed that all substances were composed of the four earthly elements arranged in different proportions. This supposition could be verified by any number of simple demonstrations. For instance, earth mixed with water became liquid; when exposed to air, it became dust; and when heated with fire, it became hard. Such examples are numerous and easy to demonstrate. Such demonstrations gave credence to the idea that all substances could be altered by manipulation of one or more of the basic elements. This notion is the foundational thesis of alchemy.

Another aspect of alchemy received special attention during the Hellenistic period. Metallurgy was an art practiced from the earliest times, especially in Egypt where methods of gold mining and extraction were guarded secrets. It was, however, during the speculative period of human culture, a period beginning roughly in 500 B.C.E. that metallurgy melded with Greek philosophy. Archimedes (c.290–280 to 211–212 B.C.E.), a Greek mathematician and inventor, was responsible for a number of metallurgical innovations during the Hellenistic period. He developed, for example, a process for measuring the purity of gold by determining its weight based on water displacement. "In Hellenistic period the art of metal working, knowledge of which spread abroad and in which the interest has been raised to almost scientific character, was penetrated by the philosophical theories of the Greeks."[106]

Chinese Alchemy

It seems that Chinese alchemy is the oldest of the Eastern branches, and may even predate Western alchemy. (The Chinese word for elixir, chin-je, may be the root of the Arabic *kimia*.) The Yellow Emperor Huang Ti (2704–2595 B.C.E.) is the legendary first alchemist in China, who learnt the art from three immortal women, who also generously saw fit to instruct him in the arts of love.[107]

The founder of Chinese alchemy, as it is known today involving the search for immortality, is believed to be Tsou Yen at a time during the fourth century before the Common Era. Alchemy as a process of gold making appeared at a later date. The concern of the Chinese alchemist in the beginning was transformation of the physical being, that is, the quest for health and longevity. The first historical reference to alchemy in connection with the making of gold is in 144 B.C.E. when an imperial edict declared the punishment of public execution for anyone caught counterfeiting gold.[108]

It is generally acknowledged that Taoist alchemy developed in parallel with the rise of Taoist mysticism. "Alchemical Taoism [reflecting its origin] is concerned with cultivating health, longevity, and immortality, and is divided into external and internal alchemy."[109] It is possible China was influenced by Indian alchemic practices or the influence may have gone from China to India. The record is unclear. It seems certain, however, that China had an early mystical and alchemic tradition that spread to Tibet during the first millennium of the current era. The basic principles of Chinese (Taoist) alchemy emphasized the correspondence of above and below, and of inner and outer, the interrelationship of all things and the subsequent ability to transform.

"The general term [often] used for alchemy in Chinese literature is '*lien tan*.'"[110] The words lien tan meaning pill or drug of transformation gives insight into the initial attitude of the Chinese toward alchemy. "The concepts of Chinese alchemy were, at first, more closely aligned with medicine than metallurgy. When the issue of physical immortality was considered in the fourth century B.C.E., the magical drug (elixir) was acknowledged about that time. A magical elixir was subsequently identified early in the first century B.C.E. (see Chapter One).[111]

Ored Simon Johnson wrote in *A Study of Chinese Alchemy* (1974 [1928]), "Prolongation of the physical life — with immortality as the ultimate goal — was the aim of the first phase of alchemy."[112] The essential nature of Chinese alchemy was divided from early times. The general term for alchemy was *lien tan*, as noted, however *nei tan* was used to refer to the alchemic practices for prolonging life while *wai tan* identified the alchemy of transmuting metals as a primary endeavor.[113]

Much of what is known about early alchemical practice in China comes from the period of the Warring States, the fifth to the third century before the current era. Alchemy as physical transformation was associated with Taoism, the mystical religion founded by Lao-tzu (Laozi) in the sixth century B.C.E. However, the Chinese quest for immortality probably started during the eighth century B.C.E. Belief in the possibility of obtaining unending existence either in body or spirit with the use of drugs gained greater notice in the fourth century B.C.E. The magical drug (elixir of life) referred to as drinkable gold was mentioned at about that time.

A social class of specialized individuals with skills in alchemic practices developed during the Ch'in dynasty in China (221–207 B.C.E.), and continued into the Han dynasty (206 B.C.E. — 219 C.E.). These specialists were the *fang-shin* or masters of the formulae. The group was divided into two areas of expertise. One group concentrated on magic, divination, and healing, while the other group focused on the arts of longevity and immortality. The *fang-shih* who specialized in magic employed a form called talismanic magic, because it used symbols and words of power to invoke the spirits to heal and to protect.[114]

Taoist alchemy is sometimes called physiological alchemy because its goal is to transform the physiological structure and functions of the body.[115] It is concerned with cultivating health and immortality. Physiological alchemy is also divided into two methodologies: one external and the other internal. Those persons following the external school believed that immortality could be achieved by ingesting a pill or elixir composed of the appropriate minerals and herbs. The methods of external alchemy were concerned with building a furnace, gathering minerals and herbs, and compounding substances. Internal alchemists followed a less invasive approach.

Taoist alchemy introduced the concept of *ch'i* (internal vitality and spirit) according to legend, and gave Taoism a reputation as an art of health and longevity. The Taoist approach is concerned with the transformation of human beings to give them both longer life and a closer relationship with the Tao. This process was approached with both internal and external techniques. External alchemy (*wai-dan*) included diet as well as the ingestion of minerals and herbs. This practice was known as external alchemy because it involved adding something to the body from outside. Internal alchemy did not include consuming amalgams, herbs, or elixirs. It probably evolved slightly later than external alchemy (possibly because so many patients died of ingested compounds). Both forms of alchemy were practiced together for many years.

The essence of internal alchemy, that is, to become immortal, relies "not solely by our own efforts, but by achieving harmony — unity — with the eternal Way."[116] Internal alchemy gives attention to diet, sleep, sexual activity, exercise, and a range of other items related to physical health and well-being. There is also a strong emphasis on spiritual health. This sentiment is echoed by Taoist yoga, which emphasizes that all humans are endowed with physical and spiritual energies, but they are undeveloped, and consequently, underutilized. "The metaphysical and ethical elements [as described in the *Tao Te Ching*], however, are of basic importance as being the soil in which the seed thoughts of Chinese alchemy found root and flourished."[117]

Many ideas about alchemy were affixed to Taoist canon, therefore much of the information relating to alchemy is the result of that connection. The mystical practices found their way into early Taoist writings. For example, the earliest surviving medical book, the *Huang Ti nei Ching* or "The Yellow Emperor's Esoteric Classic" written in the third century B.C.E. is theoretically based on the dualistic cosmic concept of the yin and yang. This book and the *Yün chi ch'i ch'ien (Seven Tablets in a Cloudy Satchel)* dated 1023 are sources of alchemic information. The oldest known Chinese alchemical writing is said to be the "*Chou-i ts'an t'ung ch'i* (Commentary on the I Ching)."[118] The most famous Chinese book on alchemy is the *Tan chin yao chüeh (Great Secrets of Alchemy)*.[119] This book was probably written by Sun Ssu-miao during the middle years of the sixth century of the current era. This document expounds on the process for creating elixirs made of mercury, sulfur, and the salts of mercury and arsenic to attain immortality.[120] An earlier book attributed to Wei Po-yang of the Eastern Han dynasty (25 — 220 C.E.) titled *T'san-tung-chi (The Triplex Unity)* is considered by Taoists the ancestor of all texts of alchemy.[121]

The *Ts'an T'ung Ch'i* (or *Chou-i ts'an t'ung ch'i*), is a document that appears to describe "an alchemic process for transmuting base metals into gold."[122] Some persons consider the work to be exactly what it seems to be, however others contend it contains "instructions for compounding a golden pill able to confer perennial youth, immense longevity, and perhaps flesh-and-blood immortality."[123] It explains to other readers "a method of creating, by sexual or non-sexual means, a spirit-body capable of enjoying eternal life."[124] It is for the mystics "the key to that shining apotheosis whereby one becomes pure spirit, free to plunge into the luminous undifferentiated ocean of the Tao."[125] A fifth interpretation contends the document is a manual of the art of government and war.

Gold, as a primary element in all aspects of alchemy (internal and external), is believed to come from the center of the earth and to have mystical connections with *jue* (sulphur), yellow quicksilver (mercury), and the future life.[126] The celebrated Chinese alchemist Pao P'u Tzu (pseudonym of Ko Hung, 254–334) insisted alchemical gold was superior to real gold because it is the "very essence of a variety of ingredients."[127] Ko Hung said, "If with this alchemical gold you make dishes and bowls, and eat and drink out of them, you shall live long."[128] He believed made gold was better for the sake of longevity than natural gold. The Chinese considered substances found in the ground "impure and that they needed 'preparation,' just like foodstuffs, in order to be assimilable."[129]

Taoist alchemy often presents information in an indirect way using analogies, metaphors, and symbolic language. The Taoist Great Triad of Heaven-Man-Earth, for instance, is not as it seems. It states, "Heaven represents the Spirit or Essence, Earth the Substance, and Man the synthesis of both and mediator between them, himself partaking of the dual nature of Heaven and Earth."[130] The triad also represents sulphur, quicksilver and salt, terms that convey a double meaning — material and spiritual. J.C. Cooper, *Taoism: The Way of the Mystic,* explains that sulphur "as *yang*, solar, fire, symbolizes the Will of Heaven, the active principle. Quicksilver as *yin*, lunar, the waters, is the passive and limiting power."[131] The third element, salt, "the 'crystallization,' as the result of the action and reaction of the yin-yang, is the neutral zone in which the contrary forces are stabilized and reconciled"[132] **(see figure 7.3)**.

The *Arts from the Garden of Secrets* described alchemical methods in conjunction not only with longevity techniques, but also the rites for "conjuring spirits"[133] in similarly imprecise terms. The use of such abstract writing, as well as using alchemistic signs that became symbols of psychological processes is an approach close to the original ideas of Lao Tzu.[134]

John Blofeld wrote about "The Secret Yogic Alchemy" in his book, *Taoism: The Road to Immortality* (1985). He emphasized, "Born of the Tao and permeating the cosmos are three marvelous energies — *ching* [essence], *ch'i* [vitality], and *shên* [spirit]."[135] He identifies these three treasures as "the life-giving powers wherewith the Tao sustains the universe, causing within the limitless void the coming into being, the rise and fall of the myriad entities that constitute the realm of appearance."[136] In their subtle cosmic and original forms,

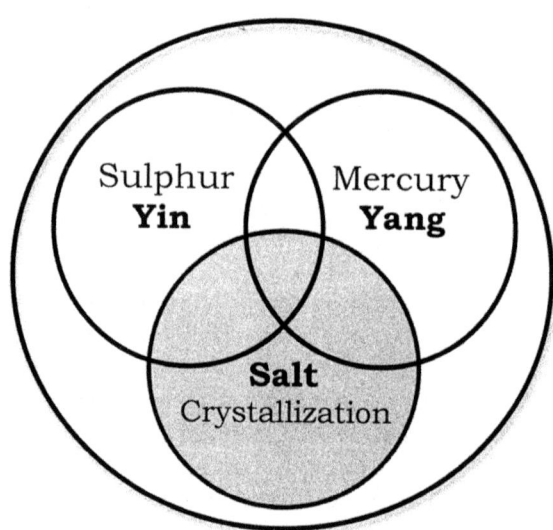

Figure 7.3: The theory that dominated the alchemic thinking beyond the Middle Ages in much of the Western world involved mercury (or quicksilver) and sulphur in various combinations. It was reasoned that mercury, liquid metal, mixed with sulphur, a stone that burned, in proper proportions would produce gold or silver. A third ingredient, salt was added later as a crystallization element. Taoist also included salt in their alchemic experimentation at some point in history. They viewed it as a way of bringing together the yin and yang elements inherent in mercury and sulphur.

Blofeld explains, "these energies are pure and holy, the very source of light and life, creative powers that bring about stupendous transformation. Only a sage of the highest attainment can gauge their unsullied perfection."[137]

Alchemy is closely related to other belief systems throughout the East, and the relationship of those practices is particularly important in China. This inclusive way of thinking is especially observable in the teaching practices and medical attitudes advocated by Taoism. The alchemical work was seen as a way to break free from time and its associated ravages — old age, illness, and death.[138] Alchemy for the Taoist "consists first in controlling the heart (the seat of fire) so that it cannot be stirred by the seven emotions [pleasure, anger, sorrow, joy, love, hate and desire]."[139] It is important that the heart is not "upset by the five thieves [the eye, ear, nose, tongue and body]; the six sense organs are immobilised and the generative force cannot be easily aroused."[140]

Immortality as the outcome of the Chinese alchemic process had a specialized meaning that does not concern itself with a clear distinction between spirit and matter. The Taoist idea of the Oneness of all creation recognized the difference between soul and body as only being one of quality and material or kind. The Taoist considered the soul "the finer essence of the human organism,"[141] therefore it did not enter into the issue of immortality. "By virtue of its fine essence it [the soul] was, 'by nature' immortal. Death was simply the separation of the finer — soul — essence from the coarser — physical — essence of the organism."[142] This separation was viewed as undesirable because it involved the loss of the physical senses and therefore placed distinct limitations upon the quality of life.[143]

Consistent with this thinking, the internal alchemists believed all the ingredients of immortality are found inside the body. These substances had to be refined and transformed by practice of calisthenics, meditation, and sexual yoga. The methods of internal alchemy are therefore concerned with cultivating the energy of life in the body (*ch'i*) without the aid of external substances. Early Taoist alchemists practiced internal alchemy (the slow method of achieving immortality) while they pursued the research and manufacturing of elixirs (the more immediate path to long life).[144]

Eva Wong wrote about Chinese internal alchemy in *The Shambhala Guide to Taoism* (1997). "Chang San-feng, the originator of *t'ai-chi ch'uan* [T'ai chi, "Grand Ultimate Fist" in the Western martial arts], began to incorporate the practice of internal martial arts into internal alchemy."[145] *T'ai-chi ch'uan* draws upon *T'ai Chi* (Chinese: "Great Ultimate") as described in the *I Ching*. *T'ai Chi* is the source and union of the two primary aspects of the cosmos, *yang* (active) and *yin* (passive). *T'ai Chi* was associated with *li*, the highest rational principle of the universe during the Sung dynasty (906–1279 C.E.). *Li* in turn engenders *ch'i*, which "is transformed through the *yin and yang* modes of development into the Five Elements (wood, earth, fire, metal, and water),"[146] the basic components of the physical universe.

The physical expressions of *yin* and *yang* are water and fire; therefore, "knowing how to use fire and water and when to apply heat and when to cool are crucial to cultivating energy and renewing life."[147] The *yin* and yang are opposing forces; therefore, they constituted the wholeness of the universe and the completeness of all things. Because it was from these two forces that the universe was created, this principle of dualism is an important factor in Chinese thought, for it permeated both the material and the moral worlds. This concept of dualism became a central element of Confucianism, and consequently, it is an influential element in Chinese thinking and alchemy. Taoist support the notion, "Since man was a part of the Universe, it was a logical conclusion that he shared in the properties and manifestations of the *yin* and *yang*. He was considered to be a product of the two forces, combining in himself the respective qualities of each."[148]

The Tantric tradition found in India, China, and Tibet promotes the search for immortality by giving advice on the proper way to prolong the adherent's life span and vitality. The medical Tantras promote the practices of inner alchemy. They rely on elixirs concocted from the purified essences of mercury and gold, as well as the skills of a perfectly qualified (sexual) companion.[149] The prescribed blend of elements differed but the basic components were often the same. The medicine of the immortals, of the highest rank is cinnabar (mercury sulfide: HgS), next is gold, then silver, followed by various species of the *chih* [divine herbs], and finally the five species of jade.[150] The medicine considered most effective in attaining immortality was a mixture of cinnabar and gold.

Many Taoist alchemists saw no conflict between the methods of ingesting of minerals and transforming the body and mind from within. They found, at various times, no need to distinguish between external and internal techniques. "It was only when the two methods were regarded as incompatible [especially after the T'ang dynasty, 618–906 C.E.] that it became necessary to distinguish between them."[151] The Tantric adherents also gradually moved away from ingesting potentially harmful materials, relying more on herbal compounds, meditation, and physical activities.

> When passion and nature unite this is called the union of the elements of metal (*chin*) and wood (*mu*). When the generative forces of spirit unite this is called the mingling of the elements of water and fire. When thought is stabilized this is the fullness of the five elements (metal, wood, water, fire, and earth).[152]

Although the Taoist tradition is divided into two branches, the philosophical and the religious, a commonality of purpose connects the two parts. Both branches endorse the "fundamental belief in immortality and ascension into heaven [the cosmic realm]."[153] The philosophical Taoist doctrine includes a theoretical interpretation of human life as well as practical instructions on how to pursue the Tao and thereby to attain the cosmic state, whereas the goal of Taoist religious thinkers is to "make people overcome the narrow confines of ordinary life, to attain longevity and immortality."[154]

The underlying principles of Chinese alchemy are those relating to understanding the formation and functions of the cosmos. This knowledge is necessary to support the idea that the cosmos and humanity obey common laws, and that humanity is the cosmos in miniature. "The same laws rule for the one as for the other, and from the one a way leads into the other. The psyche and the cosmos are related to each other like the inner and outer worlds."[155] It is understood, therefore, that "man participates by nature in all cosmic events, and is inwardly as well as outwardly interwoven with them."[156] The concept of transformation (fulfilling) is both an inward and outward process. It is with this fulfillment (transformation) that the alchemist can transcend space and time.

The internal art of the Taoists was to "prolong life, promote health, preserve youth, nurture vitality, and enhance awareness. Attaining all of these goals is not easy, but diligent practitioners are able to achieve most of them."[157] In other terms, on the highest level, the goal was to attain celestial immortality. Although physical exercise may appear to be contrary to the Taoist attitude of no action (*wu-wei*), properly regulated it is conducive to health and longevity. The Taoist writer Lü Pu-wei (d. 237) "advocated physical exercise as a health measure, because of its aid in acquiring the 'vital' breath."[158] Only when action interferes with harmony and oneness is it evil. The restful period following physical exercise exemplifies those qualities of inaction and indifference characteristic of Tao.[159]

Eva Wong states, "practitioners combined meditation and calisthenics, and some even incorporated the *Shang-ch'ing* methods of absorbing the essence of the sun, moon, and stars in their practice of cultivating health and longevity."[160] Although external alchemy declined in the tenth century, some internal alchemists reintroduced the use of herbs to supplement the internal methods. It is important to note as Wong explains, "These internal alchemists, however, had one thing in common: they all acknowledged that internal alchemy involved both physical and psychological transformation. In this respect, all were proponents of the dual cultivation of body and mind."[161]

The nurturing of physical and mental energies relates to the idea of shape — the absolute void taking shape. The shaping of the void is the "sublimation of the spirit; this is the sublimation both within and without."[162] This is the union of the positive and negative. Lu K'uan Lü wrote in *Taoist Yoga: Alchemy and Immortality* (1973), quoting an unidentified immortal master, "Shape is formed by Tao (immortality) and life is made eternal through alchemy which consists of borrowing boundless prenatal vitality to continue (the existence of) limited bodily form."[163] Lu reinforced his statement, "in other words," he wrote, "this boundless prenatal vitality which is the true essence of the positive and negative principles between heaven and earth, is used to create the immortal foetus which now has shape."[164]

"The human body is like a rootless tree and relies solely on the breath as root and branches. A lifetime is just a dream, like an out breath which does not guarantee the in breath after it."[165] The body, heart, and thought are called the three families (*san chia*) in alchemic thinking, and the generative force, (vital) breath, and spirit are the three treasures (*san pao*).[166] Body, heart, and thought represent the principal (*chu*), and the generative force, (vital) breath, and spirit are the function (*gung*). The union of these elements into one whole produces the elixir of immortality.[167] The control and return of these three elements (or factors) to the one source can only occur in the condition of serene voidness. "When the heart is empty of externals spirit and nature unite, and when the body is still, the generative force and passions are extinct. When thought is reduced to the state of serenity, the three factors mingle into one."[168]

Taoism compared the refinement of the human body with the processing of metals. "There is an exact parallel between the transmutation of the gross powers of body and mind into pure spirit and that of base metals into the pure element, gold."[169] The Tao alchemist considered the location in the body where energy is refined and collected to be the cauldron. "When the impurities are burned off, the golden pill, or the elixir of immortality, emerges. The elixir, in Taoist alchemy, is also called the sacred fetus, because, like a fetus in a womb, to mature it has to be incubated for a period of time."[170]

The alchemist in his or her essential being "is the product of the attributes of Heaven and Earth, by the interaction of the dual forces of nature, the union of the animal and the intelligent soul, and the finest subtle matter of the five elements."[171] Taoism focused outward on this attitude toward nature. A part of this belief accommodated the natural transformation of metals. This concept promoted the thesis that all metals will eventually become gold if allowed to properly mature. The time of maturation was thought to be long and the alchemists simply claimed to accelerate the process. Time for the alchemist was transcended, thereby allowing the adept to access the realm of timelessness. The same was true with space. The alchemist placed himself or herself and his or her work at the center, at a point devoid of dimension. "From this spaceless and timeless point he [the alchemist] is able to move along the axis that connects the higher and lower levels of being."[172]

Anne Bancroft wrote in *Religions in the East* (1974), "The actual practice of Taoism came more and more to be identified with alchemy and yoga practices, the search for the drug of immortality, and with spells and charms to ward off demons." Bancroft continued, "The true mystics of Taoism felt the power of natural scenery and were deeply moved by moments of ineffable beauty, such as the mysterious grace of a willow tree seen against the sky, or water reeds bending in the breeze."[173]

Taoism alchemy degenerated during the Han period [206–219 C.E.]. It evolved into an external wizardry. The Taoist court magicians, however, continued to seek the philosopher's stone to create gold out of the baser metals and gain for people physical immortality.[174] Various mixtures were made and tested. Nonetheless, years later, "toward the end of the Southern dynasties [c. 580 C.E.], the Taoist alchemists were having doubts about ingesting compounds made from lead, mercury, cinnabar, and sulphates. Many alchemists and their patrons died eating elixirs concocted from poisonous materials."[175]

Alchemy had resurgence during the T'ang dynasty (616–906 C.E,). This era is sometimes called the "Golden Age of External Alchemy." Royal patronage promoted the creation of a new group of Taoist alchemists. These individuals focused on external alchemy and consequently worked exclusively in the research and development of the elixir of immortality. Taoists who experimented with the external pill prior the T'ang dynasty also practiced other techniques for prolonged existence. However, with the increased interest in the pills of immortality by T'ang dynasty emperors, a greater number of Taoists were exclusively involved with external alchemy.

As the Taoist view changed, the values associated with life and personal being were transformed or reformed to reflect the values advocated by Lao Tzu. The emphasis was upon becoming one with the inner way of the universe.[176] The notion of greatness or fulfillment had a double meaning. First, it involved "*inner greatness*, which is a magnitude of spirit reflected in the peace and contentment of the individual in his or her completeness."[177] Second, it involved "*outer greatness*, which is manifested in the ability to live well practically, dignifying the social context of one's ordinary day-to-day existence."[178]

> See nothing; hear nothing; let your soul be wrapped in quiet; and your body will begin to take proper form. Let there be absolute repose and absolute purity; do not weary your body nor disturb your vitality — and you will live forever.[179]

Indian Alchemy

> The oldest Indian writings, the *Vedas* (Hindu sacred scriptures), contain the same hints of alchemy that are found in evidence from ancient China, namely vague references to a connection between gold and long life.[180]

Many beliefs and practices come from the complex religious and mystical concepts of India. The celestial vista includes countless gods and demons encountered in social and spiritual manifestations that are but illusions and not reality. These psychosomatic apparitions are dispelled once the soul attains fully liberated knowledge, therewith achieving an un-shadowed view of reality. An acknowledged intellectual objective of Hinduism is to be absorbed into the Infinite, thus, fulfilling the desire for transcendence from the material world. This path to transformation is pursued through self-examination, the termination of physical powers, and belief in the spiritual guidance of a mystical adept.

The Hatha yogis and the Tantrists view their transformation goal as transmuting their bodies into incorruptible ones, which are called "'divine body' (*divya-deha*), 'body of gnosis' (*jñâna-deha*), 'perfect body' (*siddha-deha*) or, in other contexts, the body of 'the one delivered in life' (*jivan-mukta*)."[181]

Although the word alchemy is commonly used in the West (based on the nomenclature assigned by Latin Europe in the twelfth century), the Greeks, Chinese, and Indians, normally spoke of The Art to describe the quest for knowledge of divine transformation. This term was used to express the idea of change or transmutation whether speaking of metals or humans. Another term, *Rasâyana* (the way of the *rasas*), is a Sanskrit word used in India for alchemy after about the tenth century C.E. It was use before that time in classical Indian medicine to mean "rejuvenation therapy."[182] The term *rasa-rasayana* first appeared in Buddhist and Hindu tantric texts in about the eighth century in reference to the supernatural power (*siddhi*) relating to magical elixir.[183] (*Siddhi* is a Sanskrit word that can be translated to mean perfection or attainment.) *Raseshvara darshana* is translated as "the science of mercury."[184]

Rasâyana is an art that includes certain operations, drugs, and compound medicines, most of which come from plants. It restores the "health of those who [are] ill beyond hope, and gives back youth to fading old age, so that people become again what they were in the age near puberty."[185] Following the prescribed regimen is said to make white hair black again, restore the keenness of the senses, rejuvenate juvenile agility, and even revitalize sexual energy.[186]

The *Mahâbhârata*, an important Sanskrit epic of ancient India, contains a great quantity of philosophical and devotional information including a description of the "four goals of life"— right action, purpose, pleasure, and liberation. The *Bhagavad-Gita*, the instructive dialogue between Lord Krishna and Arjuna (see Chapter One) is a part of the *Mahâbhârata*. The authorship of the *Mahâbhârata* is generally attributed to Vyasa (also called Veda Vyasa as the compiler of the Vedas or Krishna Dwaipayana). Krishna is an important character in the *Mahâbhârata*.

Although the quest for gold is a part of Indian alchemy, much of alchemy focuses on physical and spiritual transformation through right action, meditation, and body control. These elements are formulated within the practice of yoga (see Chapter Six). The *Vedas* are viewed as a social and cultural reminder of these aspects of life. Writing in *The Forge and the Crucible*, Mircea Eliade states, "In India, too, there is an abundance of evidence for the existence of alchemy as a spiritual technique.... First, there is the 'popular' tradition ... concerning the yogi-alchemists."[187] Eliade goes on to say, "These [yogi-alchemists], by means of the rhythmic control of the breathing (prânâyâma) and the use of vegetable and mineral remedies, are said to have succeeded in prolonging their youth indefinitely and in transmuting ordinary metals into gold."[188]

Alchemic practice is associated with Hatha-yoga and Tantrism; therefore, the notion of transformation of base metals into gold is considered more of a symbolic concept than a true objective. Liberation, the fourth of the four goals, requires self-purification and separation from material bondage that causes repeated birth and death in the material world. True liberation includes control of mental desires and the tendencies to indulge in sensual pleasures. Attaining liberation is viewed as the highest path to salvation from the recycling existence of death and rebirth in the material environment. These practices, though alchemic in nature, are inherent within the yoga tradition. Liberation from rebirth, however, is uniquely a part of Buddhism as the elimination of psychological attachments by extinguishing desire, which results in subduing karma and the prevention of rebirth.

The Indian Buddhist monk-philosopher Nâgârjuna (c.150 – c.250 C.E.) is regarded as the author of a large number of alchemistical treatises. He is the founder of Mâdhyamika, the Middle Path school of Mahâyâna Buddhism. His concept of emptiness (sûnyatâ) is considered an intellectual and spiritual achievement. He wrote "critical analyses of views about the origin of existence, the means of knowledge and the nature of reality."[189] His writings questioned the assumptions about the existence of stable substances. Such concepts lend themselves to ideas of transmutation. Nâgârjuna promoted the notion of change or transformation by proposing liberation through showing the interconnectedness of all things. This view included the perspective in which human life evolves in the natural and social worlds. His central concern is the emptiness of all things, which in turn acknowledges the constantly changing and therefore the variable nature of all phenomena.

Nâgârjuna sought to understand all philosophical assessments of reality and found them self-contradictions. He subsequently developed a theory of knowledge based on two sets of criteria — between two orders of truth.[190] That he is referred to as a magician and alchemist in the early fourteenth century Jainas author, Merudtunga's *Prabandhacintamani* may relate more to his philosophical activities than alchemical. Nonetheless, one legend proclaims he concocted an elixir that enabled him to fly through the air, and another tells "when famine was ravaging the land, he [Nâgârjuna] made gold and exchanged it for grain imported from distant countries."[191]

Nâgârjuna, an advocate of dialectical thinking, is recognized as the author of important works: the *Mûlamadhyamakakârikâ* (more commonly known as *Ma dhya me ka Karika*; in English: "Fundamentals of the Middle Way") and *Vigrahavyavadtani* ("Averting the Arguments"). Both these texts are critical analyses of views about the origin of existence, the means of knowledge, and the nature of reality.[192] There are, in addition, a number of Tantric (magical) texts attributed to Nâgârjuna.

Early Indian natural philosophy includes theories of nature based on the five material elements (fire, wind, water, earth, and space). These texts dating from the fifth to third centuries B.C.E. also include the concept of vitalism ("animated atoms"), as well as the duelist nature of love and hate, and action and reaction.[193] Vitalism, a concept investigated by Aristotle, considers the balance and imbalance in the vital energies that distinguish living matter from non-living matter. Vitalism is associated with the yogic concept of *prâna* (breath; the body's vital airs or energies) in the eastern traditions. This principle may be applied alchemically to all matter. Consequently, the material elements and notion of vitalism play an important role in alchemy and subsequently in chemistry.

The concept of vitalism is instrumental in determining the distinction between organic and inorganic substances. This principle states that organic materials possess vital forces while inorganic materials do not; consequently, organic materials cannot be synthesized from inorganic components. This concept follows Aristotle's distinction between the mineral kingdom and the animal and vegetative kingdoms.

The concept of vitalism in alchemic application requires non-living matter to be putrefied before revitalized is possible. The notion of putrefaction is a part of making the matter more refined and stable. Putrefaction, in this sense, is the disintegration or decomposition of matter as a temporary regression because the seed must rot, and the body must die before new growth and resurrection is possible.[194] Metal, for example, is converted into an inert mass or powder by heat, grinding, or pulverizing before it is given new form — resurrected.

The concept of organic and inorganic material has a direct application in alchemy. Inorganic matter can be melted and can be restored to its previous condition when removed from the heat. Organic matter, in contrast, is cooked when heated thereby transforming it into new forms that cannot be restored. Cooking or heating is often required for purification. Arthur Waite wrote in *The Hermetic Museum* 1990 [1893], "Quicksilver is the mother of all metals, on account of its coldness and moistness; and if it be once purified and cleaned of all foreign matter it cannot be mixed any more with grossness of any kind, neither can it changed back into an imperfect metal."[195]

The primary purpose of Indian alchemy, like Yoga and Tantrism, is to "cleanse the body and mind, aiming for the so-called 'glorified body' that is impervious to time and decay."[196] The alchemists' intention was to prolong youth by the release of "hidden energies that are latent within the body in order to gain enlightenment and absolute liberty."[197] Nevertheless, interest in making gold was an element of Indian alchemy. The text *Mahâprajnâpâramitopadesa* (translated in 402–405 C.E.) states, "By drugs and incantations one can change bronze into gold. By skilful use of drugs silver can be changed into gold, and gold into silver."[198] Kumârajîva translated this important document, by Nâgârjuna, into Chinese in (344–413 C.E.) fixing the time of writing in the fourth century and well ahead of the alchemic activity of the Arab Abâ Mûsâ Jâbir iba Hayyân.

The *Vedas*, as noted, contain a number of references to alchemy including those that connect gold and long life. Mercury, an element vital to alchemy everywhere is first mentioned in *Arthasâstra* (The Handbook of [the King's] Profit) in the fourth to third century B.C.E. (Mercury, however, seemed to have less importance to Indian alchemists than to adepts in China and the Western world.) The *Arthasâstra* is an important Indian manual on the art of politics. Attributed to Kautilya, it relates to the "science of artha, or material prosperity, which is one of the four goals of human life."[199]

There are texts acknowledging the idea of transmuting base metal to gold, as well as those that proposed other uses for precious metals. The Indian alchemist on occasion gave primary attention to making gold, but is believed to give little importance to that achievement. Instead, "the six metals (gold, silver, tin, iron, lead, and copper), each further subdivided (five kinds of gold, etc.), were 'killed' (i.e., corroded) but not 'resurrected,' as was the custom of Western alchemy. Rather, they were killed to make medicines."[200]

The alchemy of medicine and immortality may have come to India from abroad, or the practice may have moved in the other direction. Gold making appears to have been a minor concern in either case. Medicine was the major focus of experimentation. The elixir of immortality, however, was of minor importance in India; instead, the Indian elixirs were remedies for specific diseases.[201] Indian alchemy pursued other means to immortality. It gave attention to transformation of the body through the means of yoga (see Chapter Six). "The body thus built up in the course of time by the Hatha yogins, tantrists, and alchemists corresponded in some measure to the body of a 'man-god'—a concept that ... has a long prehistory, both Indo-Aryan and pre–Aryan."[202]

Alchemy in both China and India had a clearly defined association with religious mysticism. Eliade wrote in *Yoga: Immortality and Freedom* (2009 [1958]), "The 'mystical body' which will allow the yogin to enter the transcendent mode of being, plays a considerable part in all forms of Yoga, and especially tantrism and alchemy."[203] There is a list of special powers (*siddhis*) connected with yoga including "the power of transmuting iron and other baser metals into gold by smearing with the yogin's urine and excreta."[204]

> When a man looks into a mirror, he sees therein reflected an image of himself. If, however, he tries to touch it, he will find that it is not palpable, and that he has laid his hand upon the mirror only. In the same way, the spirit which must be evolved from this Matter is visible, but not palpable.[205]

Arabic Alchemy

Alchemic investigation changed following the Christian riots in Alexandria in 400 C.E. The Roman influence increased as the Greek role decreased, and with that change, there was a different attitude about alchemy that caused the practice to become less open. The Greco-Roman city shifted its attention to the theological dispute over the nature of Christ's divinity that divided the early church causing it to form different sects. One sect, called Nestorians, the followers of the Syrian monk Nestorius (d. c.451 C.E.), fled to Persia in 489 C.E. to avoid persecution by the orthodox Christians of Constantinople. The Nestorians took with them much of the Greek attitude of intellectual inquiry into philosophy and nature including alchemy.

The Arabs experienced a practical application of Greek learning (science) when they besieged Constantinople (673 C.E.) and were repulsed by Greek fire, a chemical mixture that burned intently and could not be extinguished with water. The fire destroyed the wooden ships of the Arabic fleet. Legend tells that Callinicus an alchemist (chemist) who left Egypt ahead of the invading Arab army in 641 C.E. prepared the fire.[206]

The Arabs, although repulsed at Constantinople, defeated the Byzantines (Eastern provinces of the old Roman Empire), occupied major cities in Syria and Palestine, and looked to the west, to the enormous wealth of Egypt. 'Ami ibn al-'Ās led an army into Egypt in 639 and completed the conquest in 642 C.E. The Arabs moved from North Africa into Spain in 711 and defeated the Visigothic ruler, King Roderick. They established Muslim states in Spain that remained until 1492. The movement west by the Arabs, especially their activities in Spain, marked a new era for alchemy in the western world as well as opening an intellectual path to the east.

Ibn al-Nadim, a biographer of the second half of the tenth century, wrote, "The first Muslim to interest himself in alchemy was the Umayyad prince Khalid ibn Yazid, who died about 704."[207] Khalid (also written Halid) was reportedly the student of the Syrian monk Morienus or Marianus in Alexandria.[208] Ibn al-Nadim, wrote, "Khalid had a general love for the sciences but was particularly attracted to that of alchemy; so he ordered some Greek philosophers to be summoned from Egypt and instructed them to translate alchemical books from Greek and Coptic languages into Arabic."[209] Morienus supposedly told his secret for transmutation to Khalid, who committed the information to verse. "Among the works bearing his name are *The Book of Amulets, The Great and Small Books of The Scroll, The Book of the Testament on the Arts,* and *The Paradise of Wisdom.*"[210] These writings started the spread of Hellenistic alchemy to the Islamic world and for the next three centuries, the Arabs were the leading advocates of the Art.[211]

A second person widely associated with Arabic alchemic practice was Geber (see Chapter One), who flourished around 778 C.E. (Other sources place his alchemic life as early as 760 C.E., and some references say he was active much later, possibly during the fourteenth century. Some historians dispute his existence, believing him to be an imaginary character composed of different individuals.) His Arab name is thought to be Abâ Mûsâ Jâbir iba Hayyân, but he reportedly adopted the Westernized name Geber to give more authority to his writings. The *Encyclopædia of Religion and Ethics* (1980) noted that at times the epithet sufi was coupled with the name Geber. The reason for this connection was his reported zeal for Islam.[212]

Jâbir was believed to be an alchemist at the court of Hârûm ar-Rashîd in Baghdad. (Others contend he lived in Kufa [also spelled Kûfah] in Iran that was a center of Arab culture from the eighth to tenth centuries. It is agreed however, that he lived in Kufa for some time and maintained a laboratory there.) He was an important link between the Christian and Muslim worlds during the Middle Ages. More than two thousand books are attributed to Jâbir, and many of those books were known and read outside the Arab world. (A number of his books relating to Arabic alchemic practices were translated into Latin during the eleventh to thirteenth centuries.[213] Some of these books were possibly the work of Jâbir's students.) Regardless of authorship, these documents were extremely influential in a field where mysticism, magic, secrecy, and obscurity were the usual rule.

It is sometimes thought that Jâbir lived and worked in Spain during the eighth or ninth century because of the great influence of his writing on Latin Europe. This belief is inconsistent with available information. His writings were carried into Moorish Spain and from that location found their way into the hands of Western Europeans. Jâbir's works were subsequently translated into Latin, and thereby, contributed to the spread of alchemy in the western world.

There is no evidence of any truly major accomplishments to validate the high regard in which later alchemists held Jâbir. His standing seems to rely primarily on the merits of his metaphysical philosophy of nature and perhaps his advancement of the theory of matter. Jâbir endorsed the earlier Greek belief that all things are made of fire, earth, water, and air. He also promoted the concept that the four elements combined to make mercury and sulfur and that all metals are formed from these two substances when combined in various proportions.[214] Jâbir seemingly understood that the common mixture of mercury and sulfur produced the red compound called cinnabar, but he theorized that the correct proportion would produce gold. This was perhaps the beginning of the so-called mercury and sulfur theory that was widely endorsed and was a major influence on early chemistry.[215]

Jâbir pursued many interests. His theories about alchemy included the idea that metals had external and internal compositions. He said that "lead is cold and dry externally and hot and moist internally; gold, on the other hand, is hot and moist externally and cold and dry internally."[216] This assessment was an elaboration on Aristotle's concept of the four elements, and was a part of Jâbir's scheme for calculating the ratio of mercury and sulfur for transmutation of one metal into another. Jâbir also emphasized the mysticism importance of numbers relating to the quantities and lengths of time for processes. "He said that everything in the world is governed by the number 17 — metals, for instance, have 17 'powers.'"[217] The number 17 is composed of 1, 3, 5, and 8. These numbers relate to the magic square of the first nine digits[218] (see figure 7.4).

The alchemic doctrine of the Arabs was very philosophical in its approach, and implied certain concepts on the nature of physical matter

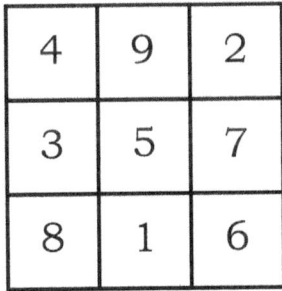
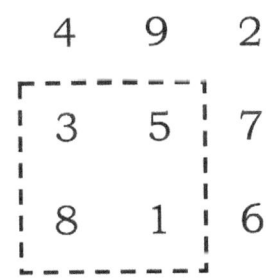

Figure 7.4: The Arab alchemist Jâbir gave special attention to numbers in his consideration of alchemic theory. Element proportions, time of processing, temperature, and related laboratory activities had numerical values. He believed that by proper calculation, the correct proportions of mercury and sulphur could be determined, as well as the correct time of processing to ensure the production of gold. Everything, according to Jâbir, was based on the magic number 17. Use of the Magic Square was later adapted for other purposes such as divining.

that were derived from general philosophy.[219] There was in this approach a humanizing notion regarding the life of metals. Jâbir expounded on this issue in his *Book of Mercy*. He applied anthropomorphic concepts to mineralogy. This approach included the idea of marriage, pregnancy, and gestation. These conditions were believed necessary for metals "the same as in the case of a human being."[220]

The Chinese alchemists view this idea similarly by contending their activities contribute to Nature's work by accelerating the growth of metals. Western alchemists also believe that all ores will, in time, become gold, but first the metals must go through a proper gestation period. According to alchemistic traditions, "the formation and life of metals require time ... to bring the metal in the womb of the earth to it perfect state, which is the state of gold, nature takes a very long time, more than a thousand years."[221] Based on this alchemic perspective, "the 'nobility' of gold is thus the fruit [of the earth] at its most mature; the other metals are 'common' because they are crude, 'not ripe.'"[222] It is the role of the alchemist to work with nature while seeking the means for accelerating the maturing process.

The anthropomorphic concept applied to metals also included the idea of life and death, body and soul, matter and mind. This attitude assigns mystical properties to minerals and their action or interaction with other elements. Tangible and intangible spiritual qualities inhabit the minerals giving them a sense of life or death. There are some substances that are considered "earthly and gross, and others pure and light; the former are called 'dead' and the latter 'living;' these notions of death and life are also employed in a relative way."[223] As an example of the relative nature of this concept, "sulphur and arsenic are [considered] living when they are mixed with substances inferior to them, such as talc; but they appear earthly and dead when they are united with live mercury."[224]

The Arab alchemists believe there is a material element and a spiritual element to all minerals, and therefore, to all combinations. The notion of resident spirits is not unique to Arabic thinking. A similar practice was found in China. This belief is clearly noted in the Chinese legends of Yu the Great, the piercer of mountains. The legend maintains, "Yu was a happy miner who gave health to the earth instead of disease."[225] He reportedly knew the proper way to placate the spirits of the mine and the earth. Comparable practices are found in Europe and Africa where it is commonly believed that without assistance from the spirits the minerals being sought will not be found. The treasures of the earth — its children — belong to certain people and their beliefs and practices authorized access to them. It may have been the "encounter with the symbolisms, myths, and techniques of the miners, smelters, and smiths which ... gave rise to the first alchemical operations."[226]

In addition to reading and analyzing Greek philosophy, the Arab alchemists sought the elusive elixir (*al iksir*), a living substance that could be combined with imperfect metals to transform those materials into a perfect state. The alchemists used different means and sought this purifying substance in different locations. They did not consider this material to be an exclusive mineral; consequently, they made use of various organic bodies in its preparation. Their experimentation included such substances as "excrement, blood, hair, and egg."[227] (The egg was a popular alchemic substance because it was viewed as androgynous — a complete entity.) Jâbir reported experimented with "marrow, blood, bones, lion's urine, onions, peppers, and pears."[228]

The *elixir vitae* is often described symbolically as a stone, the Philosopher's Stone. The stone, in some descriptions, is an actual hard substance that can be ground into a powder and mixed with water and other substances. The result of this concoction is the coveted elixir. Other accounts are less specific about the nature of the stone, and how it is to be prepared and used. Some alchemists reportedly used various combinations of ingredients and particular methods of heating, grinding and mixing, together with other rituals to create the elixir.

Jâbir wrote about the Philosopher's Stone: "Our stone is one, one medicine, to which we add nothing, from which we take nothing away, only removing that which is superfluous."[229] The philosopher's stone (Latin: *lapis philosophorum*) was a central element of alchemy symbolizing perfection, enlightenment, immortality. It is most often described in terms that have a religious nature. Words are used to praise its unique spiritual quality and transcendental nature.

> It is a Stone, and not a stone in the sense of having the nature of any one stone; it is fire, yet it has not the appearance, or properties, of fire; it is air, yet neither has it the appearance, or properties, of air; it is water, but has no resemblance, or affinity, to the nature of water. It is earth, though it has not the nature, or appearance, of earth, seeing that it is a thing by itself.[230]

A later Islamic alchemist and writer was Abu Bakr Muhammad ibn Zakariyya, known as Al-Razi [or Rhazes], "the man of Rayy" (ancient Rhagae), from his birthplace near Teheran. His lifetime extended from 866 [some writers believe he was born between 850 or 865] to 925. He is considered an alchemist, philosopher, and perhaps the greatest physician of the Islamic world. His most important medical writings are the *Kitab al-Mansuri* and the *Kitab al-hawi*. The latter work was translated into Latin as the *Comprehensive Book*. It is a survey of Greek, Syrian, and early Arabic medicine, and includes Indian medical knowledge.[231] He also wrote on alchemy *Compendium of Twelve Treatises* and *Book of Secrets*.

Al-Razi was especially important in the history of science (alchemy) because he carefully classified observations and verified facts regarding chemical substances, reactions, and apparatus. He maintained meticulous records of his experiments and described his findings in language free from mysticism and ambiguity.

The concepts of philosophy and science were viewed as synonyms during the early years of this era, and in this equation, alchemy was a science. Al-Razi, as a philosopher, has eight alchemical titles ascribed to him. Two titles attributed to him, *Concerning Alums and Salts* and *The Light of Light*, were translated into Latin in the twelfth century.[232] "His works show an interest in the classification and taxonomy of chemical substances and display the range of the laboratory equipment, substances and processes by this time available to the alchemist."[233]

Another important Islamic scholar was Avicenna. His full name was Abû 'Alî al-Husayn ibn 'Abd Allâh ibn Sînâ (980–1037 C.E.). He was an Iranian physician known through out Islam as a philosopher-scientist. Said to be an avid reader, he mastered Islamic law, medicine, and metaphysics at a young age. His most famous written work is *Kitâb ash-shifâ (Book of Healing)*, a philosophical and medical encyclopedia, is among the largest text ever undertakings by one person. It includes commentary on logic, the natural sciences, the *quadrivium* (geometry, astronomy, arithmetic, and music), and metaphysics.[234] His book *al-Qânûn fi at-tibb (The Canon of Medicine)* is considered the "most famous single book in the history of medicine in both East and West."[235] He also investigated Islamic philosophy as it related to mystical theosophy.

Although the background of Islamic philosophical interests is found in early phases of theology, its origins and inspirations are quite different from those of theology. Islamic philosophy "developed out of and around the nonreligious practical and theoretical sciences; it recognized no theoretical limits other than those of human reason itself; and it assumed that the truth found by unaided reason does not disagree with the truth of Islâm when both are properly understood."[236] Islamic philosophy was not subservient to religion or religious theory. The two disciplines were related, because both followed the paths of reason and logic and disassociated themselves from traditional religious practices and from mysticism. One important difference was that Islamic theology used only Arabic as a linguistic medium, whereas philosophy accommodated all participants who divided themselves into philosophic groups according to interests instead of religious beliefs or linguistic preferences.[237]

The origins of Islamic philosophy and subsequently its interest in alchemy and science can be traced to early translations of Greek documents. There were adequate translations of scientific and philosophic texts in the Islamic world by the middle of the ninth century to demonstrate that scientific and philosophic investigation was more than a series of discussions based on what the religious leaders called sound reasoning. The Arabic quest for knowledge was inclusive in that it was not limited to one topic or one way of thinking. Translated documents related to the study of logic, the sciences of nature (psychology and biology), the mathematical sciences (music and astronomy), metaphysics, ethics, and politics, as well as those related to alchemy. Islam seemingly accepted the Greek alchemical tenets fully because there are a large number of Greek technical terms transliterated into Arabic and Hellenic treatises.[238]

Although the Arabs added to the alchemic practices of the Western world, they were most likely the "preservers of Greek-Hellenistic knowledge."[239]

European Alchemy

> The goal of Western alchemy was the production of the Philosopher's Stone, which would enable the alchemist to turn base metals such as lead into silver and gold. This however, was merely the test employed to check whether the Stone was genuine, and its real purpose was to bestow spiritual wealth and prolong life.[240]

There was an atmosphere of superstition and ignorance in Europe during the Middle Ages. Learned persons offering observations or achievements beyond the norm were thought to communicate with devils. The rewards for visionary thinking and experimentation were often accusations of heresy followed by excommunication and imprisonment or torture. The Fourth Lateran Council of 1215 reconstituted the papal state, following a long period of conflict with temporal authority. The prevailing mood among the clergy was to establish a European nation with the papacy as a universal power. The medieval papacy collapsed because of corruption and Pope Boniface VIII forced the papal court to move to Avignon. It was in this climate that mixed distrust, confusion, and piety that alchemy was introduced into Latin Europe.

Most western Europeans had their first contact with the Islamic world because of the Crusades to take possession of the Holy City of Jerusalem. The First Crusade was in 1096, and for nearly two centuries (until 1291), a Christian enclave existed in the area of Jerusalem (often identified as the Kingdom of Jerusalem). This was a time (the Middle Ages) of significant social, economic, and institutional growth in Western Europe. It was also a time in which Christians returning to Western Europe from the Middle East carried the knowledge and appreciation of Arabic science and learning. It was in this environment that the center of alchemy shifted to Spain, and from there, the Art was introduced into Latin Europe.

The history of alchemy in Latin Europe is similar to other mythic attitudes in western culture. There were obvious historical connections with Greece and Egypt, but the stronger influence came from the Moors in Spain.[241] The Europeans scholars gained a better understanding of the Moorish civilization thereby learning that the libraries of the rulers and nobles often numbered 400,000 volumes. They learned that the Arabs possessed books that had been translated from the Greek, and subsequently, they sought to translate many of those works into Latin to make them available to Latin-speaking scholars.

Although Kabbalists (Jewish mystics), Rosicrucians (the secret Brotherhood of the Rosy Cross), and astrologers were instrumental in spreading alchemy throughout the Western world during medieval and Renaissance times, much of its early development can be traced to a few individuals who invested time and energy in translating important books from Arabic and Greek into Latin. Persons such as Robert of Chester, Gerbert of Aurillac, Adelard of Bath, Michael Scott, Gerard of Cremona, Arnald de Villanova, Ramón Lull, Fulbert of Chartres, Hermann of Germany, Albertus Magnus, Thomas Aquinas, and Roger Bacon helped to introduce alchemy to Latin Europe. Most of these individuals were primarily scholars stimulated by the quest for knowledge rather than alchemists. Many were members of the clergy pursuing the notion that science and religion were not contradictory concepts. Their investigation of alchemy, and in some cases their practice in the Art, was seldom generated by the pursuit of wealth.

The French scholar and monk Gerbert of Aurillac (c.940–1003) went to Spain in 967 and lived there for three years. It was during his time at Santa Maria de Ripoll that he studied astronomy along with geometry, and music. He is also believed to have had exposure to various documents relating to alchemy at that time. Gerbert was consecrated pope in 999 and chose the name Pope Sylvester II. Perhaps because of his personal experience in Spain, he was an advocate for the study of Arab material by Latin scholars during his papacy. Interestingly, rumor circulated after his death in 1003 that he learned magical arts during his time in Spain. Some believed he was assisted in his learning by the devil, and others insisted he relied upon an artificial head that answered his questions. (The story related in *Alchemy and Alchemists* by Sean Martin notes that Gerbert allegedly "made [the] talking head through magical means and seven or eight years before election to the pontificate [he] had to swear before a council at Amiens that he wasn't a sorcerer."[242])

While living in Spain studying alchemy and astronomy, the English scholar Robert of Chester was among the first to translate an Arabic work of alchemy into Latin. He wrote in the preface to his translation of Morienus's *The Book of the Composition of Alchemy* (1144), "What alchemy is and what is its composition, your Latin world does not yet know truly."[243] (E. J. Holmyard believes the completed translation of the *Book of the Composition of Alchemy* from Arabic into Latin, 11 February 1144, establishes the date that alchemy was introduced into Latin Europe. Thus, the earliest figure in Muslim alchemy, Morienus, becomes also the earliest of European alchemy.[244])

Another twelfth century publication that had an influence upon European scholars was that of the Spaniard Artephius. The book titled *The Art of Prolonging Human Life* made reference to alchemic practices and the use of special techniques for sustaining the human body. The book's author professes to have been "moved by pity and good conscience" as an aid to "persons unable to perfect these techniques for long life." The author reports he lived for one thousand years and claimed this secret to long life could be learned from his book "provided one [the reader] be not stiff-necked and have a little experience." The idea of such physical longevity had an appeal to members of European learned society.

The acceptance of publications translated into Latin inspired others to translate Arab authors, and over the next century a number of books found their way into Europe.[245] Probably the greatest translator of Arabic works was Gerard of Cremona (c. 1114–1187). Gerard reportedly went to Toledo, Spain, to learn Arabic so he could read the *Almagest*, written by the second century Greek mathematician and astronomer Ptolemy. He is said to have remained in Spain for the remainder of his life. He is credited with translating ninety-two Arabic works, some of them extremely long.

Michael Scott (1175–1235) was a primary contributor to bringing alchemy into prominence in Europe. He learned Arabic in Sicily and traveled to Spain and Italy to study and to translate books on philosophy and medicine. He worked under the patronage of Frederick II in Sicily and served as his teacher. He returned to Spain where he translated Aristotle's treatise on Natural History, as well as books on magic and astronomy.[246] It is also believed that during his time in Toledo, Spain, he studied black magic and experimented with alchemy.

Alchemy was familiar enough in Europe by 1250 that books were written and information exchanged. Albertus Magnus (c.1193–1280) promoted alchemy as a branch of philosophy. He was a dominant figure in learning and the natural sciences in the thirteenth century. Albertus set himself the extraordinary task of making Aristotelian knowledge and philosophy intelligible to Latin readers.[247] It was through his efforts that the writings of Aristotle were recognized for their scholastic value in the later Middle Ages and thereafter into modern times. Albertus was also the most prolific writer of his century. His book *Libellus de Alchimia* includes a practical discourse on the transformation of metals, the structure of furnaces, and the different approaches to be used in the study of alchemy. He is reported to have said, "Alchemy, cannot change species but only imitate them.... I have myself tested alchemical gold and found that after six or seven ignitions it was converted into powder."[248]

The English scholar and monk Roger Bacon (1214–1292) was a contemporary of Albertus Magnus. He was a philosopher and educational reformer who is best known for his belief in experimental science and the application of mathematical techniques to scientific investigation. He studied mathematics, astronomy, alchemy, and languages, and was known as a "devotee of tangible knowledge." Bacon endeavored to write a *Summa Scientire* that was an encyclopedic summary of all the sciences including alchemy. He defined alchemy "as the Science of a certain Medicine or Elixir by which metals are transformed into other metals and those which are imperfect are raised into a perfect state."[249]

Bacon, a Franciscan monk and teacher, was often accused of going beyond the accepted norms in his teaching. His ideas include notions about flying machines, submarines, ships without rowers, shaped lenses to correct faulty vision, a reformed calendar, as well as the transformation of base metals into gold (see plate B). His prodigious knowledge earned him a position at Oxford in 1250, but shortly thereafter, he was placed on suspension by the authorities. Some accounts state that he was exiled to Paris where he was placed under strict supervision for ten years. He was imprisoned in 1277 where he spent 14 years.

"Except for the fact that he minimized the importance of the Aristotelian 'prime matter' and made fuller use of the theory of the four elements, Bacon differs very little from the other alchemists in his ideas about metallic constitution and transmutation."[250] He wrote, "Nature has always had for an end and tries ceaselessly to reach perfection, that is gold."[251] He reportedly believed that speculative (theoretical) alchemy was the science of the producing of things from elements and that practical alchemy "which teaches how to make the noble

Plate B: This engraving of Roger Bacon possibly conducting an experiment is the work of Michael Maier (1568?–1622). Bacon in monastic robe holds a balance with two containers one of which is burning. Bacon points to the balance of the parts indicating a figurative concern — the right proportions — in the alchemic process. The possible explanation of the print is the balancing of sulphur (the stone that burns) with mercury (quicksilver). At the time the print was created (1617) the sulphur/mercury theory was still in vogue among European alchemists. It is possible Maier drew upon this concept to create this print.

metals and colours, and other things better or more abundantly by art than they are made in nature."[252]

Thomas Aquinas (1224–1274) was a student of Albertus Magnus at Cologne and Paris. Aquinas as a theologian produced two major publications, the *Summa contra gentiles* and the *Summa theologiae*.[253] His writings include references to alchemy specifically mentioning the transmutation of metals. He seemed to believe that "alchemical gold is usually not the same thing as real gold, though again he just allows the possibility that alchemy can also produce the real thing."[254] Aquinas, a Dominican monk, contended that only God was immutable and that everything else was mutable, this is to say that only God is unchangeable. Six alchemical treatises name him as their author.

Thomas Aquinas is reported to have endorsed the notion that "the generation of metals requires also the occult operations of a celestial virtue not always under alchemical control, so that the aim of the worker should be to arrange conditions under which the virtue will be likely to function."[255]

Arnald de Villanova (c.1240–1311) and Ramón Lull (1233–1316) were considered the most prominent names among the alchemists of the last part of the thirteenth century. A number of works of a mystical approach are attributed to the two men, however their authorship is questionable. Arnald was educated in a Dominican convent and studied medicine in Naples and at Montpellier; consequently, much of his writings are medical.[256] He also wrote about alchemy, and endorsed the "sulphur-mercury theory of metallic constitution."[257] He regarded mercury as much the more significant of the two, noting, "ordinary sulphur is harmful to metals, and the sulphur that is envisaged by Arnald is that already hidden in the mercury."[258]

The sulphur-mercury theory was endorsed by most Latin alchemists of the time. Europeans influenced by Arab alchemists practicing the Art believed gold grew in the body of the earth and the methods they employed were intended to speed up the natural process.

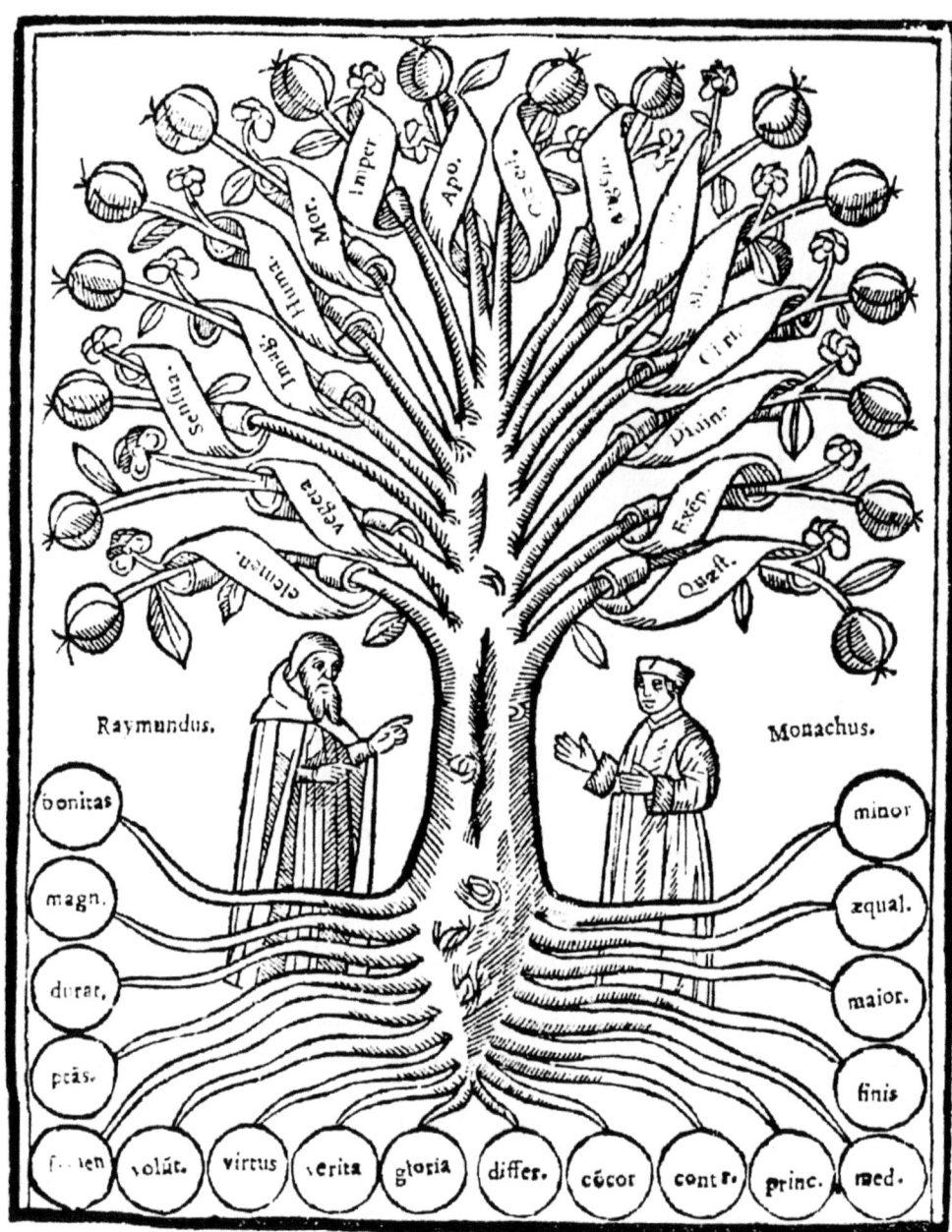

Plate C: A woodblock print showing Ramon Lull, identified as Raymundus standing under the tree of knowledge. The second figure in religious attire may be the French cardinal Jean Lemoine (Johannes Monachus) who was sent to France by Pope Boniface VIII as his representative. Lull was dead by the time Boniface was being challenged by the monarchies of Europe, but the two figure, each of which challenged and support the Catholic Church were an appropriate illustration for book on alchemy. This print was produced in 1515.

Many European alchemists supported the idea that gold, the perfect metal, as well as silver and all the imperfect metals were developed out of mercury. "[G]old was thought to contain the first principles of mercury and sulphur in the purest form."[259] Roger Bacon argued that "nothing other than these two are able to bring them to perfection or transmute them, and hence mercury and sulphur are 'the matter of our stone' [the philosopher's stone]."[260]

Ramón Lull (also written Llull and Lully or Raymundus Lullus) was a Spanish philosopher, mystic, poet, and Christian missionary to the Moors. He is credited with influencing mysticism throughout medieval Europe. He is known as the "inventor of an 'art of finding truth' (*ars inveniendi veritatis*) that was primarily intended to support the Roman Catholic faith in missionary work but was also designed to unify all branches of knowledge."[261] He studied oriental languages and Arabian philosophy to further his conversion efforts. Lull's writings were numerous (about 290), and most expounded on Christian theology (**see plate C**).

Lull's fundamental thesis was that theology and philosophy were identical in concept. He, like other scholastics of the time, argued that the two sciences agreed, so that what was true in philosophy was also true in theology and vice versa. He acknowledged that the two were different in some instances in that theology depended on revelation as a source while philosophy relied on reason. A number of alchemic works were attributed to Lull following his death in 1316; however, none can irrefutably be assigned to him. He is reported to have taught the king of England (which king is unclear) how to make gold, but history does not confirm this story.

The pursuit of practical science and alchemy was often viewed as heresy by traditional elements of the church. Latin Europe had not yet entered a time of enlightenment instead it was attempting to structure itself politically on a spiritual basis. The scholastics and alchemists had to establish themselves as a subculture in medieval Christianity because they originated in a pre–Christian cultural world. "Here they occupied a strange position, religiously as well as scientifically."[262] Their position was made more precarious by the assertion that "the same principles of evolution hold for human souls as for nature."[263] The alchemists believed, "Both partake of a single universal process typified by the transmutation of lead into gold. Such is the transformation for the sick body into health, and the exaltation of the soul into Christ."[264]

The Christian church was not eager to endorse the ideas and practices of alchemists. Practicing the Art was considered black magic and a threat to the dogma of the Holy Church. Consequently, Pope John XXI (1210–1277) condemned both Thomas Aquinas and Roger Bacon among others in a papal bull of 1277. (Aquinas was already dead, but Bacon was put in prison for his heretical activities.) Forty years later, in 1317, Pope John XXII initiated a papal edict condemning alchemy. Once again, as under Diocletian (a Roman emperor) a thousand years before, the study of alchemy was forbidden, and it came more than fifteen hundred years after an edict issued in 144 B.C.E. during the Han Dynasty in China forbidding the counterfeiting of gold.[265]

The more familiar alchemy became to Latin Europe, the more it was used for gold making despite the efforts of the church, and Europeans, monarchs and commoners proved no more resistant to the lure of the shining metal than their Arabic predecessors. Numerous alchemical treatises were produced by 1350, and fake alchemists, called blowers, were preying on a gullible and greedy public. (Fake alchemists were given the name blowers perhaps after the bellows used in firing the furnace. It is likely synonymous with hot air.)

Alchemists made important discoveries during the thirteenth century that offered new methods for the gold search. The discovery of the mineral acids was of extraordinary importance, but it took almost three hundred years before there was a clear division of the acids into three kinds: nitric, hydrochloric, and sulfuric. These three centuries saw enormous changes in European alchemy. The reactive and highly corrosive acids opened a whole new venue of research, however, the experiments tended to pursue the old objectives of separating the base metals into their elements, making elixirs, and other traditional procedures.

Practicing the Art of Alchemy

Alchemy in Europe, as elsewhere, existed on two levels: the practical and the spiritual. Those persons of a more practical attitude sought the ability to convert base metals into gold. Alchemists pursuing the spiritual aspired to purify themselves by removing the base elements of the self and attaining enlightenment. Many alchemists believed that the spiritual purification was necessary to accomplish the transformations of metals. Those persons pursuing a path that combined the practical and spiritual endeavored to reach into the regions of spirituality in pursuit of essential knowledge and thereby to understand the forces that influenced the tangible environment.

The European scholars and alchemists found anthropomorphic connections with minerals, as did the Arabs. Ores and metals were commonly regarded as living organisms. They were considered in terms of their gestation, growth, birth, and marriage. Nicolas Flamel (1330–1418) wrote, "Now all metals have been formed out of sulphur and quicksilver [the sulphur-mercury theory], which are the seeds of all metals, the one representing the male and the other the female principle."[266] The alchemical blending of sulphur and mercury was spoken of in terms of marriage, however it was also viewed as a mystical union between two cosmological principles.[267] Flamel explains the meaning of this union: "These two varieties of seed are, of course, composed of elementary substances; the sulphur, or male seed, being nothing but fire and air, while the quicksilver, or female seed, is nothing but earth and water."[268] (Flamel claimed to have succeeded in his gold making efforts. He reportedly became rich and made contribution to various hospitals and churches.)

Writing about the alchemic process employed in Europe, M.A. Atwood wrote in 1850, "It is not species that they profess to transmute; nor do they even teach in theory that lead as lead, or mercury as mercury specificate, can be changed into gold."[269] Atwood acknowledged that such transformations were not proposed any more than changing "a dog into a horse, a tulip into a daisy, or vice versa, in this way anything of unlike kind."[270] However, she states speaking of metals, "the radical moisture of which they are uniformly composed, that they say may be withdrawn by art and transported from inferior forms, being set free by the force of a superior ferment or attraction."[271]

Practicing the art of alchemy had many applications, and one that had a lasting impact on the field of medicine was the work of the German-Swiss physician and reformer Paracelsus (1493–1541). His self-bestowed name "para Celsus" was to place himself above Celsus (the renowned first century Roman medical writer and practitioner). Paracelsus is said to have graduated from the University of Vienna with a baccalaureate in medicine in 1510, at the age of seventeen. It is believed he earned his doctoral degree from the University of Ferrara in 1516. The prevailing theory in medicine at that time was that the stars and planets controlled all part of the human body. Paracelsus rejected this thesis preferring instead to advocate the healing power of nature. His practice is viewed as the origination of modern homeopathy.

Paracelsus claimed to have been taught medicine and alchemy by his father early in life. He worked for a year in a metallurgy shop in Tyrol where it is said he acquired technical knowledge about precious metals and alchemy.[272] He allegedly used his metallurgical knowledge to prepare and use new chemical remedies that contained mercury, sulfur, iron, and copper sulfate later in life as a physician and alchemist. E.J. Holmyard quotes Paracelsus as saying, "Many have said of alchemy that it is for making gold and silver. For me such is not the aim, but to consider only what virtue and power may lie in medicines."[273]

Paracelsus reportedly wandered through Western Europe, Egypt, Arabia and possibly further to the east. He is said to have worked in Russia as an army surgeon and was held captive by the Tartars. He returned to Hungary, and in time he was appointed lecturer in medicine at the University of Basel. Many books are attributed to Paracelsus but there are no authenticated volumes specifically on alchemy. However, his views of the subject can be found in his voluminous medical and philosophical works.[274] He was an advocate of medicines made from minerals as opposed to herbs, and a proponent of the notion of astral influences upon human health. He believed "there are heavens within us, too, and during illness, these need to be realigned with the greater heavens in order to restore hearth."[275]

> God has made all things, and these have a natural end to which they will come by the power of nature within them; but God has also assigned to man the power of transforming things from this natural or raw state to a condition fit for man's use.[276]

CHAPTER EIGHT

Prima Materia

"Want feeds on satisfaction of want."[1]

Alchemy has been described as the art of transformation. The task or "Great Work," of the alchemist was to transform a raw and unrefined base material or First Substance (*Prima Materia*)—either the human soul or physically, a mysterious metallic substance that was rarely identified—into something pure and perfect.[2]

Alchemists pursued perfection. They contemplated the nature of reality, sought the eternal, pondered the conflict between good and evil, and pursued the purest outcome. Alchemy for many was filled with the same idealism that permeated mystical religions. It sought to free humanity, individually or collectively, from the confines of a restrictive environment—material, physical, or spiritual. Alchemy had practical significance for Kabbalists, Christians, Gnostics, Muslims, Coptics, Taoists, Buddhists, Sufis, and atheists. It involved no specific religious belief nor did it exclude any belief; yet, all adepts acknowledged the presence of God in the alchemic process. "Grant me this gift," the Greek philosopher Democritus pleaded 2,400 year ago. "I know the diversity of matter, but how do I bring its natures into harmony?"[3]

A legend tells that a fragment of writing by an Egyptian alchemist called Kleopatra was found that included symbolic diagrams. "One of the images showed a serpent swallowing its tail to form a ring. The phrase 'The One is the All' was inscribed within the circle."[4] The image *Uroboro* or *Ouroboro* (**see drawing 8.a**) symbolically reinforces the alchemic concept of cosmic unity "in which the world above suffused the world below and all matter was interchangeable. According to some traditions, the serpent represented a sexual union between humankind and God—or at least an ecstatic penetration by the Divine Spirit."[5] Consequently, the *prima materia* is often identified with the tail eater.

"The alchemist's initial encounter with the prima materia is characterized by feelings of frustration, bewilderment, disassociation and disintegration."[6] This statement from Johannes Fabricius, *Alchemy: The Medieval Alchemists and Their Royal Art* (1976), expresses an attitude typical, so we are told, of alchemists for the earliest times. The idea of bringing nature into harmony had particular significance and particular challenges for alchemists. They reasoned it was necessary to "free the essence of the noble metal" from the base metals that imprisoned it to release the gold, whereas, in the East it was freeing the egocentric nature of humanity to unfetter the divine spirit or soul. Alchemists established laboratories or centers and devised numerous ingenious methods to accomplish this process of liberation. The purified metal laboratory work was usually performed in one of two ways, the "Dry Way or the Wet Way; some even spoke of further methods, called the Mixed Way and the

Brief Way. The different methods refer to the length of time of the work, and the temperatures required to heat the matter."[7]

Sean Martin in *Alchemy and Alchemists* (2006), describes the Wet Way as the noblest of the ways. Martin explains this method usually took the most time to accomplish because it required lower temperatures. He indicates, "Much of the work is said to be carried out at body temperature, or at the temperature of a hen sitting on her eggs [blood-warm]."[8] The Dry Way, in contrast, requires higher temperatures and greater expertise. The time required for the process ultimately depended upon the number of challenges the alchemist had to work through to achieve a sense of harmony and balance.[9]

Since the *prima materia* is difficult to define, it is difficult to discover. Jay Ramsey describes it as lying very deep. He indicates that it is the most physical and mysterious thing, and that it is, in itself, "deeper than concepts, words, or ideas. It has been given many names (among which are 'sea,' 'seed of things,' and 'basic moistness'), and we cannot precisely define it — but it clearly exists on two levels."[10] Ramsey wrote in *Alchemy: The Art of Transformation* that *prima materia* "is the original ground, the original state"[11] at the deepest and purest level, "a state deeper than chaos."[12] He describes it as "the first of all things, its substance [for alchemists] is Divine, and it is extremely fertile."[13]

Drawing 8.a: The Ouroboro (or Uroboro) is an emblematic serpent of ancient Egypt and Greece represented with its tail in its mouth continually devouring itself and being reborn from itself. The Ouroboro expresses the unity of all things material and spiritual. "One is the Serpent which has its poison according to two compositions, and One is All and through it is All and by it is All, and if you have not All, All is nothing." The Ouroboro is labeled "One is All."

There is no definitive definition of *prima materia*. This is because alchemists had personal definitions for the materials they used and the methods they employed in the search to discover it. The *materia* tended to be partly chemical, partly mythical, and partly philosophical. "It is incorrect to maintain that the alchemists never said what the *prima materia* was; on the contrary, they gave all too many definitions and so were everlastingly contradicting themselves."[14] The identified materials included quicksilver, sulphur, salt, vinegar, water, blood, urine, excreta, dew, hair, and a variety of animal and plant parts.

The Philosopher's Stone is an "invisible symbol, and perhaps one of the most interesting and mysterious, because it has given rise to many visible symbols, great thoughts, and discoveries in the realms of philosophy and science."[15] Lama Anagarika Govinda wrote in the *Foundations of Tibetan Mysticism* (1969), "The eternal vision behind it [the Philosopher's Stone] is that of the prima materia. The original substance, the ultimate principle of the world."[16]

Pliny the Elder (23–79 C.E.) spoke of the philosopher's stone in his *Natural History*, an encyclopedic work on scientific matters, published in 77 C.E. The writing describes "the fundamental practices of workers in metal and of the emperor Caligula extracting gold from orpiment (trisulfide of arsenic; As_2S_3)."[17] An often stated premise from Aristotle's time was that the "prima materia of metals is humid exhalation enclosed in crass earth, that mercury and sulphur 'are the parents of all other metals,' (mercury was called the womb or mother of all metals) that lead and other materials would be gold if they had time, and that alchemy helps that process along."[18]

Paracelsus, the sixteenth century physician and alchemist (see Chapter Seven), wrote, "This unique (*unica*) *materia* is a great secret having nothing in common with the elements."[19] He said it was the "mother of the elements and of all created things."[20] The female mercurial principle represents the mutable aspect of natural processes, their fluid changeability. "The necessary counterforce to mercury, a force that also defines and shapes, is represented by male sulphur."[21] Other alchemists believed the *prima materia* could be found in the manipulation of the elements. They contended the material of the stone must pass from one nature into another, causing the elements to be gradually extracted, and thereby relinquish their powers (energy). The process was continued until all the elements were inverted (reversed) and sedentary.

Some researchers contend the *prima materia* is ubiquitous. It can be found always and everywhere; consequently, projection can take place always and everywhere.[22] Whereas, Thomas Aquinas (1224/25–1274) is reported to have written, "It is Mercury alone which perfects in our work, and we find in it all we have need of [and] nothing different must be added."[23] Dom Antonio Joseph Pernety wrote in the *Dictionnaire mytha-hermétick* (1787), "The Ancients commonly employed fables [to identify the *prima materia* and its location], and those of the Egyptians and of the Greeks have been invented solely with regard to the Great Work [alchemy], if we are to believe the Philosophers who have often quoted them in their works."[24]

Mircea Eliade quotes George Ripley (c.1415–1490) as saying, "The philosophers say that the birds and fishes bring the Stone to us, each man possesses it, it is everywhere, in you, in me, in all thing, in time and space."[25] Ripley, a fifteenth century English alchemist who studied the Art in Rome and on the Isle of Rhodes, wrote extensively on the topic of alchemic process. He was a proponent of the idea that the progress of the work could be followed by the succession of colors. Ripley described many of his ideas in *Compound of Alchemie* (1470–71). This treatise was written in English and dedicated to Edward IV. It gave a sense of currency to alchemic research and reinforced Ripley's reputation as an accomplished alchemist.[26]

Another prominent Englishman, Elias Ashmole (1616–1692), was known in his time as both an alchemist and a scholar. He collected and edited a volume of early alchemical texts, published in 1652 under the title *Theatrum Chemicum Britannicum*. Ashmole is better known for founding the Ashmolean Museum in the University of Oxford despite his important contributions to alchemy. The Ashmolean Museum opened in 1683, and is the oldest public museum of art, archaeology, and natural history in Great Britain.

Alchemy, as a concept, describes the process of chemical or physical change. Both practices may be viewed as relating to the transmutation of elements (component parts), and both can apply to the transformation of the human mind and body (the physical as well as spiritual). The interrelationship of these two approaches must have seemed obvious to early practitioners. The idea of transforming base metal into gold and the consumption of drinkable gold for longevity were collateral concepts — the quest for purity. C. G. Jung[27] asserts the allegorical (symbolic) aspects of the process probably occupied the thinking of some alchemists to such an extent that they believed their only concern was with chemical substances. Jung notes there were, however, a few persons "for whom laboratory work was primarily a matter of symbols and their psychic effect. As the texts show, they were quite conscious of this, to the point of condemning the naïve goldmakers as liars, frauds, and dupes."[28]

The most enduring goals of alchemy are, undoubtedly, the prolongation of life and the transmutation of base metals into gold. (This is to exclude the manufacture of fake gold and silver, imitation gems, and fraudulent health tonics.) The pursuit of the honest goals took different forms and followed different paths. Alchemy in ancient Egypt often fell to persons with skills in embalming, medicine, and magic. The earliest practitioners were seemingly priests who performed many services. This association between religion and alchemy continued into sixteenth century Europe. A similar relationship is found in Persia, India, China, Tibet, and other regions. Hinduism, Taoism, Buddhism, Islam, and Judaism all had alchemic and mystical elements.

There is nothing more representative of alchemy than the Philosopher's Stone (also called the Powder of Projection, The Tincture, the Stone of Wisdom, and the Stone of Live Metal. It was also known as the Red Stone and the White Stone. The Red Stone was used to transmute base metal to gold, and the White Stone, also known as the White Daughter, had the power to confer immunity from disease[29]). It was considered "the highest, most pure perfection of matter, the First Matter elevated to Godhead. The Philosopher's Stone has the power to transform other matter with which it comes in contact and to raise it to its own perfection. It is capable of 'transforming lead into gold.'"[30] Zosimos of Panopolis (Egypt), an early alchemist who postdates Bolos of Mendes, pursued the concept of alchemy giving particular attention to the fundamental elements of the processes employed in transformation. He wrote about the "composition of waters, movement, growth, embodying and disembodying, drawing the spirits from bodies and binding the spirits within bodies."[31] His process for ennobling (transforming to gold) base metals included killing and resurrecting. His methods for purification included extensive distillation and sublimation.

M. A. Atwood writing in *Hermetic Philosophy and Alchemy* quotes Paracelsus, "We must not limit an element to a bodily substance or quality. That which we see in only the receptacle; the true element is a spirit of life and grows in all things, as the soul in the body of man."[32] Despite the fact that Hermes Trismegistus is said to have called the stone the orphan,[33] it has the power to reconcile irreconcilable opposites by virtue of possessing the power of both.[34] "To suggest that something cannot be true because it is not communicable is poor reasoning; we depend on other people's accounts for most of our knowledge of places and events."[35] Accordingly, "one should never lose sight of the fact that the Philosopher's Stone, elusive goal of the alchemical quest, is both a material and a spiritual realization."[36]

The elixir of life (*elixir vitae*) was a frequently used name for the Philosopher's Stone. The elixir was believed to have restorative powers including the healing of the deficiencies and imperfections of base metals so they can be transmuted into perfect metals. The elixir also repaired the imperfections in humans, granting longevity and potentially immortality.[37] The Philosopher's Stone was described by Paracelsus as "the Tincture and the Lili of Alchemy and Medicine; he said that it was a 'Universal Medicine and consumes all diseases, by whatever name they are called, just like an invisible fire.'"[38]

M.A. Atwood wrote, "Thus obscure [the substance of the stone] ... is the true Master of the Alchemists; [it] is the simple generated substance of life and light, immanifestly flowing throughout nature."[39] Atwood continues "without which nothing that exists is able to be, we are not for this yet wiser how to obtain or work it apart; nor are words sufficient to convey a just notion where there is no ground of apprehension...."[40]

The Philosopher's Stone (*lapis philosophorum*) is described as "that perfect and incorrupt substance or 'noble Tincture,' never found upon our imperfect earth in its natural state, which could purge all baser metals of their dross, and turn them to pure gold."[41] The Stone is said to have no beginning and no end; it will exist in eternity. "To understand this properly, one must open wide the eyes of the soul and the spirit and observe and discern accurately by means of the inner light."[42] George Ripley believed the "prima materia is water; it is the material principle of all bodies, including mercury. It is the *hyle* which the divine act of creation brought forth from the chaos as a dark sphere."[43]

The fifteenth century monk Basil Valentine wrote in *The 'Azoth' Series*, translated by Adam McLean (2000), "The Stone from which our volatile Fire is extracted is not among the most precious."[44] Valentine spoke further about the Stone. "This same Stone," he wrote, "is made from this Fire, of a white colour and red, and nevertheless it is not a stone."[45] Valentine says the Stone produces "a clear fountain, that suffocates in its own waters its father already coagulated, and it swallows him until the soul is not returned to him and the volatile mother has not been assimilated into the Kingdom."[46] The latter statement is a proper example of anthropomorphic influence on alchemic practice.

Zosimos also gave credence to the idea that alchemic theory focused on the belief there was a substance that could bring about the desired transformation of metals instantly.[47] He is said to have called this substance the tincture. It was also called the powder (*xerion*), which was translated into Arabic and back to Latin as elixir and eventually (signifying its inorganic nature) as the philosopher's stone. The processes that were more physical, than spiritual, called it a medicine or a "drug for the rectification of human maladies."[48] Zosimos acknowledged, "When the objective of alchemy became human salvation, the material constitution of the elixir became less important than the incantations that accompanied its production."[49]

Sean Martin wrote in *Alchemy and Alchemists* (2006), "The goal of Western alchemy was the production of the Philosopher's Stone, which would enable the alchemist to turn base metals such as lead into silver and gold."[50] Gold and silver were joined with the sun and moon respectively and the divine kinship acknowledged by that relationship. The sun was thought to nurture physical life during the day, and at night, the moon safeguarded the soul.

The Philosopher's Stone was equated with the Holy Grail and Christ himself as alchemy began to spread through Christian Europe during the Middle Ages. It was described "not as a cup or chalice, as is traditional [for the Grail], but as a stone beyond price, the stone 'which the builders rejected, but which has become the corner stone.'"[51] Arnaud de Villanova, the twelfth century scholar and translator, wrote that the "Stone and Grail were one and the same thing. Like the prima materia which is said to be everywhere and despised by all."[52] Arnaud is said to have written, "the Stone/Grail is an 'insignificant stone ... of trifling value/it is despised by fools, the more cherished by the wise.' And like the Grail, the Stone was famously difficult to attain."[53]

Emerald Tablet

The Emerald Tablet (as described in Chapter Seven) is believed inscribed with the essence of Egyptian philosophy, including the magical secrets of the universe. The true origin of the Tablet is not known since no original exists. It is only known in translations, and consequently has been attributed to different authors include various seventh century Arabic and Chinese alchemists. "The Tablet probably first appeared in the West in editions of the pseudo–Aristotlean *Secretum Secretorum*, a translation of the *Kitab Sirr al-Asrar*, a book of advice to the kings which is thought to date to the ninth century."[54]

The writings of Hermes Trismegistos, the legendary author of the Emerald Tablet, were primarily on astrology to which treatises on medicine and alchemy were later added. The *Tabula Smaragdina* (Emerald Table) was a favorite source for medieval alchemists and magic.[55] Although the principles described in these writings were basic to the occult sciences, it was necessary to know the laws of sympathy and antipathy by which the parts of the universe were related to make these assumptions effective in practice. That these principles did not exist and could not be discovered by normal scientific practices was reason to rely upon divine revelation. Following this thinking to a logical conclusion, the objective of Hermetism was the deification or rebirth of man through the knowledge of the one transcendent God, the world, and men.[56]

The Emerald Tablet is not a lengthy document as preserved in translation. When it was first introduced in Latin Europe during the Middle Ages it was erroneously believed to be of great antiquity.[57] The text offers little instruction on alchemic process, but it was viewed as the most influential document relating to alchemy. The second sentence of the tablet is considered of major importance. It is translated, "That which is above is like to that which is below, and that which is below is like that which is above."[58] Alchemists believe this statement means "that just as there are elements that make up physical reality in the Below, so must there be similar elements in the Above through which the godhead operates. They saw these heavenly elements as universal principles, a trinity of forces acting on everything."[59] The next sentence expounds on the message of the first. It states, "And just as all things have come from this One Thing, through the mediation of One Mind, so do all created things originate from this One Thing, through Transformation."[60] The one thing and the one mind are one. They are different aspects of the same thing. "Mind and matter appear as two in the mirror of existence, but they flow into one another as One."[61]

Writing in *The Emerald Tablet: Alchemy for Personal Transformation* (1999) a contemporary book by Dennis Hauck, the author states, "The Hermetic tradition emphasized the existence of a supreme force called the One Thing which has no perceptible form until it is grounded or expressed in material reality."[62] Hauck believes, "The expression of that force is guided by the One Mind, the mind of the supreme being, and is a process responsible for the creation of the universe."[63]

"Cultivating the Nourishing Life Arts of spiritual alchemy has but one secret, diligent discipline, in which wealth and high position are of no use…. Why?"[64] Stuart Olson, writing in *The Jade Emperor's Mind Seal Classic: The Taoist Guide to Health, Longevity, and Immortality* (2003), asks and answers this question. He maintains wealth and high position have no value, "Because the techniques and means for attaining immortality lie in a person's genuine desires to attain tranquility, to achieve freedom from avarice, to see and hear internal functions, and to be totally absorbed in freedom from emotions."[65]

The Laboratory

> Preparation begins with a quest for the prima materia, literally the material which is to be transformed, and alchemists have pictured this as a journey to a mine — a place that is under the surface and is dark.[66]

Plate D: *Alchymist im laboratorium* a print made from a painting by Thomas Wiick (1616–1677) shows the alchemist and his assistant in the laboratory. The alchemist is using a bellows to increase the heat of the fire under a caldron that is being used to distill a liquid. The spout of the upper part of the caldron has a spout that extends to a smaller container. The liquid in the caldron is heated to boiling temperature and the steam is directed through the spout into the smaller container where is condenses. An alchemic balance is achieved: liquid (water) plus heat produced steam (air) that condenses, thus returning to liquid (water).

The alchemist, seeking immortality, must carefully consider the relevance of space and time — the two main features of the cosmos — to the work performed. The quest involves attempts to suspend time or to transcend it, thereby gaining access to timelessness. "The same is with space: its centre, where the alchemist places himself and his work, is a point devoid of dimension."[67] The alchemist is able to move from this spaceless and timeless realm along a line that connects the higher and lower levels of being[68] (see plate D).

As described in Chapter One, the concept of the four earthly elements was identified in the fifth century B.C.E. by the Greek philosopher Empedocles, endorsed by Plato, refined by Aristotle, and reinforced by Jâbir (see also Chapter Seven). Earth, water, fire, and air, the four elements have two qualities — hot or cold, wet or dry (see figure 8.1). "In each element, one of the qualities predominates: in earth, it is dryness; in air, wetness; in fire, heat; and in water, coldness. The elements can change, according to properties they have in common with other elements."[69] Consistent with this concept, "Fire can become air through heat, or become earth by drying out. Implicit in this is the possibility of transmutation: lead could become gold through the manipulation of the metal's qualities."

Aristotle traced all elements back to a common, *prima materia*. The alchemists called this matter as "our chaos" or the "dark lump" that "resulted from the fall of Lucifer and Adam."[70] Alexander Roob wrote, "[T]he *prima materia* conjoins with the four qualities of

Eight. Prima Materia

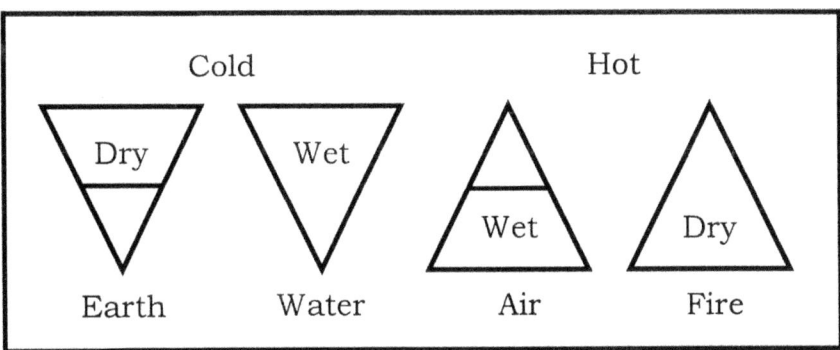

Figure 8.1: Each of the four elements is dominated by one quality—hot or cold, wet or dry. It is possible for elements to change utilizing qualities they share with other elements. The quality of each element also has an important role in the transformation of one element to another. The quality also influences the process by which that transformation is possible. For example, water and air are wet; therefore, transferring energy from water to air through the quality of wetness is an easily performed step.

dryness, coldness, moisture, and heat, thus developing to form the four elements"[71] as Aristotle describes the alchemic process. "By manipulating these qualities, it [is] ... possible," he believed "to change the elemental combinations of materials, thereby bringing about their transmutation."[72]

Roob quotes the writing of J. d'Espagnet in considering the statement of Aristotle about alchemic activities ("Das Geheime Werk," in: *Deutsches Theatrum chemicum*, Nuremberg, 1728), "Accordingly, the work of the alchemist lies 'only in the rotation of the elements. For the material of the stone [Philosopher's Stone] passes from one nature into another, the elements are gradually extracted, and in turn relinquish their powers [...] until all are turned downwards together and rest there.'"[73]

The mercury-sulphur theory developed by Jâbir ibn Hayyân continued to be the endorsed alchemic concept into the seventeenth century. Jâbir (in the person of Geber or pseudo–Jâbir) claimed that the "cause of perfection in metals in nature [that is, gold and silver] is a properly proportionate mixture of mercury and sulphur and long and temperate maturing by heat in the bowels of the earth until the mixture is eventually rendered fusible and malleable."[74] Geber advocated the notion that "gold was made from a combination of the most subtle, fixed, and brightest mercury with a little clear, fixed, red sulphur. Silver was made from a combination of mercury and white sulphur...."[75] The mixing and matching of materials in the laboratory attempted to imitate the natural process but with greater rapidity. The idea being that since all metals are composed of the same elements — mercury and sulphur — imperfect bodies could be changed by removing impurities and augmenting perfect elements.

Alchemy was from the beginning a secret art. "[T]he Greek language was used in Egypt in writing about the art refers to the need for preventing unseemly dissemination of the more profound aspects of alchemic knowledge."[76] "Alchemists [from the beginning] concerned themselves with theory and speculation, often in figurative language [...] Writers on alchemy used language in ways that were not exclusively, and perhaps not even primarily, confined to expressing the production of change in metals."[77] Alchemic writing employed riddles, metaphor, analogy, signs, and symbols to record activities, ideas, theory, and practice for references. The writings, especially the symbols, were intricately woven into an individual's or group's ongoing insight into practices or activities. The symbols had, or appear to have, a certain capacity that defined the reality of a particular individual or group. The alchemist used symbols as abstractions of the values assigned to the things they used.

The language employed by alchemists was partly allegorical, and though particular markings might convey information to other adepts, they often had little relation to actual fact. Any list of signs, symbols, or marks used to identify specific substances might as a result represent the thinking of only one person or one laboratory. There are some identifiable exceptions to this generalization. Gold was generally identified with the sun and represented by a circle or a circle with a dot in the middle. Ether (atmosphere) was at times also designated by a circle, and in Taoism, the circle is also the diagram for *Wu-chi* (the limitless) — coming into existence and the return to the Tao. Silver was identified with the moon and shown as the crescent opening to the left; whereas, air might be represented as a crescent moon opening to the right.

Garth Roberts wonders whether the allegorical instructions provided by the alchemists "are figurative expressions concealing practical processes from the vulgar, and revealing them through a veil to the initiate, or whether the medium is the message and the allegory is meant to reveal some other meaning."[78]

The symbols used for substance identification were, according to E. J. Holmyard, a "kind of shorthand designed perhaps to save time more than to puzzle the vulgar [the uninitiated], but there was little uniformity in the schemes adopted by different alchemists ... [a] practitioner might use several distinct signs for a single substance or operation."[79] There is a symbolic relationship between the planets and certain metals in alchemy and astrology. The practice among writers on alchemic subjects was to identify metals with the planets. Gold, as noted above, corresponded with the sun and silver with the moon. Other metals, mercury, iron, tin, and lead, were associated respectively with Mercury, Mars, Jupiter, and Saturn. This association has a long history in western alchemy. It was used by the Muslims and passed to the Europeans.

"Countless are the symbols with which the adepts embellished their secret. 'Explain the unknown by the more unknown' is one of the alchemic theorems."[80] Some of the symbols used in alchemic practice are shown in **figure: 8.2**. This list is drawn from different sources but references the list noted by Holmyard in *Alchemy* (1990 [1957]).[81]

The contemporary chemical symbol for mercury is Hg derived from the Latin *Hydrargyrum*, liquid silver. Mercury was known and used in Egypt perhaps as early as 1500 B.C.E. and was a critical element in alchemy for centuries before the current era. It was probably known in the China at about the same time. The name mercury originated in 6th century alchemy when the sign for the planet was used to represent the metal. The primary source of mercury is cinnabar or mercury sulfide. Cinnabar was a common ingredient in Chinese alchemic processes.

Sulphur (also spelled sulfur), "the stone that burns" was also an early element in the alchemic processes. The chemical symbol for sulphur is S, which is derived from the scientific name for the element. It was known from prehistoric times, and is called brimstone in Genesis. "Suddenly the Lord rained burning sulphur on the cities of Sodom and Gomorrah and destroyed them and the whole valley, along with all the people there and everything that grew on the land" (Genesis 19:23, 24, 25).[82]

Like the universe at the beginning of creation (Genesis 1:2), work in the laboratory is

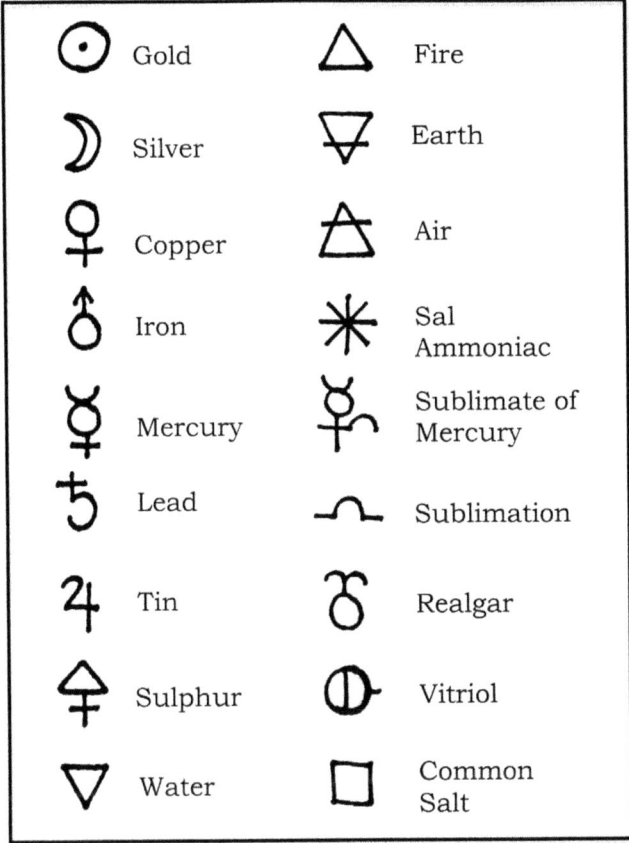

Figure 8.2: Various symbols were employed by alchemists to indicate the substances used in their experiments. Often the persons working in a particular laboratory were the only ones who knew the exact meaning of each symbol. The cause for this lack of communication was not always secrecy, but the fact that no standard list of minerals and metals was established until the nineteenth century. The Swedish scientist J.J. Berzelius proposed in 1813 that chemical symbols be based on the Latin names of the elements.

said to begin in darkness. Preparing the *prima materia* is the first stage of the Lesser Work, the *nigredo*—the black stage of the process.[83] The essence of this part of the process is blackening and putrefying. It is called *calcinario* (to burn) and *mortificatio* (to mortify).[84] This stage of the alchemic process is known as black because it deals with initial raw material. It is said to allude to the black soil of the Egyptian Delta. It may also refer to the killing of the *prima materia* in that life follows death through transformation. Psychologically the first stage relates to spiritual death and the elimination of the ego. The second stage of the Lesser Work is the *albedo*—the whitening.[85] ("Then God commended, 'Let there be light'—and light appeared" [Genesis 1:3]). The matter is cleaned, and mind and body are prepared for a spiritual and physical reunion by fasting and observation of the proper rituals. The final stage of the process is the Greater Work: the *rubedo*.[86] This is the red stage.[87] It is the culmination of the alchemist's work at which time the Stone or Elixir is achieved. It is in spiritual terms, the mystical union of the soul and the body.[88]

> Know ye, therefore, Enquirers into the rumour, and Children of Wisdom, that the vulture standing upon the mountain crieth out with a loud voice, I am the White of the Black, and the Red of the White, and the Citrine of the Red; and I speak the very truth.[89]

The colors are a very important part of the alchemic process because of the lack of specific knowledge (rules) about the transformation from raw material to stone or elixir. The sequence of black, white, and red (some said purple) color was generally considered correct; therefore, when the black or red appeared out of the proper sequence it signaled failure. The work was repeated until the desired colors were achieved. A yellow stage was identified between the white and red stages by some alchemists.⁹⁰ The French alchemist Nicholas Flamel (c.1330–1417) reported a list of colors including "citrine, green, red, yellow and blue preliminary to the white stage."⁹¹ This multi-color progression was often referred to as the rainbow or peacock feather effect.

Emphasizing the issue about color in laboratory work, Mircea Eliade wrote in *The Forge and The Crucible* (1978 [1956]), "Transmutation, the *magnum opus* which culminated in the Philosopher's Stone, is achieved by causing matter to pass through four phases, named, from the colours taken on by the ingredients."⁹² Eliade uses the Greek terms to identify the colors: "melansis (black) [portrayed as a dead man or a crow], leukosis (white) [symbolized by the pelican piercing its breast with its beak], xanothosis (yellow) [the sower sowing seeds in a field], and iosis (red) [the wedding of the king and queen or the starry lion]."⁹³ The issue of color, that is, the references to the four phases of the laboratory process was mentioned "in the pseudo-Domocritean [writing] *Physika kai Mystika* (fragment preserved by Zosimos)—that is, in the first alchemical writing proper (second to first century B.C.E.)"⁹⁴

The exact number and shades of colors varied according to the author and the records maintained. Equally ambiguous was the length of time required for the laboratory process. The duration of the work and the sequence of stages differed depending on the logic and mystical reasoning of the alchemist. The number of day, weeks, or months was often of numerologically significant. The time for the work might be seven days to correspond with the days of the week, or twelve days reflecting the number of months in a year, or nine months relating to the period of gestation of the human embryo.⁹⁵

Gareth Roberts quotes Sir George Ripley, canon at Bridlington in Yorkshire, England, "Equally important and equally debated [referring to the number of days required for the process] was the nature of the vessel(s) for the [laboratory] work. Alchemists were fond of the axiom that just as the work and its matter were one, so only one vessel was needed, 'one thing, one glasse, one furnace, and no more.'"⁹⁶ Different types and sizes of furnaces were used as well as different degrees of heat depending on the individual and the process. The primary fuel used to heat the furnace was charcoal according to E.J. Holmyard.⁹⁷ Other fuels, "wood, peat, rushes, oil, wax, pitch, coal, and dried dung," were also employed

Drawing 8.b: Success in the alchemical search for the "stone" often depends on the quality of the furnace, bellows, and cauldron. Alchemists invested a great deal of time and study in developing a furnace to provide temperature hot enough to soften or melt (transform) the ingredients. The fire was regulated by the amount of air available to enhance ignition; therefore, bellows were used to produce accurate temperatures at different stages of refining. A leak-proof cauldron (crucible) was needed to contain the tempered substances after they were purified.

depending on availability.[98] Alchemists were obsessed with the idea that if they could get a sufficiently high temperature, transmutation would be easy.[99] Bellows of different sizes and shapes were used to provide the air necessary for attaining higher temperatures.

The design and construction of the furnace was an important element of the laboratory process, and details were often included in the alchemic treaties (**see drawing 8.b**). Each adept seemingly had a different idea about the making of the furnace, the number of furnaces needed for the various steps in the refining process, and the design, shape, and material of the crucible in which the material was placed for smelting. Selecting the proper furnace and vessel was as difficult as finding the correct substance with which to begin the quest.

Fire is one of the alchemist's essential tools. Although the earliest unquestionable use of fire was about 500,000 B.C.E. some evidence suggest it was used at a much earlier date. The fire and heat used in making the elixir was given great attention. Dry heat and wet heat as well as high and low temperature was required depending on the different stages

Plate E. This image produced in 1652 was a chapter frontispiece in ***Theatrum chemicum britannicum*** by Elias Ashmole. The central image shows the alchemist and his assistant in the laboratory. They are working with seven different furnaces, and each furnace appears to be dealing with a different part of the alchemic process. The regulation of temperature was believed a critical factor in the transmutation process. The boarder with birds, plants, and bugs is a style use in much of this book by Ashmole. It may demonstrate the influence of Arabic illustrations, which used abstract arabesque designs to embellish book pages.

of the operation. "Four degrees of heat — according to some authorities, water, ashes, sand and flame — were likened to the four seasons of the year."[100] The four grades of fire may also refer to the various states of consciousness that must be understood and purified[101] (**see plate E**).

The dramatic elements of the laboratory process such as the sufferings, death and resurrection of matter has a significant role in alchemic practice. It is identified and acknowledged in the very beginnings of Greco-Egyptian alchemistical literature (perhaps drawing upon the Hellenistic mystery religions such as belief in the goddess Isis[102]). This practice acknowledges association with the mystical drama of God and his or her passion, death, and resurrection — "which is projected on to matter in order to transmute it."[103]

Physical Alchemy

> In fine, it is your mind that becomes the Buddha, nay, it is your mind that is indeed the Buddha. The ocean of true and universal knowledge of all the Buddhas derives its source from one's own mind and thought.[104]

Once humans moved beyond the level of basic survival, they began to question why they came into the world and what happened when they died. They wanted to know whether death was the end of everything or was there a paradise waiting for those persons who lived a proper life. The issue of afterlife took precedence over most other issues in many cultures. The need for reassurance that some aspect of life, not necessarily in a corporal sense, continued after physical death generated various belief practices. Renewal, resurrection, life after death, and immortality were ways to address this persistent concern.

The idea of a mystical means for achieving immortality was an early and common notion. Divine intervention, a magic pill, self-sacrifice, and prayer were but a few of the means conceived to achieve the desired renaissance. The alchemist's laboratory was typically devoted to both labor and prayer. "The art of alchemy is divided into two equal and essential parts: manual labor, on one hand, and prayer, meditation, and study on the other," according to Stanislas Klossowski de Rola.[105] This division of physical and spiritual activity reflected the eternal quest for immortality. Early burials included the accouterments for life in the next world, and rituals from blood sacrifices to self-mortification appealed to greater beings for help in achieving extended life. Religions promised life everlasting for the righteous, and the elixir of life — the golden pill — offered a shortcut to eternal existence. Alchemy declared, "Life is renewed when impurities in the body are purged."[106]

The *prima materia* could be called "the ground of the soul."[107] Human existence on earth is fragile. It is imperfect and impermanent. It has evolved, or some would say declined, from the time of creation. The Hindu have the four *yugas* (world ages) that symbolically represent four throws of a dice game. The *yugas* are viewed as descending — though in repetitive cycles — from perfection to moral chaos.[108] The mythology of other people, Chinese, Polynesians, American Indians, have similar beliefs relating to their view of existence. The epic poet Hesiod, a native of Greece during the eighth century before the current era, also considered the ages of the world as four in number. He believed the ages were symbolized by gold, silver, bronze, and iron, and that each period successively declined in morality.[109]

> The mind is the alchemical mercury that must be transmuted into pure gold. It is also the cauldron in which this process of transformation occurs. The yogis are great spiritual alchemists whose secret work is their own metamorphosis.[110]

The Taoist sought the pill of immortality and developed techniques such as meditation, breathing exercises, diet, and other forms of internal alchemy that were believed to confer immortality. Taoists believed it is not possible to enter the alchemic process without meditation and concentration; they assist every step of the way. "They help us towards where we need to go ... which is into the flask itself: what alchemists call 'the closed body of the house.'"[111]

Ko Hung (283–343 C.E.), a celebrated writer on the technical methods for prolonging life, wrote in the *Pao-p'u-tzu (He Who Holds to Simplicity)* the alchemical formulas for immortality. The book is divided into two parts. The first twenty chapters describe alchemical practices and include a recipe "for an elixir called gold cinnabar and recommends sexual hygiene, special diets, and breathing and meditation exercises. He even prescribes a method for walking on water and for raising the dead."[112] The rest of the book deals with Confucianism and ethics. Ko Hung was careful to distinguish the gold elixir (potable gold) that leads to immortality from the counterfeiting of the metal.[113] "The Taoists believes that it takes a human being about one year to enter this earthly realm and that it should take no longer to become an immortal, as both are just a transformation and birthing process."[114]

Taoists continued to pursue a divided path in the quest for immortality after the fourth century; however, the extremes, except for noticeable lapses, were less severe. "On the left are sorcery, alchemy, sexual practices, and demon enslavement. Roughly, it is a path that believes in external methods. The right-handed path advocates asceticism, celibacy, and meditation. Roughly, it is an internal path."[115] The two paths differed in their methodology and interpretation of the Taoist principles.

Chinese alchemy as a path to immortality followed its own course against a backdrop of changing times and mounting influences. Whereas the Western world, with its various religious promises of immortality, never seriously believed alchemy would satisfy that objective, the shortcomings of Chinese religions in regard to immortality left that goal open to the alchemists.[116] The reliance on alchemic means to gain immortality was somewhat lessened as the Chinese adopted Buddhism, which offered other, less dangerous ways for achieving the goal, but the Taoist influence remained strong.

Taoist alchemists during the T'ang Dynasty (618–906 C.E.) believed one type of elixir occurred naturally and was found in "minerals and stones that have absorbed the yin and yang vapors of the universe."[117] They reasoned, "when correct amounts of sunshine and moonlight have been absorbed over a period of four thousand three hundred and twenty years, substances like lead and mercury will be transformed into cinnabar, and will eventually crystallize into a pill with a golden color."[118] A person fortunate enough to find and ingest the golden pill was granted instant immortality.

Much of the alchemic research during the T'ang Dynasty focused on the building of furnaces and cauldron for controlling the heating of the *prima materia*. The alchemists reasoned that if the golden pill evolved naturally, humans using a technique that emulated the natural process could synthesize it. "The rationale was that if the *yang* heat and *yin* cooling could be simulated in laboratory conditions, it might be possible to create the immortal elixir under controlled conditions."[119] The Chinese theorized the heating and cooling of the furnace should "follow the movement of the sun, moon, and stars."[120] The process of modulating the temperature of the furnace, consequently, lasted for months following the seasons as well as the solar sequence.

Logical as the process seemed, many individuals died from ingesting pills and elixirs concocted from mercury, lead, sulphur, arsenic, zinc, and various other ingredients. Probably because of the lack of success, alchemists began to question during the late years of the T'ang Dynasty, whether immortality was possible. This state of mind led to a rethinking of the meaning of immortality.[121]

> The essence of perfect Tao is profoundly mysterious; its extent is lost in obscurity. See nothing; hear nothing; let your soul be wrapped in quiet; and your body will begin to take proper form.[122]

The Taoists used the term *chen-jen* to identify the fully perfected being—the acknowledged self. Many people believe the physical body lives and acts on its own inhabiting spirit-soul, and the activities of the world are thought to be the responsibility of other spirits. The world is inhabited by an abundance of spirits, and their presence is discernable in every aspect of human existence. There is no distinction between spirit and matter for the Taoist. "Metals and all Minerals, are endured and possessed with their own incomprehensible Spirit, in which, the power and virtue of all their possible effects consist. For whatsoever is without Spirit, wants Life, and contains in itself no vivifying Virtue."[123] Between spirit and body, the distinction is one of quality — not of material or kind.[124]

Mystic realization does away with the distinction between the self and the world. The pursuit of individual salvation (enlightenment or immortality) often requires initiation (Sanskrit, *abhiseka*; Tibetan, *wong*) consisting of some form of purification (comparable to the activities in the laboratory). Such cleansings may include examination of essential belief and personal values. This procedure requires the individual to undergo a form of transformation, and to be initiated into life phases that are often inexplicable. The initiation ritual requires enduring a symbolic rites of passage, as well as the related social obligations.[125] The objective of these activities, in alchemic terms, is to rid the individual of a disruptive thinking that includes the ego (**see plate F**).

The initiation practice is exemplified by the legendary experience of Gautama, who practiced austerity for six months until he became physically wasted before he realized the unity of mind and body — the first step toward transformation and enlightenment. The Taoist contends that under such circumstances, "Internal and external [are] blended into Unity. After that, there [is] no distinction between eye and ear, ear and nose, nose and mouth: all [are] the same."[126] The mind is fixed, the body is in suspension, and the flesh and bones melt together in this attitude of concentration to form a physical and mental whole — Oneness.

Meditation is for Buddhists an intermediary step in the initiatory process. Meditation, like prayer, is an example of seeking the right attitude for transformation. Alchemists endorse the concept of prayer, "and as many alchemists have stated, the [purification] process can only be accomplished with God's help and completed with God; in other words, through what is higher than ourselves."[127] This type of prayer is petitional in form but general in direction. It seeks that

Plate F: This woodblock print showing a man with a sword and a dismembered body was produced in 1599. It offers what might be described as a gruesome image, particularly the man holding the sword and the head of the fallen individual. The picture is not, however, the message. As is often repeated in the myths of the world the savior must suffer death and separation before purification is possible. Spiritually, the physical body died, the bones or innards removed, cleaned, and restored before resurrection. The alchemic practice required purification of materials before they could the combined and transformed. The cleaving of the human form in this print represents that purification process.

which is presumably unattainable by personal efforts — sanity and wholeness.[128] "A second aspect of purification follows on from this and is a more active expression. It is simply commitment — commitment that follows a choice to actually do something."[129]

The pursuit for physical and spiritual transformation is a very old search. It has its beginning in the earliest years of human existence. The methods differed, but the objectives were similar — to gain the essence of perfection and to limit the passage of time. Individuals pursued a mystical relationship with their gods by assuming a spiritual nature or by acquiring the likeness, physically or mentally, of the Absolute. The Egyptians, for example, gave great attention to the preparation for death and the transformation from one existence to another. They endorsed the myth of a dying and rising savior god who could grant immortality to devotees. The concept of a transformation reality was common in much of the world. It had its beginning in the earliest beliefs of humanity and was manifest in the shamanic practices where guardian spirits aided in travel to regions beyond the physical world.

Jung equated immortality, or the quest for immortality, to "a clock that never runs down."[130] He envisioned a relationship between immortality and "a *mandala* [sometimes called the magic circle] that revolves eternally like the heavens."[131] Immortality is more than long-life; it is an attitude relating to emotional and spiritual existence, a sense of self-discovery that may be exemplified by the mandala. The "*mandala* (Tibetan: *dkyil 'khor*) is a strongly symmetrical diagram concentrated about a center."[132] It represents a secure existence safe from outside intrusions though surrounded by a troublesome world. The circle marks the center of social order — the safe zone, and symbolically defined the center of the human — the soul. The consecrated circle of the mandala (see figure 8.3) is present in many belief systems in North American, Australia, Tibet, India, China, Mexico, Egypt, the Middle East, part of Africa, and other locations. The microcosmic, magic circle or cosmic center is exemplified by the sacred places of the Eastern and Western worlds.

Figure 8.3: The mandala (Tibetan: *dkyil 'khor*) is described in different ways perhaps because it serves different purposes. It is a design involving concentric circles that radiate out from the center (*dkyil*). The square or triangle is sometimes at the center of the mandala. It is the central part of the design is important as a point of concentration for meditation. The center of the mandala is said to correspond with nirvâna and the surrounding circles represent the world. Martin Brauen writes in *Mandala: Sacred Circles in Tibetan Buddhism* (2009), "a mandala can belong to one of four main categories on the basis of its center; lotus, wheel, disk divided into nine cells, and triangle."

A concept present in ancient India included the belief that humanity possessed a divine spark but due to ignorance was unaware of this endowment. It was also believed that man and the universe were identical, and that revelation took place not on earth but at the cosmic center of the universe by virtue of the cosmic soul. Alexander Roob wrote in *The Hermetic Museum: Alchemy & Mysticism* (2006), "This cosmic soul reflected the ideas of the higher, transcendental sphere of the divine intellect, and through the influence of the stars these ideas imprinted they eternal 'symbols' on the lower, physical transient sphere."[133]

Just as all religions have a mystical foundation, all religious beliefs reinforce the notion of transformation — the leaving behind of the bad or unacceptable — the alchemy of human life. The speaking of words, mantra, prayers, chants, and oaths for mystical and alchemic purposes is common practice. Such activities are based on choices made by the human mind.

"As to the true man, he makes gold because he wishes by the medicinal use of it to become an immortal."[134] It is neither mystical nor magical for individuals to seek the golden pill or to possess the supernatural qualities ascribed to the Philosopher's Stone. To say that it is human nature trivializes the merit and in some instances the value of such a rare commodity. Nevertheless, the elixir of immortality or the essence of self-realization, by any name, is a constant feature of every person from an early age. The *prima materia* is the human intellect, the *latent goldness* is the human will or wisdom, and *immortality* is human achievement.

It may be said that every person possesses the essential elements to produce the golden pill of immortality. A primary ingredient of the alchemic process is the spiritual principle identified with mercury, "which is far from being the metal which we ordinarily know by that name. The Mercury which the alchemists sought — often in strange places — is a hidden and powerful substance."[135] However, the mercury sought by the alchemist is that unique element hidden within the human body. In fact, it was called "Mercury of the Wise." It was said that he who can discover it is on the way toward [alchemic] success.[136]

> If life is passed aimlessly with death ever coming unexpectedly, the bones of the body will dispense, the four elements (of metal, wood, water, and fire) will scatter and the deluded consciousness will transmigrate through another realm of existence without knowing what form it will take in another life.[137]

Material Alchemy

C. G. Jung had a particular interest in alchemy and the alchemic process. His book *Psychology and Alchemy* (1980 [1952]) includes the following: "Alchemy," he wrote, "describes a process of chemical transformation and gives numberless directions for its accomplishment. Although hardly two authors are of the same opinion regarding the exact course of the process and the sequence of its stages."[138] Jung believes that most alchemists agreed on the principal points of transformation, and were of similar opinion, at least in the Western World since the beginning of the current era.

The alchemic process in the Western World gave primary attention to the process of transformation and each adept had a different notion about how this was accomplished. "The idea of the production of gold was so dominant in alchemy [in the Western World] that it was actually spoken of as the gold maker's art. It meant the ability to make gold out of baser materials, particularly out of other metals."[139]

The Chinese alchemists during the early millennium of the current era may be divided into three groups in contrast with the approach of their western colleagues. The most idealistic Chinese were seekers of knowledge. "They were sincere followers of Lao Tzü, and, as such, they had a genuine and unselfish interest in his teaching. To them the question of the transmutation of metals presented the challenge of the unknown."[140] The solution of this mysterious problem was of an intellectual nature instead of material. "The alchemists of this order were largely recluses or anchorites, pursuing their researches in the solitude of the mountains."[141] Success was viewed as elevation and perfection by solving the riddle, not obtaining the product.

A second group of Chinese alchemists were the seekers of favor. Persons of this pursuit frequented the imperial courts. "The motive in their case was personal glory and honor, for in case of the success of their efforts, their names would become imperishable by reason of their connection with the imperial throne."[142] This association ended when the T'ang dynasty was replaced by the period known as the Five Dynasties and Ten Kingdoms (907–960 C.E.). The political and social chaos that marked this half-century caused many intellectuals to abandon political life and became recluses.[143]

The third group of Chinese alchemists was seekers of riches. The motive that activated this group was the desire to acquire wealth. "For, whether life was considered as endless, or as only of normal duration, the possession of material means marked the difference between affluence and want."[144] The desire for gold was a potent incentive in the search for process of transmutation. Unlike the first group where the process was the motivation, for these individuals, the purpose was the product — gold.

Within each of the groups was also the potential of discovering medicine to prolong life. This purpose had greater or lesser importance based on the group, time, and circumstantial motivation. The first group saw immortality as an integral part of Taoism, whereas, the second group recognized the potential of imperial favor that would accompany discovery of the golden pill. The third group understood the financial benefit of the finding the means to ensure long-life. Taoists were also of the opinion that man-made gold was more valuable than native gold. It was believed that the alchemic process imbued the gold with a special quality that could be transmitted to humans. This added to the possibility of personal enrichment that appealed to the second and third groups of alchemists, but meant little to the first group.

Ko Hung, a prominent fourth century Chinese alchemist, wrote, "[H]ow is it that it [transmutation] does not exist? Take the case of the human body. Normally it is visible, yet there are methods by which it can be made invisible. Spirits are normally invisible, but there are devices whereby they may be seen."[145] The foundation of the belief in transmutation is reflected in the philosophy of Taoism, which proclaims the entire cosmos is identical in substance. Taoists contend the universe is energized and regulated by a cosmic soul that identifies itself in the forces of *yin* and *yang*. All objects of the mineral kingdom are therefore essentially the same, but they differ in quality based on the proportion to their infusion with *yin* and *yang*.[146]

The challenge of transmutation of metal, east or west, was refining the essence — the purification process. The Chinese sought to transmute base metal into "precious metal by the dual method of eliminating the more material *Yin* qualities in their composition, and by augmenting, or refining, the more spiritual *Yang* (Tao) qualities."[147] It is this context that the Chinese spoke of the red component, called cinnabar or mercury, and the white part, called lead, as the primary components for turning base metals into gold.[148] The Western alchemist pursued the purification process by an often complicated, multi-step process that might include, sublimation, fixation, calcination, solution, distillation, and coagulation.[149]

The seven metals, gold, silver, copper, tin, lead, zinc, and iron (metals known very early in the rise of alchemy) were thought by many early alchemists to be of the same species. Assuming this hypothesis were true, it should be possible to dissect the impure metals, remove the impurities and reconnect the remaining elements to form the perfect metal. It was in this context that the mercury-sulphur theory was applied. "Amalgams may be made of mercury with lead, tin, gold, silver, and copper [but] an amalgam of iron cannot be prepared directly."[150] It is also understood that when mercury is converted into a solid, the product is of a shining color.

The alchemist had only to look to nature for proof that transmutation was possible. Metals were believed (as noted) to grow and mature within the earth and when the "metal reached its final perfection and not extracted from the earth, which was no longer providing it with nourishment, it may well, at this stage, be compared to an old and decrepit man."[151] It was believed the "alchemical art was minister to and follower of nature, indeed Albertus Magnus ... said that it was the art that most closely imitated nature."[152] Albertus elaborated on this concept, "starting with the same first principles of 'our mercury' and 'our sulphur,'" he stated, and, "imitating nature's heat—in the alchemical furnace—and nature's enclosed, dryly compacting space beneath the earth where gold is formed—in the sealed alchemical vessel."[153]

The alchemic thinking in the Western World was for many years dominated by the mercury-sulphur theory. This composition concept was expanded by the sixteenth century, possibly beginning with Paracelsus, to include salt (see Chapter Seven). Thereafter, materials, particularly minerals, were thought composed of three ingredients each of which had an anthropomorphic relationship: mercury (life force), sulphur (soul or individualized essence), and salt (physical body). This compositional theory was implemented in many (perhaps most) laboratories of western alchemists. These components were separated and recombined until they were in perfect proportion and in harmony with each other (chemically and spiritually). Most alchemists consider mercury (life force) "not only as the first matter, but in particular as the first matter of metals, since all the philosophers seemed to cry with one voice—'O our Mercury, our Mercury.'"[154]

Both the elixir and gold were thought to be composed of mercury and sulphur, or from mercury alone that was believed to contain internal sulphur. The "importance of mercury and the idea that gold could be made from mercury alone, seems to have prevailed in the fourteenth and fifteenth centuries."[155] The users of mercury in the alchemic process often identified "our" mercury, which appears to mean, "our mercury is not the mercury of the common people."[156] The alchemists stress it is called "philosophers' mercury," or as George Ripley said, "But not the common [mercury] called quicksilver by name."[157] Arthur E. Waite notes, "Common quicksilver [mercury, *argent vive*], however carefully prepared, can never become the quicksilver of the Sages, for common quicksilver can only stand the test of fire by the aid of some other dry and more highly digested quicksilver."[158]

Alchemists discovered a number of new substances in their search for the *prima materia*. Among those discoveries were sal ammoniac, saltpeter, alcohol, and the mineral acids. They used corrosive salts and mineral acids to modify (liquefy) metals. (The alchemists sought to reduce all elements to a liquid state. "One of the alchemists' maxims was: 'Perform no operation till all be made water.'"[159]) The first acid used was probably nitric acid (*aqua fortis*) made by distilling together saltpeter (potassium nitrate, KNO_3) and vitriol or alum.[160] The discovery of the vitriol (hydrated sulfates and sulfuric acid H_2SO_4) alums (aluminum sulfate

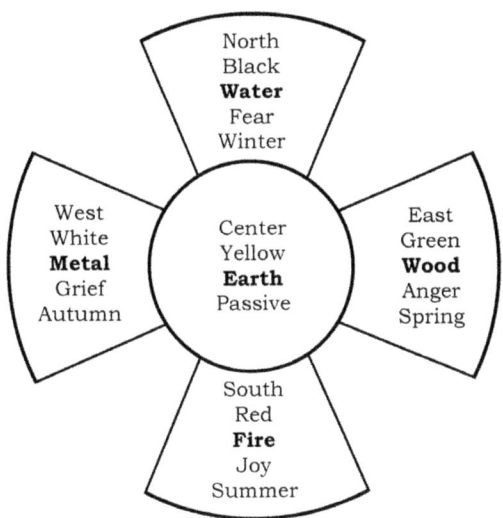

Figure 8.4: The Chinese concept of the cosmos arranged according to the five elements, five directions, five emotions, four seasons, and five significant colors. China, the middle kingdom — earth — is assigned to the center where it assists the other elements in the "rule" of the seasons. It is the place of passivity where all directions and emotions merge into one.

with sulfates of univalent cations of potassium, sodium or ammonium), and the chlorides of sodium and ammonium was an important achievement for the laboratory activities of the alchemist. Arsenic was already in use since before the present era for coloring metals (see Chapter Seven).

"The hermetic view of the elements was mystical, too. Air was seen as a magical element, full of imagination and spirits, while water was the link between air and earth, as well as 'above' and 'below.'"[161] The earth, in this context, "was the ground of Creation, like a womb or matrix in which all generation takes place, receiving all the cosmic influences from the stars."[162] These concepts found validation in nature. The human body, like many other substances, is composed of air and water plus a few minerals that are found in most places including soil. Life was associated with breath (air). The challenge for the alchemist was to rearrange the elements in such a way to generate a different metal or a disease and age resistant human body.

Alchemy considers nature as powerful, intelligent, and creative, but slow. The alchemist worked to accelerate the process of inner and outer evolution of the three realms of mineral, plant, and animal by imitating nature's methods. The alchemic design is not intended to violate Nature's laws, but to perform the process the same as nature, only quicker and more efficiently.[163] The alchemist treats his (or her) materials as God was treated in the mystery plays during the Middle Ages; the minerals substances suffer, die, or are reborn to another form of being, that is, they were transmuted.[164]

The belief that the alchemists could influence their environment through their discipline is a Hermetic concept that echoes its historic origins. Hermetic writings (also called *Hermetica*) address topics on occult, theological, and philosophical subjects including alchemy, astrology, and magic. The message of the Hermetic writing is that "Humanity is created by God like God and lives under the aegis of Nature. Destinies are ruled by the heavenly bodies, the microcosm, or Earth, is a reflection of the macrocosm or heaven."[165] The concept of alchemical transmutation according to Mircea Eliade "is the fabulous consummation of a faith in the possibility of changing Nature by human labours (labours which always had some liturgical significance)."[166]

Western alchemists endorsed the notion of four elements — earth, water, fire, and air (called essence by adepts) — from the time of Empedocles, the fourth century B.C.E. (see Chapter Seven); whereas, in Chinese cosmology there are five agents or elements (*Wu hsing*). Each of the elements relates to the *Yin-Yang* concept, and, thereby, refers to the Chinese understanding the nature of the cosmos (**see figure 8.4**). Interaction of the two principles associated with the five elements causes them to activate, thus enabling change to take place within the world. The elements are not physical substances; they represent cyclic movement. Each element is associated with a quarter of the world, a season, and a color; "wood to the East, spring, and green; fire to the South, summer, and red; metal to the West, autumn, and white; water to the North, winter, and black, while earth, at the center, is yellow."[167] China, the middle kingdom — earth — is assigned to the center where it assists the other elements in the rule of the seasons.

The art of the alchemist, whether spiritual or physical, consists of completing the work of perfection, bringing forth and making dominant, as it were, the "latent goldness" that "lies obscure" in metal or man.[168] It is, therefore, that matter has both spirit and body, and that the two are blended to be one. This ideal was found in the earthly elements, thus calling forth the alchemists' challenge — the concept of unity. Fire cannot become water without air, and earth cannot become air without water. Fire, a volatile and subtle element, cannot unite with the earth which is corporeal and fixed, because the volatile will abandon the fixed and return to its chaotic state.[169] "This is so in all Natural things that the most Volatile principle, cannot unite with the most fixt without its proper medium. An Artist [alchemist] ought to observe this constantly that he may not lose his time, his Matter, and Expenses."[170] Unity is evasive.

Gold ... is the symbol of immortality. In Egypt the flesh of the Gods was believed to be of gold. By becoming God, the flesh of Pharaoh also became gold. Alchemical transmutation is therefore equivalent to the perfecting of matter or, in Christian terminology, to its redemption.[171]

CHAPTER NINE

Secret Messages of the Mind

"Images, symbols and myths are not irresponsible creation of the psyche."[1]

The alchemic symbols, especially as applied to the mystic life, are full of an often deliberate obscurity; which makes their exact interpretation a controversial matter at the best. Moreover, the authors of the various Hermetic writings do not always use them in the same sense....[2]

"Alchemy is too closely related to the aspirations of mankind in general to be confined to any one race or nation."[3] The East and West share this common legacy that probably started with shamanic practices, the likely forerunner to alchemy. Shamans during the Bronze Age (beginning before 3000 B.C.E.) in China used spells and magical practices, to bring rain. Shamanism was an established practice in China by the early part of the Chou Dynasty (1122–225 B.C.E.). Shamans were employed at that time as advisers, diviners, and healers, and they were expected to use their talents as directed by the court or their employers.

The shaman sought to divide the paranormal forces into matter and spirit when humanity was at the mercy of the extraordinary powers of nature. The external challenges were consequently confronted on a psychological basis instead of on an intellectual or emotional one. Transformation and transference were interconnected parts of this process of change and sublimation because they included the involvement of a mythical element that fell within the accepted norms of the people.

"Shamanism is one of the most general human institutions,"[4] as observed by Ruth Benedict in *Patterns of Culture* (1959 [1934]). Most early cultures embraced some form of shamanistic practice. Shamanism, like other societal institutions, did not originate at any location as a fully developed belief system, and, as previously noted, undoubtedly included alchemic (transformation) practices from earliest times. The beginning of shamanism may be represented by certain socio-magical activities, but like other culturally significant behavior, shamanic belief undoubtedly evolved from superstitions, beliefs, and necessities.

Mysticism as a ubiquitous but loosely patterned practice of an animistic and pantheistic approach to life has no identifiable beginning; therefore, it can have no end. It is old and new at the same time. The approach to mysticism that evolved as a Western tradition around the beginning of the current era is associated with secret philosophy that is derived from Hellenistic styled magic and alchemy. This philosophical attitude was influenced by Jewish mysticism, astrology, and other occult sciences, as well as spiritual renewal.[5] Belief systems such as these that recognize a socially defined spiritual order expect individuals living within that environment to comply with the essential nature of that order. Human behavior is regulated by a set of practice that are based on the same principle, to act and to be in harmony with the order of the world, which is natural and divine at the same time.

Life and death are common aspects of human existence just as they are common expression found within alchemy. The impure is killed (or made to die) before it can be resurrected (given renewed life). The impure must undergo the ritual of fire to burn away the impurities, before it can be transformed into a new and purer form. This analogy is but one of many that are apparent in both the written texts of alchemy and the pictorial representations that illuminate those writings.

The similarities between East and West narratives—shamanism, mysticism, and alchemy—are many. Tantric practitioners often relied upon hymns to summarize the essence of their beliefs, whereas Western alchemists used poetry and song. The Tantric narratives combined "ancient Vedic rituals along with sectarian practices and popular legends."[6] Alchemists in the West referenced to Hellenic legends, wrote in ciphers, and anthropomorphized the materials and procedures. There is however no consistency of system or name from one text to another in either the East or West.

"In Western Europe, during the so-called Dark Ages, there was also a magical, as well as a mystical tradition; but it had little in common with Hermeticism [as evolved during the Hellenistic period]. Among the Slavic and Teutonic people, there was the conventional shaman."[7] Shamanic practices were also found in regions of Northern and Eastern Europe where they were an integral part of every hunting-gathering culture and an important force for maintained traditional values. Mircea Eliade described the activities of the shaman as essential to the "psychic integrity of the community."[8]

Just as the alchemic intellectual stimulants were lost in Alexandria by the destruction of the library and museum, much of the record of Greek learning that remained in Constantinople was lost in 1204 when western European Crusaders sacked the city. Although the Greeks recovered the city in 1261, a significant part of the intellectual community was gone and for the following two centuries, only a remnant of Greek learning remained intact. Finally, when Turkish armies overran Constantinople in 1453, resident Greek scholars fled to Western Europe taking with them potions of their libraries. The Greek learning made available to the West was a stimulant to philosophical and science thinking. It helped to move away from superstition and irrational belief, thus, prepare the way as Europe moved beyond the Middle Ages and into the Renaissance.

The Furnace and Anvil

The metallic ages, Copper, Bronze, and Iron, although occurring at different times in different locations, involved the use of a smelting furnace to melt metal so it could be shaped. This achievement was a major step forward for the production of weapons and implements used for defending and cultivating the land. Copper, a relatively soft yellow metal, was found in natural deposits and sometime after 6000 B.C.E. it was discovered the metal could be melted at relatively low temperatures and formed into different shapes. Copper was extensively used in Egypt for weapons and grave implements as early as 5000 B.C.E., and in 3700 B.C.E. the oldest known piece of bronze was produced, also in Egypt. Bronze is an alloy of copper and tin that is harder than copper and can be sharpened to a fine edge. The amalgamation of two metals involving heat was an important step forward in metallurgy. Copper was used in China as early as 2500 B.C.E., and it is acknowledged that bronze vessels were being cast during the Shang dynasty, 1766–1122 B.C.E.

The basic alchemic principles were resident from the beginning in the working of the furnace and the anvil. The transformation of metal required the skills of the practitioner and the aid of the gods. The shaman delivered the message to the deity, performed the ritual sacrifice, and interpreted the responses that allowed the metallurgical process to take place. The shaman in some cultures was also considered the master of fire. European folklore includes the story of rejuvenation through the furnace fire. The story identifies Jesus Christ with the blacksmith "who heals the sick and rejuvenates the old by putting them in a heated oven or forging them on an anvil."[9] Another story tells that Jesus resurrected the victims of an imprudent smith from his bones or ashes.[10]

A story in *The Forge and the Crucible* (1956) by Mircea Eliade relates that Jesus while visiting a blacksmith threw "into the furnace an old woman (wife or mother-in-law of the smith) and, by forging her on the anvil, transform[ed] her into a beautiful maiden."[11]

There was no clear division between mystical metallurgy and alchemy in China. It was in the realm of metallurgy that cinnabar (mercury sulfide) as a longevity drug was processed. ("Cinnabar also could be made inside the body mainly by distillation of sperm. The Taoist, imitating animals and vegetables, [suspended] himself upside down causing the essence of his sperm to flow ... to his brain."[12]) This self-realizing concept of rejuvenation and longevity is a common theme of Taoist alchemy. The return to the uterus — the embryonic state, the untarnished nature of the newborn — was an acknowledged goal. The alchemist sought to achieve this state by the smelting of various ingredients in his or her own furnace internally or by external means.

C.A. Burland wrote, "The alchemical idea was bound to arise from observation of the world and the life of the human being, as soon as metallurgy was developed."[13] Smelting was often associated with sexual union or the sacred marriage of male and female ores. Fire was the agent of unification. Chinese alchemists believed duplicating the gestational process by which a child is engendered would generate the Philosopher's Stone. This analogy is implicit in the writings of Western alchemists (they say, for example, that the fire under the receptacle or container must burn continuously for forty weeks — the period necessary for the gestation of the human embryo).

Religion in both the Eastern and Western worlds had a role in the development, spread, and decline of alchemy. Taoism in the East must be credited with being a major contributor to alchemic appreciation and practice. The search for immortality was a primary motivation among the Taoists and when Buddhism offered a different concept of immortality available to everyone through meditation, proper diet, and observance of fundamental canons, the Taoists' exclusive approach decreased in importance. It continued to be a recognized religion that endorsed the value of immortality.

The Western religious environment was unfocused in the Hellenistic Era. A number of different cults, gods, and practices loosely associated with Roman religion allowed the spread of the Hermetic doctrine not as a sustaining force but as a "special group of ideas developed within religious societies which aimed at the attainment of individual salvation for their members."[14] Christianity viewed the alchemist and the related doctrine as heresy early in the current era, and condemned those individuals who pursued the Art. Immortality or salvation was a Christian incentive not to be circumvented by alchemists or mystics. Kabbalah and Sufi adherents secretly practiced their mysticism and acknowledged the spiritual nature of the universe that evolved into alchemy.

The development of alchemy was veiled in allusion. The quest of the alchemists often relied on the beliefs and practices of the ancients that were obscured by analogy and mystical rhetoric. Early writings, formulas, and ideas were interpreted, tried, and retried. The proper proportion of materials, the correct heat and time to ensure complete amalgamation, and the appropriate attitude were necessary to ensure the desired transformation. This cycle of analysis, experimentation, and repetition (life, death, and resurrection) is exemplified by the *Ouroboros*, the snake eating its tail (**see figure 9.1** and drawing 8.a).

C.A. Burland wrote in *The Arts of the Alchemists* (1967), "The alchemist firmly believed that a power from above enlightened him at the moment when he was at last fit to receive the knowledge."[15] Burland contends the making of the gold was in fact, "a seal of approval set on a lifetime of work and study. In terms of our civilization, those ingots of alchemical gold were produced at an expense far in excess of the material value of the metal."[16]

Western Messages

Western hermetic tradition is based on philosophical and religious beliefs generally configured upon the Hellenistic Egyptian documents ascribed to Hermes Trismegistus. These beliefs greatly influenced the Western alchemic practice and were considered to be of great importance during the late Middle Ages and into the European Renaissance. That these documents actually included little information about alchemy or the alchemic process did not alter their importance.

The gibberish (so called because of the writing style of the Arab alchemist Jâbir ibn Hayyân) of Western alchemic writing was often used to disguise the transformation that the church condemned as heretical practice. The church believed (correctly) that alchemy was based upon the idea that the "individual could raise himself or herself toward salvation without the agency of established religion."[17] Whether alchemy is more about transformation of the inner being or transmutation of base metal is an issue determined by the individual alchemist; nevertheless, the indirect and often nonsensical writing style as well as the generally complex imagery are not easily understandable.

The early texts relating to alchemy in Egypt and Latin Europe have already been described in the preceding chapter. The Emerald Tablet, probably written between the first and third centuries of the current era, is thought to be the first Hermetic writing (also called *Hermetica*). "The riddling and oracular style, and also brevity, characterize the maxims of the 'Emerald Table' of Hermes Trismegistus which may be one of the oldest Arabo-Latin texts and was perhaps translated into Latin some time around 1211 C.E."[18] The tablet is considered by many as the most definitive summary of Hermetic thought up to the Middle Ages.[19]

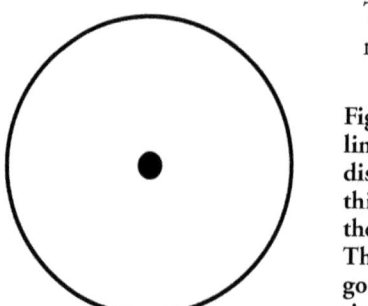

Figure 9.1: The circle as represented by the Ouroboros is a curved line that includes all the points of a plane that are within a fixed distance from a particular point. The center (fixed) point is, in this case, the goal of the alchemic process and the points along the plane are the steps or stages of the process of transformation. The circle presupposes the process may be repeated until the goal is achieved. The circle with a dot in the center is a traditional symbol for gold.

Evelyn Underhill wrote in *Mysticism: A Study in the Nature and Development of Spiritual Consciousness* (2002 [1911]), "Of all the symbolic systems in which ... truth has been enshrined none is so complete, so picturesque, and now so little understood as that of the 'Hermetic Philosophers' or Spiritual Alchemists."[20] Nevertheless, the philosophical thinking advocated by Hermes can hardly be considered as "just a clever intellectual exercise. It is about focusing the mind in deep meditation on *Atum* (an ancient Egyptian name for God). Such pure philosophy is about rising above mere opinions to experience directly the Mind of the Universe."[21]

The essential nature of alchemy may lie hidden in the minds of the adepts identified with the *Turba Philosophorum*. This "parliament of alchemy"[22] offered all shades of opinions and conduct, ranging from one extreme to the other. Alchemy, according to this text, could degenerate into the depths of fraud, or "reach sublime heights under the stimulus and inspiration of philosophy and religion."[23] Other important writings attributed to Hermes are the seventeen treatises of the *Corpus Hermeticum*. These philosophical texts represent most of the theological writings of Hermes. (There were eighteen books originally, but the fifteenth is currently missing.) It is commonly believed these books were collated from ancient material that was available to scholars in Alexandria.

The first person to record his thoughts on the alchemic arts was Bolos of Mendes (see Chapter Eight). His book is titled *Phusika kai mustika*. *Phusika* refers to things in nature and *mustika* denotes mysticism. Sean Martin suggests the proper translation of the book title should be *On Nature and Initiatory Things*.[24] (Bolos of Medes is identified with Democritus. Both were alchemists and many believe they are the same person; historical reference seems to indicate Bolos was a follower of Democritus.)

The Hermetic Art may be viewed as fundamentally a magical application of the highest order, because it presupposed the absolute in science and selection and uses chemistry as a secondary instrument. The Art is a search for the Absolute because the "Absolute is that which admits of no errors; it is the fixation of the volatile; it is the immutable law of reason and truth — the Absolute Reason which is essential to being."[25] The writings speak of life and work, nature and salvation. They often include elaborate instructions on how to prepare the stone, but they are generally unintelligible in any practical sense. Alchemical texts are designed to effectively mask the issue of exactitude.

Jung wrote in *Psychology and Alchemy* (1980 [1952]), "The alchemist was quite aware that he writes obscurely. He admits that he veils his meaning on purpose, but nowhere ... does he say that he cannot write in any other way."[26] Jung believes alchemists made obfuscation "a virtue of necessity" by claiming that "mystification is forced on him for one reason or another, or that he really wants to make the truth as plain as possible, but cannot proclaim aloud just what the prima materia or the lapis is."[27]

The visionary aspect of European alchemy was symbolically represented by the winged dragon perhaps to acknowledge the joining of Hermetic philosophy and Christian dogma. The alchemic dragon is in itself a hybrid, a mixing of elements that may foretell different messages. It combines the underworld principle of the serpent and the aerial principle of bird — above and below, the beginning and the end — as a winged creature may also represent mercury (Latin: *Mercurius*) — the god identified with Hermes (**see Plate G**). "When the alchemist [spoke] of Mercurius, on the face of it he means quicksilver, but inwardly he means the world-creating spirit concealed or imprisoned in matter."[28] This manipulation of possible meanings is common in alchemic literature and art.

The European alchemists had greater freedom in their artwork and the use of images to illustrate their texts than was available to Islamic scholars. "Thus, the Islamic alchemist was usually restricted to a world of words and symbols within which his thoughts had to be expressed. On the other hand, the way was open for the Europeans to escape into another method of expression."[29] C.A. Burland believes the "possibilities of pictorial expression may have inhibited the need of scholars for a system of practical philosophy to give them a spiritual release."[30] He reasons that "as the western Europeans acquired a deeper education they were to find that their studies of alchemy, learned from the Arabs, were to be greatly enriched by their pictorial traditions"[31] (**see plates E and H**).

The early alchemist would seem to be an individual devoted to the pursuit of understanding the ultimate question of existence. The search for the secrets of matter, its purification, and transformation was accompanied by an equally challenging search within the alchemist himself or herself (**see plate I**). This quest, similar to that of the mystic, would be a comprehension of the nature of the Absolute and creation. This mission fit well with certain beliefs, but most Western Europeans found it difficult to grasp the concept of studying the natural (material) world to gain a "wider understanding than that revealed in the Scriptures."[32]

"Emblems (allegorical images) of alchemy entered at many points into the ... art of the Middle Ages."[33] Alchemical symbols often found an expression in decorative architecture and stone, as well as in the pictorial media. The work of art could do more than just exemplify the Hermetic principle of harmonious propor-

Plate G: Two putti are holding the philosopher's stone containing the image of Hermes in the upper section of the engraving while a man and woman kneel before a furnace waiting for transmutation in the lower section. Birds with fly about the feet of the putti and the sun shines benevolently. Each part of the illustration has a specific alchemic message. The birds, for example convey information through the sprigs they carry. The sprig carried by the bird on the left has the sign of sublimation and the rays of the sun indicate an enhanced degree of fire. The man appears to be in prayer while the woman is gesturing upward. The print was created in 1652.

Plate H: This image is the title page of Andreas Libavius,' *Alchymia*, produced in Frankfort in 1606. The figure on the left of the title plate is Galen and to the right is Aristotle. The figures above seemingly in prayer are Hippocrates and Hermes. Galen was a Greek physician and philosopher who was a predominant influence on medical theory and practice in Europe from the Middle Ages until the mid-seventeenth century; hence, the association with Hippocrates. Hermes and Aristotle are connected by alchemy. The activities below the title plate show figures busy at the practice of medicine and alchemy.

tion and balance. "Once pictorial imagery had entered alchemy it was set on a course of advancement which made it almost like a religion."[34] It could act as a talisman. "In other words, it could be an active agent, a dynamic element, in the magical operation — could indeed constitute in itself a magical act."[35]

The reliance on symbolism draws upon the early practices of western alchemy. The Egyptian Horapollo (also sometimes called Horus Apollo) is identified as a fifth century grammarian from Phanebytis (or Nilopolis), Egypt. It is to him that the *Hieroglyphica*, a work that explained the hidden meaning of the mysterious Egyptian hieroglyphs, is attributed. (There are differing opinions about whether Horapollo is the actual author of the manuscript, but his authorship is commonly reported.) The document was eventually discovered by the Florentine monk Cristoforo Buondelmonti and acquired for Cosimo de' Medici.[36] The *Hieroglypica*, consisting of two books, and is said to have reached Florence in 1422 where it was received with considerable enthusiasm.

The *Hieroglypica* includes almost 189 chapters (70 in one book and 119 in the second) explaining Egyptian hieroglyphs.[37] The commentaries were ultimately found to be a mixture of fact and fantasy, and leaning heavily toward the latter. Nevertheless, the book was copied numerous times during the fifteenth century and widely circulated. The most interesting copy of the *Hieroglypica* was prepared for Emperor Maximilian I and included illustrations by the German artist Albrecht Dürer (1471–1528).[38] This document helped to inspired the allegorical images and style of future books relating to mysticism and alchemy. Dürer is

Plate I: This image is a reproduction of a painting of the alchemist and assistant in the laboratory by the artist Thomas Wiick (1616–1677). He created the feeling of the solitary nature of the alchemist's quest. The disarray of the furnace area and the papers scattered on the floor suggest a time of theorizing and search instead of mixing and testing. Alchemists spend much time reviewing and analyzing the writings of earlier practitioners. They believed others had succeeded in the search for the philosopher's stone, and reasoned that by accurately interpreting the writing of their predecessors they could also find the secret to making gold.

Plate J: This print, Melencolia I, by Albrecht Dürer (1471–1528) was in the book *Hieroglypica* prepared for Emperor Maximilian I. Dürer is said to use "underlying pentagonal geometry based on the Golden Section" in this work produced in 1514. The print shows a female figure with wings representing Melancholy. She is wearing a wreath and sitting among a number of objects, including a bell, hourglass, scales, and a magic square. There is a putto sitting on a grindstone and a dog is sleeping nearby. There is a ladder and various other tools scattered about the image. A bat carries a sign in the background with the word "Melancolia I." The structure of the print is complex and includes a number of related geometric shapes — squares, circles, and triangles. © The Trustees of the British Museum. All rights reserved.

said to use "underlying pentagonal geometry based on the Golden Section" in his work titled *Melancholia* (**see plate J**).[39]

Hermeticism endorsed the notion of the interconnectedness of all things. This concept of interrelationship was believed to extend into art, music, and architecture. Numbers and measurements can be traced to hermetic concepts that influenced composition, structure, and cadence. The Golden Mean, also called the Golden Section as found in the work of Leonardo da Vinci. It was considered a "confirmation of the harmonious relationship between microcosm and macrocosm — humanity and the universe. Its significance was deemed all the greater by virtue of the fact that it could be found, like a divine signature, in nature...."[40]

The Golden Section considers the scale of human environment as it relates to the human body. The concept of proportion is an important consideration in art and architecture. The notion of the Golden Mean also includes the Hindu ideal of the four noble truths that follow the path between the two extremes of sensual indulgence and ascetic self-torture.[41] Gautama rejected the two extremes in his search for enlightenment. He followed the Middle Way consisting of the Eightfold Path: (1) right views, (2) right intention, (3) right speech, (4) right action, (5) right livelihood, (6) right effort, (7) right mindfullness, and (8) right concentration.

Plate K: The blood of the lion and the tears of the eagle are intertwined with the sun and moon. It is the conflict between and joining of the occult (alchemy) and philosophy, male and female principles, mercury and sulphur, gold and silver. It may represent the union of all matter. The image relies upon symbolic reference and the metaphorical world, and like many references to alchemy the image may be interpreted differently according to the interest and intent of the viewer. This image, an engraving, is from the "*Azoth*" series of Basil Valentine. It was produced between 1728 and 1732.

The alchemic tradition of reliance on ancient works changed as scientific endeavors increased in understanding and importance in Europe. The first book in the emblem genre was *Emblemata*, by Andrea Aleiato and published in 1531. Alciato, an Italian lawyer and humanist, is identified as the "father of emblem literature."[42] The hieroglyphic and graphic tradition of the emblem continued to develop into the seventeenth century, and it continued to serve the interests of mystics and alchemists. "Horapollo's interpretation of hieroglyphs contributed to a perennial tradition which saw all religious myths and imagery as the cloak of a hidden allegory."[43]

Stanislas Klossowski de Rola describes the *Emblemata* of the sixteenth century as "'hieroglyphs' directly inspired by Horapollo."[44] De Rola maintains the "allegorical images accompanied by a few cryptic lines of prose or verse, emblems presented to the learned a kind of pictorial riddle containing a solution of a moral nature."[45] Emblems were recognized as a perfect means for the sharing of esoteric information, and as such, were put into practice by the alchemists.

The alchemists included "every classical myth, every ancient fable and every conceivable allegorical figure, emblem, symbol — or 'hieroglyph'— in a complex system of multiple correspondences constituting a formidable initiatory challenge for every aspiring Son of Hermes."[46] De Rola wrote in *The Golden Game*, "These so-called 'Hieroglyphicall Figures' and 'Hermetick Emblems' constitute an independent pictorial language which, in silence but not without eloquence, conveys the secret language of alchemy to those aspiring 'Sons of the Art' ... [alchemy disciples] who alone can discover them."[47]

The mystical alignment between concept and comment demonstrates the close connection between the material and metaphorical worlds (**see plate K**). Both the non-literal character of the writing and the images that illustrated the material confirmed the secret nature of alchemic texts. The images "came into being because of the difficulty alchemists found in expressing their understanding in words."[48] The images preserve secrecy in scope and content, message and meaning; nevertheless, the "visual language of alchemy is just as important as its verbal expression, and is sometimes more accessible."[49]

> [T]he transient entities known as sentient beings (gods, humans, animals, etc.) are held to consist of five aggregates — namely forms, feelings, perceptions, impulses, and consciousness — apart from which they are nothing but pure, undifferentiated non-substance.[50]

The symbolic images that easily conceal more than one meaning were ideal means for the secret communication; consequently, alchemists adopted the practice. Western alchemic documents included "images of dragons, lions, snakes, ravens, pelicans, skeletons, suns, and moons, Sol and Luna, king and queen, and the ever-present Mercurius are a call to our own expression of what we feel in the depths of our own physical being."[51] The alchemist was "bound by secrecy and obscurity so that the great secret should not be betrayed to unsuitable people. Yet he really preferred the whole practical process to be part of the pictorial myth."[52]

Garth Roberts wrote in *The Mirror of Alchemy* (1994), "It may prove useful to think of alchemy's languages in four ways: its characteristic use of language and the 'rhetoric' of alchemy; its narratives; other discourses which (to use alchemical metaphors) it 'amalgamated' or perhaps 'fermented,' and its recurrent images and metaphors."[53] It should be remembered that when the alchemist speaks of gods and goddesses, plants, animals, and astrological elements those connections do not necessarily refer to actual substances but to spiritual essence.

Alchemists, for instance, support the notion that metals possessed a body and a soul like humans,[54] and the anthropomorphic element is very strong in the illustration associated with alchemy. The androgyny or the "double thing," the conjunction of the twin principle, appears in many illuminations and epitomizes the complex message of alchemy. A "Y" sometimes symbolically represents this combination of forces or powers.[55] Two become one in this idealized equation. Quoting Michael Maier (1617), "All are united in one, which is divided into two parts."[56] Mercury and sulphur, for example, are often represented as male and female figures joined or being joined to become one unified factor.

The unification of elements is the symbolic sexual act (coition). This anthropomorphic conjoining results in conception, pregnancy, and birth as symbolic elements of alchemy and as represented in many belief systems. This union of principles had its "social aspect in alchemical images of marriage and there are endless references to the marriage of the red man and the white woman ... the chemical weddings of male sulphur and female mercury."[57] **(see plate L)**.

The idealistic and esoteric nature of alchemy and mysticism inspired poetry, image making (painting and prints), and music in both the East and West. The images like the words are often difficult to interpret and often seem to include disassociated figures, objects, and meanings. The documents composed by Western alchemists are often an obstacle to the uninitiated person wishing to obtain information about practices, procedures, or products. The symbolic terms and references offer little insight into actual conditions or thinking. This type of symbolic reference is found in Christian art of the Renaissance. It was a prevailing aspect of Chinese art into the twentieth century. Tibetan art also offers a complex arrangement of symbols and discrete references that are wholly unrecognizable to the uninitiated.

"The alchemists themselves were aware of the infinite number of discourses, metaphors, and analogies that alchemy could appropriate ... [T]he Stone [for example] may be compared, by analogy, with all things in the world: creation, animals, vegetables, conception, and death."[58] The Western alchemist's world is a world of illusions fostered by belief, single mindedness, and imagination that has a religion foundation. "[A]lchemy is a microcosm in which the artistic trends in the greater macrocosm can be traced." [59] John Read writing in *The Alchemist in Life, Literature and Art* (1947) gives an example of this trend. "[I]n alchemical engraving," Read wrote referring to traditional printmaking techniques, "there is a slow movement from the woodcut to the copper plate and etching, and from the copper plate to the stipple engraving and mezzotint."[60]

Plate L: There are numerous images of the "King and Queen" in alchemic illustration. This picture showing a crowned man standing on the sun and a crowned woman standing on the moon is similar to others images. The joining of flowers with the descending dove represents marriage and the union of two substances—mercury and sulphur.

The relative meaning of any art form depends on the culture of which it is a product. The real differed from the imagined, and art conveys imagination that often exceeds belief. Dance, for example, is an ancient form of magic. The dancer was expanded into a being equipped with supra-normal power **(see drawing 9.a)**. His or her personality is transformed. "Like yoga, the dance induces trance, ecstasy, the experience of the divine, the realization of one's own secret nature, and, finally, mergence into the divine essence."[61]

The difference between that which is perceived as real and unreal in a mystical context is never clear and perhaps it is not meaningful when everything is believed "a creation of mind, when imaginings, dreams, and material objects are seen to be much more alike than would otherwise be the case."[62] Notions relating to reality are marginally relative for Tantric Buddhists. The uncertainty about degrees of reality or forms of existence are pointless to persons who are certain that nothing exists except as the object of erroneous perception. All that is important is the level at which something appears to be real. Such beliefs confirmed that, to the knowledgeable adept, the deity he or she routinely calls upon is more real than his or her family, friends, or surroundings.

Alchemy as a universally acknowledged practice was from the beginning partly concerned with material practices that were to produce change in substances, especially minerals. Many alchemists immersed themselves in the study of theory and conjecture, often in figurative language. The visual narratives were a way to remind adepts of the practices of the past as well as assigning pictorial references to ideas, beliefs, and concerns. "One of the most characteristic aspects of artistic activity is the investment of particular meaning in certain objects, which can in turn exert a powerful influence on other individuals"[63]

Two are one and the one is Absolute. "The Macrocosm is not separable from the Microcosm," according to W.Y. Evens-Wentz, "neither the One nor the Many can have any real existence apart from each other. As being the individualized, or personal aspect which the microcosmic mind (or consciousness) assumes in its own eyes, the ego, or self, is illusory."[64] The unenlightened or spiritually unawakened person is dependent for his or her illusory personal character upon a sense of separateness and the interminable stream of sensuous impressions derived from contact with the external universe.[65]

The phenomenon of the internal and external universes is exemplified by the differences between Eastern and Western attitudes toward religion. Western humanity is often ego-bound, thing-bound, and unaware of the essence of his or her being. Eastern humanity, in contrast, generally experiences the world of particulars, and even his or her ego is fixed on the essential nature of being. This connection is often so

Drawing 9.a: Dancer represents one form of ecstatic activity found in different spiritual devotions. The movements of the dance transform the dancer until a sense of ecstasy is achieved. This Dancer, made in the fifteenth century of painted wood is a remarkable image that demonstrates the important role of dance in early Eastern cultural life. Female dancers are often depicted in Indian sculptures, nonetheless, this figure, a male, is shown in a dance posture and with bells tied around his calves. Shiva, as Nataraja, the Lord of Dance, regulates the universe with his dance and tramples ignorance. Possible drawing from the same tradition, Sufi dancers, Dervishes, follow an intricate pattern as they step and whirl around the floor. The Dervishes attain a hypnotic state and ecstatic trance through recitation of a devotional formula and through their ritualized dance.

strong, as demonstrated by the self-mortification associated with some esoteric religious practices. The Westerner tends to consider the outward aspects of religious belief and deemphasize the inner being. The Easterner recognizes the inner nature of religious belief and gives far less attention to the external facets of faith.[66]

Because alchemy was an oral tradition based on information passed from master to student, signs and symbols were often used as a type of alchemic shorthand. Consequently, no two alchemic manuscripts agree on the order, nature, or processes of laboratory work. Evelyn Underhill wrote in the book *Mysticism: A Study in the Nature and Development of Spiritual Consciousness* about the issue of the "symbols which have been adopted by those mystics in whom temperamental consciousness of their own imperfection, and of the unutterable perfection of the Absolute life for which they longed, has overpowered all other aspects of man's quest for reality."[67]

"[A]lchemists," according to Alastair Baxter, "were often abused, even persecuted for introducing into their works so much religious imagery expressed in symbolic language. Yet we must concede that a high sense of sincere veneration often inspired these allegorical conceptions, many of which are beautiful."[68] Baxter wrote in *A Survey of the Occult* (1935) the religious references "reveal the profound earnestness with which the alchemists approached the subject."[69]

Edward Kelley, [1555–1597] a pseudo-alchemist and alleged scoundrel, is quoted by Michael Poll in *The Stone of the Philosophers* as saying, "[N]othing is more ancient, excellent, or more desirable than truth, and whoever neglects it must pass his whole life in the shade."[70] The alchemists, much like the mystics, strongly believed, "Man is spirit, body and mind in one with physical nature.... Spirit is no external, isolated thing, but is reality itself: inherent in all matter animate and inanimate."[71]

> And certainly he to whom the whole course of Natures lyes open rejoyceth not so much that he can make Gold or Silver or the Divells to become subject to him, as that hee sees the Heavens open, the Angells of God Ascending and Descending, and that his own name is fairly written in the Book of Life [Quoting Elias Ashmole's *Prolegmena* in *Theatrum Chemicum Britannicum*, London, 1652].[72]

Eastern Messages

> Alchemy is a journey of dying and being born or reborn. In modern terms this translates into a journey from the ego-state or "me-state" to the Self–"I" that I truly am, my true being and identity.[73]

Gold is the natural son of the Mother Nature. "[A]lthough she wishes to produce only one metal, she find herself constrained to create several. Gold and only gold is the child of her desires. Gold is her legitimate son because only gold is a genuine production of her efforts."[74]

The alchemic concept of mind (spiritual) and body (physical) are often combined in Eastern practices and offer a range of images and literature that extends into the early history of humanity. The types and styles of images associated with mystical activities are varied and extraordinary. The earliest images found in the Indus Valley were small terra-cotta figurines of women similar to those found in the Mediterranean area and in western Asia from Neolithic times. There were male figures presumed to be in sacerdotal poses, possible yogic in nature. Seals with religious and legendary themes discovered at Mohenjo-daro reinforce the notion of mystical practices (see Chapter Six).[75]

Religion, mysticism, and alchemy, along with the related visual references, are intermingles and often inseparable. Art and religion are generated from the same core values. The comingling of art (storytelling) and religion is exemplified by the early written records of India, the *Vedas (Knowledge)*, a collection of Hindu sacred texts. The *Vedas* are considered the creation of neither human nor god; rather, they are regarded as the eternal Truth revealed in ancient time directly to inspired seers (*rishis*) who transcribed them into the perfect human language — Sanskrit.[76] The *Vedas* are the documentation of all Indian religion before Buddhism and early classical Hindu texts.

The *Rigveda (Wisdom of the Verses)* is the oldest Vedic text. It is composed of 1,028 hymns and was written about 1,400 B.C.E. The *Rigveda* is a reflection of a polytheistic attitude concerned with the propitiation of deities related to the sky and the atmosphere. It also gives definition to certain gods, such as Indra, and describes the creation of the universe and the importance of the cosmic order.[77] The *Rigveda* attends to the activities of both mundane and spiritual life. A special element of *Rigvedic* doctrine is the *muni*. These individuals (*muni*) were a type of shaman, a person having healing and psychic transformation powers and trained in various magic arts. The *muni* were believed capable of supernatural feats, such as levitation.[78]

The Hindu written record included metaphors, verse, and ideological commentary. It gives instructions, explains results, and encourages proper action. "Perhaps the defining characteristic of Hindu belief is the recognition of the *Veda*, the most ancient body of religious literature, as an absolute authority revealing fundamental and unassailable truth."[79] Hindu generally endorse the concept of transmigration and rebirth, the cyclical notion of human existence including belief in karma. The process of rebirth, *samsâra*, has no beginning and no end. This belief "encourages the view that mundane life is not true existence and that human endeavour should be directed toward a permanent interruption of the mechanism of karma and transmigration."[80] The transformational, alchemic, or mystical aspect of this process is deliverance from "the impermanence that is an inescapable feature of mundane existence."[81]

The impermanent nature of existence as reflected by the measurement of time may be referred to as dreamtime or that time. It may be identified as the mythic beginning of "Once upon a time," which the Arabic language genially registers as "It was and was not so."[82] This Arabic expression "identifies the principal feature of sacred mythic time, its paradoxical nature: both super-real and unreal, alive and dead, ordered and disordered, serious and playful."[83] The perception of time in that way configures the thought processes of individuals and defines the transfer of information and images. The physical and mental worlds overlap and in some instances, they seem to be the same. It is on these occasions that art, regardless of its form, becomes real, and that reality is particularly applicable for adherents of mysticism and alchemy.

Although the alchemist puts himself or herself in the place of time, he or she takes care not to assume its role. The alchemists' aspiration is to increase the tempo of things, and thereby, to make gold more quickly than Nature. He or she is nonetheless, as a mystic or philosopher, afraid of Time. Mircea Eliade believes the alchemist "did not admit himself to be an essentially temporal being, he longed for the beatitude of paradise, aspired to eternity and pursued immortality, the *elixir vitae*."[84] Eliade cautions, "Above all we must bear in mind that the alchemist became master of Time when, with his various apparatus, he symbolically reiterated the primordial chaos and the cosmogony or when he underwent initiatory 'death and resurrection.'"[85] Time appears to have been a common concern for most alchemists; for instance, an underlying goal of Indian alchemy was to free the alchemist from the constraints of time.

> Hermes ultimately points to a deeper understanding of time. The past has gone and does not exist. The future has yet to happen and does not exist. The present moment passes so quickly that it has no permanence. Before we have even said "now" the moment has gone.[86]

The wheel of life, the cycle of birth, life, death and re-birth, is a commonplace concept in Eastern thought as well as a fundamental theme of philosophy, myth and symbol, religion, politics, and art.[87] It is the reoccurring process of transformation from one stage to another with renewal proclaiming life is eternal until the practitioner is released from the wheel. "Death abolishes historical time and allows entrance into the 'open existence' of timeless Reality. It ends the old order of existence, making it possible to begin life anew, regenerated."[88]

The *Vedas* addressing existence and the associated challenges are primarily philosophical. Their verse is often a search for knowledge that speaks of truth in stories, hymns, and word pictures. The last part of the *Vedas*, called the *Upanishads*, is considered more philosophical than the previous portions.[89] The *Vedas* expound the principles and virtues of yoga as a means of analyzing the self and how the pure Self is realized. The *Vedas* include references to the connection between gold and long life. Mercury, a vital element of alchemy, is first mentioned in the *Artha-sàstra* (*Handbook of [the King's] Profit*). The manual on the art of politics is attributed to Kautilya and believed written during the third century before the current era.[90] Two later alchemical texts of importance, attributed to Nagarjuna, a Buddhist monk (150–250 C.E.), are the *Mûlamadhyama kakârikâ* and the *Vigrahavyâvartanî*. These documents analyze the origin of existence, the means of knowledge, and the nature of reality.[91]

Hindu alchemy, "like its Chinese counterpart, is [often] concerned with the production of elixirs to prolong life."[92] The Hindu alchemist's pursuit of this objective included the ritual cleansing of the body and mind to ensure a prolongation of youth. "The flow of energy throughout the body was thought to directly affect consciousness, so, to the Indian alchemist, to control the breath was to gain control over the way one received the world."[93] Shiva and his consort epitomize dynamic energy; therefore, they are important in Indian alchemy as symbols of both spiritual and physical attitude. Shiva is the constant, passive, male energy—the primordial matter from which all things emerge and his consort the Shakti is the active Mother-Destroyer, the endless changing of the world. They are twin principles found in Hinduism and in the Tantra.[94] They represent the union of opposites in Tantric tradition.

Belief systems (Christian, Buddhist, Hindu, Jain, or Muslim as examples) seldom remain without some material expression — in the form of ritual vessels, sanctuaries, pictures, sacrificial, or votive gifts. "Art has always been used in the service of religion."[95] The visual arts of India, as in the rest of Asia and much of Western Europe through the Renaissance, relied upon symbolic representations of myth and religion for subject matter; consequently, "alchemy was indissolubly linked with medieval art."[96] As noted above, the art of European alchemy made extensive use of traditional imagery — traditional in the sense of conventional figures and circumstances but arranged in non-traditional configurations. Animals played an important roll in European and Asian art (**see drawings 9.b and 9.c**) while Asian art often included an array of figures and symbols arranged in a narrative relationship. The art of the time was used to illustrate the human element of metaphysical concepts.

Left: Drawing 9.b: Yu Giang, God of the North from the 2,200-year-old fabled geographical and cultural account of early Chinese mythology. This mythical being has a bird body and human head. He has wings, bird feet, and snakes around his ankles and coming from his ears, yet he has the tranquil appearance and expression of youth. *Right:* Drawing 9.c: The creature (God) Ying-Chao is the protector of the Eerduosigaoyuan, Ordos Plateau in Inner Mongolia, China. It has humanized face, horse body, bird wings and tiger stripe. Mystical beings are often represented as an element that joins human, animal, and natural elements. Documents such as Mountain Ocean Sutra describe the deed of gods and demons as "morality lessons" to guide human behavior.

Indian art drew upon hundreds of gods and goddesses for inspiration. A wide range of representative images was developed and integrated into temple (religious) art as Hinduism evolved over the last 4,000 years. The gods most commonly depicted are Brahma (the Creator), Shiva (the destroyer and the restorer; the ascetic and the symbol of sensuality), and Vishnu (the protector and preserver of the world). Each of the deities may have numerous avatars (incarnations)—human or animal—with which they are identified. Vishnu, for example, has one thousand names that are often repeated as an act of devotion.

Shiva is shown in a variety of forms. He is, at time, shown in his androgynous union with his consort in one body, half-male and half-female. This form relates to the European androgynous combining of mercury and sulphur, the male and female elements denoting both physical and theoretical unification. "Mercury [in Western art], like the Hermaphrodite, possesses the double nature of the alchemical Male, hot and dry, and of the alchemical Female, cold and wet, which is why he is the medium of all transformation."[97] (Mercury in Latin is Mercurius, god of merchandise and merchants. He is commonly identified with the Greek god Hermes.) Such sexual symbols play an important part in alchemic art. "Hindu Tantra proclaims everything, the crimes and miseries as well as the joys, to be the active play of a female creative principle, the Goddess of many forms, sexually penetrated by an invisible, indescribable, seminal male."[98]

Although Indian art is often "expressed with startling sensuality," according to Jung, "they [works of art] are, in their truest essence, unsensual, not to say suprasensual."[99] He declares, "It is not the world of the senses, of the body, or colours and sounds, not human passions that are born anew in transfigured forms, or with realistic pathos, through the creativity of the Indian soul."[100] Jung suggests it is "an underworld or an overworld of a metaphysical nature, out of which strange forms emerge into the familiar earthly scene."[101] Philip Rawson comments in *The Art of Tantra* (1973), "The objective coloured surface was never meant to challenge comparison with any sensuously derived image of external reality. It was meant to stimulate radiant inner icons, whose bodies and features could be quite unrealistic in any ordinary sense of the word."[102]

Most Tantric practitioners, like the alchemists, contend there are parts of the process that cannot be put into writing because Tantra cannot be learned from books, but only from a competent teacher or guru.[103] A code-language used when writing was necessary to disguise critical passages. "Virtually all [Tantric documents] use symbolisms which can only be partly understood by the outsider." The point of the process (ritual or rite), for the Tantric, "is that the symbolisms of which they are composed open in his own mind vistas of feeling and meaning which change him, obliterating his materialist view of the world."[104]

While the Western alchemist views the *prima materia* as a necessary ingredient to begin the quest for gold, the Tantric views desire and enjoyment as transformations of the raw material. No Tantric rite will function unless the essential elements — enjoyment and desire — are present. The anthropomorphic recognition of the principles of enjoyment and desire relate to sexual intercourse that is connected to its spiritual ends and thereby considered a form of divine ecstasy. Hence, "sexual energy of humanity is identified in India with the cosmic energy, [therefore] images which represent the outward appearance of sexual energy are worshipped as its emblems."[105] The outward sexual energy is most apparent in the *yab-yum* figures.

The *yab-yum* figure is found in the Buddhist art of India, Nepal, and Tibet. It is a representation of the male deity in sexual embrace with his female consort. The pose is to represent the mystical union of the active force (*upâya*, the masculine), with wisdom (*prajna*, the female). This interaction is thought necessary to "overcome the false duality of the world of appearance in the striving toward spiritual enlightenment"[106] (see photograph 7). One of the pair, usually the male, may be in bestial form, although the female also may be in angry form; thereby, representing a basic concept of Buddhism, "the essential process of joining insight with compassion.... The *yab-yum* image is linked to fundamental aspects of the unconscious, serving to identify and sublimate conscious and unconscious instincts into a potent visual metaphor."[107]

The *yab-yum* figures have led to the belief that Tantric Buddhism is closely linked with eroticism and sexuality. Martin Brauen writing in *Mandala Sacred Circle in Tibetan Buddhism* (2009), believes this perspective "overlooks the fact that the sexual union of a male deity, or yogin, with his partner, or of a female deity with her partner, is a symbol of *unio mystica*, the mystical union of wisdom."[108] Brauen contends the *yab-yum* figures offer "insight into the emptiness of everything (in the form of the female deity) and method or compassion (in the form of the male deity)."[109]

Rawson wrote in *The Art of Tantra* (1973), "Tantra art may seem to have no clear limits; one cannot easily say such and such is Tantrick, and such and such is not. But this does not mean that the unity is unreal."[110] Rawson notes, "In practice, Tantra has adopted and adapted images from different sources, remodeling its significance and weaving the strands of tradition together into a complex pattern of symbolism."[111] Although there are many variants in practice, this joining of parts is a form of emotional and spiritual reality. The colors used in Tantric illuminations include a standard repertoire of hues, all of which have a specific purpose and three-dimensional forms all include the same plastic metaphors.[112]

As integral elements of the transformational process and its symbolic representation, myths and magic are closely interwoven and they are often influenced by selective memory. The past has two distinct parts: the temporal one that passes and is gone, and the metaphorical one that remains in the memories and traditions of a society and its surroundings.[113] The alchemist expressed thoughts from deep within himself or herself, of which he or she saw only the outward manifestations. The alchemic thoughts appeared as references to traditional imagery, such as, "the green dragon and the white or red lions [that] were, at the same time, material substances, and visionary figures."[114]

Western alchemists might embellish their ideological or perhaps fanciful documents with the persona of Lady Alchymia, the beautiful woman in a flowing robe representing the humanization of Nature.[115] Taoism, however, sought its principles and rules for "human life not within humanity, but within nature itself. Consequently, instead of emphasizing human society, this philosophy emphasizes the metaphysical foundations of nature."[116] Taoism give emphasis to the notion that people are in tune with the universe when their actions are the actions of the universe flowing through them.[117] The sympathetic alignment of the microcosm and the macrocosm is often depicted in Chinese art as exemplified by the majestic landscape with diminutive figures representing humanity.

"Taoist literature manifests such richness and variety that scholars tend naturally to seek the symbolic modes of expression that served as points of unity within its historical diversity. No image is more fundamental to all phases of Taoism than that of the child."[118] This humanized reference had specific ideological references. The logic for endorsing this ideal is the new-born child possesses a sense of completeness, but that natural state is only discernable before the initial emergence of his or her ego consciousness.[119] The original ignorance (non-ego state) of the child is distinguished from the no-knowledge of the sage who can "sit in forgetfulness."[120]

Although the Chinese made frequent use of symbolism in alchemic writings and in their preparation for the transmutation of metals, there are about 100 books that are part of the Taoist canon relating to alchemy. The use of esoteric language for inscribing their practice was probably due to the desire of the alchemists to keep their group exclusive and their art a secret as was the practice in Europe. O.S. Johnson notes some examples of the code language in the book *A Study of Chinese Alchemy:* "Yin was 'white tiger,' Yang 'green dragon,' realgar 'masculine yellow,' orpiment 'feminine yellow,' mother-of-pearl 'cloud-mother,' and vermilion 'fairy lady.' The sun was called the 'golden crow' and the moon was the 'golden mirror.'"[121]

As noted, the earliest record of attempts to transmute metal in Chinese history occurred during the reign of Emperor Wu Ti (140–86 B.C.E.). This boastful performance was the result of influence by the court alchemist, Li Shao-chün.[122] The emperor became interested in the mysteries of alchemy because of the claims of the alchemist. Li Shao-chün reportedly boasted that he knew how to transform cinnabar into gold. He claimed he could ride the "flying dragon to the extremities of the earth,"[123] and straddle the "hoary crane and soar above the nine degrees of Heaven."[124] There are no records to document his success or failure to achieve these imaginative goals.

The Chinese royal court favored alchemic activities for some time, but gradually it decreased in importance as Buddhism exerted greater influence. The concept of immortality was changed by Buddhist ideals and the method of attaining the ultimate goal did not rely on external remedies. The doctrine of Buddhism was not written until almost four hundred years after his death at about the time the Buddhist age began in China. The messages of the Buddha were transmitted during his lifetime in the form of instructions to individuals. The collecting and compiling of these lectures into a permanent record by King Asoka (see Chapter Two), and the dispatching of proselytizing monks, spread the message of Buddhism across Asia.

Sacred Impressions

> The Tibetan people's active engagement with the spiritual world existed on several levels. The most constant and mundane involvement was the daily manipulation of objects to magically protect the individual and the community.[125]

"Buddhist art is an elaborate assemblage of images of divinities and objects, ranging from a humble teacher and compassionate saviours to multi-headed, ferocious deities and extending to mysterious images and objects of bewildering complexity."[126] It is described as being of a temporary nature. It is useful to help people still caught in the trap of a world of objects that "they either desire or hate — both of which feelings constitute attachment."[127] It is a reminder to support and reinforce the "eternal truths of the religion, and its development and style remain integral to the history of the religion, the two not being easily separated."[128]

Art brings an object, attitude, expression, or belief to mind in much the same way as the symbol. Louis Frédéric wrote in *Buddhism: Flammarion Iconographic Guide*, "If, according to the Judaeo-Christian concept, God created humanity in his image, humanity, at all times and in all places, has tried to retrieve the image of this God."[129] Frédéric notes that sometimes humanity finds the desired image in one form and at other time the images (deities) created (or the images imposed upon them, by intuition or by revelation) are impersonal and abstract, idols, fetishes, supports or symbols that are "rudimentary or, on the contrary, highly evolved. In most cases, the very idea of divinity has been the object of representations, concrete or symbolic."[130]

"Art is not sacred by virtue of its quality but of its content."[131] The message conveyed by the art or location stimulates indwelling beliefs and thereby generates a positive, generally spiritual response. Traditional locations such as stupas, cave sanctuaries, and monasteries provide sanctified places for meetings between devotees and awakened beings. These structures and institutions, some of which are architectural wonders, are either immanent as relics or festooned with sculptural symbols. The use of paintings, sculptures, and other objects believed to, for example, "represent the wisdom of the Buddha and his followers provide both a focus for devotion and a visual definition of the ineffable state of being that is enlightenment."[132]

The stupa, often embellished with carvings and symbolic motifs in keeping with the Mahâyâna doctrine, was the primary Buddhist structure of sanctity. It is a solid, hemispherical mount, originally of earth and later of masonry. Early stupa were said to contain relics of the Buddha or bodhisattvas. They were constructed in sacred places especially locations associated with the Buddha's life. "Adjusting to the vagaries of Buddhist doctrine, the stupa went through many metamorphoses in different latitudes: in Ceylon it became the *dogoba*, in Siam the *chedi*, and in Tibet the *chörten*."[133] The Tibetans frequently used *chörten* as receptacles for offerings or as tombs for important spiritual leaders.

Relics of saints and other religious persons are objects of worship or veneration related to the concept of transcendence. Often the relic consists a skeletal fragment, a lock of hair, or a fragment of clothing. These objects of veneration are placed in reliquaries such as Tibetan *chörten* and thereby made available for public ceremonies. Some of the relics are used in ritual activities and associated with transformation of physical as well as the spiritual attitudes. Large-scale repositories such as towers, stupas, or sarcophagi may be constructed on a location associated with a particular religious occurrence.

Smaller *chörtens*, or reliquary towers, implied the presence of the Buddha (see Chapter Five and photograph 15). They were repositories for precious objects — mementos, prayers, or the remains of important persons. (When an important person or spiritual leader is cremated, the residual ash is thoroughly checked for small pearl-like bits of bone. These remnants are considered very precious, as they are the essence of the individual and the source of concentrated energy. These pearls are placed in *chörten* or small figurative sculptures and serve as valued centers of devotion.)

A sect of Tibetan monks uses kapāla, skull cups, in Buddhist rituals as transformational objects. The upper section of the human cranium is removed for use in ritual activities acknowledging life and the transitory nature of existence (see Chapter Five). The skull cup is often a carefully decorated object that rests on a triangular pedestal symbolizing a sacrificial fire. The *kapâla* is used in ritual offerings to the *dharmapala*, defender of the faith. It may be filled with wine to represent blood or dough cakes that resemble human ears, eyes, and tongues.[134] *Kapâla* are made from the skulls of various persons including shamans and lamas. (Chapter Five has a notation identifying other skull sources.) Each *kapâla* source is thought to impart certain qualities.

Use of the *kapâla* is a very ancient practice and one that is of particular importance to shamans. The shamans use the "spiritual skull bowl for their invocations and meditations. The skull cup is very important to the Tantrikas for destroying demons, and likewise to the *kâpâlika*, the skull carrying sadhus."[135] The *kâpâlika* are an extremist Tantric order whose members carry the upper part of a human skull (*kapâla*) as a begging bowl.

It is believed that early Buddhism prohibited depictions of the Buddha in bodily form but allowed representation by certain symbols. This idea is based in part on the lack of instructions for depicting the Buddha in early texts.[136] Representative relics, including his footprints (see drawing 5.j), were venerated after the death of the Buddha. Anthropomorphic images of the Buddha were not produced until about the beginning of the common era. These images were placed with other objects as focal points for worshiping the Buddha. "Buddha-images and power objects, scriptural texts and *chörtens* are sacred in so far as there is no distinction between the work of art and the reality it symbolizes."[137]

"There was a progression, from the earliest symbolic images (the pillars, trees, thrones, wheels, animals, and *stupas*), to the fertility and donor figures and finally to human images of the Buddha and bodhisattvas."[138] Although the practice of honoring and worshiping the Buddha figure is central to Buddhism, the images of the Buddha differ significantly from place to place. The Western world saw a similar transformation in the image of Jesus Christ. The Christ figure evolved from an esoteric symbol, to a putti-like angle, to the miniature adult, and eventually the crucified anthropomorphic figure. The sacred nature of the image, and not the physical manifestations, inspired reverence.

The cross was not commonly used as a Christian symbol until after the time of Constantine in the fourth century. Constantine abolished crucifixion as a death penalty, and subsequently the cross was promoted as a symbol of the Christian faith. The swastika is another often seen design that can be found on Buddhist monasteries and temples. It is a traditional symbol of good luck for the Buddhists. The swastika is a spiritual symbol of auspiciousness and eternal life in China (called *wan tzu*), and in Western Europe, it is recognized as *cruz gammata*—composed of four Greek capitals of the letter gamma. The swastika is found on many early Christian tombs.[139]

Although no instructions were given for the anthropomorphic depiction of the Buddha, rules were established four centuries after his death. "The proportions of the Buddha-figures are created according to the Buddhist canon of aesthetics to approximate an ideal form that can arise spontaneously in the mind of an adept in his realization of the Buddha-nature."[140] Similarly, other objects used in Buddhist rituals were "made according to canonical rules in the monasteries by the monks themselves or by artists traveling from one monastery to another. For this reason there is very little free expression in the handling of subject matter."[141]

The images of the Buddha have a special function for the tantric practitioner. "In the creative phase of his meditation the yogi practices the invocation of the Buddhas through visualization, and in the early stages of that practice sculptured images and paintings can provide models for visualization."[142] The yogi allows his or her imagination to fulfill the visualization need in later stages of practice. Such visions arise directly from the unconscious or subconscious mind without necessary allusion to the natural or spiritual worlds. These visions can seldom be explained in common terms causing the yogi (mystic or shaman) to rely of abstract references.

Symbols are needed to convey the essence of spiritual ecstasy because it is too abstract to be expressed in representative terms. John Blofeld wrote about different uses of symbols in *The Tantric Mysticism of Tibet*. "The Tantric use of symbols involves a mystery, one that is rare and curious."[143] Blofeld acknowledges that it is "possibly not without parallel in other form of mysticism. There are symbols and symbols, those employed to covey knowledge to others and those required for penetrating to the utmost depths of one's own consciousness."[144] According to Blofeld, Vajrayâna symbols as found in Tibetan Buddhism "range from straight forward diagrams, shapes and objects devised for teaching purposes to something altogether different—symbols seemingly endowed with life which hover on the frontier between symbolic entities and actual beings that are scarcely distinguishable from god and goddesses."[145]

A symbol and ritual element of special importance to Tibetan Buddhism is the *vajra* (see photographs 1 and 13). The word *vajra* (Tibetan: *dordje*) in Vajrayâna is itself a symbolic reference denoting the diamond, a substance so hard that nothing can break or even chip it. (The vajra is sometimes called a thunderbolt.) It is the transcendental Reality itself. "The way of the Vajrayâna is the Way of Power which leads to the mastery of good and evil. It is also the Way of Transformation whereby inward and outward circumstances are transmuted into weapons [thunderbolt] by the power of mind."[146] John Blofeld affirms the ways of transformation and power. He wrote in *The Tantric Mysticism of Tibet* (1974), "Manipulation of the forces of good and evil provides the power. Wisdom and compassion are the means. The adamantine jewel enfolded by the lotus is the symbol."[147]

The Vajrayâna or Adamantine Vehicle, the school of Mahâyâna Buddhism practiced in Tibet and Mongolia, is a practical form of mysticism. It includes techniques for reaching a level of insight that negates the ego and allows the practitioner to enter a state of bliss.[148]

It is in this realm that the symbolic reference in art often acquires a particularly abstract nature; however, the origin or reality of the iconic references in this Buddhist art is secondary to the spiritual and emotional values according to author Lumir Jisl author of *Tibetan Art* (1957). Jisl declares, "Even the uninitiated observer — granted aesthetic sensibility — senses, without understanding the ideas behind a Tibetan painting or sculpture or the emotions that gave rise to it, and appreciates that he is viewing a true work of art."[149] Jisl suggests, "Only in the second place does such an observer enquire into the iconographic origin and try to discover the purposes for which the work was created and the conditions under which it arose."[150]

Art carries different messages, and it is valued for the message, secret or overt, it conveys to the viewer. An imagery or object includes not only a symbol or image, but also a dynamic representation of the relationship between object and event. When an object or symbol adequately matches the imagined image stored in the viewer's memory, a graphic association is established, and the related information is intuitively understood. The notion of perceptional memory, that is, the recognition and interpretation of sensory stimuli based primarily on memory, is an important element of culturally motivated activities, as well as a decisive factor in determining the shape and design of objects.

Robert Fisher wrote in *Buddhist Art and Architecture* (1993), "The basic difference between the art of the Theravada and Mahâyâna schools [is] in subject-matter, with the celestial Buddhas and bodhisattvas dominant in Mahâyâna art."[151] Fisher explains, "For Theravadins, images of the historical Buddha, Sakyamuni, and of his former lives, the *jatakas*, were of primary significance, for they viewed him more as a human role-model."[152] The Theravadins (a school of Hinayâna or Less Vehicle Buddhisms) prefer activities that demonstrate "virtuous behaviour, acts of meditation, and teaching that revealed the inner strength needed to triumph over evil and illusion."[153]

The Tantric Buddhist process of mind control that produces levels of consciousness deeper than conceptual thought cannot be described in words; in experiencing them, logical thought is transcended — thus the need for symbols.[154] Tibetan art includes numerous depictions of *Dharmapalas* (Dharma Protectors) as symbolic reference. These terrifying characterizations are often draped with severed heads and holding blood-filled cups made from human skulls. *Dharmapalas* (see drawings 4.f and 5.c) are "important in Tantric practice as symbols of the 'anger without hatred' with which the practitioner must confront disturbing forces within the mind, such as greed, hatred, and delusion."

Tibetan art images such as the *Yamantaka* (see photograph 8) are associated with wisdom. They are believed to subdue obstacles and transform the understanding of death. This horrific bull-headed creature is credited with transforming death from a seemingly stable existence to an unstable one. Tibetan Buddhism recognizes that each passing moment represents the death of the past moment and the birth of the next one.

The mystic pattern of the mandala (Tibetan, *dkyil 'khor*) is a favorite subject of Buddhist art (see Chapter Eight, figure 8.3). The mandala (a cosmic diagram) is often painted on the walls and ceilings of Buddhist temples. Tibetans have a particular preference for colored devotional painting on cloth called *thangkas* that are used as the focus of meditation and other rites.[155] The brightly colored designs on the thangkas may be painted, embroidered, or appliquéd. The mandala is a favored design, but the range of images includes most of the gods and goddess in the Tibetan belief system. Other forms of Tibetan art range "from tiny molded clay *tsha-tshas* (votive talismans) and cloth prayer flags block-printed with sacred prayers and mantras, to exquisite wood and metal sculptures of Tibet's innumerable deities in all their forms and attributes."[156] Many of these objects have mystical as well as spiritual significance (see photograph 18).

The relations of cosmic sacrality are primordial revelations; "they take place in the most distant religious past of humanity,"[157] and later innovations have not had power to abolish them. This perspective of the cosmic web has an important role in Buddhism. The central element, one of the primary scriptures of Mahâyâna Buddhism, the *Avatamsaka Sutra*, is the "description of the world as a perfect network of mutual relations where all things and events interact with each other in an infinitely complicated way."[158] The universal nature of this interrelatedness is the subject of numerous Buddhist allegories and symbols. Even so, the universal interwovenness found in Eastern mysticism "always includes the human observer and his or her consciousness."[159]

"The art of a culture[ly endorsed symbol] is not merely the art that it brings into the world; it consists also of the repertory of previous figures that it draws on."[160] Tantric Buddhism gives special attention to the concept of the cosmic web. The scriptures of this school of Buddhism, the Tantras, a word whose Sanskrit root means to weave, refers to the interwoven nature of all things and events.[161] It is in this setting that the cosmic soul reflects the "ideas of the higher, transcendental sphere of the divine intellect, and through the influence of the stars these ideas imprinted their eternal 'symbols' on the lower, physical sphere."[162]

Buddhist works of art in their purest forms were concerned with organizing experience and providing information. They expressed an order for veneration in ways that is acceptable to their cultural setting and by means that could be repeated. As symbolic references to

Photograph 18: Tsha-tshas are small votive pieces made by pressing clay into a mold. The clay is dried and sometimes fired in a low temperature kiln. The small sculptures are painted or stained after hardening and placed on home or temple shrines. A variety of images are represented by the tsha-tsha with the Buddha being the most common. This piece appears to show the figure of Vajravarahi with a skull cup in her left hand, a moon shaped knife (chopper) in her right hand, and a garland of skulls around her neck. She is standing on a supine body and surrounded by flames.

various reverential and physiological activities of both social and psychological importance, they portrayed order in a chaotic environment. "Tibetan art is [in this way] almost entirely religious in form and meaning. The mystic realm of Buddha-vision is described in shapes and symbols which provide the motifs for religious artefacts and domestic decorations."[163] The symbolic messages of Buddhist art, like those of Medieval Christian art, are practical ways of reminding believers against venturing too far from the preconscious and harmonious relationship with the larger mystical world that religion holds.

> In every temple, whether a sanctuary or not, the function of both carvings and paintings was to bode forth the *forms of Truth* in a place created to that end.[164]

The concept of transformation when viewed from the Buddhist perspective includes the idea of *anâtmatâ*. This concept acknowledges "non-selfhood, the absence of limiting self-identity in people and things."[165] *Anâtmatâ* identifies a way of thinking that sets aside the generally accepted idea that the world is composed of separate entities, and that each entity has its own natural existence apart from common perception. It suggests that humanity must go beyond the self-imposed perspectives that incorrectly interpret the reality we experience as separate things defined by preconceived concepts, symbols, and words. This notion is consistent with the ideas fostering alchemy, that is, the commonalty of materials, and the false imposition of traditional ideas and practices.

History does not modify the basic concepts of an archaic symbol or practices. History may add new meanings, but the changes generally do not destroy the structure or character of the belief, although spontaneous insight may promote different interpretations of traditional symbols and practices. Much of this creative process is done subconsciously, and it emerges automatically. This intuitive creative progression may be equally true of the activities of alchemists, mystics, artists, and philosophers. The great religion, discovery, invention, or work of art often owes its inception to a sudden perception or conception for which the individual cannot account; its execution to power is so far beyond the control of that self, it seem to "come from beyond."[166]

> All veritable and first-hand apprehensions of the Divine obtained by the use of symbols, as in the religious life; all the degrees of prayer laying between meditation and the prayer of union; many places of poetic inspiration and "glimpses of truth," are activities of the illuminated mind.[167]

Chapter Ten

Transformation and Transcendence

"Ignorance, or delusion, is the erroneous perception of things."[1]

> We tend to think of transformation ... as a kind of guaranteed promise of change, without recognizing that for change to be real, it also has to be physical — it has to be in the body and at a subtle level of energy. That is transmutation and it comes before transformation itself can take place. Otherwise, we may experience release or relief, but not a permanent change.[2]

The most fundamental aspect of alchemy is transformation, and it is acknowledged in different ways. The changes are most commonly identified as being either chemical or physical. The chemical (or material) change refers to the transformation of metals or other similar elements; whereas, the physical change acknowledges the sought after transformation from old age to youth, for example, or even the transcendence from a natural to a supernatural existence. The projected outcome of alchemic change is normally positive and seldom includes degradation except as a transitional step in a process to attain a positive result. Alchemy is generally believed to focus on those elements that appeal the most to people: wealth, longevity, and immortality.

Alchemy was perhaps not the first practice to seek these goals. Depending on the location and the development of the particular society, religion, medicine, and metallurgy may predate alchemic practices. Early metallurgists, blacksmiths, and smelters, were closely affiliated with mystical and wish fulfilling traditions. The smith held a special social position within much of the early world because he was viewed as being clever, capable with his hands, and closely association with the fire god, a central deity in most cultures. The forging and shaping of metals were viewed as being spiritually or supernaturally inspired; consequently, the blacksmith was often a member of an occult or secret society. The smith as a respected member of the occult community also carved masks in parts of Africa, and in Siberia, he shaped metal fetishes to attach to the shaman's ritual coat.

The practice of transforming metal is believed to have begun very early (New Stone Age) particularly in regions of central Russia along the middle reaches of the Yenisei River. Perhaps earlier people found gold nuggets in streams and flattened them to make ornaments. Anthropologists speculate that people soon discovered that the bright yellow metal could be agglomerated into larger pieces by hammering.[3] The transformation of metal later had a close association with fire, a sacred element, and that connection gave the blacksmith alchemic identity. The line between societal relevance, functional skills, and spiritual affiliation was blurred and the smith often had influence in all areas.

The transformation of copper and tin into bronze occurred about 3,500 B.C.E., but its use in the making of sculpture and religious artifacts did not take place until much later. The process of smelting, that is, the mixing of metals, required a furnace, crucible, and fire, the primary elements of the alchemist's laboratory. The ideal blending of copper and tin required experimentation and the resulting metal (bronze) was a new metal bright and shiny like gold. It was harder than copper yet easier to melt and to form into other shapes. It is also harder than pure iron and did not corrode. The possible connection of this transformational process to alchemy is difficult to estimate; however, it is known that metallurgy was introduced into Egypt at a very early time. The metalworkers made bowls and vessels by the raising technique involving beating on wooden anvils. The raising technique is a subtle transformational process that required a certain skill.

The smelting furnace was from early times a sacred object that required special attention. The Asur people of India were traditionally iron-smelters and their mythology speaks of offering sacrifices to the furnace. Mircea Eliade wrote in the *Forge and the Crucible* (1978), "The smelting of metal is regarded as a sinister operation requiring the sacrificing of a human life."[4] Because certain objects, such as the furnaces, had an existence that extended beyond human knowledge, they possessed universal importance. Complete understanding of the requirements of the spirit world was not always possible; therefore, people turned to ritual means for cajoling and placating the seemingly fickle deities. The stimulants of belief, hope, and anxiety were often only transcendental aspects of the material world.

Generations of humans have strived to reach into the realm of the spiritual by seeking the knowledge to understand the forces that influence the natural world. Objects in nature — plants or animals — had an identity that existed outside their physical being and that reality had a universal meaning. Human existence, therefore, could not be measured just by the principles that applied to reality and everyday life. It required new standards that identified with the transcendental world of belief and tradition. A distinction was made between the spiritual and the mundane based on belief, and the acceptance of that separation was necessary because it allowed the supernatural and the natural to be acknowledged. The concept of the supernatural could not exist without the development of a clear concept of the natural.

Taoism, pursuing the course of nature, "seeks its principles and rules for human life not within humanity, but within nature. Consequently, instead of emphasizing human society, this philosophy emphasizes the metaphysical foundations of nature."[5] The philosophy of nature or natural philosophy (*philosophia naturalis*), as it was later called, is the study of nature and the physical universe. Historically, the word philosophy has meant different things, and the idea of natural philosophy is believed to have originated in Greece in the sixth century B.C.E. Knowledge of the natural world called upon deduction, that is, reason and logic. It was in this vein that alchemists reasoned that all metals were composed of different arrangements and amounts of the same properties, and that by simple adjustment they could be transformed.

The Chinese, Indian, and Greek natural philosophy systems acknowledged five almost identical basic elements (see Chapter Eight), and endorsed a view in which nature comprised opposite forces — hot and cold, male and female. This concept recognizing the relationship of positive and negative acknowledged the principle of energy. China and Egypt also shared an assumption of cosmic order based on belief in numerous benevolent gods. "The Chinese considered the universe a vast organism in which all elements were connected."[6] This cosmic perspective was reinforced by the study of astronomy, which was a particularly important factor for mystics and alchemists. Its relationship with religion gave it a ritual dimension. Astronomy facilitated the calculation of times, a critical factor for alchemists.

The outer world, the space above the surface plane, was the place of the gods and because occurrences in that realm were thought to foretell earthly disasters, they were carefully observed. It was from this perspective that early natural philosophers deemed the stars and planets divine. This assumption also placed the heavenly bodies within the sphere of the mystic. Observation of the changing alignment of some stars and the constant relationship of others bolstered the idea that all things were composed of similar elements in different arrangements. Mystics and alchemists, particularly those in the West, generally embraced a similar astrological concept drawing upon the work and vision of early astronomers that extended to 1800 B.C.E. Babylon. It this context, "an elaborate theory was developed, linking the energies of individual stars and planets with material objects such as precious stones and metals, and with parts of the human body."[7]

Astronomy continued to be an important element in the cultural and medical life of Western Europe into the sixteenth century. Michel De Notredame was a widely recognized astrologer and physician. He gained renown for his prophecies that he published in 1555. Because of the book's cryptic style that mingled French, Spanish, Latin, and Hebrew words, as well as its four-line rhyming configuration, the prophecies were subject to interpretation. Some persons believed the prophecies were plausible predictions while others viewed them as having no apparent meaning.

Life evolved in stages; therefore, it was not possible to know all phases or aspect of life at one time. Taoists sought "to understand [those] phases or stages ... and the way in which life works through all of them to attain its ends."[8] Believers with sufficient pre-knowledge might begin to live life more wisely. Many traditional societies endorsed the belief that the first step of transformation or rebirth is death. As the alchemist found it necessary to kill the minerals (or metals) before they could be transformed, the same was true of life. The process of transmutation could not occur as a direct transformation from a living creature to another. The aspects of physical and psychological death awakened the divine forces that transcended time and space.

The emphasis in this practice is not on death itself but on rebirth or the renewal of life—the generation of new compassion and energy. Death, however, is a necessary part of the process followed by the return to life—the reemergence from chaos. It is an attitudinal demise involving the figurative destruction of the ego and the end of a profane existence to allow rebirth (transformation) of an ego-free manifestation—a form of emotional immortality.

A similar experience can be identified with Jesus, Buddha, and Mohammed. Each underwent a period of trial in which they were figuratively denied their true existence and after a time they each reemerged as sanctified beings. Early gods followed this process according to myth and legend; whereas, death, whether real or figurative, is for many people an archetypal metaphor or symbol for an unimaginable transformation that penetrated the barriers of the rational mind. The loss of Self is often a complex and generally difficult process. It may be viewed as a necessary step to end one part of life (physical or intellectual) and the beginning of a new life (spiritual), or the conclusion of existence as is commonly known. People very often appeal to the supernatural for assistance to deal with these concerns and to provide a measure of protection against the malevolent forces that might jeopardize transposition of the Self to a doctrine identified paradise.

Death puts one in touch with something hidden from consciousness — some treasure or secret knowledge or special wisdom veiled by an interior darkness symbolized by the underworld, womb, belly of a whale or giant, or interior of a mountain. To enter this darkness is to discover the secrets of life and its destiny.[9]

The Transformational Nature of Time

Time is a reoccurring aspect of mysticism, alchemy, and transformational processes. It is the ultimate vehicle of impermanence. "Time itself, its course, division, and fixed points, is both an illusion and the bearer and mediator of the sacred or holy."[10] The human begins life with the illusion that a long time and a whole world lie before him or her. The individual believes he or she has time for all imagined activities,[11] but time has a measured pace that bypasses anticipation and aspiration. Transformation progresses through time in an orderly manner from childhood to old age and eventually death. The impermanence of time becomes a reality too soon, and with too obvious an outcome. The Western mind requires a cosmology with a beginning and a goal in an attempt to regulate time. "The Occidental cannot accept a cosmology with a beginning and mere end, just as he cannot accept the idea of a static, self-contained, eternal cycle of events."[12]

Life in all forms is a captive of time. All aspects of existence are regulated, in some way, by the conditions emanating from the passage of hours, days, weeks, and months. Deterioration and destruction are inherent in all things. The Buddhist and the Yogi pursue a concept of transformation by means of meditation, mystical techniques, and philosophies to attain spiritual mastery and liberation. These objectives and the associated processes seek the same end — relief from the suffering of existence in Time.[13] The law of karma prolongs worldly existence by a series of transmigrations constituting the endless return to existence and thus to suffering.[14] Taoists seeking liberation from the constraints of time are comparable to being restored to health as physical harmony, whereas, Buddhists pursue deliverance from the karmic cycle (nirvâna) as a relief from time.

The concept of immortality necessitated the cancellation of time, because the passage of time promotes deterioration of the human mind and body, whereas discontinuing the advancement of time facilitates longevity. The prerequisite for Taoist immortals was that they should be in good health; consequently, a physical *status quo* was achieved with the halting of time. Taoism advocated returning to the physical and mental purity and undiminished vitality of the newborn child. The supposition being that the child is without the physical habits and maladies as well as an ego and assumptions of self-importance acquired during an adult's lifetime. Taoists considered the essential nature of the newborn child as the ideal status on which to imprint the ideals of the Tao. The newborn child is the beginning of time.

"Chuang-tzu's image for creation was that of the activity of the potter and the bronze caster: 'to shape and to transform' (*tsao hua*)."[15] These two critical activities were considered two phases of the same process. Chuang-tzu contended the indiscernible Tao formed and reformed the universe constantly out of primeval chaos — a return to the starting point of time. The continual transformation of the universe by the altering the complementary energies of yin and yang, is an external facet of the Tao.

A similar idea of the two phases of one process is reflected in the Buddhist notion of selfhood and universe. These assumptions of existence are only the inside and outside of the same illusion.[16] The mystery of unity and diversity may be symbolized, for example, by the image of mirrors that reflect the different aspect of the divine, or as prisms coloring the pure light.[17] These idyllic references are a unification of form, content, and sometimes desire — the comingling of vision, belief, and aspiration.

> Alchemy was like other aspects of the faith, especially its eschatology. The sixth century theologian Aeneas of Gaza invoked alchemical ennobling of metals to demonstrate the transfiguration of resurrected bodies. In the white stage, the stone will be brought to Paradise after its pains in Purgatory.[18]

Yogic practice provided an opportunity for profane time to be rejuvenated. The practice is to retrace time and to allow the advocate to arrive at the beginning. There the individual "joins that paradoxical instant before which Time was not, because nothing had been manifested."[19] The individual in this position can relive and forget past experiences and symbolically embrace the primordial chaos that existed before the beginning of the world and just as the world was created, so in the repetition of that event, the present is regenerated. The suspension of normal existence (the Self) expresses the unconditioned nature of belief.

Immortality is for mystics and alchemists alike a literal idea, since some people hope to live forever, and a metaphorical one in which the spirit is purified and comes closer to unity with the universe (**see drawing 10.a**). "The immortality of the soul insisted upon by dogma exalts it above the transitoriness of mortal man and causes it to partake of some supernatural quality."[20] The Tao alchemist tried to initiate the union of the two cosmological principles, Heaven and Earth, in his own body by emulating the fusion of metals. He or she sought to gain the primordial chaotic status that existed before Creation by completing the transformational process.[21] The alchemist endeavored to reach this status by meditation or by embryonic breathing.[22] This inhalation technique represents the concept of return to the origin that was favorably valued in China. Taoism places considerable importance on embryonic breathing, a practice of reciprocal respiration like that of the fetus. The practitioner is said to imitate "the circulation of blood and breath between mother and child and vice versa."[23]

The universe is in a perpetual change according to Chinese belief. This fluctuation corresponds to a pattern either of continual movement between seemingly opposite poles or a recurring movement in a closed orbit. The movement between the yin and yang forms a relationship in all phenomena — time, space, numbers, and ethics.[24] This oscillation configuration is identified with the yin-yang manifestations of Taoism, whereas the recurring or cyclical movement is identified with the five elements, earth, wood, metal, fire, and water. The five elements, in turn, correspond with the third month of summer and with spring, autumn, summer, and winter, respectively. These elements also define the five directions, and the five primary colors (see figure 8.4). No conscious activity is required to acknowledge the changing nature of the universe, because according to Chinese tradition the cyclical movement produces both the practical and abstract forms of the cosmos.

The soul trapped in *samsâra* (the finite world of change) is doomed endlessly to repeat itself, that is, its karmic pattern repeats until it finds release from past deeds. Everything in *samsâra* is transient, and everything is subject to suffering.[25] The soul is born in any creature and continues to be reborn once it falls from its original state of self-consciousness and bliss. Buddhists believe this unsatisfactory state of being is the result of ignorance and delusion, and that the quest for self-emancipation from the physical and spiritual activities of the mundane world acknowledges a time and place that can be identified. The victims of *samsâra* "revolve through innumerable cycles of existence, ignorant of their exalted nature. Clinging to the notion of an ego and restlessly striving to satisfy its wants, they add momentum to the process of causation by which they are enchained."²⁶ The opposite to *samsâra* is *nirvâna*, the state of undistorted reality.

> [E]very sentient being is capable of attaining enlightenment which is not so much a change from one extreme, Samsâra, to another Nirvâna, but the ineffable experience in which both have ceased to dominate the thought of man[kind] so that he begins to live his life as transformed by pure transcendence (quoting *sGam.po.pa*, Tibetan philosopher-saint).²⁷

Time continued to be an element of spiritual concern into the medieval period. The medieval philosophers viewed the universe as being finite in time. This approach represented prevalent Christian thinking that dominated the reasoning of that era. Some Muslim and Jewish philosophers also supported the concept of a finite cosmology, but other persons such as Fakir al-Din al-Razi (Abû 'abd Allâh Muhammad Ibn 'umar Ibn Al-husayn Fakhr Ad-dîn Ar-râzî) believed there existed an infinite outer space beyond the known world — the place of a transcendent God. (Fakir al-Din al-Razi was a Muslim theologian and scholar. He is acclaimed as an authority on the Qur'an.)

The Western notion of finite time required a definable life span, that is, a certain birth and death. This notion did not endorse the concept of transformation by resurrection that allowed physical existence beyond the identified human limits to accommodate religious belief. Although viewed in different ways and with different objectives, resurrection is found in most cultures. The real and the imagined, the mundane and spiritual, are aspects of human existence that give substance to such beliefs. Greco-Roman religion included resurrection of the soul, but not the resurrection of the body. The Christian Bible includes a description of resurrection in Ezekiel 37:4–6 (among others). "He [the Lord] said, Prophesy to the bones. Tell these dry bones to listen to the word of the Lord. 'Tell them that I, the Sovereign Lord, am saying to them: I am going to put breath into you and bring you back to life. I will give you sinews and muscles, and cover you with skin."²⁸ Theoretically, life was renewed by transformation. Ideologically, it continued due to belief.

Mystical union with the divine forces of

Drawing 10.a: Shou-Leo is the popular name for Shou-xing (Shou Shen), the Taoist God of Longevity. He has been known by many names and identified with various activities throughout the centuries. He is sometimes called the Old Man of the South Pole and Star God of Longevity. He is usually portrayed with a long beard and carrying a staff. He is often shown holding the peach of immortality and a gourd containing the elixir of life. Shou-Leo is often portrayed accompanied by a deer and crane as corresponding symbols of immortality. The current location of this object has not been confirmed.

the universe requires conduct imbued with compassion and infallible skill to transform the passion that forces humanity downward into delusion so that the direction of that force is reversed and transposed into an upward progression in the direction of Enlightenment.[29] Mystic realization does away with the distinction between the self and the world. All beings and all things are fundamentally one in Taoist terms. Any willful human intervention into this union is believed to ruin the harmony of the natural transformation process.[30]

The concept of transformation (change) is fundamental to humanity. Transformational rites gain their meaning from the core of tradition, in that humanity's existence is constantly changing. This certainty is found in all settings and extends beyond the documented record. It acknowledges the belief that mystics (shamans) can transcend the normal human conditions and overcome circumstances that could harm ordinary persons. The mystic (shaman) is believed to have conquered death. This same sense of transformation is found in Hermetic tradition as well as in Gnostic texts that describe the possibility of attaining divine status.

Instances of self-transformation (based on concentration, meditation, and dedication) are often for the positive purpose of spiritual fulfillment — transcendence. Although the wish to rise above the mundane is a common aspiration, the self-defined revelation of transcendence (moving above the ego–Self) cannot be identified in space and time. It is believed that any Self so disclosed does not entirely end (thereby remaining both transcendent and immanent at the same time). There may be, however, a claim for personal immortality, though it can only be expressed in terms of continuing personal life values. This notion is apparent in Christianity with resurrection of the body, as with Jesus Christ, and in Hinduism and Buddhism with reincarnation in this world. Consideration of future life, whether in Christianity or other religions, is a means of referencing the belief in humanity's transcendence above the here and now. It is expressed in language that maintains a transcendental potential that is not extinguished by death.

Yungdrun Bön (Old Bön; *bon mying ma*) identified three precepts or cycles for overcoming the ambiguities that trouble the individual in his or her pursuit of transformation and enlightenment. The doctrine for fulfilling this goal is divided into meaning and expression, while the final cycle of precepts are identified as three: outer, inner, and secret.

- The Path of Renunciation (The Outer Precepts)
- The Path of Transformation (The Inner Precepts)
- The Path of Liberation (The Secret Precepts)

Each of the precepts has different layers of information, use, and purpose. The Path of Renunciation, for example, includes the inner or secret aspect of Bön philosophy, the Path of Transformation holds the Secret Mantras (sacred sounds), and the Path of Liberation expresses the Bön of Great Perfection or *Dzogchen*.[31]

These paths may differ depending on the particular school of Buddhism. The Lesser Way (Hinayâna) basis for pursuit of transformation and liberation includes the Base, the Path, and the Fruit. It requires the realization of the emptiness of an independent self. Pursuit of this goal consists of the "three-fold training of morality, meditation, and wisdom."[32] The Fruit (anticipated result) of this approach is attainment of the status of *Arhat* ("one who is worthy") (see drawing 2.a).

The Greater Way of the Mahâyâna tradition also includes the Base, the Path, and the Fruit. The base requires understanding the emptiness of an independent existence, and practicing the six (or ten) *pâramitâs* (perfections or transcendental virtues): generosity, morality, patience, vigor, meditation, wisdom, skill, resolution, perfection, and knowledge.[33]

"The first six levels are preliminary representing the true practice of the six perfections. Irreversibility occurs as soon as the seventh stage is reached. The bodhisattva, from this moment, assumes the true Buddha nature."[34] The Fruit of this approach is attainment of the status of *trikaya* (three bodies). This status reflects the modes of being of the Buddha: the *dharmakaya* (body of essence), the *sambhogakaya* (body of enjoyment), and *nirmanakaya* (body of transformation).[35]

The words or expressions of these Paths (following the Bön practice) are described in the four portals plus the Treasury that is the fifth.[36]

- The Bön of "the White Waters": This portal focuses on certain "wrathful or fierce mantra associated with various meditation deities."[37]
- The Bön of "the Black Waters": This collection includes "various magical rituals, funeral rites, ransom rites, divination practices, and so on, necessary for the process or purifying and counteracting negative energies."[38]
- The Bön of the Extensive *Prajñâpâramitâ* (Perfection of Wisdom): This portal is a body of moral precepts, vows, rules, and ethics for monks and ordained lay people.[39]
- The Bön of the Scriptures and the Secret Oral Instructions of the Masters: This is a "collection of the oral instruction and the written scriptures of various masters."[40]
- The Bön of the Treasury: This collection includes "essential material from all Four Portals of Bon."[41]

Stuart Alve Olson, author of *The Jade Emperor's Mind Seal Classic: The Taoist Guide to Health, Longevity, and Immortality* (2003), wrote, "The middle level is that of the earthly immortal, and is achieved mainly through methods of internal alchemy — namely — the practice of meditation, which leads to tranquility, and breathing exercises, which form the Elixir of Immortality and the Spiritual Fetus."[42] Olson explains, "This method immortalizes the spirit but not the physical body. The difference between the earthly immortal and the corpse-freed immortal is that the earthly immortal can create transformation bodies and exist wherever and as whomever he chooses."[43]

Transformation, as a process considered by alchemists, had a range of theoretical and practical applications that influenced the results of their Great Work. The Chinese believed all elements of the universe were subjected to periodical transformation. This concept is reflected in the theory of the five phases (*wu-hsing*) and in the 64 hexagrams of the *I Ching*.[44] The changing principle was observable in nature. Earth, for example, could be transformed into a hard rock-like substance through the intermediate step of heat (fire), and it can be transformed into a wet softness through the transitional step of wetness (water). The other aspect of the transformation process that was equally important to early alchemists was the idealistic notion of truth and liberation. This superior virtue as described by Taoism is the latent power that never lays claim to achievements.

Alchemists, East and West, gave a great deal of attention to natural processes while pursuing their elusive goal. They assumed there was a relationship between the microcosm (little world) of the human–Self and the macrocosm (large world) of the world–Self. The analogy between the whole and its parts was fundamental to the development of alchemic theory. It was also pertinent to astrology and other fields in which belief in a metaphysical relationship between humanity and the rest of nature is projected. The alchemic quest was viewed as evidence of this concept. It also identifies with the alchemist's effort to "transcend his natural life in order to attain consciousness of God, he conceives of God as essentially transcendent to the natural world."[45]

The humanization of spirits to introduce a level of reassuring reality to a seemingly unreal situation was a common and persistent practice. (With this in mind, the question arose as to whether God created humanity in his image or people created God in their image.) The assignment of human characteristics to deities made them more approachable as well as more understandable. However, the transformation of the gods is not always complete. Only the body was human for many Egyptian gods, for example, while the head was that of an animal, or the combination might be reversed (see drawings 1.d. 4.b, and 7.a). The guise was one of human and animal or avian unification. This transformation was not necessarily based on the belief that the spirit being had the physical appearance of an animal, but that they embodied the cultural or spiritual characteristics of particular zoomorphic or anthropomorphic entities.

Within this emotive model, the imagination, although defined by a variety of terms, is a field for psychic conjecture allowing deified beings to be present in a self-defining and protective environment. The transcendent and immanent come together in the form of a god or goddess that are believe motivated by prayer and sacrifice to give and to prevent events. The Egyptian Maat (also spelled Mayet), a goddess and the daughter of Re, the creator god, appeared in a personalized form. As a personification of the cosmic order, she was both transcendent and immanent — above and within. She had a critical role in human life and embraced notions of reciprocity, justice, truth, and moderation.[46] Her domain includes not only the order of the nature, but also the social and ethical orders. Maat's purpose in mystic tradition involved judgment of the dead. She weighed the heart of the deceased against the truth. She was thought to create continuity between religion, politics, and morality, and to represented order.

Re, the creator god and founder of the cosmic order, is represented by Maat. The welfare of man has its appointed place within the cosmic realm. This arrangement is usually viewed as a divine order that is well intentioned toward humanity and working for humanities' wellbeing as long as people are willing to insert themselves into this arrangement. The Hindu *Rigveda* includes the idea that the universe continues for about 311 trillion and 40 billion years, a time that represents 100 years of the cosmic creator Brahma. The Hindus believe the universe cycles between expansion and total collapse. The universe is a living entity according to Hindu belief, and it is endowed with a perpetual cycle of life — birth, death, and rebirth.[47]

One of four basic concepts fundamental to Indian spirituality is *karma*. The other three are *mâyâ* (cosmic illusion), *nirvâna* (absolute reality), and *yoga* (technique for gaining liberation). The law of karma is the law of universal causality, which connects humanity with the cosmos and condemns individuals to transmigrate indefinitely.[48] It is the quest for liberation and transformation — to free oneself from the cycle of life. Mircea Eliade writes, "To free oneself is equivalent to forcing another plane of existence, to appropriating another *mode of being* transcending the human condition."[49]

"Mystical states of consciousness can have a profound effect on the nervous system and the rest of the body. After all, the experience of ecstatic union occurs in the embodied state."[50] A person may be transformed or renewed by mystical experience. Spiritual and emotional emancipation is an acknowledged goal of most transformation efforts. "A further form of transformation is achieved through a rite used directly for this purpose. Instead of the transformation experience coming to one through participation in the rite, the rite is used for the express purpose of effecting the transformation."[51] This type of activity is exemplified by the taking of communion. The belief in unification with the body of Christ can have a transformational influence on the spirituality of supplicants.

Humanity often imagines the supernatural to validate everyday reality. He or she seeks escape (or deliverance) from the mundane. Many such activities encountered in life are about transformation — the leaving behind of the old and acquiring of the new. "Consumed by craving, enraged by hatred, blinded by delusion, overwhelmed and despairing, man contemplates his own downfall, that of others, and both together."[52] Greed, hatred, and delusion are the primary faults of humanity according to Buddhist doctrine. These are motivating factors for escapist thinking because it is from this inferior state of being that humanity seeks release — liberation by transformation. It is, however, only at times of crisis that the average human is motivated to pursue a course of redemption, whereas the mystic seeks a direct experience of the reality of the divine.

The mystic, as a communicant with a world beyond the normal plane, might achieve temporary transcendence; however, the primary focus of the mystical event is the human need for communication with God (or gods). The need for contact with the divine source, whether external or internal, may be achieved through a period of ascetical contemplation. "In its most specific mystical sense, contemplation denotes ecstatic rapture — a short lived experience, a moment of insight, in which the soul enjoys immediate contact with God."[53] The unity of the deity and the mystic may be so complete that there was no sense of other — no duality.

Symbolic renewal is associated with the transition in an individual's life identified by cultural traditions. These activities do not combine the societal initiation process with religious dogma or secular group-consciousness; instead they are to fuse the individual's physical substance (energy) with the prime matter of the universe. The initiatory activities point to humanity's need for liberation from a state of existence that is too final or too restrictive. They are concerned with deliverance from — or transcendence of— restrictive patterns of existence, as the individual progresses toward a superior or more mature stage of development. The symbol is the void, the unconsciousness, or the womb from which the renewed individual will emerge.

Mysticism is generally acknowledged as a quest for hidden wisdom that in India is built upon the way of knowledge (*jnâna*), actions (*karma*), and devotion (*bhakti*). It is believed to transcend the temporal divisions of understanding in its pursuit of union with the divine. Mysticism is a search for that nonphysical element within the human psyche that is fundamental to the quest for equilibrium in a chaotic world. The nature of mysticism is a value shared with life — the reality of consciousness. It involves elevation to a transcendent state in which the mystic or layperson can satisfy his or her craving for absolute truth.[54] It is a form of living beyond the mundane plane of existence and the joining of various levels of transcendent reality. The mystic, while in that realm, may communicate with spirits to convey messages about mundane issues for which spiritual intervention offers a pragmatic approach to the necessities of survival.

The ideal of spiritual transformation for many persons identifies with the notion that heaven is the place of the spiritual (the good and saintly), and earth is the place of the corporal (the physical and mundane). The two worlds are viewed as opposite physical localities. Jakob Boehme, however, contended that "heaven and hell [perhaps synonymous with the earthly world] are found within. Both are present in this world, and as a consequence of the exercise of the will, a person lives in love or in wrath."[55] Central to Boehme's understanding of the cosmos and its essential unity is "that all three worlds — the fire-world of wrath, the light-world of love, and the present earthly world — mutually dwell in one another."[56]

Belief in an ideal world, an ageless physical being, and the ability to transform base metal to gold have universal appeal. Perhaps because the human body is subject to observable transformation in the conventional states of childhood, youth, maturity, and old age, the process of change is both fascinating and frightening to most people. Nothing is immune to change. Myths tell of the world being created out of the body of a primordial deity and how the human race came into being. Often the beginning relates to the sacrifice and resurrection of a deity in human form. It is from that transformed being (sometimes female and other times male) that the existing race of humanity emerges. Nothing is created without sacrifice.

Transformation of the ordinary — the commonplace — into the extraordinary gave greater importance to socio-cultural activities and supported the initiation of events and practices. The tripartite division of the small world of man (microcosm) into body, soul, and spirit[57] maintains the idea of a cosmic soul that dwells in the transcendent realm. The process of transformation, the rebuilding of the self on a higher level calls for establishment within the sphere of consciousness certain spiritual perceptions that are the primary material of mystical understanding.[58] The goal of spirituality whether for Self- or God-realization, must be founded on self-transcendence.

Transformation, mystical, spiritual, or alchemic, has its beginning in the center (center of the universe, center of being, center of creation), and this positioning is commonly associated with the womb — the place of origin. The uterus is generally identified as a place of security and in India; it is symbolically represented by the *yoni*. The ancient Chinese placed the feminine element within the *yin* as the counterpart to the masculine *yang*. The uterus or *vas* has an important role in Western alchemy where it identifies the cauldron or vessel in which the alchemist cooks his or her materials. The *vas* is tightly closed to allow a proper gestation period before the golden child is born. "Nothing enters into it (the stone) that did not come from it; since, if anything extraneous were to be added to it, it would at once be spoilt."[59] The Golden egg and Hermetic egg are other references to the transformed matter (prima materia) compounded by the alchemist and placed in the *vas hermeticum*, the tightly sealed womb (in this case the distillation apparatus).

The *vas Hermetis* that contains the materials to be transformed is a critical part of the alchemic process. "It is a kind of matrix or uterus from which the ... miraculous stone, is to be born."[60] The *vas* may be figurative and identified with the concept of creation. The symbolic womb (*vas*) as a cauldron from which life emerges is also viewed as a reference to the immaculate conception of Jesus as well as Sakyamuni Buddha. The womb as the center of creation, "The seeding place of the diamond body"[61] is repeated in reference to Shiva and his manifestation, the *lingam*. This symbol of the masculine energy is often seen in association with the *yoni*, the female energy. The symbolic unification of the male and female forces is found in a space identified as the womb room (*garbha-griha*), the life center of the sacred space.[62]

References to the womb, uterus, and vulva as sources of life figuratively and actually are numerous. Ritual coitus (Sanskrit: *maithuna*) was practiced in India from Vedic times, but "tantrism transformed it into an instrument of salvation."[63] Sexual union as a ritual act, described in Vedic text, was performed for two purposes before being incorporated into Tantric practice: (1) a sacred or priestly union, or (2) an orgiastic union to gain universal fecundity or to create a "magical defense."[64] The idealized transformation resulting from sacred union is described in the *Brhadaranyaka Upanisad* and reported in the book *Yoga: Immortality and Freedom* by Mircea Eliade. Speaking of the woman the *Upanisad* states:

"Her lap is a sacrificial altar; her hairs, the sacrificial grass; her skin, the *somapress*. The two lips of the vulva are the fire in the middle."[65] The ritual nature of sexual intercourse can be traced to many cultures where belief endorsed the sacred act of procreation. (The pressing of *soma*, a plant grown in the mountains of India, is associated with the fertilizing rain. Soma was known as the master of plants, the healer of disease, and the bestower of riches.[66])

Kundalini yoga also incorporates the creative energy of the male-female elements. The *Svâdhisthâna-Cakra* that controls the organs of elimination and reproduction is associated with all reproductive activities — sexual and pre-sexual.[67] The Root Center, *Mûlâdhâra-Cakra*, located in the pelvic region, includes the kundalini (serpent) symbol wound around the lingam and placed within the Yoni triangular with its apex pointed down (see figure 10.1). The triangle symbolizing the regenerative vulva and identifies with the mysteries of the cosmos.

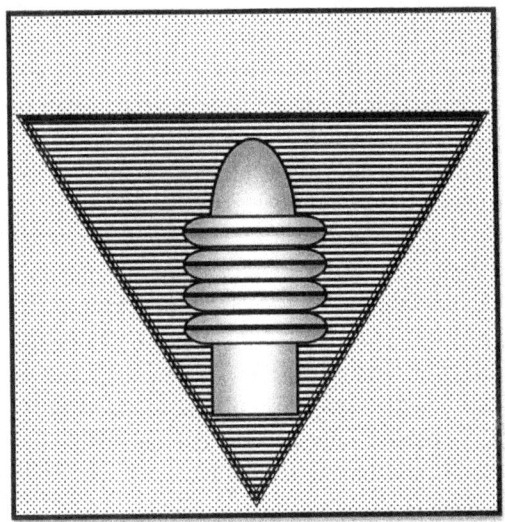

Figure 10.1: The serpent energy of the kundalini (female) is wound around the lingam (male) and placed within the "Yoni" triangular with its apex pointed down. The triangle symbolizing the regenerative vulva and identifies with the mysteries of the cosmos. The "V." as a graphic representation of the pubic triangle and is associated with fertility and birth. It is a mark recognized in many areas of the world and is incorporated into designs or design sequences as "V's" and "X's." The "X" design is connected with regeneration — new crops, springtime, and birth; it also symbolizes marriage or mating. The kundalini is associated with the yoni in the cakra as a symbol of feminine energy that is released through yogic practice. The yoni, a Sanskrit word, is often used to identify the female genitalia. It is the counterpart of the male phallus. The yoni is interpreted to mean source or origin of life, place of birth, and is described as the female sexual principle and to identify a particular object of worship. The Vedas refer to the yoni in different ways and different forms of yoni veneration.

Ritual intercourse was a personal act that recognized the power and authority of a particular deity. The act was believed to have a direct influence of the actions of that god or goddess. Such acts of devotion are possible between the individual and his or her god or gods, but may fall outside the cosmic order. This type of association may exist (emotionally not sexually), for example, between a person and the Egyptian goddess Maat. This manifestation of the cosmic order is personal and not of a general nature. However, the connection experienced by an individual and an intermediary figure, such as the Iranian *Asha*, the Indian *rta* (divine order), or the Chinese *Tao* are highly impersonal. This type relationship denies contact with the Godhead, and thereby adheres to the cosmic order.

Taoism represents cosmic order. It is the concept that gives existence meaning, and the primeval power that forms the foundation of all that is. Taoism expresses the state of being that "is characterized by total tranquility and transcendence of self, through which individual consciousness is believed to become one with the Tao."[68] The endorsement of the Tao constitutes "absolute reality and cannot be defined or understood in human terms except through individual experience of *hsü* [emptiness or purity]."[69] Taoism is about total order. It is composed of not only natural elements but also social and moral rules.

The perspective of the universe inherent to all Chinese philosophy can be defined as magical or even alchemical. It is not materialistic or animistic (belief based on soul substances). The Tao universe is envisioned as a hierarchically ordered environment in which every part replicates the whole. Humanity as a microcosm (small universe) corresponds to the macrocosm (large universe). This universal relationship acknowledges the human body as a replica of the cosmos. There is a system of correspondence and participation between humanity and the universe that mystics, philosophers, alchemists, and shamans may describe but did not invent. The feeling of unity between humanity and the natural order is characteristic of Chinese mentality, and Taoists, in particular, have elaborated upon it.[70]

"Immortality is not thought of as a function of the group, the race, the species, but of the individual."[71] Personal anticipation or expectation is not an acceptable emotion in the search for transformation. Such thinking demonstrates the continuing presence of the ego — the Self. The individual must transcend, must rise above, such thinking, and release the ego, the Self-I before proceeding along the path toward enlightenment or immortality. "It is the impermanence of the object of craving that causes disappointment and sorrow."[72]

There is a parallel between Tantrism and Western mysteriosophic, a religious practice (cult), that was active at the beginning of the Christian era. (Mysteriosophic refers to the "'wise' reinterpretation of mysteries wherein the divine soul replaces the dying god in the soul's descent from a superior world into the corporeal world."[73]) This dualistic nature also reflects the life and death principle found in Hinduism. Mysteriosophic thinking arose in the West from the "confluence of Gnosticism, Hermetism, Greco-Egyptian alchemy and the traditions of the Mysteries."[74] A movement that embraced a fundamental nature, mysteriosophic sought the wisdom of secret mystic and cultic doctrines.

As noted, union with God is a fundamental element of mysticism, but the nature of this union has no uniform conception. The Western devotee (mystic) seeks direct communion with God, the omnipotent deity that has the power and the wisdom to create and to destroy. The God of the West can be both benevolent and vengeful. The realm of this God is high above the ceiling of the world. The Eastern devotee (mystic and lay person) is aware of the immanence of their gods, therefore, communication, although a mystical objective, is more routine and a part of traditional physical and spiritual practice.

Transcendent Thinking

> The mystic is less concerned with doing and believing than with *being* and *becoming*.[75]

Erik Erikson wrote in *The Life Cycle Completed* (1998), "'Transcendence' is a word one is reluctant to use freely, for it has the tone, the imprint of the special, the holy."[76] He states that according to the dictionary, "'to transcend' simply means 'to rise above or go beyond a limit, exceed, excel; also go beyond the universe and time.'"[77] "Transcendence," Erikson writes, "has placed itself in the domain of religion, where it is on holy ground and protected from casual usage. That the word is used in all religions is unsurprising since it covers an area passing human knowledge, while expressing the hopes and expectations of all true believers."[78]

Giuseppe Tucci considered the issue of transcendent consciousness in his book *The Religion of Tibet* (1988). Tucci wrote, "This transcendent consciousness emanates from a mental body, which in its described structure travels from life to life, driven by its karmic inheritance and by the defilements which burden it."[79] Tucci believes that in terms of its nature, transcendent consciousness "cannot be distinguished from the innate mind. The yogin can transform this mental body into a body of transcendent cognition through his meditation, experience, and practice."[80]

John A. Stewart, in the book *Myths of Plato*[81] (1970 [1905]), refers to "transcendental consciousness" that occurs in a variety of fields, in numerous ways, and with all degrees of depth and inclusiveness. A special appreciation of beauty, enjoyment of music, communion with nature, an insight into the meaning of a truth, and the enjoyment of life in the pursuit of duty illustrate some types of experience that transcend consciousness. They are experiences in which subject and object are fused into wholeness in which self is identified with object.

"[T]he body of transcendent consciousness is free from any kind of defilement, and it is not perceptible to an ordinary man."[82] No other force is equivalent to the impact upon the existence of individuals and communities as that generated by acknowledgment of the transcendental world. Phenomena that occur outside the rule of natural law are both wondrous and terrifying because they reinforce the belief that life as a transcendental concept has meaning.[83] "This transcendental realization of undifferentiated being is also the objective and substance of sacred sexual intercourse. It is in this practice that the 'jewel in the lotus,' the eternal embrace of the male and female aspect of infinite Reality, is discovered."[84]

There is a difference between the transcendent attitudes as they relate to religion and religious thinking in the East and West. The source of those differences can be traced to tradition, attitude, and belief. The attitudinal shift started to change with the spread of Catholicism and Islam in the West. Although both of these religions had a mystical foundation, that basis was gradually displaced by dogma. The Eastern religions acknowledged and embraced the mystical belief system. The West recognized a creator God that transcended the universe, whereas the East had indwelling gods that were immanent. The Western mystic and alchemist appealed to the Creator God for assistance when dealing with issues of transformation, while the Eastern counterparts looked to karma, personal dedication, and correct physical and mental practices to achieve similar goals.

Transcendence as a state of being that exceeds physical existence is a form of spiritual freedom that often occurs during reverential expression, meditation, and paranormal activities. It is acknowledged in the manifestation of the divine, and contrasts with the notion of God, or the Absolute, existing completely in the physical order, or interchangeable with it. Transcendence can be credited to the celestial in both its being and its knowledge. God therefore can be said to transcend the universe, and to transcend knowledge (exceeding human understanding). This status disallows the immanence or omnipotence of God (existence in all part of the universe), and is contrary to some religious practices.

The limitless nature to the transcendent state addresses a need that originates in the psyche. The ability to cross supernatural frontiers thereby to visit the place of the gods transforms the real and imagined worlds into one inseparable spiritual realm. This ideological combination is reinforced by hope and belief. The transcendent being is viewed as being free and above the "universe of everyday experience."[85] This is a very old concept that is documented on rock overhangs and stone faces (**see drawing 10.b**). The ancient god ascended to the upper world, the shaman took flight, and the yogi levitated. Tibetan lamas were believed capable of flight (trans-positioning) that is, projecting their mind and body from one location to another. Both freedom and transcendence are associated with flight. The shaman's power resides in his supposed ability to leave his body and fly about the universe as a bird.[86] "[T]he desire for absolute freedom ranks among the essential longings of man, irrespective of the stage his culture has reached and of its forms of social organization."[87]

The transcendent God exists over and beyond the universe, and when the distance between god and humanity becomes too great, there is the possibility of loss of communication with the Absolute—the divine. This possibility of separation is inherent in Western and Middle-Eastern dogma, whereas for Buddhism, Taoism, Confucianism, Shinto, and other Eastern religions this viewpoint is not a factor. Buddhism denies the existence of a supreme deity. Buddhism teaches there are no gods in the full sense of the word. The gods, according to Buddhist doctrine, are higher beings, but they belong to the cosmos and are as much in need of salvation as humanity. Taoism, Confucianism, and Shinto have no fixed dogma that includes a divine power. Christianity, Judaism, and Islam view the supreme divinity as a being; Eastern religions consider the Absolute as a "state of being."[88]

The Greeks, Arabs, and medieval alchemists in Europe based their alchemic theory on transmutation of metals and other materials and experimentally attempted to prove it, whereas, the mystics in India applied the alchemic principle to their own spiritual development. They believed that the person who could penetrate to the ultimate principle of unity within himself, could not only transform the elements of the external world, but also those of his own being. The power sought by the Indian mystic was equally meaningful in the spiritual as well as the material worlds.[89] Indian contemplation, from about 400 C.E. onward, focused on defining and arranging the manifestations of reality, life, and experience within one single imaginative whole. "It attempted to comprehend the history of each individual in relation to the entire cosmos."[90]

Belief, as psychological continuity in the transcendental practice, ranges beyond commonplace experience and allowed emotional interpretation to modify an imperfect reality. The acceptability of this practice on both the physical and mental levels is often modified to accommodate group tradition and experience. A sympathetic understanding must exist between all elements of the transformational process for it to be effective. It must recognize the temporary nature of all things, as well as the vulnerability of all humanity.

Drawing 10.b: Shaman in bird-like attire attesting to the unity of humans and nature. "The universe, the earth, human, animal and the plant world form an indivisible unity. The earth is the center, the focus of the cosmos." The worship of the sky, as supreme god is a very archaic element of the religions ideology of Turkic people; therefore, the "bird" affiliation by the shaman is natural. This art is from the second millennium B.C.E. It is located in the Karakol, Altal region, Kyrgyzstan.

Recognition of the doctrine of impermanence is a step on the Buddhist's spiritual path toward enlightenment. It is a critical facet of opening the mind to know things not known to others. "The loosening of the knots" is reportedly a simile used by Buddha, "when explaining that the process of liberation consists merely in the untying of the knots of our own being, through which we have fettered ourselves and have become slaves of our confused illusions."[91] Opening the mind to greater understanding or knowledge — enlightenment — is an inbuilt objective of Buddhism and Hinduism.

> [W]e draw conclusions about the inner world from our wealth of outward impressions. We even derive its content from outside on the principle that nothing is in the mind which was not previously in the senses.[92]

The connection between the inner and outer worlds is often viewed as coincidence and ignored. These worlds represent two sides of one reality that can be seen by shamans, mystics, and visionaries.[93] This reasoning relates to the transcendental or mystical state that is not experienced in a physical way but known nevertheless. "Spirits constantly appear to men in dreams or simply as daylight apparitions and communicate freely, without the aid of a shaman; and the conditions under which they required a shaman as a necessary intermediary are not at all clear."[94] Dreams, among many cultural groups, are given a status of reality but that does not necessarily imply that the two, dreams and reality, are indistinguishable. The dream may be differentiated from reality, but given special status in relation to the activities of daily existence.

The world as we know it is a façade, whereas reality is often most accessible by dreams. Legend maintains the Frenchman Nicholas Flamel (see Chapter Seven) was visited by an angel in a dream and shown an "old book with magnificent illustrations. Flamel reached out to touch the book, but both the book and the angel vanished before he could hold it in his hands."[95] He bought a book some years later, in 1357, and recognized it as the one he had seen in his dream. "The book was written by a certain Abraham Eleazar, and it appeared that he was describing the art of transmuting metals into gold."[96] Flamel studied the book, an ancient Kabbalistic text, for years and supposedly brought his dream to fruition in April of 1382 when it is believed he and his wife, Perenelle, successfully performed the experiment to transmute base metal to gold.

Legend states that over the following several years the Flamels gave away large sums of money to churches and hospitals, and most observers assumed the source of the funds was in the laboratory. The Flamels died without sharing the secret of their success, and no records were found in their home. Some versions of the story say the couple did not die in France, but went to India where they lived on the gold from the alchemist's furnace.

> If there is something we cannot know, we must necessarily abandon it as an intellectual problem. For example, I do not know for what reason, the universe has come into being, and shall never know. Therefore, I must drop this question as a scientific or intellectual problem. But if an idea about it is offered to me — in dreams or in mystic traditions — I ought to take note of it. I even ought to build up a conception on the basis of such hints, even thought it will forever remain a hypothesis which I know cannot be proved.[97]

Chapter Notes

Preface

1. Tucci, G. *Tibet: Land of Snow*, translated by J. E. Stapleton Driver (New York: Stein and Day, 1967), p. 14.
2. Bennett, C. A. *A Philosophical Study of Mysticism* (New Haven: Yale University Press, 1923), p. 108.
3. Edson, G. *Shamanism: A Cross-Cultural Study of Beliefs and Practices* (Jefferson, NC: McFarland, 2005), p. 1.
4. Edson, G. *Masks and Masking: Faces of Tradition and Belief Worldwide* (Jefferson, NC: McFarland, 2009), p. 1.
5. Underhill, E. *Practical Mysticism* (New York: P. P. Dutton, 1960), p. 4.

Chapter One

1. Venerable Sujiva. *The First Step in Insight Meditation* (Nadimala, Dehiwala, Sri Lanka: Buddhist Cultural Centre, 1986) p. 68.
2. "mysticism," Encyclopædia Britannica, from *Encyclopædia Britannica Deluxe Edition 2005 CD*. Encyclopædia Britannica (accessed January 2, 2009).
3. Russell, B. *Mysticism and Logic* (New York: W. W. Norton, 1929), p. vi.
4. Underhill, E. *Mysticism: The Natural and Development of Spiritual Consciousness* (Mineola, NY: Dover, 2002 [1911]), p 3.
5. Paul, R. A. *The Tibetan Symbolic World: Psychoanalytic Explorations.* (Chicago: University of Chicago Press, 1982), p. 43.
6. Govinda, Lama Anagarika. *The Way of the White Clouds* (London: Rider, 1974 [1966]), p. 54.
7. *Ibid.*
8. *Ibid.*, p. 23.
9. *Ibid.*
10. Sauvage, G. M. "Mysticism," Transcribed by Elizabeth T. Knuth. *The Catholic Encyclopedia*, Vol. X. (New York: Robert Appleton Company, 1911). <http://www.newadvent.org/cathen/index.html>. (Accessed April 21, 2010).
11. Stillman, J. M. *The Story of Alchemy and Early Chemistry* (New York: Dover, 1960 [1924]), p. 1.
12. *Ibid.*
13. H. H. The Dalai Lama, Tsong-ka-pa, and Jeffrey Hopkins. *Tantra in Tibet,* translated and edited by Jeffrey Hopkins (Ithaca, NY: Snow Lion, 1987) p. 47.
14. Govinda, Lama Anagarika. *The Way of the White Clouds,* p. 123.
15. Conrad, J. *Heart of Darkness* (New York and Toronto: Alfred A. Knopf, 1967), p. 50.
16. Burt, C. "Judgment of the Dead" in R. Cavendish, R. ed. *Man, Myth & Magic: The Illustrated Encyclopedia of Mythology, Religion and the Unknown*, vol. 11, pp. 1447–1462 (North Bellmore, NY: Marshall Cavendish Corporation, 1995), p. 1459.
17. *Ibid.*
18. Govinda, Lama Anagarika. *The Way of the White Clouds,* p. 37.
19. "mysticism," Encyclopædia Britannica, from *Encyclopædia Britannica Deluxe Edition 2005 CD*. Encyclopædia Britannica (accessed January 2, 2009).
20. *The Heart Sutra,* Translation and commentary by Red Pine (Bill Porter) (Berkeley: Counterpoint, 2004), p. 32.
21. *Ibid.*
22. *Ibid.*
23. Rinpoche, H. E. Kalu. *Foundations of Tibetan Buddhism* (Ithaca, NY: Snow Lion, 1999), p. 193.
24. Lommel, A. *World of the Early Hunters*, translated by M. Bullock (London: Paul Hamlyn, 1967), pp. 26–27.
25. Sumegi, A. *Dreamworlds of Shamanism and Tibetan Buddhism: The Third Place* (New York: State University Press, 2008), p. 5.
26. Evens-Wentz, W. Y., ed. *Tibetan Yoga and Secret Doctrines*, 2d. Translated by Chen-Chi Chang (London, Oxford, and New York: Oxford University Press, 1967 [1958]), ff. 1, p. 115.
27. Paolucci, H. *Hegel: On The Arts* (New York: Frederick Unger, 1979), p. 11.
28. Islamic Mysticism (Sufism) http://philtar.ucsm.ac.uk/encyclopedia/islam/sufi/index.html (accessed April 23, 2008)
29. "Hinduism," Encyclopædia Britannica, from *Encyclopædia Britannica Deluxe Edition 2005 CD*. Encyclopædia Britannica (accessed June 12, 2010).
30. Johnson, S. *The Book of Tibetan Elders: The Life Stories and Wisdom of the Great Spiritual Masters of Tibet* (New York: Riverhead Books, 1996), p. 188.
31. Rinpoche, S. *The Tibetan Book of Living and Dying*, edited by P. Gaffney and A. Harvey (San Francisco: HarperSanFrancisco, 1992), p. 46.
32. Blofeld, J. *The Tantric Mysticism of Tibet: A Practical Guide* (New York: Causeway Books, 1974), p. 191.
33. Johnson, S. *The Book of Tibetan Elders,* p. 185.
34. Blofeld, J. *The Tantric Mysticism of Tibet,* p. 41.
35. *Ibid.*
36. Rinpoche, H. E. Kalu. *Foundations of Tibetan Buddhism* 3 ed. (Ithaca, NY and Boulder, CO: Snow Lion, 2004), p.192.
37. Wong, E. *The Shambhala Guide to Taoism* (Boston & London: Shambhala, 1997), p. 99.
38. Arendt, H. *The Human Con-*

dition (Chicago: University of Chicago Press, 1958), p. 137.
39. David-Neel, A. *My Journey to Lhasa* (Boston: Beacon Press, 1986 [1927]), p. 301.
40. *Ibid.*
41. Hastings, J., ed. "Tibet," in: *Encyclopædia of Religion and Ethics*, vol. XI, pp. 331–334 (New York: Charles Scribner's Sons, 1951), p. 332.
42. Blofeld, J. *The Tantric Mysticism of Tibet*, p. 25.
43. H. H. Dalai Lama. *The Universe in a Single Atom: The Convergence of Science and Spirituality* (New York: Morgan Road Books, 2005), p. 119.
44. Edson, G. *Shamanism: A Cross-cultural Study of Beliefs and Practices* (Jefferson, NC: McFarland, 2008), p. 14.
45. Humphrey, C. and Urgunge, O. *Shamans and Elders: Experience, Knowledge, and Power among the Daur Mongols* (Oxford: Clarendon Press, 1996), p.315.
46. Edson, G. *Masks and Masking* (Jefferson, NC: McFarland, 2005), p. 177.
47. "Taoism" Encyclopædia Britannica, from *Encyclopædia Britannica Deluxe Edition 2005 CD*. Encyclopædia Britannica (accessed June 16, 2010).
48. "Taoism," *Encyclopaedia Britannica Library*, from Encyclopaedia Britannica 2005 Deluxe Edition CD-ROM. Encyclopaedia Britannica (accessed May 2, 2007).
49. Frazer, J. G. *The Golden Bough: A Study of Magic and Religion*, vol. 1 (New York: Macmillan, 1958), p. 624.
50. Cavendish, R. (ed.) *Man, Myth & Magic: The Illustrated Encyclopedia of Mythology, Religion and the Unknown*, vol. 17 (New York, London and Sydney, 1995), p. 2354.
51. Govinda, Lama Anagarika. *The Way of the White Clouds*, p. 115.
52. "karma," Encyclopædia Britannica, from *Encyclopædia Britannica Deluxe Edition 2005 CD*. Encyclopædia Britannica, May 30, 2004 (Accessed June 8, 2010).
53. Powell, A. *Living Buddhism*. (Berkeley: University of California Press, 1995), p. 191.
54. Kirkland, R. *Taoism: The Enduring Tradition* (New York and London: Routledge, 2004), p. 184.
55. Waley, A. *The Nine Songs: A Study of Shamanism in Ancient China* (London: George Allen and Unwin Ltd., 1955), p. 9.
56. Johnson, O.S. *A Study of Chinese Alchemy* (New York: ARNO Press, 1974), p. 43.
57. Alchemy "Chinese alchemy," Encyclopædia Britannica, from *Encyclopædia Britannica Deluxe Edition 2005 CD*. Encyclopædia Britannica (accessed January 7, 2009).
58. *Ibid.*
59. *Ibid.*
60. "Vajrayana," Encyclopædia Britannica, from *Encyclopædia Britannica Deluxe Edition 2005 CD*. Encyclopædia Britannica (accessed April 27, 2010).
61. Walker, B. "Tantrism" in: Cavendish, R., ed. *Man, Myth & Magic: The Illustrated Encyclopedia of Mythology, Religion and the Unknown*, Vol. 18, pp. 2556–2561(New York, 1995), p. 2558.
62. Oman, J. *The Natural & the Supernatural* (New York: Macmillan, 1931), p. 377.
63. *Ibid.*
64. Cavendish, R. (ed.) *Man, Myth & Magic: The Illustrated Encyclopedia of Mythology, Religion and the Unknown*, p. 558.
65. Frazer, J. G. *The Golden Bough: A Study of Magic and Religion*, vol. I. (New York: Macmillan, 1958), p. 624.
66. Kehoe, A. B. *Shamans and Religion* (Prospect Heights, IL: Waveland Press, 2006), p. 14.
67. Gareth, R. *The Mirror of Alchemy* (Toronto: University of Toronto Press, 1994), p. 45.
68. "alchemy," Encyclopædia Britannica, from *Encyclopædia Britannica Deluxe Edition 2005 CD*. Encyclopædia Britannica, May 30, 2004 (April 2, 2010).
69. "Hermetic writings," Encyclopædia Britannica, from *Encyclopædia Britannica Deluxe Edition 2005 CD*. Encyclopædia Britannica, May 30, 2004 (April 4, 2010).
70. *Ibid.*
71. Sauvage, G.M. "Mysticism." Transcribed by E.T. Knuth. In: *The Catholic Encyclopedia*, vol. X. (New York: Robert Appleton Company, 1911). <http://www.newadvent.org/cathen/index.html>. (Accessed April 21, 2010).
72. "Religion of the East," Encyclopædia Britannica, from *Encyclopædia Britannica Deluxe Edition 2005 CD*. Encyclopædia Britannica, May 30, 2004 (July 19, 2010).
73. "Aristotle." Encyclopædia Britannica, from *Encyclopædia Britannica Deluxe Edition 2005 CD*. Encyclopædia Britannica, May 30, 2004 (April 6, 2010).
74. Gareth, R. *The Mirror of Alchemy* (Toronto: University of Toronto Press, 1994), p. 45.
75. *Ibid.*
76. Silberer, H., and S. E. Jelliffe. *Problems of Mysticism and Its Symbolism* (Whitefish, MT: Kessinger Publishing, 2009 [1917]), p. 112.
77. Stillman, J. M. *The Story of Alchemy and Early Chemistry* (New York: Dover, 1960 [1924]), p. 5.
78. Gareth, R. *The Mirror of Alchemy*, p. 45.
79. *Ibid.*
80. Roob, A. *The Hermetic Museum: Alchemy and Mysticism*. Köln, London, and Paris: Taschen, GmbH, 2009), p. 144.
81. Fabricius, J. *Alchemy: The Medieval Alchemists and Their Royal Art* (Copenhagen: Rosenkilde and Bagger, 1976), p. 8.
82. *Ibid.*
83. *Ibid.*
84. Huang, K., and R. Huang. *I Ching* (New York: Workman Publishing, 1987, p. 8.
85. Hutin, S. *A History of Alchemy* (New York: Walker, 1963) p. 11.
86. Johnson, S. *The Book of Tibetan Elders: The life Stories and Wisdom of the Great Spiritual Masters of Tibet* (New York: Riverhead Books, 1996), p. 119.
87. Johnson, S. *The Book of Tibetan Elders*, p. 119.
88. H.H. Dalai Lama. The Universe in a Single Atom, p. 52.
89. *Ibid.*
90. *Ibid.*
91. Gareth, R. *The Mirror of Alchemy*, pp. 47–48.
92. Aristotle. *Metaphysics,* translated with Commentaries and Glossary by Hippocrates G. Apostle (Bloomington: Indiana University Press, 1966), p.143:1045a.
93. Sauvage, G. M. "Mysticism" Transcribed by E.T. Knuth. In: *The Catholic Encyclopedia*, vol. X. (New York: Robert Appleton Company, 1911). <http://www.newadvent.org/cathen/index.html>. (Accessed April 21, 2010).
94. Cochren, A. *History of Alchemy* http://www.alchemylab.com/history_of_alchemy.htm (accessed April 9, 2010.
95. "Egyptian religion," Encyclopædia Britannica, from *Encyclopædia Britannica Deluxe Edition 2005 CD*. Encyclopædia Britannica, May 30, 2004 (April 9, 2010).
96. Cavendish, R., ed. *Man, Myth & Magic*, p. 557.
97. Radin, P. *Primitive Religion: Its Nature and Origin*, 2d (New York: Dover, 1957), p. 214.
98. Hatab, L. J. *Myth and Philosophy: A Contest of Truths* (La Salle, IL: Open Court, 1990), p. 51.

99. Silberer, H., and S. E. Jelliffe. *Problems of Mysticism and its Symbolism* (Whitefish, MT: Kessinger Publishing, 2009 [1917]), p. 113.
100. *Ibid.*
101. Alchemy "Arabic alchemy," Encyclopædia Britannica, from *Encyclopædia Britannica Deluxe Edition 2005 CD*. Encyclopædia Britannica, May 30, 2004 (April 2, 2010).
102. Alchemy "Hellenistic alchemy" Encyclopædia Britannica, from *Encyclopædia Britannica Deluxe Edition 2005 CD*. Encyclopædia Britannica, May 30, 2004 (April 3, 2010).
103. Alchemy "Hellenic alchemy," Encyclopædia Britannica, from *Encyclopædia Britannica Deluxe Edition 2005 CD*. Encyclopædia Britannica, May 30, 2004 (April 4, 2010).
104. *Ibid.*
105. Alchemy "Hellenic alchemy," Encyclopædia Britannica, from *Encyclopædia Britannica Deluxe Edition 2005 CD*. Encyclopædia Britannica, May 30, 2004 (April 30, 2010).
106. Alchemy "Arabic alchemy" Encyclopædia Britannica, from *Encyclopædia Britannica Deluxe Edition 2005 CD*. Encyclopædia Britannica, May 30, 2004 (April 4, 2010).
107. Alchemy "Arabic alchemy" Encyclopædia Britannica, from *Encyclopædia Britannica Deluxe Edition 2005 CD*. Encyclopædia Britannica, May 30, 2004 (April 2, 2010).
108. Hutin, S. *A History of Alchemy*, p. 13.
109. *Ibid.*, pp. 13–14
110. Johnson, S. *The Book of Tibetan Elders*, pp. 265–266.

Chapter Two

1. Radha, S. S. *Kundalini Yoga for the West* (Spokane, WA: Timeless Books, 1978), p. 12.
2. H. H. The Dalai Lama. *Becoming Enlightened*, translated and edited by Jeffrey Hopkins (New York: Atria Books, 2009), p. 232.
3. Jung, C. G. *Psychology and Religion: West and East*, 2d. Translated by R.F.C. Hull. Bollingen Series XX (Princeton, NJ: Princeton University Press, 1969, p. 475.
4. *Ibid.*, p. 476.
5. *Ibid.*, p. 477.
6. Smart, J. J. C. "Time and its role in the history of thought and action" Encyclopædia Britannica, from *Encyclopædia Britannica Deluxe Edition 2005 CD*. Encyclopædia Britannica, May 30, 2004 (accessed May 2, 2010).
7. Chen, R. S. *Asian Thought and Culture: A Comparative Study of Chinese and Western Cyclic Myths* (New York, Berlin, and Paris: Peter Lang, 1992), p. 35.
8. *Ibid.*, p. 36.
9. Eliade, M. *Images and Symbols: Studies in Religious Symbolism* Translated by Philip Mairet (Princeton, NJ: Princeton University Press, 1991), p. 57.
10. *Ibid.*, pp. 57–58.
11. Ferguson, J. *Encyclopedia of Mysticism and Mystery Religions* (New York: Crossroad, 1982, [c1976]), p. 69.
12. Blofeld, J. *The Tantric Mysticism of Tibet: A Practical Guide* (New York: Causeway Books, 1974, p. 52.
13. *Ibid.*
14. Bechert, H., and R. Gombrich eds. *The World of Buddhism: Buddhist Monks and Nuns in Society and Culture* (New York and Bicester, UK: Facts on File, 1984), p. 24.
15. *Ibid.*
16. Heller, A. *Tibetan Art: Tracing the Development of Spiritual Ideals and Art in Tibet 600–2000 A.D.* (Suffolk, UK and Milano, Italy: Jaca Books, Antique Collectors' Club, 1999), p. 15.
17. Lewis, I. M. *Ecstatic Religion: A Study of Shamanism and Spirit Possession*. 2nd. ed. (New York and London: Routledge, 1989), p. 5.
18. H. H. The Dalai Lama, *Becoming Enlightened*, translated and edited by Jeffrey Hopkins (New York: Atria Books, 2009), p. 248.
19. Feuerstein, G. *Tantra: The Path of Ecstasy* (Boston and London: Shambhala, 1998), p. 2.
20. David-Neel, A. *My Journey to Lhasa* (Boston: Beacon Press, 1986 [1927]), p. 302.
21. *Ibid.*, p. v.
22. David-Neel, A. *Magic and Mystery in Tibet* (New Hyde Park, NY: University Books, 1965), p. v.
23. Tucci, G. *Tibet: Land of Snow*, translated by E. J. Stapleton Driver (New York: Stein and Day, 1967), p. 74.
24. Govinda, Lama Anagarika. *The Way of the White Clouds* (London: Rider, 1974 [1966]), p. 54.
25. *Ibid.*
26. Tucci, G. *Tibet: Land of Snow*, p. 79.
27. Govinda, Lama Anagerika. *The Way of the White Clouds*, p. xiv.
28. Underhill, E. *Mysticism: A Study in the Nature and Development of Spiritual Consciousness* (Mineola, NY: Dover, 2002 [1911]), p. 234.
29. Halifax, J. *Shaman: The Wounded Healer* (London: Thames and Hudson, 1982), p. 5.
30. Jung, C. G. *Psychology and Religion: West and East*, p. 489.
31. Hutin, S. *A History of Alchemy* (New York: Walker, 1963), p. 15.
32. Jung, C. G. *Psychology and Religion: West and East*, p. 183.
33. Tucci, G. *Tibet: Land of Snow*, p. 68.
34. Blofeld, J. *The Tantric Mysticism of Tibet*, p. 63.
35. Rambach, P. *The Secret Message of Tantric Buddhism* (New York: Rizzoli International, 1979), p. 11.
36. Snellgrove, D. *Buddhist Himalaya: Travels and Studies* (Oxford: Bruno Cassirer, 1957), p. 52.
37. Rambach, P. *The Secret Message of Tantric Buddhism*, p. 11.
38. Cavendish, R. (Ed.) *Man, Myth & Magic: The Illustrated Encyclopedia of Mythology, Religion and the Unknown* (New York, London and Sydney: Marchall Cavendish, 1995), p. 296.
39. Stone, R. *Indian Mythology: Myths and Legends of India, Tibet and Sri Lanka* (London: Lorenz Books, 2000), p. 90.
40. Blofeld, J. *The Tantric Mysticism of Tibet*, p. 63.
41. Waddell, L. A. *Buddhism of Tibet or Lamaism*, 2d ed. (Cambridge: W. Heffer & Sons, Limited, 1939 [1854]), pp. 6–7.
42. Gordon, A. K. *Tibetan Religious Art* (New York: Columbia University Press, 1952), p. 4.
43. Blofeld, J. *The Tantric Mysticism of Tibet*, pp. 48–49.
44. *Ibid.*, p. 54.
45. *Ibid.*, p. 47.
46. *Ibid.*, p. 46.
47. *Ibid.*, p. 46.
48. *Ibid.*, p. 49.
49. Stone, R. *Indian Mythology: Myths and Legends of India, Tibet and Sri Lanka*, p. 90.
50. "Buddhist council," Encyclopædia Britannica, from *Encyclopædia Britannica Deluxe Edition 2005 CD*. Encyclopædia Britannica, May 30, 2004 (accessed April 23, 2010).
51. Rambach, P. *The Secret Message of Tantric Buddhism*, p. 17.
52. Waddell, L. A. *Buddhism of Tibet or Lamaism*, p. xx.
53. *Ibid.*, p. xxiv.
54. *Ibid.*, pp. xxv–xxvi.
55. *Ibid.*, p. xxix.
56. Rinpoche, Kalu. *Foundations of Tibetan Buddhism*, 3ed (Ithaca, NY and Boulder, CO: Snow Lion, 2004), p. 19.
57. *Ibid.*, p. 18.
58. Tucci, G. *Tibet: Land of Snow*, p. 72.
59. Rinpoche, Kalu. *Foundations of Tibetan Buddhism*, p. 189.
60. Snelling, J. *The Buddhist*

Handbook: A Complete Guide to Buddhist Teaching and Practice (London: Rider, 1998), p. 81.
61. Heller, A. *Tibetan Art: Tracing the Development of Spiritual Ideals and Art in Tibet 600–2000 A.D.* (Suffolk: Jaca Books, Antique Collectors' Club, 1999), p. 15.
62. Waddell, L. A. *Buddhism of Tibet or Lamaism*, p. 13.
63. *Ibid.*
64. Snellgrove, D. "Tibet" in: Cavendish, R. (Ed.) *Man, Myth & Magic: The Illustrated Encyclopedia of Mythology, Relition and the Unknown*, Vol 19, pp. 2619–2625 (New York: Marshall Cavendish, 1995), p. 2621.
65. Thurman, R. A. F. *Essential Tibetan Buddhism* (Edison, NJ: Castle Books, 1997), p. 291.
66. Waddell, L. A. *Buddhism of Tibet or Lamaism*, p. 14.
67. *Ibid.*, p. 12.
68. *Ibid.*, p. 14.
69. Gordon, A. K. *Tibetan Religious Art*, p. 11.
70. *Ibid.*, p. 13.
71. Samuel, G. *Civilized Shamans: Buddhism in Tibetan Societies* (Washington and London: Smithsonian Institution Press, 1993), p. 408.
72. *Ibid.*, pp. 408–409.
73. Rambach, P. *The Secret Message of Tantric Buddhism*, p. 19.
74. Samuel, G. *Civilized Shamans: Buddhism in Tibetan Societies*, pp. 408–409.
75. Snellgrove, D. *Buddhist Himâlaya*, p. 51–52.
76. *Ibid.*, p. 52.
77. Waddell, L. A. *Buddhism of Tibet or Lamaism*, p. 16.
78. Jung, C. G. *Psychological Reflections: A New Anthology of His Writings 1905–1961*, 2d. Selected and edited by Jolande Jacobi. Bollingen Series XXXI (Princeton, NJ: Princeton University Press, 1970 [1953]), re: 72:104; p. 11.
79. *Ibid.*, re: 69:78, p. 9.
80. *Ibid.*
81. Heller, A. *Tibetan Art: Tracing the Development of Spiritual Ideals and Art in Tibet 600–2000 A.D.*, p. 15.
82. Snellgrove, D. *Buddhist Himâlaya: Travels and Studies*, p. 54.
83. *Ibid.*
84. *Ibid.*
85. *Ibid.*
86. *Ibid.*
87. *Ibid.*, p. 55.
88. David-Neel, A. *My Journey to Lhasa*, p. xix.
89. David-Neel, A. *Magic and Mystery in Tibet*, p. 7.
90. Blofeld, J. *The Tantric Mysticism of Tibet*, p. 64.

91. David-Neel, A. *Magic and Mystery in Tibet*, p. 7.
92. *Ibid.*
93. Snellgrove, D. "Tibet" in R. Cavendish, R. (ed.) *Man, Myth & Magic: The Illustrated Encyclopedia of Mythology, Religion and the Unknown*, p. 2620.
94. Tucci, G. *Tibet: Land of Snow*, p. 68.
95. Rinpoche, Kalu. *Foundations of Tibetan Buddhism*, p. 193.
96. Blofeld, J. *The Tantric Mysticism of Tibet*, p. 9.
97. David-Neel, A. *Magic and Mystery in Tibet*, p. 7.
98. Waddell, L. A. *Buddhism of Tibet or Lamaism*, p. xiii.
99. Snellgrove, D. L. (general editor) *The Image of the Buddha* (San Francisco: Kodansha International/UNESCO, 1978), p. 462.
100. Tucci, G. *The Religions of Tibet*, translated by Geoffrey Samuel (Berkeley and Los Angeles: University of California Press, 1980), p. 1.
101. Samuel, G. *Civilized Shamans: Buddhism in Tibetan Societies* (Washington and London: Smithsonian Institution Press, 1993), pp. 406–407.
102. Kvaerne, P. "The Religions of Tibet," in: Kitagawa, J. *The Religious Traditions of Asia*, pp. 195–205 (London: RoutledgeCurzon, 1987), p. 199.
103. Waddell, L. A. *Buddhism of Tibet or Lamaism*, p. 15.
104. "Vajrayâna." *Encyclopædia Britannica*, from *Encyclopædia Britannica Deluxe Edition 2005 CD*. Encyclopædia Britannica, May 30, 2004 (accessed March 10, 2010).
105. "Vajrayâna." *Encyclopædia Britannica*, from *Encyclopædia Britannica Deluxe Edition 2005 CD*. Encyclopædia Britannica, May 30, 2004 (accessed March 10, 2010).
106. Rambach, P. *The Secret Message of Tantric Buddhism*, p. 17.
107. Tucci, G. *Tibet: Land of Snow*, p. 72.
108. David-Neel, A. *My Journey to Lhasa*, p. 250.
109. Das, C. S. *A Tibetan-English Dictionary with Sanskrit Synonyms* (Stirling: New Delhi, 1985, reprint Calcutta, 1903), p. 372.
110. *Ibid.*
111. David-Neel, A. *My Journey to Lhasa*, p. 250.
112. Kvaerne, P. "The Religions of Tibet," in: Kitagawa, J. *The Religious Traditions of Asia*, p. 197.
113. *Ibid.*
114. Kvaerne, P. "Bon," in: L. Jones, Editor in chief. *Encyclopedia of Religion*, 2d ed, Vol. 2. pp. 1007–1010

(New York: Thompson Gale, 2005), p. 1008.
115. Murthy, K. K. *Buddhism in Tibet* (Delhi: Sundeep Prakashan, 1989), pp. 2–3.
116. *Ibid.*, p. 3.
117. Snellgrove, D., and H. Richardson. *A Cultural History of Tibet* (Boston: Shambhala, 1995 [1968]), p. 59.
118. *Ibid.*
119. Murthy, K. K. *Buddhism in Tibet*, p. 3.; Also see A. David-Neel, *My Journey to Lhasa*, p. 250.
120. Storm, R. *Indian Mythology: Myths and Legends of India, Tibet and Sri Lanka* (London: Lorenz Books, 2000), p. 24.
121. Snellgrove, D., and H. Richardson, *A Cultural History of Tibet*, p. 73.
122. Pearlman. E. *Tibetan Sacred Dance* (Rochester, VT: Inner Traditions, 2002), p. 15.
123. Waddell, L. A. *Buddhism of Tibet or Lamaism*, p. 24.
124. Snellgrove, D., and H. Richardson, *A Cultural History of Tibet*, p. 73.
125. Pearlman, E. *Tibetan Sacred Dance*, p. 17.
126. Murthy, K. K. *Buddhism in Tibet*, p. 19.
127. Tucci, G., H. Nakamura, and F. Reynolds. "Suffering, impermanence, and no-self" *Encyclopædia Britannica*, from *Encyclopædia Britannica Deluxe Edition 2005 CD*. Encyclopædia Britannica, May 30, 2004 (accessed May 5, 2010).
128. "Tibet, Mongolia, and the Himalayan Kingdoms" *Encyclopædia Britannica*, from *Encyclopædia Britannica Deluxe Edition 2005 CD*. Encyclopædia Britannica, May 30, 2004 (accessed March 13, 2010).
129. Murthy, K. K. *Buddhism in Tibet*, p. 20.
130. *Ibid.*, p. 25.
131. Blofeld, J. *The Tantric Mysticism of Tibet*, pp. 40–41.
132. Murthy, K. K. *Buddhism in Tibet*, p. 58.
133. David-Neel, A. *Magic and Mystery in Tibet*, p. 21.
134. Snellgrove, D. "Tibet" in R. Cavendish, R. (Ed.) *Man, Myth & Magic: The Illustrated Encyclopedia of Mythology, Religion and the Unknown*, p. 2620.
135. Waddell, L. A. *Buddhism of Tibet or Lamaism*, p. xxxi.
136. Powell, A. *Living Buddhism* (Berkeley: University of California Press, 1995), p. 124.
137. Rambach, P. *The Secret Message of Tantric Buddhism*, p. 160.

138. Blofeld, J. *The Tantric Mysticism of Tibet*, p. 52.
139. Govinda, Lama Anagarika. *The Way of the White Clouds*, p. 115.
140. *Ibid.*
141. *Ibid.*
142. Snellgrove, D. L. *The Image of the Buddha*, p. 352.
143. *Ibid.*
144. Tucci, G. *Tibet: Land of Snow*, p. 98.
145. Fisher, R. E. *Art of Tibet* (London: Thames and Hudson, 1997), p. 29.
146. *Ibid.*
147. Snellgrove, D. L. (general editor) *The Image of the Buddha*, p. 352.
148. Fisher, R. E. *Art of Tibet*, p. 12.
149. Murthy, K. K. *Buddhism in Tibet*, p. 57.
150. Fisher, R. E. *Art of Tibet*, p. 29.
151. *Ibid.*
152. Heller, A. *Tibetan Art: Tracing the Development of Spiritual Ideals and Art in Tibet 600–2000 A.D.*, p. 15.
153. Hoppál, M. *Studies on Mythology and Uralic Shamanism* (Budapest: Akadémiai Kiadó, 2000), p. 4.
154. Gordon, A. K. *Tibetan Religious Art*, p. 10.
155. *Ibid.*
156. Rinpoche, Kalu. *Foundations of Tibetan Buddhism*, p. 10.
157. Fisher, R. E. *Art of Tibet*, p. 90.
158. David-Neel, A. *Magic and Mystery in Tibet*, p. 186.
159. *Ibid.*
160. Gordon, A. K. *Tibetan Religious Art*, p. 10.
161. Tucci, G. *Tibet: Land of Snow*, p. 109.
162. De Nebesky-Wojkowitz, R. *Oracles and Demons of Tibet: The Cult and iconogrdaphy of the Tibetan Protective Deities* (Varanasi, India: Book Faith India, 1993), p. 343.
163. Fisher, R. E. *Art of Tibet*, p. 93.
164. *Ibid.*, p. 92.
165. *Ibid.*
166. Govinda, Lama Anagarika. *The Way of the White Clouds*, p. 117.
167. Fisher, R. E. *Art of Tibet*, p. 92.
168. *Ibid.*, p. 22.
169. *Ibid.*, p. 96.
170. *Ibid*, pp. 98–99.
171. Tucci, G., H. Nakamura, and F. Reynolds. "suffering, impermanence, and no-self" Encyclopædia Britannica, from *Encyclopædia Britannica Deluxe Edition 2005 CD*. Encyclopædia Britannica, May 30, 2004 (accessed May 5, 2010).

Chapter Three

1. Brinton, H. H. *The Mystic Will: Based on a Study of the Philosophy of Jacob Boehme* (New York: Macmillan, 1930), p. 17.
2. Hastings, J. ed. "Mysticism" In: *Encyclopædia of Religion and Ethics* (Edinburgh: T. & T. Clark, 1980), p. 83.
3. Underhill, E. *Mysticism: A Study in the Nature and Development of Spiritual Consciousness* (Mineola, NY: Dover, 2002 [1911]), p. 70.
4. *Ibid.*
5. *Ibid.*
6. Quispel, G. "Gnostic Man: The Doctrine of Basilides" pp. 210–246, in: J. Campbell ed., *The Mystic Vision: Papers from the Eranos Yearbooks*, Bollingen Series XXX-6 (Princeton, NJ: Princeton University Press, 1982), 210.
7. Birket-Smith, K. *The Paths of Culture*, translated by Karin Fennow (Madison: University of Wisconsin Press, 1965), p. 351.
8. Underhill, E. *Mysticism: A Study in the Nature and Development of Spiritual Consciousness*, p. 140.
9. Mysticism, "Basic patterns," Encyclopædia Britannica, from *Encyclopædia Britannica Deluxe Edition 2005 CD*. Encyclopædia Britannica, May 30, 2004 (accessed July 28, 2010).
10. Underhill, E. *Mysticism: The Nature and Development of Spiritual Consciousness*, p. 63.
11. Birket-Smith, K. *The Paths of Culture*, p. 350.
12. Blofeld, J. *The Tantric Mysticism of Tibet: A Practical Guide* (New York: Causeway Books, 1974), 213.
13. Gimello, R. M. "Mysticism in Its Contexts" in: S. T. Katz, ed. *Mysticism and Religious Traditions*, pp. 61–88 (Oxford: Oxford University Press, 1983), p. 61.
14. Kohn, L. *Taoist Mystical Philosophy: The Scripture of Western Ascension* (Albany, NY: State University Press, 1991), p. 15.
15. Mysticism, "Relation of mystical experience to other kinds of experience," Encyclopædia Britannica, from *Encyclopædia Britannica Deluxe Edition 2005 CD*. Encyclopædia Britannica, May 30, 2004 (accessed July 28, 2010).
16. *Ibid.*
17. Taoism, "Western mysticism and religion," Encyclopædia Britannica, from *Encyclopædia Britannica Deluxe Edition 2005 CD*. Encyclopædia Britannica, May 30, 2004 (accessed July 30, 2010).
18. Freke, T., and P. Gandy. *The Complete Guide to World Mysticism* (London: Judy Piatkus Lnc., 1997), p. 17.
19. Child, A., and I. Child. *Religion and Magic in the Life of Traditional Peoples* (Englewood Cliffs, NJ: Prentice Hall, Ltd., 1993), p. 37.
20. Underhill, E. *Mysticism: A Study in the Nature and Development of Spiritual Consciousness*, p. 81.
21. Blofeld, J. *The Tantric Mysticism of Tibet*, p. 70.
22. Gillette, D. *The Shaman's Secret* (New York and London: Bantam Books, 1997), p. 108.
23. Hastings, J. ed. "Mysticism" In: *Encyclopædia of Religion and Ethics*, p. 83.
24. Plato, *Myths of Plato*, translated with introductory and other observations, by J. A. Stewart and edited by G. R. Levy (New York: Barnes and Nobles, 1970 [1905]).
25. Mysticism, "other experiences and definitions of mysticism," Encyclopædia Britannica, from *Encyclopædia Britannica Deluxe Edition 2005 CD*. Encyclopædia Britannica (accessed January 2, 2009).
26. *Ibid.*
27. Freke, T., and P. Gandy. *The Complete Guide to World Mysticism*, p. 18.
28. Webster, H. *Magic: A Sociological Study* (Stanford, CA: Sanford University Press, 1948), p. 39.
29. Sauvage, G. M. "Mysticism" in: *Catholic Encyclopedia*, Volume X, Transcribed by Elizabeth T. Knuth. (New York: Robert Appleton Company, 1911 <http://www.newadvent.org/cathen/index.html> (accessed September 21, 2008.
30. Kohn, L. *Early Chinese Mysticism: Philosophy and Soteriology in the Taoist Tradition* (Princeton, NJ: Princeton University Press, 1992), p. 83.
31. *Ibid.*
32. Besserman, P. *Kabbalah and Jewish Mysticism* (Boston and London: Shambhala, 1997), p. 1.
33. Happold. F. C. *Mysticism: A Study and an Anthology* (New York: Penguin Books, 1985 [1963].) p. 19.
34. *Ibid.*, p. 20.
35. Scholem, G. G. *Major Trends in Jewish Mysticism* (New York: Schocken Books, 1972 [1941]), p. 6.
36. "mysticism" Encyclopædia Britannica, from *Encyclopædia Britan-*

nica Deluxe Edition 2005 CD. Encyclopædia Britannica, May 30, 2004 (accessed October 16, 2010).
37. *Ibid.*
38. Eliade, M. *Shamanism: Archaic Techniques of Ecstasy*, translated by Willard R. Trask (Bollingen Series LXXVI, Princeton, NJ: Princeton University Press, 1974), p. 508.
39. *Ibid.*, p. xix.
40. Watts, A. *The Supreme Identity: An Essay on Oriental Metaphysic and Christian Religion*, 2d (New York: Pantheon Books, 1972), p. 45.
41. Hoppál, M. "Shamanism: Universal Structures and Regional Symbols" pp. 181–192. in: *Shamans and Cultures*, ed. Mihály Hoppál and Kieth Howard (Budapest: Akadémiai Kiadó and Los Angeles: International Society for Trans-Oceanic Research, 1993), p. 190.
42. Bancroft-Hunt, N., and W. Forman. *People of the Totem* (New York: G. P. Putnam's, 1979), p. 76.
43. Walter, M. N., and E. J. N. Fridman, eds. *Shamanism: An Encyclopedia of World Beliefs, Practices, and Culture*, vol. I (Santa Barbara, CA and Oxford: ABC CLIO, 2004), p. xi.
44. Dow, J. *The Shaman's Touch: Otomi Indian Symbolic Healing* (Salt Lake City: University of Utah Press, 1986), p. 7.
45. Sumegi, A. *Dreamworlds of Shamanism and Tibetan Buddhism: The Third Place* (New York: State University of Press, 2008), p. 6.
46. Taoism, "The microcosm-macrocosm concept," Encyclopædia Britannica, from *Encyclopædia Britannica Deluxe Edition 2005 CD*. Encyclopædia Britannica, May 30, 2004 (accessed July 30, 2010).
47. McGhee, R. *Ancient People of the Arctic* (Vancouver: UBC Press, published in association with the Canadian Museum of Civilization, 1996), p. 157.
48. *Ibid.*
49. Underhill, E. *Mysticism: A Study in the Nature and Development of Spiritual Consciousness*, p. 63.
50. Eliade, M. *Shamanism: Archaic Techniques of Ecstasy*, p. 88.
51. Gimello, R. M. "Mysticism in Its Contexts," p. 63.
52. Campbell, J. *The Masks of the Gods: Primitive Mythology* (New York: ARKANA, published by Penguin Books USA, 1976), p.109.
53. *Ibid.*
54. *Ibid.*, pp.109–110.
55. *Ibid.*
56. Scholem, G. G. *Major Trends in Jewish Mysticism*, p. 5.
57. Hinduism, "Mysticism," Encyclopædia Britannica, from *Encyclopædia Britannica Deluxe Edition 2005 CD*. Encyclopædia Britannica, May 30, 2004 (accessed September 14, 2010).
58. Hinduism, "Mysticism," Encyclopædia Britannica, from *Encyclopædia Britannica Deluxe Edition 2005 CD*. Encyclopædia Britannica, May 30, 2004 (accessed October 21, 2010).
59. "Tantra." Encyclopædia Britannica, from *Encyclopædia Britannica Deluxe Edition 2005 CD*. Encyclopædia Britannica, May 30, 2004 (accessed October 14, 2010).
60. Eliade, M. *Shamanism: Archaic Techniques of Ecstasy*, p. 416.
61. Campbell, J. *The Mask of God: Primitive Mythology*, p. 437.
62. Eliade, M. *Shamanism: Archaic Techniques of Ecstasy*, pp. 416–417.
63. Jung, C.G. *Psychology and Religion: West and East*, 2d, translated by R.F.C. Hull (Bollingen Series XX, Princeton, NJ: Princeton University Press, 1973), p. 508.
64. Evans-Wentz, W.Y., ed. *The Tibetan Book of the Dead* (New York: A Galaxy Book, Oxford University Press, 1960 [1927]), p.102.
65. Underhill, E. *Mysticism: A Study in the Nature and Development of Spiritual Consciousness*, p. 386.
66. Maddox, J. L. *The Medicine Man: A Sociological Study of the Character and Evolution of Shamanism* (New York: Macmillan, 1923), p.141.
67. Lu, K'uan Yu. *Taoist Yoga: Alchemy and Immortality* (New York: Samuel Wiser, 1972), p. 27.
68. Eliade, M. *Shamanism: Archaic Techniques of Ecstasy*, p. 417.
69. Iyengar, B. K. S. *Yoga: The Path to Holistic Health* (London, New York: Dorling Kindersley, 2001), p. 10.
70. Govinda, Lama Anagarika. *The Way of the White Clouds* (London: Rider, 1974 [1966]), p. 94.
71. *Ibid.*
72. Harvey, A., ed. *The Essential Mystics: The Soul's Journey into Truth* (Edison, NJ: Castle Books, 1998), p. 17.
73. Bancroft, A. *Religions of the East* (London: William Heinemann, 1974), p. 183.
74. Merton. T. *Thoughts on the East* (New York: New Directions Bibelot, 1995 [1965]), p. 10.
75. Taoism, "Western mysticism and religion," Encyclopædia Britannica, from *Encyclopædia Britannica Deluxe Edition 2005 CD*. Encyclopædia Britannica, May 30, 2004 (accessed July 30, 2010).
76. Merton. T. *Thoughts on the East*, p. 10.
77. Taoism, "The microcosm-macrocosm concept," Encyclopædia Britannica, from *Encyclopædia Britannica Deluxe Edition 2005 CD*. Encyclopædia Britannica, May 30, 2004 (accessed July 30, 2010).
78. Monroe, C. R. *World Religions: An Introduction* (Amherst, NY: Prometheus Books, 1995), p. 76.
79. Kirkland, R. *Taoism: The Enduring Tradition* (New York and London: Routledge, 2004), p. 2.
80. Bancroft, A. *Religions of the East*, p. 183.
81. *Ibid.*
82. Kohn, L. *Early Chinese Mysticism: Philosophy and Soteriology in the Taoist Tradition* (Princeton, NJ: Princeton University Press, 1992), p. 8.
83. *Ibid.*, p. 46.
84. *Ibid.*, p. 8.
85. Taoism, "The microcosm-macrocosm concept," Encyclopædia Britannica, from *Encyclopædia Britannica Deluxe Edition 2005 CD*. Encyclopædia Britannica, May 30, 2004 (accessed July 30, 2010).
86. Fung, Y. *A Short History of Chinese Philosophy*, ed. Derk Bodde (New York: The Free Press, A Division of Macmillan Publishing, 1948), p. 7.
87. Lao Tzu. *Tao Te Ching*, translated by James Legge (New York: Metro Books 2008), p. 11.
88. Kohn, L. *Taoist Mystical Philosophy*, p. 7.
89. Jung, C. G. *Mysterium Coniunctionis*, 2d, translated by R.F.C. Hull, Bollingen Series XX (Princeton, NJ: Princeton University Press, 1970), p. 223.
90. *Ibid.*
91. Bancroft, A. *Religions of the East*, p. 192.
92. Blofeld, J. *I Ching: The Book of Changes*, A translation (London and Wellington: Unwin Paperbacks, 1989 [1965]), p. 38.
93. "providence" Cosmic order, *Encyclopaedia Britannica Library*, from Encyclopaedia Britannica 2005 Deluxe Edition CD-ROM. Encyclopædia Britannica (accessed August 10, 2010)
94. Kohn, L. *Taoist Mystical Philosophy: The Scripture of Western Ascension*, pp. 5–6.
95. Taoism, "The microcosm-macrocosm concept," Encyclopædia Britannica, from *Encyclopædia Britannica Deluxe Edition 2005 CD*. Encyclopædia Britannica, May 30, 2004 (accessed July 30, 2010).
96. *Doctors, Diviners, and Magi-*

cians of Ancient China, translated by Kenneth J. DeWoskin (New York: Columbia University Press, 1983), p. 2.

97. Richards, C. gen. ed. *The Illustrated Encyclopedia of World Religions* (Shaftesbury, Dorset, Rockport, MA, and Melbourne, Victoria: Element Books, Ltd., 1997), 207.

98. Underhill, E. *Mysticism: The Nature and Development of Spiritual Consciousness*, p. 63.

99. Tucci, G., H. Nakamura, and F. E. Reynolds. "suffering, impermanence, and no-self" Encyclopædia Britannica, from *Encyclopædia Britannica Deluxe Edition 2005 CD.* Encyclopædia Britannica, May 30, 2004 (accessed May 5, 2010).

100. ben Shimon Halevi. *The Work of the Kabbalist* (York Beach, ME: Samuel Weiser, 1985), p. xiii.

101. Monroe, C. R. *World Religions: An Introduction*, pp. 74–75.

102. Bancroft, A. *Religions of the East*, p. 211.

103. Fortune, D. *Mystical Qabalah* (York Beach, ME: Samuel Weiser, 1997 [1935]), p. 2.

104. *Ibid.*, p. 29.

105. Gellman, J. "Mysticism," *Stanford Encyclopedia of Philosophy* <http://plato.stanford.edu/cgi-bin/encyclopedia/archinfo.cgi (accessed November 18, 2009).

106. Matt, D. *The Essential Kabbalah: The Heart of Jewish Mysticism* (Edison, NJ: Castle Books, 1997), p. 1.

107. Ariel, D. *The Mystic Quest: An Introduction to Jewish Mysticism* (Northvale, NJ: Jason Aronson, 1988), p. 123.

108. *Ibid.*

109. ben Shimon Halevi. *The Work of the Kabbalist* (York Beach, ME: Samuel Weiser, 1985), p. 1.

110. *Ibid.*, p. 3.

111. "Merkava," Encyclopædia Britannica, from *Encyclopædia Britannica Deluxe Edition 2005 CD.* Encyclopædia Britannica, May 30, 2004 (accessed October 15, 2010).

112. Scholem, G. G. *Major Trends in Jewish Mysticism*, p. 5.

113. ben Shimon Halevi, Z. *The Work of the Kabbalist* (York Beach, ME: Samuel Weiser, 1985), p. 36.

114. Besserman, P. *Kabbalah and Jewish Mysticism* (Boston and London: Shambhala, 1997), p. 1.

115. Wilson, C. *The Occult: A History* (New York: Random House, 1971), p. 204.

116. Partridge C., gen. ed. *Introduction to World Religions* (Minneapolis: Fortress Press, 2005), p. 278.

117. Shah, I. A. S. *Occultism: Its Theory and Practice* (New York: Dorset Press, 1993), p. 11.

118. Franck, A. *The Kabbalah: The Religious Philosophy of the Hebrews* (New York: Bell, 1940), p. 224.

119. *Ibid.*

120. *Ibid.*, p.224.

121. Jung, C. G. *Psychological Reflections: A New Anthology of His Writings 1905–1961*, 2d. Selected and Edited by Jolande Jacobi. Bollingen Series XXXI (Princeton, NJ: Princeton University Press, 1970 [1953]), re: 47:10, p. 25.

122. Jang, N. H. *Shamanism in Korean Christianity* (Seoul and Edison, NJ: Jimoondang, 2004), p. 51.

123. Addison, C. M. *The Theory and Practice of Mysticism 1918* (New York: E. P. Dutton, 1918), p. 28.

124. Knowles, D. *What Is Mysticism* (London: Burns & Oates, 1967), p. 13.

125. *Ibid.*, p.126.

126. Jung, C. G. *Mysterium Coniunctionis*, p. 375.

127. Underhill, E. *Mysticism: The Nature and Development of Spiritual Consciousness*, p. 344.

128. *Ibid.*

129. Jang, N. H. *Shamanism in Korean Christianity*, p. 51.

130. Underhill, E. *Mysticism: The Nature and Development of Spiritual Consciousness*, p. 104.

131. Happold. F. C. *Mysticism: A Study and an Anthology*, p. 21.

132. Freke, T., and P. Gandy. *The Complete Guide to World Mysticism*, p. 9.

133. Eliade, M. *Shamanism: Archaic Techniques of Ecstasy*, p. 508.

134. "paradise" in: Encyclopædia Britannica, from *Encyclopædia Britannica Deluxe Edition 2005 CD.* Encyclopædia Britannica, May 30, 2004 (accessed September 17, 2010).

135. "Eucharist" Encyclopædia Britannica, from *Encyclopædia Britannica Deluxe Edition 2005 CD.* Encyclopædia Britannica (accessed October 25, 2010).

136. Spencer, S. Rev., and B. J. McGinn. "Christianity," Encyclopædia Britannica, from *Encyclopædia Britannica Deluxe Edition 2005 CD.* Encyclopædia Britannica, May 30, 2004 (accessed October 18, 2010).

137. Lewis, I. M. *Ecstatic Religion: A Study of Shamanism and Spirit Possession*, 2d (London: Routledge, 1989), p. 35.

138. Spencer, S. Rev., and B. J. McGinn. "Christianity," Encyclopædia Britannica, from *Encyclopædia Britannica Deluxe Edition 2005 CD.* Encyclopædia Britannica, May 30, 2004 (accessed October 18, 2010).

139. Jones, R. *Studies in Mystical Religion* (New York: Russell & Russell, 1970 [1909]), p. xxi.

140. Spencer, S. Rev., and B. J. McGinn. "Christianity," Encyclopædia Britannica, from *Encyclopædia Britannica Deluxe Edition 2005 CD.* Encyclopædia Britannica, May 30, 2004 (accessed October 18, 2010).

141. "Roman Catholic" Encyclopædia Britannica, from *Encyclopædia Britannica Deluxe Edition 2005 CD.* Encyclopædia Britannica, May 30, 2004 (accessed October 18, 2010).

142. Jones, R. *Studies in Mystical Religion*, p. xxi.

143. *Ibid.*

144. *Ibid.*

145. "Sufism" Encyclopædia Britannica, from *Encyclopædia Britannica Deluxe Edition 2005 CD.* Encyclopædia Britannica (accessed October 26, 2010).

146. Happold, F. C. *Mysticism: A Study and an Anthology*, p. 96.

147. *Ibid..*

148. Nicholson, R. A. *The Mystics of Islam* (London: Routledge and Kegan Paul Ltd., 1970 [1914]), p. 68.

149. Fadiman, J., and R. Frager, eds. *Essential Sufism*, p. 1.

150. Sufism "Classical mysticism," Encyclopædia Britannica, from *Encyclopædia Britannica Deluxe Edition 2005 CD.* Encyclopædia Britannica, May 30, 2004 (accessed April 6, 2008).

151. Bancroft, A. *Religions of the East* (London: William Heinemann, 1974), p. 211.

152. Partridge C. *Introduction to World Religions*, p. 366.

153. "Sufism," Encyclopædia Britannica, from *Encyclopædia Britannica Deluxe Edition 2005 CD.* Encyclopædia Britannica, May 30, 2004 (accessed September 12, 2010).

154. *The Religion of the Sufis*, translated by David Shea and Anthony Troyer (London: The Octagon Press, 1979), p. 27.

155. Freke, T., and P. Gandy *The Complete Guide to World Mysticism*, p. 108.

156. Harvey, A., ed. *The Essential Mystics: The Soul's Journey into Truth*, p. 137.

157. Fadiman, J., and R. Frager, eds. *Essential Sufism*, pp. 1–2.

158. Nicholson, R. A. *The Mystics of Islam*, pp. 79–80.

159. "Sufism History: Classical mysticism" In: Encyclopædia Britannica, from *Encyclopædia Britannica Deluxe Edition 2005 CD.* Encyclopædia Britannica, May 30, 2004 (ac-

cessed September 12, 2010).
160. Nicholson, R. A. *The Mystics of Islam*, p. 44.
161. Fadiman, J., and R. Frager, eds. *Essential Sufism*, p. 3.
162. Katz, S. *Mysticism and Religious Traditions* (Oxford: Oxford University Press, 1983), p. 140.
163. Bancroft, A. *Religions of the East*, p. 219.
164. Fadiman, J., and R. Frager, eds. *Essential Sufism*, p. 1.
165. "Sufism" In: Encyclopædia Britannica, from *Encyclopædia Britannica Deluxe Edition 2005 CD*. Encyclopædia Britannica, May 30, 2004 (accessed September 12, 2010).
166. Noss, D. *A History of the World's Religions*, 12d (Upper Saddle River, NJ: Pearson Education, 2008), p. 583.
167. Bancroft, A. *Religions of the East*, p. 221.
168. *Ibid.*.
169. *Ibid.*, pp. 221–222.
170. Eliade M. *Yoga; Immortality and Freedom*, translated by Willard R. Trask (Bollingen Series LVI, Princeton, NJ: Princeton University Press, 1990 [1958]), p. 5.
171. Nicholson, R. A., ed. *Kitab al-Luma,'* (The Book of Flashes) (London: Luzac, 1947), p. 34–35.

Chapter Four

1. Bennett, C. A. *A Philosophical Study of Mysticism* (New Haven, CT: Yale University Press, 1923), p. 108.
2. d'Aquili, E., and A. B. Newberg. The Mystical Mind: Probing the Biology of Religious Experience (Minneapolis, MN: Fortress Press, 1999), p. 80.
3. *Ibid.*
4. Hefner, A. G. *The Mystica*. (last modified June 12, 2008) http://www.themystica.com/mystica/default.html. (accessed December 11, 2010).
5. Hastings, J. ed. "Mysticism," *Encyclopedia of Religion and Ethics* (Edinburgh: T&T Clark, 1994), p. 108.
6. *Ibid.*
7. Happold, F. C. *Mysticism: A Study and An Anthology.* (New York: Penguin Books, 1985 [1963]), p. 37.
8. Kohn, L. *Early Chinese Mysticism: Philosophy and Soteriology in the Taoist Tradition* (Princeton, NJ: Princeton University Press, 1992) p. 38.
9. Brinton, H. H. *The Mystic Will: Based on a Study of the Philosophy of Jacob Boehme* (New York: Macmillan, 1930), p. 15–16.
10. *Ibid.*
11. Arberry, A. J. *Sufism: An Account of the Mystics of Islam* (London: George Allen & Unwin Ltd., 1968 [1950]), p. 12.
12. "mysticism" Encyclopædia Britannica, from *Encyclopædia Britannica Deluxe Edition 2005 CD*. Encyclopædia Britannica, May 30, 2004 (accessed March 3, 2011).
13. Happold. F. C. *Mysticism: A Study and an Anthology*, p. 20.
14. Eliade, M. *Yoga: Immortality and Freedom*, translated by Willard R. Trask. (Bollingen Series LVI, Princeton NJ: Princeton University Press, 2009 [1958]), p. 15.
15. Freke, T., and P. Gandy. *The Complete Guide to World Mysticism* (London: Judy Piatkus, 1997), p. 37.
16. Eliade, M. *Yoga: Immortality and Freedom*, p. 15.
17. Johnson, O. S. *A Study of Chinese Alchemy* (Shanghai: The Commercial Press, Limited, 1928 reprinted from a copy in the Columbia University Library, New York: Arno Press, 1974), p. 22.
18. Fung, Y-L. *A Short History of Chinese Philosophy*, edited by D. Bodde (New York: The Free Press, A Division of Macmillan, 1948), p. 77.
19. *Ibid.*
20. "Mencius" contributed by Yi Pao Mei, Encyclopædia Britannica, from *Encyclopædia Britannica Deluxe Edition 2005 CD*. Encyclopædia Britannica, May 30, 2004 (accessed February 20, 2011).
21. McKechnie, J. L. gen. super. *Webster's New Twentieth Century Dictionary of the English Language*, 2d. (New York: William Collins+World, 1977), p. 1190.
22. *Ibid.*
23. Mencius" contributed by Yi Pao Mei, Encyclopædia Britannica, from *Encyclopædia Britannica Deluxe Edition 2005 CD*. Encyclopædia Britannica, May 30, 2004 (accessed February 20, 2011).
24. "mysticism" Encyclopædia Britannica, from *Encyclopædia Britannica Deluxe Edition 2005 CD*. Encyclopædia Britannica, May 30, 2004 (accessed March 3, 2011).
25. McKechnie, J. L. *Webster's New Twentieth Century Dictionary of the English Language*, p. 1132.
26. "Aristotle" Encyclopædia Britannica, from *Encyclopædia Britannica Deluxe Edition 2005 CD*. Encyclopædia Britannica, May 30, 2004 (accessed February 20, 2011).
27. Eliade, M. *Yoga: Immortality and Freedom*, p. 13.
28. *Ibid.*
29. Hastings, J., ed. "Mysticism," *Encyclopedia of Religion and Ethics*, p.114.
30. Russell, B. *Mysticism and Logic* (New York: W.W. Norton, 1929), p. 9.
31. Underhill, E. *Mysticism: A Study in the Nature and Development of Spiritual Consciousness* (Mineola, NY: Dover, 2002 (unaltered reproduction of the 12th edition, 1930, published by E. P. Dutton, of the work originally published in 1911), p. 81.
32. Bancroft, A. *Religions of the East* (William Heinermann Ltd., 1974), p. 130.
33. King, U. *Christian Mystics* (Mahwah, NJ: HiddenSpring, 2001), p.17.
34. Ariel, D. S. *The Mystic Quest: An Introduction to Jewish Mysticism* (Northvale, NJ and London: Jason Aronson, 1988), p. 48.
35. Hefner, Alan G. *The Mystica* (last modified June 12, 2008) http://www.themystica.com/mystica/default.html (accessed December 11, 2010).
36. Hastings, J., ed. "Mysticism," *Encyclopedia of Religion and Ethics*, p.114.
37. *Ibid.*
38. Blofeld, J. *The Tantric Mysticism of Tibet: A practical Guide to the Theory, Purpose, and Techniques of Tantric Meditation* (New York: Causeway Books, 1974, p. 52.
39. Bancroft, A. *Religions of the East*, p. 211.
40. d'Aquili, E., and A. B. Newberg. *The Mystical Mind: Probing the Biology of Religious Experience*, p. 159.
41. *Ibid.*, p. 157.
42. Porter, B. *Road to Heaven: Encounters with Chinese Hermits* (Berkeley: Counterpoint, 1993), p. 1.
43. "hermit" Encyclopædia Britannica, from *Encyclopædia Britannica Deluxe Edition 2005 CD*. Encyclopædia Britannica, May 30, 2004 (accessed February 23, 2011).
44. "Essene" Encyclopædia Britannica, from *Encyclopædia Britannica Deluxe Edition 2005 CD*. Encyclopædia Britannica, May 30, 2004 (accessed Marh 4, 2011).
45. Eliade, M. *Yoga: Immortality and Freedom*, p. 140.
46. *Ibid.*
47. Waddell, L. A. *Tibetan Buddhism with its Mystic Cults, Symbolism and Mythology* (New York: Dover, 1972 [1895].), p. 224.
48. Govinda, L. A. *The Way of White Clouds: A Buddhist in Tibet*, 5th

imp. (London: Rider, 1974 [1966]), p. 99.

49. "*dukkha*" Encyclopædia Britannica, from *Encyclopædia Britannica Deluxe Edition 2005 CD*. Encyclopædia Britannica, May 30, 2004 (accessed May 5, 2010).

50. King, U. *Christian Mystics* (Mahwah, NJ: HiddenSpring, 2001), p.17.

51. Buonaiuti, E. "Symbols and Rites in the Religious Life of Certain Monastic Orders," in J. Campbell, ed. *The Mystic Vision*, pp. 168–209 (Bollingen Series XXX-6, Princeton, NJ: Princeton University Press, 1982), p. 183.

52. Kohn, L. *Early Chinese Mysticism: Philosophy and Soteriology in the Taoist Tradition* (Princeton, NJ: Princeton University Press, 1992), p. 61.

53. *Ibid.*, p. 121.
54. *Ibid.*
55. Eliade, M. *Yoga: Immortality and Freedom*, p. 5.
56. *Ibid.*, p. 73.
57. *Ibid.*, p. 74.
58. *Ibid.*, p. 133.
59. *Ibid.*
60. Hastings, J. ed. "Mysticism," *Encyclopedia of Religion and Ethics*, p.85.
61. Halifax, J. *Shamanic Voices* (New York: E. P. Dutton, 1979), p. 5.
62. Eliade, M. *Shamanism: Archaic Techniques of Ecstasy*, translated by Willard R. Trask (Bollingen Series LXXVI, Princeton NJ: Princeton University Press, 1964), p. 508.
63. Eliade, M. *Shamanism: Archaic Techniques of Ecstasy*, p. 508.
64. Lewis, *Ecstatic Religion*, p. 5.
65. Wong, E. The Shambhala Guide to *Taoism* (Boston and London: Shambhala, 1997), p. 14.
66. *Ibid.*
67. Blofeld, J. *The Tantric Mysticism of Tibet*, p. 66.
68. Hastings, J., ed. "Mysticism," *Encyclopedia of Religion and Ethics*, p. 86.
69. Stoddart, W. *Sufism: The Mystical Doctrines and Methods of Islam* (St. Paul, MN: Paragon House, 1985), pp. 22–23.
70. Blofeld, J. *The Tantric Mysticism of Tibet*, p. 52.
71. Eliade, M. *Yoga: Immortality and Freedom*, p. 167.
72. Bennett, C. A. *A Philosophical Study of Mysticism*, p. 109.
73. Underhill, E. *Practical Mysticism*, p. 91.
74. *Ibid.*
75. *Ibid.*, p. 82.
76. Freke, T., and P. Gandy. *The Complete Guide to World Mysticism* (London: Judy Piatkus, 1997), p. 37.

77. Johnson, S. *The Book of Tibetan Elders: Life Stories and Wisdom from the Great Spiritual Masters of Tibet.* (New York: Riverhead Books, 1996) pp. 265–266.

78. "magic," Encyclopædia Britannica, from *Encyclopædia Britannica Deluxe Edition 2005 CD*. Encyclopædia Britannica, May 30, 2004 (December 23, 2010).

79. Malinowski, B. *Sex, Culture, and Myth* (London: Rupert Hart-Davis, 1963), p. 188.
80. *Ibid.*
81. *Ibid.*, p. 189.
82. *Ibid.*
83. Guiley, R. E. *The Encyclopedia of Magic and Alchemy* (New York: Facts on File an imprint of Infobase Publishing, 2006), p. xii.
84. *Ibid.*, p. 175.
85. Webster, H. *Magic: A Sociological Study* (Stanford, CA: Sanford University Press, 1948), p. 39.
86. Guiley, R. E. *The Encyclopedia of Magic and Alchemy*, p. xii.
87. Feuerstein, G. *The Yoga Tradition: It History, Literature, Philosophy and Practice* (Prescott, AZ: Hohm Press, 1998), p. 39.
88. Frazer, J. G. *The Golden Bough: A Study in Magic and Religion*, Vol. 1 (New York: MacMillan, 1958), p.12.
89. *Ibid.*
90. Lowie, R. H. *Primitive Religion* (New York: Liveright, 1952 [1924]), p. 138.
91. Guiley, R. E. *The Encyclopedia of Magic and Alchemy*, p. 175.
92. Webster, H. *Magic: A Sociological Study*, p.38.
93. Maringer, J. *The Gods of Prehistoric Man*, edited and translated by Mary Ilford (New York: Alfred A. Knopf, 1960), p. 250.
94. "dhamapāla," Encyclopædia Britannica, from *Encyclopædia Britannica Deluxe Edition 2005 CD*. Encyclopædia Britannica, May 30, 2004 (December 25, 2010).
95. Monroe, C. R. *World Religions: An Introduction* (Amherst, NY: Prometheus Books, 1995), p. 76.
96. *Encyclopedia of Magic & Superstition: Alchemy, Charms, Dreams, Omans, Rituals, Talismans, Wishes* (London: Octopus Books Limited, 1974) p. 188.
97. *Ibid.*, p. 188.
98. Gordon, S. *The Paranormal: An Illustrated Encyclopedia* (London: Headline Book Publishing PLC, 1992), p. 178.
99. *Ibid.*, p. 56.
100. *Ibid.*, p. 178.

101. *Ibid.*
102. Guiley, R. E. *The Encyclopedia of Magic and Alchemy*, p. xi.
103. *Ibid.*, p. xii.
104. Wong, E. The Shambhala Guide to *Taoism* (Boston and London: Shambhala, 1997), p. 5.
105. *Ibid.*
106. Malinowski, B. *Sex, Culture, and Myth*, p. 190.
107. Child, A. B., and I. L. Child. *Religion and Magic in the Life of Traditional Peoples* (Englewood Cliffs, NJ: Prentice Hall, 1993), p. 81.
108. "divination," Encyclopædia Britannica, from *Encyclopædia Britannica Deluxe Edition 2005 CD*. Encyclopædia Britannica, May 30, 2004 (accessed December 27, 2010).
109. Child, A. B., and I. L. Child. *Religion and Magic in the Life of Traditional Peoples*, p. 99.
110. *Ibid.*
111. de Nebesky-Wojkowitz, Réne. *Oracles and Demons of Tibet* (Varamasi, India: Book Faith India an imprint of Pilgrims Book House, 1993), p. 409.
112. "dreams as a source of divination," Encyclopædia Britannica, from *Encyclopædia Britannica Deluxe Edition 2005 CD*. Encyclopædia Britannica, May 30, 2004 (accessed December 27, 2010).
113. Blofeld, J. *I Ching: The Book of Changes*, a translation (London, Sydney, and Wellington: A Mandala Book, Unwin Paperbacks, 1989 [1965]), p. 3.
114. Malinowski, B. *Sex, Culture, and Myth*, p. 190.
115. Tucci G. *The Religions of Tibet*, translated by Geoffrey Samuel (Berkeley and Los Angeles: University of California Press, 1980), p. 8.
116. Fenton, P. *Tibetan Healing: The Modern Legacy of Medicine Buddha* (Wheaton, IL and Chennai, India: Quest Books, 1999), p. 168.
117. *Ibid.*, pp. 168–169.
118. Lévi-Strauss, C. *Structural Anthropology* (New York: Basic Books, A Division of HarperCollins, 1963), p. 168.
119. Kurtz, P. *The Transcendental Temptation: A Critique of Religion and the Paranormal* (Buffalo, NY: Prometheus Books, 1991), p. 449.
120. *Effortless Being: The Yoga Sutras of Patanjali*, translated by Alistair Shearer (London, Boston, and Wellington: Mandala, Unwin Paperbacks, 1982), p. 10.
121. Campbell, J. *Transformations of Myth Through Time* (New York, London, and Toronto: Perennial Library, Harper & Row, 1990), p. 1.

122. Ariel, D. S. *The Mystic Quest: An Introduction to Jewish Mysticism*, p. 136.
123. *Ibid.*, pp. 136–137.
124. Forty, J. *Mythology: A Visual Encyclopedia* (London: PRC Publishing Ltd., 2001), p. 8.
125. *Ibid.*, p. 14.
126. Partridge C., gen. ed. *Introduction to World Religions* (Minneapolis: Fortress Press, 2005), p. 20.
127. Malinowski, B. *Sex, Culture, and Myth*, p. 253.
128. Forty, J. *Mythology: A Visual Encyclopedia*, p. 18.
129. Lévi-Strauss, C. *Structural Anthropology*, p. 207.
130. Burland, C. A. *Myths of Life and Death* (New York: Crown, 1974), p. 6.
131. *Ibid.*
132. Kluckhohn, C. "Myths and Rituals: A General Theory," pp. 137–167 in: R. A. Georges, ed. *Studies on Mythology* (Homewood, IL: The Dorsey Press, 1968), p. 137.
133. Topitsch, E. "World Interpretation and Self-Interpretation: Some Basic Patterns," pp. 157–173, in: H. A. Murray, ed. *Myth and Mythmaking* (New York: George Braziller, 1960), p. 157.
134. Birket-Smith, K. *The Paths of Culture: A General Ethnology*, translated by Karin Fennow (Madison and Milwaukee: University of Wisconsin Press, 1965), p. 59.
135. "Christianity," Encyclopædia Britannica, from *Encyclopædia Britannica Deluxe Edition 2005 CD*. Encyclopædia Britannica, May 30, 2004 (accessed February 11, 2011).
136. *Good News Bible* (New York: United Bible Societies, 2007), p. 4.
137. Johnson, O. S. *A Study of Chinese Alchemy*, p. 14.
138. *Ibid.*
139. Roberts, J. *Japanese Mythology A to Z* (New York: Facts on File, 2004), pp. 53–54.
140. *Ibid.*, pp. 20–21.
141. *Essential Visual History of World Mythology* (Washington, DC: National Geographic, 2008), pp. 100–101.
142. *Ibid.*, p. 335.
143. *Ibid.*, p. 394.
144. Ferguson, G. *Signs and Symbols of Christian Art* (New York: Oxford University Press, 1959), p. ix.
145. "*Avalokitesvara*," Encyclopædia Britannica, from *Encyclopædia Britannica Deluxe Edition 2005 CD*. Encyclopædia Britannica, May 30, 2004 (accessed February 14, 2011).
146. Palmer, M., and J. Ramsay, with M-H. Kwok. *The Kuan Yin Chronicles: The Myths and Prophecies of the Chinese Goddess of Compassion* (Charlottesville, VA: Hampton Roads, 2009), p. xiv.
147. "Great Mother of the Gods," Encyclopædia Britannica, from *Encyclopædia Britannica Deluxe Edition 2005 CD*. Encyclopædia Britannica, May 30, 2004 (accessed February 8, 2011).
148. Hackin, J., et al. *Asiatic Mythology: A detailed Description and Explanation of the Mythologies of All the Great National of Asia* (New York: Crescent Books, 1963), p. 148.
149. Edson, G. *Shamanism: A Cross-Cultural Study of Beliefs and Practices* (Jefferson, NC: McFarland, 2009), p. 199.
150. Jung. C. G. *Psychology and Alchemy*, 2d, translated by R.F.C. Hull (Bollingen Series XX, Princeton, NJ: Princeton University Press, 1980 [1952]), p. 25.
151. Edson, G. *Shamanism: A Cross-Cultural Study of Beliefs and Practices*, p. 201.
152. "Christianity" Encyclopædia Britannica, from *Encyclopædia Britannica Deluxe Edition 2005 CD*. Encyclopædia Britannica, May 30, 2004 (accessed August 18, 2011).
153. Edson, G. *Shamanism: A Cross-Cultural Study of Beliefs and Practices*, p. 200.
154. Walker, B. *The Woman's Dictionary of Symbols and Sacred Objects* (Edison, NJ: Castle Books, 1988), p. 195.
155. *Ibid.*, pp. 195–196.
156. Hackin, J, et al. *Asiatic Mythology: A detailed Description and Explanation of the Mythologies of All the Great National of Asia* (New York: Crescent Books, 1963), pp. 126–127.
157. *Ibid.*
158. "Tara," Encyclopædia Britannica, from *Encyclopædia Britannica Deluxe Edition 2005 CD*. Encyclopædia Britannica, May 30, 2004 (accessed February 10, 2011).
159. Czaja M. *Gods of Myth and Stone* (New York and Tokyo: Weatherhill, 1974), p. 163.
160. Hagen, R-M, and R. Hagen *L'Egypte: Les homes, les dieux, les pharaons* (Köln: Taschen Verlag GmbH, 1999), p. 147.
161. Beane, W. C., and W. G. Doty, eds. *Myths, Rites, Symbols: A Mircea Elliade Reader*, vol. I (New York and London: Harper Colphon Books, Harper & Row, 1976), p. 250.
162. Mackenzie, D. A. *Myths and Legends Series: China and Japan* (London: Bracken Books, 1985), p. 261.
163. *Ibid.*, p. 260.
164. Pinch, G. *Magic in Ancient Egypt* (Austin: University of Texas Press, 1994), p. 23.
165. *Ibid.*
166. Campbell, J. *Transformations of Myths Through Time*, p. 93.
167. Feuerstein, G., S. Kak and D. Frawley. *In Search of the Cradle of Civilization: New Light on Ancient India* (Wheaton, IL and Adyar, Madras: Quest Books, The Theosophical Publishing House, 1995), p. 235.
168. Campbell, J. *Transformations of Myths Through Time*, p. 74.
169. Middleton, J., ed. *Gods and Rituals: Readings in Religious Beliefs and Practices* (Austin: University of Texas Press, 1981), p. 115.
170. "Hinduism," Encyclopædia Britannica, from *Encyclopædia Britannica Deluxe Edition 2005 CD*. Encyclopædia Britannica, May 30, 2004 (accessed January 10, 2011).
171. Malinowski, B. *Sex, Culture, and Myth*, p. 253.
172. "Yama," Encyclopædia Britannica, from *Encyclopædia Britannica Deluxe Edition 2005 CD*. Encyclopædia Britannica, May 30, 2004 (accessed January 10, 2011).
173. "Mictlantecuhtli," Encyclopædia Britannica, from *Encyclopædia Britannica Deluxe Edition 2005 CD*. Encyclopædia Britannica, May 30, 2004 (accessed February 17, 2011).
174. Pope, J. A., ed. director. *Mysteries of the Ancient Americas* (Pleasantville, NY and Montreal: The Reader's Digest Association, 1986), p. 294.
175. *Essential Visual History of World Mythology*, p. 382.
176. Oakes, L., and L. Gahlin. *Ancient Egypt* (New York: Barnes & Noble, 2006), p. 289.
177. Mackenzie, D. A. *Myths and Legends Series: China and Japan* (London: Bracken Books, 1985), p. 222.
178. Fleming, F., and A. Lothian. *The Way to Eternity: Egyptian Myths* (London: Duncan Baird, 1997), p. 105.
179. Mackenzie, D. A. *Myths and Legends Series: China and Japan*, p. 213.
180. *Ibid.*, p. 214.
181. *Ibid.*, p. 215.
182. Blofeld, J. *Taoism: The Road to Immortality* (Boston: Shambhala, 1985), p. 72.
183. "Taoism," Encyclopædia Britannica, from *Encyclopædia Britannica Deluxe Edition 2005 CD*. Encyclopædia Britannica, May 30, 2004 (accessed January 21, 2011).

184. Leeming, D. A. *The World of Myth*, p. 68.
185. "reincarnation," Encyclopædia Britannica, from *Encyclopædia Britannica Deluxe Edition 2005 CD*. Encyclopædia Britannica, May 30, 2004 (accessed February 16, 2011).
186. "Pyramid Texts," Encyclopædia Britannica, from *Encyclopædia Britannica Deluxe Edition 2005 CD*. Encyclopædia Britannica, May 30, 2004 (accessed February 16, 2011).
187. "mysticism" Encyclopædia Britannica, from *Encyclopædia Britannica Deluxe Edition 2005 CD*. Encyclopædia Britannica, May 30, 2004 (accessed August 18, 2011).
188. Evans-Eentz, W. Y. *The Tibetan Book of the Dead or The After-Death Experience on the Bardo Plane, according to Lama Kazi Dawa-Samdup's English Rendering* (New York: A Galaxy Book, Oxford University Press, 1960 [1927]), p. 2.
189. Eliade, M. *Images and Symbols: Studies in Religious Symbolism*, pp. 57–59.
190. Turner, V. *The Forest of Symbols: Aspects of Ndembu Ritual* (Ithaca and London: Cornell University Press, 1967) p. 45.
191. Edson, G. *Shamanism: A Cross-Cultural Study of Beliefs and Practices*, p. 28.

Chapter Five

1. *Harmonizing Yin and Yang: The Dragon—Tiger Classic*, translated and introduced by E. Wong (Boston and London: Shambhala, 1997), p. 1.
2. Simpkins, C. A., and A. M. Simpkins. *Meditation for Therapists and their Clients* (New York and London: W.W. Norton, 2009), p. 150.
3. Jung, C. G. ed. *Man and His Symbols*, J. Freemen coordinating editor (Garden City, NJ: Doubleday, 1964), p. 23.
4. Whitehead, A. N. *Symbolism, Its Meaning and Effect* (New York: Fordham University Press, 1955 [1927]), p. 1.
5. *Ibid.*, p. 2.
6. *Ibid.*
7. Huxley, F. *The Way of the Sacred* (Garden City, NY: Doubleday, 1974), p. 85.
8. *Ibid.*
9. Chile, H., and D. Colles. *Christian Symbols Ancient & Modern* (London: G. Bell and Sons, 1971), p. 1.
10. Eliade, M. *Images and Symbols: Studies in Religious Symbolism*, translated by Philip Maier (Princeton, NJ: Princeton University Press, 1991), p. 12.
11. Eliade, M. *Symbolism, the Sacred, and the Arts*, edited by Diane Apostolos-Cappadona (New York: Continuum, 1992), p. 18.
12. Renou, L. ed. *Hinduism* (New York: George Braiziller, 1962), p. 32.
13. Underhill, E. *Mysticism: A Study in the Natural and Development of Spiritual Consciousness* (Mineola, NY: Dover, 2002 [1911]), p. 79.
14. *Ibid.*
15. Radha, Swami S. *Mantras: Words of Power* (Kootenay Bay, BC: timeless books, 2005), p. 25.
16. Partridge C., gen. ed. *Introduction to World Religions* (Minneapolis: Fortress Press, 2005), p. 20.
17. Eliade, *Images and Symbols*, p. 9.
18. Hyman, J. *The Imitation of Nature* (New York and Oxford: Basil Blackwell Ltd., 1989), pp. 66–67.
19. Young, D. *Origins of the Sacred* (New York: St. Martin's Press, 1991), p. 169.
20. von Franz, M-L. *Alchemy: An Introduction to the Symbolism and the Psychology* (Toronto: Inner City Books, 1980), p. 15.
21. Needham, R. *Symbolic Classification* (Santa Monica, CA: Goodyear Publishing Company, 1979), p. 5.
22. Cirlot, J. E, *A Dictionary of Symbols*, translated by Jack Sage (New York: Philosophical Library, 1962), p. xiv.
23. Dissanayake, E. *What Is Art For?* (Seattle and London: University of Washington Press, 1988), p. 126.
24. Jung. C. G. *Psychology and Religion: West and East*, 2d, translated by R. F. C. Hull (Bollingen Series XX, Princeton: Princeton University Press, 1973), p. 312.
25. Cohen, A. "Symbolic Action and Structure of the Self" in: I. Lewis, ed. *Symbols and Sentiments: Cross-cultural Studies in Symbolism* (London, New York, and San Francisco: Academic Press, a subsidiary of Harcourt Brace Jovanovich, 1977), p. 117.
26. Eliade, M. *Images and Symbols*, p. 9.
27. Hyman, J. *The Imitation of Nature*, pp. 66–67.
28. Partridge C. *Introduction to World Religions*, p. 20.
29. Radha, S. S. *Kundalini Yoga for the West* (Spokane, WA: Timeless Books, 1993), p. 47.
30. Sufism "Symbolism in Sufism," Encyclopædia Britannica, from *Encyclopædia Britannica Deluxe Edition 2005 CD*. Encyclopædia Britannica, May 30, 2004 (accessed September 12, 2010).
31. *Ibid.*
32. Underhill, E. *Mysticism: The Nature and Development of Spiritual Consciousness* (Mineola, NY: Dover, 2002), p. 80.
33. Jung, C. G. *Symbols of Transformation*, Vol 5. (Bollingen Series XX, New York: Pantheon Books, a Division of Random House, 1956), p. 12.
34. Whitehead, A. N. *Symbolism Its Meaning and Effect*, pp. 10–11.
35. *Ibid.*, p. 11.
36. Partridge C., gen. ed. *Introduction to World Religions*, p. 20.
37. Radha, S. S. *Mantras: Words of Power*, p. 23.
38. Bancroft, A. *Religions of the East* (London: William Heinemann, 1974), p. 45.
39. Radha, S. S. *Mantras: Words of Power*, pp. 23–24.
40. *Ibid.*, p. 26.
41. *Ibid.*, p. 30.
42. Too, L. *Mantras and Mudras: Meditations for the Hands and Voice to Bring Peace and Inner Calm* (London: HarperCollins, 2002), p. 32.
43. "Om," Encyclopædia Britannica, from *Encyclopædia Britannica Deluxe Edition 2005 CD*. Encyclopædia Britannica (accessed November 13, 2010).
44. Cirlot, J. E. *A Dictionary of Symbols*, translated by Jack Sage (New York: Phiosophical Library, 1962), p. xxxvi.
45. Bancroft, A. *Religions of the East*, p. 47.
46. Fisher, R. E. *Art of Tibet* (London: Thames and Hudson, 1997), p. 217.
47. Müller-Ebeling, C., C. Rätsch, and S. B. Shahi. *Shamanism and Tantra in the Himalayas* (London: Thames & Hudson, 2002), p. 73.
48. *Ibid.*
49. *Ibid.*, p. 74.
50. "The soul-body relationship," metaphysics, Encyclopædia Britannica, from *Encyclopædia Britannica Deluxe Edition 2005 CD*. Encyclopædia Britannica (accessed November 29, 2010).
51. "Shamanism," Encyclopædia Britannica, from *Encyclopædia Britannica Deluxe Edition 2005 CD*. Encyclopædia Britannica (accessed November 29, 2010).
52. Frazer, J. G. *The Golden Bough: A Study in Magic and Religion*, vol. 1 (New York: The MacMillan Company, 1958), p. 342.
53. "Soul," Encyclopædia Britannica, from *Encyclopædia Britannica*

Deluxe Edition 2005 CD. Encyclopædia Britannica (accessed November 29, 2010).
  54. "Symbols of sacred time and space," Encyclopædia Britannica, from *Encyclopædia Britannica Deluxe Edition 2005 CD*. Encyclopædia Britannica, May 30, 2004 (accessed November 20, 2010).
  55. Muni S. R. *Yoga: The Ultimate Spiritual Path* (St. Paul, MN: Llewellyn, 2001), p. 11.
  56. *Ibid.*
  57. *Ibid.*
  58. Blofeld, J. *The Tantric Mysticism of Tibet: A practical Guide to the Theory, Purpose, and Techniques of Tantric Meditation* (New York: Causeway Books, 1974), p. 119.
  59. Feuerstein, G. *Tantra: The Path of Ecstasy* (Boston and London: Shambhala, 1998), p. 24.
  60. Fisher-Schreiber, I., F-K Ehrhard, K. Friedrichs, and M. S. Diener. *The Encyclopedia of Eastern Philosophy and Religion* (Boston: Shambhala, 1994), p. 298.
  61. Feuerstein, G. *Tantra: The Path of Ecstasy*, p. 24.
  62. Eliade, M. *Images and Symbols*, p. 57.
  63. Feuerstein, G. *Tantra: The Path of Ecstasy*, p. 35.
  64. *Ibid.*, p. 38.
  65. *Ibid.*
  66. *Ibid.*
  67. Müller-Ebeling, C., C. Rätsch, and S. B. Shahi. *Shamanism and Tantra in the Himalayas*, p. 90.
  68. Bancroft, A. *Religions of the East*, p. 186.
  69. Maringer, J. *The Gods of Prehistoric Man*. (New York: Alfred A. Knopf, 1960), p. 279.
  70. "Judaism." Encyclopædia Britannica, from *Encyclopædia Britannica Deluxe Edition 2005 CD*. Encyclopædia Britannica (accessed November 14, 2010).
  71. Ferguson, G. *Signs and Symbols in Christian Art* (New York: Oxford University Press, 1959), p. 66.
  72. *Ibid.*
  73. Beer, R. *The Handbook of Tibetan Buddhist Symbols* (Boston: Shambhala, 2003), p. 263.
  74. *Ibid.*
  75. *Ibid.*
  76. *Ibid.*
  77. *Ibid.*
  78. Ferguson, G. *Signs and Symbols in Christian Art*, p. 69.
  79. Cirlot, J. E. *A Dictionary of Symbols*, p. 135.
  80. Bayley, H. *The Lost Language of Symbolism*, Vol. II (London: Bracken Books, 1996 [1912]), p. 341–342.
  81. Guiley, R. E. *The Encyclopedia of Magic and Alchemy* (New York: Facts on File an imprint of Infobase Publishing, 2006), p. 131.
  82. "hands, imposition of," Encyclopædia Britannica, from *Encyclopædia Britannica Deluxe Edition 2005 CD*. Encyclopædia Britannica (accessed December 1, 2010).
  83. "sacrament," Encyclopædia Britannica, from *Encyclopædia Britannica Deluxe Edition 2005 CD*. Encyclopædia Britannica (accessed December 1, 2010).
  84. *Ibid.*
  85. Bruce-Mitford, M. *The Illustrated Book of Signs & Symbols* (Westmount, Quebec: Reader's Digest Association [Canada] Ltd., 1996), p. 75.
  86. *Ibid.*, p. 110.
  87. Guiley, R. E. The Encyclopedia of Magic and Alchemy, p. 130.
  88. Shah, S. I. A. *Occultism Its Theory and Practice* (New York: Dorset Press, 1993), p. 138.
  89. Bancroft, A. *Religions of the East*, p. 223.
  90. Müller-Ebeling, Rätsch, and Shahi. *Shamanism and Tantra*, pp. 227–228.
  91. Mullin, G. H., and A. Weber. *The Mystical Arts of Tibet* (Atlanta, GA: Longstreet Press, 1996), p. 72.
  92. Baumer, C. *Bön: Tibet's Ancient Religion*, translated by Michael Kohn (Trumbull, CDT: Weatherhill, 2002), pp. 166–168.
  93. "arts, Central Asia," Encyclopædia Britannica, from *Encyclopædia Britannica Deluxe Edition 2005 CD*. Encyclopædia Britannica (accessed December 7, 2010).
  94. "rosary" Encyclopædia Britannica, from *Encyclopædia Britannica Deluxe Edition 2005 CD*. Encyclopædia Britannica (accessed November 21, 2010).
  95. Radha, S. S. *Mantras: Words of Power*, p. 34.
  96. Levenson, C. Symbols of Tibetan Buddhism (New York: Barnes and Noble Books, 2002), p. 36.
  97. *Ibid.*
  98. Müller-Ebeling, C., C. Rätsch, and S. B. Shahi. *Shamanism and Tantra in the Himalayas*, p. 224.
  99. *Ibid.*
  100. de Nebesky-Wojkowitz, Réne. *Oracles and Demons of Tibet* (Varamasi, India: Book Faith India an imprint of Pilgrims Book House, 1993), p. 456.
  101. Flesher, P. Buddhist Glossary, Religious Studies Program. University of Wyoming, http://uwacadwib.uwyo/religionet/er/default.htm (accessed November 23, 2010).
  102. Kohn, L. Early *Chinese Mysticism: Philosophy and Soteriology in the Taoist Tradition* (Princeton, NJ: Princeton University Press, 1992), p. 8.
  103. Johnson, O.S. *A Study of Chinese Alchemy*, reprint edition (New York: ARNO Press, 1974 [1928]), p. v.
  104. "yin-yang," Encyclopædia Britannica, from *Encyclopædia Britannica Deluxe Edition 2005 CD*. Encyclopædia Britannica (accessed November 19, 2009).
  105. *Ibid.*
  106. Bancroft, A. *Religions of the East*, p. 200.
  107. *Ibid.*, p. 198.
  108. Blofeld, J. *Taoism: The Road to Immortality* (Boston: Shambhala, 1985), p. 7.
  109. *Ibid.*
  110. *Ibid.*
  111. Bayley, H. *The Lost Language of Symbolism*, vol. II (London: Bracken Books, 1996 [1912]), p. 267.
  112. *Ibid.*
  113. *Ibid.*, p. 270.
  114. Campbell, J. *The Mystic Image* (Bollingen Series C, Princeton, NJ: Princeton University Press, 1974), p. 193.
  115. *Ibid.*
  116. *Ibid.*, p. 192.
  117. Scholem, G. G. *Major Trends in Jewish Mysticism* (New York: Schocken Books, 1972 [1941]), p. 214.
  118. Müller-Ebeling, C., C. Rätsch, and S. B. Shahi. *Shamanism and Tantra in the Himalayas*, p. 110.
  119. *Ibid.*
  120. *Ibid.*, p. 73.
  121. Huxley F. *The Way of the Sacred*, p. 140.
  122. *Ibid.*
  123. Johnson, O. S. *A Study of Chinese Alchemy*, p. 11.
  124. *Ibid.*
  125. Guiley, R. E. The Encyclopedia of Magic and Alchemy, p. 81.
  126. *Ibid.*
  127. Snellgrove, D. L., gen. ed. *The Image of the Buddha* (San Francisco and Paris: Kodansha International and UNESCO, 1978), p. 429.
  128. Müller-Ebeling, C., C. Rätsch, and S. B. Shahi. *Shamanism and Tantra in the Himalayas*, p. 10.
  129. *Ibid.*
  130. *Ibid.*, p. 218.
  131. Fisher, R. E. *Art of Tibet* (London: Thames and Hudson, 1997), pp. 91–92.
  132. Snellgrove, D. L. *The Image of the Buddha*, p. 455.
  133. Müller-Ebeling, C., C. Rätsch, and S. B. Shahi. *Shamanism*

and Tantra in the Himalayas, p. 220.
   134. Harvey, G., ed. *Readings in Indigenous Religions* (London and New York: Continuum, 2002), p. 152.
   135. Lee, S. E. *A History of Far Eastern Art* (Englewood Cliffs, NJ: Prentice-Hall, and New York: Harry N. Abrams, 1973), p. 76.
   136. *Ibid.*
   137. Fortune, D. *The Mystical Qabalah* (York Beach, ME: Samuel Weiser, 1997 [1935]), p. 5.
   138. Partridge C. *Introduction to World Religions*, p. 21.
   139. Wilson, F. A. *Art as Revelation* (Fontwell (Sussex: Centaur Press Ltd., 1961), p. 4.
   140. Jung, C. G., ed. *Man and His Symbols*, p. 23.
   141. "The sacred," Encyclopædia Britannica, from *Encyclopædia Britannica Deluxe Edition 2005 CD*. Encyclopædia Britannica (accessed November 15, 2010).
   142. Eliade, M. *Symbolism, the Sacred, and the Arts*, p.13.

Chapter Six

   1. Levenson, C. *Symbols of Tibetan Buddhism* (New York: Barnes & Noble Books, 2000), p. 20.
   2. Feuerstein, G. *The Yoga Tradition: It History, Literature, Philosophy and Practice* (Prescott, AZ: Hohm Press, 1998), p. 123.
   3. Brinton, H. H. *The Mystic Will: Based on a Study of the Philosophy of Jacob Boehme* (New York: Macmillan, 1930), p. 17.
   4. *Effortless Being: The Yoga Sutras of Patanjali*, translated by Alistair Shearer (London, Boston, and Wellington: Mandala, Unwin Paperbacks, 1982), p. 9.
   5. *Ibid.*, p. 16.
   6. Frawley, D. *Yoga & Ayurveda: Self-Healing and Self-Realization* (Twin Lakes, WI: Lotus Press, 1999), p. 87.
   7. Evans-Wentz, W. Y., ed. *Tibetan Yoga and Secret Doctrines or Seven Books of Wisdom of the Great Path, According to the Late Lama Kazi Dawa-Samdup's English Rendering*, 2d. Translated by Chen-Chi Chang (London, Oxford, and New York: Oxford University Press, 1967 [1958]), p. 25.
   8. Desikachar, T. K. V. *The Heart of Yoga: Developing A Personal Practice* (Rochester, VT: Inner Traditions International, 1995), p. xxvi.
   9. *Ibid.*, p. 13.
   10. Prabhupada, A. C. B. S. *Bhagavad-gītā as It Is* (New York, London, Bombay: The Bhaktivedanta Book Trust, 1972), p. 145.
   11. *Ibid.*, p. 106.
   12. *Ibid.*, p. 107.
   13. *Ibid.*
   14. *Ibid.*, p. 36.
   15. Muni, S. R. *Yoga: The Ultimate Spiritual Path* (St. Paul, MN: Llewellyn, 2001), p. 19.
   16. *Ibid.*, p. 20.
   17. Newell, Z. *Downward Dogs & Warriors: Wisdom Tales for Modern Yogis* (Honesdale, PA: Himalayan Institute Press, 2007), p. 10.
   18. Feuerstein, G., ed. Teaching of Yoga, p. xix.
   19. Worthington, V. *A History of Yoga* (London and New York: ARKANA, 1982), p. 1.
   20. *Ibid.*
   21. Feuerstein, G. *The Yoga Tradition*, p. 319.
   22. Campbell, J. *Myths of Light: Eastern Metaphors of the Eternal*, D. Kudler, ed. (Joseph Campbell Foundation, Novato, CA: New World Library, 2003), p. 25.
   23. Iyengar, B. K. S. *Yoga: The Path to Holistic Health* (London, New York, and Delhi: Dorling Kindersley Publishing, 2001), p. 46.
   24. Varenne, J. *Yoga and the Hindu Tradition*, translated by Derek Coltman (Chicago and London: University of Chicago Press, 1976), p. 78.
   25. *Ibid.*
   26. *Ibid.*
   27. *Ibid.*
   28. *Ibid.*, p. 79.
   29. *Ibid.*
   30. Muni, S. R. *Yoga: The Ultimate Spiritual Path*, p. 1.
   31. Underhill, E. *The Way of the Spirit*, edited by Grace A. Brame (New York: Crossroad Publishing Company, 1990), p. 126.
   32. *Ibid.*
   33. Stone, M., ed. *Freeing the Body Freeing the Mind: Writings on the Connections Between Yoga & Buddhism* (Boston and London: Shambhala, 2010), p. 4.
   34. Feuerstein, G., ed. *Teachings of Yoga*, p. xv.
   35. Ravindra, R. *Yoga and the Teaching of Krishna: Essays on the Indian Spiritual Traditions*, edited by Priscilla Murray (Adyar, India and Wheaton, IL: The Theosophical Publishing House, 1998), p. 66.
   36. Varenne, J. *Yoga and the Hindu Tradition*, p. 195.
   37. "Patanjali," Encyclopædia Britannica, from *Encyclopædia Britannica Deluxe Edition 2005 CD*. Encyclopædia Britannica, May 30, 2004 (accessed December 20, 2010).
   38. Boccio, F. J. "Mindfulness Yoga" in M. Stone ed. *Freeing the Body, Freeing the Mind: Writings on the Connection Between Yoga & Buddhism*, pp. 144–164 (Boston and London: Shambhala, 2010), p. 150.
   39. Stone, M., ed. *Freeing the Body, Freeing the Mind: Writings on the Connection Between Yoga & Buddhism*, p. xiii.
   40. Boccio, F. J. "Mindfulness Yoga," p. 150.
   41. Newell, Z. *Downward Dogs & Warriors: Wisdom Tales for Modern Yogis* (Honesdale, PA: Himalayan Institute Press, 2007), pp. ix–x.
   42. Taimni, I. K. *The Science of Yoga: The Yoga-sutra of Patanjali in Sanskrit with translation in Roman, Translation in English and Commentary* (Wheaton, IL, Madras and London: The Theosophical Publishing House, 1967), p. 17.
   43. Feuerstein, G. *The Shambhala Guide to Yoga* (Boston and London: Shambhala, 1996), p. 51.
   44. *Ibid.*
   45. *Ibid.*, p. 49.
   46. Lu, K. Y. *Taoist Yoga: Alchemy and Immortality* (New York: Samuel Wiser, 1972), p. 28.
   47. *Ibid.*, p. 29.
   48. *Ibid.*
   49. Stone, M., ed. *Freeing the Body Freeing the Mind: Writings on the Connections between Yoga & Buddhism*, p. 8.
   50. Ravindra, R. *Yoga and the Teaching of Krishna*, p. 61.
   51. *Ibid.*
   52. Iyengar, B. K. S. *The Tree of Yoga* (Boston: Shambhala, 2002), p. 127.
   53. *Ibid.*
   54. Constable, G., ed. *Eastern Mysteries* (Alexandria, VA: Time-Life Books, 1991), p. 40.
   55. Varenne, J. *Yoga and the Hindu Tradition*, p. 11.
   56. Lindemans, M. F. "Yogini" in Encyclopedia Mythica. http://www.pantheon.org/articles/y/yogini.html (accessed February 9, 2011).
   57. Iqbal, M. *The Development of Metaphysics in Persia: A Contribution to the History of Muslim Philosophy* (Lahor: Bazm-Iqbal, 1964), p. 86.
   58. *Ibid.*
   59. Stephens, M. *Teaching Yoga: Essential Foundations and Techniques* (Berkeley, CA: North Atlantic Books, 2010), p. 55.
   60. Iyengar, B. K. S. *Yoga: The Path to Holistic Health*, p. 57.
   61. Breaux, C. *Journey into Consciousness: The Chakras, Tantra, and*

Jungian Psychology (York Beach, ME: Nicolas-Hays, 1989), p. xi.

62. Evens-Wentz, W. Y., ed. *The Tibetan Book of the Dead or the After-Death Experiences on the Bardo Plane, According to Lama Kazi Dawa-Samdupu's English Rendering* (London, Oxford, and New York: Oxford University Press, 1960 [1927]), p. 216.

63. Woodroffe, J. *The Serpent Power* (Madras: Ganesh, 1973), p. 109.

64. *Ibid.*, p. 19.

65. *Ibid.*

66. Iyengar, B. K. S. *Yoga: The Path to Holistic Health*, p. 37.

67. "mind, philosophy of," Encyclopædia Britannica, from *Encyclopædia Britannica* Deluxe Edition 2005 CD. Encyclopædia Britannica, May 30, 2004 (accessed January 07, 2011).

68. Blofeld, J. *Taoism: The Road to Immortality* (Boston: Shambhala, 1985), p. 9.

69. *Ibid.*, pp. 148–149.

70. Lu, K'uan Yü. *Taoist Yoga: Alchemy and Immortality*, p. 27.

71. Campbell, J. *Myths of Light: Eastern Metaphors of the Eternal*, D. Kudler, ed. (Joseph Campbell Foundation, Novato, CA: New World Library, 2003), p. 25.

72. Feuerstein, G. *The Shambhala Guide to Yoga*, p. 45.

73. Woodroffe, J. *The Serpent Power*, pp. 22–23.

74. Iyengar, B. K. S. *The Tree of Yoga*, p. 127.

75. *Ibid.*

76. *Ibid.*, p. 90.

77. "thought," Encyclopædia Britannica, from Encyclopædia Britannica Deluxe Edition 2005 CD. Encyclopædia Britannica, May 30, 2004 (accessed January 24, 2011).

78. Breaux, C. *Journey into Consciousness: The Chakras, Tantra, and Jungian Psychology*, p. 175.

79. *Ibid.*

80. Radha, S. S. *Kundalini Yoga for the West* (Seattle, WA: Timeless Books), 1978), p. 46.

81. Tucci, G. *The Religions of Tibet*, translated by Geoffrey Samuel (Berkeley and Los Angeles: University of California Press, 1988), p. 71.

82. Blofeld, J. *Taoism: The Road to Immortality*, p. 9.

83. Iyengar, B. K. S. *Yoga: The Path to Holistic Health*, p. 37.

84. Muni, S. R. *Yoga: The Ultimate Spiritual Path*, p. 2.

85. *Ibid.*

86. Newell, Z. *Downward Dogs & Warriors: Wisdom Tales for Modern Yogis*, p. 11.

87. Singleton, M. *Yoga Body: The Origins of Modern Posture Practice* (Oxford: Oxford University Press, 2010), p. 28.

88. Vishnu-Devananda, S. *Hatha Yoga Pradipika: The Classic guide for the Advanced Practice of Hatha Yoga (Kundalini Yoga)*, Reprinted from the 1893 edition containing the Commentary Jyotsna of Brahmananda (New York: Om Lotus Publishing Company, 1987), p. 7.

89. Feuerstein, G. *The Yoga Tradition: Its History, Literature*, Philosophy and Practice, p. 39.

90. Varenne, J. *Yoga and the Hindu Tradition*, p. vii.

91. Radha, S. S. *Kundalini Yoga for the West*, p. 17.

92. *Ibid.*

93. *Ibid.*

94. Vishnu-Devananda, S. *Hatha Yoga Pradipika: The Classic guide for the Advanced Practice of Hatha Yoga (Kundalini Yoga)*, p. 10.

95. "pranayama" Encyclopædia Britannica, from Encyclopædia Britannica Deluxe Edition 2005 CD. Encyclopædia Britannica, May 30, 2004 (accessed January 28, 2011).

96. Scholem, G. G. *Major Trends in Jewish Mysticism*, 6d (New York: Schocken Books, 1972 [1941]), p. 139.

97. Vishnu-Devananda, S. *Hatha Yoga Pradipika: The Classic guide for the Advanced Practice of Hatha Yoga (Kundalini Yoga*, p. 37.

98. Ravindra, R. *Yoga and the Teaching of Krishna: Essays on the Indian Spiritual Traditions*, p. 285.

99. Feuerstein, G. *The Shambhala Guide to Yoga*, p. 51.

100. Gordon, S. *The Paranormal: An Illustrated Encyclopedia* (London: Headline Book Publishing PLC, 1992), p. 306.

101. Bancroft, A. *Religions of the East*, p. 41.

102. Jones, L., ed. in chief. *Encyclopedia of Religion*. 2d, Vol. 14; Masaaki, Hattori ed.(1987 & 2005) "Yog c ra" (USA: Macmillan Reference), p. 9897.

103. "Yogâcâra," Encyclopædia Britannica, from *Encyclopædia Britannica* Deluxe Edition 2005 CD. Encyclopædia Britannica, May 30, 2004 (accessed January 02, 2011).

104. Waddell, L. A. *Tibetan Buddhism with its Mystic Cults, Symbolism and Mythology* (New York: Dover, 1972 [1895]), p. 129.

105. Rambach, P. The Secret Message of Tantric Buddhism (New York: Rizzoli International, 1979), p. 69.

106. Radha, S. S. *Kundalini: Yoga for the West*, p. 26.

107. Stone, M., ed. *Freeing the Body, Freeing the Mind*, p. 212.

108. "Hinduism," Encyclopædia Britannica, from *Encyclopædia Britannica* Deluxe Edition 2005 CD. Encyclopædia Britannica, May 30, 2004 (accessed January 07, 2011).

109. Bancroft, A. *Religions of the East*, p. 39.

110. *Ibid.*

111. Feuerstein, G. *Tantra: The Path of Ecstasy* (Boston & London: Shambhala, 1998), p. 18.

112. *Ibid.*

113. *Ibid.*

114. *Ibid.*

115. Worthington, V. *A History of Yoga*, p. 113.

116. Woodroffe, J. *The Serpent Power*, p. 24.

117. Tucci, G. *The Religions of Tibet*, p. 85.

118. Eliade, M. *Yoga Immortality and Freedom*, p. 274.

119. Radha, S. S. *Kundalini Yoga for the West*, p. 18.

120. Eliade, M. *Yoga Immortality and Freedom*, p. 274.

121. *Ibid.*, p. 272–273.

122. Worthington, V. *A History of Yoga*, p. 41.

123. Iyengar, B.K.S. *The Tree of Yoga*, p. 121.

124. Woodroffe, J. *The Serpent Power*, pp. 55–56.

125. Iyengar, B.K.S. *Yoga: The Path to Holistic Health*, p. 46.

126. *Ibid.*

127. Eliade, M. *Yoga: Immortality and Freedom*, p. 339.

128. *Ibid.*

129. Baker, I. A. *The Tibetan Art of Healing* (San Francisco: Chronicle Books, 1997), p. 119.

130. Tulku, T. *Tibetan Relaxation: The Illustrated Guide to Kum Nye Massage and Movement—A Yoga from the Tibetan Tradition* (London: Duncan Baird, 2007), p. 8.

131. *Ibid.*

132. *Ibid.*

133. *Ibid.*

134. Chopra, D. "Preface: The Art of Healing," pp. 8–11, in Ian A. Baker, *The Tibetan Art of Healing* (San Francisco: Chronicle Books, 1997), p. 8.

135. *Ibid.*, p. 11.

136. Govinda, Lama Anagarika. *The Way of the White Clouds* (L.ondon: Rider, 1974 [1966]), p. 94.

137. Chopra, D. "Preface: The Art of Healing," p. 11.

138. Tulku, T. *Tibetan Relaxation: The Illustrated Guide to Kum Nye Massage and Movement—A Yoga from the Tibetan Tradition*, p. 15.

139. Baker, I. A. *The Tibetan Art of Healing*, p. 18.

140. *Ibid.*, p. 25.
141. *Ibid.*
142. *Ibid.*, p. 46.
143. *Ibid.*, p. 163.
144. Blofeld, J. *Taoism: The Road to Immortality*, p. 132.
145. Blofeld, J. *The Tantric Mysticism of Tibet: A Practical Guide to the Theory, Purpose, and Techniques of Tantric Meditation* (New York: Causeway Books, 1974), p. 229.
146. Thich, N. H. *The Heart of Buddha's Teaching* (New York: Broadway Books, 1999), p. 209.
147. *Effortless Being: The Yoga Sutras of Patanjali*, p. 21.
148. Woodroffe, J. *The Serpent Power*, p. 23.
149. *Ibid.*, p. 25.
150. Ravindra, R. *Yoga and the Teaching of Krishna: Essays on the Indian Spiritual Traditions*, p. 110.
151. *Ibid.*, p. 109.
152. Vishnu-Devananda, S. *Hatha Yoga Pradipika: The Classic guide for the Advanced Practice of Hatha Yoga (Kundalini Yoga)*, p. 83.
153. Fisher, R. E. *Art of Tibet* (London: Thames and Hudson, 1997), p. 90.
154. Chang, C-Y. *Original Teachings of Ch'an Buddhism: Selected from The Transmission of the Lamp* (New York: Pantheon Books, a Division of Random House, 1969), p.23.
155. Varenne, J. *Yoga and the Hindu Tradition*, 83.
156. "pranayama" Encyclopædia Britannica, from *Encyclopædia Britannica* Deluxe Edition 2005 CD. Encyclopædia Britannica, May 30, 2004 (accessed January 29, 2011).
157. *Effortless Being: The Yoga Sutras of Patanjali*, p. 9.
158. Feuerstein, G. *The Yoga-Sutra of Patanjali: A New Translation and Commentary*, p. 96.
159. Taimni, I. K. *The Science of Yoga: The Yoga-sutra of Patanjali in Sanskrit with translation in Roman, Translation in English and Commentary*, p. 275.
160. *Ibid.*, pp. 85–86.
161. *Ibid.*, p. 275.
162. *Ibid.*
163. Feuerstein, G. *The Yoga Tradition: It History, Literature, Philosophy and Practice*, p. 127.
164. *Ibid.*
165. Varenne, J. *Yoga and the Hindu Tradition*, p. 181.
166. *Ibid.*
167. Desikachar, T. K. V. *The Heart of Yoga: Developing A Personal Practice*, p. 161.

Chapter Seven

1. Baxter, A. "Alchemy," in: *Survey of the Occult*, ed. Julian Franklyn. pp. 2–34 (London: Arthur Barker Limited, 1935), p. 29.
2. Blofeld, J. *The Tantric Mysticism of Tibet: A practical Guide to the Theory, Purpose, and Techniques of Tantric Meditation* (New York: Causeway Books, 1974), p. 56.
3. Constable, G., ed. *Secrets of the Alchemists* (Alexandria, VA: Time-Life Books, 1990), p. 16.
4. *Ibid.*
5. Ransay, J. *Alchemy: The Art of Transformation* (London: Thorsons, 1997), p. 18.
6. Roberts, G. *The Mirror of Alchemy* (Toronto and Buffalo: University of Toronto Press, 1994), p. 13.
7. Stavish, M. *The Path of Alchemy: Energetic Healing and the World of Natural Magic* (Woodbury, MN: Llewellyn, 2006), p. 4.
8. Eliade, M. *Yoga: Immortality and Freedom*, translated by Willard R. Trask (Bollingen Series LVI, Princeton, NJ and Oxford: Princeton University Press, 2009 [1958]).
9. Constable, G., ed. *Secrets of the Alchemists*, p. 19.
10. Eliade, M. *The Forge and the Crucible*, 2d, translated by Stephen Corrin (Chicago and London: University of Chicago Press, 1978b [1956]) p. 192.
11. Baxter, A. "Alchemy," in: *Survey of the Occult*, p. 3.
12. *American Journal of Chinese Medicine.* "Alchemy, Chinese versus Greek, an etymological approach: a rejoinder," 1988;16 (1–2):83–6. http://www.ncbi.nlm.nih.gov/pubmed/3064584?dopt=Abstract (accessed December 26, 2010).
13. *Ibid.*
14. *Ibid.*
15. *Ibid.*
16. Origin of the Name "Chemistry" http://hilltop.bradley.edu/~rbg/Origin.html (accessed December26, 2010.
17. Holmyard, E. J. *Alchemy* (New York: Dover, 1990 [1957]), p. 25.
18. Stavish, M. *The Path of Alchemy: Energetic Healing and the World of Natural Magic*, p. 2.
19. *Ibid.*
20. *Ibid.*
21. Hutin, S. *A History of Alchemy* (New York: Walker, 1963), p. 12
22. *Ibid.*
23. *Ibid.*
24. Holmyard, E. J. *Alchemy*, p. 15.
25. *Ibid.*, p. 15–16.
26. *Ibid.*, p. 16.
27. Hutin, S. *A History of Alchemy*, p.123.
28. *Ibid.*, p.15.
29. Stillman, J. M. *The Story of Alchemy and Early Chemistry* (New York: Dover 1960 [1924]), p. 1.
30. *Ibid.*
31. Atwood, M. A. *Hermetic Philosophy and Alchemy* (New York: The Julian Press, 1960 [1850]), p. 144.
32. *Ibid.*
33. Hutin, S. *A History of Alchemy*, p. 11.
34. Atwood, M. A. *Hermetic Philosophy and Alchemy*, p. 72.
35. Cockren, A. *History of Alchemy.* http://www.alchemylab.com/history_of_alchemy.htm (accessed January 7, 2009).
36. Stavish, M. *The Path of Alchemy*, p. 4.
37. Pinch, G. *Magic in Ancient Egypt* (Austin: University of Texas Press, 1994), p. 47.
38. *Ibid.*, p. 80.
39. *Ibid.*
40. Budge, W. *Egyptian Religion* (New York: Dover, 1971.), pp. 103–104.
41. *Ibid.*
42. "earth" Encyclopædia Britannica, from *Encyclopædia Britannica Deluxe Edition 2005 CD*. Encyclopædia Britannica (accessed March 24, 2011).
43. "ba" Encyclopædia Britannica, from *Encyclopædia Britannica Deluxe Edition 2005 CD*. Encyclopædia Britannica (accessed March 24, 2011).
44. "death" Encyclopædia Britannica, from *Encyclopædia Britannica Deluxe Edition 2005 CD*. Encyclopædia Britannica (accessed March 24, 2011).
45. *Ibid.*
46. Oaks, L., and L. Gahlin. *Ancient Egypt* (New York: Barnes & Noble, 2006), p. 397.
47. *Ibid.*, p. 303.
48. Holmyard, E. J. *Alchemy*, p. 25.
49. "Hellenistic alchemy" Encyclopædia Britannica, from *Encyclopædia Britannica Deluxe Edition 2005 CD*. Encyclopædia Britannica (accessed January 7, 2009).
50. Pinch, G. *Magic in Ancient Egypt*, p. 169.
51. *Ibid.*
52. *Ibid.*
53. Constable, G., ed. *Secrets of the Alchemists*, p. 19.
54. Stavish, M. *The Path of Alchemy*, p. 4.
55. Constable, G., ed. *Secrets of the Alchemists*, p. 19.
56. *Ibid.*

57. Pinch, G. *Magic in Ancient Egypt*, p. 167.
58. Holmyard, E. J. *Alchemy*, p. 97; See also: Constable, G. ed. *Secrets of the Alchemists*, p. 20; and "alchemy" Encyclopædia Britannica, from *Encyclopædia Britannica Deluxe Edition 2005 CD*. Encyclopædia Britannica.
59. Holmyard, E. J. *Alchemy*, p. 99.
60. *Ibid*, p. 98.
61. Fromm, J. R. "Alchemy." http:/www.3rd1000.com/history/alchemy.htm (accessed April 9, 2008).
62. Roberts, G. *The Mirror of Alchemy*, p. 32.
63. Stavish, M. *The Path of Alchemy*, p. 5.
64. Silberer, H., and S. E. Jelliffe. *Problems of Mysticism and its Symbolism* (Whitefish, MT: Kessinger Publishing, 2009 [1917]), p. 112.
65. *Ibid*.
66. Constable, G., ed. *Secrets of the Alchemists*, p.17.
67. *Ibid*.
68. Martin, S. *Alchemy and Alchemists* (Harpenden, Herts, UK: Pocket Essentials, 2006), p. 46.
69. *Ibid*.
70. Roberts, G. *The Mirror of Alchemy*, p. 23.
71. Ramsay, J. *Alchemy: The Art of Transformation*, p.18; see also, Roberts, G. *The Mirror of Alchemy*, p. 45.
72. Constable, G., ed. *Secrets of the Alchemists*, p. 23.
73. Hastings, J. *Encyclopædia of Religion and Ethics*, Vol. 1 (Edinburgh: T. & T. Clark, 1980), p. 288.
74. Oaks, L., and L. Gahlin. *Ancient Egypt*, p. 442.
75. *Ibid*.
76. Pinch, G. *Magic in Ancient Egypt*, p. 169.
77. "Iamblichus" Encyclopædia Britannica, from *Encyclopædia Britannica Deluxe Edition 2005 CD*. Encyclopædia Britannica (accessed March 24, 2011).
78. Gareth, R. *The Mirror of Alchemy*, p. 19.
79. Oliver, M. *History of Philosophy: Great Thinkers from 600 B.C. to the Present Day* (London: Prospero Books, 1999), p. 12.
80. *Ibid*.
81. Bennett, C. A. *A Philosophical Study of Mysticism* (New Haven: Yale University Press, 1923), p. 110.
82. *Ibid*.
83. Fabricius, J. *Alchemy: The Medieval Alchemists and Their Royal Art* (Copenhagen: Rosenkilde and Bagger, 1976), p. 6.

84. Gareth, R. *The Mirror of Alchemy*, pp. 19–21.
85. *Ibid*., p. 26.
86. Oliver, M. *History of Philosophy: Great Thinkers from 600 B.C. to the Present Day*, p. 12.
87. "mystery religion" Encyclopædia Britannica, from *Encyclopædia Britannica Deluxe Edition 2005 CD*. Encyclopædia Britannica, May 30, 2004 (accessed March 31, 2011).
88. "Mitra" Encyclopædia Britannica, from *Encyclopædia Britannica Deluxe Edition 2005 CD*. Encyclopædia Britannica, May 30, 2004 (accessed March 30, 2011).
89. *Ibid*.
90. "Mithraism" Encyclopædia Britannica, from *Encyclopædia Britannica Deluxe Edition 2005 CD*. Encyclopædia Britannica, May 30, 2004 (accessed March 30, 2011).
91. Gareth, R. *The Mirror of Alchemy*, p. 45.
92. "Empedocles" Encyclopædia Britannica, from *Encyclopædia Britannica Deluxe Edition 2005 CD*. Encyclopædia Britannica, May 30, 2004 (accessed March 31, 2011).
93. "Heracleitus" Encyclopædia Britannica, from *Encyclopædia Britannica Deluxe Edition 2005 CD*. Encyclopædia Britannica, May 30, 2004 (accessed March 31, 2011).
94. *Ibid*.
95. "philosophy, history of" Encyclopædia Britannica, from *Encyclopædia Britannica Deluxe Edition 2005 CD*. Encyclopædia Britannica, May 30, 2004 (accessed March 30, 2011).
96. Oliver, M. *History of Philosophy: Great Thinkers from 600 B.C. to the Present Day*, p. 20.
97. "Aristotle" Encyclopædia Britannica, from *Encyclopædia Britannica Deluxe Edition 2005 CD*. Encyclopædia Britannica, May 30, 2004 (accessed March 30, 2011).
98. Gareth, R. *The Mirror of Alchemy*, p. 45.
99. *Ibid*.
100. Stillman, J. M. *The Story of Alchemy and Early Chemistry*, p. 5.
101. Gareth, R. *The Mirror of Alchemy*, p. 45.
102. *Ibid*.
103. Holmyard, E.J. *Alchemy*, p. 22.
104. Gareth, R. *The Mirror of Alchemy*, pp. 47–48.
105. Aristotle. *Metaphysics*, translated with Commentaries and Glossary by Hippocrates G. Apostle (Bloomington: Indiana University Press, 1966), p.143:1045a.
106. Silberer, H., and S. E. Jelliffe.

Problems of Mysticism and its Symbolism, p. 112.
107. Martin S. *Alchemy and Alchemists*, p. 80.
108. Eliade, M. *Yoga: Immortality and Freedom*, p. 236.
109. Wong, E. *Taoism* (Boston and London: Shambhala, 1997), p. 4.
110. Johnson, O. S. *A Study of Chinese Alchemy* (Shanghai: The Commercial Press, Limited, 1928 reprinted from a copy in the Columbia University Library, New York: Arno Press, 1974), p. 43.
111. "alchemy" Encyclopædia Britannica, from *Encyclopædia Britannica Deluxe Edition 2005 CD*. Encyclopædia Britannica (accessed March 7, 2011).
112. Johnson, O. S. *A Study of Chinese Alchemy*, p. 43.
113. *Ibid*.
114. Wong, E. *Taoism*, p. 32.
115. *Ibid*., p. 66.
116. Blofeld, J. *Taoism: The Road to Immortality*, p. 133.
117. Johnson, O. S. *A Study of Chinese Alchemy*, p. 22.
118. "alchemy" Encyclopædia Britannica, from *Encyclopædia Britannica Deluxe Edition 2005 CD*. Encyclopædia Britannica (accessed January 7, 2009).
119. "Chinese alchemy" Encyclopædia Britannica, from *Encyclopædia Britannica Deluxe Edition 2005 CD*. Encyclopædia Britannica (accessed January 7, 2009).
120. *Ibid*.
121. Wong, E. *Taoism*, p. 68.
122. Blofeld, J. *Taoism: The Road to Immortality*, p. 116.
123. *Ibid*.
124. *Ibid*.
125. *Ibid*.
126. Eliade, M. *Yoga: Immortality and Freedom*, p. 287.
127. Martin S. *Alchemy and Alchemists*, p. 85.
128. Eliade, M. *Yoga: Immortality and Freedom*, p. 285.
129. *Ibid*.
130. Cooper, J. C. *Taoism: The Way of the Mystic* (New York: Samuel Weisner, 1972), p. 81.
131. *Ibid*, p. 85.
132. *Ibid*.
133. Pregadio, F. *Great Clarity: Daoism and Alchemy in Early Medieval China* (Stanford, CA: Stanford University Press, 2006), p.32.
134. Wilhelm, R., translated and explained. *The Secret of the Golden Flower: A Chinese Book of Life*, translated to English by Cary Baynes (London: Routledge & Kegan Paul Ltd., 1931), p. 7.

135. Blofeld, J. *Taoism: The Road to Immortality*, p. 130.
136. *Ibid.*
137. *Ibid.*
138. Martin S. *Alchemy and Alchemists*, p. 81.
139. Lu, K. Y. *Taoist Yoga: Alchemy and Immortality* (New York: Samuel Weiser, 1973), p. xii.
140. *Ibid.*
141. Johnson, O. S. *A Study of Chinese Alchemy*, p. 40.
142. *Ibid.*, pp. 40–41.
143. *Ibid.*, p. 41.
144. Wong, E. *Taoism*, p. 67.
145. Wong, E. *The Shambhala Guide to Taoism* (Boston and London: Shambhala, 1997), p. 79.
146. "T'ai Chi" Encyclopædia Britannica, from *Encyclopædia Britannica Deluxe Edition 2005 CD*. Encyclopædia Britannica, May 30, 2004 (accessed December 31, 2010).
147. Wong, E. *Taoism*, p. 69.
148. Johnson, O. S. *A Study of Chinese Alchemy*, p. 15.
149. Baker, I. A. *The Tibetan Art of Healing* (San Francisco: Chronicle Books, 1997), p. 118–119.
150. Johnson, O. S. *A Study of Chinese Alchemy*, p. 59.
151. Wong, E. *Taoism*, p. 67.
152. Lu, K. Y. *Taoist Yoga: Alchemy and Immortality*, p. 30.
153. Kohn, L. *Taoist Mystical Philosophy: The Scripture of Western Ascension* (Albany, NY: State University of New York Press, 1991), p. 4.
154. *Ibid.*
155. Wilhelm, R., translated and explained. *The Secret of the Golden Flower: A Chinese Book of Life*, translated to English by Cary Baynes (London: Routledge & Kegan Paul Ltd., 1931), p. 11.
156. *Ibid.*
157. Blofeld, J. *My Journey in Mystic China: Old Pu's Travel Diary*, translated by Daniel Reid (Rochester, VT: Inner Traditions, 2008 [1990]), p. 201.
158. Johnson, O. S. *A Study of Chinese Alchemy*, p. 49.
159. *Ibid.*
160. Wong, E. *The Shambhala Guide to Taoism*, p. 79.
161. *Ibid.*
162. Lu, K. Y. *Taoist Yoga: Alchemy and Immortality* (New York: Samuel Weiser, 1973), p. 158.
163. *Ibid.*
164. *Ibid.*
165. *Ibid.*, p. 27.
166. *Ibid.*, p. 30.
167. *Ibid.*
168. *Ibid.*
169. Blofeld, J. *Taoism: The Road to Immortality*, p. 117.
170. Wong, E. *Taoism*, p. 71.
171. Johnson, O. S. *A Study of Chinese Alchemy*, p. 15.
172. Pregadio, F. *Encyclopedia of the History of Science, Technology and Medicine in Non-Western Countries*, 2d, ed. Helaine Selin (Berlin and New York: Springer, c2008). http://www.goldenelixir.com/jindan/jindan_intro.html
173. Bancroft, A. *Religions of the East* (London: William Heinemann Ltd., 1974), p. 203.
174. Wilhelm, R. *The Secret of the Golden Flower: A Chinese Book of Life*, p. 6.
175. Wong, E. *Taoism*, p. 73.
176. Koller, J. M. *Oriental Philosophies*, 2d. (New York: Charles Scribner's Sons, 1985), p. 245.
177. *Ibid.*
178. *Ibid.*, pp. 245–246.
179. Johnson, O. S. *A Study of Chinese Alchemy*, p. 39.
180. "alchemy" Encyclopædia Britannica, from *Encyclopædia Britannica Deluxe Edition 2005 CD*. Encyclopædia Britannica, May 30, 2004 (accessed April 05, 2011).
181. Eliade, M. *The Forge and the Crucible*, p. 129.
182. White, D. G. "*Rasayana* (Alchemy)" *Oxford Bibliographies Online* Oxford: Oxford University Press http://www.oxfordbibliographies.com/display/id/obo-9780195399318-0046 (accessed April 6, 2011).
183. *Ibid.*
184. Eliade, M. *The Forge and the Crucible*, p. 128.
185. Eliade, M. *Yoga: Immortality and Freedom*, p. 278.
186. *Ibid.*
187. Eliade, M. *The Forge and the Crucible*, p. 127.
188. *Ibid.*
189. "Nâgârjuna" Encyclopædia Britannica, from *Encyclopædia Britannica Deluxe Edition 2005 CD*. Encyclopædia Britannica, May 30, 2004 (accessed March 10, 2011).
190. "Indian philosophy" Encyclopædia Britannica, from *Encyclopædia Britannica Deluxe Edition 2005 CD*. Encyclopædia Britannica, May 30, 2004 (accessed April 07, 2011).
191. Eliade, M. *Yoga: Immortality and Freedom*, p. 277.
192. "Nâgârjuna" Encyclopædia Britannica, from *Encyclopædia Britannica Deluxe Edition 2005 CD*. Encyclopædia Britannica, May 30, 2004 (accessed April 06, 2011).
193. "alchemy" Encyclopædia Britannica, from *Encyclopædia Britannica Deluxe Edition 2005 CD*. Encyclopædia Britannica, May 30, 2004 (accessed March 10, 2011).
194. Roberts, G. *The Mirror of Alchemy*, p. 59.
195. Waite, A. E. *The Hermetic Museum* (Boston, MA and York Beach, ME: Weiser Books, 1990 [1893]), p. 249.
196. Martin, S. *Alchemy and Alchemists*, p. 88.
197. *Ibid.*
198. Eliade, M. *Yoga: Immortality and Freedom*, p. 279.
199. "Artha-sâstra" Encyclopædia Britannica, from *Encyclopædia Britannica Deluxe Edition 2005 CD*. Encyclopædia Britannica, May 30, 2004 (accessed March 10, 2011).
200. "alchemy" Encyclopædia Britannica, from *Encyclopædia Britannica Deluxe Edition 2005 CD*. Encyclopædia Britannica, May 30, 2004 (accessed April 07, 2011).
201. "alchemy" Encyclopædia Britannica, from *Encyclopædia Britannica Deluxe Edition 2005 CD*. Encyclopædia Britannica, May 30, 2004 (accessed March 10, 2011).
202. Eliade, M. *Yoga: Immortality and Freedom*, p. 235.
203. *Ibid.*, p. 6.
204. *Ibid.*, p. 130.
205. Waite, A. E. *The Hermetic Museum*, p. 334.
206. Fromm, J. R. "Alchemy." www.3rd1000.com/history/alchemy.htm (accessed April 09, 2008).
207. Holmyard, E. J. *Alchemy*, pp. 63–64; also see Hastings, J. *Encyclopædia of Religion and Ethics*, Vol. 1 (Edinburgh: T. & T. Clark, 1980), p. 289.
208. Hastings, J. *Encyclopædia of Religion and Ethics*, Vol. 1 (Edinburgh: T. & T. Clark, 1980), p. 289.
209. Holmyard, E. J. *Alchemy*, p. 64.
210. Martin, S. *Alchemy and Alchemists*, p. 49.
211. *Ibid.*
212. Hastings, J. *Encyclopædia of Religion and Ethics*, Vol. 1, p. 290.
213. "Geber" Encyclopædia Britannica, from *Encyclopædia Britannica Deluxe Edition 2005 CD*. Encyclopædia Britannica, May 30, 2004 (accessed March 10, 2011).
214. "Jabir ibn Hayyan, Abu Musa" Encyclopædia Britannica, from *Encyclopædia Britannica Deluxe Edition 2005 CD*. Encyclopædia Britannica, May 30, 2004 (accessed April 02, 2011).
215. *Ibid.*
216. Holmyard, E. J. *Alchemy*, p. 75.
217. *Ibid.*
218. *Ibid.*, p. 76.
219. Hastings, J. *Encyclopædia of Religion and Ethics*, Vol. 1, p. 290.

220. Ibid., p. 291.
221. Ibid.
222. Eliade, M. *The Forge and the Crucible*, p. 51.
223. Hastings, J. *Encyclopædia of Religion and Ethics*, Vol. 1, p. 291.
224. Ibid.
225. Eliade, M. *The Forge and the Crucible*, p. 53.
226. Ibid., p. 148.
227. Hastings, J. *Encyclopædia of Religion and Ethics*, Vol. 1, p. 291.
228. Fernando, D. *Alchemy: An Illustrated A to Z* (London: Blandford, A Cassell Imprint, 1998), p. 64.
229. Waite, A. E. *The Hermetic Museum*, p. 12.
230. Ibid., p. 172.
231. "razi, ar-" Encyclopædia Britannica, from *Encyclopædia Britannica Deluxe Edition 2005 CD*. Encyclopædia Britannica, May 30, 2004 (accessed April 02, 2011).
232. Roberts, G. *The Mirror of Alchemy*, p. 27.
233. Ibid.
234. "Avicenna" Encyclopædia Britannica, from *Encyclopædia Britannica Deluxe Edition 2005 CD*. Encyclopædia Britannica, May 30, 2004 (accessed April 05, 2011).
235. Ibid.
236. "Islâm " Encyclopædia Britannica, from *Encyclopædia Britannica Deluxe Edition 2005 CD*. Encyclopædia Britannica, May 30, 2004 (accessed April 03, 2011).
237. Ibid.
238. Holmyard, E. J. *Alchemy*, p. 67.
239. Silberer, H., and S. E. Jelliffe. *Problems of Mysticism and its Symbolism*, p. 113.
240. Martin, S. *Alchemy and Alchemists*, pp. 21–22.
241. Holmyard, E. J. *Alchemy*, p.105.
242. Martin, S. Alchemy and Alchimists, p. 14.
243. Roberts, G. *The Mirror of Alchemy*, p. 29.
244. Holmyard, E. J. *Alchemy*, p.106.
245. Martin, S. *Alchemy and Alchemists*, p. 52.
246. Fernando, D. *Alchemy: An Illustrated A to Z*, p. 151.
247. Roberts, G. *The Mirror of Alchemy*, p. 31.
248. Holmyard, E. J. *Alchemy*, p. 116.
249. Fernando, D. *Alchemy: An Illustrated A to Z*, p. 20.
250. Holmyard, E. J. *Alchemy*, p. 121.
251. Roberts, G. *The Mirror of Alchemy*, p. 51.
252. Holmyard, E. J. *Alchemy*, p. 120.
253. "Aquinas, Thomas, Saint" Encyclopædia Britannica, from *Encyclopædia Britannica Deluxe Edition 2005 CD*. Encyclopædia Britannica, May 30, 2004 (accessed March 17, 2011).
254. Roberts, G. *The Mirror of Alchemy*, p. 33.
255. Holmyard, E. J. *Alchemy*, p. 117.
256. Roberts, G. *The Mirror of Alchemy*, p. 37.
257. Holmyard, E. J. *Alchemy*, p. 125.
258. Ibid.
259. Roberts, G. *The Mirror of Alchemy*, p. 62.
260. Ibid.
261. "Llull, Ramon" Encyclopædia Britannica, from *Encyclopædia Britannica Deluxe Edition 2005 CD*. Encyclopædia Britannica, May 30, 2004 (accessed March 18, 2011).
262. Fabricius, J. *Alchemy: The Medieval Alchemists and Their Royal Art*, p. 7.
263. Brinton, H. H. *The Mystic Will Based on a Study of the Philosophy of Jacob Bohme* (New York: Macmillan, 1930), p. 87.
264. Ibid.
265. Pregadio, F. *Great Clarity: Daoism and Alchemy in Early Medieval China*, p. 27.
266. Waite, A. E. *The Hermetic Museum* (Boston, pp. 141–142.
267. Eliade, M. *The Forge and the Crucible*, p. 151.
268. Waite, A. E. *The Hermetic Museum*, p. 142.
269. Ibid., p. 73.
270. Ibid.
271. Ibid.
272. Holmyard, E. J. *Alchemy*, p. 165.
273. Ibid., p. 170.
274. Ibid.
275. Martin, S. *Alchemy* and Alchemists, p. 71.
276. Holmyard, E. J. *Alchemy*, p. 173.

Chapter Eight

1. Blofeld, J. *The Tantric Mysticism of Tibet: A practical Guide to the Theory, Purpose, and Techniques of Tantric Meditation* (New York: Causeway Books, 1974), p. 55.
2. Fontana, D. *The New Secret Language of Symbols: An Illustrated Key to Unlocking their Deep and Hidden Meaning* (London: Duncan Baird, 2010), p. 60.
3. Constable, G. ed. *Secrets of the Alchemists* (Alexandria, VA: Time-Life Books, 1990), p. 23.
4. Ibid., p. 24.
5. Ibid.
6. Fabricius, J. Alchemy: The Medieval Alchemists and Their Royal Art (Copenhagen: Rosenkilde and Bagger, 1976), p. 20.
7. Martin, S. *Alchemy and Alchemists* (Harpenden, Herts, UK: Pocket Essentials, 2006), p. 25.
8. Ibid.
9. Ibid.
10. Ramsay, J. *Alchemy: The Art of Transformation* (London: Thorsons, 1997), p. 50.
11. Ibid.
12. Ibid.
13. Ibid.
14. Jung, C. G. *Psychology and Alchemy* 2d, translated by R. F. C. Hull (Bollingen Series XX, Princeton, NJ: Princeton University Press, 1980 [1952]), p. 317.
15. Govinda, L. A. *Foundations of Tibetan Mysticism* (York Beach, ME: Samuel Weiser, 1969), p. 51.
16. Ibid.
17. Roberts, G. *The Mirror of Alchemy* (Toronto and Buffalo: University of Toronto Press, 1994), p. 18.
18. Ibid., p. 53.
19. Jung, C. G. *Psychology and Alchemy*, p. 321.
20. Ibid.
21. Roob, A. *The Hermetic Museum: Alchemy & Mysticism* (Köln, London, and Tokyo: Taschen, 2006), p. 26.
22. Jung, C. G. *Psychology and Alchemy*, p. 323.
23. Atwood, M.A. *Hermetic Philosophy and Alchemy* (New York: The Julian Press, 1960 [1850]), p. 77.
24. de Rola, S. K. *The Golden Game: Alchemical Engravings of the Seventeenth Century* (London: Thames and Hudson, 1997), p. 16.
25. Eliade, M. *The Forge and the Crucible*, 2d, translated by Stephen Corrin (Chicago and London: University of Chicago Press, 1978b [1956]), p. 163.
26. Holmyard, E. J. *Alchemy* (New York: Dover, 1990 [1957]), p. 187.
27. Jung, C. G. *Psychology and Alchemy*, p. 34.
28. Ibid.
29. Baxter, A. "Alchemy," in: *Survey of the Occult*, ed. Julian Franklyn. pp. 2–34 (London: Arthur Barker Limited, 1935), p. 7.
30. Wasserman, J. *Art and Symbols of the Occult* (London: Tiger Books International, 1993), p. 93.
31. "alchemy" Encyclopædia Bri-

tannica, from *Encyclopædia Britannica Deluxe Edition 2005 CD*. Encyclopædia Britannica (accessed April 16, 2011).
32. Atwood, M. A. *Hermetic Philosophy and Alchemy*, p. 85.
33. Jung, C. G. *Psychology and Alchemy*, p. 319.
34. de Rola, S. K. *The Golden Game: Alchemical Engravings of the Seventeenth Century, p. 181.*
35. Blofeld, J. *The Tantric Mysticism of Tibet*, p. 66.
36. de Rola, S. K. *The Golden Game: Alchemical Engravings of the Seventeenth Century, p. 19.*
37. Guiley, R. E. *The Encyclopedia of Magic and Alchemy* (New York: Facts on File an imprint of Infobase Publishing, 2006), pp. 88–89.
38. *Ibid.*, p. 245.
39. Atwood, M. A. *Hermetic Philosophy and Alchemy*, p. 90.
40. *Ibid.*.
41. Underhill, E. *Mysticism: A Study in the Nature and Development of Spiritual Consciousness* (Mineola, NY: Dover, 2002), p. 142.
42. Jung, C.G. *Psychology and Alchemy*, p. 322.
43. *Ibid.*, pp. 324–325.
44. *The "Azoth" Series of Basil Valentine*, translated and colored by A. McLean (Glasgow: Hermetic Studies No. 7, 2000), p. 12.
45. *Ibid.*
46. *Ibid.*
47. "alchemy" Encyclopædia Britannica, from *Encyclopædia Britannica Deluxe Edition 2005 CD*. Encyclopædia Britannica (accessed April 16, 2011).
48. *Ibid.*
49. *Ibid*).
50. Martin, S. *Alchemy and Alchemists* (Harpenden, Herts, UK: Pocket Essentials, 2006), pp. 21–22.
51. *Ibid.*, p. 37.
52. *Ibid.*, p. 38.
53. *Ibid.*.
54. Guiley, R. E. *The Encyclopedia of Magic and Alchemy*, p. 89.
55. "Hermetic writings" *Encyclopædia Britannica*, from Encyclopædia Britannica Deluxe Edition 2005 CD. Encyclopædia Britannica, May 30, 2004 (accessed April 13, 2010).
56. *Ibid.*
57. Martin, S. *Alchemy and Alchemists*, p. 30.
58. Holmyard, E. J. *Alchemy* (New York: Dover, 1990 [1957]), p. 97.
59. Hauck, D. W. *The Emerald Tablet: Alchemy for Personal Transformation* (London: Penguin Compass, 1999), p. 105.
60. *Ibid.*, p. 45.

61. *Ibid.*
62. *Ibid.*, p. 9.
63. *Ibid.*
64. Olson, S. A. *The Jade Emperor's Mind Seal Classic: The Taoist Guide to Health, Longevity, and Immortality*, p. 54.
65. *Ibid.*
66. Ramsay, J. *Alchemy: The Art of Transformation*, p. 50.
67. Pregadio, F. *Encyclopedia of the History of Science, Technology and Medicine in Non-Western Countries*, 2d, ed. Helaine Selin. Berlin and New York: Springer, c2008. http://www.goldenelixir.com/jindan/jindan_intro.html
68. *Ibid.*
69. Martin, S. *Alchemy and Alchemists*, p. 23.
70. Roob, A. *The Hermetic Museum: Alchemy & Mysticism*, p. 28.
71. *Ibid.*, p. 30.
72. *Ibid.*
73. *Ibid.*
74. Roberts, G. *The Mirror of Alchemy*, p. 51.
75. *Ibid.*
76. Federmann, R. *The Royal Art of Alchemy*, translated by Richard H. Weber (Philadelphia, New York and London: Chilton Book, 1964), p. 24.
77. Roberts, G. *The Mirror of Alchemy*, p. 65.
78. *Ibid.*, p. 66.
79. Holmyard, E. J. *Alchemy*, p. 153.
80. Federmann, R. *The Royal Art of Alchemy*, p. 37.
81. Holmyard, E. J. *Alchemy*, p. 153.
82. *Good News Bible* (New York: United Bible Societies, 2007), p. 21.
83. Martin, S. *Alchemy and Alchemists*, p. 26.
84. Ramsey, J. *Alchemy: The Art of Transformation*, p. 61.
85. Martin, S. *Alchemy and Alchemists*, p. 27.
86. *Ibid.*
87. Roberts, G. *The Mirror of Alchemy*, p. 55.
88. Martin, S. *Alchemy and Alchemists*, p. 27.
89. Atwood, M.A. *Hermetic Philosophy and Alchemy*, pp. 109–110.
90. Roberts, G. *The Mirror of Alchemy*, p. 55.
91. *Ibid.*, p. 56.
92. Eliade, M. *The Forge and the Crucible*, p. 149.
93. *Ibid.*
94. *Ibid.*
95. Roberts, G. *The Mirror of Alchemy*, p. 56.
96. *Ibid.*, p. 60.
97. Holmyard, E. J. *Alchemy*, p. 46.

98. *Ibid.*
99. *Ibid.*
100. Roberts, G. *The Mirror of Alchemy*, p. 60.
101. Hauck, D. W. *The Emerald Tablet: Alchemy for Personal Transformation*, p. 145.
102. "resurrection" *Encyclopædia Britannica*, from Encyclopædia Britannica Deluxe Edition 2005 CD. Encyclopædia Britannica, May 30, 2004 (accessed April 30, 2010).
103. Eliade, M. *The Forge and the Crucible*, p. 150.
104. Jung, C. G. *Psychology and Religion: West and East*, 2d, translated by R. F. C. Hull (Bollingen Series XX, Princeton: Princeton University Press, 1973), p. 563.
105. de Rola, S. K. *The Golden Game: Alchemical Engravings of the Seventeenth Century, p. 42.*
106. Wong, E. *Taoism* (Boston and London: Shambhala, 1997), p. 69.
107. Ramsay, J. *Alchemy: The Art of Transformation*, p. 50.
108. "Christianity, The ages of the world" *Encyclopædia Britannica*, from Encyclopædia Britannica Deluxe Edition 2005 CD. Encyclopædia Britannica, May 30, 2004 (accessed April 09, 2010).
109. *Ibid.*
110. Feuerstein, G. ed. *Teachings of Yoga*, p. xiv.
111. Ramsay, J. *Alchemy: The Art of Transformation*, p. 55.
112. "Ko Hung" *Encyclopædia Britannica*, from Encyclopædia Britannica Deluxe Edition 2005 CD. Encyclopædia Britannica, May 30, 2004 (accessed April 30, 2010).
113. "Taoism" *Encyclopædia Britannica*, from Encyclopædia Britannica Deluxe Edition 2005 CD. Encyclopædia Britannica, May 30, 2004 (accessed April 23, 2010).
114. Olson, S. A. *The Jade Emperor's Mind Seal Classic*, p. 131.
115. Deng, M-D. *Chronicles of Tao: The Secret Life of a Taoist Master* (San Francisco: HarperSanFrancisco, a Division of HarperCollins, 1993), p. 209.
116. "alchemy" *Encyclopædia Britannica*, from Encyclopædia Britannica Deluxe Edition 2005 CD. Encyclopædia Britannica, May 30, 2004 (accessed April 23, 2010).
117. Wong, E. *The Shambhala Guide to Taoism* (Boston and London: Shambhala, 1997), p. 74.
118. *Ibid.*
119. *Ibid.*
120. *Ibid*
121. *Ibid.*, p. 75.
122. Johnson, O.S. *The Study of*

Chinese Alchemy, translated by Stephen Corrin (New York: ARNO Press, 1974 [1928]), p. 39.
123. Valentine, B. "Triumphal Chariot of Antimony" pp. 174–280 in: M. R. Poll, ed. *The Stone of the Philosophers* (Lafayette, LA: Cornerstone Books, 2007), p. 182.
124. Johnson, O.S. *The Study of Chinese Alchemy*, p. 40.
125. Norman, D. *The Hero: Myth/Image/Symbol* (New York and Cleveland: The World Publishing Co., 1969), pp. 4–5.
126. Johnson, O.S. *The Study of Chinese Alchemy*, p. 44.
127. Ramsay, J. *Alchemy: The Art of Transformation*, p. 52.
128. Bennett, C. A. *A Philosophical Study of Mysticism* (New Haven: Yale University Press, 1923), pp. 142–143.
129. Ramsay, J. *Alchemy: The Art of Transformation*, p. 52.
130. Jung, C.G. *Psychology and Alchemy*, p. 181.
131. *Ibid*.
132. Brauen, M. *Mandala: Sacred Circle in Tibetan Buddhism* (New York: Rubin Museum of Art and Stuttgart: Arnoldsche Art, 2009), p. 11.
133. Roob, A. *The Hermetic Museum: Alchemy & Mysticism*, p. 19.
134. Johnson, O.S. *The Study of Chinese Alchemy*, p. 71.
135. Underhill, E. *Mysticism: A Study in the Nature and Development of Spiritual Consciousness* (Mineola, NY: Dover, 2002), p. 145.
136. *Ibid*.
137. Lu, K. Y. *Taoist Yoga: Alchemy and Immortality* (New York: Samuel Wiser, 1972), p. 27.
138. Jung, C.G. *Psychology and Alchemy*, pp. 228–229.
139. Silberer, H., and S. E. Jelliffe. *Problems of Mysticism and its Symbolism* (Whitefish, MT: Kessinger Publishing, 2009 [1917]), p. 113.
140. Johnson, O.S. *The Study of Chinese Alchemy*, p. 69.
141. *Ibid*.
142. *Ibid.*, p. 70.
143. *Ibid*.
144. *Ibid.*, p. 71.
145. *Ibid.*, p. 72.
146. *Ibid.*, p. 73.
147. *Ibid.*, p. 74.
148. Olson, S.A. *The Jade Emperor's Mind Seal Classic: The Taoist Guide to Health, Longevity, and Immortality*, p. 90.
149. Roberts, G. *The Mirror of Alchemy*, p. 59.
150. Holmyard, E. J. *Alchemy*, p. 137.
151. Eliade, M. *The Forge and The Crucible*, p. 46.
152. Roberts, G. *The Mirror of Alchemy*, p. 54.
153. *Ibid*.
154. Waite, A. E. The Hermetic Museum, Vol II (Boston, MA/York Beach, ME: WeiserBooks, 1990 [1893]), p. 116.
155. Roberts, G. *The Mirror of Alchemy*, p. 62.
156. *Ibid.*, p. 63.
157. *Ibid*.
158. Waite, A. E. The Hermetic Museum, Vol II, p. 27.
159. Eliade, M. *The Forge and The Crucible*, p. 153.
160. "alchemy" Encyclopædia Britannica, from *Encyclopædia Britannica Deluxe Edition 2005 CD*. Encyclopædia Britannica (accessed May 3, 2011).
161. Ramsay, J. *Alchemy: The Art of Transformation*, p. 36.
162. *Ibid*.
163. Hauck, D. W. *The Emerald Tablet: Alchemy for Personal Transformation*, p. 17.
164. Eliade, M. *The Forge and The Crucible*, p. 150.
165. Guiley, M.E. *The Encyclopedia of Magic and Alchemy*, p. 135.
166. Eliade, M. *The Forge and The Crucible*, p. 150.
167. Campbell, J. *The Mythic Image* (Bollingen Series C, Princeton, NJ: Princeton University Press, 1974), p. 165.
168. Underhill, E. *Mysticism: A Study in the Nature and Development of Spiritual Consciousness*, p. 143.
169. Kirchweger, A. "Golden Chain of Homer" in: *The Stone of the Philosophers: An Alchemical Handbook*, edited by Poll, M. R. (Lafayette, LA: Cornerstone Book, 2007), p. 22.
170. *Ibid*.
171. Eliade, M. *The Forge and the Crucible*, p. 151.

Chapter Nine

1. Eliade, M. *Images and Symbols: Studies in Religious Symbolism*, translated by Philip Mairet (Princeton, NJ: Princeton University Press, 1991), p. 12.
2. Underhill, D. *Mysticism: A Study in the Nature and Development of Spiritual Consciousness* (Mineola, NY: Dover, 2002 [1911]), p. 141.
3. Johnson, O.S. *A Study of Chinese Alchemy* (Shanghai: Commercial Press, Limited, 1928 reprinted from a copy in the Columbia University Library, New York: Arno Press, 1974), p. 111.
4. Benedict, R. *Patterns of Culture*, 2nd ed. (Boston: Houghton Mifflin, 1959 [1934]), p. 96.
5. "occultism" Encyclopædia Britannica, from *Encyclopædia Britannica Deluxe Edition 2005 CD*. Encyclopædia Britannica (accessed June 10, 2011).
6. Rawson, P. *The Art of Tantra* (London: Thames and Hudson Ltd., 1973), p. 26.
7. Baigent, M., and R. Leigh. *The Elixir and the Stone: A History of Magic and Alchemy*, p. 45.
8. Eliade, M. *Shamanism: Archaic Techniques of Ecstasy*, translated by Willard R. Trask (Bollingen Series LXXVI, Princeton, NJ: Princeton University Press, 1964), p. 508.
9. Eliade, M. *The Forge and the Crucible*, translated by Stephen Corrin (Chicago and London: University of Chicago Press, 1978), p. 107.
10. *Ibid*.
11. *Ibid*.
12. *Ibid.*, p. 117.
13. Burland, C.A. *The Arts of the Alchemists* (London: Weidenfeld and Nicolson, 1967), p. 18.
14. *Ibid.*, p. 17.
15. *Ibid.*, p. 1.
16. *Ibid.*, p. 1.
17. Fontana D. *The Secret Language of Symbols* (San Francisco: Chronicle Books, 1994), p. 146.
18. Roberts, G. *The Mirror of Alchemy* (Toronto and Buffalo: University of Toronto Press, 1994), p. 68.
19. Baigent, M., and R. Leigh. *The Elixir and the Stone: A History of Magic and Alchemy*, p. 22.
20. Underhill, E. *Mysticism: A Study in the Nature and Development of Spiritual Consciousness*, p. 141.
21. Freke, T., and P. Gandy. *The Hermetica: The Lost Wisdom of the Pharaohs* (New York: Tarcher Cornerstone Editions, Penguin Group, 1999), p. 1.
22. Read, J. *The Alchemist in Life, Literature and Art* (London, Toronto, and New York: Thomas Nelson and Sons Ltd., 1947), p. 69.
23. *Ibid*.
24. Martin, S. Alchemy and Alchemists (Harpenden, Herts, UK: Pocket Essentials, 2006), p. 44.
25. Baxter, A. "Alchemy," in: *Survey of the Occult*, ed. Julian Franklyn. pp. 2–34 (London: Arthur Barker Limited, 1935), p. 7.
26. Jung, C. G. *Psychology and Alchemy* 2d, translated by R. F. C. Hull (Bollingen Series XX, Princeton, NJ: Princeton University Press, 1980 [1952]), p. 289.
27. *Ibid*.
28. *Ibid.*, pp. 292–293.

29. Burland, C. A. *The Arts of the Alchemists*, p. 36.
30. *Ibid.*, pp. 36–37.
31. *Ibid.*, p. 36.
32. *Ibid.*, p. 39.
33. Read, J. *The Alchemist in Life, Literature and Art*, p. 56.
34. Burland, C. A. *The Arts of the Alchemists*, p. 37.
35. Baigent, M., and R. Leigh. *The Elixir and the Stone: A History of Magic and Alchemy*, pp. 208–209.
36. De Rola, S. K. *The Golden Game: Alchemy Engravings of the Seventeenth Century* (London: Thames and Hudson, 1997), p. 9.
37. *Ibid.*, p. 10.
38. *Ibid.*
39. Baigent, M., and R. Leigh. *The Elixir and the Stone: A History of Magic and Alchemy*, p. 208.
40. *Ibid.*, p. 207.
41. "Indian philosophy" Encyclopædia Britannica, from *Encyclopædia Britannica Deluxe Edition 2005 CD*. Encyclopædia Britannica (accessed September 7, 2011).
42. "emblem book" Encyclopædia Britannica, from *Encyclopædia Britannica Deluxe Edition 2005 CD*. Encyclopædia Britannica (accessed April 10, 2011).
43. De Rola, S. K. *The Golden Game: Alchemy Engravings of the Seventeenth Century*, p. 16.
44. *Ibid.*, p. 11.
45. *Ibid.*.
46. *Ibid.*, p. 17.
47. *Ibid.*, p. 8.
48. Ramsay, J. *Alchemy: The Art of Transformation* (London: Thorsons, 1997), p. 32.
49. *Ibid.*, pp. 32–33.
50. Blofeld, J. *The Tantric Mysticism of Tibet: A Practical Guide* (New York: Causeway Books, 1974), p. 62.
51. Ramsay, J. *Alchemy: The Art of Transformation*, p. 33.
52. Burland, C.A. *The Arts of the Alchemists*, p. 77.
53. Roberts, G. *The Mirror of Alchemy*, p. 66.
54. Baxter, A. "Alchemy," in: *Survey of the Occult*, p. 3.
55. De Rola, S. K. *The Golden Game: Alchemical Engravings of the Seventeenth Century*, p. 114.
56. Roberts, G. *The Mirror of Alchemy*, p. 32.
57. *Ibid.*, p. 84.
58. *Ibid.*, p. 66.
59. Read, J. *The Alchemist in Life, Literature and Art*, p. 21.
60. *Ibid.*.
61. Zimmer, H. *Myths and Symbols in Indian Art and Civilization*, edited by Joseph Campbell (Bollingen Series VI, Princeton: Princeton University Press, 1974), p. 151.
62. Blofeld, J. *The Tantric Mysticism of Tibet* (New York: Causeway Books, 1974), p. 98.
63. Gardner, H. *The Arts and Human Development* (New York: BasicBooks, a subsidiary of Perseus Books, L.L.C., 1994 [1973]), p. 83.
64. Evens-Wentz, W. Y. *Tibetan Yoga and Secret Doctrines*, translated by Chen-Chi Chang (Oxford: Oxford University Press, 2000), p.16.
65. *Ibid.*
66. Jung, C. G. *Psychology and Alchemy*, p. 8.
67. Underhill, D. *Mysticism: A Study in the Nature and Development of Spiritual Consciousness*, p. 140.
68. Baxter, A. "Alchemy," in: *Survey of the Occult*, p. 6.
69. *Ibid.*
70. Poll, M. R. ed. *The Stone of the Philosophers* (Lafayette, LA: Cornerstone Books, 2007), p. 1.
71. Baxter, A. "Alchemy," in: *Survey of the Occult*, p. 5.
72. De Rola, S. K. *The Golden Game: Alchemical Engravings of the Seventeenth Century*, p. 22.
73. Ramsay, J. *Alchemy: The Art of Transformation*, p.10.
74. Eliade, M. *The Forge and the Crucible*, p. 50.
75. "Hinduism" Encyclopædia Britannica, from *Encyclopædia Britannica Deluxe Edition 2005 CD*. Encyclopædia Britannica (accessed May 11, 2011).
76. *Ibid.*
77. *Ibid.*
78. *Ibid.*
79. *Ibid.*
80. *Ibid.*
81. *Ibid.*
82. Young, D. *Origins of the Sacred: The Ecstasies of Love and War* (New York: St. Martin's Press, 1991), p. 164.
83. *Ibid.*
84. Eliade, M. *The Forge and the Crucible*, p. 174.
85. *Ibid.*, pp. 174–175.
86. Freke, T., and P. Gandy. *The Hermetica: The Lost Wisdom of the Pharaohs*, p. 42.
87. Zimmer, H. *Myths and Symbols in Indian Art and Civilization*, ed. J. Campbell, p. 13.
88. Eversole, F. *Art and Spiritual Transformation: Seven Stages of Death and Rebirth* (Rochester, VT: Inner Traditions, 2009), p. 67.
89. Koller, J. *Oriental Philosophies*, 2d (New York: Charles Scribner's Sons, 1985), p. 26.
90. "Artha-sâstra" Encyclopædia Britannica, from *Encyclopædia Britannica Deluxe Edition 2005 CD*. Encyclopædia Britannica (accessed March 18, 2011).
91. "Nâgârjuna" Encyclopædia Britannica, from *Encyclopædia Britannica Deluxe Edition 2005 CD*. Encyclopædia Britannica (accessed March 18, 2011).
92. Martin, S. *Alchemy and Alchemists*, p. 87.
93. *Ibid.*, p. 88.
94. *Ibid.*, p. 87.
95. Maringer, J. *The Gods of Prehistoric Man*, edited and translated by Mary Ilford (New York: Alfred A. Knopf, 1960), p. vii.
96. Read, J. *The Alchemist in Life, Literature and Art*, p. 56.
97. De Rola, S. K. *The Golden Game: Alchemical Engravings of the Seventeenth Century*, p. 181.
98. Rawson, P. *The Art of Tantra*, p. 11.
99. Jung. C. G. *Psychology and Religion: West and East*, p. 559.
100. *Ibid.*
101. *Ibid.*
102. Rawson, P. *The Art of Tantra*, p. 25.
103. *Ibid.*, p. 26.
104. *Ibid.*
105. *Ibid.*, p. 77.
106. "yab-yum" Encyclopædia Britannica, from *Encyclopædia Britannica Deluxe Edition 2005 CD*. Encyclopædia Britannica (accessed May 21, 2011).
107. Fisher, R. E. *Art of Tibet* (London: Thames and Hudson, 1997), p. 56.
108. Brauen, M. *Mandala Sacred Circle in Tibetan Buddhism* (New York: Rubin Museum of Art, Stuttgard: Arnoldsche Art, 2009), p. 174.
109. *Ibid.*
110. Rawson, P. *The Art of Tantra*, p. 7.
111. *Ibid.*
112. *Ibid.*, p. 16.
113. Stone, P. G., and B. Molyneaux, eds. *The Presented Past* (London and New York, Routledge, 1994), p. 2.
114. Burland, C. A. *The Arts of the Alchemists*, p. 71.
115. Martin, S. *Alchemy and Alchemists*, p. 3.1
116. Koller, J. *Oriental Philosophies*, 2d (New York: Charles Scribner's Sons, 1985), p. 283.
117. *Ibid.*, pp. 284–285.
118. "Taoism" Encyclopædia Britannica, from *Encyclopædia Britannica Deluxe Edition 2005 CD*. Encyclopædia Britannica (accessed March 8,

2011).

119. Jung, C. G., ed. *Man and His Symbols*. John Freemen coordinating editor (Garden City, NY: Doubleday, 1964), p. 146.
120. "Taoism" Encyclopædia Britannica, from *Encyclopædia Britannica Deluxe Edition 2005 CD*. Encyclopædia Britannica (accessed May 25, 2011).
121. Johnson, O. S. *A Study of Chinese Alchemy*, p. 76.
122. *Ibid.*
123. *Ibid.*
124. *Ibid.*
125. Reynolds, V. *Tibet A Lost World: The Newark Museum Collection of Tibetan Art and Ethnography* (New York: The American Federation of Arts, Bloomington and London: Indiana University Press, 1979), p. 57.
126. Fisher, R. E. *Buddhist Art and Architecture* (London: Thames and Hudson Ltd., 1993), p. 11.
127. Rawson, P. *Sacred Tibet*, p. 10.
128. Fisher, R. E. *Buddhist Art and Architecture*, p. 8.
129. Frédéric, L. *Buddhism: Flammarion Iconographic Guides* (Paris and New York: Flammarion, 1995), p. 9.
130. *Ibid.*
131. Dowman, K. *The Sacred Life in Tibet* (San Francisco: Thorsons, An imprint of HarperCollins, 1997), p. 90.
132. Leidy, D. P. *The Art of Buddhism: An Introduction to Its History and Meaning* (Boston and London: Shambhala, 2008), p. 5.
133. Levenson, C. B. Symbols of Tibetan Buddhism, translated by Nissin Marshall (New York: Barnes and Noble Books, 2000), p. 28.
134. "*kapala*" Encyclopædia Britannica, from *Encyclopædia Britannica Deluxe Edition 2005 CD*. Encyclopædia Britannica, May 30, 2004 (accessed June 15, 2011).
135. Müller-Edeling, C., C. Rätsch, and S. B. Sihahi. *Shamanism and Tantra in the Himalayas*, translated by Annabel Lee (London: Thames & Hudson Ltd, 2002), p. 223.
136. "Buddha" Encyclopædia Britannica, from *Encyclopædia Britannica Deluxe Edition 2005 CD*. Encyclopædia Britannica (accessed May 23, 2011).
137. Dowman, K. *The Sacred Life in Tibet*, p. 91.
138. Fisher, R. E. *Buddhist Art and Architecture*, p. 11.
139. "cross" Encyclopædia Britannica, from *Encyclopædia Britannica Deluxe Edition 2005 CD*. Encyclopædia Britannica (accessed May 23, 2011).
140. Dowman, K. *The Sacred Life in Tibet*, p. 91.
141. Gordon, A. *Tibetan Religious Art* (New York: Columbia University Press, 1952), p. viii.
142. Dowman, K. *The Sacred Life in Tibet*, p. 91.
143. Blofeld, J. *The Tantric Mysticism of Tibet*, p. 94.
144. *Ibid.*
145. *Ibid.*
146. *Ibid.*, p. 9.
147. *Ibid.*, p. 82.
148. *Ibid.*, p. 9.
149. Jisl, L. *Tibetan Art*, translated by Ilse Gottheiner (London: Spring Books, 1957), p. 7.
150. *Ibid.*
151. Fisher, R. E. *Buddhist Art and Architecture*, p. 12.
152. *Ibid.*
153. *Ibid.*
154. Blofeld, J. *The Tantric Mysticism of Tibet*, p. 95.
155. Lowenstein, T. *Treasures of the Buddha: The Glories of Sacred Asia* (London: Duncan Baird, 2006), pp. 182–183.
156. *Ibid.*
157. Eliade, M. *The Sacred and the Profane: The Nature of Religion*, translated by Willard R. Trask (New York and London: A Harvest Book, Harcourt, 1987), p. 138.
158. Capra, F. *The Tao of Physics* (Boston: Shambhala, 2000), p. 139.
159. *Ibid.*, p. 140.
160. Malraux, A. *The Metamorphosis of the Gods*, translated by Stuart Gilbert (Garden City, NY: Doubleday, 1960), p.20.
161. Capra, F. *The Tao of Physics*, p. 139.
162. Roob, A. The Hermetic Museum: Alchemy & Mysticism (Köln, London, and Tokyo: Taschen, 2006), p. 19.
163. Dowman, K. *The Sacred Life in Tibet*, p. 89.
164. Malraux, A. *The Metamorphosis of the Gods*, p.19.
165. Rawson, P. *Sacred Tibet*, p. 10.
166. Underhill, E. *Mysticism: The Nature and Development of Spiritual Consciousness*, p. 63.
167. *Ibid.*, p. 234.

Chapter Ten

1. Thich, N. H. *Transformation & Healing: Sutra on the Four Establishments of Mindfulness* (Berkeley, CA: Parallax Press, 1990), p. 98.
2. Ransay, J. *Alchemy: The Art of Transformation* (London and San Francisco: Thorsons an imprint of HarperCollins, 1997), p. 96.
3. "metallurgy" Encyclopædia Britannica, from *Encyclopædia Britannica* Deluxe Edition 2005 CD. Encyclopædia Britannica, May 30, 2004 (accessed July 04, 2011).
4. Eliade, M. *The Forge and The Crucible*, 2d, translated by Stephen Corrin (Chicago and London: University of Chicago Press, 1978b [1956]), p. 67.
5. Koller, J. M. *Oriental Philosophies*, 2d (New York: Charles Scribner's Sons, 1985), p. 283.
6. "science, history of" Encyclopædia Britannica, from *Encyclopædia Britannica* Deluxe Edition 2005 CD. Encyclopædia Britannica, May 30, 2004 (accessed July 15, 2011).
7. Pinch, G. *Magic in Ancient Egypt* (Austin: University of Texas Press, 1994), pp. 167–168.
8. Eversole, F. *Art and Spiritual Transformation: The Seven Stages of Death and Rebirth* (Rochester, VT: Inner Traditions, 2009), p. 64.
9. *Ibid.*, p. 67.
10. "Symbols of sacred time and space" Encyclopædia Britannica, from Encyclopædia Britannica Deluxe Edition 2005 CD. Encyclopædia Britannica, May 30, 2004 (accessed July 12, 2011).
11. James, J. ed. *The Way of Mysticism* (London: Jonathan Cape, 1950), p. 108.
12. Jung. C. G. *Memories, Dreams, Reflections*, edited by Aniela Jaffé, translated by Richard and Clare Winston (New York: Vintage Books, a Division of Random House, 1965), pp. 316–317.
13. Eliade, M. *Myth and Reality*, translated by Willard R. Trask (New York: Harper Torchbooks, Harper & Row, 1963), p. 85.
14. *Ibid.*
15. "Taoism" Encyclopædia Britannica, from *Encyclopædia Britannica* Deluxe Edition 2005 CD. Encyclopædia Britannica, May 30, 2004 (accessed July 09, 2011).
16. Govinda, L. A. *Foundations of Tibetan Mysticism* (York Beach, ME: Samuel Weiser, 1969), p. 81.
17. Sufism "Symbolism in Sufism" Encyclopædia Britannica, from *Encyclopædia Britannica* Deluxe Edition 2005 CD. Encyclopædia Britannica, May 30, 2004 (accessed September 12, 2010).
18. Roberts, G. *The Mirror of Alchemy* (Toronto and Buffalo: University of Toronto Press, 1994), p. 82.
19. Eliade, M. *Myth and Reality*, p.

86.
20. Jung. C. G. *Psychology and Religion: West and East*, 2d, translated by R. F. C. Hull (Bollingen Series XX, Princeton, NJ: Princeton University Press, 1973), p. 10.
21. Eliade, M. *Myth and Reality*, pp. 83–84.
22. *Ibid*, p. 83.
23. *Ibid*.
24. "creation myth" Encyclopædia Britannica, from *Encyclopædia Britannica* Deluxe Edition 2005 CD. Encyclopædia Britannica, May 30, 2004 (accessed May 28, 2011).
25. Blofeld, J. *The Tantric Mysticism of Tibet: A Practical Guide* (New York: Causeway Books, 1974), 48.
26. *Ibid.*, 57.
27. Gard, R. A., ed. *Buddhism* (New York: George Braziller, 1962), p. 19.
28. *Good News Bible* (New York: United Bible Societies, 2007), pp. 837–838.
29. Blofeld, J. *The Tantric Mysticism of Tibet*, 213.
30. "Taoism" Encyclopædia Britannica, from *Encyclopædia Britannica* Deluxe Edition 2005 CD. Encyclopædia Britannica, May 30, 2004 (accessed July 09, 2011).
31. Lopön, T. N. R. "The Condensed Meaning of an Explanation of the Teachings of Yungdurng Bon," translated by John Reynolds (Kathmandu, Nepal: Bonpo Foundation, 1991) http://bon-encyclopedia.wikispaces.com/lopon+yungdrung+condensed (accessed May 31, 2011.
32. *Ibid*.
33. "pâramitâ" Encyclopædia Britannica, from *Encyclopædia Britannica* Deluxe Edition 2005 CD. Encyclopædia Britannica, May 30, 2004 (accessed June 01, 2011).
34. "Buddhism" Encyclopædia Britannica, from *Encyclopædia Britannica* Deluxe Edition 2005 CD. Encyclopædia Britannica, May 30, 2004 (accessed May 31, 2011).
35. "trikaya" Encyclopædia Britannica, from *Encyclopædia Britannica* Deluxe Edition 2005 CD. Encyclopædia Britannica, May 30, 2004 (accessed May 31, 2011).
36. Reynolds, J. M. "The Bonpo Traditions of Dzogchen" (http://www.vajranatha.com/teaching/BonpoDzogchen.html, accessed February 7, 2011).
37. *Ibid*.
38. *Ibid*.
39. *Ibid*.
40. *Ibid*
41. *Ibid*.
42. Olson, S. A. *The Jade Emperor's Mind Seal Classic: The Taoist Guide to Health, Longevity, and Immortality* (Rochester VT: Inner Traditions, 2003), p. 15.
43. *Ibid*.
44. "Taoism" Encyclopædia Britannica, from *Encyclopædia Britannica* Deluxe Edition 2005 CD. Encyclopædia Britannica, May 30, 2004 (accessed July 15, 2011).
45. Underhill, E. *Mysticism: The Nature and Development of Spiritual Consciousness* (Mineola, NY: Dover, 2002 [unaltered reproduction of the 12th edition, 1930, published by E. P. Dutton, of the work originally published in 1911]), p. 102.
46. "Egyptian religion" Encyclopædia Britannica, from *Encyclopædia Britannica* Deluxe Edition 2005 CD. Encyclopædia Britannica, May 30, 2004 (accessed June 06, 2011).
47. "Cosmology" Encyclopædia Britannica, from *Encyclopædia Britannica* Deluxe Edition 2005 CD. Encyclopædia Britannica (accessed June 10, 2011).
48. Eliade, M. *Yoga: Immortality and Freedom*, translated by Willard R. Trask. (Bollingen Series LVI, Princeton NJ: Princeton University Press, 2009 [1958]), p. 3.
49. *Ibid.*, p. 4.
50. Feuerstein, G. *The Yoga Tradition: It History, Literature, Philosophy and Practice* (Prescott, AZ: Hohm Press, 1998), p. 38.
51. Yates, J. ed. *Jung on Death and Immortality* (Princeton, NJ: Princeton University Press, 1999), p. 50.
52. Bowker, J. *World Religions: The Great Faiths Explored & Explained* (London: DK Publishing Books, 1997), p. 64.
53. Fairweather. W. *Among the Mystics* (Freeport, NY: Books for Libraries Press, 1968 [1936]), p. 125.
54. Underhill, E. *Mysticism: The Nature and Development of Spiritual Consciousness*, p. 3.
55. Boehme, J. *Genius of the Transcendent: Mystical Writings of Jakob Boehme*, translated by M. L. Birkel and J. Bach (Boston & London: Shambhala, 2010), p. 30–31
56. *Ibid*.
57. Roob, A. *The Hermetic Museum: Alchemy & Mysticism* (Köln, London: Taschen, 2006), p. 19.
58. Underhill, E. *Mysticism: The Nature and Development of Spiritual Consciousness*, p. 102.
59. Jung, C. G. *Psychology and Alchemy* 2d, translated by R. F. C. Hull (Bollingen Series XX, Princeton, NJ: Princeton University Press, 1980 [1952]), p. 167.
60. *Ibid.*, p. 237.
61. *Ibid.*, p. 108.
62. Zimmer, Heinrich. *Myths and Symbols in Indian Art and Civilization*, edited by Joseph Campbell (Bollingen Series VI, Princeton, NJ: Princeton University Press, 1972), p. 127.
63. Eliade, M. *Yoga: Immortality and Freedom*, p. 254.
64. *Ibid*.
65. *Ibid.*, p. 255.
66. "soma" Encyclopædia Britannica, from *Encyclopædia Britannica* Deluxe Edition 2005 CD. Encyclopædia Britannica (accessed July 15, 2011).
67. Govinda, L. A. *Foundations of Tibetan Mysticism* (York Beach, ME: Samuel Weiser, 1969), p. 140s.
68. "hsü" Encyclopædia Britannica, from *Encyclopædia Britannica* Deluxe Edition 2005 CD. Encyclopædia Britannica (accessed May 30, 2011).
69. *Ibid*.
70. "Taoism" Encyclopædia Britannica, from *Encyclopædia Britannica* Deluxe Edition 2005 CD. Encyclopædia Britannica, May 30, 2004 (accessed May 28, 2011).
71. Campbell, J. *Masks of the Gods: Primitive Mythology* (New York: ARKANA, Penguin Books USA 1976) p. 291.
72. Tucci, G., H. Nakamura, and F. E. Reynolds. "suffering, impermanence, and no-self" Encyclopædia Britannica, from *Encyclopædia Britannica* Deluxe Edition 2005 CD. Encyclopædia Britannica (accessed May 5, 2010).
73. "dualism" Encyclopædia Britannica, from *Encyclopædia Britannica* Deluxe Edition 2005 CD. Encyclopædia Britannica, May 30, 2004 (accessed June 6, 2011)
74. Eliade, M. *Yoga: Immortality and Freedom*, p. 202.
75. Blofeld, J. *The Tantric Mysticism of Tibet*, p. 30.
76. Erikson, E. H. *The Life Cycle Completed* (New York: W. W. Norton, 1998 [1982]), p. 124.
77. *Ibid*.
78. *Ibid*.
79. Tucci, G. *The Religions of Tibet*, translated by Geoffrey Samuel (Berkeley: University of California Press, 1988), p. 59.
80. *Ibid*.
81. Stewart, J. A. *Introduction and Observations: The Myths of Plato* (New York: Barnes and Noble 1970 [1905]).
82. Tucci, G. *The Religions of Tibet*, p. 59.
83. Edson, G. *Shamanism, A Cross-Cultural Study of Beliefs and*

Practices (Jefferson, NC: McFarland, 2009), p. 24.

84. Feuerstein, G. *The Yoga Tradition: It History, Literature, Philosophy and Practice*, p. 238.

85. Jung. C. G. *Memories, Dreams, Reflections*, p. 106.

86. Jung. C. G. *Man and His Symbols*, p. 151.

87. Jung. C. G. *Memories, Dreams, Reflections*, p. 106.

88. Blofeld, J. *The Tantric Mysticism of Tibet*, 213.

89. Govinda, L. A. *Foundations of Tibetan Mysticism*, p. 52.

90. Rawson, P. *Sacred Tibet* (London: Thames and Hudson, Ltd., 1991), p. 30.

91. Govinda, L. A. *Foundations of Tibetan Mysticism*, p. 167.

92. Jung. C. G. *Psychology and Religion: West and East*, p. 559.

93. Matthews, C., and J. Matthews. *Walkers Between the Worlds: The Western Mysteries from Shaman to Magus* (Rochester, VT: Inner Traditions, 2003 [1985]), p. 107.

94. Waley, A. *The Nine Songs: A Study of Shamanism in Ancient China* (London: George Allen and Unwin Ltd., 1955), p. 10.

95. Martin, S. *Alchemy and Alchemists* (Harpenden, Herts, UK: Pocket Essentials, 2006), p. 64.

96. *Ibid*.

97. Jung. C. G. *Memories, Dreams, Reflections*, pp. 301–302.

Bibliography

Abraham, Lyndy. *A Dictionary of Alchemical Imagery.* Cambridge: Cambridge University Press, 1998.

Ackerman, Diane. *A Natural History of the Senses.* New York: Random House, 1990.

Adamson, Stephen, ed. *The Way to Eternity: Egyptian Myth.* London: Duncan Baird Publishers, 1997.

Addison, Charles M. *The Theory and Practice of Mysticism.* New York: E. F. Dutton, 1918.

Ager, John C. *The Path of Life,* compiled from the writings of Emanuel Swedenborg. New York: New-Church Press, 1912.

Aldhouse-Green, Miranda, and Stephen Aldhouse-Green. *The Quest for the Shaman: Shape-Shifters, Sorcerers and Spirit-Healers of Ancient Europe,* London: Thames & Hudson, 2005.

American Journal of Chinese Medicine. "Alchemy, Chinese versus Greek, an etymological approach: a rejoinder." http://www.ncbi.nlm.nih.gov/pubmed/3064584?dopt=Abstract.

Ankarloo, Bengt, and Stuart Clark, eds. *Witchcraft and Magic in Europe: The Eighteenth and Nineteenth Centuries.* Philadelphia: University of Pennsylvania Press, 1999a.

_____. *Witchcraft and Magic in Europe: The Twentieth Century.* Philadelphia: University of Pennsylvania Press, 1999b.

Anonymous. *Alchemy, Medicine, Religion: In the China of A.D. 320,* translated by James R. Ware. Cambridge, MA: M.I.T. Press, 1966.

Antropova, V. V., and V. G. Kuznetsova "The Chukchi" In: Levin, Mikhail Grigor and Leonid Pavlovich Potapov, eds. *The Peoples of Siberia,* pp. 799–835, translated by Scripta Technica, English translation edited by Stephen Dunn. Chicago: University of Chicago Press, 1956

Arberry, A. J. *Sufism: An Account of the Mystics of Islam.* London: George Allen & Unwin Ltd., 1968 [1950].

Arendt, Hannah. *The Human Condition.* Chicago: University of Chicago Press, 1958.

Ariel, David S. *The Mystic Quest: An Introduction to Jewish Mysticism.* Northvale, NJ: Jason Aronson, 1988.

Arieti, Silvano. *Creativity: The Magic Synthesis.* New York: Basic Books, 1976.

Aristotle. *Meteorologica.* Translated by H.D.P. Lee. Cambridge, MA: Harvard University Press, 1952.

_____. *Metaphysics,* translated with Commentaries and Glossary by Hippocrates G. Apostle. Bloomington: Indiana University Press, 1966.

Ashmole, Elias. *Theatrum Chemicum Britannicum.* Reprint of the London Edition 1652 with a new Introduction by Allen G. Debus. The Source of Science, No. 39. New York: Johnson Reprint Corporation, 1967.

Atwood, Mary Anne. *Hermetic Philosophy and Alchemy.* New York: Julian Press, 1960 [1850].

Baigent, Michael and Richard Leigh. *The Elixir and the Stone: A History of Magic and Alchemy.* London: Random House Group, 1997.

Baker, Ian A. *The Tibetan Art of Healing.* San Francisco: Chronicle Books, 1997.

Balzar, Marjorie M., ed. *Shamanism: Soviet Studies of traditional Religion in Siberia and Central Asia.* Armonk, New York: M.E. Sharpe, 1990.

_____. ed. *Shamanic Worlds: Ritual and Lore of Siberia and Central Asia.* Armonk, NY: North Castle Books, 1997.

Bancroft, Anne. *Religions of the East.* London: William Heinemann Ltd., 1974.

Bancroft-Hunt, Norman and Werner Forman. *People of the Totem.* New York: G. P. Putnam's, 1979.

Bansal. B. L. *Bon: Its Encounter with Buddhism in Tibet.* Delhi, India: Eastern Books Linkers, 1994.

Barton, George A. *The Religions of the World,* 4th ed. Chicago: University of Chicago Press, 1937.

Baumer, Christoph. *Bön: Tibet's Ancient Religion,* translated by Michael Kohn. Trumbull, CT: Weatherhill, 2002.

Baxter, Alastair. "Alchemy," in: *Survey of the Occult,* ed. Julian Franklyn. pp. 2–34, London: Arthur Barker Limited, 1935.

Bayley, Harold. *The Lost Language of Symbolism,* vol. 2. London: Bracken Books, 1996 [1912].

Beane, Wendell C. and William G. Doty, eds. *Myth, Rites, Symbols: A Mircea Eliade Reader,* vol. I. New York: Harper and Row, 1976.

Bechert, Heinz, and Richard Gombrich eds. *The World of Buddhism: Buddhist Monks and Nuns in Society and Culture.* New York: Facts on File Publications, 1984.

Beer, Robert. *The Handbook of Tibetan Buddhist Symbols.* Boston: Shambhala, 2003.

Bell, Charles. *The Religion of Tibet.* Oxford: The Clarendon Press, 1931.

Bellezza, John Vincent. *Spirit-Mediums, Sacred Mountains and Related Bon Textural Traditions in Upper Tibet: Calling Down the Gods*. Leiden, 2005.

ben Shimon Halevi, Z'ev. *The Work of the Kabbalist*. York Beach, ME: Samuel Weiser, 1985.

Benedict, Ruth. *Patterns of Culture*, 2d edition. Boston: Houghton Mifflin, 1959 [1934].

Bennett, Charles A. *A Philosophical Study of Mysticism*. New Haven, CT: Yale University Press, 1923.

Berglie, Per-Arne. "Tibetan Shamanism," in: Walter, M. N. and E. J. N. Fridman, eds. *Shamanism: An Encyclopedia of World Beliefs, Practices and Culture*, pp. 790–798. Santa Barbara, CA: ABC-CLIO, 2004.

Besserman, Perle. *Kabbalah and Jewish Mysticism*. Boston and London: Shambhala, 1997.

Bettelheim, Bruno. *Symbolic Wounds*. Glencoe: The Free Press, 1954.

Birket-Smith, Kaj. *The Paths of Culture: A General Ethnology*, translated by Karin Fennow. Madison: University of Wisconsin Press, 1965.

Blanshard, Brand. *Reason and Belief*. New Haven, CT: Yale University Press, 1975.

Blau, Tatjana and Mirabai Blau. *Buddhist Symbols*. New York: Stirling, 2003.

Bloch, Maurice, and Jonathan Parry, eds. *Death and the Regeneration of Life*, Cambridge: Cambridge University Press, 1982.

Blofeld, John. *The Tantric Mysticism of Tibet: A Practical Guide to the Theory, Purpose, and Techniques of Tantric Meditation*. New York: Causeway Books, 1974.

_____. *Bodhisattva of Compassion: the Mystical Tradition of Kuan Yin*. Boston: Shambhala, 1988.

_____. *I Ching: The Book of Change*. London: Unwin Hyman, 1989 [1965].

_____. *My Journey in Mystic China: Old Pu's Travel Diary*, translated by Daniel Reid. Rochester, VT: Inner Traditions, 2008 [1990].

Boehme, Jakob. *Genius of the Transcendent: Mystical Writings of Jakob Boehme*. Translated and edited by Michael L. Birkel and Jeff Bach. Boston: Shambhala, 2010.

Bouisson, Maurice. *Magic: Its History and Principal Rites*, translated by G. Almayrac. New York: Dutton, 1961.

Bowker, John. *World Religions: The Great Faiths Explored & Explained*. London: DK Publishing Books, 1997.

Bradley, Richard. *Ritual and Domestic Life in Prehistoric Europe*. London: Routledge, 2005.

Brandon, S. G. F. *Man and God in Art and Ritual: A Study of Iconography, Architecture and Ritual Action as Primary Evidence of Religious Belief and Practice*. New York: Charles Scribner's Sons, 1975.

Brauen, Martin. *Mandala: Sacred Circle in Tibetan Buddhism*. New York: Rubin Museum of Art, 2009.

Breaux, Charles. *Journey into Consciousness: The Chakras, Tantra, and Jungian Psychology*. York Brach, ME: Nicholas-Hays, 1989.

Briggs, John. *Fire in the Crucible: The Alchemy of Creative Genius*. New York: St. Martin's Press, 1988.

Brinton, Howard H. *The Mystic Will: Based on a Study of the Philosophy of Jacob Boehme*. New York: Macmillan, 1930.

Bronkhorst, Hohannes. *Buddhist Teaching in India*. Boston: Wisdom Publications, 2009.

Bruce-Mitford, Miranda. *The Illustrated Book of Signs & Symbols*. Westmount: Reader's Digest Association (Canada) Ltd., 1996.

Budge, E. A. Willis. *Osiris and the Egyptian Resurrection*, 2 vols. London: P. L. Warner and G. P. Putnam's Sons, 1911.

_____. *Egyptian Magic*. New York: Dover Publications, 1971.

Buonaiuti, Ernesto. "Symbols and Rites in the Religious Life of Certain Monastic Orders," in J. Campbell, ed. *The Mystic Vision*, pp. 168–209. Bollingen Series XXX-6, Princeton, NJ: Princeton University Press, 1982.

Burckhardt, Titus. *Alchemy*. Translated by William Stoddart. Longmead, UK: Element Books Ltd., 1986.

Burkert, Walter. *Ancient Mystery Cults*. Cambridge, MA: Harvard University Press, 1987.

Burland, Cotttie A. *The Magical Arts: A Short History*. London: Arthur Barker Limited, 1966.

_____. *The Arts of the Alchemists*. New York: MacMillan, 1967.

_____. *Beyond Science: A Journey into the Supernatural*. New York: Grossett & Dunlap, 1972.

_____. *Myths of Life and Death*. New York: Crown Publishers, 1974.

Burt, Cyril. "Judgement of the Dead" in R. Cavendish, ed. *Man, Myth & Magic: The Illustrated Encyclopedia of Mythology, Religion and the Unknown*, pp. 1447–1462. North Bellmore, NY: Marshall Cavendish Corporation, 1995.

Butler, Dom B. *Western Mysticism: The Teaching of Augustine, Gregory and Bernard on Contemplation of the Contemplative Life*. London: Constable, 1967 [1922].

Cabezón, José Ignacio, ed. *Tibetan Ritual*. Oxford: Oxford University Press, 2010.

Campbell, Joseph. *The Masks of God: Oriental Mythology*. New York: The Viking Press, 1962.

_____. *The Mystic Image*. Bollingen Series C. Princeton NJ: Princeton University Press, 1974.

_____. *The Masks of the Gods: Primitive Mythology*. New York: Penguin Books USA, 1976.

_____. *Transformations of Myths Through Time*. New York: Perennial Library, Harper & Row Publishers, 1990.

_____. *Myths of Light: Eastern Metaphors of the Eternal*, Edited by David Kudler. Joseph Campbell Foundation. Navato, CA: New World Library, 2003.

Capra, Fritjof. *The Tao of Physics*. Boston: Shambhala, 2000.

Cavendish, Richard, ed. *Man, Myth & Magic: The Illustrated Encyclopedia of Mythology, Religion and the Unknown*. New York: Marshall Cavendish, 1995.

Chamalún, Luis Espinoza. *The Gate of Paradise: Secrets of Andean Shamanism*, translated by Hilary Dyke. Bath, UK: Gateway Books, 1998.

Chen, Robert Shanmu. *Asian Thought and Culture: A*

Comparative Study of Chinese and Western Cyclic Myths. New York: Peter Lang, 1992.

Chang, Chung-Yuan. *Original Teachings of Ch'an Buddhism: Selected from The Transmission of the Lamp*. New York: Pantheon Books, 1969.

Chernetsov, Valeriy Nikolayevich. "Concepts of the Soul Among the Ob Ugrians" In: Henry N. Michael, ed. *Studies in Siberian Shamanism*, pp. 3–45. Toronto: Arctic Institute of North America by University of Toronto Press, 1963.

Child, Alice B. and Child Irvin L. *Religion and Magic in the life of Traditional Peoples*. Englewood Cliffs, NJ: Prentice-Hall, 1993.

Child, Heather and Dorothy Colles. *Christian Symbols Ancient and Modern*. London: G. Bell and Sons, 1971.

Chkashige, Masumi. *Chinese Alchemy*. New York: Samuel Weiser, 1974.

Chopra, Deepak. "Preface: The Art of Healing," pp. 8–11, in Ian A. Baker, *The Tibetan Art of Healing*. San Francisco: Chronicle Books, 1997.

Christie, Anthony. *Chinese Mythology: Library of the Worlds Myths and Legends*. New York: Peter Bedrick Books, 1983.

Cirlot, Juan Edwardo. *A Dictionary of Symbols*, translated by Jack Sage. New York: Philosophical Library, 1962.

Clément, Olivier. *The Roots of Christian Mysticism*, translated by Theodore Berkeley and Jeremy Hummerstone. New York: New City Press, 1995.

Cochren, A. *History of Alchemy*. http://www.alchemylab.com/history_of_alchemy.htm (accessed April 9, 2010.

Codd, Edward. *Magic in Names and Other Things*. Detroit, MI: Singing Tree Press, 1968.

Collins, John J. *Primitive Religion*. New York: Rowman and Littlefield, 1978.

Conrad, Joseph. *Heart of Darkness*. New York: Alfred A. Knopf, 1967.

Constable, George ed. *Secrets of the Alchemists*. Alexandria, VA: Time-Life Books, 1990.

Conze, Edward, ed. *Buddhist Wisdom Books: The Diamond Sutra and the Heart Sutra*. London: George Allen & Unwin, 1975 [1958].

Coomaraswamy, Ananda K. *Buddha and the Gospel of Buddhism*. New Delhi: Munshiram Manoharlal Publishers Private, Ltd., 1985 [1972].

Cooper, J. C. *Taoism: The Way of the Mystic*. New York: Samuel Weiser, 1972.

Copleston, Reginald S. *Theravāda Buddhism*, edited by Harcharan Singh Sobti. Delhi: Eastern Books Linkers, 1993 [1892].

Crapanzano, Vincent and Vivian Garrison. *Case Studies in Spirit Possession*. New York: Wiley, 1977.

Dan, Joseph. *Jewish Mysticism and Jewish Ethics*. Northvale, NJ: Jason Aronson, 1996.

Das, C. S. *A Tibetan-English Dictionary with Sanskrit Synonyms*. New Delhi: Guarav, 1985 [1903].

David-Neel, Alexandra. *My Journey to Lhasa*. Boston: Beacon Press, 1986 [1927].

_____. *With Mystics and Magicians in Tibet*. London: John Lane, 1931.

_____. *Magic and Mystery in Tibet*. London: Mandala, 1965.

d'Aquili, Eugene G., C. D. Laughlin, and J. McManus. *The Spectrum of Ritual: A Biogenetic Structural Analysis*. New York: Columbia University Press, 1979.

_____, and A. B. Newberg. *The Mystical Mind: Probing the Biology of Religious Experience*. Minneapolis, MN: Fortress Press, 1999.

De Harlez, Charles. "Laotze, le premier philosophe chinois" In: *Mémoires couronnés et autres de l'Académie* (Brussels: Académie Royale de Belgique, January, 1886), In: Sauvage, G. M. "Mysticiam" In: Catholic Encyclopedia, Volume X., Transcribed by Elizabeth T. Knuth. (New York: Robert Appleton, 1911. http://www.newadvent.org/cathen/index.html

de Nebesky-Wojkowitz, Réne. *Oracles and Demons of Tibet*. Varamasi, India: Book Faith, 1993.

Deng, Ming-Dao. *Chronicles of Tao: The Secret Life of a Taoist Master*. San Francisco: HarperSanFrancisco, 1993.

de Rola, Stanislas K. *The Golden Game: Alchemical Engravings of the Seventeenth Century*. London: Thames and Hudson, 1997.

Desikachar, T.K.V. *The Heart of Yoga: Developing A Personal Practice*. Rochester, VT: Inner Traditions International, 1995.

de Waal Malefijt, Annemarie. *Religion and Culture: An Introduction to Anthropology of Religion*. New York: Macmillan, 1968.

Dhonden, Yeshi. *Healing from the Source: The Science and Lore of Tibetan Medicine*. Edited and Translated by B. Alan Wallace. Ithaca, NY: Snow Lion Publications, 2000.

Dissanayake, Ellen. *What is Art For?* Seattle: University of Washington Press, 1988.

Doctors, Diviners, and Magicians of Ancient China. Translated by Kenneth J. DeWoskin. New York: Columbia University Press, 1983.

Doig, James. C. *Aquinas on Metaphysics: A Histroico-Doctrinal Study of the Commentary on the Metaphysics*. The Hague: Martinus Nijhoff, 1972.

Douglas, Mary. *Natural Symbols: Explorations in Cosmology*, New York: Pantheon Books, 1982.

Douglas, Nik. *Tibetan Tantric Charms and Amulets*. New York: Dover Publications, 1978.

Dowman, Keith. *The Sacred Life of Tibet*. San Francisco: Thorsons, 1997.

Drury, Nevill. *Dictionary of Mysticism and the Esoteric Traditions*. Santa Barbara, CA: ABC-CLIO, 1992.

Durkheim, Émile. *The Elementary Forms of the Religious Life*. Glencoe, IL: The Free Press, 1954.

_____. *The Rules of Sociological Method*, George E. G. Catlin, ed., translated by Sarah A. Solovay and John H. Mueller. New York: Free Press, 1966.

Edson, Gary. *Shamanism: A Cross-Cultural Study of Beliefs and Practices*. Jefferson, NC: McFarland, 2009.

Effortless Being: The Yoga Sutras of Patanjali. Translated by Alistair Shearer. London: Unwin Paperbacks, 1982.

Eliade, Mircea. *Myths, Dreams, and Mysteries*, translated by Philip Mairet. New York: Harpers & Brothers Publishers, 1960.

_____. "Recent Works on Shamanism." In: *History of Religion*, I, 1961. Chicago: University of Chicago Press, 1961.

_____. *Myth and Reality*, translated by Willard R. Trask. New York: Harper Torchbooks, 1963.

_____. *Shamanism: Archaic Techniques of Ecstasy*. Translated by Willard R. Trask. Bollingen Series LXXVI, Princeton NJ: Princeton University Press, 1964.

_____. *A History of Religious Ideas*, vol. 1. Translated by Willard R. Trask. Chicago: University of Chicago Press, 1978a.

_____. *The Forge and The Crucible*, 2d, translated by Stephen Corrin. Chicago and London: University of Chicago Press, 1978b [1956].

_____. *The Sacred and the Profane: The Nature of Religion*, translated by Willard R. Trask. New York: A Harvest Book, Harcourt, 1987 [1957].

_____. *Images and Symbols: Studies in Religious Symbolism*, translated by Philip Mairet. Princeton, NJ: Princeton University Press, 1991 [1952].

_____. *Symbolism, the Sacred, and the Arts*, edited by Diane Apostolos-Cappadona. New York: Continuum, 1992.

_____. *Yoga: Immortality and Freedom*, translated by Willard R. Trask. Bollingen Series LVI, Princeton NJ: Princeton University Press, 2009 [1958].

Ellwood, Robert S. Jr. *Mysticism and Religion*. Englewood Cliffs, NJ: Prentice_Hall, 1980.

Ember, Carol R., and Melvin Ember. *Anthropology*. 9th ed. Upper Saddle River, NJ: Prentice Hall, 1999 [1973].

Encyclopaedia Britannica Library. From Encyclopaedia Britannica 2005 Deluxe Edition CD-ROM. Encyclopaedia Britannica, 1994–2003.

Encyclopedia of Magic & Superstition: Alchemy, Charms, Dreams, Omans, Rituals, Talismans, Wishes. London: Octopus Books Limited, 1974.

Ennemoser, Joseph. *History of Magic*, vol. II, translated by William Howitt. New York: University Books, 1970.

Epstein, Perle. *Oriental Mystics and Magicians*. Garden City, NY: Doubleday, 1975.

Erikson, Erik. H. *The Life Cycle Completed*. New York: W. W. Norton, 1998 [1982].

Essential Visual History of World Mythology. Washington, D.C.: National Geographic, 2008.

Evens-Wentz, W. Y., ed. *The Tibetan Book of the Dead or the After-Death Experiences on the Bardo Plane, according to Lama Kazi Dawa-Samdupu's English Rendering*. London: Oxford University Press, 1960 [1927].

_____, ed. *Tibet's Great Yogi, Milarepa*. 2d. ed. London: Oxford University Press, 1969 [1928].

_____, ed. *Tibetan Yoga and Secret Doctrines or Seven Books of Wisdom of the Great Path, According to the Late Lama Kazi Dawa-Samdup's English Rendering*, 2d. Translated by Chen-Chi Chang. London: Oxford University Press, 2000 [1958].

Eversole, Finley. *Art and Spiritual Transformation: The Seven Stages of Death and Rebirth*. Rochester, VT: Inner Traditions, 2009.

Fabricius, Johannes. *Alchemy: The Medieval Alchemists and Their Royal Art*. Copenhagen: Rosenkilde and Bagger, 1976.

Fadiman, James, and Robert Frager, eds. *Essential Sufism*. San Francisco: HarperSanFrancisco, 1987.

Fairweather, William. *Among the Mystics*. Freeport, NY: Books for Libraries Press, 1968 [1936].

Fanning, Steven. *Mystics of the Christian Tradition*. London: Routledge, 2001 [1936].

Fardon, Richard, ed. *Power and Knowledge: anthropological and sociological approaches:* proceedings of a conference held at the University of St. Andrews. Edinburgh: Scottish Academic Press, 1985.

Federmann, R. *The Royal Art of Alchemy*, translated by Richard H. Weber. Philadelphia: Chilton Book, 1964.

Fenton, Peter. *Tibetan Healing: The Modern Legacy of Medicine Buddha*. Wheaton, IL: Quest Books, 1999.

Ferguson, George. *Signs and Symbols of Christian Art*. New York: Oxford University Press, 1959.

Ferguson, John. *Encyclopedia of Mysticism and Mystery Religions*. New York: Crossroad, 1982 [c1976].

Fernando, Diana. *Alchemy: An Illustrated A to Z*. London: Blandford, a Cassell Imprint, 1998.

Feuerstein, Georg. ed. *The Yoga-Sutra of Patanjali: A New Translation and Commentary*. Rochester, VT: Inner Traditions International, 1989.

_____. *Teachings of Yoga*. Boston and New York: Shambhala, 1997.

_____. *Tantra: The Path of Ecstasy*. Boston: Shambhala, 1998a.

_____. *The Yoga Tradition: It History, Literature, Philosophy, and Practice*. Prescott, AZ: Hohm Press, 1998b.

_____, Subhash Kak, and David Frawley. *In Search of the Cradle of Civilization: New Light on Ancient India*. Wheaton, IL: Quest Books, 1995.

Fisher, Robert E. *Buddhist Art and Architecture*. London: Thames and Hudson, 1993.

_____. *Art of Tibet*. London: Thames and Hudson, 1997.

Fisher-Schreiber, Ingrid, Franz-Karl Ehrhard, Kurt Friedrichs, and Michael S. Diener. *The Encyclopedia of Eastern Philosophy and Religion*. Boston: Shambhala, 1994.

Flaherty, Gloria. *Shamanism and the Eighteenth Century*. Princeton, NJ: Princeton University Press, 1992.

Fleming, Fergus and Alan Lothian. *The Way to Eternity: Egyptian Myths*. London: Duncan Baird Publishers, 1997.

Flesher, P. Buddhist Glossary, Religious Studies Program. University of Wyoming, http://uwacad wib.uwyo/religionet/er/default.htm (accessed November 23, 2010).

Fontana, David. *The Secret Language of Symbols*. San Francisco: Chronicle Books, 1994.

_____. *The New Secret Language of Symbols: An Illustrated Key to Unlocking their Deep and Hidden Meaning*. London: Duncan Baird Publishers, 2010.

Forsyth, James. *A History of the Peoples of Siberia: Russia's North Asian Colony 1581–1990*. Cambridge: Cambridge University Press, 1992.

Fortune, Dion. *The Mystical Qabalah*. York Beach, ME: Samuel Weiser, 1997 [1935].

Forty, Jo. *Mythology: A Visual Encyclopedia*. London: PRC Publishing Ltd., 2001.

Franck, Adolphe. *The Kabbalah: The Religious Philosophy of the Hebrews*. New York: Bell, 1940.

Frawley, David. *Yoga & Ayurveda: Self-Healing and Self Realization*. Twin Lakes, WI: Lotus Press, 1999.

Frazer, James George. *The Magic Art*. 3d ed. vols. I and II. London: Macmillan, 1922.

_____. *Fear of the Dead in Primitive Religion*, vol. III. London: Macmillan, 1936.

_____. *The Golden Bough: A Study of Magic and Religion*, vol. I. New York: Macmillan, 1958.

Frédéric, Louis. *Buddhism: Flammarion Iconographic Guides*. Paris and New York: Flammarion, 1995.

Freke, Timothy and Peter Gandy. *The Complete Guide to World Mysticism*. London: Judy Piatkus Publishers, 1997.

_____. *The Hermetica: The Lost Wisdom of the Pharaohs*. New York: Tarcher Cornerstone Editions, Penguin Group, 1999.

Fried, Martha N., and Morton H. Fried. *Transitions: Four Rituals in Eight Cultures*. New York: W. W. Norton, 1980.

Fromm, James R. "Alchemy." *Third Millenium Online*. http:/www.3rd1000.com/history/alchemy.htm

Fung, Yu-Lan. *A Short History of Chinese Philosophy*, ed. Derk Bodde. New York: The Free Press, 1948.

_____. *Chaung-Tzu: A New Selected Translation with an Exposition of the Philosophy of Kuo Hsiang*. Beijing: Foreign Languages Press, 1997 [1931].

Gaisseau, Pierre-Dominique. *The Sacred Forest: Magic and Secret Rites in French Guinea*, translated by Stephen Becker. New York: Alfred A. Knopf, 1954.

Gard, Richard A. ed. *Buddhism*. New York: George Braziller, 1962.

Gardner, Harold. *The Arts and Human Development*. New York: BasicBooks, 1994 [1973].

Gardner, Joseph L., ed. *Mysteries of the Ancient Americans: The New World before Columbus*. Pleasantville, NY: Reader's Digest Association, 1986.

Gayheart, Robert B. "Origin of the Name 'Chemistry'" http://hilltop.bradley.edu/~rbg/Origin.html.

Gellman, Jerome, "Mysticism," Stanford Encyclopedia of Philosophy http://plato.stanford.edu/cgi-bin/encyclopedia/archinfo.cgi (accessed November 18, 2009).

George, Robert A. ed. *Studies in Mythology*. Homewood, IL: Dorsay Press, 1968.

Gilbert, Robert A. "Occultism." Encyclopædia Britannica, from *Encyclopædia Britannica Deluxe Edition 2005 CD*. Encyclopædia Britannica, 1994–2004.

Gillette, Douglas. *The Shaman's Secret: The Lost Resurrection Teachings of the Ancient Maya*. New York: Bantam Books, 1997.

Gimello, Robert M. "Mysticism in Its Contexts" in: Steven T. Katz, ed. *Mysticism and Religious Traditions*, pp. 61–88. Oxford: Oxford University Press, 1983.

Gombrich, E. H. *Art and Illusion: A Study in the Psychology of Pictorial Representation*, 2d. ed. Bollingen Series XXXV-5, Kingsport, TN: Kingsport Press, 1961.

Goodman, Falicitas D. *Ecstasy, Ritual, and Alternate Reality: Religion in a Pluralistic World*. Bloomington: Indiana University Press, 1988.

Good News Bible. New York: United Bible Societies, 2007.

Gordon, Antoinetta K. *Tibetan Religious Art*. New York: Columbia University Press, 1952.

_____. *The Iconography of Tibetan Lamaism*. New Delhi: Munshiram Manoharlal Publishers Pvt. Ltd., 1998

Goudsblom, Johan, Eric Jones, and Stephen Mennell. *The Course of Human History*. New York: M.E. Sharpe, 1996.

Govinda, Lama Anagarika. *Foundations of Tibetan Mysticism*. York Beach, ME: Samuel Weiser, 1969.

_____. *The Way of White Clouds: A Buddhist in Tibet*, 5th imp. London: Rider, 1974 [1966].

Graf, Fritz. *Magic in the Ancient World*, translated by Franklin Philip. Cambridge, MA: Harvard University Press, 1997.

Grant, Patrick. *Literature of Mysticism in Western Tradition*. New York: St. Martin's Press, 1983.

Guenther, Herbert V. *The Life and Teaching of Naropa*. London: Oxford University Press, 1963.

Guiley, Rosemary E. *The Encyclopedia of Magic and Alchemy*. New York: Facts on File an imprint of Infobase Publishing, 2006.

Hackin, J, Clement Huart, Raymonde Linossier, H. de Wilman-Grabowska, Charles-Henri Marchal, Henri Maspero, and Serge Eliseev. *Asiatic Mythology: A detailed Description and Explanation of the Mythologies of All the Great Nations of Asia*. New York: Crescent Books, 1963.

Hagen, R-M, and R. Hagen *L'Egypte: Les homes, les dieux, les pharaons*. Köln: Taschen Verlag GmbH, 1999.

Halifax, Joan. *Shamanic Voices*. New York: E. P. Dutton, 1979.

_____. *Shaman: The Wounded Healer*. London: Thames and Hudson, 1982.

Hall, Manly Palmer. *The Guru: By his Disciple*. Los Angeles: Philosophical Research Society, 1944.

Happold. F. C. *Mysticism: A Study and an Anthology*. New York: Penguin Books 1985 [1963].

Hare, William Loftus. *Mysticism of East and West: Studies in Mystical and Moral Philosophy*. New York: Harcourt, Brace, 1923.

Harmonizing Yin and Yang: The Dragon–Tiger Classic, translated and introduced by Eve Wong. Boston: Shambhala, 1997.

Harpur, James, ed. *The World's Religions: Understanding the Living Faiths*. New York: Reader's Digest Association, 1993.

Harrison, Jane Ellen. *Ancient Art and Ritual*. New York: Henry Holt, 1913.

Hart, George. *A Dictionary of Egyptian Gods and Goddesses*. London: Routledge, 1996.

Harvey, Andrew, ed. *The Essential Mystics: Selections from the World's Great Wisdom Tradition*. San Francisco: HarperSanFrancisco, 1997.

_____. ed. *The Essential Mystics: The Soul's Journey into Truth*. Edison, NJ: Castle Books, 1998.

Harvey, Graham, ed. *Readings in Indigenous Religions*. London: Continuum, 2002.

Hastings, James, ed. *Encyclopædia of Religion and Ethics*, vol. XI. New York: Charles Scribner's Sons, 1951.

———. ed. *Encyclopædia of Religion and Ethics*. Edinburgh: T. & T. Clark, 1980.

———. ed. *Encyclopædia of Religion and Ethics*. Edinburgh: T. & T. Clark, 1994.

Hauck, Dennis W. *The Emerald Tablet: Alchemy for Personal Transformation*. New York: Penguin Compass, 1999.

Hayden, Brian. *Shamans, Sorcerers and Saints: A Prehistory of Religion*. Washington D.C.: Smithsonian Books, 2003.

Hefner, Alan G. *The Mystica*. Last modified June 12, 2008. http://www.themystica.com/mystica/default.html

Heidegger, Martin. *The Fundamental Concepts of Metaphysics: World, Finitude, Solitude*, translated by William McNeill and Nicholas Walker. Bloomington: Indiana University Press, 1995.

Heinze, Ruth-Inge, ed. *The Nature and Function of Rituals: Fire from Heaven*. Westport, CT: Bergin & Garvey, 2000.

Heissig, Walter. *The Religions of Mongolia*, translated by Geoffrey Samuel. Berkeley: University of California Press. 1980.

Heller, Amy. *Tibetan Art: Tracing the Development of Spiritual Ideals and Art in Tibet 600–2000 A.D.* Suffolk, UK: Jaca Book, Antique Collectors' Club, 1999.

H. H. The Dalai Lama. *A Simple Path*, translated by Geshe Thupten Jinpa, edited by Dominique Side. London: Thorsons, 2000.

———. *The Universe in a Single Atom: The Convergence of Science and Spirituality*. New York: Morgan Road Books, 2005.

———. *The Middle Way: Faith Grounded in Reason*, translated by Thupten Jinpa. Boston: Wisdom Publications, 2009.

———. *Becoming Enlightened*, translated and edited by Jeffrey Hopkins. New York: Atria Books, 2009.

———, Tsong-ka-pa, and Jeffrey Hopkins. *Tantra in Tibet*, translated and edited by Jeffrey Hopkins. Ithaca, NY: Snow Lion Publications, 1987.

Hill, Douglas. *Magic and Superstition*. London: Hamlyn Publishing Group Ltd., 1968.

Hindsley, Leonard. *The Mystics of Engelthal: Writings from a Medieval Monastery*. New York: St. Martin's Press, 1998.

Hitchcock, John T. and Rex L. Jones, eds. *Spirit Possession in the Napal Himalaya*. London: Warminster, 1976.

Hoebel, Edward Adamson. *Man in the Primitive World*, 2d ed. New York: McGraw-Hill Book, 1958.

Holmyard, Eric John. *Alchemy*. New York: Dover Publications, 1990 [1957].

Hopfe, Lewis M. *Religions of the World*, 6th ed. Lavinia R. Hopfe and Lewis M. Hopfe, Jr., ed. New York: Maxwell Macmillan International, 1994 [1970].

Hopkins, Arthur J. *Alchemy Child of Greek Philosophy*. New York: AMS Press, 1967.

Hopkins, Jeffrey. *Tantric Techniques*. Ithaca, NY: Snow Lion Publications, 2008.

Hoppál, Mihály. "Shamanism: Universal Structures and Regional Symbols" pp. 181–192. in: *Shamans and Cultures*, ed. Mihály Hoppál and Kieth Howard. Budapest: Akadémiai Kiadó, 1993.

———. *Studies on Mythology and Uralic Shamanism*. Budapest: Akadémiai Kiadó, 2000.

———, and Gábor Kósa. *Rediscovery of Shamanic Heritage*. Budapest: Akadémiai Kiadó, 2003.

———, and Kieth D. Howard, eds. *Shamans and Cultures*. Budapest: Akadémiai Kiadó. 1993.

Horne, James R. *The Moral Mystic*. Waterloo: Canadian Corporation for Studies in Religion/Corporation Canadienne des Sciences Religieuses by Wilfrid Laurier University Press, 1983.

Howells, William. *The Heathens: Primitive Man and His Religion*. Garden City, NY: Doubleday, 1948.

Huang, Kerson and Rosemary Huang. *I Ching*. New York: Workman, 1987.

Hultkrantz, Åke. "Shamanism: A Religious Phenomenon? In: G. Doore, ed. *Shaman's Path: Healing, Personal Growth and Empowerment*, pp. 33–42. Boston: Shambhala, 1988

———. "The Place of Shamanism in the History of Religions," In: Mohály Hoppál and Otto van Sadovszky. *Shamanism Past and Present*, Part 1. Budapest: Ethnographic Institute, Hungarian Academy of Sciences, 1989.

Hummel, Siegbert. Die *Lamanistische Kunst in der Umwelt von Tibet*. Leipzig: Otto Harrassowitz, 1955.

Humphrey, Caroline with Urgunge Onon. *Shamans and Elders: Experience, Knowledge and Power among the Daur Mongols*. Oxford: Clarendon Press, 1996.

Hutin, Serge. *A History of Alchemy*. New York: Walker, 1963.

Hutton, Ronald. *Shamans: Siberian Spirituality and the Western Imagination*. London: Hambledon and London, 2001.

Huxley, Francis. *The Way of the Sacred*. Garden City, NY: Doubleday, 1974.

Hyman, John. *The Imitation of Nature*. New York: Basil Blackwell Ltd., 1989.

Ions, Veronica. *The World's Mythology*. London, New York and Toronto: 1974.

Inayat Khan, Pir Vilayat. *Awakening: A Sufi Experience*, edited by Pythia Peay. New York: Jeremy P Tarcher—Putnam, 1999.

Iqual, Muhammad. *The Development of Metaphysics in Persia: A Contribution to the History of Muslim Philosophy*. Lahore: Bazm-Iqbal, 1964.

Iyengar, B.K.S. *Yoga: The Path to Holistic Health*. London: Dorling Kindersley, 2001.

———. *The Tree of Yoga*. Boston: Shambhala, 2002.

James, Joseph, ed. *The Way of Mysticism*. London: Jonathan Cape, 1950.

James, William. *The Varieties of Religious Experience*. New York: Collier Books, 1961.

———. *The Will to Believe and Other Essays in Popular Philosophy*. New York: Barnes and Noble Books, 2005 [1897].

Jang, Nam Hyuck. *Shamanism in Korean Christianity*. Seoul: Jimoondang, 2004.

Jisl, Lumir. *Tibetan Art*, translated by Ilse Gottheiner. London: Spring Books, 1957.

Jensen, Adolf E. *Myth and Cult Among Primitive Peo-*

ples. Translated by M. T. Choldin and W. Weissleder. Chicago: University of Chicago Press. 1963 [1951].

Johnson, Sandy. *The Book of Tibetan Elders: Life Stories and Wisdom from the Great Spiritual Masters of Tibet.* New York: Riverhead Books, 1996.

Johnson, Obed S. *A Study of Chinese Alchemy.* Shanghai: Commercial Press, Limited, 1928 reprinted from a copy in the Columbia University Library, New York: Arno Press, 1974.

Jones, Lindsay, ed. *Encyclopedia of Religion.* 2d, Vol. 14; Masaaki, Hattori (Ed.) (1987 & 2005) "*Yogācāra*": p. 9897. Detroit: Macmillan Reference, USA.

Jones, Rufus M. *Studies in Mystical Religion.* New York: Russell & Russell, 1970 [1909].

Jung, Carl G. *Psyche & Symbol,* edited by Violet S. de Laszlo. Garden City, NY: Anchor Original, Doubleday Anchor Books, 1958.

———, ed. *Man and His Symbols.* John Freemen coordinating editor. Garden City, NY: Doubleday, 1964.

———. *Memories, Dreams, Reflections,* Edited by Aniela Jaffé, translated by Richard and Clare Winston. New York: Vintage Books, 1965.

———. *Psychology and Religion: West and East,* 2d. ed. Translated by R.F.G. Hull. Bollingen Series XX, Princeton, NJ: Princeton University Press. 1969.

———. *Mysterium Coniunctionis,* 2d. ed. Translated by R.F.C. Hull, Bollingen Series XX. Princeton, NJ: Princeton University Press, 1970a.

———. *Psychological Reflections: A New Anthology of His Writings 1905–1961,* 2d. Selected and Edited by Jolande Jacobi. Bollingen Series XXXI. Princeton, NJ: Princeton University Press, 1970b [1953].

———. *Mandala Symbolism.* Translated by R.F.G. Hull. Bollingen Series. Princeton, NJ: Princeton University Press, 1973 [1959].

———. *Psychology and Alchemy,* 2d. ed. translated by R.F.C. Hull. Bollingen Series XX, Princeton, NJ: Princeton University Press, 1980 [1952].

Kakar, Sudhir. *Shamans, Mystics & Doctors: A Psychological Inquiry into India and Its Healing Traditions.* Chicago: University of Chicago Press, 1991.

Kalweit, Holger. *Shamans, Healers, and Medicine Men,* translated by Michael H. Kohm. Boston: Shambhala, 1992.

Kant, Immanuel. *Groundwork of the Metaphysic of Morals,* translated and analysed by H. J. Paton. New York: Harper Touchbooks/the Academy Library, 1964 [1948].

Kapferer, Bruce. *The Feast of the Sorcerer: Practices of Consciousness and Power.* Chicago and London: University of Chicago Press, 1997.

Kapstein, Matthew T. *The Tibetans.* Malden, MA: Blackwell, 2006.

———, ed. *Buddhism Between Tibet and China.* Boston: Wisdom Publications, 2009.

Karmay, Samten G. and Jeff Watt, eds. *Bon: The Magic Word.* New York: Rubin Museum of Art, London: Philip Wilson Publishers, 2007.

Katz, Steven T., ed. *Mysticism and Religious Tradition.* Oxford, New York: Oxford University Press, 1983.

Kehoe, Alice Beck. *Shamans and Religion: An Anthropological Exploration in Critical Thinking.* Prospect Heights, IL: Waveland Press, 2000.

Kharitidi, Olga. *Entering the Circle: Ancient Secrets of Siberian Wisdom Discovered by a Russian Psychiatrist.* London: Thorsons, 1996.

Kiev, Ari, ed. *Magic, Faith, and Healing: Studies in Primitive Psychiatry Today.* London: The Free Press of Glencoe, Collier-Macmillan Limited, 1964.

———. *Transcultural Psychiatry.* New York: The Free Press, 1972.

King, Ursula. *Christian Mystics: Their Lives and Legacies throughout the Ages.* Mahwah, NJ: HiddenSpring, 2001.

Kirk, Geoffrey. S. *Myth: Its Meaning and Functions in Ancient and Other Cultures.* Berkeley: University of California Press, 1970.

Kirkland, Russell. *Taoism: The Enduring Tradition.* New York and London: Routledge, 2004.

Kirchweger, Anton Josef. "Golden Chain of Homer" in: *The Stone of the Philosophers: An Alchemical Handbook,* Edited by Poll, M. R. Lafayette, LA: Cornerstone Book Publishers, 2007.

Kister, David A. *Korean Shamanist Ritual: Symbols and Dramas of Transformation.* Budapest: Akadémiai Kiadó, 1997.

Kitagawa, Joseph M. *Religion in Japanese History.* New York: Columbia University Press, 1966.

———. *The Religious Traditions of Asia: Religion, History and Culture.* London: Routledge Curzon, 1987.

Kluckhohn, C. "Myths and Rituals: A General Theory," pp. 137–167 in: R. A. Georges, ed. *Studies on Mythology.* Homewood, IL: The Dorsey Press, 1968.

Knappert, Jan. *The Encyclopedia of Middle Eastern Mythology & Religion.* Shaftesbury, UK: Element Books, 1993.

Knowles, David. *What Is Mysticism.* London: Burns & Oates, 1967.

Kohn, Livia. *Taoist Mystical Philosophy: The Scripture of Western Ascension.* Albany: State University of New York Press, 1991.

———. *Early Chinese Mysticism: Philosophy and Soteriology in the Taoist Tradition.* Princeton, NJ: Princeton University Press, 1992.

Koller, John M. *Oriental Philosophies,* 2d. ed. New York: Charles Scribner's Sons, 1985.

Koyré, Alexandre. *Mystiques, Spirituels, Alchimistes.* Paris: Librairie Armand Colin, 1955.

Kuper, Adam. *The Invention of Primitive Society.* London: Routledge, 1988.

Kurtz, Paul. *The Transcendental Temptation: A Critique of Religion and the Paranormal.* Buffalo, NY: Prometheus Books, 1991.

Kvaerne, Per. *The Bon Religion of Tibet: The Iconography of a Living Tradition.* Boston: Shambhala, 1996.

———. "Bon," in: L. Jones, Editor in chief. *Encyclopedia of Religion,* 2d ed, vol. 2. pp. 1007–1010. New York: Thompson Gale, 2005.

La Fontaine, J.S. *Initiation: Ritual Drama and Secret Knowledge Across the World.* Harmondsworth, UK: Penguin Books, 1985.

Lam, Susan Y. Y., ed. *Ancient Taoist Art from Shanxi Province.* Hong Kong: University Museum and Art Gallery, University of Hong Kong, 2003.

Lopön, Trnzin Namdak Rinpoche. "The Condensed Meaning of an Explanation of the Teachings of

Yungdurng Bon," Translated by John Reynolds (Kathmandu, Nepal: Bonpo Foundation, 1991) http://bon-encyclopedia.wikispaces.com/lopon+yung drung+condensed (Accessed June 1, 2011).

Lang, Andrew. *Myth, Ritual and Religion*, vols. I & II. New York: Longmans, Green and Co., 1913.

Lao Tzu. *Tao Te Ching*, translated by Ralph Alan Dale. New York: Barnes & Noble, 2002.

Leclant, Jean, director. *Le Mode Égyptien: Les Pharaons*. Paris: Editions Gallimard, 1979.

Lee, Sherman. E. *A History of Far Eastern Art*. Englewood Cliffs, NJ: Prentice-Hall, 1973.

Leeming, David. A. *The World of Myth*. New York: Oxford University Press, 1990.

_____. *A Dictionary of Asian Mythology*. Oxford: Oxford University Press, 2001.

Leidy, Denise Patry. *The Art of Buddhism: An Introduction to its History and Meaning*. Boston: Shambhala, 2008.

Leuba, James, H. *The Psychology of Religious Mysticism*. London: Kegan Paul, Trench, Trubner Ltd. 1928.

Levenson, Claude. *Symbols of Tibetan Buddhism*, translated by Nissin Marshall. New York: Barnes and Noble Books, 2003.

Lévi-Strauss, Claude. *Structural Anthropology*, translated by Claire Jacobson and Brooke G. Schoepf. New York: Basic Books, 1963.

Levin, Mikhail Grigor and Leonid Pavlovich Potapov, eds. *The Peoples of Siberia*, translated by Scripta Technica, English translation edited by Stephen Dunn. Chicago: University of Chicago Press, 1956.

Lewis, I. M. *Symbols and Sentiments*. New York: Academic Press, 1977.

_____. *Ecstatic Religion: A Study of Shamanism and Spirit Possession*. 2d ed. New York: Routledge, 1989.

Lin, Yu Tang, ed. *The Wisdom of China and India*. New York: Random House, 1942.

Lindemans, Micha. F. "Yogini." *Encyclopedia Mythica*. http://www.pantheon.org/articles/y/yogini.html (accessed February 9, 2011).

Linden, Stanton J. *Mystical Metal of Gold: Essays on Alchemy and Renaissance Culture*. New York: AMS Press, 2007.

Lindsay, Jack. *A Short History of Culture*. New York: Citadel Press, 1963.

_____. *The Origins of Alchemy in Graeco-Roman Egypt*. New York: Barnes & Noble, 1970.

Little, Stephen. *Taoism and the Arts of China*. Chicago: The Art Institution of Chicago, 2000.

Lommel, Andreas. *The World of the Early Hunters*. Translated by Michael Bullock. London: Evelyn, Adams & MacKay, 1967.

Lopez, Jr., Donald S., ed. *Asian Religions in Practice*. Princeton, NJ: Princeton University Press, 1999.

Lowell, Percival. *Occult Japan or The Way of the Gods*. Boston: Houghton, Mifflin, 1895.

Lowenstein, Tom. *Treasures of the Buddha: The Glories of Sacred Asia*. London: Duncan Baird Publishers, 2006.

Lowie, Robert. H. *Primitive Religion*. New York: Liveright Corporation, 1952 [1924].

Lu, K'uan Yü. *Taoist Yoga: Alchemy and Immortality*. New York: Samuel Weiser, 1973.

Lubar, Steve, and W. David Kingery, eds. *History from Things: Essays on Material Culture*, Washington, D.C.: Smithsonian Institution Press, 1993.

Lubbock, John. *Prehistoric Times*. London: Williams & Norgate, 1865.

_____. *The Origin of Civilization and the Primitive Condition of Man*. London: Longman, 1870.

Mackenzie, D. A. *Myths and Legends Series: China and Japan*. London: Bracken Books, 1985.

Maddox, John Lee. *Medicine Man: A Sociological Study of the Character and Evolution of Shamanism*. New York: Macmillan, 1923.

Malinowski, Bronislaw. *A Scientific Theory of Culture*. Chapel Hill: University of North Carolina Press, 1944.

_____. *Sex, Culture, and Myth*. London: Rupert Hart-Davis, 1963.

Malraux, André. *The Metamorphosis of the Gods*, translated by Stuart Gilbert. Garden City, NY: Doubleday, 1960.

Marcotty, Thomas. *Dagger Blessing The Tibetan Phurpa Cult: Reflections and Materials*. Delhi: B. R. Publishing Corporation, 1987.

Maringer, Johannes. *The Gods of Prehistoric Man*. Edited and translated by Mary Ilford. New York: Alfred A. Knopf, 1960.

Markman, Roberta H., and Markman Peter T. *The Flayed God: The Mesoamerican Mythological Tradition*. New York: HarperCollins Publishers, 1992.

Marshack, Alexander. *The Roots of Civilization*. New York: McGraw-Hill Book, 1972.

Martin, Sean. *Alchemy and Alchemists*. Harpenden, Herts, UK: Pocket Essentials, 2006.

Maskarinee, Gregory G. *The Rulings of the Night: An Ethnography of Nepalese Shaman Oral Text*. Madison: University of Wisconsin Press, 1995.

Matt, Daniel C. *The Essential Kabbalah: The Heart of Jewish Mysticism*. Edison, NJ: Castle Books, 1997.

Matthews, Caitlin, and John Matthews. *Walkers Between the Worlds: The Western Mysteries from Shaman to Magus*. Rochester, VT: Inner Traditions, 2003 [1985].

Mauss, Marcel. *A General Theory of Magic*, translated by Robert Brain. London: Routledge, 1972 [1902].

McGhee, Robert. *Ancient People of the Arctic*. Vancouver: UBC Press, Published in Association with the Canadian Museum of Civilization, 1996.

McGill, Ormond. *The Mysticism and Magic of India*. South Brunswick, NJ: A.S. Barnes, 1977.

McGinn, Bernard. *The Foundations of Mysticism*. London: SCM Press, 1992.

McKechnie, Jean L. gen. super. *Webster's New Twentieth Century Dictionary of the English Language*, 2d. New York: William Collins+World, 1977.

McMillan. David W. *Emotion Rituals*, New York: Routledge, 2006.

Merton, Thomas. *Mystics and Zen Masters*. New York: Noonday Press, 1967.

_____. *Thoughts on the East*. New York: New Directions Bibelot, 1995 [1965]).

Meyer, Marvin and Paul Mirecki. *Ancient Magic and Ritual Power*. Leiden: E. J. Brill, 1995.

_____. *Magic and Ritual in the Ancient World*. Leiden: E. J. Brill, 2002.

Middleton, John, ed. *Gods and Rituals: Readings in Religious Beliefs and Practices.* Austin: University of Texas Press, 1981.

Monroe, Charles R. *World Religions: An Introduction.* Amherst, NY: Prometheus Books, 1995.

Morris, Richard. *The Last Sorcerers: The Path from Alchemy to the Periodic Table.* Washington, D.C.: Joseph Henry Press, 2003.

Müller, Klaus. E., U. Ritz-Müller, and Christoph, Henning. *Soul of Africa: Magical Rites and Traditions.* Cologne: Könemann Verlagsgesellschaft mbH, 2000.

Müller-Edeling, Claudia, Christian Rätsch, and Surendra Bahadur Sihahi. *Shamanism and Tantra in the Himalayas,* translated by Annabel Lee. London: Thames & Hudson Ltd, 2002.

Mullin, Glenn H., and Andy Weber. *The Mystical Arts of Tibet.* Atlanta, GA: Longstreet Press, 1996.

Muni Swami Rajarshi. *Yoga: The Ultimate Spiritual Path.* St. Paul, MN: Llewellyn Publications, 2001.

Murray, Henry A., ed. *Myth and Mythmaking.* New York: George Braziller, 1960.

Murthy, K. Krishna. *Buddhism in Tibet.* Delhi: Sundeep Prakashan, 1989.

Nairn, Rob. *Living, Dreaming, Dying.* Boston: Shambhala, 2004.

Needham, Rodney. *Symbolic Classification.* Santa Monica, CA: Goodyear, 1979.

Newell, Zo. *Downward Dogs & Warriors: Wisdom Tales for Modern Yogis.* Honesdale, PA: Himalayan Institute Press, 2007.

Nicholson, Raymond. A., ed. *Kitab al-Luma'* (The Book of Flashes). London: Luzac, 1947.

_____. *The Mystics of Islam.* London: Routledge and Kegan Paul, Ltd., 1970 [1914].

Nivendita, Sister and Ananda K. Coomeraswamy. *Hindus and Buddhists.* London: Bracken Books, 1985.

Noel, Daniel C., ed. *Paths of the Power of Myth.* New York: Crossroad, 1990.

Noss, David S. *A History of the World's Religions,* 12d. Upper Saddle River, NJ: Person Education, 2008.

Norbeck, Edward. *Religion in Primitive Society.* New York: Harper & Row, Publishers, 1961.

Oakes, Lorna and Lucia Gahlin. *Ancient Egypt.* New York: Barnes and Noble, 2006.

O'Keefe, Daniel. L. *Stolen Lightning: The Social Theory of Magic.* New York: Continuum, 1982.

Oliver, Martyn. *History of Philosophy: Great Thinkers from 600 B.C. to the Present Day.* London: Prospero Books, 1999.

Olson, Stuart Alve. *The Jade Emperor's Mind Seal Classic: The Taoist Guide to Health, Longevity, and Immortality.* Rochester, VT: Inner Traditions, 2003.

Oman, John. *The Natural & the Supernatural.* New York: Macmillan, 1931.

Pal, Pratapaditya. *The Sensuous Immortals: A Selection of Sculptures from the Pan-Asian Collection.* Los Angeles: Los Angeles County Museum of Art, 1977.

_____, and Amy Heller. *Himalayas: An Aesthetic Adventure.* San Francisco: University of California Press, 2003.

Palmer, Martin, and Jay Ramsay, with Man-Ho Kwok. *The Kuan Yin Chronicles: The Myths and Prophecies of the Chinese Goddess of Compassion.* Charlottesville, VA: Hampton Roads, 2009.

Pant, Jitendra, ed. *Himalayan Mysteries.* New Delhi: Roli & Janssen BV, 2001.

Paolucci, Henry. *Hegel: On The Arts.* New York: Frederick Unger, 1979.

Parman, Susan. *Dream and Culture: An Anthropological Study of the Western Intellectual Tradition.* New York: Praeger, 1991.

Partridge, Christopher, gen. ed. *Introduction to World Religions.* Minneapolis, MN: Fortress Press, 2005.

Paul, Robert. A. *The Tibetan Symbolic World: Psychoanalydtic Explorations.* Chicago: University of Chicago Press, 1982.

Pearlman. Ellen. *Tibetan Sacred Dance: Journey into the Religious and Folk Traditions.* Rochester, VT: Inner Traditions, 2002.

Pearson, James L. *Shamanism and the Ancient Mind: A Cognitive Approach to Archaeology.* Walnut Creek, New York: AltaMira Press, 2002.

Petry, Ray C., ed. *Late Medieval Mysticism.* The Library of Christian Classics, vol. XIII. Philadelphia: The Westminster Press, 1957.

Pinch, Geraldine. *Magic in Ancient Egypt.* Austin: University of Texas Press, 1994.

Plato, *Myths of Plato,* translated with introductory and other observations, by John A. Stewart and edited by G. R. Levy. New York: Barnes and Nobles, 1970 [1905].

Poll, Michael R., ed. *The Stone of the Philosophers: An Alchemical Handbook.* Lafayette, LA: Cornerstone Book Publishers, 2007.

Pope, John A. ed. director. *Mysteries of the Ancient Americas.* Pleasantville, NY: The Reader's Digest Association, 1986.

Porter, Bill. *Road to Heaven: Encounters with Chinese Hermits.* Berkeley, CA: Counterpoint, 1993.

Powell, Andrew. *Living Buddhism.* Berkeley: University of California Press, 1995.

Prabhupada, Swami A.C. Bhaktivedanta. *Bhagavad-gītā as It Is.* New York: The Bhaktivedanta Book Trust, 1972.

Pregadio, Fabrizio. *Encyclopedia of Taoism.* Richmond, VA: Curzon, 2000.

_____. *Great Clarity: Daoism and Alchemy in Early Medieval China.* Stanford, CA: Stanford University Press, 2006.

_____. *Encyclopedia of the History of Science, Technology and Medicine in Non-Western Countries,* 2d. ed. Helaine Selin. Berlin: Springer, c2008. http://www.goldenelixir.com/jindan/jindan_intro.html

Price, John R. *The Alchemist's Handbook.* Carlsbad, CA: Hay House, 2000.

Principe, Lawrence M. and Lloyd DeWitt. *Transmutations: Alchemy in Art.* Philadelphia: Chemical Heritage Foundation, 2002.

Quispel, Gilles. "Gnostic Man: The Doctrine of Basilides" pp. 210–246, in J. Campbell, ed., *The Mystic Vision: Papers from the Eranos Yearbooks,* Bollingen Series XXX-6. Princeton, NJ: Princeton University Press, 1982.

Radha, Swami Sivananda. *Kundalini Yoga for the West.* Spokane, WA: Timeless Books, 1978.

_____. *Mantras: Words of Power*. Kootenay Bay, BC: Timeless Books, 2005.

Radin, Paul. *Primitive Religion: Its Nature and Origin*, 2d. ed. New York: Dover Publications, 1957 [1937].

_____. *The World of Primitive Man*. New York: Grove Press, 1960.

Rambach, Pierre. *The Secret Message of Tantric Buddhism*, translated by Barbara Bray. New York: Rizzoli International Publications, 1979.

Ramsay, Jay. *Alchemy: The Art of Transformation*. London: Thorsons, 1997.

Ratzel, Friedrich. *History of Mankind*, translated by A. J. Butler. New York: Macmillan, 1896.

Ravindra, Ravi. *Yoga and the Teaching of Krishna: Essays on the Indian Spiritual Tradition*, translated by Priscilla Murray. Adyar, India: The Theosophical Publishing House, 1998.

Rawson. Philip. *The Art of Tantra*. London: Thames and Hudson, Ltd., 1973.

_____. *Sacred Tibet*. London: Thames and Hudson, Ltd., 1991.

Read, John. *Prelude to Chemistry: An Outline of Alchemy its Literature and Relationships*. New York: MacMillan, 1937.

_____. *The Alchemist in Life, Literature and Art*. London: Thomas Nelson and Sons Ltd., 1947.

Read, Carveath. *Man and His Superstitions*. London: Senate, an imprint of Studio Editions Ltd., 1995 [1925].

Renou, Louis, ed. *Hinduism*. New York: George Braziller, 1962.

Reynolds, John Myrdhin. "The Bonpo Traditions of Dzogchen." http://www.vajranatha.com/teaching/BonpoDzogchen.html

Reynolds, Valrae. *Tibet A Lost World: The Newark Museum Collection of Tibetan Art and Ethnography*. New York: The American Federation of Arts, 1979.

Richards, Chris, gen. ed. *The Illustrated Encyclopedia of World Religions*. Shaftesbury, Dorset, Rockport, MA: Element Books, Ltd., 1997.

Rinpoche, H.E. Kalu. *Foundations of Tibetan Buddhism*, 3d. ed. Ithaca, NY: Snow Lion Publications, 2004.

Rinpoche, Khenchen Thrangu. *Medicine Buddha Teachings*, translated by Lama Yeshe Gyamtso and edited by Lama Tashi Namgyal. Ithaca, NY: Snow Lion Publications, 2004.

Rinpoche, Sogyal. *The Tibetan Book of Living and Dying*, edited by P. Gaffney and A. Harvey. San Francisco: HarperSanFrancisco, 1992.

Roberts, Gareth. *The Mirror of Alchemy; Alchemical Ideas And Images In Manuscripts And Books From Antiquity To The Seventeenth Century*. Toronto: University of Toronto Press, 1994.

Roberts, Jeremy. *Japanese Mythology A to Z*. New York: Facts on File 2004.

Roob, Alexander. *The Hermetic Cabinet: Alchemy and Mysticism*. Köln: Taschen, GmbH, 2009.

Ross, Nancy Wilson. *Three Ways of Asian Wisdom*. New York: Simon and Schuster, 1966.

Ruffing, Janet K., ed. *Mysticism and Social Transformation*. Syracuse, NY: Syracuse University Press, 2001.

Russell, Bertrand. *Mysticism and Logic*. New York: W. W. Norton, 1929.

_____. *Our Knowledge of the External World*. New York: W. W. Norton, 1929.

_____. *Mysticism and Logic and Other Essays*. London: George Allen & Unwin Ltd., 1963 [1918].

Ryan, Robert. E. *Shamanism and the Psychology of C. G. Jung*. London: Vega, 2002.

Sagalayev, A. M. and I. V. Okryabr'skaya. *Traditional World View of the Turks of Southern Siberia: Sign and Ritual*. Nauka: Novosibirsk, 1990,

Sahlins, Marshall. *Culture and Practical Reason*. Chicago: University of Chicago Press, 1976.

Samuel, Geoffrey. *Civilized Shamans: Buddhism in Tibetan Societies*. Washington, D.C.: Smithsonian Institution Press. 1993.

Sandner, Donald F. and Wong, Stephen H., eds. *The Sacred Heritage: The Influences of Shamanism on Analytical Psychology*. New York: Routledge, 1997.

Sargent, Denny. *Global Ritualism: Myth and Magic Around the World*. St. Paul, MN: Llewellyn Publications, 1994.

Sauvage, George. M. "Mysticiam" In *Catholic Encyclopedia*, vol. X., Transcribed by Elizabeth T. Knuth. New York: Robert Appleton, 1911. http://www.newadvent.org/cathen/index.html

Scarpari, Maurizio. *Ancient China: Chinese Civilization from its Origins to the Tang Dynasty*. New York: Barnes and Noble, 2006.

Scholem, Gershom. *Major Trends in Jewish Mysticism*, 6d. ed. New York: Schocken Books, 1972 [1941].

Schimmel, Annemarie. *Mystical Dimensions of Islam*. Chapel Hill: University of North Carolina Press, 1975.

Schuon, Frithjof. *Logic & Transcendence: A New Translation with Selected Letters*. ed. James S. Cutsinger. Bloomington, IN: World Wisdon, 2009.

Schusky, Ernest. and Culbert, Patrick. *Introducing Culture*, 3d ed. Englewood Cliffs, NJ: Prentice-Hall, 1978.

Seligmann, Kurt. *The History of Magic*. New York: Pantheon Books, 1948.

Service, Elman. R. *Profiles in Ethnology*. New York: Harper & Row, Publishers, 1963.

Shaughnessy, James D. ed. *The Roots of Ritual*. Grand Rapids, MI: William B. Eerdmans, 1973.

Scharfstein, Ben-Ami. *Mystical Experience*. Baltimore, MD: Penguin Books 1974.

Schuhmacher, Stephan and Gert Woerner eds. *The Encyclopedia of Eastern Philosophy and Religion*. Boston: Shambhala, 1989.

Shah, Ikbal Ali, Sirdar. *Occultism: Its Theory and Practice*. New York: Dorset Press, 1993.

Shah, Sayed Idries. *Oriental Magic*. New York: Philosophical Library 1957.

Shore, Bradd. *Culture in Mind: Cognition, Culture, and the Problem of Meaning*. New York: Oxford University Press, 1996.

Silberer, Herbert, and Smith E. Jelliffe. *Problems of Mysticism and its Symbolism*. Whitefish, MT: Kessinger, 2009 [1917].

Simpkins, C. Alexander, and Annellen M. Simpkins. *Meditation for Therapists and their Clients*. New York: W.W. Norton, 2009.

Singleton, Mark. *Yoga Body: The Origins of Modern Posture Practice*. Oxford: Oxford University Press, 2010.

Sivin, Nathan. *Chinese Alchemy: Preliminary Studies*. Cambridge, MA: Harvard University Press. 1968.

Smart, John J. C. "Time and its role in the history of thought and action." Encyclopædia Britannica, from *Encyclopædia Britannica Deluxe Edition 2005 CD*. Encyclopædia Britannica, 1994–2004.

Snellgrove, David. *Buddhist Himalaya: Travels and Studies in a Quest of the Origins and Nature of Tibetan Religion*. Oxford: Bruno Cassirer, 1957.

_____. *Himalayan Pilgrimage: A Study of Tibetan Religion*. Oxford: Bruno Cassirer, 1961.

_____. *Four Lamas of Dolpo*, vol. I. Cambridge, MA: Harvard University Press, 1967.

_____, gen. ed. *The Image of the Buddha*. San Francisco: Kodansha International/UNESCO, 1978.

_____. *The Nine Ways of Bön: Excerpts from "gZibrjid."* Boulder, CO: Prajna Press, 1980.

_____. "Tibet" in: R. Cavendish, R., ed. *Man, Myth & Magic: The Illustrated Encyclopedia of Mythology, Religion and the Unknown*, vol. 19, pp. 2619–2625. New York: Marshall Cavendish, 1995.

Snellgrove, David and Richardson, Hugh. *A Cultural History of Tibet*. Boston: Shambhala, 1968.

Snelling, John. *The Buddhist Handbook: A Complete Guide to Buddhist Teaching and Practice*. London: Rider, 1998.

Sopa, Geshe Lhundup and Jeffery Hopkins. *Practice and Theory of Tibetan Buddhism*. New York: Grove Press, 1976.

Spencer, Sidney Rev. and Bernard J. McGinn. "Christianity," Encyclopædia Britannica, from *Encyclopædia Britannica Deluxe Edition 2005 CD*. Encyclopædia Britannica, 1994–2004.

Spiro, Melford. E. *Burmese Supernaturalism*. Englewood Cliffs, NJ: Prentice-Hill, 1967.

Spineto, Natale. *Les Symboles dans l'Historire de l'Humanité*. Milano: Editoriale Jaca Book spa, 2002.

Stace, W. T. *Mysticism and Philosophy*. Philadelphia: J. B. Lippincott, 1960.

Stavish, Mark. *The Path of Alchemy: Energetic Healing and the World of Natural Magic*. Woodbury, MN: Llewellyn Publications, 2006.

Steiner, Rudolf. *Mysticism at the Dawn of the Modern Age*, 2d. ed., translated by Karl E. Zimmer. Blauvelt, NY: Steinerbooks, 1980.

Stephens, Mark. *Teaching Yoga: Essential Foundations and Techniques*. Berkeley, CA: North Atlantic Books, 2010.

Stevens, Edeard. *Oriental Mysticism*. New York: Paulist Press, 1973.

Stewart, John Alexander. *The Myths of Plato*. New York: Barnes and Noble Inc. 1970 [1905].

Stillman, John Maxson. *The Story of Alchemy and Early Chemistry*. New York: Dover Publications, Inc. 1960 [1924].

Stoddart, William. *Sufism: The Mystical Doctrines and Methods of Islam*. St. Paul, MN: Paragon House, 1985.

Stone, Michael, ed. *Freeing the Body, Freeing the Mind: Writings on the Connections Between Yoga & Buddhism*. Boston: Shambhala, 2010.

Stone, Peter G., and Brian L. Molyneaux, eds. *The Presented Past*. London: Routledge, 1994.

Storm, Rachel. *Indian Mythology: Myths and Legends of India, Tibet and Sri Lanka*. London: Lorenz Books, 2000.

_____. *Mythology of Asia and the Far East*. London: Southwater, 2006.

Sullivan, Lawrence E. *Icanchu's Drum: An Orientation of Meaning in South American Religion*. New York: Macmillan, 1988.

Sumegi, Angela. *Dreamworlds of Shamanism and Tibetan Buddhism*. Albany: State University of New York, 2008.

Sun, X. G., and H. G. Wang, eds. *Haiwaibei jing* (Classic of Regions Beyond the Seas: North). Beijing: CTPC, 1997.

Suzuki, D. T. *Swedenborg: Buddha of the North*, translated and with an Introduction by Andrew Bernstein. West Chester, PA: Swedenborg Foundation, 1996 [1913].

_____. *Mysticism: Christian and Buddhist*. London: Routledge, 2002 {1957}.

Swedenborg, Emanuel. *Apocalypse Revealed: The Arcana There Foretold, Which have Hitherto Remained Concealed*. Philadelphia: J. B. Lippincott 1884.

_____. *Heaven and its Wonders and Hell from Things Heard and Seen*. Philadelphia: J. B. Lippincott, 1890.

Taimni, I. K. *The Science of Yoga: The Yoga-sutra of Patanjali in Sanskrit with translation in Roman, translation in English and commentary*. Wheaton, IL: The Theosophical Publishing House, 1967.

Tambiah, S. J. *Buddhism and the Spirit Cults in Northeast Thailand*, Cambridge: Cambridge University Press, 1970.

Taylor, F. Sherwood. *The Alchemists: Founders of Modern Chemistry*. New York: Henry Schuman, 1949.

The 'Azoth' Series of Basil Valentine, translated and coloured by Adam McLean. Glasgow: Hermetic Studies No. 7, 2000.

The Diamond Sutra, translated by A. F. Price and Wong, Mou-Lam http://tw.myblog.yahoo.com/jw!so3qZkWTExbaL_GEr7EePezdqA—/article?mid=10915&next=10258&l=f&fid=5&sc=1

The Heart Sutra, Translation and commentary by Red Pine (Bill Porter). Berkeley, CA: Counterpoint, 2004.

The Religion of the Sufis. Translated by David Shea and Anthony Troyer. London: Octagon Press, 1979.

The Serpent Power, 3d. ed., translated and edited by A. Avalon. London: Ganesh & Co. 1981 [1913].

Thich, Nath Hanh. *Transformation & Healing: Sutra on the Four Establishments of Mindfulness*. Berkeley, CA: Parallax Press, 1990.

_____. *The Heart of Buddha's Teaching*. New York: Broadway Books, 1999.

Thomas, Keith. *Religion and the Decline of Magic*. Oxford: Oxford University Press. 1971.

Thompson, Charles J. S. *Magic and Healing*. London: Rider, 1946.

Thurman, Robert. *Essential Tibetan Buddhism*. Edison, NJ: Castle Books, 1997.

_____. *The Jewel Tree of Tibet: The Enlightenment*

Engine of Tibetan Buddhism. New York: Free Press, 2005.
Too, Lillian. *Mantras and Mudras: Meditations for the Hands and Voice to Bring Peace and Inner Calm*. London: HarperCollinsPublishers, 2002.
Topitsch, Ernst. "World Interpretation and Self-Interpretation: Some Basic Patterns," pp. 157–173, in: H. A. Murray, ed. *Myth and Mythmaking*. New York: George Braziller, 1960.
Torgovnick, Marianna. *Primitive Passions: Men, Women, and the Quest for Ecstasy*. New York: Alfred A. Knopf, 1997.
Torrance, Robert M. *The Spiritual Quest: Transcendence in Myth, Religion, and Science*. Berkeley: University of California Press. 1994.
Tresidder, Jack. *Dictionary of Symbols: An Illustrated Gide to Traditional Images, Icons and Emblems*. San Francisco: Chronicle Books, 1999.
Tso Te Ching and Hua Hu Ching. *The Complete Works of Lao Tzu*, Translation and Elucidation by Hua-Ching Ni. Los Angeles: Tao of Wellness, 1979.
Tsultem, N. *Mongolian Sculpture*. Ulan-Bator: State Publishing House, 1989.
Tucci, Giuseppe. *Tibet: Land of Snow*, translated by J. E. Stapleton Driver. New York: Stein and Day Publishers, 1967.
_____. *The Religions of Tibet*, translated by Geoffrey Samuel. Berkeley and: University of California Press, 1988.
Tucci, Giuseppe, Hajime Nakamura, and Frank E. Reynolds. "Suffering, impermanence, and no-self" Encyclopædia Britannica, from *Encyclopædia Britannica Deluxe Edition 2005 CD*. Encyclopædia Britannica, 1994–2004.
Tulku, Tarthang. *Tibetan Relaxation: The Illustrated Guide to Kum Nye Massage and Movement—A Yoga from the Tibetan Tradition*. London: Duncan Baird Publishers, 2007.
Turner, Victor. *The Forest of Symbols: Aspects of Ndembu Ritual*. Ithaca, NY: Cornell University Press, 1967.
Underhill, Evelyn. *Practical Mysticism*. New York: P. P. Dutton & Co., 1960.
_____. *Mystics of the Church*. New York: Schocken Books, 1964.
_____. *The Way of the Spirit*, edited by Grace A. Brame. New York: Crossroad, 1990.
_____. *Mysticism: A Study in the Nature and Development of Spiritual Consciousness*. Mineola, NY: Dover, 2002 (unaltered reproduction of the 12th edition, 1930, published by E. P. Dutton, of the work originally published in 1911).
Underhill, Ruth. *Red Man's Religion: Beliefs and Practices of the Indians North of Mexico*. Chicago: University of Chicago Press, 1965.
Underwood, Horace. G. *The Religions of Eastern Asia*. New York: The Macmillan, 1910.
Valentine, Basil. "Triumphal Chariot of Antimony" pp. 174–280 in M. R. Poll, ed. *The Stone of the Philosophers*. Lafayette, LA: Cornerstone Books Publishers, 2007.
Van Deusen, Kira. *Singing Story, Healing Drum*. Montreal & Kingston and London: McGill-Queen's University Press, 2004.
Van Over, Raymond, ed. *Chinese Mystics*. New York: Harper & Row, Publishers, 1973.
Varenne, Jean. *Yoga and the Hindu Tradition*, translated by Derek Coltman. Chicago: University of Chicago Press, 1976.
Venerable Sujiva. *The First Step in Insight Meditation*. Nadimala, Dehiwala, Sri Lanka: Buddhist Cultural Centre, 1986.
Vetter, George B. *Magic and Religion: Their Psychological Nature, Origin, and Function*. New York: Philosophical Library, 1973.
Vishnu-Devananda, Swami. *Hatha Yoga Pradipika: The Classic guide for the Advanced Practice of Hatha Yoga (Kundalini Yoga)*, Reprinted from the 1893 Edition containing the Commentary Jyotsna of Brahmananda. New York: Om Lotus, 1987.
von Franz, Marie-Louise. *Alchemy: An Introduction to the Symbolism and the Psychology*. Toronto: Inner City Books, 1980.
Waddell, L. Austine. *The Buddhism of Tibet or Lamaism*, 2d. ed. Cambridge: W. Heffer & Sons, Limited, 1939 [1854].
_____. *Tibetan Buddhism With its Mystic Cults, Symbolism and Mythology*. New York: Dover Publications, 1972 [1895].
Waite, Arthur Edward. *The Book of Ceremonial Magic*. New York: University Books, 1961.
_____. *The Hermetic Museum*. Boston: Weiser Books, 1990 [1893].
Waley, Arthur. The *Nine Songs: A Study of Shamanism in Ancient China*. London: George Allen and Unwin Ltd. 1955.
_____. *The Way and Its Power: A Study of the Tao Té Ching and Its Place in Chinese Thought*. London: George Allen & Unwin Ltd., 1956 [1934].
Walker, Barbara. *The Woman's Dictionary of Symbols and Sacred Objects*. Edison, NJ: Castle Books, 1988.
Walker, Benjamin. "Tantrism" in: Cavendish, R., ed. *Man, Myth & Magic: The Illustrated Encyclopedia of Mythology, Religion and the Unknown*, vol. 18, pp. 2556–2561. New York: M. Cavendish, 1995.
Wallis, Wilson. D. *Religion in Primitive Society*, New York: F. S. Crofts & Co., 1939.
Walter, Mariko Nambe, and Eva Jane Neumann Fridman, eds. *Shamanism: An Encyclopedia of World Beliefs, Practices and Culture*. Santa Barbara, CA: ABC-CLIO, 2004.
Wang, Keping. *The Classic of the Dao: A New Investigation*. Beijing: Foreign Languages Press, 1998.
Wangyal, Tenzin. *Wonders of the Natural Mind: The Essence of Dzogchen in the Native Bon Tradition of Tibet*, Edited by Andrew Lukianowicz. Barrytown, NY: Station Hill Press, 1993.
Wasserman, James. *Art and Symbols of the Occult*. London: Tiger Books International, 1993.
Watts, Alan. *The Supreme Identity: An Essay on Oriental Metaphysic and Christian Religion*, 2d. ed. New York: Pantheon Books, 1972.
Weber, Max. *The Sociology of Religion*. London: Methuen & Co. Ltd., 1922.
Webster, Hutton. *Magic: A Sociological Study*. Stanford, CA: Stanford University Press, 1948.
White, David G. *The Alchemical Body: Siddha Tradi-*

tions in Medieval India. Chicago: University of Chicago Press, 1996.

———. "Rasayana (Alchemy)" *Oxford Bibliographies Online*. Oxford: Oxford University Press, 2010. http://www.oxfordbibliographies.com/display/id/obo-9780195399318-0046

White, Leslie A. *The Science of Culture: A Study of Man and Civilization*. New York: Grove Press, 1949.

Whitehead, Alfred North. *Symbolism: Its Meaning and Effect*. New York: Fordham University Press, 1955 [1927].

Wilhelm, Richard, trans. *The Secret of the Golden Flower: A Chinese Book of Life*, English translation by Cary Baynes. London: Routledge & Kegan Paul Ltd., 1931.

Wilkinson, Katherine, ed. *Signs and Symbols*. London: Dorling Kindersley Ltd. 2008.

Wilkinson, Philip. *Mythologies: Personnages & Légendes du Monde Entier*. Montreal: Sélection du Reader's Digest (Canada) Limitée, 1999.

———. *Buddhism*. London: Dorling Kindersley Ltd., 2003.

Williams, Paul. "Bodhisattva Path," in: L. Jones, Editor in chief. *Encyclopedia of Religion*, 2d ed, vol. 2, pp. 996–1000. New York, London, and Munich: Thompson Gale, 2005.

Wilson, Colin. *The Occult: A History*. New York: Random House, 1971.

Wilson, Frank Avray. *Art as Revelation*. Fontwell, Sussex, UK: Centaur Press Ltd., 1961.

Wolf, Arthur. P., ed. *Religion and Ritual in Chinese Society*. Stanford, CA: Stanford University Press, 1974.

Wong, Eve. *Shambhala Guide to Taoism*. Boston: Shambhala, 1997

Woodroffe, John. *The Serpent Power: being the Ṣaṭcakra-nirūpana and Pādukā-pañcaka*. Madras: Ganesh & Co. Publishers, 1973.

Worthington, Vivian. *A History of Yoga*. London: ARKANA, 1982.

Yang, Erzeng. *The Story of Han Xiangzi: The Alchemical Adventures of a Daoist Immortal*. A China Program Book, translated and introduced by Philip Clart. Seattle: University of Washington Press, 2007.

Yates, Jenny, ed. *Jung on Death and Immortality*. Princeton, NJ: Princeton University Press, 1999.

Yearout, Floyd, ed. *Myths*. Maidenhead, UK: McGraw-Hill Co. 1976.

Young, Dudley. *Origins of the Sacred: The Ecstasies of Love and War*. New York: St. Martin's Press, 1991.

Zaehner, Robert. C. *Mysticism, Sacred and Profane*, London: Oxford University Press, 1957.

Zeller, Eduard. *Aristotle and The Earlier Peripatetics*, vol. I, translated by Costeliloe, B. F. G. and J. H. Muirhead. New York: Russell & Russell, Inc, 1962.

Zimmer, Heinrich. *Myths and Symbols in Indian Art and Civilization*, Edited by Joseph Campbell. Bollingen Series VI, Princeton, NJ: Princeton University Press, 1972.

About the Illustrations

About the Drawings

1.a Yama, God of Death: This drawing is after an illustration in Tsultem N. 1989:plates 178, 179, and 180.
1.b Thoth, God of Wisdom: This drawing is after an illustration in Wasserman, J. 1993:62, see also Ions, V. 1974: 50; Forty, J. 1999: 69 and 117; Burland, C. 1967:9; and Oaks and Gahlin, 2006:301, 286, and 395.
1.c Dance of Death: This drawing is after an illustration in Rawson, P. 1991:34; see also Levenson, 2003:117.
1.d Anubis, Lord of Sacred Land: This drawing is after an illustration in Forty, J. 1999: 69; see also Oaks and Gahlin, 2006:135 and 397; Ions, V. 1974: 50; Adamson, S. 1997:97; and Edson, 2009: drawing 9.13, p. 205.
2.a Arhat: This drawing is after an illustration in Sun, X. G. and Wang, H. G. 1997:323.
2.b Om mani padmi hum: This drawing is reproduced in numerous locations. Two examples are Too, 2002:131, and Levenson, C. 2003:35.
4.a Khnum, Egyptian Ram headed creation god: This drawing is after an illustration in Forty, J. 2001:91; see also Oaks and Gahlin, 2006: 346–347; Burland, C. 1967:9; and Adamson, S. 1997, 102.
4.b Ganesha: This drawing is after an illustration in Bruce-Mitford, M. 1996:20; also see, Ross, N. 1966:36: Pal, P. 1977, plate 57, Wilkinson, P. 1999:40.
4.c Garuda: This drawing is after an illustration in Pal, P. 1977:176, plate 104; see also, Edson 2009: drawing 4.4, page 79.
4.d Christian cross: This drawing is after an illustration in Bruce-Mitford, M. 1996:18; also see, Wilkinson, K. 2008:178.
4.e Wadjet, Eye of Horus: This drawing is after an illustration in Oaks and Gahlin, 2006:285 and 431; see also: Forty, J. 1999: 101; Bruce Mitford, M. 1996:100; Ions, V. 1974:35; Fontana, D. 1993:57; Spineto, N. 2002:55, and Huxley, F. 1974:54.
4.f Mythical demon Vajrapâni: This drawing is after an illustration in a kapala in the collection of Chiang Min-Chi.
4.g Mictlantecuhti: This drawing is after an illustration in Philip, N. 2004:117; see also: Pope, J. A. 1986:294. Fontana, D. 2010:109; and Tresidder, J. 1998:62.

5.a Om: This drawing is after an illustration in Blau, T. & M. 2003:66; see also: Bruce-Mitford, M. 1996: 21.
5.b Wheel of Life: This drawing is after an illustration in Bowker, J. 1997: 54 and 64; Wilkinson, K. 2008:174; Bechert, H. and R. Gombrich 1984:29, and 51; and Rawson, P. 1991:66–67.
5.c Mahâkâla: This drawing is from an object in the collection of Mr. Chiang Min-Chi.
5.d 'Chum mask: This drawing is after an illustration in Lowenstein, T. 2006:206
5.e Wheel of Law: This drawing is after an illustration in Frederic, L. 1995:66; also see, Gordon, A. 1998:9; Bowker, J. 1997:54; Beer, R. 2003: 14 and 15; and Bechert, H. and R. Gombrich, 1984:51.
5.f Eight Trigrams: This drawing is after an illustration in Spineto, N. 2002:179; see also, Wong, 1997:104, 125, and 128; Harpur, J. 1993:179; Pregadio, F. 20001165; Storm, R. 2006:24–25; Wilkinson, K. 2008:170; Yearout, F. 1976: 64.
5.g Modern Yin-Yang symbol: This drawing is after illustrations in many publications; Spineto, N. 2002:179; see also, Bruce-Mitford, M. 1996:102; and Wilkinson, K. 2008:170.
5.h Old Yin-Yang symbol: This drawing is after an illustration in Wong, 1997:125; also see Harpur, J. 1993:183; Pregadio, F. 2000:935–936.
5.i Taoist Dragon: This drawing is after an illustration in Yearout, F. 1976:47; also see Beer, R. 2003:98; Ions, V. 1974:192, Lee, S. 1973:422; Bruce-Mitford, M. 2004:30.
5.j Footprints (Buddhapada): This drawing is after an illustration in Bowker, J. 1997:63; also see, Bower, J. 1998:62–63; and Wilkinson, K. 2008:118–119.
6.a Shanti mudra: This drawing is of the author's hand.
6.b Yoga Tree: This drawing is based in part on the "stump" in de Rola, S.K. 1997: 26. Also see: Wasserman, J. 1993:29.
6.c Chakra: This drawing is after an illustration in Rawson, P. 1973:157 with permission of Thames and Hudson Ltd., London.
7.a ba, human headed hawk: This drawing is after an illustration in the *Encyclopedia of Magic & Superstition: Alchemy, Charms, Dreams, Omans, Rituals, Talismans, Wishes*, 1974:73; see also, Fontana, D. 1993:87; Campbell, J. 1990:81; Oaks and Gahlin 2006:418.

8.a Ouroboros: This drawing is after an illustration in Constable, G. 1990:25; see also Yearout, F. 1976:181.
8.b Furnaces: This drawing is a composite of furnaces from different publication. Furnaces were selected and altered to demonstrate different types and styles.
9.a Dancer: This drawing is after an illustration in Pal, P. 1977, plate 39.
9.b Yu Giang, God of the North Sea: This drawing is after an illustration in Sun, X. G. and Wang, H. G., ed. 1997:510.
9.c Tiger horse: This drawing is after an illustration in Sun, X. G. and Wang, H. G. ed. 1997:105
10.a Shou-lao: This drawing is after an illustration in Christie, A. 1983:67; see also, Ions, V. 1974:186.
10.b Birdman: This drawing is after an illustration in Hoppál, M. and K. Howard, 1993:269.

Vajra (Thunderbolt) Scepter Master Chiang Min-Chi
Indian Couple reproduction granted by ©The Trustees of the British Museum. All rights reserved.
Conch, Master Chiang Min-Chi
Skulls, Master Chiang Min-Chi
Mala from the author's collection
Oracle Skull, Master Chiang Min-Chi
Yab-Yum, Master Chiang Min-Chi
Protector figure on Kapala, Master Chiang Min-Chi
Mahakala, Master Chiang Min-Chi
Prayer wheel (Tibetan: 'khor-lo)
Tibetan Drum, Master Chiang Min-Chi
Phurba, Master Chiang Min-Chi
Vajra Skull Design, Master Chiang Min-Chi
Vajra Scepter and Bell, Master Chiang Min-Chi
Bone Trumpet, Master Chiang Min-Chi
Chörten, Master Chiang Min-Chi
Cakra Painting reproduction granted by Thames & Hudson.
Tsha-tsha, Master Chiang Min-Chi

About the Figures

1.1 4 elements and 4 related conditions: Roberts, G. 1994: 47.
2.1 Four cardinal points: Blofeld, J. 1974:108
3.1 Kabbalah Tree of Life: Halevi Z. ben S. 1985:32 and 60; see also, Wasserman, J. 1993:32; Fontana, D. 1993:153.
5.1 Chörten Structure: Bechert, H. and R. Gombrich, 1984:221.
7.1 Three Substances: "Aristotle" in: Encyclopædia Britannica
7.2 Four elements: Stillman, J. 1960 [1924]:5.
7.3 Three Ingredients: Wasserman, J. 1993:93.
7.4 Numbers: Runes, D. D. 1959:171; also see, Burland, C.A. 1967:33; Laing and Wire, 1993:233; Martin, S. 2006:51; Wong, E. 1997:130.
8.1 Four Elements: Roberts, G. 1994: 47; also see, Burland, C.A. 1967:209; Poll, M. R. 2007:21–23.
8.2 Chemical Symbols: Holmyard, E. J. 1990 [1957]:153; also see, Roberts, G. 1994:67.
8.3 Mandala: Campbell, J. 1990:147.
8.4 Directions: No reference
9.1 Circle: No reference
10.1 Yoni: No reference

About the Photographs

All photographs are from the collection of Master Chiang Min-Chi except 2, 5, and 17.

About the Plates

A. Parvaati reproduction granted by ©The Trustees of the British Museum. All rights reserved
B. Roger Bacon, from the Library of Congress, LC-USZ62-110316
C. Ramón Lull, from the Library of Congress, LC-USZ62-110315
D. Alchemist in Laboratory, from the Library of Congress, LC-USZ62-80071
E. Frontispiece in *Theatrum chemicum britannicum* by Elias Ashmole, from the Library of Congress, LC-USZ62-95262
F. Purification, from the Library of Congress, LC-USZ62-95265
G. Philosopher's stone containing the image of Hermes as Mercury, from the Library of Congress, LC-USZ62-75101
H. Title page of Andreas Libavius' *Alchymia*, from the Library of Congress, LC-USZ62-95269
I. Alchemist and assistant in laboratory, from the Library of Congress, LC-USZ62-96982
J. Melencolia I by Albrecht Dürer, reproduction granted by ©The Trustees of the British Museum. All rights reserved
K. Lion and Eagle, from the Library of Congress, LC-USZ62-95266
L King and Queen marriage, from the Library of Congress, LC-USZ62-95264

Index

Numbers in ***bold italics*** indicate pages with photographs.

Adamantine 38, ***40***, 133, 147, 234
Addison, Charles Morris 69
al Adawiyah, Râbi'ah 73
Albertus Magnus 185–187, 210
Aleiato, Andrea 222
Alexandria 17, 21, 156, 164–167, 180, 214, 217
al-Razi 183, 243
anâtmatâ 237
Aquinas, Thomas 185, 187, 189, 194
Arhat 34, ***35***, 244
Ariel, David 67
Aristotle 17–19, 21, 79, 165–169, 178, 181, 186, 194, 198, 199, ***219***
âsana 142, 144, ***148***, 154
Ashmole, Elias 194, ***203***, 226
âtman 52, 116, 144, 147, 148
Atwood, Mary Ann 158, 190, 195, 196
Avalokitesvara 98, 100
Avicenna 183

Bacon, Roger 185–***187***, 189
Baker, Ian 152
Bancroft, Anne 64, 66, 150, 175, 176
Baxter, Alastair 156, 226
Bayley, Harold 129
Beer, Robert 121
Benedict, Ruth 95, 213
Bennett, Charles A. 165
ben Shimon Halevi, Z'ev 67
Bhagavad-Gita 61, 101, 131, 138, 141, 177
Birket-Smith, Kaj 51
Blofeld, John 13, 147, 172, 173, 234
blood 47, 71, 97, 119, 122, 136, 159, 161, 166, 171, 182, 193, 204, ***222***, 233, 235, 242
Bodhisattva 5, 29, 34, 35, 38, 43, ***47***, 98, 100, ***104***, 232, 233, 235, 245
Boehme, Jakob 77, 247
Bolos of Mendes 25, 161, 162, 195, 217

Bön 38, 40–42, 83, 87, 103, 124, 136, 244, 245
bone 24, 47, 48, 70, 82, 87, ***88***, 90, 91, 120, 121, 125, 126, ***128***, 134, 157, 182, 206, 208, 215, 233, 243
Bön-po 41, 42, 83
Brahma 32, 81, 82, 96, 115, 125, 141, 144, ***148***, 229, 246
Brauen, Martin ***207***, 230
Brinton, H. H. 77
Buddha 19, 32–38, 41, 43–***47***, 49, 52, 84, 88, 95, 98, 103, 114, 118, 123, 127, 130, 132, 134, 135, 141, 142, 144, 232–237, 240, 245, 248, 253
Buddhism 1, 3, 9–13, 15, 16, ***17***, 20, ***22***, 23, 27, 29, 30–49, 53, 58, 60–62, 71, 76, 78, 80, 81–84, 87–89, 92, 93, 95, 96, 98, ***99***, 100, ***101***, 103, ***104***, 106, 112, 114–117, ***121***, 123–***127***, 130–135, 139, 141, 142, ***143***, 145, 146, 149–152, 154, 177, 178, 195, 205, 206, ***207***, 215, 227, 228, 230, 232–237, 241, 244, 247, 252, 253
Budge, Sir Wallis 160
Burland, Cottie A. 96, 215, 216, 218

cakra (chakra) 117, 127, 134, 141, 143–145, 149, 153, 249
Callinicus 180
Campbell, Joseph 60, 130
'chem 124
ch'i 128, 145, 171, 172, 173
Ch'in Dynasty 170
China 9, 14–***17***, 19, 21, 25, 28, 35, 38, 39, 42–45, 53, 62–65, 78, 80–84, 90, 96–98, 102, 105, 106, 113, 114, 116, 122, 127, 128, 131, 136, 149, 151, 154–156, 161, 162, 169–174, 176, 177, 179, 182, 189 195, 197, 200, 204, 205, 207, 209, ***211***–215, 224, 228, ***229***, 231, 232,
234, 239, 242, 245, 248, 249, 250
Chinese cosmology 131, 211
chörten 134, ***135***, 233
Chou Dynasty 83, 213
Christian mysticism 64, 69, 70, 72, 80
Christianity 9, 29, 33, 37, 45, 52, 56, 66, 69–72, 76, 80, 81, 82, 88, 93, 95, 98, 99, ***103***, 110, 116, 120, 121, 122, 125, 130, 131, 140, 166, 180, 181, 184, 189, 196, 212, 215, 217, 224, 232, 234, 237, 243, 244, 250, 252
Chung-tzu 241
cinnabar 156, 174, 176, 181, 200, 204, 205, 209, 215, 232
Confucius 118, 131
Cooper, J.C. 172
Corpus Hermeticum 162, 217

d'Aquili, Eugene 80
Das, S. C. 40
David-Neel, Alexandra 13, 30, 38, 39, 41, 46
death 2, 10–***17***, 22–24, 27–29, 33, 37, 47, 48, 52, 57–60, 62–64, 67, 73, 76, 80, 83, 84, 86, 88, 90, 93, 96, 101–107, 116–121, 125, 126, ***132***, 134, 136, 140, 150, 152, 156, 159, 160, 166, 173, 177, 182, 185, 189, 201, 203, 204, ***206***–208, 214, 216, 224, 227, 228, 232–235, 240, 241, 244, 246, 250
Democritos 156, 161
de Rola, Stanislas Klossowski 204, 223
dervish 73, 75, 123
dharma 33, 35, 45, 49, 77, ***134***, 135, 153, 235
dharma-cakra 127, 135
dharmapala 87, ***105***, 123, 233, 235
di Villanova, Arnald (de Villanova) 158, 159, 185, 187, 196
divination 58, 65, 78, 84–86, 90–92, 122, 126, 159, 170, 245

divine spirit 79, 192
dragon 61, 128, 130–132, 217, 231
dream 19, 59, 62, 90–92, 145, 175, 253
duḥkha 32, 81
Dürer, Albrecht 220, **221**

ecstasy 5, 6, 12, 29, 54, 56, 57, 59, 62, 69, 79, 82, 83, 119, 123, 142, 149, 151, 152, 225, 230, 234
Emerald Table 18, 25, 162, 196, 197, 216
Egypt 12, 15, 17, 18, 19, 23–26, 67, 68, 70, 81, 91, 97, 99, 101, 102, **103**–106, 116, 122, 130, 155, 156, 159–167, 169, 180, 185, 191, 192, **193**–196, 199, 200, 207, 201, 203, 212, 214, 216, 217, 220, 239, 246, 249, 250
Eightfold Path **127**, 135, 142, 153, 222
Eliade, Mircea 28, 56, 59, 62, 77, 81, 83, 84, 111, 113, 151, 155, 177, 179, 194, 202, 211, 214, 215, 227, 239, 246, 248
elixir 3, 8, 15, 16, 21, 22, 65, 88, **100**, 142, 146, 151, 156, 163, 169–171, 173–179, 182, 183, 186, 190, 195, 196, 201, 203–205, 208, 210, 227, 228, **243**, 245
Emblemata 222, 223
enlightenment 1, 11, 12, **17**, 32, 34, 39, **41**, 45, 60, 62, 149, 153, 179, 183, 189, 190, 206, 222, 230, 232, 243, 244, 250, 253
Evens-Wentz, W.Y. 225

Fabricius, Johannes 19, 20, 165, 192
Fadiman, James 73, 74
fang-shin 170
fêng-shui 128
Feuerstein, George 102, 119, 142, 150
Fisher, Robert 47, 235
Flamel, Nicholas 190, 202, 253
Fortune, Dion 66
Frazer, James George 85, 86
Frédéric, Louis 232
Fung, Yu-Lan 78
furnace 152, 161, 171, 189, 202, 203, 205, 210, 214, 215, **218**, **220**, 239, 253

Ganesha 99, 100
garuda **91**, 100
Gautama 32–34, 45, 98, 144, 206, 222
Geber 25, 180, 199
Gerard of Cremona 185, 186

ghost 9, 70, 107, 126, 159
gold 6, 8, 15, 19–22, 25, 26, 31, **40**, 106, 113, 134, **135**, 138, 140, 151, 155–158, 161, 163, 165, 169–172, 174–179, 181, 182, 184, 186, 187, 189–192, 194–196, 198–200, 204, 205, 208–210, 212, 216, **220**, **222**, 226–228, 230, 231, 238, 239, 248, 253
Golden Mean 222
Gordon, Antoinetta 45
Govinda, Lama Anagarika 44, 193
Greece 15, 17–19, 21, 25, 82, 96, 102, **103**, **127**, **128**, 130, 131, 155, 156, 161, 162, 164–167, 169, 180–186, 192, **193**, 198, 199, 202, 204, 214, **219**, 229, 234, 239
Guiley, Rosemary 87, 131
guru 42, 111, 114, **139**, 141, 230

Halifax, Joan 31
Han Dynasty 52, 106, 119, 170, 171, 189
Happold, Frederick C. 73, 77
hatha yoga 62, 140, 144, 147, 148, 150, 153, 177
Hauck, Dennis 197
Hebrew 66, 67, 99, 120, 240
Hermes 18, 25, 26, 102, 155, 158, 161, 162, 166, 195, 216–**219**, 223, 228, 229
Hermes Trismegistus 18, 161, 162, 195, 197, 216
hermit 51, 81
Hieroglypica 220, **221**
Hinayâna 34, 39, 42, 149, 235, 244
Hinduism 11, 15, 19, 27, 34, 35, **40**, **47**, 58, 60, 61, 64, 71, 77, 78, 80, 82, 88, 89, 96, 100, **101**, 103, 106, 114–116, 118, 125, **133**, 134, **139**–141, 143, 145, 149, 150, 155, 176, 177, 194, 204, 222, 227–229, 244, 246, 250, 253
Holmyard, Eric J. 157, 158, 162, 185, 191, 200, 202
Holy Spirit 9, 72
Horace **104**
Horapollo 220, 222, 223
Huxley, Francis 109

I Ching 16, 64, 65, 68, 92, 128, 171, 173, 245
ibn Hayyân, Jâbir (Geber) 25, 162, 179–183, 198, 199, 216
immortality 1, 3, 6, 8, 12, 14–16, 21–24, 52, 56, 65, 81, 85, **100**, 104, 106, 107, 116, **131**, 147, 150, 156–158, 160, 170–176, 179, 183, 195, 197, 198, 204–209, 212, 215, 227, 232, 238, 240–245, 248, 250

India 11, 16, 19, 25, 32, 33, 35–37, 39, **41**–47, 60–62, 73, 81, 82, 87, 96, 101–103, 114, 122, **127**, 138, 145, 147, 149–151, 154, 156, 162, 164, 170, 174, 176, 177, 179, 195, 207, 208, 227, 228, 230, 239, 247–249, 252, 253
Islam 33, 37, 56, 66, 71, 73, 74, 88, 93, 118, 122, 125, 156, 180, 183, 184, 195, 218, 251, 252
Isis 5, 70, 101, 161, 162
Iyengar, B.K.S. 139, 143, 146, 151

James, William 80
Jesus Christ 19, 23, 45, 52, 70–72, 88, 95, 98, **103**, 118, 120, 125, 140, 154, 155, 189, 196, 215, 233, 234, 244, 246
Jewish mysticism 52, 56, 66, 67, 95, 120, 148, 185, 213
Jisl, Lumir 235
Johnson, Ored Simon 131, 170, 231
Jones, Rufus 72
Judaism 33, 66–68, 71, 93, 94, 99, 120, 122, 125, 185, 195, 243, 252
Jung, Carl G. 8, 27, 31, 37, 64, 70, 98, 112, 113, 195, 207, 208, 217, 230

Kabbalah 66–69, 130, 185, 192, 215
Kak, Subhash 102
Kali 118, 119, 133, 149
kapâla 47, 87, 120, 121, **133**, 233
kâpâlika 233
karma 13, 15, 85, 116, 118, 126, 177, 227, 241, 246, 247, 251
Kehoe, Alice Beck 17
Kelley, Edward 226
Khnum 97
Kluckhohn, Clyde 96
Knowles, David 70
Ko Hung 172, 204, 205, 209
Kohn, Livia 63
Krishna 101, 102, 110, 131, 138, 177
kundalini 61, 130, 141, 143, 144, 149, 249
Kuan-yin 98

laboratory 157, 163, 164, 181, 183, 192, 195, 197–206, 211, **220**, 226, 239, 253
lama 12, 42, 45, 49, 91, 92, 94, 107, 124, 134, 233, 252
Lao-tzu 15, 64, 97, 118, 119, 131, 170, 172, 176, 209
lataif 75
Leonardo Da Vinci 222
Levenson, Claude **22**, 125
Lévi-Strauss, Claude 96
Lewis, I. M. 29

Index

Li Shao-chün 231
liberation 29, 31, 33, 48, 52, 61, 62, 64, 66, 79, 81–83, 85, 106, *117*, 118, 139, 140–142, 147, 150, 151, 177, 178, 192, 241, 244–247, 253
light 6, 8, 9, 43, 62, 64, 68, 69, 75, 95–97, 113, 120, 128, *129*, 130, 143, 152, 155, 157, 166, 173, 182, 183, 195, 196, 201, 242, 247
Lowenstein, Tom 123
Lu, K'uan Yü 142, 175
Lü, Pu-wei 174
Lull, Ramón 185, 187–189

Maddox, John Lee 62
magic 6, 8, 10, 13, 15, 18, 21, 24, 30, 35, 37, 38, 39, 44, 46, 49, 50, 51, 52, 55, 57, 58, 59, 62, 64–67, 70, 76, 82, 83, 85–94, 102, 106, 107, 109, 120, 121, 122, 131, 132, 137, 140, 149, 150, 153, 155, 159–161, 163–166, 170, 177, 178, 181, 185, 186, 189, 195, 196, 197, 204, 207, 208, 211, 213, 214, 217, 220, *221*, 224, 227, 231, 245, 248, 250
mahâkâla 88, 103, 123
Mahâyâna 34–39, 42–44, 48, 84, 92, *104*, 118, 149, 178, 232, 234–236, 244
Maier, Michael *187*, 223
mala 87, *88*, 125, 126
Malinowski, Bronislaw 85, 95
mandala *43*, 61, 115, 123, 132, 207, 230, 235
mantra 16, *46*, 49, 61, 82, *88*, 89, 94, *104*, 109–111, 114, 115, 123, 125, 126, *135*, 138, 140, *143*, 145, 153, 208, 235, 244, 245
mantrayâna 16, 38
Maria "the Jewess" 163, 164
Martin, Sean 185, 193, 196, 217
McGhee, Robert 59
meditation 29, 31–35, *43*, 46, *47*, 61, 63, 66, 78–84, 89, 110, 114, 115, 123, 125, 127, 134–136, 138, 139, 142, 144–149, 151–154, 173–175, 177, 204–207, 215, 217, 234, 235, 237, 241, 242, 244, 245, 251
Melancholia *221*, 222
Mencius 78
mercury 16, 18, 20, 26, 151, 152, 158, 171, 172, 174, 176, 177, 179, 181, 182, 187, 189–191, 194, 196, 199, 200, 204, 205, 208–210, 215, 217, *222*–224, 228, 229
metaphysics 6, 13, 15, 19, 22, 27, 28, 31, 35, 50–52, 54, 56, 70, 71, 76, 78, 79, 82, 87, 107,

132, 136, 138, 140, 141, 143, 146, 153, 167, 171, 181, 183, 184, 228, 230, 231, 239, 245
Mictlantecuhti 104, *105*
Mohenjo-daro 139, 226
Mongolia 12, 38, 43, 45, 58, 100, *124*, 154, *229*, 234
monk 9, 33, 34, 49, 81, 112, 126, 177, 180, 185–187, 196, 220, 228, 233
Moors 185, 189
Morienus (Marianus) 180, 185
mudrâ 61, 82, 94, 119, 123, 139
Muni, Swami Rajarshi 117, 140
Muslim 25, 36, 43, 73–75, 116, 143, 180, 181, 185, 192, 200, 228, 243
mythology 14, *17*, 19, 24, 28, 32, 37, 39, 88, 89, 94–107, *131*, 133, 138, 143, 159, 162, 165, 166, 204, 207, 223, 228, *229*, 239, 240

Nâgârjuna 177–179, 228
Nâlandâ 36
Nepal 33, 38, 39, 43, 44, 100, 101, 115, 230
New Testament 71, 72, 95, 122
nirvâna 12, 29, 33, 34, 37, 45, 84, 118, *207*, 241, 243, 246

occult 18, 21, 27, 30, 68, 77, 83, 121, 157, 162, 187, 197, 211, 213, *222*, 226, 238
Old Testament 72, 91, 95, 116, 122, 130
Oliver, Martyn 165
Olson, Stuart Alva 197, 245
oracle 28, 91
Osiris 70, 101, 102, 105, 159, 160
ouroboro 192, *193*

Padmasambhava 42, 88
Paracelsus 190, 191, 194, 195, 210
Parvati 99, *100*, 139, 147, *148*, 150
Patanjali 61, 82, 138, 141, 142, 151
philosopher's stone 10, 121, 131, 163, 176, 182–184, 189, 193, 195, 196, 199, 202, 208, 215, *218*, *220*
phurba 124, 132
Pinch, Geraldine 159, 161
Plato 17, 19, 54, 116, 165–168
Porter, Bill 81
prajna 9, *40*, 230
prânâyâma 82, 142–144, 146–148, 154, 177
prayer wheel 126
prima materia 131, 150, 186, 192–194, 196–198, 201, 204, 205, 208, 210, 217, 230, 248
primal matter 97, 131
Prophet Muhammad 73, 103, 106, 118

Quetzalcoatl 104, 105
quicksilver 172, 179, *187*, 190, 193, 210, 217

Radha, Swami Sivnanda 114, 125, 147
raga 114
raja-yoga 140, 147, 148, 153
Ramsey, Jay 155, 193
rasâyana 147, 177
Rawson, Philip 230
Read, John 224
reincarnation 12, 13, 24, 48, 62, 94, 104, 106, 244
Rigveda 85, 138, 227, 246
Ripley, Sir George 194, 196, 202, 210
ritual 6, 10, 14, 24, 28, 36, 37, 39, *40*, 45–49, 58, 59, 61, 86, 87, 92–94, 97, 101, 107–109, 111, 112, 120–125, 130, 132, 133, 136, 150, 153, 156, 166, 206, 214, 215, 228, 230, 233, 234, 238–240, 248, 249
Robert of Chester 185
Roberts, Garth 155, 200, 202, 223
Roob, Alexander 198, 199, 208
Rosicrucians 185

Sakta Tantras 61
Sakyamuni 32, 43, 45, 98, *104*, 235, 248
samadhi 82, 142, 149, 151
samsâra 12, 37, 39, 118, 126, 227, 242, 243
sangha 9, 33, 134, 135
Scholem, Gershom G. 56, 61
Scott, Michael 185, 186
shakti (sakti) 35, 61, 118, 130, 143, 144, 149, 150, 228
shamanism 8, 10, 11, 19, 23, 28, 29, 31, 40, 42, 54–63, 68–70, 83, 84, 92, 94, 101, 102, 122, 124, 130–132, 134, 146, 150, 151, 155, 213–215, 227, 234, 244, 252, 253
Shang Dynasty 215
Shiva (Siva) 35, 82, 96, 99, 100, 103, 119, 125, 134, 138, 139, 144, 147–150, *225*, 228, 229, 248
Siddhartha 32
siddhi 42, 177
Silberer, Herbert 163
skull 46–*48*, 87, 88, 91, 104, *105*, 119–121, 124, 125, *132*, 143, 146, 233, *236*
soul 5, 7, 11–13, 18, 23, *48*, 51–55, 57, 59, 60, 62, 64, 67–75, 77, 79, 80, 94, 95, 97, 98, 104–107, 112, 113, 116, 120–122, 127, 136, 140, 143, 146, 153, 158, 160, 173, 175, 176, 182, 189, 192, 195, 196, 201, 204,

205, 207–210, 223, 230, 236, 242, 243, 247, 248, 250
spirit 5–7, 9, 10, 12–15, 20, 23, 24, 29–31, 35, 39, 45, 47–49, 51–63, 69, 70, 72, 73, 75–77, 79, 82, 85, 86, 88, 107, 109, 112, 114, 120, 121, 131, 137, 139, 140, 145, 149, 151, 153, 158, *160*, 166, 170–176, 179, 192, 195, 196, 206, 212, 213, 217, 218, 226, 239, 242, 245, 246, 248
Stavish, Mark 155, 156
Stewart, John Alexander 54, 251
Stillman, John Maxxon 7, 158
Storm, Rachel 32
stupa 35, 45, 134, *135*, 232, 233
Sufism 11, 73–75, 113, 123, 143, 180, 215, *225*
sulphur 158, *172*, 182, *187*, 189, 190, 193, 194, 199, 200, 205, 210, 222–224, 229
sulphur-mercury theory 20, 181, 187, 190, 199, 210
Sung Dynasty 173
supernatural 5, 6, 9–14, 16, 23, 27–31, 34, 36, 38, 50, 52, 54, 56–58, 60, 66, 71, 72, 77, 78, 80, 83, 86–88, 90, 91–95, 97, 101, 102, 107, 120, 134, 142, 159, 163, 177, 208, 227, 238–240, 242, 247, 251
sutra 34, 37, 61, 118, 138, 141, *229*, 236
symbol 10, 28, 31, 36, 38, 40, 44–46, 49, 58, 66, 68, 89, 96, 100, *103*, *104*, 108–117, 119–123, 125–136, 139, 155, 157, 163, 193, 200, *201*, 212, 220, 223, 228–237, 240, 247–249

T'ai Chi 97, 173
T'ang Dynasty 174, 176, 205, 209
Tanjur 43, 46
Tantrism 7, 13, 16, 30, 32, 35, 36, 37, 39, *41*, 42, 47, 58, 61, 78, 81, 87, 91, *101*, 110, 115, 118–121, 125, *132*–134, 136, 137, 140, 143, 144, 149–152, 174, 176, 177, 178, 179, 214, 225, 228–236, 248, 250
Tao-te Ching 63, 64, 78, 128, 171
Taoism 9, 14, 15, 20, 52, 58, 63–65, 68, 78, 90, 93, 106, 119, 127–*128*, *129*, *131*, 142, 145, 147, 155, 161, 162, 170–176, 195, 197, 200, 204–206, 209, 210, 215, 231, 239, 241–242, *243*–245, 249–250, 252; alchemy 170–172, 175, 215; mysticism 14, 63, 106, *131*, 170; yoga 145, 171, 175
Târâ 98, 100
thangka *100*, 115, 132
Theravâda 33, 34, 37, 149, 235
Thoth 18, 25, 26, 102, *104*, 155, 161, 162, 166
Tibet 5, 7, 11–13, 15–*17*, 20, *22*, 23, 29–32, 34, 35, 37–*48*, 49, 58, 62, 68, 81, 83, 86–89, 92, 98, 100, 101, 102, 103, *105*, 106, 114, 116, 117, 120, *121*, 123, 125, 126, 128, *132*–136, 149, 151–154, 170, 174, 193, 195, 206, *207*, 224, 230, 232–235, 237, 243, 251, 252
Tonpa Shenrap 41
Topitsch, Ernst 96
transcendental consciousness 50, 54, 251
transcendentalism 5, 6, 8, 9, 13, 14, 30, 50, 51, 53, 57, 58, 72, 77, 91, 93, 118, 139, 140, 143, 148–150, 154, 183, 208, 234, 236, 239, 244, 251–253
transmigration 12, 24, 95, 227
truth 5–11, 14, 27, 29–32, 38, 39, 46, 50, 51, 54–56, 58, 63, 66, 67, 69–72, 74, 76, 77, 79, 81, 84, 85, 89, 93, 95, 105, 113, 114, 130, 133, 136, 157, 178, 184, 189, 201, 217, 226–228, 237, 245–247, 251
tsha-tsha 235, *236*
Tucci, Giuseppe 30, 38, 39, 44, 251
tulku 42, 48

Underhill, Evelyn 50, 51, 59, 62, 70, 84, 110, 140, 217, 226
universal spirit 35
Upanishads 80, 114, 141, 228

Valentine, Basil 196, *222*
vajra 39, *40*, 132, 133, 147, 234
vajrâ-cârya 39
Vajrapâni *104*, 133

Vajrayâna 16, 38, 39, 42, *104*, 120, 150, 234
Varenne, Jean 139–140, 154
Vedas 17, 89, 93, 103, 176, 177, 179, 227, 228, *249*
Vikramasila 36
Vishnu 82, 96, 100, 101, 115, 134, 144, *148*, 229

Waddell, Austine L. 39, 43
wadjet 103, *104*
wai-dan 171
Waite, Arthur 179, 210
Walter, Mariko Namba 57
warring states 15, 155, 170
Watts, Allan 56
Webster, Hutton 55
Wheel of the Law 103, *134*
Whitehead, Alfred North 109, 113
Wiick, Thomas *198*, 220
Wilson, Collin 68
Wong, Eva 173, 175
Woodroffe, Sir John 153
Worthington, Vivian 139
wu 15, 83

yab-yum 39, 40, *101*, 149, 230
Yama 16, *17*, 103–*105*, *117*, *121*, 124, 126, 142, 154, 235
Yamantaka 88, 104, *105*, *121*, 235
yantra 115
Yellow Emperor 169, 171
yin-yang 53, 127–129, 131, *172*, 209, 211, 242
Ying-Chao *229*
yogâcâra 149
Yogâeârya 35
Yoga-Sutra 61, 82, 138, 140–143, 151, 153, 154
yogi 35, 40, 60–62, 75, 82–84, 87, 110, 117, 137–139, 141–153, 172, 176–178, 204, 226, 234, 241, 242, *249*, 252; mysticism 60–62
yoni 133, 150, 248, 249
Yu Giang *229*
Yu the Great 182

Zen 154
Zeus 15, 18, 101, 102, 131, 155
Zosimos of Panopolis 26, 163, 195, 196, 202

www.ingramcontent.com/pod-product-compliance
Ingram Content Group UK Ltd.
Pitfield, Milton Keynes, MK11 3LW, UK
UKHW050541150426
5217IPUK00026B/2023